Maya™ 6
The Complete Reference

About the Authors

Tom Meade is a San Francisco–based 3D effects artist, instructor, and writer. Meade earned his BA in film production from Boston University and worked on several interactive CD-ROM games as a 2D production artist before making the leap to 3D. He has produced 3D illustrations for *Wired* magazine and worked previously as a 3D technician for Pulse Entertainment, a company that creates web-based animations for such high-profile clients as AOL/Time Warner, NBC Online, and Warner Brothers/WB Online. Meade currently teaches Maya at San Francisco State University's Multimedia Studies Program and the Academy of Art University. For the past three years, he has worked at dvGarage, a 3D/FX training company, building video-based 3D training products, including the dvGarage 3D Toolkit and Maya Lab. Meade was a contributing author on Cat Woods's *Mastering 3ds max 4* (Sybex, 2001).

Shinsaku Arima is a 3D VFX artist and instructor who has been actively working on heavy effects–driven movies such as *The Matrix: Revolutions*, *The Day After Tomorrow*, and *Sky Captain and the World of Tomorrow*. After earning his BFA from the University of Southern California in sculpture and photography, Arima worked for several years as a professional sculptor, creating and selling large-scale metal sculptures. For the past six years he has taught Maya and 3D animation at such well-respected institutions as the Academy of Art University, Mesmer Animation Labs, and DeAnza College. Arima's past positions have included working as manager of Mesmer Animation Labs, as a full-time instructor at Academy of Art University, and as a trainer and technical director for ESC Entertainment. He is currently working as FX technical director at The Orphanage in San Francisco. Arima is co-author (with Anthony Rossano) of *XSI Illuminated: Foundation 2* (Mesmer Press, 2000).

About the Technical Editor

Alex Tang has worked in 3D graphics for more than 15 years. He spent several years as a technical consultant and certified trainer at Alias, providing Maya and other consulting and production services to clients such as Digital Domain, Big Idea, and Boeing. He has also been a course developer and Maya instructor at the Academy of Art University and San Francisco State University's Multimedia Studies Program. In previous years, Alex developed graphics and other software while on the technical staff at SGI, Oracle, and IBM Watson Research. He currently works as technical editor at Industrial Light & Magic.

Maya™ 6

The Complete Reference

Tom Meade
and Shinsaku Arima

 O S B O R N E

New York Chicago San Francisco
Lisbon London Madrid Mexico City
Milan New Delhi San Juan
Seoul Singapore Sydney Toronto

*The **McGraw·Hill** Companies*

McGraw-Hill/Osborne
2100 Powell Street, 10th Floor
Emeryville, California 94608
U.S.A.

To arrange bulk purchase discounts for sales promotions, premiums, or fund-raisers, please contact **McGraw-Hill**/Osborne at the above address. For information on translations or book distributors outside the U.S.A., please see the International Contact Information page immediately following the index of this book.

Maya™ 6: The Complete Reference

234567890 CUS CUS 01987654

Book p/n 0-07-222719-2 and CD p/n 0-07-222720-6
parts of
ISBN 0-07-222718-4

Publisher
Brandon Nordin

**Vice President
& Associate Publisher**
Scott Rogers

Acquisitions Editor
Marjorie McAneny

Project Editors
Lisa Theobald, Madhu Prasher

Technical Editor
Alex Tang

Copy Editor
Lisa Theobald

Proofreader
Marilyn Smith

Indexer
Karin Arrigoni

Composition
Tara Davis, Elizabeth Jang,
Jean Butterfield

Illustrators
Kathleen Edwards, Melinda Lytle

Series Designers
Lyssa Wald, Peter F. Hancik

Cover Designer
Jeff Weeks

Cover Illustration
Ping Xie

This book was composed with Corel VENTURA™ Publisher.

Contents at a Glance

Contents

II 3D Modeling

4   Advanced NURBS Modeling **87**

5   Polygon Modeling **137**

6   Organic Modeling **161**

III Animation

9   Character Setup: Joints, Connections, and Kinematics 241

10 Character Setup: Character Controls 275

11 Character Setup: Binding Skin 299

12 Character Animation 327

IV   Texturing, Lighting, and Rendering

V   Particles, Emitters, and Fields

17   Particles and Fields 471

18   Advanced Particle Systems and Effects 509

Foreword

by Alex Lindsay

Maya is not only one of the most powerful 3D software packages available, it's one of the most complicated. The possibilities are as limitless as the paths to get to them. This maze of tools can be very difficult to traverse for those looking to begin "high-end 3D" work. I think your guides, Tom and Shin, will make this journey much easier.

I met Tom when he was my student. I was still with Industrial Light & Magic, and Tom was just beginning his 3D work. Along with a handful of other students, we began to work on projects that required us to approach the work not from a student or teacher perspective, but as a production artist. While this may seem like a subtle difference, production is a completely different world. The saying, "The map is not the territory" perfectly describes the 3D market. So many things seem to make sense in theory and work in isolated cases, but they quickly fall apart under the weight of the "Real World."

When thinking about graphics, production, or life in general, this is one of the most important things to remember. We often think of learning as a set of skills, a collection of "tricks up our sleeve." Many classes and books provide many of these tidbits. But this rarely leads us to a profound understanding of our art that truly provides a foundation for inspiring work. Small problems become days of frustration or failure. We follow what we are "supposed" to do for weeks when the most effective, and often unconventional, solution is days away.

The key is to understand the underlying principles of the process. With these principles in mind, one has the agility to handle the issue at hand with a solid footing and clear vision. Through true understanding of the art in which we are immersed, we can have a bird's eye view of the process to help us make intelligent and grounded decisions.

So how do we get there?

- *Observe.* Would you like to know the fastest way to add realism to your work? Take a digital camera and shoot 10 photos a day of everyday items. Shoot door knobs, street signs, old cars. Watch not only how the light interacts with the object but how the camera interacts with the scene. I still do this constantly.

- *Fail.* Push yourself outside your boundaries. If you aren't failing, you aren't pushing.

- *Study.* When something doesn't work, find out why it doesn't work. Don't just figure out how to get around the problem—find out why the problem exists.

- *Experiment.* Playing with ideas is very important. You need to keep what you do fun. Experimentation gives you the space to play and is especially useful if you just failed at something.

- *Work with others.* Working by yourself is a nearly guaranteed way to fall behind. You can't learn everything and your eye is not perfect. You need a second opinion and a different perspective constantly to progress.

- *Work on real projects.* It is important, probably more important than anything else, to find real clients with real problems—even if it's work for free at first. People rarely do their best work for themselves. A client's needs help you mold your work and push you to perform. We often think we want to be a great artist like the masters in the art museums, rarely thinking about how much of their work was for contract—not art for art's sake. If you don't have any clients, find them. Give your work to non-profits or trade your work for services, but whatever you do, *do not* hide away to "work on your demo tape." I've seen many a computer artist get lost on this path.

With that, I will leave you with Tom and Shin. Their combined experience in production will provide a real grounding for the content presented here. I have worked with Tom for years, and Shin's background speaks for itself. This book is a place to start—and a good one. The rest of the path will be up to you.

Alex Lindsay
dvGarage
San Francisco, California
June 2004

Acknowledgments

Our greatest thanks goes to Margie McAneny for giving us the opportunity to write this book and advising and encouraging us all of the way through the end of the project. Thanks to Lisa Theobald for taking on the monstrous task of editing this project and constantly reminding us that it would soon be over. Many more thanks to the people at Osborne/McGraw-Hill: Roger Stewart, Madhu Prasher, Tana Allen, Carolyn Welch, and the many others who put time into producing this book. A special thanks to Cat Woods for helping us through the initial stages of preparing this book.

Tom: Thank you, Alex Lindsay, for introducing me to the world of 3D and always emphasizing "the details." Thanks to Dan Meblin and Young Harvill for giving me the opportunity to work in this industry and learn from it. Thanks to all of the Maya Masters: Chris Landreth, Jason Schleifer, Steven Stahlberg, and many others who have presented their discoveries and experience to the community over the years. Thanks to the Gnomon Workshop for the resources you've made available. Another round of applause to the students at the Academy of Art University in San Francisco, many of whom submitted much of the artwork used in these pages. An honorable mention goes to Ping Xie for his hard work in designing the cover. And thank you Mom, Dad, Kelly, Chris, Pamela, and all of my friends for your love and support during this project. It would not have been possible without you.

Shin: I'd like to thank my mother and father for endless support; Rodney Iwashina for being the most amazing and efficient supervisor during *Matrix* production; Remo Balcells for being a very patient and wise VFX supervisor during *Day After Tomorrow* production; Rudy Grossman for being an extremely friendly and assuring supervisor for *Sky Captain*; all my students for teaching me how to teach and supplying me with beautiful 3D images; Wenchin Hsu for taking care of me with whole-hearted love; Steven, Cara, David, Jesse, Rachel, and Juan for being a great company; and Gabriela and Rachel for giving me great joy in my life.

Introduction

If you have gone to the movies lately or played a video game on an Xbox system, you are familiar with the types of animation that Maya can produce. Maya is currently the industry-standard application for producing animation and effects for film, television, video games, and the Internet. This book was written to demonstrate how the program works and how it is used to produce content for these industries.

Not so many years ago, access to Maya by someone outside of the animation industry was limited. The software cost tens of thousands of dollars and the hardware required to run it was just as expensive. Attending a school was just about the only option for anyone interested in learning about this exciting new technology.

As computer hardware became faster and cheaper, software companies began to realize that they could sell these high-end applications to smaller studios, independent artists, and students if they made the price more appealing to those markets. Today you can purchase Maya Complete for under $2000, or you can download a free version, called the Personal Learning Addition, from the Alias Web site. The final obstacle, once you have the software installed, is learning how to use it. That's where this book comes into play.

Learning an application as large and powerful as Maya can be overwhelming, to say the least. While Maya 6's online documentation provides an excellent resource for learning about each and every little piece inside the program, it was not really designed to show you how all of the pieces fit together so that you can go about designing and completing a project. Knowing how to use a hammer does not necessarily mean that you can build a house. This book teaches you many of the tools in Maya *in the context of using them in a real-world production environment.*

This book was designed to cover the basics of the program and to demonstrate how Maya can be used to create projects. What you will gain from reading this book is a knowledge of specific workflows that are common to most 3D productions. Whether it be modeling a head for animation or rendering a vehicle for integration into a live-action plate, this book will direct you through processes that have been tried and tested in production environments. Successfully building a project that is free of errors and can be easily edited at any time during a production is beyond the scope of what any manual can teach you, but it is something that reading and working through the tutorials in this book can help you achieve.

Who Should Read This Book

This book is intended for CG artists, engineers, filmmakers, or hobbyists who are serious about using Maya to create high-quality images and animations. Some of the information here is very basic, while much of it is more advanced. Beginners will be happy to know that we've detailed where to find each and every tool or window as you follow along the tutorials. Advanced users will find plenty of information within these pages that you won't find in other books. We believe we have created a book that will be useful to anyone with a genuine interest in Maya.

While the book covers the fundamental aspects of Maya, such as the user interface and navigation, some knowledge or experience with 3D animation techniques will be necessary before you attempt to complete the tutorials. If you are migrating to Maya from another 3D package, it is suggested that you complete the introduction and Project One tutorials in the *Learning Maya 6 Foundations* book that ships with the software.

How the Book Is Organized

We have organized this book into six parts that begin with an overview of Maya and then follow the order of a typical production workflow. However, this does not mean that you have to read this book in order. Users with previous experience in Maya will have no problems jumping right to the character-rigging chapters in Part III or building explosions in Part IV.

For people with less experience, it is recommended that you try and follow the book in the order in which it has been laid out. We took extra care to explain how to execute basic tasks in the beginning of the book. These tasks, such as setting tool options and executing commands, are used throughout the entirety of the book but are not explained in such detail in later chapters.

Part I is designed especially for people new to the 3D production process or to Maya. It outlines the different processes used in a production and explains how they fit together. The overview of Maya's user interface is followed by a tutorial that directs you through a simple project, showing how to navigate through the interface and introducing some basic 3D concepts.

Part II covers modeling with all three of the geometry types available in Maya: NURBS, polygons, and subdivision surfaces. The NURBS and polygonal modeling chapters concentrate on hard-surface modeling techniques, and the subdivision surface chapter shows how to build a humanoid head. Beginners should beware that some of these exercises, particularly the spaceship tutorial, may be difficult to complete if you are not totally comfortable using Maya. If you find you are having difficulties with one of these projects, there is no harm in skipping it and continuing on with the rest of the book. You can always return to missed sections and complete them at a later time.

Part III is dedicated to animation, with a strong emphasis on character animation. After covering the basics of keyframe animation and some basic deformation tools, the setup for a character is explained in detail in three chapters so that it can be easily animated in Chapter 12.

Part IV begins with an in-depth study of how to use Maya's Hypershade interface to build materials and control the lighting in a Maya scene. Advanced texture-mapping techniques are demonstrated, along with an approach to building a realistic skin shader. Workflows for using Maya's Paint Effects toolset are also covered in this section. Finally, we practice different rendering techniques in both Maya's software renderer and the Mental Ray for Maya renderer.

Part V explores Maya's Dynamics toolset. This includes particles, fields, expressions, and rigid and soft body dynamics for creating realistic effects and animation by running simulations based on natural phenomena. Maya's hardware renderer is also covered here.

Part VI focuses on completing a single project of a spaceship landing. Camera mapping, multipass rendering, command-line rendering, and compositing techniques are all explained in detail.

The appendix offers some brief information about Maya's scripting language, MEL (Maya Embedded Language). This concludes with a tutorial that supplements one of the exercises in Chapter 10, where we make a button that switches an inverse kinematics control to a forward kinematics control.

Conventions Used in This Book

A few conventions are used in this book. One has to do with choosing a command from a menu and opening its Options window. When we direct you to choose a command from the menu, we use the | symbol to signify a submenu. For example, if we say "create a polygonal sphere by choosing Create | Polygon Primitives | Sphere," that means you need to click the Create menu in the menu bar, mouse over Polygon Primitives from the resulting list, and then choose Sphere from the submenu.

Most of the tools and commands in Maya have options that can be edited and set before executing the tool or command. These options are usually accessed by clicking the little box next to a tool or command in the menu items. This book uses the ❐ symbol to denote the Options window command. For example, to open the Options window for the Sphere command, we say "choose Create | Polygon Primitives | Sphere ❐."

Another convention used throughout this book are icons appearing in the margin of some pages. Maya offers several ways to execute tools and commands. We will always direct you to execute these tools and commands via the main menus, but you may also choose to click a button on a Shelf or toolbar. For this reason, we provide the button icon in the margin when introducing a tool or command for the first time. The margin icons that look like CDs are explained next.

Finally, keyboard combinations are included for both the Windows and Mac platforms. Windows combinations appear first, and Mac combinations follow in parentheses.

 ## About the CD

This book includes a CD that contains Maya scene files and other resources that are used throughout the book. Many tutorials will instruct you to open a certain CD file to use at the start of a project. This is emphasized with a CD icon in the text margin.

> **NOTE** *Most of the files included with the book CD were designed to open in Maya 5 or later. However, some of the files use features that are specific to Maya 6 and therefore will not open in Maya 5 or earlier versions.*

Introduction
to Maya

Core Concepts

Maya is the state-of-the-art, industry standard application that is widely used for 3D modeling, animation, and effects. Users of the program produce content for film and television production, video game development, web design, and print production.

Maya is a culmination of technologies created by Alias and Wavefront, the premiere computer graphics software companies of recent decades. It is the largest commercial computer application ever written, with levels of complexity and functionality exceeding other high-end 3D animation packages.

Within the last five years, film effects companies including Industrial Light & Magic (ILM), Pixar, Imageworks, and Digital Domain have adopted Maya as their standard for producing 3D animated effects. Recognizing its technological superiority to its competitors, Sony and Microsoft have helped to define Maya as the industry standard for video game graphics as well, developing content for their PlayStation and Xbox. Web, print, and industrial designers are also poised to adopt Maya as an industry standard because of a new, significantly lower price point.

In 2003, the Academy of Motion Picture Arts and Sciences recognized these achievements and the software's impact in the movie industry by awarding Alias with an Oscar for Technical Achievement.

Maya comprises a complete, integrated set of practical, easy-to-use tools for creating complicated special effects. These tools enable 3D modeling; animating; texturing, lighting, and rendering capabilities; and dynamics. Maya's scripting language, MEL (Maya Embedded Language) allows users the flexibility to create and modify existing toolsets to create their own custom functions and streamline their production processes. The unique level of integration of Maya's tools prevents compatibility problems often caused in competing applications that rely on plug-in technologies or that require additional software packages to create all elements of an animated 3D image.

So now that you have Maya installed on you computer, how do you begin releasing your imagination onto the screen in front of you? Before we get into the specifics, it is important that you understand the concepts and processes behind a 3D production. In this chapter, we will define these processes and explain how Maya handles them.

Production Workflow

In almost everything we do, we can choose from a variety of available options to accomplish the task. Maya is no different. In fact, Maya often offers so many options that it can take days, months, or even years to discover the most efficient processes to use for completing a project. This book is designed to share and suggest certain processes, often called *workflows*, that are used in many professional 3D productions.

To illustrate the importance of an efficient workflow, consider the manufacture of an automobile. During the design and engineering process, the most critical decisions are made: What will this car need to do? Who is it for? How will it be used? After answering these questions, the designers and engineers get busy, and the design of the car begins to take shape. Now, what would happen if all the components—the frame, the engine, and the interior—were constructed, and the team that finished first went ahead and started putting the car together with the parts they had created? The car would be a disaster. As each new component became ready, employees would have to take the car apart and reassemble it. This process could go on forever.

A 3D production is not much different. If you build and animate your skeleton without knowing what the model looks like, you might put the legs in the wrong place. If you begin the layout of the texture coordinates but then find that the character is not deforming properly and the model will have to be modified, the work done on texturing will have to be trashed.

At this time, whether or not you understand texture coordinates or how they are affected by a model is not important. The main thing to realize is that a certain workflow needs to be followed for scenes to be completed quickly and efficiently. In general, a good workflow should begin by planning in preproduction, and then the necessary objects are modeled. If characters are included in the scene, they must be set up so that they can be animated in the next phase.

A lot happens during the animation phase. In addition to the keyframed animation techniques you'll learn about in Chapter 7, effects such as fire, smoke, and water can be added into the scene through the use of particles. Finally, the objects are textured, the scene is lit, and the animation is rendered to create the final sequence of images.

Depending on the type of production, the last phase of the workflow will involve some kind of post-production process. In film and television, this might include using compositing software to combine live-action footage shots with the elements rendered from Maya. In a video game production, post-production might involve the programming of the game within a game engine.

Let's look at some specific workflows within the production process to learn more about them.

Preproduction

Preproduction is not necessarily a workflow particular to Maya, but it is one of the most important phases of any 3D production workflow. Even in a world of advanced technology, a 3D project should begin on pencil and paper. Storyboarding, conceptual sketches, and character design are truly essential to any successful 3D project.

> _NOTE_   _**Remember that the object of your animation is to tell a story visually. Use traditional filmmaking techniques to enhance your idea. Color, lighting, camera angles, and composition are all important elements that help to convey a mood. Plan to incorporate these elements into your shots so that every frame tells a story of its own.**_

For *Star Wars: Episode 1*, George Lucas and his team of computer graphics artists at JAK Films pioneered the idea of using computers to previsualize scenes in the movie once the storyboards were complete. The resulting *animatics* enabled Lucas to use basic geometry, animation, and lighting to set up and experiment with the shots that the storyboard artists had conceived. It also provided the perfect channel for communication with the visual effects artists at Industrial Light & Magic. These artists not only received the drawn storyboards, but they had an idea of exactly how the objects and the camera moved though the scenes. Since then, previsualization has become popular in the film industry as a method for designing complicated shots involving effects. Even as a solo artist, "previz" can help you quickly figure out if your shot, or sequence of shots, is working.

> _NOTE_   *Many books are available to aid you in designing your animations through a series of shots. One in particular,* Film Directing Shot by Shot, *by Steven D. Katz (Michael Wiese Productions, 1991), is full of information about previsualization and visual storytelling techniques. You can also visit http://www.thestoryboardartist.com for more information on storyboarding.*

Modeling

Before you can begin animating, you need to have created objects to animate. Modeling is the process of building the characters, props, and environments in the scene. These objects are constructed from 3D geometrical surfaces so that they can be rotated around and viewed from all angles. One of the biggest advantages of using 3D over more traditional 2D techniques for animation is that the 3D objects, a character for example, needs to be built only once, while a character created in 2D needs to be re-created for every frame of the animation. Figure 1-1 shows an example of a 3D model in its *wireframe* view.

In terms of workflow, the most important thing for you to know before you begin is how much of the model will be seen in the animation and how close the camera will get to the model. It is important that you figure out how a model will be used in the project in the preproduction process. For example, spending a week to model a detailed cell phone that will only be seen sticking out of someone's pocket from a distance is a waste of time. If you plan ahead in preproduction, you can avoid spending time on unimportant details and focus on the important ones.

Once you have determined the types of scenes and camera shots that will be needed for a model, you then need to consider what will happen with the model downstream. In the case of a character, its geometry must be modeled so that it will *deform*, or bend, properly when it is animated. In most cases, the geometry must be complete before the texture coordinates, known as *UV coordinates*, are laid out for texture mapping. The model's complexity will also have a direct affect on the amount of time it takes to render.

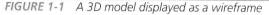

FIGURE 1-1   *A 3D model displayed as a wireframe*

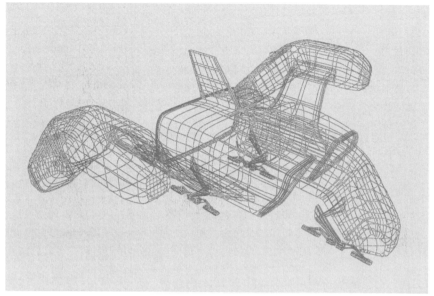

Maya offers three different modeling toolsets: NURBS (Non-Uniform Rational B-Splines), polygonal, and subdivision surface modeling. Chapters 3, 4, 5, and 6 cover these toolsets and demonstrate work flows for using them.

Character Setup

Character setup, also called *rigging,* is the process of preparing a character so that it can be animated. Typically, you begin by creating a skeleton that matches the scale and features of a model. For example, the character's hip joint needs to be placed at the hip, the knee joint at the knee, the ankle joint at the ankle, and so on. Figure 1-2 shows an example of a rig for a humanoid character.

Control objects are created and connected to the skeleton. These controls will enable the animator to move and pose the skeleton intuitively, simlilar to the controls on a puppet. A properly rigged skeleton can be handed off to an animator who might not be technically proficient but will still be able to operate the skeleton, making the animation process go much faster.

FIGURE 1-2   *A typical character rig*

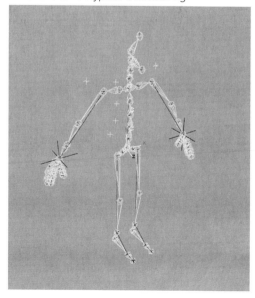

Ultimately, you bind on skin to the character—or you connect the skeleton to the character's model so that when a joint rotates, the geometry will bend, or deform, with it. Some of the more complicated character rigs even use a system of muscles that drive the skin models. This creates deformations that are more physically correct.

You will learn techniques for character rigging in Chapters 8 through 11.

Animation

Animation workflow is what will finally let your character zip through time and space. Effective animation is achieved through orderly *keyframing*—the process of recording an object's placement, rotation, scale, shape, and such in a specific time.

The most efficient animation workflow is using what is known as a *block and refine* technique. The first pass at the animation should attempt to do nothing more than position the character in some of its key poses over the duration of the scene. This pass should attempt to establish the timing of each pose or position in the scene. At this point, usually no keyframe *interpolation* is involved—that is, no movement exists to transition between the keyframes, and the character merely pops into position, holds, and then pops into the next pose.

During the next few passes, you block out some of the secondary poses that fall between those you set in the previous pass. Once all of the significant poses have been set, interpolation is turned on and the process of refining the motion between these poses begins. Because this process can take a long time, much patience is required as you do pass after pass, adding more and more detail to the motion.

> _TIP_   **To help make sure your animations are lifelike, act out the animation yourself and time the action using a stopwatch. Better yet, videotape yourself for reference.**

Chapter 7 will introduce you to some basic animation techniques on simple objects. You will then apply these techniques to a character in Chapter 12.

Shading and Texturing

Shading and texturing is the process that adds realistic or stylized surface elements to your models; otherwise, they would all render out to be the same textureless, flat color. For every surface or group of surfaces, a material is created that determines the surface's characteristics—what color, or how transparent, shiny, bumpy, or reflective it is. 3D artists usually say that the material determines how the object *shades*. Figure 1-3 shows a teapot that has been set up to reflect its environment.

Bitmapped images, such as those that you might create in an external image editing or illustration program such as Adobe Photoshop, can be used to control the various shading characteristics. In most cases, much of the finer detail of an object's surface can be added via these texture maps. The creases in skin or the panels on an airplane's wing are usually added with texture maps.

Chapter 13 will teach you the basics of shading and texturing. In Chapter 14, these techniques will be put into practice in two tutorials.

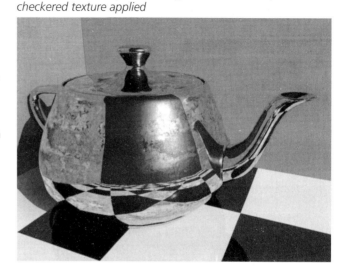

FIGURE 1-3   *A teapot reflecting the wall and floor, with a checkered texture applied*

Lighting and Rendering

The final piece of the 3D production process is the lighting and rendering of the scene. Lights are added and used in Maya just as they might be in the real world. In filmmaking, lights are used not just to illuminate the scene, but also to create or enhance a mood. This is done though the placement, intensity, and color of the lights used.

To see the results of your lighting, you must first render the scene. *Rendering* is the process of creating an image from all of this 3D data. For a single frame, the rendering engine draws each pixel by finding an object in front of the camera and drawing it based on the direction of the surface, the surface characteristics, and the lighting information. Once the scene has been set up and the rendering settings determined, the rendering process does not involve anymore input from the user. Instead, it is accomplished by the computer and can take a few seconds to hours— or days—to render, depending on the complexity of the scene.

Figure 1-4 shows a rendered scene that has been lit with various types of lights. While some lights are set up simply to illuminate the scene overall, you will also notice that some of the light beams are visible because they have been rendered with a fog effect. You will learn all about how to set up and use all kinds of lights in Chapters 13, 14, and 16.

Post-Production

After every frame of the animation has been rendered, the footage will usually be brought into another software package so that the 3D elements can be combined with other elements shot on video or film. It is also common for the 3D elements in the scene to be rendered separately.

FIGURE 1-4   *A rendered scene that uses lights with fog*

For example, each character might be rendered as a separate element and then integrated at the *compositing* stage.

In some cases, the various surface characteristics are rendered in a separate pass for each object. This gives the compositor absolute control over the entire image. With this method, the reflectivity, shininess, and color can be changed easily without the artist having to go back and correct it in 3D and re-render the image. We will explore these techniques in Chapters 20 and 21.

Now that you have an idea of the different workflows involved in the 3D production process, you should be able to map out a good plan for how to attack your animation in the most efficient and least frustrating way possible.

> NOTE   *Keep in mind that you will make mistakes while you are learning the workflow process. Hopefully, though, by practicing the methods taught in this book, your mistakes will be minimal and you can concentrate on the art.*

Nodes, Attributes, and Dependencies

If you are a race car driver, you may not be expected to know how to build a car from scratch, but you should at least have a good understanding of how your car works. Knowing how the gearbox works will help you shift gears more efficiently while you are racing. A Maya user should approach Maya in the same way. The Maya user interface is designed so that it is possible for someone to use it to complete a project without knowing much about what's going on "under the hood." However, to harness its power and work more efficiently, you should understand the basics of how Maya works.

If you've read the documentation for Maya, or you've read about it on the Internet, you might be familiar with a Maya scene being described as "a collection of nodes with attributes that are connected." But what does this mean, exactly?

A *node* is the basic building block for anything in Maya. A node contains *attributes,* or *channels,* that are specific to that particular node. Many node types are used in Maya, including shape nodes, transform nodes, and nodes that contain algorithms for certain operations. To understand this better, let's look at what nodes make up a NURBS sphere. (NURBS is a type of geometry in Maya where the surface is defined mathematically. This results in an infinitely smooth surface, regardless of how curvy it is.)

Any object in Maya, be it a piece of geometry, a texture map, a light, or even an operation, can be defined in one or a group of nodes. Figure 1-5 shows the nodes that make up a primitive NURBS sphere in Maya, as displayed in Maya's Hypergraph. The Hypergraph window shows a graphical representation of the relationship among objects. In Figure 1-5, the Hypergraph is graphing the flow of the connected attributes between the nodes that make up this sphere. Although this might not make much sense to you now, you'll learn more about using Hypergraph in almost all of the chapters in this book. For now, you should know that the lines that appear between nodes show that the attributes of the nodes are connected, and the arrows show the direction of these connections. In other words, in this example, Maya handles the information contained in the first node, makeNurbSphere1, and outputs that information though an attribute that is connected to an input attribute on the next node, nurbsSphereShape1. It then moves to the initialShadingGroup node and processes the attributes contained within it to display the final shape on your computer screen.

All the information about the sphere's size, *sweep* angle (where it begins and ends), and resolution is stored in unique *attributes* as some value inside the makeNurbSphere1 node. The values for these attributes can be an integer (a whole number), a float (a decimal), a Boolean (on or off), or a string (text). You as the user can edit the values for the attributes on this node in Hypergraph to modify its size and shape.

The *input* attributes are *output* from the makeNurbSphere1 node's output surface attribute. This attribute from the makeNurbSphere1 node feeds into the nurbsSphereShape1 node's create attribute. The nurbsSphereShape1 node contains attributes that deal mostly with how the rendering engine will interpret this shape at render time. For example, the

FIGURE 1-5 *Maya's Hypergraph displaying the nodes that make up a NURBS sphere*

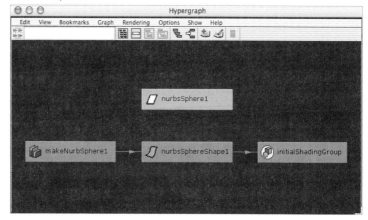

shape node contains attributes that determine whether the object will cast a shadow, receive a shadow, cast a reflection, or will even be rendered at all.

Now that Maya knows what the shape is, it needs to know how the object will shade so that it can render it properly. The initialShadingGroup node takes the output from the shape node and the output from the material node to decide the surface properties for this sphere. It then outputs that information, along with any other information based on its own attributes, and feeds the sphere into the render partition—where the information from the shading group and the lights are calculated together for the renderer to do its job. (The renderPartition node is not displayed in Figure 1-5.)

A node that has another node feeding into it (as indicated by the lines in the Hypergraph) has a relationship known as a *dependency*. As we continue to perform more operations on the shape node and modify it further, Maya creates another node "on top" of the shape node for that operation (see the section "Node Hierarchies" to see how this works). However, because this topmost node is still dependent on all of the nodes that are feeding into it, you could say that the node on top has *history*.

Transform Nodes

While literally hundreds of types of nodes are available in Maya, one in particular is worth noting here. This is the *transform node*, which contains attributes whose values determine the translation (position), rotation, scale, and visibility of the objects connected to it.

When an object is transformed—that is, moved, rotated, or scaled—the transformation occurs from the object's *pivot* point. By default, this pivot point is at the center of an object's *bounding box*, an invisible cube that is scaled to hold the volume of the object. In the case of a wheel on a car, the pivot point is at the center and the wheel rotates in one axis around that point. However, in many instances, you will want to edit the position of that pivot point, since many objects don't rotate exactly around their centers. For example, consider the Earth rotating around the sun: the pivot point for the Earth's orbit would be at the center of the sun. If you were to set this up in Maya, as we will do in Chapter 2, you would need to move the pivot point from the center of the Earth sphere to the center of the sun sphere, so that the Earth rotates around the sun instead of around its own center.

Node Hierarchies

If you refer back to Figure 1-5, you'll see that the *transform node*, named nurbsSphere1, does not display any lines connecting it to the other nodes in the sphere's network. The reason that the connections are displayed differently for this node is because none of the attributes from any of the other nodes shown in the Hypergraph are connected to the transform node. Instead, they share a different type of relationship, called a *hierarchical* relationship. In Figure 1-5, the transform node nurbsSphere1 is higher in the *hierarchy* than the three nodes below it.

When you work with 3D modeling and animation, you often use a hierarchy to create relationships among objects. For example, to have multiple objects follow one object's movement, you need to create a hierarchical relationship. Say you're working with a car object. You want to be able to select the car's body and have the wheels, doors, trunk, and hood all move with it. The car body object, in this case, would the *parent object,* and the other objects would be the *children* of the car body. The way children follow a parent is called *hierarchical transformation*.

This hierarchical concept is useful while grouping many objects into one model or for animating several objects efficiently. Figure 1-6 shows a simple hierarchy for some of the planets in our solar system. Notice how the Hypergraph is displaying the nodes in this example. No colored lines with arrows connect them. This is because we are viewing a hierarchy showing how several objects, or nodes, are grouped together in dependencies—not a single object's dependencies.

The structure of a hierarchy is known as a *tree,* because of its resemblance to that natural phe-nomenon—except it's upside down. The top, or base level, of the hierarchy is called the *root,* while the objects below the root hierarchy are called the *branches*. Sometimes you'll see the terms *parent* and *child* used to describe the hierarchy. Basically, the parent is the root, and the children are the branches.

Now, how does this relate to the discussion of nodes, attributes, and dependencies? Well, when you select an object in Maya, whether it is in the Hypergraph, the Outliner, or in the view window (all of these windows will be discussed in Chapter 2), you are actually selecting the object's transform node and all of its attributes and dependencies. And this is important to keep in mind as you're creating and animating objects.

FIGURE 1-6 *A group of objects are displayed as a hierarchy in Maya's Hypergraph window*

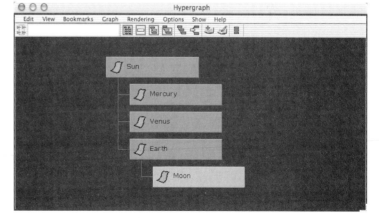

Summary

It is important that you remember the core concepts presented in this chapter as you read the rest of the book and work with Maya. They will help you understand how 3D animation is created and how Maya behaves. We'll take a look at the Maya interface in Chapter 2, where you will get an opportunity to apply some of the concepts discussed here.

The Maya
User Interface

Maya's interface hasn't changed much
since its conception, probably because the
development team at Alias created a functional
and easy-to-grasp user interface from the start.
In this chapter, we explore the Maya interface by
first learning the placement of the useful buttons
and windows and then by using them in a simple
step-by-step tutorial.

A Tour of the Maya Interface

Figure 2-1 shows Maya's default arrangement of the user interface elements. This arrangement is called a *layout*. Here is a quick tour of each element of this layout from top to bottom, left to right.

> NOTE *The exact location and style of the menu bar, title bar, and the minimize, maximize, and close buttons will differ between platforms. (Figure 2-1 is from a Mac.) Everything else within the Maya user interface will be the same whether you're using Windows or a Mac.*

The Title Bar

The title bar displays the Maya version number, the name of the scene you are working on, and the name of any object you have selected. It also includes standard minimize and maximize buttons and a close button.

FIGURE 2-1 *The Maya interface with the default Mac user interface*

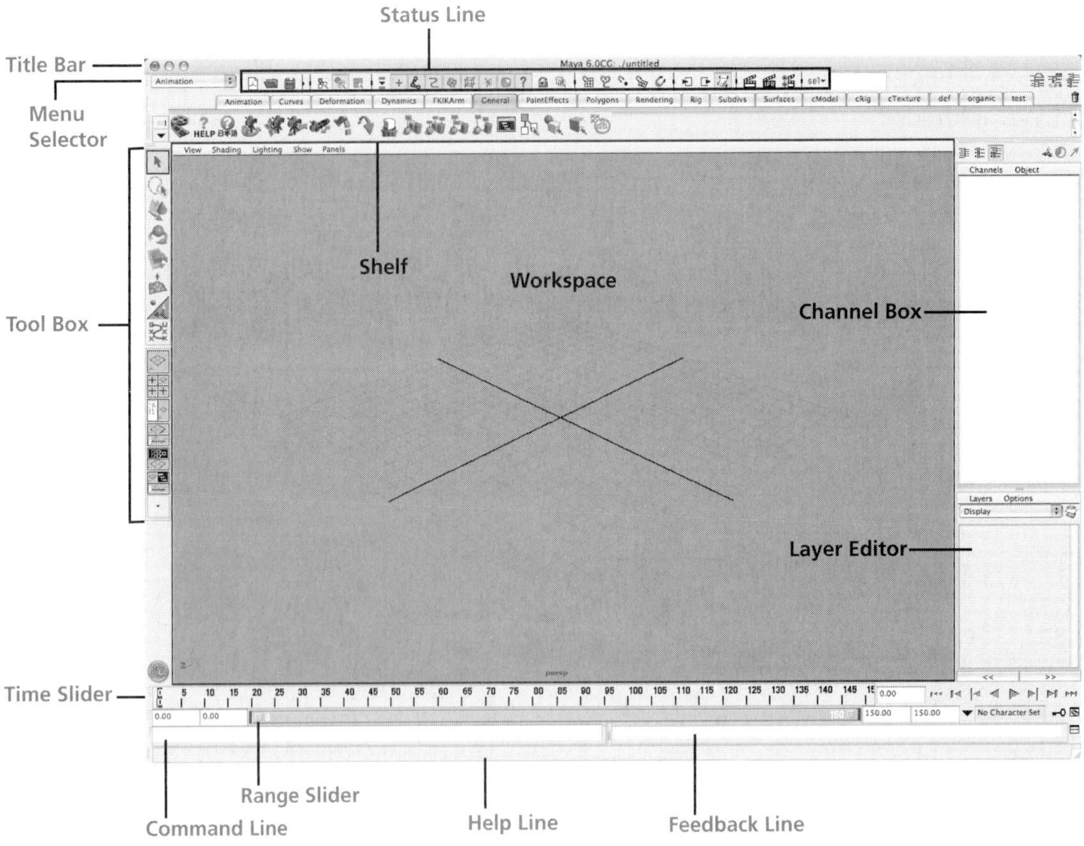

The Menu Bar

The menu bar lets you quickly access numerous functions in Maya via pull-down menus. The contents of each pull-down menu give you access to related tools, commands, and settings, and, when available, the menu lists the keyboard shortcuts for executing tools or commands.

Menu Sets

Because Maya has so many menus, they won't all fit in a single-row menu bar. The Maya interface solves this space problem by separating menus into modules, called *menu sets*, that let you see only the tools and commands related to your particular workflow.

Four menu sets are used in Maya Complete: Animation, Modeling, Dynamics, and Rendering. Six menu sets are used in Maya Unlimited: Animation, Modeling, Dynamics, Rendering, Cloth, and Maya Live. You can access these menu sets from the menu selector's drop-down list in the Status Line, as shown in the illustration. After you have selected a menu set, you will notice that some of the options in the menu bar will change according to the set you chose.

> TIP   *By using the Hotbox, discussed later in this chapter, you can view all the menus at once.*

You can also access these menu sets by pressing keyboard commands, or *hot keys*, as shown in Table 2-1.

You can also choose a menu set by pressing the H key while you hold down the left mouse button in the view window. A *marking menu* will appear, containing each menu set, as shown in the next illustration. You can choose the set you want by releasing the left mouse button when the cursor is over the appropriate set.

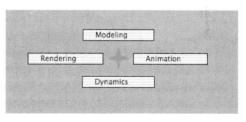

TABLE 2-1   Keyboard Commands for Menu Sets

HOT KEY	MENU SET
F2	Animation
F3	Modeling
F4	Dynamics
F5	Rendering
F6	Maya Live

> *NOTE* *Marking menus are used throughout the Maya interface. If you hold down a specific hot key and left-click in a window, or if you right-click anywhere in a window (without using a hot key), a marking menu will appear.*

Regardless of the menu sets you're using, the File, Edit, Modify, Create, Display, Window, and Help menu options will always appear in the menu bar. These items are not specific to any particular workflow. Instead, they give you access to many of the common editing commands found in most software packages (such as Cut, Copy, Paste, Save, and Close) and allow you to create new objects (the Create menu), modify these objects (the Modify menu), access different windows (the Window menu), and choose how objects are displayed in the view window (the Display menu).

Tools and Commands

Tools and commands are two different things in Maya. As you browse though Maya's menus, you'll notice that some of the items listed include the word *tool* and others do not. The differences between a *tool* and a *command* are subtle. For example, the Create menu includes a tool called the CV Curve Tool. When the tool is selected from the menu, Maya enters a mode in which that tool is active. In the case of the CV Curve tool, a control vertex is created each time you click your mouse button in the view window. To finish using the tool, you must press the ENTER (RETURN) key.

A command, on the other hand, can require some sort of input before it can be selected from a menu. The Edit | Duplicate command is a good example. Before you can select the Duplicate command from the Edit menu, you first must select an object or objects that you wish to duplicate. After the selections have been made, you can choose the command from the Edit menu and it is executed. The result, of course, is a duplicate of the selected object(s), and that's it—the operation executed by the Duplicate command did its job and you can move on to your next task. Some commands don't require any input—they simply create an object when they're executed. For example, the Create | Locator command simply creates a locator.

Tool Options and Command Settings

Another element that can be found next to some of the tools and commands in the menus is a rectangular box icon (❐). Selecting this icon will open either the Options window for a command or the Tool Settings window for tools. The Options window will always open as a floating window. Here you can modify the settings for the specified command and then execute it. Figure 2-2 shows the Duplicate Options window, where you would be able to specify how many duplicates should be created and how each duplicate should be moved, rotated, or scaled from the original position. To open this window, choose Edit | Duplicate ❐.

When the ❐ icon is selected for a tool, the Tool Settings window will open on the right side of the Workspace. This interface was designed to allow you to modify the tool's settings as you

FIGURE 2-2   The Duplicate Options window

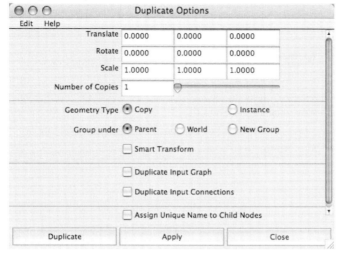

work with it. For example, Figure 2-3 shows the Tool Settings window for the 3D Paint tool (discussed in Chapter 15). This window opens when you choose Texturing | 3D Paint Tool ❐. When this tool is active and you are painting an object in the view window, you can easily adjust settings such as color and brush size.

> **NOTE**   **As we progress through this book, these menu items will be covered in detail as they relate to the toolsets discussed in each chapter.**

The Status Line

The Status Line includes valuable tools you can use while you are working, such as selection masks, snapping modes, and a rendering button. We will explore some of these tools and buttons in the tutorial later in this chapter. We'll use others throughout the book. Figure 2-4 shows arrangements of useful buttons on the Status Line.

FIGURE 2-3   The 3D Paint Tool Settings window

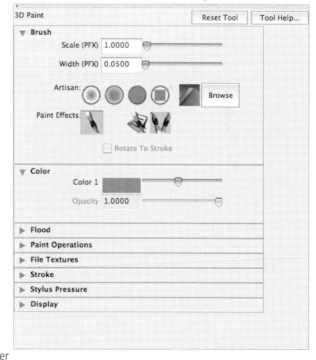

FIGURE 2-4   *The arrangement of buttons on the Status Line*

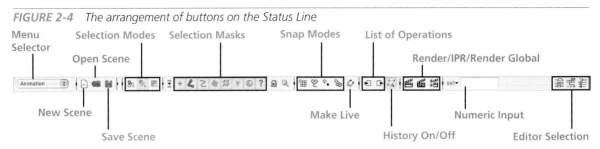

Probably the most widely used buttons in the Status Line are the Selection Modes and Selection Masks. The Selection Modes section gives you three different options for selecting objects in the view windows. From left to right, these are Select by Hierarchy, Select by Object Type, and Select by Component Type. Once one of these options is toggled on by clicking it in the Status Line, the Selection Masks section will update to display the relevant selection types for that mode.

Notice in Figure 2-4 that the middle Selection Mode button, Select by Object Type, is depressed. Therefore, the Selection Masks section displays a collection of buttons that have icons representing different object types. In this case, the selection types available for Select by Object type are (from left to right) Handles, Joints, Curves, Surfaces, Deformers, Particles, Rendering Nodes, and miscellaneous objects.

These selection modes and masks can make selecting objects in the view window much easier when the scene becomes crowded. For example, your scene may have hundreds of surfaces very close to one another with a curve tucked among them. Selecting that curve without also selecting a surface could be tricky. In such a case, you could click the Surfaces button in the Selection Masks section to disable surface selection. Now when you click the curve in the view window, you will be unable to select the surfaces, making it much easier to select just the curve.

The Shelf

The Shelf, located under the Status Line, contains buttons for accessing your most frequently used commands and tools. Figure 2-5 shows the buttons and tabs located on the Shelf. These buttons have been organized into tabs respective to certain workflows. Choosing a tab will display Shelf items in that tab. By clicking a button on the Shelf, you can execute commands or launch tools without having to choose them from a menu. As you become more experienced in Maya, you will no doubt want to customize your Shelf with tools or commands that execute custom settings.

FIGURE 2-5   *The buttons and tabs on the Shelf*

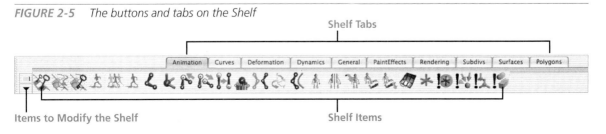

If you find that a command or tool is available from the menu bar but it is not on a Shelf, you can add it to the Shelf. Hold down the SHIFT-CTRL (SHIFT-CONTROL) keys and then select the command or tool that you want to add from the menu in the menu bar. As soon as you release the mouse button, the item you selected will be added to the Shelf.

You can create a new Shelf, delete the currently selected Shelf, load a Shelf from your hard disk, or open the Shelf Editor by clicking the little black arrow to the left of the Shelf. This opens a list of items that modify the shelf. Using these options, you can organize Shelf buttons in individual tabs, such as a Modeling tab, Animation tab, Lighting tab, and so on, to accommodate different workflows.

We will make custom Shelf buttons throughout many chapters in this book. For a detailed example, see Chapter 4.

The Tool Box

The tool box, shown in Figure 2-6, contains shortcuts to the most commonly used tools for all workflows.

The first two tools in the tool box are the basic *selection* tools. You can select an object in the view window by clicking the Selection tool and then clicking the object in the view window. To select multiple objects, you can either hold down the SHIFT key while clicking objects in the view window or choose the Lasso tool in the tool box and drag a selection around all of the objects that you want included in your selection.

The next three tools in the tool box are called *transform* tools—the Move, Rotate, and Scale tools. Select an object in the view window and then choose the tool from the tool box. Figure 2-7 shows a sphere that has been selected, and the Move tool is active. Notice that a *transform manipulator* appears at the sphere's pivot point. Three arrows extend from the manipulator tool: one red, one green, and one blue. By clicking and dragging the red, green, or blue arrow, you can constrain the sphere's movements to the X, Y, or Z axis, respectively. The Rotate and Scale tools have their own unique manipulators whose colors correspond to the same three axes. You will get plenty of practice using these tools in every chapter of this book.

The Soft Modification tool is new to Maya 6. This tool lets you quickly manipulate the shape of an object, similar to sculpting in clay. By clicking any object, you are able to move the manipulator and modify a region of the object. The range of the effect and the falloff can be adjusted in the tool's settings. We will cover this tool in great detail in Chapter 6.

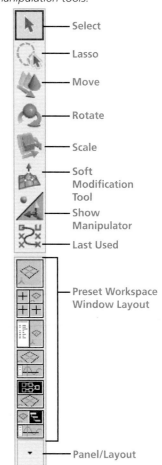

FIGURE 2-6 *The tool box contains basic selection and manipulation tools.*

Select

Lasso

Move

Rotate

Scale

Soft Modification Tool

Show Manipulator

Last Used

Preset Workspace Window Layout

Panel/Layout

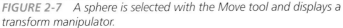

FIGURE 2-7   A sphere is selected with the Move tool and displays a transform manipulator.

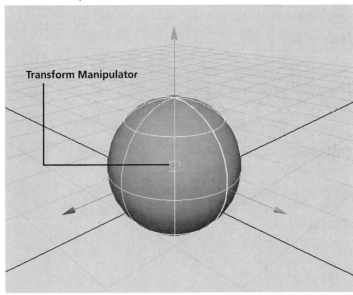

The Show Manipulator tool can be used interactively to edit the attributes of certain kinds of nodes. Its exact functionality depends on what is selected. A common use for the Show Manipulator tool is to place a spotlight and set its direction. If a light is created and the Show Manipulator tool is chosen, two transform manipulators will show up in the view windows: one to control the position of the light and the other to control the light's target. We will use the Show Manipulator tool to edit attributes of various types of nodes throughout this book.

Continuing down the tool box is a varying option that will show the last tool used. This can be useful when you are using a tool repeatedly. It saves you from having to select the tool from the menu or from the Shelf.

The last part of the tool box contains shortcut buttons to access various layouts for the Workspace. These buttons activate common preset layouts. Since we have not yet discussed all of the windows that are available in these layouts, we won't go into specifics here. However, you will be directed to use some of these buttons to change the layouts throughout many tutorials in this book.

The Workspace

The Workspace is composed of one or more *view panels* used to access different parts of the user interface. By default, only one panel is displayed when you start up Maya. This is the Perspective view and is shown back in Figure 2-1. Take a look at Figure 2-8. This shows the Maya window with three panels loaded: the Perspective view, the Hypergraph, and the Graph Editor. Use of these panels is discussed later in this chapter in the tutorial section.

The Channel Box

You should remember from Chapter 1 that attributes of nodes are also referred to as *channels*. The Channel Box, shown in Figure 2-9, lets you view, edit, and keyframe all of the keyable attributes on any node of the object that is selected. A *keyable* attribute is an attribute that a

FIGURE 2-8   *The Maya window with a three-panel layout containing (top left) the Perspective view, (top right) the Hypergraph, and (bottom) the Graph Editor*

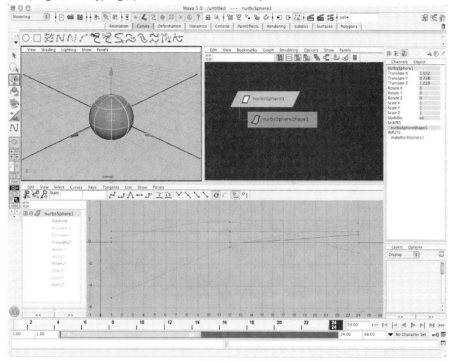

keyframe can set to enable that attribute to be animated. You will soon learn that most nodes contain a lot more attributes than those displayed in the Channel Box. However, by default, only certain attributes are set up to be animatable.

> **NOTE**   *Non-keyable attributes can be edited in the Attribute Editor, which is discussed later in the chapter. In Chapter 7, you will learn how to edit a node's attributes in the Channel Control window to make it keyable or non-keyable.*

You can edit the values for the attributes in the Channel Box in two ways. You can click in the field containing the current value, type in a new value, and press ENTER (RETURN). Or you can click the attribute's name in the Channel Box to highlight it, and then middle-mouse-button-drag (*MMD-drag* from here on) anywhere in the view window. The value will change as if it were being controlled by an invisible slider.

FIGURE 2-9   *The Channel Box displays the attributes for the object called nurbsSphere1.*

Channels	Object
nurbsSphere1	
Translate X	0
Translate Y	1
Translate Z	0
Rotate X	4
Rotate Y	5
Rotate Z	4
Scale X	1
Scale Y	2
Scale Z	1
Visibility	on
SHAPES	
nurbsSphereShape1	
INPUTS	
makeNurbSphere1	
Radius	1
Start Sweep	0
End Sweep	360
Degree	Cubic ▼
Sections	8
Spans	4
Height Ratio	2

The Layer Editor

Just below the Channel Box is the Layer Editor, shown in Figure 2-10. You can use the Layer Editor to organize your scene by grouping objects into layers. Layering provides you with a quick and easy way to hide or show groups of objects by making a layer invisible or visible,

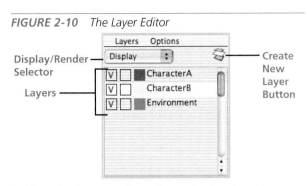

FIGURE 2-10   The Layer Editor

or by making it renderable or unrenderable. What happens depends on whether the objects are grouped to a *display* layer or to a *render* layer.

Click the Create New Layer button in the Layer Editor to create a new layer. Each layer is named and listed in the Layer Editor. Left-click the boxes to the left of the layer name to turn on or off the visibility of the layer (V) and to cycle through Selectable (the blank box), which makes the layer selectable; Template (T), in which the object can be seen as a wireframe and is not selectable; and Reference (R), in which the object can be seen as shaded and can be rendered but is not selectable.

You can double-click a layer in this list to bring up the layer Properties window. This window lets you rename the layer and assign a color to it. When a color is assigned to a layer, the objects in that layer will display in that color in the view window. This does not, however, affect the color of any geometric surfaces in the view window.

We will use display layers to group geometric types when we model the cell phone and space-ship in Chapter 4.

The Time Slider and the Range Slider

Figure 2-11 shows both the Time Slider and Range Slider, along with other controls located along the bottom of the Maya Workspace window. You can scrub through an animation by clicking and dragging the Time Slider along the timeline. To play the animation forward or in reverse, you can use the VCR-like playback controls (the usual arrow buttons).

FIGURE 2-11   The controls along the bottom of the interface

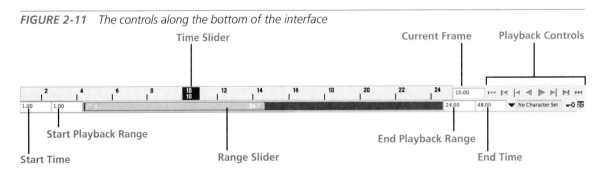

You can set the total length of the animation by keying in the start and end times in their respective fields. The Range Slider sets the range of frames that will be displayed in the Time Slider. Use the Range Slider to limit how much of the total animation time you want to play back. This is especially helpful when you want to work on a small section of a longer animation.

The Command Line and Script Editor Button

You use the command line near the bottom of the Maya window, shown next, to type in Maya Embedded Language (MEL) commands. If you are more of a programmer type than an artist type, the command line is a real plus. You type the commands on the left side, and any error message or feedback is displayed at the right. The tiny box icon to the right of the feedback line is the Script Editor button, which lets you create and edit long MEL scripts. The Script Editor also shows all the errors and warnings for a particular piece of script.

Command Line　　　　　　　Feedback Line　　　　　　Script Editor

> *NOTE*　**Basic MEL scripting is discussed in the appendix.**

The Help Line

The light-gray bar across the bottom of the Maya window is the help line, shown next. If you move your mouse cursor around Maya's user interface, the help line displays what each part of interface does. When you use actions and tools, the help line will tell you which tool you are using and what you should do next.

Move Tool: Use manipulator to move object(s). Use edit mode to change pivot (HOME).　Ctrl+LMB to move perpendicular.

The Hotbox

If you hold down the SPACEBAR, the Hotbox will open, as shown in Figure 2-12. The Hotbox is a group of menus that provides an easy-to-access interface that you can place anywhere on your screen. The Hotbox is highly customizable to meet your particular needs. You can click Hotbox Controls in the Hotbox and then choose Show All to show all the menus available in Maya at once.

Because you can potentially access all of Maya's tools and commands from the Hotbox, you could conceivably hide all of the other interface elements by choosing Display | UI Elements and disabling all of the checked items in that list. This means that you could display just the Workspace and nothing else. We won't be doing that in this book, but if you are short on screen real estate, it might be helpful to hide your menus and anything else you don't need and access them through the Hotbox instead.

FIGURE 2-12   *The Hotbox is useful for accessing all the menus quickly.*

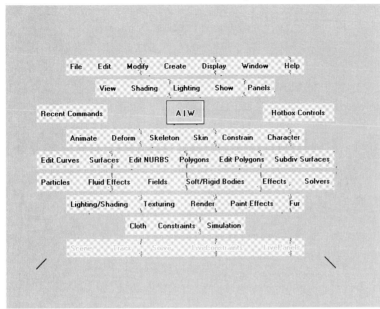

Tutorial: Working with the Maya Interface

Now that you have some idea of where helpful tools, buttons, boxes, and bars are located in the interface, it's time to start a project and put them to use. Here's a small exercise you can use to practice working with the user interface.

In this tutorial, we create a scene that contains three NURBS spheres that represent the Sun, the Earth, and the Moon. We will create these objects and edit attributes on their transform nodes to place them in the scene. Next, we will group these objects together in a hierarchy and animate them. After that, we will create some materials for these objects and edit their colors. Finally, we'll set up lighting and render the animation.

As you work through this tutorial, remember that its real purpose is to let you practice using the interface. Don't get hung up on the specifics of keyframing the animation or editing the materials. It is more important that you pay attention to general concepts, such as where the various elements are located and how they can be used. This tutorial includes the following aspects of working with Maya:

- How to create projects and manage files
- How to use the Workspace window
- How to work with interface elements
- How to use the transform manipulators to edit objects' transform attributes

Open Maya and Set Up a Project

A *project* is an assemblage of folders and subfolders that are set up on your hard drive to organize you Maya projects. It is likely that your Maya project will contain other files in addition to your Maya scene file, such as texture maps or cached animation data. It is therefore helpful for

each project if you first set up a directory that contains subdirectories for all
of the different elements the project
includes. Fortunately, setting up this
structure from Maya is easy—in fact,
Maya does it for you.

Let's start a new project.

1. Launch Maya, and choose
File | Project | New. Figure 2-13
shows the New Project window.

2. Type in a name for your project.
For this example, enter
firstProject.

3. Set the Location where you
want to save your Maya
projects. You can type in the
exact path or click the Browse
button and navigate to the
folder in which you want to
save your project. The default
path will be in a Maya directory in your user directory.
This is generally a good place to store all of your Maya projects.

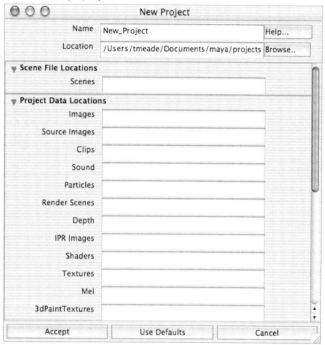

FIGURE 2-13 *The New Project window is where you start work on a new Maya project.*

4. Click the Use Defaults button at the bottom of the window. For this project, we'll be
using the predefined folder names assigned automatically by Maya. However, if you
want to customize the names of these directories, you can type in a name for each
folder in the text fields under Scene File Locations and Project Data Locations.

5. Click the Accept button to create the project.

After you create the project, the project folder will appear in the location you chose in step 3.
Figure 2-14 shows our firstProject folder in the default location. To open this window, choose
File | Project | Set. Highlight the project folder you want to access and click Choose. Now, as you
save your scene, Maya will automatically place the scene file in the scenes directory inside the
firstProject directory.

> *TIP It's a good idea to make a habit of creating a project folder whenever you
> start a new project. This will help you keep your project components intact.*

FIGURE 2-14   *The new project appears in the default location.*

Create and Place Geometry

Now we'll create some objects and place them in the scene using some of the transform tools.

NOTE   *You'll learn how to manipulate or view objects in the view window so that you can zoom in on objects and orbit around the scene. Since these are some of the most common actions you will use in every project, Maya offers some keyboard shortcuts to access them quickly. These will be discussed in various sections throughout the rest of this chapter.*

1.   To create a NURBS sphere object from the menu bar, choose Create | NURBS Primitives | Sphere. A sphere will appear at the origin of your scene in the view window.

2.   Currently, this object is named nurbsSphere1. Let's rename it to make sure that our project is well organized. Look on the right side of the Maya window and find the Channel Box. The first line in the Channel Box, nurbsSphere1, should be highlighted in gray. This is the name of the object's transform node. Click in that field and type in **Sun**. Then press ENTER (RETURN). The node will now be named Sun, as shown in the following illustration, and Maya will update the shape node name to SunShape.

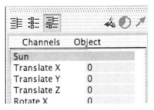

3.   The Sun model will remain at the origin of the scene, just as the real sun sits at the center of our solar system. However, we will scale it up in all directions to make it larger. With the Sun still selected in the view window, choose the Scale tool in the tool box by clicking it. The scale manipulator will appear in the view window, extending from the pivot point at the center of the sphere.

4.   Click-and-drag the light-blue cube at the center of the manipulator. Dragging your mouse to the right will uniformly increase the scale values in X, Y, and Z. Watch the scale values in the Channel Box change as you drag the manipulator. Now scale the Sun object to 3 units in X, Y, and Z. When you see the scale values reach 3 in the Channel Box, let go of your mouse. You have successfully edited the scale for this object interactively with the manipulator.

5. In the Channel Box, you will also see a node called SunShape, and underneath that will be a field named Inputs. This contains a list of all of the nodes that are connected to the input attributes of this shape node. All of the inputs into the SunShape node will be shown here, with the last one—that is, the one directly connected to the SunShape node—listed at the top. In this case, only one input node is connected to the SunShape node, and it is called makeNurbSphere1. (Refer to the "Nodes, Attributes, and Dependencies" section of Chapter 1 for more information on these nodes.) Select the makeNurbSphere1 node in the Channel Box, and all of the keyable attributes for this node will appear in a list.

Using the Hypergraph Window

The Hypergraph window, shown in Figure 2-15, can display all of the nodes in a Maya scene and depict how they are related.

As mentioned in Chapter 1, nodes can share two different relationships: a dependent relationship, when the attributes are connected, and a hierarchical relationship, when the transform nodes are grouped. The Hypergraph can display the scene to show either of these two relationships. By default, the Hypergraph will display the scene as a hierarchy. If you want to see the dependencies for any object shown in the hierarchical view, you can select the object and click the Input and Output Connections tool in the Hypergraph's toolbar. When you're attempting to edit

FIGURE 2-15   The Hypergraph window

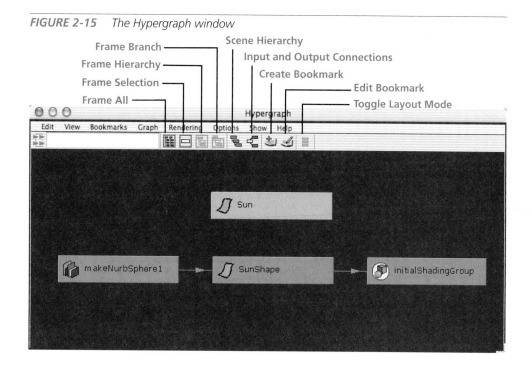

the attributes of certain nodes in a scene, the Hypergraph provides an easy way to select specific nodes directly. Let's open the Hypergraph and view the dependencies on the Sun (the SunShape node).

1. To open the Hypergraph, choose Window | Hypergraph. The Hypergraph will appear in its own separate floating window.

2. When you initially open the Hypergraph, you will see a rectangular block called Sun. This is the Sun object's transform node. To view its dependencies, click the Input and Output Connections icon in the Hypergraph's toolbar. Now all three nodes that make up the Sun object will appear with lines connecting the nodes.

3. Select the makeNurbSphere1 node. Notice that after you select a node, its attributes are listed in the Channel Box.

4. While we could edit some of these attributes to make only a half sphere or change its resolution, the existing, default attributes will work fine for our Sun. Since we no longer need the information here to determine the current shape of our Sun, we can delete the Sun object's history. This will get rid of all of the SunShape node's dependencies. With the makeNurbSphere1 node selected, choose Edit | Delete By Type | History. Notice that the makeNurbSphere1 node is no longer listed in the Inputs section in the Channel Box. At this point, the SunShape node has no dependencies. You can close the Hypergraph window.

Now let's create the Earth and the Moon. We could do this by creating another two spheres from the Create menu, but since we really don't need to modify the makeNurbSphere1 node, we can just duplicate the Sun, move it, scale it, and rename it.

1. To duplicate the Sun, first select it in the view window and choose Edit | Duplicate. (You can also press the shortcut, CTRL-D [COMMAND-D], on your keyboard.) At first, you may not notice anything different in your view window; don't worry—this is because the duplicate is sitting right on top of the original. Once you move the duplicate, you will see that two identical spheres now appear in the scene.

2. Choose the Move tool in the tool box. You will notice that the move manipulator appears in the view window and extends from the sphere's pivot point. Click-and-drag the red manipulator to move the sphere out along the X axis. You will see that you indeed have two separate sphere objects.

3. With the sphere copy still selected, go to the Channel Box and rename this object from nurbSphereCopy1 to **Earth**. Now duplicate the Earth and move the duplicate out along the X axis to separate it from the original. Name this third object **Moon**.

To place and scale these objects more precisely, we will change our Workspace to display some different views. We will change the layout of the Workspace to the Four View layout.

Using the Four View Layout

Keep your cursor on top of the Perspective view and quickly tap the SPACEBAR. The Workspace will now show the Four View layout, which includes the Top view, Perspective view, Front view, and Side view, as shown in Figure 2-16.

Let's take a moment to understand these view windows and navigate inside them. The window at the top right is the *Perspective* view. This view uses *perspective correction*, which works just like our eyes or a camera—that is, objects farther away from you look smaller than closer objects. Perspective view is good for visualizing how a final rendering will look, since that's how a rendering camera will see the scene. Moving counterclockwise from Perspective view is the Top, Front, and Side orthographic views.

Orthographic views (the Front, Top, and Side) have no perspective correction. If two objects of matching size appear, and one is placed "farther away" from the object in front, they both will appear to be the same size in an orthographic view. Orthographic views are good for analytically viewing your models and scenes. For example, you can compare object sizes, place objects, and check alignments in these views without accounting for the distortion caused by perspective correction.

FIGURE 2-16   Four view windows appear.

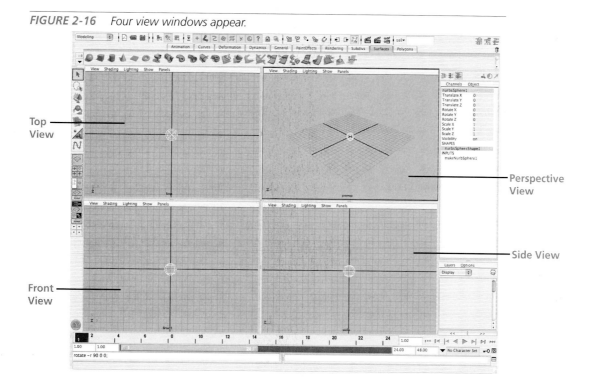

Top View

Front View

Perspective View

Side View

Maya's Cameras

As you look at your scene through one of the view windows, it is important to realize that you are actually looking through one of Maya's *cameras*. While cameras will be discussed in detail in Chapter 13, it is imperative that you learn right from the start how to manipulate your view as you look through them. The three most common tools used to manipulate a camera are Tumble, Track, and Dolly. The illustration here depicts these three actions as a camera that is viewing a cone object in the scene.

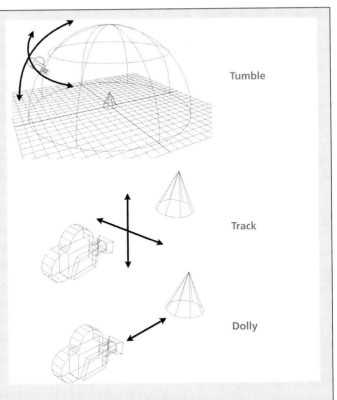

Tumble

Track

Dolly

The Tumble tool allows you to orbit, or rotate, around the camera's center of interest. This tool will work only in Perspective view, because, for example, if you were to tumble in the Front view, you would no longer be looking at the object's front—right? This tool can be accessed from the view window by choosing View | Camera Tools | Tumble Tool.

The Track tool will move, or *pan*, the camera from side to side or up and down. It can be accessed by choosing View | Camera Tools | Track Tool.

The Dolly tool moves toward or away from the center of interest. This tool can be accessed by choosing View | Camera Tools | Dolly Tool.

While these tools are all available from the view window's menu bar, you will probably find it much more efficient to use keyboard/mouse button combinations to access them. The following table describes the shortcuts for accessing these tools. (Note that the Macintosh actions appear in parentheses.)

ACTION	TOOL	FUNCTION
ALT-LMB-click (OPTION-LMB-click) and drag—Perspective view only	Tumble	View your scene from all around by orbiting
ALT-MMB-click (OPTION-MMB-click) and drag	Track	Move a view horizontally and vertically
ALT-LMB-click-MMB-click (OPTION-LMB-click-MMB-click) and drag; or ALT-RMB-click (OPTION-RMB-click) and drag	Dolly	Move the view forward and back

NOTE *This book uses the following shortcuts for button clicks and drags: LMB (left mouse button), RMB (right mouse button), and MMB (middle mouse button).*

Focus and Shade in the View Window

You'll often work with dozens, or even hundreds, of objects in a scene. Every time you want to adjust the view to move closer to, or *focus* on, one or more objects, you may find it cumbersome to use the Tumble, Track, or Dolly tool. Instead, you can use hot keys from the keyboard that let you focus on a selected object or group of objects. Focusing on objects will frame or fit them to the bounds of your view window. It also sets the camera's center of interest at the center of the selected object or objects. This feature is especially helpful when you select the Tumble tool in the Perspective view, because this tool orbits the camera around this center point.

The hot keys available for these focusing actions are shown here:

HOT KEY	FUNCTION
F	Focus on a selected object in a selected window.
SHIFT-F	Focus on a selected object in all windows.
A	Focus on all objects in a selected window.
SHIFT-A	Focus on all objects in all windows.

Let's focus on all of the objects in all of the windows of the view.

1. In the Perspective view, left-click to select a sphere. Hold down the SHIFT key and left-click the other spheres to add them to your selection.

2. Press the F key to focus on the spheres. The three spheres should zoom in closer to the camera.

3. Try tumbling the camera in Perspective view. Hold down the ALT (OPTION) key and LMB-drag. You'll notice that the camera is orbiting around the *center of the three objects*, not the scene's origin, as it was earlier.

Display Options

So far, you have been viewing these objects in *wireframe* mode. You can change the way a piece of geometry will display in a view window by setting the display options for that window. These options can be accessed via the View menu in the view window. You can also press a hot key to choose a view mode, as shown in Table 2-2. These display modes will activate your computer's hardware shading engine built into your video card and let you view the objects in your scene as shaded; shaded and textured; and shaded, textured, and lit.

These display options can also let you view certain types of geometry at different levels of detail. Both NURBS and subdivision surfaces, two of the three geometry types in Maya, are mathematical representations of surfaces. Although these geometric types are discussed in

TABLE 2-2   *Hot Keys for Display Modes*

HOT KEY	MODE
1	Rough, NURBS, and subdivision only
2	Medium
3	Fine
4	Wireframe
5	Smooth shade, default light
6	Smooth shade with hardware texturing, default light
7	Smooth shade with lighting, hardware rendering lights if you have created lights; otherwise objects shown in black

detail in Chapters 3, 4, and 6, for now, you should realize that these types of surfaces can be displayed at varying levels of detail. For example, if you have a lot of objects in your scene and are displaying them at their finest level, your computer's performance could suffer as you manipulate your camera or objects through the scene and your computer attempts to render the complex objects. Displaying surfaces in less detail will help to improve this performance. This is where changing view modes comes in particularly handy.

Spheres in rough, medium, fine, wireframe, smooth shade, and texturing modes are shown in Figure 2-17.

FIGURE 2-17   *Display options in Maya*

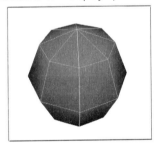
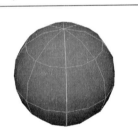

| Rough | Medium | Fine |

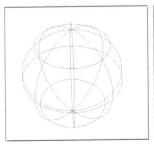

| Wireframe | Smooth Shade | Texturing |

NOTE *Be aware that when you use hot keys, any changes you make affect only the objects in the active window.*

Let's take a look at the spheres with a fine level of detail and smooth shaded in the Perspective view. Press 3 (which is the default detail level) to view the spheres at fine detail, and then press 5 to see them smooth shaded. This gives you a better idea of how these objects might look when rendered. But before we start rendering, let's work on placement and scale.

Transform Objects

Here we'll concentrate on the exact placement and scale of each object. We won't worry about the precise distances and proportions to make our planets match the scale of the solar system elements in our own universe. However, we do want to depict that the Sun is the largest object in our model solar system while the Moon is the smallest. We also want to arrange the objects so that the distance between the Sun and the Earth is greater than the distance between the Earth and the Moon.

While we already practiced moving and scaling in the first step of this tutorial, we used the transform tools in the tool box. To get you moving along faster, you should learn and use the hot keys to select the items in the tool box. From now on, try to get in the habit of using the hot keys to access these tools, as shown in Table 2-3.

TIP *You may find it helpful to rest your left hand on the keyboard with your pinky finger on top of the Q key and the rest of the fingers on your left hand on the W, E, and R keys. This will give your fingers quick access to all of these tools, regardless of where your cursor is located on the screen.*

TABLE 2-3 *Tool Box Hot Keys*

HOT KEY	TOOL
Q	Select tool
W	Move tool
E	Rotate tool
R	Scale tool
T	Manipulator tool
Y	Last used tool

1. To place our three planetary objects in the scene, we will use the Top view. Select the Earth object and press the W key to activate the Move tool.

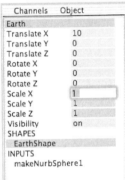

2. Let's place this object so that it sits at 10 units on the X axis. To make sure you place the object exactly at 10 units on X, turn on grid snapping to enable you to snap any object to specific grid units. On the Status Line, click the Snap to Grid button.

3. Now that grid snapping is enabled, return to the Top view and click inside the yellow box at the origin of the Manipulator tool. This will let you move the object in any direction relative to the axis of the current view. Since we are snapping to the grid, it should be easy not to slip the object out onto the Z axis.

4. Move the Earth object out in the X direction to 10 units. You can confirm that the Earth is at 10 units in X by checking the values in the Channel Box. The field labeled Translate X should show a value of 10.

5. Now scale the Earth object down so that it is smaller than that Sun. For the purpose of this tutorial, you will set the Earth's scale to 1 unit in X, Y, and Z. Instead of using the Manipulator tool, practice editing the scale attributes by entering values directly into the Channel Box. You could also enter the values separately in the fields one by one, but a quicker way is to click in one of the fields and LMB-drag down over all of the input fields in the Channel Box for Scale X, Y, and Z, as shown in the illustration.

Channels	Object
Earth	
Translate X	10
Translate Y	0
Translate Z	0
Rotate X	0
Rotate Y	0
Rotate Z	0
Scale X	1
Scale Y	1
Scale Z	1
Visibility	on
SHAPES	
EarthShape	
INPUTS	
makeNurbSphere1	

6. After the input fields are selected, a cursor will appear in the last field chosen. Type in a value of **1** and press ENTER (RETURN). Notice that all three fields will update to contain a value of *1*.

7. With the Sun and the Earth in place, focus your attention on the Moon. Use the techniques just discussed to edit the translate and scale attributes of the moon in the Channel Box. Place the moon at 13 units in X and enter a scale of **0.25** for is scale values in X, Y, and Z.

TIP   *The default size of the Manipulator tool is appropriate for most of applications. If you want to change the size of the Manipulator tool, however, you can do so by using hot keys. Pressing the minus key (–) will make the Manipulator tool appear smaller, and pressing the equal sign key (=) will make it larger. You can also fine-tune the appearance of the Manipulator tool. Open the Preferences window by choosing Window | Settings/Preference | Preferences; click Manipulators in the list on the left side. There you can change Global size (total size), Handle size, Line size, and other tool sizes for the Manipulator tool using sliders.*

Using Undo

Before we get too far, it's important that you know how to undo your operations. Knowing this will encourage you to experiment as much as you want, since you can make and undo mistakes with confidence.

You can press the undo hot key, CTRL-Z (COMMAND-Z), and the redo hot key, SHIFT-Z, to fix any mistakes.

The default setting for undo lets you undo only your past 10 actions. You can increase the number of actions you can undo in the Preferences window. Choose Window | Settings/ Preferences | Preferences. From the list on the left side, choose Undo. In the next dialog box, you can turn undo on or off or reset the limit of actions that you can undo. You can even set this number to Infinite—however, doing this could cause Maya to run slowly.

Create a Hierarchy

Now that the objects are placed and scaled, we need to group them together in a *hierarchy*. The Sun will be the *root* object, the Earth will be the *child* of the Sun, and the Moon will be a *child* of the Earth. To monitor this hierarchical relationship, we will view the hierarchy in the Hypergraph, but instead of opening the Hypergraph as a floating window from the Window menu, we will change the Side view in the Four View layout to display the Hypergraph instead.

Each of the four views displayed in the current layout is inside a *panel*. In our project, each of four panels displays one of the default views (see Figure 2-16). Any panel can be set to display another window, instead of having to open the window from the Window menu and view it as a floating window.

To change a panel's display, use the Panels menu in the selected panel's menu bar. In this case, we will set the panel that is currently displaying the Side view to display the Hypergraph instead.

1. Select the Side view panel, and choose Panels | Hypergraph. The Hypergraph will load into this panel and should include the three transform nodes named Sun, Earth, and Moon.

2. To parent the Earth to the Sun, MMB-drag the Earth node onto the Sun node. Notice that the Hypergraph now displays a line connecting these two nodes, which means that these two nodes are connected hierarchically.

3. Now use a different technique to link the Moon to the Earth. Move into the Top view panel. Select the Moon, and hold down the SHIFT key to select the Earth. (Pressing the SHIFT key as you click, or SHIFT-clicking, lets you add objects to your selection.)

4. With the Moon and Earth objects selected *in that order*, press the P key. If you look in the Hypergraph, you will see that the Moon is now parented to the Earth (that is, the Moon is a child of the Earth). The nodes in the Hypergraph should look like those in the illustration.

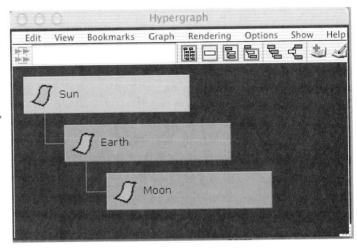

5. To see how these objects behave in their hierarchy, select the Sun in one of the view windows and choose the Rotate tool by pressing the E key. Click and drag the Rotate manipulator to rotate the Sun. Notice how the child objects behave. Press CTRL-Z (COMMAND-Z) to undo the rotation and return the objects to their original orientation.

Create a Group Node

While these objects are now arranged in the correct hierarchy, we need to make some additions so that they will animate properly. As you recall, back in Chapter 1 we discussed how every object's transform node transforms around its pivot. We know that our Earth spins around its own axis once every 24 hours. Using the current settings, we could animate this behavior now, because if you select the Earth and rotate it, it will rotate around its pivot, which is located at the Earth's center. However, we also need to account for the Earth's orbit around the Sun, so in this case, we need the Earth to pivot around the Sun. If the Earth is already using its own pivot point to rotate around its own axis, we cannot use the same pivot point for the orbit. We therefore need to create another pivot point between the Earth and the Sun and place it at the center of the Sun. The easiest way to do this is to group the Earth object to itself. This will parent the Earth to a new transform node with its own pivot.

A *group node* is simply a transform node with no shape object associated with it. Often, objects are grouped together for organizational purposes—to keep similar things grouped together. In our planetary project, we will use grouping to give us an extra transform node with an extra pivot point so we can accommodate our Earth's orbit around the Sun.

1. In Top view, select the Earth object and choose Edit | Group. This will create a group node called *group1* as the parent of the Earth. By default, a group's pivot point will always be at the origin of the scene—the 0,0,0 point. For the purpose of our Earth sphere, this is exactly where we want this pivot point to be located, since 0,0,0 also happens to be the location of the center of our Sun sphere.

2. With the group1 node still selected (use the Hypergraph to select it if you have accidentally unselected it), choose the Rotate tool and rotate the node around with its Rotate manipulator. The Earth and its child (the Moon) now rotate around the Sun.

3. In the Channel Box, change the new group name from group1 to **earthOrbit**.

4. You know that the Moon does not rotate around its own axis—it rotates around the Earth. Therefore, you need to edit the pivot point for the Moon's transform node so that it is at the center of the Earth. Press the W key to choose the Move tool. You will see that the transform manipulator is at the origin of the Moon.

5. Press the INSERT (HOME) key to edit the pivot. The transform manipulator in the view window changes, as shown in the illustration.

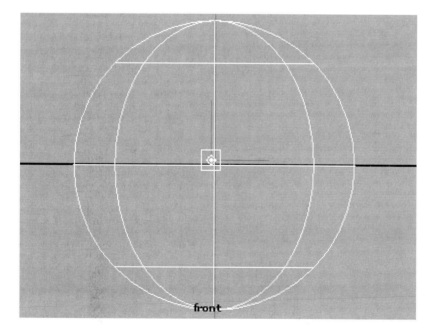

6. In the Status Line, turn on grid snapping. (You can also turn on grid snapping by holding down the X key while you move an object in the view window.)

7. Drag the pivot icon and snap it to the grid line at the center of the Earth.

8. Press the INSERT (HOME) key to return focus to the Move tool.

FIGURE 2-18 *The Hypergraph window displaying the final hierarchy of the objects*

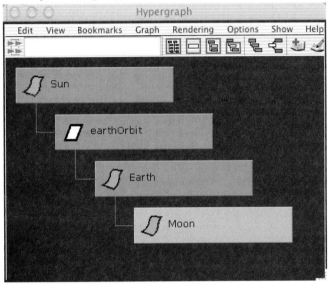

This will complete the setup of our hierarchy. The hierarchy displayed in the Hypergraph should now look like the one shown in Figure 2-18. Next, we will animate these objects.

Animate the Objects

Now we will animate these objects to resemble the behavior of the solar system. While they won't be *completely* accurate, we will attempt to animate the actions that occur during a one-month time span. What this means is that the Earth will rotate around the sun 30 degrees (360/12 = 30); the Earth will rotate around its own axis 30 times, once each day; and the Moon will rotate around the Earth 30 times (though this really happens every 27 days, but we'll round off to 30 just to make it easy).

Now we need to decide how long this animation will last. Since *30* seems to be the magic number we are using to determine orbits and rotations, let's say that the animation will be 30 seconds long. So how many frames is this? By default, Maya's frame rate (frames per second, or fps) is set to 24, which is the standard for film production. Since 30 seconds × 24 fps = 720 frames, we will set the range of the animation to 720 frames long. Let's get started.

1. Along the bottom of the Maya window you'll find the Range Slider, just below the Time Slider. Set the total animation time and Range Slider time to **720**.

2. Now you will set up the Workspace to use another layout that is especially useful for animating: the Outliner/Perspective layout. Choose the Outliner/ Perspective layout button in the tool box. The Workspace layout will change.

The Outliner
The Outliner, shown in Figure 2-19, is another way of displaying all of the objects in a scene. The objects listed here show the hierarchies in a way that's similar to that of a common Explorer (Windows) or Finder (Mac) view used to browse file directory structures. To access the Outliner, choose Window | Outliner. To unfold a hierarchy, click the plus sign (+) icon to the left of the object's name. If you want to view all of the branches and sub-branches of a hierarchy, hold down the SHIFT key and click the plus sign.

1. SHIFT-click the + icon to the left of the Sun node (and notice that the plus sign changes to a minus sign). This will expand the hierarchy to reveal all of the child objects, as shown in Figure 2-19.

2. Click and drag in the Outliner to select all the objects in the Sun's hierarchy. Be sure that the Time Slider is set to 1, and then choose Animate | Set Key. This will set a keyframe for all of the selected objects in the scene for their current positions at frame 1.

3. Move the current Time Slider to frame 720. You can do this by clicking and dragging the Time Slider to the end of the frames being displayed, or you can type **720** into the Current Frame field (see Figure 2-11).

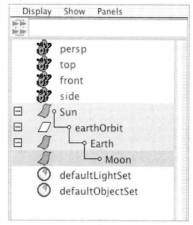

FIGURE 2-19   The Outliner lists the objects in the current scene.

4. In the Outliner, select the object named earthOrbit that you created earlier. Then, in the Channel Box, set the Rotate Y attribute to **30**.

5. Again, choose Animate | Set Key to set a keyframe for this position.

6. Now select the Earth object in the Outliner and set its Rotate Y attribute to **10800** (360 days × 30).

7. Instead of choosing Animate | Set Key, select the Rotate Y attribute in the Channel Box so that it is highlighted (make sure the actual attribute name is selected, not the value in the text field); then right-click the attribute. Choose Key Selected from the marking menu.

8. Click the Play button (see Figure 2-11). The animation will play back. The Earth will rotate around the Sun 30 degrees, or 1/12 of the way around, while it rotates around its own axis 30 times. The Moon will follow the rotation of its parent object (the Earth) and will appear to orbit the Earth.

Shading Objects

Materials give an object its shading properties. In other words, an object's material can control the color and shininess, or how reflective this object is. (We will discuss materials in depth in Chapters 13 and 14.) In this section, we will create some new materials and apply them to our geometry. Then we will edit the materials' attributes to change their colors. This section will introduce you to two new pieces of the interface: the Hypershade and the Attribute Editor.

The Hypershade Window

The Hypershade, shown in Figure 2-20, is where materials are created and edited in a Maya scene. You can open the Hypershade by choosing Window | Rendering Editors | Hypershade.

By default, the Hypershade window will contain three main sections: the Create Render Node menu, the upper tabs section, and the lower tabs section.

In the Create Render Node menu, you can browse and create various types of materials, textures, lights, cameras, and utilitlies. By clicking and holding on the arrow next to Create Materials, you can change this menu to show these other types of rendering nodes. The upper tabs section contains separate tabs for browsing any of the nodes in your current scene. By default, the Materials tab contains materials. Depending on what type of object is created in the scene, it will use the materials appropriate for it. By default, any geometry created in a scene will use the Lambert1 material until the user creates and assigns a new material.

The lower tabs section contains a Work Area tab (the Hypershade window) and another for a Shader Library. The work area is where you can view all of the connections on a selected material node. It is similar to the Hypergraph window, except that it is optimized for material editing in that the icons representing the node use pictorial representations, called *swatches,* in addition to their names. The Shader Library lets you browse though a collection of premade materials and texture maps that ship with Maya.

FIGURE 2-20   *The Hypershade window with the default layout*

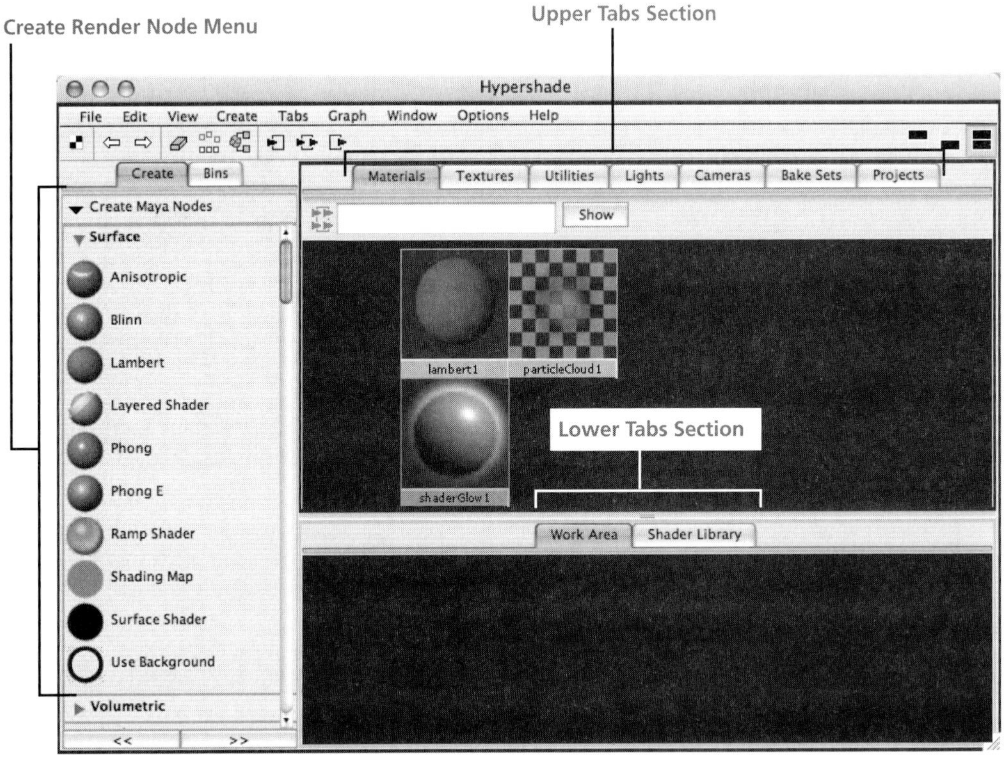

Let's create three new materials—one for each of our spherical elements. If you have opened the Hypershade, close it now. Instead of using the Hypershade in a floating window, we will modify the Workspace to display a two-panel view—one panel showing the Perspective view and another for the Hypershade window.

1. In the tool box, click the Hypershade/Perspective button to load the Workspace layout.

2. From the Create Render Node menu in the Hypershade window, click the icon labeled Lambert. This will create a new Lambert material. A Lambert swatch will appear in the Materials tab as well as in the Workspace and will be named Lambert2.

3. Select this material in the Materials tab, and rename it in the Channel Box to **mSun**. The *m* signifies that this node is a *material* node. Also, because we already have a node in our scene named Sun, we need to give this node a different name, since all nodes in a Maya scene must have a unique name. (This naming convention will be used throughout the rest of the book.)

4. Double-click the mSun material node in the Materials tab of the Hypershade window. This will automatically change the layout of the Maya window to display the Attribute Editor instead of the Channel Box.

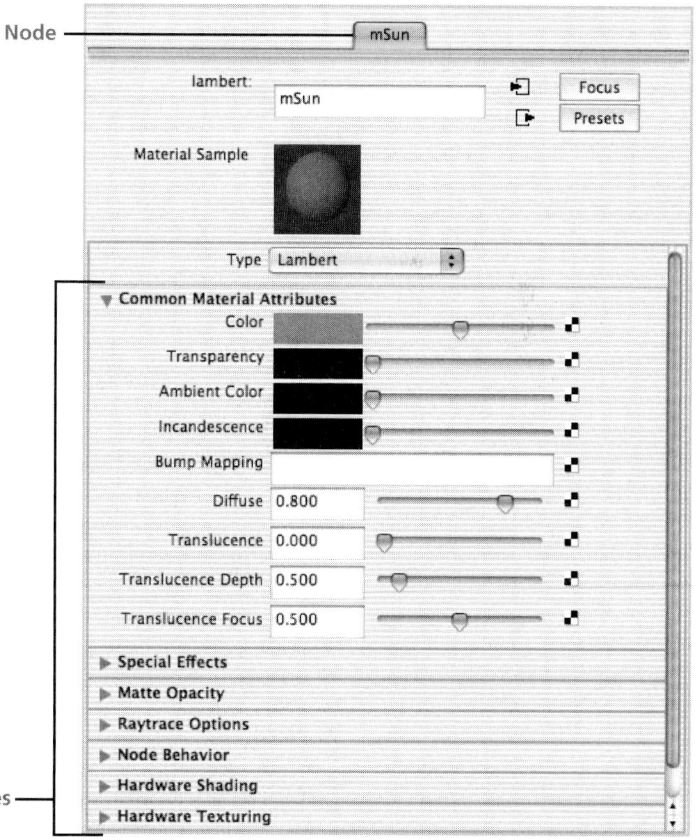

The Attribute Editor

The Attribute Editor, shown in Figure 2-21, displays all of the connected nodes and their material attributes for a selected object. Each tab represents a respective node and its attributes. Figure 2-21 shows only one node, mSun, because it's the only material node we've created so far.

FIGURE 2-21 *The Attribute Editor showing the mSun material's attributes*

Node ——

Material Attributes ——

> **NOTE** *Although the Channel Box also displays attributes, it displays only the attributes of nodes that are keyable—that is, the keyframes are able to be set on these attributes to animate them. While you can make any attribute keyable, this issue will be addressed specifically in Chapter 7.*

A great aspect of the Attribute Editor is that is contains sliders, instead of text fields, that you can use to edit attributes—so you can *see* the effects of your changes. However, because it displays all of the available attributes on any one node, this may be more than you need to work with for your current process. For material editing, however, using the Attribute Editor is recommended.

Here's how you edit attributes:

1. At the top of the Common Material Attributes list, find the attribute named Color. In Figure 2-21, this is set to a gray color in the middle of the slider. Click the gray color chip to bring up the Color Chooser, shown in Figure 2-22.

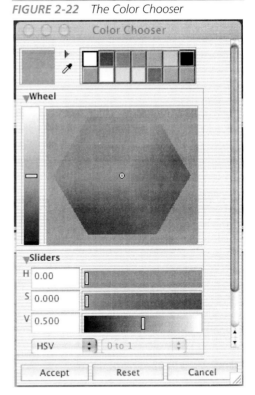

FIGURE 2-22   The Color Chooser

2. Click and drag in the color wheel (the hexgonal shape in the middle of the Color Chooser) to select a yellowish orange color for the Sun. When you are happy with the color, click Accept to close the Color Chooser.

3. To apply this material to the Sun object, MMB-drag the material from the upper tabs section of the Hypershade window onto the Sun object in the Perspective view window.

4. Now add colors for the two other objects in the scene in the same way. Make the Earth's material blue and leave the Moon's color at its default gray.

5. You need to make one more edit to the mSun node to make the Sun appear to be illuminating. You can do this by editing the mSun's Incandescence attribute in the Attribute Editor. Change the Incandescence attribute color to a bright yellow, using the slider as you did earlier. (This attribute will be explained in detail in Chapter 13.)

Add Light

So far, the existing light in the scene is illuminating from the default light, which will always sit right above the camera of the view being rendered. The default light is used for nothing more than performing quick renders as you work on your scene. It is not intended to be used as your final light source.

For this scene, we will add what is called a *point light* and place it at the origin of the scene. A point light illuminates in all directions, as opposed to something like a spot light that illuminates in one direction. Because this light source will be representing the Sun in this animation, the point light is the best choice.

1. Choose Create | Light | Point Light. A light icon will appear at the scene's origin, but since the view is displaying in shaded mode, you will not be able to see it because it is inside the Sun.

2. To see the real-time effects of the light in Perspective view, press the 7 key; this will turn on show lighting.

3. Save the scene by choosing File | Save. Name the scene **SolarSystem**. This scene file will be saved in the Scenes directory inside our firstProject directory.

> *NOTE   **If you want to move the light, you can press 4 and return to wireframe mode so that you can see the light and use the manipulator tools to move it. However, the light is already placed where we want it, so we don't need to do this right now.***

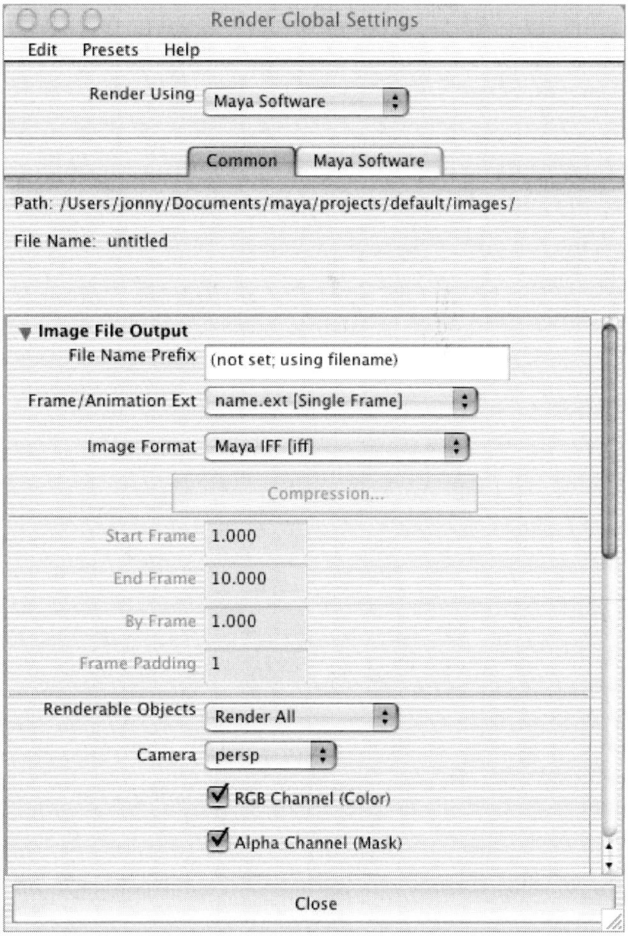

Render the Animation

In this final step of the tutorial, we will configure the renderer and render the animation. The main window for configuring the renderer is the Render Global Settings window shown in Figure 2-23. This window will be examined in detail in Chapter 16. For the purpose of this tutorial, we will make only a few modifications here before invoking the Batch Render command.

FIGURE 2-23   *The Render Global Settings window*

1. Choose Window | Rendering Editors | Render Globals to open the Render Global Settings window. You can also access this window from the Status Line by clicking the Render Globals button.

2. In the Render Global Settings window, click the arrow to open the pull-down menu in the Frame/Animation Ext field and select name_#.ext.

3. Set the End Frame of the animation to **720**.

4. Click the Maya Software tab, and scroll down to find the Anti-Aliasing Quality folder (the sections noted by the little black triangles are called *folders*). Click the arrow to the left of the folder to open it.

5. Set the Quality pull-down menu on the Maya Software tab to Production Quality. Click the Close button to close the Render Global Settings window.

6. Press F5 to change to the Rendering menu set. Choose Render | Batch Render. The Batch Render application will launch, and your animation will begin to render as a sequence of individual frames.

You can monitor the progress of your render by looking in the feedback line at the bottom of the Maya window. This will tell you the percentage of completion for each frame rendered as well as the path to the directory where the files are being written.

Use Fcheck

When the rendering is complete, open the Fcheck application found in the same directory as the Maya application to check the image sequence and playback. You can use Fcheck to view a sequence of images as an animation. After you've launched Fcheck, choose File | Open Image Sequence, and then navigate to the file that contains the first frame of the animation. This file will be called SolarSystem_01.iff and will be located in the Images directory inside the firstProject directory. Click Open and the image sequence will load and play back.

Summary

By now, you should have a good idea of how to navigate the basic Maya interface and create a simple animation. While we haven't shown you everything, you should have an idea of how to select nodes, edit their attributes, change the layout of the Workspace, use some hot keys, and access windows from the Window menu. Throughout the remainder of the book, we will explore all of these elements of the user interface in greater detail.

3D Modeling

3

Basic NURBS Modeling

The NURBS toolset is the most flexible

of the three types of modeling toolsets available

in Maya. If you are new to modeling, it's a good

idea to start with the NURBS toolset, because it is

Maya's oldest and most mature modeling toolset.

If necessary, NURBS surfaces can also be easily

converted into polygons for further editing or

for exporting to another application. While it

is especially useful for building curvy, organic

surfaces for industrial design and characters,

you can also use the NURBS toolset to create square or hard-edged models for architectural applications.

Non-Uniform Rational B-Splines is a mathematical term that sounds complicated. To understand NURBS, you should know that NURBS objects represent a mathematical description of a curve or surface. Although you don't need to be able to construct and solve polynomial equations to use the NURBS toolset, it does help if you understand a little about polygonal geometry.

Polygonal geometry, which is explained in detail in Chapter 5, is made up of finite segments called *faces*; NURBS geometry is infinitely smooth. Figure 3-1 shows a NURBS sphere (left) and a polygonal sphere (right). Look at the edges of the spheres and notice that the polygonal sphere is made up of segments and is not smooth like the NURBS sphere.

A good analogy to make for the difference between NURBS and polygons is to consider the difference between vector-based graphics used in Adobe Illustrator and Flash and pixel-based images used in Adobe Photoshop and many digital video and photography applications. Because vector lines are drawn on your screen based on a mathematical description, they will always remain smooth, no matter how close you zoom in on them or how big the window in which they are played back. Pixel-based images, on the other hand, are made up of finite rectangles, called *pixels*. While these may not be visible when you're viewing an image at its normal resolution, the image will start to break up as you zoom in and see that the image is made up of thousands, or even millions, of rectangular pixels.

What this means is that, in general, polygons make for good hard-edged surfaces, while NURBS makes for better curved surfaces. In Chapter 5, you'll learn how to convert a polygon to a NURBS object.

FIGURE 3-1   *A close-up of a NURBS sphere (left) versus a polygonal/faceted sphere (right)*

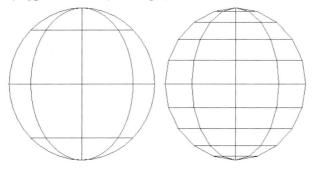

In this chapter, even though the main topic of discussion is NURBS, you will also learn a lot more about the Maya user interface. Using marking menus, setting tool options, and using tools and commands are just some of the things that are covered here. In Chapter 4, you'll learn more advanced techniques for using NURBS modeling.

Anatomy of NURBS Curves and Surfaces

Both NURBS curves and surfaces have similar components that control how they are edited. Understanding how these components relate to each other and how they are used to calculate curves and surfaces will provide you with a good foundation for transforming your simple surfaces into more complex shapes while maintaining a clean geometry that is easy to edit.

We'll first examine curves, since they have similar, but fewer, components than surfaces. You'll then learn how these components relate to surfaces and how some other components are unique to surfaces.

Components of a NURBS Curve

Figure 3-2 shows a NURBS curve displaying its components.

- **Edit points**   When a curve is drawn in Maya, the software joins together polynomial curve segments, called *spans*. The points where these segments join are called *edit points* (sometimes called *knots*). Edit points lie on a curve, and each point displays a small × that you can select and move to edit the shape of a curve. Edit points can be added to a curve by using the Insert Knot tool.

- **Control vertices (CVs)**   CVs control how the curve is "pulled" or "weighted" between edit points. CVs basically define the shape of a curve or surface. The number of CVs between edit points depends on the *degree* of the curve. (See the section entitled "Surface or Curve Degree" later in this chapter.) CVs often lie above or below a curve, in space, and are the points most commonly moved in X, Y, Z space to control the shape of the curve. CVs cannot be inserted directly into the curve but are added when an edit point is inserted.

FIGURE 3-2   *NURBS curve anatomy*

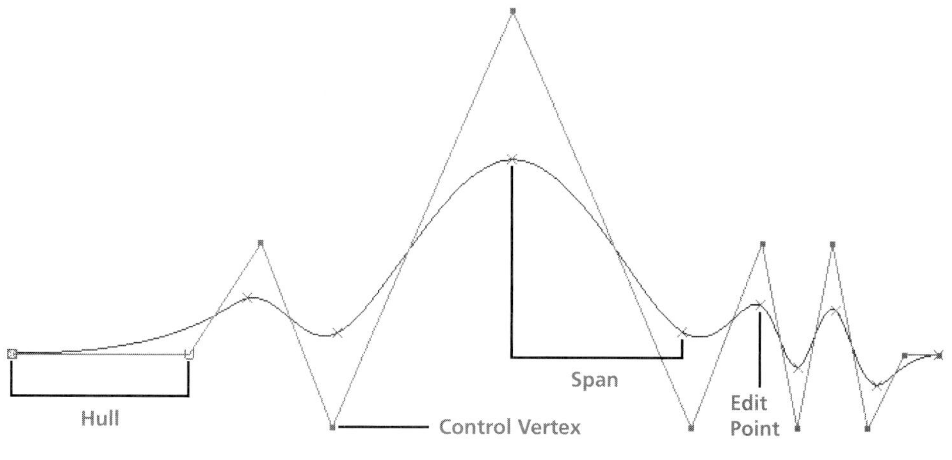

- **Curve points**   One of the many great aspects of NURBS technology is that because curves are mathematically calculated, any *curve point* along a curve can be chosen and adjusted. While a curve point cannot be edited directly, it can be chosen as the place to insert an edit point or as the point at which you want to detach a curve into two pieces. (These points are not shown in Figure 3-2.)

- **Hulls**   Hulls are straight lines that connect the CVs together. Choosing a hull will select all of the CVs in a curve.

You can display and choose curve components in several ways. Right-clicking any object in a view window will always display that object's components in a marking menu. If you want to display and choose only one of these components at a time, you can right-click the curve (or surface) and choose the desired component from the marking menu. A marking menu displaying the available components for a NURBS curve is shown in Figure 3-3.

If you want to display and choose several components at once, you can use the selection mask buttons on the Status Line. To do this, click the Select by Component Type button, and then activate the buttons for the components you want to use.

You can also right-click (RMB-click) a selection mask button and choose exactly what components you want it to show; these settings vary depending on what type of object is being chosen. (For example, clicking the Points Selection Mask button will display NURBS CVs, polygonal vertices, subdivision vertices, lattice points, and particles.) You might need to adjust these components, depending on what is included in your scene. A great thing about using these selection masks is that you can enable multiple selection masks at once. For example, your could enable the selection masks for CVs and hulls so that you are able to pick one or both component types at the same time.

If you want to view a component but not select it, you can display it by choosing an option from the Display menu. For example, to see the hulls of your object, select the object, and then choose Display | NURBS Components | Hulls. The hulls will be displayed for that object.

FIGURE 3-3   A marking menu showing the components for a NURBS curve

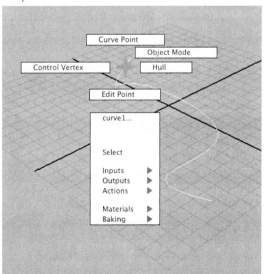

Components of a NURBS Surface

NURBS surfaces contain some of the same components as NURBS curves. Both CVs and hulls perform the same functions that they do for curves and can be chosen and edited in the same way. However, surfaces also have some unique components, as shown in Figure 3-4. These unique components are discussed next.

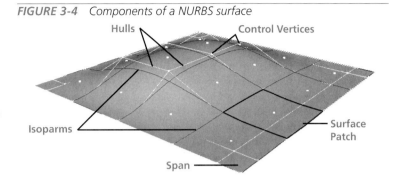

FIGURE 3-4   Components of a NURBS surface

Hulls

Control Vertices

Isoparms

Surface Patch

Span

- **Isoparms**   Isoparms lie on the NURBS surface and extend across the entire surface at a constant parametric value. (See "Parameterization of Surfaces" later in this chapter.) Just as edit points represent the ends of curve spans, isoparms represent the boundaries between *surface patches*—the regions on a surface enclosed by isoparms. Isoparms can be selected and added to a surface, but unlike their curve counterparts, they cannot be edited directly.

- **Surface Point**   Any point or parameter on a surface. This is similar to a curve point (and is not shown in Figure 3-4).

- **Surface Patch**   The region between the enclosed isoparms.

Surface or Curve Degree

The degree of a surface or a curve refers to the exponent used in the underlying polynomial equation that defines the geometry. What this means to the Maya user is that degree equates to the number of control vertices that are needed to define one span of a NURBS curve or surface. The number of control vertices needed to define one span will always equal the degree of the curve + 1. Therefore, a one-degree (linear) curve will have two control vertices—one at the beginning and one at the end. A one-degree curve is always a straight line. Maya allows NURBS objects to have one, two, three, five, and seven degrees of curvature. In Maya, a degree of three is the default and is most often used.

Curve Direction

The direction of a curve is initially determined by the order in which you draw it, which is called the curve's *U direction*—the first point at which you draw is considered the beginning of the curve and the last point is the end point. If you don't know which direction an existing curve is going, you can select it and display the components by pressing F8 (or you can enable the Select by Component Type button in the Status Line) and making sure the Points Selection Mask is activated in the Status Line. Or you can right-click the object and choose Control Vertex.

The beginning of the curve will be marked with a small box, and the second CV will be marked with a *U* to communicate that the curve is moving in the U direction. This is illustrated in Figure 3-5.

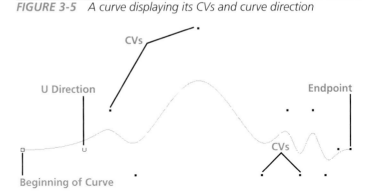

FIGURE 3-5   *A curve displaying its CVs and curve direction*

NOTE   *You can change the direction of a curve by choosing Edit Curves | Reverse Curve Direction.*

Knowing the direction of a curve is especially important during certain operations, especially those that involve connecting and merging curves. You'll see an example showing why knowing the direction of curves is important later in this chapter in the section "Cutting and Filleting Curves."

Parameterization of Curves

Parameterization describes the location of each point on a NURBS surface or curve. Each of these points has a numerical value known as a *parameter*. On a curve, this parameter gives a point's location in the curve's U direction. The first point on a curve will always have a U value of 0. This U value increases as you continue along the curve toward its end. These increasing values, or parameters, are determined by the placement of the edit points on the curve.

As you begin to generate surfaces from the curves you draw, the parameterization of the curves becomes very important for creating clean, orderly surfaces. For example, a loft operation creates a surface between two or more curves. (Lofting is discussed in detail in the section "Surfaces" later in this chapter.) To generate the cleanest surface, the parameters of the source curves must match.

Before we get into exactly how the edit points are used to determine the parameters of points on a curve, let's look at why parameterization is important.

Figure 3-6 shows two surfaces that were generated by lofting two curves together. The curves used to generate the surface on the left were created with the same number of spans (four) and as a result, they had matching parameterization. The structure of the lofted surface is clean and predictable. You can tell this by looking at the even flow of isoparms that were created by connecting the edit points on the original curves. As a modeler, you can predict exactly where these isoparms are going to intersect each curve.

The surface on the right was generated with two curves that had different parameterizations. One curve had four spans and the other had seven. When the curves were lofted together, Maya placed isoparms on the surface so that each isoparm corresponds to an edit point on each curve. The resulting surface, then, contains ten spans in the U direction to compensate for the different parameterization of the source curves. It's not as orderly as the surface on the left.

FIGURE 3-6   *The surface on the left was generated from curves with matching parameterization. The surface on the right was generated from curves that had different parameterization. The ×s indicate the edit points.*

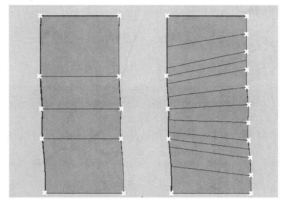

You can find the parameter value of any curve by right-clicking the curve and choosing Curve Point from the marking menu. Then click any point on the curve, and its parameter value will appear on the title bar at the top of your main Maya window, as shown here.

Maya 6.0 : ./untitled   ---   curve1.u[2.39777622504771]

You can also use the Parameter tool to find the parameter of any point on a curve (choose Create | Measure Tools | Parameter Tool) by clicking any point along a curve. The parameter value for this point will appear next to the point and remain on screen, as shown in Figure 3-7. This is perhaps a bit more convenient and useful than looking in the title bar.

Exactly how a parameter value is calculated across the curve is determined by one of two methods: the uniform method or chord-length method, both shown in Figure 3-7. You can determine the method used before the curve is drawn by selecting the option in the Knot Spacing attribute of the Curve tool's Options window (choose Create | CV Curve Tool ❑).

With uniform parameterization, integral parameter values are assigned at each edit point. To demonstrate, let's consider a curve with four spans, in which the edit points are not evenly spaced. In the uniform parameterized curve in Figure 3-7, the first four edit points fall in the first half of the curve and the last edit point is at the end of the curve. The first edit point has a parameter value of 0, the next edit point has a value of 1, the next is 2, then 3, and the last point has a value of 4. We can use the Arc Length tool (choose Create | Measure Tools | Arc Length Tool) and the Parameter tool (Create | Measure Tools | Parameter Tool) to find a parameter value for any point on the curve by clicking it. Say, for example, you wanted to find the

FIGURE 3-7 *Two, four-span curves: the top curve uses uniform parameterization and the bottom curve uses chord-length parameterization.*

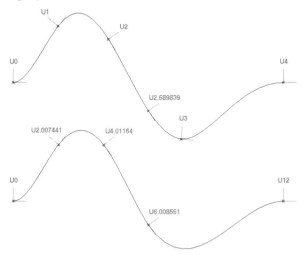

parameter value for the middle of the curve. Clicking at the center of the curve will return a value of 2.589839, also shown in Figure 3-7.

Using uniform parameterization, you can match parameterization between two curves just by figuring the total number of spans. However, determining parameters based on the length of the curves is not so straightforward. By clicking at the approximate midpoint of the four-span curve shown in Figure 3-7, the midpoint parameter shows 2.589839. This is not so intuitive if you want to insert knots at specific lengths, however—like half way, a quarter of the way, or three-quarters of the way down the curve. When these types of calculations are necessary, it's probably more useful to use chord-length parameterization.

Using chord-length parameterization, the parameter values are assigned to the edit points based on the distance of a straight line, expressed in Maya units, extended between the edit points. While this method gives the curves irregular parameter values, the values do reflect information that is relative to a point's position along the curve. So, for example, since this curve is 12 units long, it has a U parameter of 12. The middle of this curve could then be easily determined by dividing the parameterization in half. A U value of 6, then, would be the middle of the curve.

Parameterization of Surfaces

So far, we have talked about parameterization of curves that have a single parameter value in the U direction. A NURBS surface is always rectangular. Its coordinate system, therefore, must have two parameters—one in U and the other in V. With this coordinate system in place, we can then determine the parameter value of any point on the surface by describing it in terms of a UV value. You can start to see how a NURBS surface is really nothing more than a grid.

Figure 3-8 shows a uniform surface displaying its origin (at the lower-left corner) and U and V directions. As with curves, you can make these indicators display on a surface by right-clicking the surface and choosing Control Vertex from the marking menu, by pressing F8 and choosing the Points Selection Mask button in the Status Line, or by choosing Display | Nurbs Components | Surface Origins.

In Figure 3-8, the origin of the surface has a UV value of 0,0 while the
point on the opposite corner has a
UV value of 3,3. You can find the
UV parameter values for any point
on a surface by right-clicking that
surface and choosing Surface Point
from the marking menu. The point
at which you click the surface will
return the UV parameter values in
the title bar (the same way selecting
a curve point did for a curve in the
preceding section).

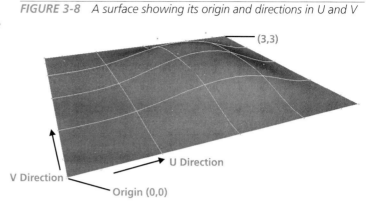

FIGURE 3-8   A surface showing its origin and directions in U and V

Using Parameterization to Build a Model

Now that you have some idea what parameterization entails, you need to decide which kind
you want to use when you build your models. One of the most important factors to consider
when making this decision is based on your overall *production pipeline*—the path that a production will follow from start to finish. For example, in larger production studios, models might
be generated in Maya but may then be exported into other software for texturing, animation,
and rendering. It is possible that somewhere along the line, one of these programs will not be
able to read a surface using chord-length parameterization, so you'd want to be sure to use
uniform parameterization instead.

After you choose a method of parameterization, you need to choose the modeling approach
you'll use. Two approaches of NURBS modeling are covered in Chapter 4: one uses *trimmed surfaces* and the other uses *patch modeling*. The patch modeling approach will require that the
different surfaces, or patches, have matching parameterization so that any seams between
the surfaces will not be visible when the image is rendered. As you will learn by following the
spaceship procedure in Chapter 4, matching parameterization will be difficult to reckon without
the use of uniform geometry.

Other approaches to modeling and the capabilities of your production pipeline might allow
for the use of chord-length parameterization. Probably the biggest advantage to using chord-
length geometry is that textures can be applied evenly across the surface without stretching or
squeezing the texture map.

Figure 3-9 shows two surfaces. The surface on the right uses uniform parameterization, whereas
the surface on the left uses chord-length parameterization. Notice the effect that the uniform
parameterization has on the checked pattern in the texture. While the texture map stretches

FIGURE 3-9   *A chord-length surface and a uniform surface; both have the same texture map applied.*

to fit evenly between the isoparms, the isoparms are not evenly spaced across the surface, so stretching occurs. The texture on the chord-length surface, however, is evenly spaced across the entire surface because its parameters are based on the length, which is even across the surface.

NOTE   **In the Attribute Editor of a NURBS object, you can enable an option called Fix Texture Warp. When enabled, the distortion of a texture map due to surface parameterization is improved at render time.**

Surface Direction

You know surfaces have U and V directions; now you'll learn about another important dimension: *surface* direction. Every surface has two sides. The surface direction that faces outward is called its *normal direction*. Every point on a surface has a *surface normal.* Think of these as lines that perpendicularly extend from any point on a surface in the normal, or outward, direction.

You can display the surface normal direction by choosing Display | NURBS Components | Surface Normals. You'll see a perpendicular line extending from the center of each surface patch.

Choose Display | NURBS Components | Surface Origins to display the surface normal as a blue line that extends from the surface *origin.* This display is a more manageable option to work with, since fewer normal lines appear that might obstruct your view of other objects in the scene.

The surface normals can be reversed by choosing Edit NURBS | Reverse Surface Direction. Since the relationship of the normal to the U and V directions of the surface is always the same, the normals of the surface will be always be reversed when either direction is changed or swapped. This relationship is illustrated in Figure 3-10.

FIGURE 3-10   *Surface displaying normal direction. The U direction of the surface on the right has been reversed.*

Advantages and Disadvantages of NURBS Modeling

NURBS modeling works well for building any smooth, curving surface—such as the body of a car or a human body. Because of its ability to represent complex shapes, NURBS is the preferred toolset used among most industrial designers. In fact, chances are that the chassis of your computer and monitor were designed using NURBS modeling.

However, the biggest drawback to using NURBS has to do with the fact that to build a complex object, you must create and link together multiple individual surfaces. Working with multiple surfaces can mean more time spent having to texture each surface individually and manage the seams between surfaces so that they match at render time.

Advantages of NURBS

Following is a discussion of some of the benefits of NURBS modeling.

Few Control Points

Using NURBS, you can create and edit smooth curving objects with few control points. This means that by editing just one control point, a subtle curve can be introduced into the surface without creating any abrupt or rough changes.

Figure 3-11 shows a NURBS sphere on the left and a polygonal sphere on the right. One of the vertices (whose location is represented by an X, Y, and Z coordinate) on each object has been pulled out from the sphere. Notice that the NURBS object remains smooth as the surface is recalculated, while the change in the surface of the polygonal object is sharp and abrupt.

Resolution Independence

The mathematical nature of NURBS surfaces enables smooth surfaces to remain smooth no matter how close the camera zooms in. However, when a NURBS surface is rendered, it is *tessellated*, which means that it is converted into polygonal faces, based on the *tessellation attributes* of the NURBS object. In plain English, this means that while the object is being cut up into triangles, the user still has the power to assign how smooth or coarse the object will render. One advantage of tessellation is that it optimizes a scene's rendering time. If the object is far away from the camera, it can be rendered with a low tessellation setting. The same piece of geometry can also be used in a close-up shot by increasing the tessellation setting. With a polygonal object, however, two separate models would have to be built to optimize the overall polygon count of the scene: one low-resolution

FIGURE 3-11   The object on the left shows a NURBS sphere with one of the vertices moved; the object on the right shows a polygonal sphere with one of the vertices moved.

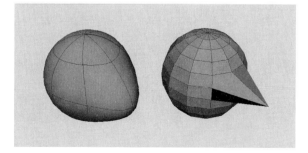

model for when the object is in the background, and a high-resolution model that will work for close-up shots.

Texture Coordinates

By its rectangular nature, any point on a NURBS surface can be defined by a coordinate in the U and V directions (remember, UV coordinates are the local coordinates for individual NURBS surfaces). Texture maps, such as bitmapped files that you might create in an image editing application like Photoshop, are also rectangular in nature, and their pixels are defined by coordinates in the X and Y directions. Because of this congruent relationship, Maya is able to fit a texture map to a surface by matching these corresponding coordinate systems, allowing the texture to fit exactly on a surface and match its curvature, no matter how many twists or turns the surface makes. Having the ability to use UV mapping coordinates gives you a powerful alternative to the projection mapping method (discussed in Chapter 13) already available for texturing surfaces in Maya.

The advantages are most evident in an example such as the one shown in Figure 3-12, where the surface is twisting so much that it would be difficult to map it using projections. Because the texture has to be projected from a place in 3D space, much like a projector will project a slide or piece of film, this will cause stretching and overlapping of the texture on curved or overlapping surfaces.

FIGURE 3-12   *A texture applied to a NURBS surface in normal (UV) mode (left) versus a texture attempting to be mapped using planar projection (right).*

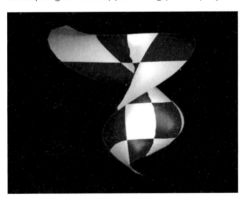 

Definition   ***projection mapping***   *A method used to apply a texture map to a surface or several surfaces at once. It uses primitive shapes to project the texture onto the geometry. For example, a planar projection (shown in Figure 3-12) uses a flat plane to project the texture onto the surface. However, you might also choose to use a cylindrical projection type if the object is cylindrical in shape, or a spherical projection if it is spherical in shape. Projections are discussed in detail in Chapter 13.*

Conversion-ability

Maya allows you to convert any geometry type to another using the Convert command (discussed in Chapter 5). Converting a NURBS model to polygons can produce the cleanest geometry, and it requires the least amount of cleanup due to the inherent orderliness and "square-patch nature" of NURBS. A conversion from NURBS to a polygon is illustrated in Figure 3-13. Notice that each square surface patch on the NURBS object is converted to a square polygonal face on the polygonal object. It is even possible to specify how many polygonal faces should be created for every one surface patch on the NURBS surface so that the resulting polygonal object will appear smooth. (Techniques for converting are covered in more detail in Chapters 5 and 6.) Many modelers prefer to build the basic surfaces with NURBS and then convert them to polygons or subdivision surfaces (another type of geometry in Maya) to add more rigid detail.

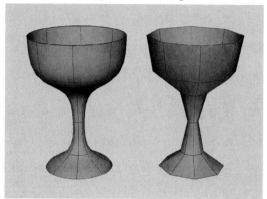

FIGURE 3-13   A NURBS surface (left) is neatly converted to a polygonal surface (right)

Definition   **subdivision surfaces**   *This type of geometry is based on the concept of subdividing polygonal faces to obtain a smooth, NURBS-like surface. Subdivision surfaces will be discussed in detail in Chapter 6.*

Disadvantages of NURBS

While you can easily model just about anything using NURBS, most of the disadvantages with NURBS stem from the fact that more complex NURBS models are often made from multiple individual surfaces. As a result, you have to deal with the following problems.

Seams

Probably the biggest problem with models built from NURBS has to do with the seams that can show between surfaces. When using trimmed surfaces, which are discussed in Chapter 4, the solution is to match the *tessellation* between adjacent surfaces manually. However, this usually results in heavy tessellation, which means a lot of polygons and hence longer render times. In Chapter 4, we will build a spaceship using a technique that minimizes this problem.

Definition   **tesselation**   *The process of creating a faceted surface. When a NURBS surface is tessellated, it is converted into polygonal faces that define the original shape.*

Branching

In modeling, *branching* refers to the parts of models that extend, or branch off, from the main surface or a group of surfaces. An example would be fingers that branch off from a hand. To build a hand that will deform, or bend, properly for animation would require that the hand and each finger be constructed with multiple surfaces. Polygonal modeling and subdivision surface modeling techniques handle these situations more efficiently than NURBS modeling. You'll understand why as you study each technique during the next four chapters.

Texture Mapping Across Multiple Surfaces

When you're creating very detailed models using NURBS, you will often end up with multiple surfaces. While this is not necessarily a bad thing, it can make managing the scene a lot more difficult, especially when it comes to having to apply texture maps across these mismatched surfaces.

Continuity

Achieving a high level of continuity between two or more curves or surfaces is one of the most difficult challenges in modeling, especially when a model is constructed with multiple surfaces. The level of continuity between surfaces determines whether an obvious change occurs where one surface ends and the adjacent one begins, or whether the transition is smooth and seamless.

Several NURBS modeling tools and commands in Maya let you achieve continuity between curves and surfaces: Align Curves, Align Surfaces, Attach Curves, Attach Surfaces, the Stitch tools, the Curve Fillet tool, and all three of the Surface Fillet tools. All of these tools will be demonstrated over the course of the next two chapters.

Levels of Continuity

Maya offers three levels of continuity, called C0, C1, and C2. Figure 3-14 shows examples of two surfaces that meet using the three levels of continuity.

FIGURE 3-14   *Two surfaces that meet, with a C0 (left), C1 (middle), and C2 (right) continuity*

- **C0—Positional**   At this level, the endpoints of a surface or curve share the exact same place in X, Y, and Z space. In other words, the objects touch but the surface connection is not seamless. C0 continuity is rarely desirable when modeling, because even the sharpest edges have some degree of smoothness to them in real life.

- **C1—Tangent**   This type of continuity offers positional continuity, plus the end tangents between the two curves or surfaces match. This means that not only are the endpoints used to calculate the continuity, but the adjacent CVs are used as well. This will create a smooth transition between the two objects without leaving a noticeable seam. It is best used when two surfaces need to join smoothly, even though the change in surface is abrupt—as in an edge or corner. An edge with less than C1 continuity will not render a specular highlight. (See Chapter 13 for more information on specular highlights.)

- **C2—Curvature**   C2 continuity has both C0 and C1 levels of continuity, plus matching curvature. This means that three control points from the edge inward on each object are used to calculate the continuity. The resulting surface will not show any changes where the object surfaces join.

Achieving Continuity Using Tools

As mentioned, several of Maya's modeling tools let you choose the level of continuity that results from joining or generating new surfaces:

- **Loft tool**   Creates a new surface between two existing surfaces with C0 continuity
- **Fillet tools**   Create a new surface between two existing surfaces with C1 or C2 continuity
- **Attach tool**   Joins together two surfaces or curves with C2 continuity
- **Stitch tools**   Give edges of objects any level of continuity
- **Align tool**   Repositions any two objects and modifies the position of the CVs to provide any level of continuity

Here's a short tutorial that demonstrates creating multiple levels of continuity between two curves using the Align Curve command:

1. Open a new scene in Maya, and press F3 to bring up the modeling menu set in the menu bar.

2. Press and hold down the SPACEBAR and left-click-and-hold on the A/W box in the middle. Choose Front from the marking menu.

3. Choose Create | EP Curve to select the EP Curve tool.

4. Click in the view window to set the first point.

5. Click again somewhere to the right of that point to set the second point, and then click again to set the third point.

6. At a slight angle to the third point, follow steps 3 through 5 to draw another curve. It should look similar to the curves shown in Figure 3-15.

FIGURE 3-15   *Two curves*

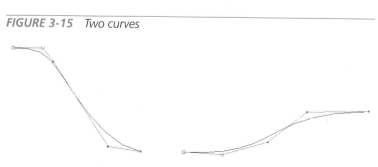

7. Select both curve objects, and choose Display | NURBS Components | Hulls. You'll see the hulls of the surfaces so you can see the effects of the continuity settings you are about to apply.

8. Select the curve on the left, and then, holding down the SHIFT key, select the curve on the right.

9. Choose Edit NURBS | Align Curves ☐.

10. In the Align Curves Options window, choose Edit | Reset Settings.

11. Choose the Position radio button in the Continuity area. The other settings should match the illustration.

12. Click the Apply button. Notice that the first curve you selected (in step 8) moved. If we had set Modify Position to Second in the Align Curves Options window, the second surface would have been moved. Notice that the positions of the hulls have not changed (Figure 3-16). This is because we are using a C0 level of continuity.

FIGURE 3-16   *The two curves after using the Align Curves command*

NOTE *Clicking the Apply button instead of the Align button will execute the Align command but will keep the Options window open.*

13. Undo the last step by Choosing Edit | Undo or by pressing CTRL-Z (COMMAND-Z).

14. In the Align Curves Options window, choose the Tangent Continuity option.

15. Click Apply to see what happens. Look at the hulls and notice that the CVs adjacent to the edges of both surfaces line up to form a straight line.

16. Select and RMB-click the first surface.

17. Select the second CV in from the edge, and then choose the Move tool from the tool box, or press the W key.

18. Try moving the CV upward in the Y direction (Figure 3-17), and you'll notice that the second CV from the edge on the other curve relocates to maintain tangency with the point that you are modifying.

Now, instead of using the Undo command to return the surfaces to their initial positions, we will edit the attributes of the Align Surface node in the Channel Box.

19. Select the alignCurve1 node under the Inputs section of the Channel Box, as shown in the illustration.

20. Click in the Field next to the Curvature Continuity attribute, and type **on** or the number **1**.

21. Now notice the hulls. Not only did the first row of CVs meet and the second align in tangency, but now the third row is also figured into the equation.

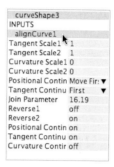

FIGURE 3-17   Moving the second CV and seeing the other curve update

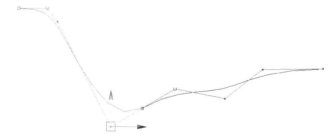

NOTE   **For on/off attributes in the Channel Box, you can also type 1 to set the attribute on or type 0 to turn the attribute off.**

Basic NURBS Modeling Tools

Now that you have some idea of how NURBS curves and surfaces work and are put together, it's time to start thinking about ways of generating these surfaces so that they begin to resemble the objects that they must represent. So where do you start? Most modelers use three basic approaches to begin fleshing out the main pieces of a model:

- Start with a primitive object, such as a plane or a sphere, and edit the positions of the CVs to sculpt it into form.

- Draw curves or one or a series of profile curves and then use one of the surface generating tools found in the Surfaces menu.

- Use a combination of both approaches.

If your surfaces are somewhat regular in shape, starting with a primitive object and sculpting it to fit the exact shape you need might be the fastest path. But if too much sculpting is needed, it might just be better to draw some good profile curves and generate the surfaces that way. As is usually the case, a combination of both methods will yield the best and quickest result.

In this section, we explore various ways to create surfaces using a variety of tools. By using these tools, you'll also start to absorb the basic workflow for modeling and using Maya in general. This involves using menus and commands to create objects, setting tool options, editing object attributes in the Attribute Editor and Channel Box, and using the basic transform tools and keyboard shortcuts.

NURBS Primitives

Primitives in Maya are objects that represent rudimentary geometric shapes. Primitive surfaces include a sphere, cube, cylinder, cone, plane, and torus. You begin modeling by creating a primitive that best matches the form and flow of an object. Then you edit its attributes to give it the desired shape and amount of control points. Only then can you begin to add detail by moving the CVs around or using other modeling tools.

Let's create a sphere and look at some of the ways we can edit its attributes:

Choose Create | NURBS Primitives | Sphere ❏ to open the NURBS Sphere Options window to create a sphere. (Alternatively, remember from Chapter 2 that you can use the Hotbox marking menu to find this option. If you press and hold down the SPACEBAR, the Hotbox will appear at your cursor's location, and you will have access to all of the same menu commands that appear in the main menu bar.)

FIGURE 3-18   *The NURBS Sphere Options window*

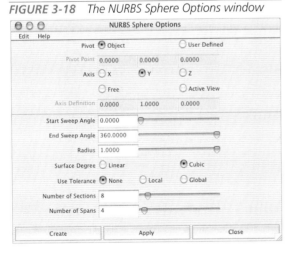

The NURBS Sphere Options window, shown in Figure 3-18, allows you to choose how your sphere will look and how it will behave when you click the Create button. The data for all of these settings are the inputs for the makeNurbSphere node that is controlling the shape. Let's take a look at the NURBS Sphere options.

- **Pivot**   By default, Object is chosen, which means that the pivot point will be located at the sphere object's center. You could also choose the User Defined option and then enter the X, Y, and Z coordinates in the fields for the Pivot Point attribute on the next line.

- **Axis**   Controls what direction the poles of the sphere will face. All of the isoparms on the surface of the sphere meet at the poles. The default sets the Axis to Y so that the poles of the sphere will point in the Y direction. Choosing the X or Z axis makes the poles of the sphere point in the X or Z direction, respectively. When the Free option is chosen, the user can define the direction of the axis in the Axis Definition attribute below. Finally, choosing the Active View option will set the axis to align with the current view window. This means that you could use the orientation of the Perspective view to align the axis of the sphere you are about to create.

- **Start Sweep Angle and End Sweep Angle**   Controls what angle the sweep of the sphere begins and ends. For example, by setting the Start Sweep Angle to 0 and the End Sweep Angle to 180, the resulting sphere will sweep 180 degrees total to make a half sphere. If the Start Sweep Angle was set at 90 and the End Sweep Angle was set at 270, the result would still be a half sphere, but it would appear to have been rotated 90 degrees from the sphere created with the 0, 180 settings.

- **Radius**   Indicates the size of the radius of the sphere, in Maya units. (Units can be set to represent centimeters, meters, inches, feet, and so on by choosing Window | Settings/Preferences.)

- **Surface Degree**   Set to Linear or Cubic. This means that the degree of the surface will be 1 or 3 (remember the discussion in "Surface or Curve Degree"?). The Linear setting will result in a rigid-looking object because the edit points of the sphere will have been connected with flat surfaces.

- **Use Tolerance**   Used to improve the precision of the sphere that is represented. This has more to do with how the sphere will be tessellated at render time. By default, the sphere is defined by a number of spans in the U and V directions. However, this can be set based on a curvature tolerance, an amount that the generated surface can deviate from the mathematical definition of the sphere. A lower tolerance value will be tessellated heavier to match the mathematical description that defines this shape.

- **Number of Sections and Number of Spans**   Settings for the number of spans in the U and V directions. Here, Maya is calling the spans in the U direction *sections*.

You may find it easier to edit the NURBS sphere's attributes after you create the primitive, because you can get visual feedback as you edit. For this reason, we'll create the sphere with the default options and then edit the attributes in the Channel Box and Attribute Editor. To make sure that you are using the default settings for this tool, you can reset it by choosing Edit | Reset Options from the NURBS Sphere Options window. Then click Create to create the sphere with these settings and click Close to close the NURBS Sphere Options window.

 If it isn't already being displayed, turn on the Channel Box either by choosing Display | UI Elements | Channel Box or clicking the Channel Box button on the Status Line.

Let's take a look at what we have so far. With the sphere selected, the Channel Box will display a list of all of the object's keyable attributes (that is, attributes that can be animated), as shown next. Under the Inputs list is a node called makeNurbSphere1. Click that node to display this input node's attributes.

Do these attributes look familiar to you? They should. These are some of the same attributes that we saw in the sphere's Options window. The "make" node of a primitive contains the algorithms used to generate a surface based on the given attributes. Clicking in the value field and typing in a new number can change any of these attributes. In the End Sweep value field, type **180**. You'll notice now that a half sphere is shown.

You can also change a value by selecting the attribute name in the Channel Box, and then dragging in the view window with the middle mouse button (MMB). This acts as a kind of invisible slider. As you MMB-drag to the right, the value increases and the sphere automatically updates in the view window. As you drag to the left, the value decreases.

 You might also choose to edit these values with the Show Manipulator tool. With the End Sweep attribute selected in the Channel Box, activate the Show Manipulator tool from the toolbar or press the T key.

A disc with a little yellow box will appear around the sphere. Dragging the yellow box will change the selected End Sweep value and update in the view window in real time. You can see an example of this in Figure 3-19.

FIGURE 3-19   Editing the End Sweep attribute with the Show Manipulator tool

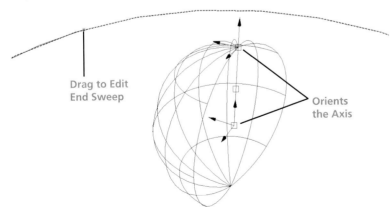

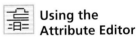 **Using the Attribute Editor**

All of the attributes in the Channel Box, and more, can also be viewed in the object's Attribute Editor. Click the Show Attribute Editor button on the Status Line or press CTRL-A (CONTROL- A) to display the Attribute Editor, shown next. With the Attribute Editor open, select the makeNurbSphere1 tab to view the makeNurbSphere1

node attributes. Again, you will see a collection of familiar attributes with sliders that can be used to set the values.

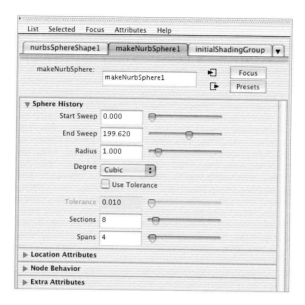

Before we move on, let's cover a few more attributes that you'll find in the Attribute Editor.

For any primitive object, the number of *sections* and *spans* can be set in the U and V directions. In the case of a sphere, the word *sections* in the Maya interface describes the number of spans in the V direction.

> NOTE   **Don't be fooled, because sections and spans are the same thing in the Maya interface.**

Channel Box versus Attribute Editor

While the Attribute Editor might allow you to display and edit many attributes, its screen size can make your display a bit cluttered, as the other open windows will be resized to accommodate the Attribute Editor. Since most of the attributes that you'll need to edit are also available in the Channel Box, you might find it more efficient to use the Channel Box while you model.

The Channel Box is a useful area to use while you're animating. Not only is it better to have the maximum screen space dedicated to the view window and Graph Editor, but in animation you are dealing with only the keyable attributes, and therefore you don't need access to the non-keyable attributes in the Attribute Editor. Other tasks in Maya, such as editing materials, are always better accomplished using the Attribute Editor. This will all become obvious as you progress through this book.

By starting with a sphere with the correct number of sections and spans for editing, you could very quickly sculpt a humanoid figure by selecting hulls and using the Move, Rotate, and Scale tools to edit their positions. Then, individual CVs or groups of CVs could be edited to add some of the more minute details. Figure 3-20 shows a humanoid torso that was sculpted by directly manipulating the CVs of a NURBS sphere.

Curves

Curves are often the starting points for models. While they are never rendered, you will probably need to work with them to some degree while building most of your objects. You might use them to trace a bitmap that you use for reference or as the input to some other operation that generates surfaces. Or you might derive a curve from a surface to duplicate and manipulate it to generate a second surface.

FIGURE 3-20 *This figure began as a sphere and was quickly sculpted into a humanoid torso and head, just by selecting rows of CVs and moving and scaling them.*

When you work with curves, most of the operations that you use will involve attaching and detaching them. A good working knowledge of curves will help you to build them efficiently, which will lead to organized surfaces that you generate from them.

Creating Curves with the Curve Tools

Maya has two different methods for creating curves—one that creates them with CVs and another that creates them with edit points (EPs). Regardless of what tool you use, keep in mind that you want to describe your curve by using the least amount of points possible. This will make it easy to edit the curves later and build efficient surfaces.

Here's how to create a curve with the CV Curve tool:

1. Choose Create | CV Curve from the main menu in the menu bar or from the Hotbox. You can also select this tool from the shelf under the Curves tab, as shown here.

2. Choose Display | UI Elements | Tool Settings ☐ to display the CV Curve Options window.

3. The default settings are set to draw a third-degree curve with uniform parameterization. If you remember from the discussion on curve degree in the "Surface or Curve Degree" section earlier in the chapter, to create one span of the curve, you take *the degree number + 1 CV.* Therefore, for example, you know that you'll need to click and set four sections of CVs to complete a curve of the third degree.

4. Hold down the SPACEBAR and click and hold the mouse over the A/W box in the center of the Hotbox. A marking menu will appear that lets you select a perspective or three orthographic views. Select Front View.

5. In the view window, left-click to set the first point of the curve.

6. Click again a few units away to set the second point.

7. Click at two places on the curve, and notice that a smooth curve now appears between the four CVs. This means that by placing those four points, you have input enough information for Maya to calculate one span of the curve (see the discussion on "Surface or Curve Degree").

8. You can continue to click and place as many CVs as you want. When you are ready to complete the curve, press ENTER.

Now we'll draw a second curve; this time, we'll use the EP Curve tool. The EP Curve tool is especially useful for tracing images or snapping and drawing a straight line between two points.

1. Choose Create | EP Curve ▢.

2. In the Curve Options window, click the Reset Tool button to set the tool to its default settings.

3. Click once in the view window to set the first point.

4. Click again in another place to set the second point. A curve will appear. Because the EP curve is completing an entire span every time a point is set, you need to set only two points to complete the curve.

EP Curve Tool		Reset Tool	Tool Help...
▼ **EP Curve Settings**			
Curve Degree ◯ 1 Linear		◯ 2	
◉ 3 Cubic		◯ 5	
◯ 7			
Knot Spacing ◉ Uniform		◯ Chord Length	

5. Before completing the curve, click again—but this time, hold down the left mouse button and drag around in the view window. You'll see that the curve is updating to follow your mouse movement, showing you how the curve will look if you release the mouse button at various points to set a new point. When you are happy with the placement of the second point, release the left mouse button.

6. Press ENTER (RETURN) to finish the curve.

From these two exercises, you can see that while it takes fewer clicks to create a curve with the EP Curve tool, you don't have as much control of the curvature since the four CVs are being created for you every time you set an edit point. It is therefore advised that you use the CV Curve tool whenever you can. The curves you create will be much more efficient, because you have used all four CVs to control the curvature over each span.

Curves on Surfaces

In addition to drawing curves on the planes in the view window, you can also draw them directly on a surface, extract them from existing curves or isoparms, create them by projecting another curve in the scene, or create them from the line of intersection between two intersecting surfaces. Most of these methods will be explored at length in the tutorials in Chapter 4.

To give you a taste of what's possible, here are some explanations for the various ways you can create curves:

 Drawing on a Live Surface   A curve can be drawn on any NURBS surface by first making the surface *live*. To do this, first select the surface on which you want to draw. Choose Modify | Make Live, or click the Make Live button in the Status Line. Once the surface is live, you can use any of the curve tools to draw onto it. This method is used to define a region for the screen piece in the cell phone tutorial in Chapter 4.

Duplicating Surface Curves   Any curve on a surface or surface isoparm can be duplicated and then edited on its own. To duplicate a curve on a surface or isoparm, first select it, and then choose Edit Curves | Duplicate Surface Curves. While the curve will still be connected to the surface through history, it will become a separate object and can be edited accordingly.

Projecting a Curve   Any curve in a scene can be projected onto a surface and a new curve created. To project a curve, select a curve and a surface and choose Edit NURBS | Project Curve On Surface. In this tool's Options window, you can specify whether the curve should be projected from the *active view* or along the *normal* of the surface. (A good example of using this tool is found in Chapter 4's spaceship tutorial, when we create the cockpit.)

Creating Curves Along Intersecting Surfaces   A curve on a surface is created along the line of intersection between any two intersecting surfaces by selecting the surfaces and choosing Edit NURBS | Intersect Surfaces.

Creating Curves on Surfaces Using Other Tool's Options   Tools such as the Circular Fillet tool have an option that allows you to create a curve on a surface when the fillet operation is performed. (In Chapter 4, see the part of the cell phone tutorial in which the fillet is made to create the speaker piece.)

Attaching and Detaching Curves

Attaching and detaching are probably the most common operations you'll use when working with curves. To attach curves, you connect or blend any two curves into a single curve. The Attach Curves command will attach two curves together based on a few settings in the Attach Curve tool's Options window, shown next. You can use two methods of attaching: connecting and blending. With the Connect option set, the end of one curve is moved to match the end of the other curve and the

curves are attached. This results in a C0 continuity between the resulting spans. When the
Blend option is selected, the curves are
blended together with C2 continuity. Each
curve will move a certain amount to blend
with the other based on the Blend Bias attribute setting. The default it 0.5000; this means
that the ends of both curves will move an equal
amount to meet and attach. Another option
allows you to keep the original curves after
the operation.

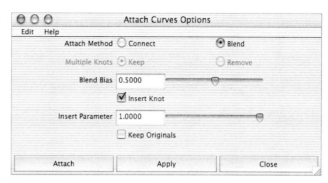

To attach two curves:

1. Draw two curves with either the CV Curve tool or EP Curve tool.

2. Choose Edit Curves | Attach Curves ❑ to bring up the Attach Curves Options window.

3. Choose Edit | Reset Settings to restore
the tool to its default settings. Then uncheck Keep Originals.

4. Click Apply to attach the curves. The two curves will be attached at the two closest
endpoints and will be blended with a bias of .5, so that each curve is moving the same
amount to attach.

Figure 3-21 shows the curves before and after attaching.

FIGURE 3-21 Curves before and after attaching

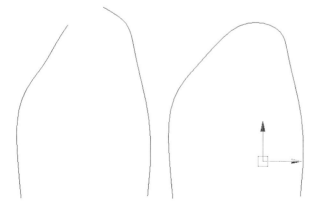

You can edit the attributes of
the resulting attached curve
to change which ends were
attached. Here's how:

1. With the attached curve
selected, select the attachCurve1
node in the Channel Box.

2. The first two attributes in
the list, Reverse1 and Reverse2,
control which points are connected.
Select the field for the Reverse1
attribute and type **on**.

3. Look at the result in the view window. The attached end of the first curve chosen before the attach operation has been reversed.

4. Now change the setting for the Reverse2 attribute. This will completely reverse the attached ends from their original orientation. Figure 3-22 shows the result.

FIGURE 3-22 *A curve with the Reverse1 attribute switched (left) and a curve with both attributes switched (right)*

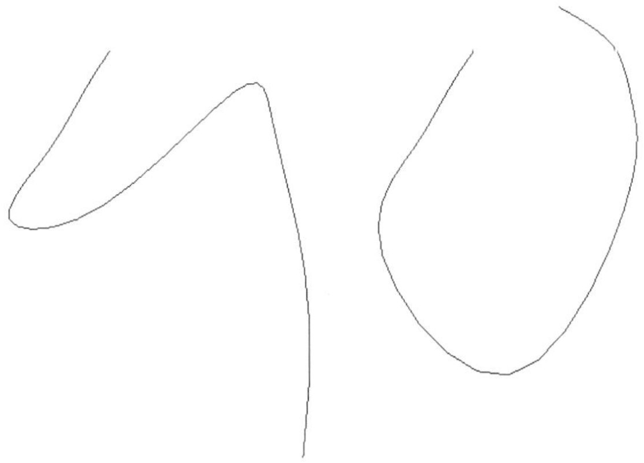

You can also choose any two points on a curve to attach:

1. Undo all changes to the point before the curves were attached.

2. Select and RMB-click the first curve, and then choose Curve Point from the marking menu.

3. Choose any point on the curve by clicking it.

4. SHIFT-click the other curve to select it. SHIFT-clicking will keep the first curve selected as you add the new selection.

5. RMB-click the second curve and choose Curve Point.

6. Shift-click the second curve to select a curve point.

7. Now, with a curve point selected on each curve, choose Edit Curves | Attach Curves, or click Apply from the Attach Curves Options window if it is still open. The curve will now attach at the chosen points.

8. To detach the curve, select it, RMB-click it, and choose Curve Point.

9. Choose Edit Curves | Detach Curves. The curve will detach at the selected curve's point. The result is two separate curves.

Detaching a curve involves choosing a point on a curve that marks the spot where the curve will be detached into two separate pieces. The only option available in the Detach Curves Options window is one to keep the original curve.

Cutting and Filleting Curves
When two curves intersect, you can use a few more options to control how they are going to meet. Cutting curves at an intersection point and then using the Attach Curves command

might achieve more predictable results than just attaching two curves regardless of where their ends are located, because the shape of the curve will not change as drastically. Furthermore, if you use a fillet to create an entirely new curve between two existing curves, you can control exactly how the new combined curve flows. Once this curve fillet is created, it can then be attached to the other curves to make one continuous curve.

A curve fillet creates a curve between two existing curves and has C1 continuity at both curves. To use the Fillet Curve command, you first select two intersecting curves.

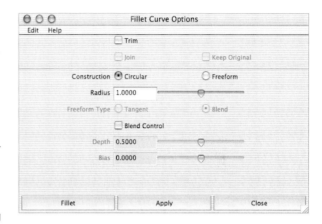

Two different construction methods can be used, Circular and Freeform, which can be set in the Fillet Curve Options window, shown next. The circular option will build a circular-shaped fillet according to the size indicated via the Radius setting. When the Freeform option is selected, the point at which the fillet begins on each curve can be set by editing the Curve Parameter attributes on the filletCurve node once the fillet has been created (in other words, you cannot set the Curve Parameter until after the fillet has been created). The Fillet Curve Options window also lets you control the depth of the fillet, or how round the fillet is, and the bias, which sets how the fillet will be weighted toward one curve or the other (similar to the Bias attribute for the Attach command).

You can also choose to trim the curves at the points where the fillet intersects by choosing the Trim option at the top of the window. If the Join option is enabled, the curves will be attached together after they are trimmed. If the Keep Original option is enabled, the curves will be dupli-cated before the command is executed. Most of the time, it is best to leave this disabled.

As you learn about cutting and filleting curves, you can combine your existing knowledge of drawing, attaching, and detaching to create the profile of a teacup that you will then use to generate surfaces in the next section.

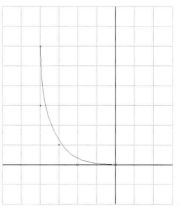

Let's begin by creating a few curves.

1. Use the CV Curve tool or EP Curve tool to create a curve that resembles the profile of a teacup. Start at the origin and move up. See the illustration shown here for help.

2. Choose Edit Curve | Offset | Offset Curve On Surface. This will create a parallel curve.

3. At the top end of the curves, use the EP Curve tool to create another curve that intersects both of the profile curves, as shown in the following illustration.

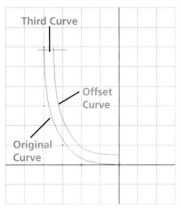

4. With both curves selected, choose Edit Curves | Cut Curves. The intersecting curves will be cut into multiple pieces. At this point, you could select any two of these curves and use the Attach Curves tool to connect or blend them.

Most intersecting curves or surfaces have some kind of transition or continuity between them. We'll explore why this is important in other chapters of this book. For now, we'll create a simple transition between two of these curves. Using Blend for the Blend Attachment Method attribute in the Attach Curves tool may not give us the amount of fine control we need. It is in these situations when the Curve Fillet tool will also come in handy.

1. Choose two of the resulting curve segments and delete the pieces of the new curve that extend beyond the intersections of the existing two curves, so that you have something that resembles this example:

2. Before using the Fillet tool to create a round corner where these curves meet, it is important that you check the direction of the curves. Maya will attempt to create this new curve in the angle of the U direction. For this reason, you may need to select one or both curves and choose Edit Curves | Reverse Curve Direction. Figure 3-23 shows the curves before and after the fillet has been created. Notice the direction of the curves in the image on the right.

FIGURE 3-23   *Curves with proper curve direction (left) and a circular fillet created between the two intersecting curves (right)*

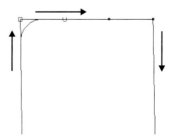

3. Now select both curves, and choose Edit Curves | Curve Fillet ❑.

4. In the Curve Fillet Options window, reset the tool's settings to use the defaults and click Apply. You should see a new circular curve that transitions between the two existing curves.

5. If the operation failed, it is either because the curves were going in the wrong direction or the radius attribute in the Fillet tool options was set too large. Undo the fillet operation and try decreasing the size of the radius.

 You may often want to attach the fillet to two other curves to make one continuous shape. You can approach this in a few different ways. If you want to continue along the path, you can use the Intersect Curves tool to determine the exact point where the two curves come together.

1. Select one of the original curves and the fillet curve. Choose Edit Curves | Intersect Curves. A marker will appear at the point where the two curves intersect.

2. RMB-click the original curve and choose Curve Point from the marking menu.

3. Click the Snap To button on the Status Line, or press and hold down the V key as you click and drag on the curve until the curve point snaps to the intersection marker.

4. Choose Edit Curves | Attach Curves ❑.

5. From the Attach Curves Options window, set the Attach method to Connect.

6. Click Apply.

7. In the Channel Box, adjust the Reverse attributes for the attachCurve1 node, until you see the effect you want, as shown in the illustration.

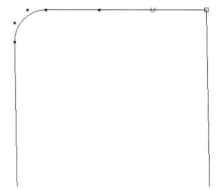

8. Repeat this process for the remaining curves.

To make this process easier, you can save some steps by using the Trim and Join options in the Fillet Options window before you create the fillet. Here we'll undo the operations we performed on the curves and use this method. The Trim option will trim away the parts of the curve not used in the end result, and the Join option will attach the fillet and original curve together.

1. Undo all of the last operations to just before you used the Curve Fillet tool so that you're back to the two curves intersecting with no fillets.

2. Choose Edit Curves | Curve Fillet ❑ and turn on the Trim and Join options by checking the appropriate boxes in the Options window.

3. Click Apply. The fillet is created, the original curves are trimmed at the intersection points, and the remaining curves are attached.

Surfaces

While curves play an important role in the modeling process, the surfaces generated from the curves are rendered to create the actual object. Surface generation in Maya begins with one or a series of source curves. These curves are used as the input objects for one of the surface-generating tools. These surface-generating tools, or modeling operations, then use their specific algorithms to generate a surface based on the attribute settings of the tool.

For example, suppose you lofted five curves together. Maya uses the five curves as the input data for a loft operation. The result is a lofted surface. This process can be illustrated by graphing the Lofted Surface's input connections in the Hypergraph, as shown in Figure 3-24.

In this section, we'll discuss some of the more common surface-generating commands and tools. You will learn ways to modify or rebuild a surface with the Rebuild Surface tool.

FIGURE 3-24   *The Hypergraph displaying the dependencies of a surface created by lofting five curves*

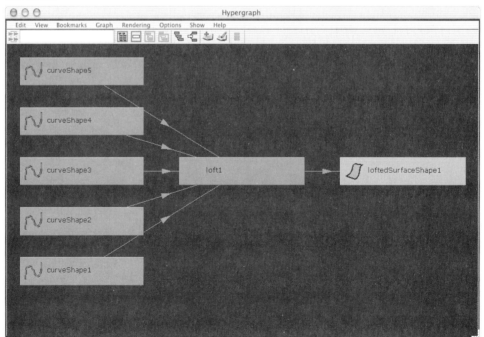

Revolve

The Revolve command is perhaps one of the simplest of the surface commands in Maya because it needs only one curve to be able to calculate the surface. But its power should not be underestimated. By modifying the surface degree or changing a pivot point, some complex surfaces can be generated that might not be so obvious from a revolve operation. (You'll see examples of this when we create the landing gears for the spaceship in Chapter 4.)

Any round, symmetrical surface is a perfect candidate for the Revolve command. In this example, we'll use the curve we created in the last section as the input for the revolve operation to make a teacup.

1. Open the scene containing your teacup profile or use the file supplied on the CD with this book.

2. In the Perspective view, select the curve, and then choose Surfaces | Revolve ❏ to open the Revolve Options window.

3. Choose Edit | Reset Settings to restore the tool to its default settings. Click Apply. The result should look like the surface shown in Figure 3-25.

    FIGURE 3-25   Revolved teacup in wireframe and shaded mode

4. Press the 6 key to display the surface in shaded mode. Press the 3 key to turn up the display smoothness. Note that it's always a good idea to look at a surface with these settings turned on as soon as it is created. You will usually be able to spot problems right away and know whether you chose the appropriate settings in the surface tool's options to get the desired result.

5. Let's examine some of the attributes of the Revolve node by selecting the surface and then selecting the revolve1 node in the Channel Box. Under the Inputs section, select the Start Sweep attribute, and then MMB-drag in the view window. The angle at which the revolve begins will change.

6. Select the surface and move it along the X axis so that it sits next to its input curve.

7. Select and RMB-click the curve, and choose Control Vertex.

8. Click one of the CVs on the curve, and then use the Move tool to change its position in the X or Y direction, as shown in Figure 3-26. Notice what happens to the surface as you tweak the CV; it updates to fit the shape of the curve. This is because the surface is still dependent on the curve to get its shape.

FIGURE 3-26 *Changing the shape of the input curve changes the resulting surface.*

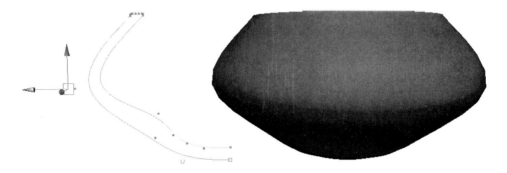

9. Undo any changes that you made to the CVs.

10. Now select the revolved surface and choose Edit | Delete By Type | History. This will delete all upstream connections to the surface—including the connection to the original profile curve and the revolve node. If you try to edit the curve again, it will have no effect on the surface. If you select the surface and look at its attributes in the Channel Box, you'll notice that the revolve1 node and all of its attributes are gone.

11. Save this scene. Choose File | Save, and name it **teacup_surface.mb** so we can use it again later.

Extrude

Another quick way to generate a surface with few input curves is to use the Extrude command. A profile curve can be extruded by any amount along its normal, or it can be extruded along a given path. The method used can be specified in the Style setting in the Extrude command's Options window. Other options can be set to determine whether the object should be extruded from its position or the path's position.

> *NOTE For an explanation of the Extrude command's many options, be sure to check Maya's online documentation under the "Extruding Surfaces" section of the NURBS modeling part.*

In this example, we will use the Extrude command to create a tube to use as a handle for our teacup. Instead of setting the options in the command's Options window, however, we will extrude the object with the default settings and then edit the Extrude node's attributes in the Channel Box.

1. Open the teacup file from the CD or use the file that you created earlier.

2. Switch to a Side view.

3. Choose the CV Curve tool with the default settings.

4. Draw a curve that resembles a handle on a teacup. It should look something like the illustration.

5. Choose Create | NURBS Primitives | Circle.

6. Move the circle out from the center so that you can see it. Press the R key to choose the Scale tool and scale it down and make it more of an elliptical shape.

7. Select the ellipse, and then select the path curve.

8. Choose Surfaces | Extrude ❑ to bring up the Extrude command's Options window. Reset these settings to their default by choosing Edit | Reset Settings, and then click Extrude.

9. The result may appear strange at first, but we will correct it by editing the attributes in the Channel Box. With the extruded surface selected, go into the Channel Box and select the extrude1 node to view its attributes.

10. Set fixed Path to **on** and Use Component to **Component Pivot**. (This is equivalent to setting Result Position to At Path and Pivot to Component in the Options window prior to the extrude.) The result should look like the surface shown here.

Loft

If a 3D modeler had to choose one surface-generating tool that he or she could not live without, it would be the Loft command. You select any number of curves to be used as *profiles* and then use the Loft command to create a surface between them. The resulting surface will pass through each of the curves in the order they were chosen.

The Loft command is particularly helpful when you are building complex, curved objects such as the body of a car. You can draw curves that match the profile at key points along the car's body, and then loft between them to generate a surface.

The curves that are used in the loft do not need to have matching spans. A surface that is generated from curves that use a different number of spans will contain the number of spans equal to the curve with the most spans. For example, suppose you have three curves—one with five spans, one with four spans, and one with three spans. The surface generated will have five spans in the U direction. While this feature is convenient, the placement of the spans in the surface will not be entirely predictable or may not even be desirable. It is recommended, therefore, that your curves all have matching parameterization before you loft them together. This can be done by duplicating and transforming curves or by using the Rebuild Curve tool to rebuild curves so that they all have matching parameterization.

We'll be making heavy use of the Loft command in the tutorials found in the next chapter, so we'll just quickly touch on the basics here.

1. Use the CV Curve or EP Curve tool to draw a curve with at least three spans.

2. While it is not required that the curves have the same number of CVs for a loft operation, it will help you to build better surfaces if the number of CVs is the same in all of the source curves. Maya will insert isoparms to compensate, but this can get messy. For this reason, we'll duplicate the curve to ensure that it has the same settings. With the curve selected, choose Edit | Duplicate ❏ to bring up the Duplicate tool's Options window.

3. Choose Edit | Reset Settings to set the tool to its defaults.

4. Enter a value of **4** for the Translate In X (the first column) and set the number of copies to **4**. Click Duplicate.

5. Make sure that all of the curves are selected, and then set the selection mode to Components and turn the CV option **on**. The Status Line, with these settings, is shown here:

FIGURE 3-27   Different shaped source curves

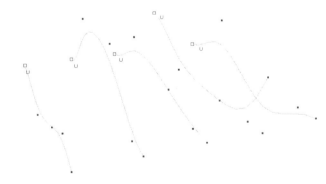

6. Use either Move tool to select and move CVs in different locations in the Y value. Also, move some of the entire curves up or down along the Y axis. Your curves should look something like the curves shown in Figure 3-27.

7. In the Status Line, click the Select Object By Type button and drag a selection around the curves to select them all at the same time.

8. Choose Surfaces | Loft ❏ to open the Loft command's Options window.

9. Choose Edit | Reset Settings to restore the tool's setting to the default.

10. Click Loft.

11. Press the 6 key and then press the 3 key to display the surface in smooth and shaded mode.

12. The surface is generated, as shown in Figure 3-28. Again, because the curves are still part of the surface's construction history, any edits made to the curves will be reflected in the surface.

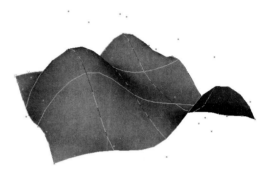

FIGURE 3-28 *A surface is generated by lofting the curves.*

13. Undo the loft operation and deselect all of the curves by clicking empty space.

14. Now choose the curves in a different order. For example, choose the first three curves in order, and then choose the last, and then the second to last.

15. Choose Surfaces | Loft. Notice how the surface flows through the curves in the order they were chosen.

Birail

Birailing works by blending one or more "profile" curves along two "rail" curves. Because birailing allows you to define all four sides of a surface, as well as any shape along that surface, it is capable of generating the most complex shapes with the fewest amount of input curves. (The Loft tool could be used to mimic surfaces generated from the birail tools but might require many source curves, and the results may not be as precise.)

Maya has three different birail tools available in the Surfaces | Birail… menu: Birail 1 Tool, Birail 2 Tool, and Birail 3+ Tool. While all of these operations require exactly two rail curves, the difference between them is the number of curves that are used as profiles.

Its simplest implementation, the Birail 1 tool works by sweeping just one profile curve along two rail curves. The following tutorial demonstrates a great workflow for using the Birail tool to create very complex surfaces. To use the Birail 1 tool, follow these steps:

1. In the Side view, use the CV Curve tool or the EP Curve tool to draw a curve that will be used as one of the rails. When you are finished drawing the curve, press ENTER (RETURN). In this example, a side profile of a car body has been drawn.

2. In the Perspective view, make sure the curve is selected, and choose Edit | Duplicate, or press CTRL-D (COMMAND-D) to duplicate the curve.

3. Select the Move tool from the tool box or press the W key and move the duplicate curve along the X axis. You now have two curves that will be used as the rail curves for the birail operation.

> *NOTE* *Since we duplicated the original curve, we know that both curves have matching parameterization. This will ensure that the resulting surface's isoparms will flow evenly across the surface once it is generated.*

4. Now to create the profile curve. One of the requirements of all the birails is that the profile curves need to intersect both of the rail curves. For this reason, we will snap the first and last CVs of the profile curve to the edit points at the end of each of the two rail curves. Select both of the rail curves and choose Display | NURBS Components | Edit Points. This will turn on the display of the edit points and enable you to snap to them when you draw your profile curve.

5. Choose the EP Curve tool (Create | EP Curve Tool). Hold down the V key to turn on point snapping and click one of the edit points on one of the rail curves. This will snap the first point of the profile curve to the end of the rail curve. While still holding down the V key, click the edit point at the end of the other rail curve. Press ENTER (RETURN) to complete the curve.

6. We now have a one-span NURBS curve whose ends are snapped to the rail curves. Now that the ends are established, we can edit the CVs of the curve to give it more shape. First we'll rebuild the curve so that it has some more CVs for us to work with. Choose Edit Curves | Rebuild

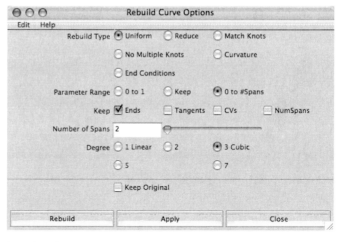

Curve ☐. We will use the Rebuild Curve command to rebuild this profile curve to have two spans instead of the one it has now. Set the Rebuild Curve Options window to match the illustration and then click the Rebuild button.

7. In the Top view window, select the profile curve, right-click, and select Control Vertex from the marking menu. Now select the three CVs in the middle of the curve and use the Move tool to move them out in the Z axis. Be careful not to select the other two CVs at either end of the curve. Doing this will break the intersection with the rail curves and we will be unable to use the Birail command with this set of curves. The next illustration shows all three curves after the editing is complete.

TIP   ***Using this process to build
the profile curve will produce a much
more precise and symmetrical curve
than if we had placed all five CVs by
hand with the CV Curve tool.***

8.   Choose Surfaces | Birail | Birail 1
Tool. The birail tools always require
that you select the profile curve(s) first and then the rail curves. In the Perspective view,
click the profile curve to select it. Now click one of the rail curves and then click the
other rail curve. Press ENTER (RETURN)
to complete the birail operation. The
illustration shows the resulting surface.

Congratulations! You've successfully generated a surface with the Birail 1 tool. If you
think about it, though, you may have been
able to build this same shape with the Extrude
command by extruding the profile curve along
a single path. However, the real power of birailing is when multiple profiles are used
in the birail operation.

For example, let's say that we want the rear profile of the car body to be rounder. To create this,
we could follow the procedure outlined in steps 5-7 above to create another profile curve at the
opposite ends of the rail curves. When using two profile curves, you need to use the Birail 2 tool
(Surfaces | Birail | Birail 2 Tool) to generate the surface.

Select each profile curve first, and then select the two profile curves and press ENTER (RETURN).
The result would look something like this:

As you can see, the shape of the first profile curve is blended into the second profile curve as it
is swept along the two rail curves. While this results in an even interpolation between these two
curves, we may want only the rear profile curve's shape to influence the surface toward the rear

of the car body. No problem. To fix this, we'll just add some more profile curves. Instead of actually drawing the curves, we will derive them from the first birail operation in step 8. Since these curves will already have their end points on the rail curves, we don't need to worry about snapping. We can then reshape these new derived curves and regenerate the surface with the Birail 3+ tool.

1. Return to the surface that was generated in step 8 using the Birail 1 tool. Hold down the right mouse button on the surface and choose Isoparms from the marking menu. Select the isoparm at the rear of the surface.

2. Hold down the SHIFT key and continue selecting other isoparms at any locations along this surface where you want to define a specific shape for the resulting surface.

3. With these isoparms still selected, choose Edit Curves | Duplicate Surface Curves. This will create curves based on the selected isoparms.

4. Select the surface and delete it.

5. Edit the CVs of each of the derived curves. Once again, be careful not to move the CVs at either end of these profile curves. Otherwise, they will no longer intersect the rail curves. The illustration shows the curves after editing the CVs of the other profile curves.

6. Choose Surfaces | Birail | Birail 3+ Tool. Select each of the profile curves. Then select the two rail curves. Press ENTER (RETURN). A new surface will be generated based on the profile curves.

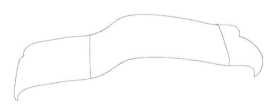

While birailing is by far the most powerful of the surface-generating tools, beginners often have problems with it. Most of the time, any errors are a result of the profile curves not intersecting the rail curves. If you are having trouble with the Birail tool, check to make sure that all of the curves intersect.

Summary

In this chapter, you learned some of the basic principals behind NURBS modeling. We have covered curve creation and editing as well as some of the more common surface-generating commands available in Maya. You have also been shown how to set the options for tools and commands found in the menu bar and edit the attributes in the Channel Box of objects once they are created. We will use many of these same techniques as we move through the tutorials in the next chapter.

Advanced
NURBS Modeling

Now that you have some understanding
of what NURBS are, it's time to practice using them
by building some models. In this chapter, we will build
two hard-surface (nonorganic) models using two
different techniques. The first model we will build
is a cell phone. We'll loft some curves to produce a
surface that will show the phone's details, such as
the holes for buttons and a trimmed-away area for
the LCD screen. The second model is a spaceship.

We will use several techniques to build the main surfaces and then use a patching technique to add the details instead of trimming.

Even if this isn't your first Maya project, be aware that building a model can take a few passes before it looks just right. If you don't like the way things look after you've completed an operation in this chapter (or anytime you work with Maya), don't get frustrated. Just undo, tweak, and try again. It's all part of the modeling process.

Modeling with Trimmed Surfaces

Modeling with trimmed surfaces is a quick way to add detail to any surface. *Trimming* involves creating a curve on a surface by drawing it, projecting it, or using a line of intersection from another intersecting surface. This curve then defines the point at which the area within that curve region can be trimmed away. *Surface fillets* are common in these kinds of models and can be used to generate continuous surfaces that blend between these edges, creating nicely rounded transitions.

Figure 4-1 depicts a plane and a cylinder blended together with a circular fillet, with the inside parts trimmed away.

We'll examine the inner workings of the Trim and Circular Fillet tools as we go through the process of building a model of a cell phone. But before we jump in and start trimming away, it is important that you consider some of the disadvantages of this modeling method. For example, if your surface is deformed in any way, trims and the fillets between them will slow down your computer while their new relationship is being calculated and rendered. Trimmed surfaces are therefore better suited for nonanimated hard-surface models. Another disadvantage when dealing with a trimmed edge is that the number of tools you can use is limited. The Attach tool, for instance, cannot attach a surface to a trimmed edge and works only with surface isoparms. Parameterization of trimmed surfaces is nearly impossible to manage and makes both texturing and converting into polygons quite tricky. Finally, a trimmed edge will produce a lot of geometry that can make your render times soar. When rendering, these heavily tessellated edges might be difficult to match, and the seams might become visible. Often, the only way to hide the seams is through tessellating the model even further. If

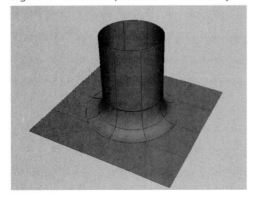

FIGURE 4-1   *A plane and a cylinder are blended together and hidden parts are trimmed away.*

the model will be used in multiple scenes of a movie, for example, the time spent on rendering might be better used in the modeling phase of the production by employing a patch modeling technique, discussed later in this chapter in the section "Modeling with NURBS Patches."

Modeling with trimmed surfaces is therefore well suited for industrial designers who prefer to realize and experiment with various forms and designs rather than achieving shorter render times.

Tutorial: Modeling a Cell Phone

In this tutorial, we'll build a model of a cell phone with trimmed surfaces. The CV Curve and Loft tools, which were covered in detail in Chapter 3, will be used to build the main body of our phone, and we'll use the Fillet and Trim tools to add detail.

We will build this cell phone as if it were to be used as an item on a desk. In other words, it will *not* be shot close-up—so we don't have to worry about the small details on the back or sides, and we won't have to close the *poles*.

Definition   ***poles***   *The point at which all of the vertices come together at either end of an object, forming a star-like pattern with their hulls.*

Set the Working Project
As always, the first step in any new project is to *set* the project from the File menu and create a directory structure that will help you organize the project's assets. A directory structure helps you ensure that all of the assets related to the project are kept in one place, which makes moving projects between computers easy.

1. Open Maya and choose File | Project | New.

2. In the New Project window, click in the Name field and type in a name for the project. For this project, type in **Cellphone Tutorial**. (Note that the project name is *not* the name of the actual scene file, but the name of the directory that will contain all of the subdirectories.)

3. Click the Use Defaults button at the bottom of this window to use the default names for all of the subdirectories.

4. Click the Accept button to accept these settings and close the window.

5. Choose File | Save. Name the file **cellphone_mdl_01**. This indicates that the file contains the cell phone and that it is the first iteration of the model file.

Now, if you go into your users\documents\maya\projects directory, you should see the new folder called Cellphone Tutorial that you created in step 2. Inside that folder are several directories. One of them, the Scenes directory, contains the cellphone_mdl_01 file you created in step 5. We will discuss the other folders as we move through tutorials throughout this book.

Set Up the Underlays

We will use two scanned images of a cell phone as visual references for this project. These images will be projected onto *image planes* and used as *underlays*. By projecting these images onto the image planes, we can match the profiles of the phone with curves drawn in Maya.

Definition   ***image plane***   *A two-dimensional backdrop that is attached to a camera and is always perpendicular to that camera.*

1. Choose Window | Saved Layouts | Four View, or click the Four View button in the toolbar. This will bring up the four panel views, with one Perspective and three Orthographic views. *Be careful not to move, pan, or scale in any of these views!* The image planes will be positioned and scaled to frame themselves within the visible region of the view window. Zooming out in one window will cause the image plane to be larger in that view than the image planes that remain at their default and will result in your underlay images being out of proportion. If you have already moved around in one of the views, you'll need to start a new project.

2. In the Top View panel, choose View | Image Plane. This brings up the file browser, where you can browse for your image file. (It will default to the Source Images directory in the current project, so if you place your image files there, they should be immediately available.)

3. Find the file named MCR_cellphone_imgPl_top.tga and click Open. The image will appear in the Top View panel.

4. Choose View | Select Camera. This will select the Top View Camera node and display its keyable attributes in the Channel Box.

5. Under the list of Input nodes in the Channel Box, select ImagePlane1 to display the image plane's attributes.

6. Set the Center Y attribute to **–10**. This will push the image plane away from our Top View camera so that it will never obstruct the geometry and will remain aligned with the view.

7. In the Top View panel, choose View | Image Plane | Image Plane Attributes to bring up the Attribute Editor for the image plane in the Top view. The following illustration shows the image plane attributes in the Attribute Editor.

8. On the imagePlane1 tab under Image Plane Attributes, set the Display attribute to Looking Through Camera so that the image plane is displayed only in the Top view. This plane will not appear in the Perspective view.

9. Repeat steps 4–8 for the Side View panel. Use MCR_cellphone_imgPl_side.tga as the image plane for the Side view. When you set the attribute for placing the image plane (as you did in step 6), be sure that you set the Center X rather than the Center Y value to **–10** so that it corresponds to the appropriate view.

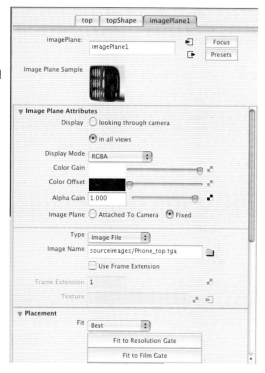

TIP _A good way to select an image plane is to use the Hypershade. Select the camera's tab in the upper tabs section of the Hypershade window and the image plane node will show up there. Select the node to edit its attributes in the Attribute Editor or Channel Box. You can delete the node by selecting it and pressing the_ DELETE _key._

TIP _You can turn off the visibility of the image planes in the view planes by choosing Show | Cameras in the view's menu bar or by creating a new layer, adding the image planes, and turning off the visibility._

Create the Profile Curves

The body of the cell phone will be constructed from a series of lofted profile curves, also known as _cross sections_. We will draw a profile curve for half of the phone body, duplicate it, and then scale it to match a profile along different parts of the phone. This process will be repeated until we have created enough curves to define the entire surface.

1. Start by drawing a profile curve for one half of the phone. This will be rectangular in form. In the Front view, choose Create | CV Curve ❒ and set the CV Curve tool's options to their default settings.

2. Start and end the curve by snapping the CVs to the closest grid lines of both ends of the phone. The second to last points should also be on those same grid lines. Note that by holding down the SHIFT key while clicking to set a point, you can constrain the placement of a point to a right angle from the last point drawn.

FIGURE 4-2   *Profile curve for half of the phone*

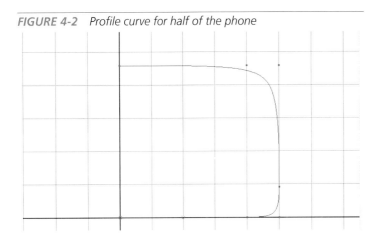

3. Press ENTER (RETURN) to complete the curve. The profile curve should look similar to the curve shown in Figure 4-2.

4. In the Side view, select the curve and move it down along the bottom edge of the phone in the underlay. Choose the Scale tool and scale the curve in the Y direction so that it matches the height of the phone in the side profile.

5. Choose Edit | Duplicate ☐ to open the Duplicate tool's Options window.

6. Choose Edit | Reset Settings to restore this tool to its default settings. Click Duplicate to duplicate the curve and close the Options window.

7. Use the Move tool to move the curve in the Side view to the next key point along the surface. A *key point* is a point that defines the shape of an object at its point of greatest change. Use the Scale tool to match the profile of the phone at that point (see Figure 4-3).

8. Press CTRL-D (COMMAND-D) to duplicate this curve and move it to the next key point along the surface. Continue duplicating, moving, and scaling the curves for the entire length of the phone.

9. Switch to the Top view and use the Scale tool to align the edges of the curves to the edges of the phone in the underlay.

FIGURE 4-3   *Placement of the second curve*

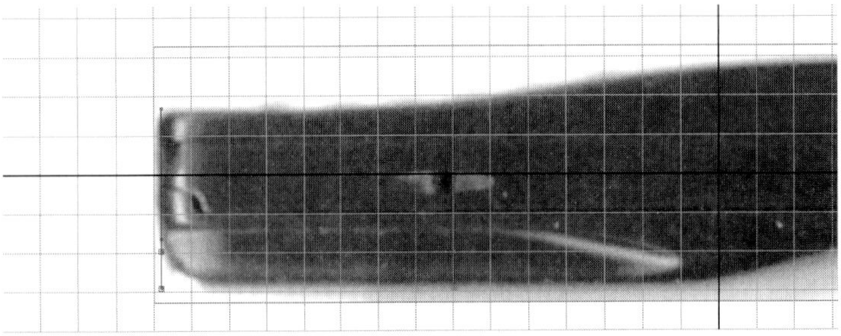

10. Select the curve at one of the ends, duplicate it, and then scale it down. You may wish to change the pivot point so that the scale happens from the center instead of the base.

11. With the curve selected and the Scale tool active, press the INSERT (HOME) key.

12. Drag the pivot point up along the Y axis so that is at about center. Press the INSERT (HOME) key again to return to the Scale tool and scale the curve down.

Figure 4-4 shows the position and scale of the seven curves that will be used to loft the surface.

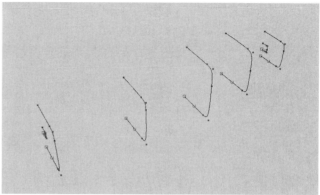

FIGURE 4-4   Position and scale of the curves

Loft the Curves

If we were to select all of the curves in the order in which we wish to execute the loft operation, the surface generated from these curves would be too wavy. This is because the surface between the curves is adjusted so that it flows through the curves evenly. It operates on the same principle that applies when you draw a curve with the EP Curve tool (Edit Point Curve tool). Choose Create | EP Curve Tool to draw a curve by placing edit points instead of CVs—that is, every time you place a new edit point, the shape of the curve adjusts to accommodate it. While we could create more cross sections with the source curves to hold the surface to the shape we want, that could end up being too much work and could create far too much geometry. Instead, we will loft the surface in segments. In this case, the surface of all of the segments will lie between the two cross sections.

1. Select the first two curves and choose Surfaces | Loft ☐ to open the Loft tool's Options window.

2. In the Options window, choose Uniform Parameterization and set Section Span to **2**.

3. Click the Loft button. Your surface will be generated. Continue this process for the rest of the curves. (The leftmost image of Figure 4-5 shows all of the surfaces after they have been lofted.)

4. Now select one of the end surfaces. In the Channel Box, select the Loft node and change the Section Spans attribute to **1**. Do this for the other end surface as well.

5. Select the first two surfaces and choose Edit Surfaces | Attach Surfaces ☐ to open the Attach Surfaces tool's Options window.

6. Choose Edit | Reset Settings from the Options window's menu to reset the tool to its default settings. With these settings, the surfaces will be blended together to create a smooth transition between all of the surfaces.

7. Click Apply to attach the selected surfaces with these settings. Do this for all of the pieces until one single surface has been created. The middle image of Figure 4-5 shows the phone once the lofted surfaces have been attached.

FIGURE 4-5 *From left to right: the curves are lofted; the lofted segments are attached; the surface is mirrored and duplicated*

 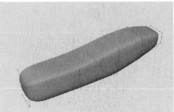 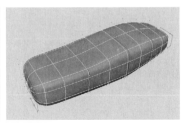

8. To mirror the surface, select it and choose Edit | Duplicate ❏ to open the Duplicate tool's Options window.

9. Set the Scale to **–1** for the X value (the first column). Click Duplicate. The rightmost image of Figure 4-5 shows the surfaces after being duplicated.

 10. Select both surfaces. In the Status Line, set the selection mask to component mode and set the type to Lines so that you can select just the isoparms. Select the edge isoparm on the top side of the phone body on each surface.

11. Choose Edit NURBS | Attach Surfaces. The surface will be attached at the selected isoparms.

> *NOTE While it is not necessary that you select the isoparms when you're attaching a surface, doing so indicates which edge isoparms will be joined. In this case, we want to attach the surface on the top of the phone to ensure that the seam appears on the back of the phone. This way, we will not run into a seam problem while drawing curves on the surface of the top of the phone later on in the tutorial.*

Create the Speaker Piece

We'll use the Circular Fillet tool to create a nice, round transition curve between two intersecting surfaces in the same way we use the Curve Fillet tool to create round transition curves between two intersecting curves. One of the Surface Fillet tool's options lets us create curves on the surfaces where the fillet surface begins and ends. This curve can then be used as a point at which we can trim the surface.

 The Trim tool is used to cut or trim away a selected region of a surface. This region is usually defined by a curve on a surface created by intersecting surfaces, fillets, drawn curves on surfaces, and other similar processes. You use the tool after you select the part of the surface you want to discard or keep. Exactly what happens to the selected region can be set in the Trim tool's Options window. If you make a mistake or want to make a change, any trimmed surface can be untrimmed by using the Untrim Surface tool.

1. To start building the speaker piece, first create a sphere and scale it to match the diameter of the speaker in the top underlay.

2. Non-uniform scale the sphere in the Y axis. Translate it in the Y direction and rotate it slightly so that it follows the surface of the phone.

3. With the sphere still selected, change to a Perspective view and press the R key to choose the Scale tool.

4. Click and drag on the green box to non-uniform scale the sphere down along its Y axis. Now rotate it slightly along the X axis and translate it down along the Y axis so that the isoparm at the equator of the sphere is somewhat tangent to the surface of the phone. Figure 4-6 shows the sphere placed in the proper position.

5. Select the sphere and the phone and choose Edit NURBS | Surface Fillet | Circular Fillet ❐ to open the Circular Fillet command's Options window.

6. Check the Create Curve On Surface check box, and set the Radius to **.3**.

7. Click Apply to create the fillet between the surfaces.

8. It is possible that the fillet will be created in the wrong direction. The Circular Fillet tool will create the fillet between the two surface normals' facing direction. If the surface normals are facing a direction other than the intended direction of the fillet, you can use the Circular Fillet tool's options to reverse these normals during the fillet operation. To do this, click the Reverse Primary Normal checkbox to reverse the surface normal direction of the fillet calculation (for the first surface selected). Click the Reverse Secondary Normal check box to reverse the direction of the second surface selected.

FIGURE 4-6 *The sphere is scaled and placed on top of the phone.*

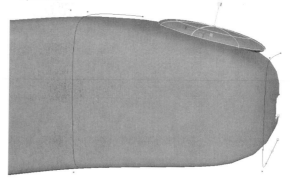

Command vs. Tool

This is a good time to bring up the difference between a *command* and a *tool* in Maya. When using a command, objects are usually selected and then the command is chosen to perform an operation based on the selected elements. The Revolve and Loft commands are examples of some commands. When using a tool, the object is not selected first. Instead, a tool is chosen and then a series of selections is made. The tool is closed by pressing the ENTER (RETURN) key. The CV Curve tool and the Trim tool are good examples of tools.

9. Examine the result in the wireframe display mode. If it does not match the example at the left in Figure 4-7, choose Edit | Undo to undo your work to before you created the fillet, and then select one of the Reverse Surface Normals check boxes in the Fillet tool's Options window and try again. Continue different combinations until it looks right.

10. Now trim away the top part of the sphere and the section of the phone that is on the inside of your new fillet. You'll need to set the Trim tool to keep the region of the surface that you select once you invoke the tool. Choose Edit NURBS | Trim Tool ❑. In the Trim tool's Options window, set the Selected State attribute to Keep. This will keep the region of the surface that you select and discard the other.

11. First trim the sphere by choosing Edit NURBS | Trim Tool and selecting the bottom part of the sphere. You will have to view the scene in wireframe to select the inside of the sphere.

12. Press ENTER (RETURN) to trim the surface. Repeat step 9 to finesse the phone surface. The right image in Figure 4-7 shows the phone after the trim operations.

Create the LED Screen

Now let's create the phone's LED screen by making the phone's surface "live" and then drawing a curve on that surface to define an enclosed region for the screen. With this area defined, we'll

---

FIGURE 4-7 *At left, a circular fillet is created around the intersection of the sphere and the phone; at right, the phone surface after trimming out the region for the speaker*

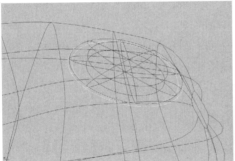
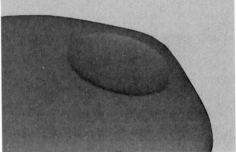

use the Trim tool to separate the phone into two pieces, the phone and the screen. We will then loft the edges of these two pieces to create a surface that can be used to produce a crease that will represent the seal around the screen.

1. In the Top view, select the main phone surface and, in the Status Line, click the Make Live button; or choose Modify | Make Surface Live.

2. Use the CV Curve tool to draw a curve on the surface of the phone that matches the shape of the screen in the underlay.

3. Open the Trim tool Options window and check the Keep Original check box. Then close the window.

4. Trim the phone's body away from the LED screen. (Since you turned on the Keep Original option, the phone's body will remain intact.)

5. Delete the history of these objects (choose Edit | Delete All By Type | History). Move the screen piece up slightly so you can see the entire phone underneath it.

6. Back in the Trim tool Options window, turn off the Keep Original check box. Then trim the screen away from the rest of the phone's body. The left image of Figure 4-8 shows the phone body about to be trimmed.

FIGURE 4-8 *The phone body about to be trimmed, and a lofted surface created between the trimmed edges*

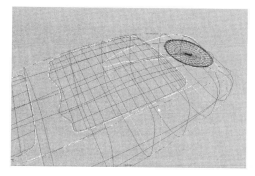
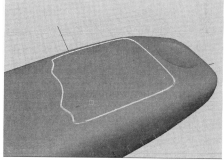

7. Slightly scale down the screen piece, and select the trimmed edge of the phone's body. To select the trimmed edge, right-click the trimmed surface and choose Trim Edge from the marking menu.

8. SHIFT-select the trimmed edge of the screen.

9. Open the Loft command's Options window and set Section Spans to **4** and apply the loft. The right image in Figure 4-8 shows a lofted surface that is created between the two trimmed edges.

10. Select the middle hull of our new loft and move it down to make a small crease appear around the screen. The image at the left in Figure 4-9 shows a close-up of this crease with the hull displaying. The image at the right shows the phone with the completed screen section.

If you'd like some more practice with drawing curves on surfaces and using the Trim tool, use the same process outlined here to create a section on the phone body for the keypad.

FIGURE 4-9   *A close-up of the crease around the screen, and the completed LED screen*

 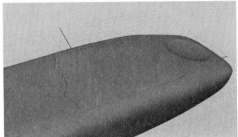

Create the Antenna

To create the antenna piece, we will use a NURBS cylinder that intersects with the phone body. A circular fillet will then be used to blend the two pieces together.

1. Create a NURBS cylinder with eight sections and three spans.

2. Place the cylinder where the antenna should appear on the cell phone body, making sure that it intersects the body. The top-left image in Figure 4-10 shows the cylinder in position.

3. Choose, Edit Surface | Circular Fillet ❑. Set the Radius to a value of **.4** to create a nice, round fillet between the pieces. The top-right image in Figure 4-10 shows the surfaces after they have been blended with a circular fillet.

4. To create some detail on the antenna, right-click the antenna and select Isoparms from the marking menu.

5. Hold down the SHIFT key and drag another isoparm about halfway between the isoparm you just placed and the isoparm at the end.

6. Choose Edit NURBS | Detach Surface. Delete the surface in the middle of the two longer pieces so that there is now a gap. It should look similar to the bottom-right image in Figure 4-10.

FIGURE 4-10 *The creation of the antenna, clockwise starting from top-left: placement of the cylinder; fillet between the phone and cylinder; cylinder detached at two places; the final antenna*

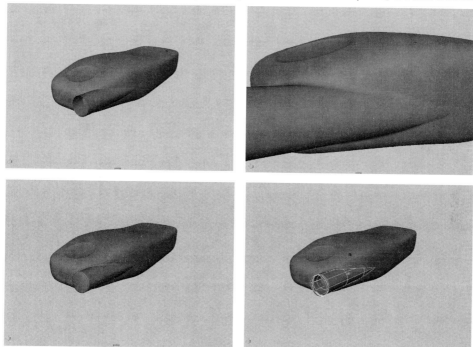

7. Now select the two isoparms on the edges, and loft the surface with two section spans between them. Doing this gives us a surface with more geometry that we can use to create tight details. Since this surface is not attached to the other parts of the cylinder, it will not disrupt them when we edit the CVs of the smaller surface.

8. Select the middle hull of this lofted surface and scale it in just a bit to create a crease.

9. Finally, select the last row of CVs at the end of the antenna and scale them all the way down to close the end. The bottom-left image in Figure 4-10 shows the phone with the completed antenna.

Model the Buttons

Now let's add the phone's number buttons.

1. In the Front view, draw a profile curve for a button with the CV Curve tool. Make sure that the two points at the top align with one another. (See the image at left in Figure 4-11.)

FIGURE 4-11 *Creating a profile curve (left), and revolving to create a button (right)*

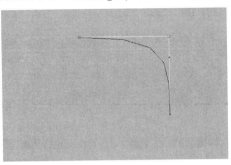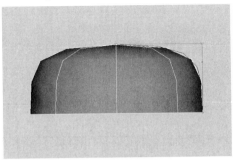

2. With the curve selected, choose Surfaces | Revolve. Make sure that the Revolve tool is set to revolve around the curve's Y axis. (See the image at right in Figure 4-11.)

3. Move the first button into position on the cell phone body. Use the Scale tool to shape it to look like the buttons in the cell phone underlay.

4. Continue to duplicate, scale, and move the buttons to match the buttons in the underlay. When you're finished, it should look similar to what's shown in Figure 4-12.

FIGURE 4-12 *Completed cell phone*

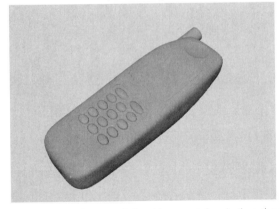

You could continue adding other details around the body of the phone if you wish. One suggestion would be to trim out areas around the buttons and then use circular fillets to round off the edges. How far you want to go with the details is up to you.

Modeling with NURBS Patches

Patch modeling involves creating a network of separate, four-sided surfaces, or *patches*, and organizing them in a way that follows the bounds of an object. The most important thing to remember when modeling these patches is that they maintain their matching surface parameterization. This will allow operations such as attaching surfaces to behave in an organized and predictable manner, resulting in well-formed surfaces. Furthermore, surfaces with related parameterization can be stitched together to create and maintain continuity among the parts of an object. Finally, if the surfaces are converted to polygons, the surfaces can be *tessellated* (converted into polygonal faces) and easily merged with the other patched surfaces adjacent to them.

Figure 4-13 shows a plane and a cylinder that have been blended together using the trim technique discussed in the section "Modeling with Trimmed Surfaces," and a plane and cylinder that

FIGURE 4-13 *A plane and a cylinder blended together through a patching technique (left) and a trim technique (right)*

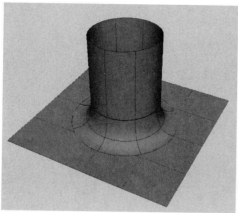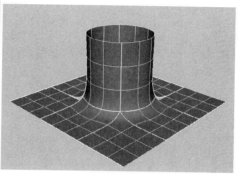

uses the multi-patch modeling technique. Notice how the surface parameterization is maintained throughout the multi-patch example shown in the figure.

In the past, the multi-patch modeling technique was most commonly used to model characters. However, with the recent advances in subdivision surface modeling, multi-patch NURBS modeling is rarely used today in organic modeling, even though it still remains the best technique for creating hard-surface models in Maya. One factor affecting this change is precision, because surfaces generated from a network of curves will usually produce very accurate results. In addition, multi-patched models can easily be converted to an organized polygonal mesh and exported to another program. Converting to polygons also gives you more options for texturing (as we'll see in Chapter 14). Finally, if the object is going to be used in several shots, the render times will be dramatically reduced, since no heavily trimmed edges will require heavy tessellation (to hide visible seams where the surfaces meet).

Tutorial: Creating a Spaceship Model

This tutorial will take you through the steps of building the spaceship model shown in Figure 4-14. Instead of using trims to cut out the holes for windows, landing gear hatches, and other elements, we'll build a network of four-sided NURBS patches that follow the contour and details of the spaceship's form.

FIGURE 4-14 *Concept drawing of the spaceship (designed and illustrated by Herold Boyesen)*

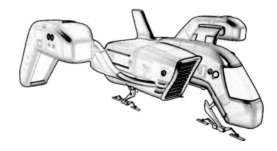

When building a model of reasonable complexity and numerous pieces, it is always best not to get hung up on the minute details at the beginning of the modeling process. Rather than building each piece separately and not moving on until each piece is absolutely finished, we are going to approach our project by building the model in "passes." In other words, we'll start by building the basic, main pieces as single surfaces and then we'll add the details in following passes.

The first pass establishes the basic shapes of the model. You can use either primitives or surfaces generated from curves. Not only will this geometry be used as the basis for the next pass, but it could also act as a low-resolution version useful for previsualizing the animation or as a stand model for better performance.

During the second pass at the model, we'll add most of the predominant detail in the surfaces. This involves breaking up the base surfaces into a bunch of individual patches and adding the details where the surfaces are supposed to break or blend with an intersecting piece of geometry.

The last pass will add the extraneous details that are either derived from surface curves or modeled as completely separate objects, as is the case with the landing gear.

> **TIP**   *Before you begin creating a model, it is important that you consider the level of detail that is needed from the model to complete the shot needed. If the model will be used in multiple shots, perhaps you can set up the production schedule to do the far and wide shots first (so that little detail is required) and the medium and close-up shots later (where more detail is required). This might give you more time to finesse the details.*

A storyboard for the shot we are trying to produce in this tutorial can be found in Appendix A. This storyboard tells us that the spaceship will be used in a medium shot, and therefore a decent amount of detail is needed. Given that we are using the patch modeling method to build the ship, we will pretend that the model will be needed in several shots with this level of detail.

Setting Up the Workspace and Custom UI

Any job in Maya can be accomplished with greater ease if the workspace is set up to fit the specific workflow. This includes setting up the panel arrangements and visible UI elements, creating Shelf buttons for frequently used tool settings and MEL scripts, and setting up keyboard shortcuts and marking menus. Although some custom Shelf buttons are suggested here, you should feel free to add your own.

The workspace should be set up to allow for the largest possible view window. Among other things, you might like to arrange the Status Line and Shelf so that their tabs are visible. On the Shelf, you can include a Rebuild Surface button with custom settings as well as a button to bring up the rebuild options for both surfaces and curves. The rest of the buttons we'll need are covered as we go along.

Let's start by setting set up the workspace for modeling:

1. Choose Display | UI Elements | Show UI Elements.

2. From the UI Elements list, uncheck Time Slider and Range Slider. Then turn on the Channel Box/Layer Editor by checking the box next to it in that list.

3. Choose Edit Surfaces | Rebuild Surfaces ❏ to open the Rebuild Surface tool Options window.

4. We need to create a setting that will be saved to a Shelf button that can be accessed quickly over and over again. The following settings should be used every time a surface is attached or detached or isoparms are inserted. This will rebuild the surface to a degree 3 surface with normal parameterization. Set the options to match those shown in the following illustration, and then click Close.

5. Click the little black arrow on the far left side of the Shelf. Choose New Shelf. Name the new Shelf **Modeling**. A new, empty Shelf is created.

6. Hold down CTRL-SHIFT (CONTROL-SHIFT) and choose Edit NURBS | Rebuild Surfaces. A Shelf button will be created that, when clicked, executes that Rebuild Surface command with the options you just set.

7. You will also be rebuilding surfaces to have different spans in U and V. For this reason, it is a good idea to create a button that brings up the Rebuild Surface Options window. Hold down CTRL-SHIFT (CONTROL-SHIFT) and choose Edit NURBS | Rebuild Surfaces ❏. This will create a Shelf button that brings up the Options window shown here.

8. Repeat steps 6 and 7 to create the Shelf button for the Rebuild Curve tool. Set the options as follows:

    - Rebuild Type: Uniform

    - Parameter Range: 0 to #Spans

    - Keep: CVs

    - Degree U and
      Degree V: 3 Cubic

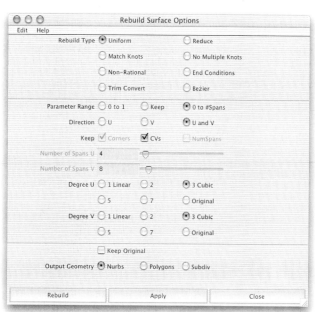

We will create more buttons and add MEL scripts to this Shelf as we advance through the tutorials in this book. For now, we've done enough, and we're ready to begin building the spaceship model.

First Pass: Building the Base Model

The goal of this first pass is to create a model that will serve as a basis for deriving the changes in all of the following passes. The model resulting from this pass will appear simple and basic in geometric form. The most important aspect of this pass is to ensure that the geometry matches the flow of the surface. In other words, the isoparms in the surfaces created in this pass should follow any turns or curves along that surface.

To create the base model, we use either sculpted NURBS primitives or surfaces generated from lofted curves. The Attach Surfaces tool will also play an important role.

Before we begin, make sure you set up your project and directory. (Review steps 1–5 in the "Set the Working Project" section of the cell phone tutorial if you need to.) We'll call this project SpaceShip_Tutorial, and we'll name the scene SpaceShip_mdl_01.mb.

The next steps deal with creating image planes that display the drawings to be used as guides as we model. Make sure the MCR_SpaceShip_imgPl_top.tga and MCR_SpaceShip_imgPl_side.tga files have been copied from the CD included with this book and are saved to your hard drive. Put them in the SpaceShip_Tutorial\Source Images directory.

For a step-by-step review of this process, refer to steps 1–7 in the "Set Up the Underlays" section of the cell phone tutorial. When set up properly, your Workspace should look like that shown in Figure 4-15.

FIGURE 4-15   *Image planes set up and ready for modeling*

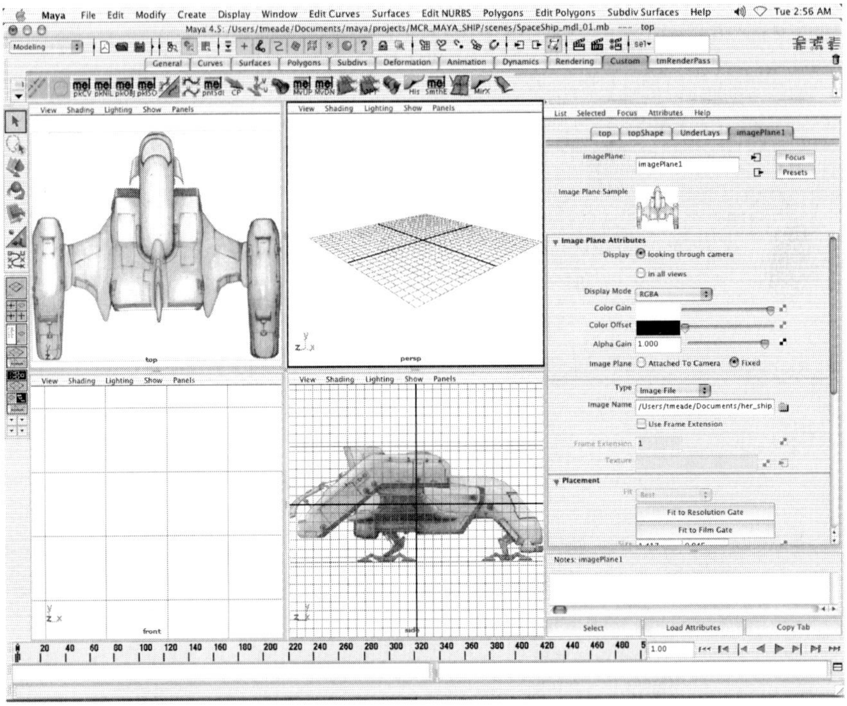

![Screenshot of Maya workspace with image planes set up for modeling a spaceship]

Drawing Profile Curves for the Engine Block   With the image planes set up, we will begin
the actual modeling process. Start by drawing and placing the curves for the large centerpiece
that houses the air intake and main thruster engines. We will then use the Loft tool to generate the
surfaces. Since the model is completely symmetrical, we'll build only half of the model. Near
the end of the process, we can mirror the geometry to create the other half.

1. Choose Create | CV Curve ☐.

2. Click the Show Tool Settings tool in the Status Line.

3. Click the Reset Tool button at the top of the tool settings panel to set the CV Curve
   tool to its defaults. This will set it up so that we can create a third-degree curve with
   uniform parameterization.

4. With your mouse cursor over the view window, hold down the SPACEBAR and left-click-hold
   the A/W box. This will bring up the view marking menu. Choose Front View.

5. Hold down the X key to toggle on grid snapping. Click at the center origin to place the
   first point.

6. Move out 5 units on the X axis and click to place the second point. Place a third point
   1 unit later at 6 units.

7. Release the X key and hold down the SHIFT key so that the next point snaps to the last
   point at a right angle. Move up about 2.5 units in Y and click to place the fourth point.
   Place the fifth point 1 unit past that.

8. Release the SHIFT key and press and hold the X key to toggle grid snapping on again.
   Snap to the grid point at 5 units in Y and 6 units in X. Place the next point at the same
   height but curve it back 1 unit in X.

9. Finally, place the last point at 0,6. Press ENTER
   (RETURN) to finish the curve. The finished curve
   should look like the one shown in Figure 4-16.

10. Switch to the Top view. Move the curve so that it
    aligns with the front edge of the thruster engine
    piece in the underlay.

11. With the curve selected, choose Edit | Duplicate ☐
    to bring up the Duplicate tool's Options window.

12. Reset the settings by choosing Edit | Reset Settings.
    Click Duplicate to duplicate the curve and close
    the Options window.

FIGURE 4-16   Profile curve displaying its CVs

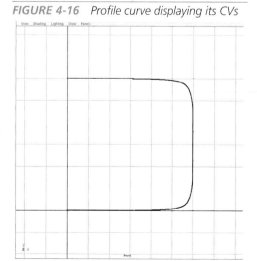

13. Choose the Move tool or press the W key and move the duplicate curve back along the Z axis to the next key point in the surface. A *key point* in a surface is the location at its greatest point of change.

14. Press CTRL-D (COMMAND-D) to duplicate the selected curve again. Move it to the next key point in the surface.

15. Continue duplicating and moving the curves to different points along the surface another five times.

FIGURE 4-17 *Scaled curves match the top profile*

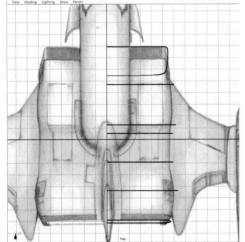

16. Starting with the first curve, select it and choose the Scale tool or press the R key. Non-uniform scale the curve along its X axis (drag the red box) so that the right edge matches the right edge of the object in the drawing. Do this for each of the curves. You should end up with something that resembles Figure 4-17.

17. Switch to the Side view. Starting with the first curve, move the curve along the Y axis so that it aligns with the base of the object in the drawing. Repeat this for the rest of the curves.

18. Now go back through and non-uniform scale the curves along the Y axis (drag the yellow box) so that the top of the curve aligns with the top of the object in the drawing.

19. We now need to bend that first curve so that it conforms to the front of the thruster object where the air intake is. Select the bottom half of the CVs in the front curve and move them back along the Z axis to the point at which the surface begins along the bottom edge. Then use the Rotate tool to make the CVs better align with the entire edge. Figure 4-18 shows the final result of all of the curves once they have been scaled and edited to match the profiles in the underlay.

FIGURE 4-18 *The curves have been scaled and edited to match the profile in the Side view.*

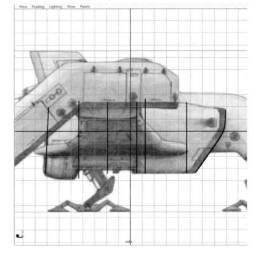

20. The rear of the thruster piece ends at a slight angle. Compensate for this in the profile curve by rotating it slightly.

Generating the Surface Now we'll loft these curves to generate the surfaces. If we were to select all of the curves and loft them at the same time with uniform parameterization, the surface would not match up properly. It would look something like Figure 4-19. It's close, but notice that the surface at the front (on the right side of the image) curves down as it leaves the first source curve. You can also see a problem in the step segment in the middle. To obtain more predictable results, we are going to loft the curves in segments just as we did with the cell phone body earlier in this chapter.

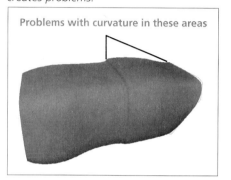

FIGURE 4-19 Lofting all the curves at once creates problems.

1. Select the first three curves. Because these curves were created in order, you can drag-select them and they will loft in the correct order.

2. Choose Surfaces | Loft □ to open the Loft tool Options window.

3. Choose Edit | Reset Settings. Click the Loft button to loft the curves. The result should look like the left image in Figure 4-20.

4. In the Select Object By Type menu in the Status Line, turn off the Surface Mask button. This way, you will not accidentally select the surface when you try to select the curves.

5. Select the third and fourth curves, and then choose Surfaces | Loft.

6. Select the fourth and fifth curves. This time, hold down the SPACEBAR to open the Hotbox and choose Recent Commands | Loft. (This might be a quicker way to invoke the loft operation, because your eyes don't have to leave that spot on the screen to go up top.)

7. Finally, select the fifth, sixth, and seventh curves and loft them together. When you are finished, you will have four separate surfaces with positional continuity. (See the right image in Figure 4-20.)

FIGURE 4-20 Lofted surfaces

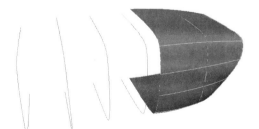 

NOTE   **You might also consider making a Shelf button in your modeling Shelf, or creating a hot key for the loft operation, using the default settings.**

Before we attach these surfaces, we can add spans to the surfaces that we want to remain more intact after the attach has occurred. Remember from our discussion of continuity that curvature continuity requires three CVs from each surface edge. Since these surfaces were lofted with only one span between each loft, almost half of the surface will change to blend with the surface next to it when the Attach command is used. Inserting more section spans will cause less of a change. The second surface is the one that we are concerned about.

8. Select the second surface from the front. In the Status Line, click the Show Attribute Editor button.

9. Choose the loft node from the tabs in the Attribute Editor. In this case, it is the second loft made, so the node is called loft2. It should look like the one shown here.

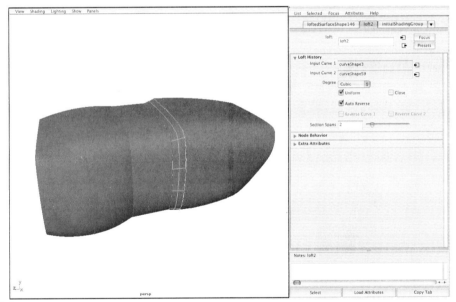

10. Under the Loft History attribute group, you will see an attribute called Section Spans. Increase this value to **2**.

Note that we could also have used the Rebuild Surface tool here, but since the Section Spans attribute is part of our construction history, it is faster to do it this way. Whenever possible, you should try to avoid adding extra nodes to objects.

11. Now we will attach the surfaces. Select the first and second surfaces. Choose Edit Surfaces | Attach Surfaces ❑ to bring up the Attach Surface tool options.

12. Choose Edit | Reset Settings to use the defaults. Click the Attach button.

13. Select that newly attached surface and the third surface and use the Attach Surface tool to attach them. Repeat this again for the last surface. Figure 4-21 shows the engine block with all of the surfaces attached.

FIGURE 4-21   All four surfaces attached

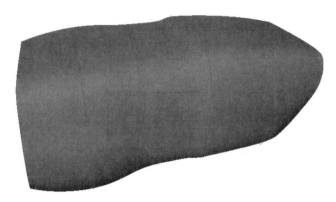

14. Every time you attach, detach, or add isoparms, you should rebuild the surface to maintain normal parameterization. With the surface selected, click the Rebuild Surface button that we set up in our modeling Shelf. You'll notice that some of the isoparms reposition themselves slightly.

Organizing the Scene with Display Layers   Let's clean up the organization of the scene a bit. The Layer Editor offers a great way to organize objects in a scene. The visibility of a layer can be toggled on and off to control the visibility of a group of objects.

1. Click the Show Channel Box/Layer Editor button in the Status Line.

2. In the Layer Editor, click the Create New Layer button. A new layer is created.

3. Double-click the new layer text area to edit it. The Edit Layer window opens, where we can rename this layer. Let's call it **baseCurves**.

4. Select all of the curves in the scene. Right-click the baseCurves layer in the Layer Editor and choose Add Selected from the marking menu.

5. Create another layer and name it **baseSurfaces**. Add the engine block surface to this layer.

6. Click in the field of the object name in that Channel Box and change it to **nMainEngine**. (The *n* prefix denotes that the object is a NURBS object.)

7. In the Layer Editor, uncheck the Visible check box for the two new layers that contain our objects. This will hide all objects in these layers while we work on new pieces of the spaceship.

Modeling the Side Thruster Engine and Fuselage Now let's build the fuselage and side thruster engine with a series of lofted curves.

1. Use steps similar to steps 1–9 of the "Drawing Profile Curves for the Engine Block" section to draw the profile curve for the side thruster engine. It should have five CVs for a total of five spans. Figure 4-22 shows how the completed curve should look.

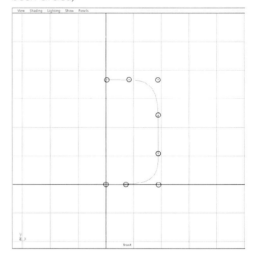

FIGURE 4-22 *Profile curve for the engine thruster engine displaying its CVs (CVs have been circled)*

2. Go through the steps of aligning the curves at the key points of the surface.

3. Use the Rotate tool to rotate and place the curves at the key points on an angle. When moving these curves, make sure that the Move tool is set to move in Object space. To access and change the Move tool's settings, double-click the Move tool in the toolbar. See Figure 4-23 for exact placement of the curves on the spaceship drawing.

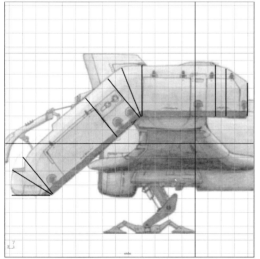

FIGURE 4-23 *Curves (highlighted in black) aligned along the surface of the thruster engine*

4. Choose Surfaces | Loft ❐ and set the number of Section Spans to **2**. For the surfaces that need only one section span, we'll make changes later in the Channel Box.

5. Loft the curves two at a time. The three curves that define the major turn in the surface can be lofted at the same time. You will end up with eight separate surfaces.

6. Select the first surface and change the Section Spans attribute on the Loft node to **1**. This can be done either in the Channel Box or in the Attribute Editor under the Loft node. Do this for the second surface as well. See Figure 4-24 for details.

7. Use the Attach tool with the default settings to attach all of these surfaces together.

FIGURE 4-24   *Separate surfaces after lofting; the Section Spans attribute of the first two lofts has been set to 1.*

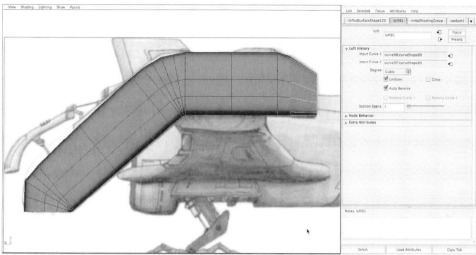

8.   With the resulting single surface selected, click the Rebuild Surface button in your custom modeling Shelf.

9.   Choose Edit | Delete By Type | History. The completed surface should look like the one shown here.

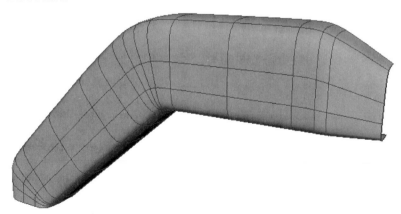

10.   In the Attribute Editor, name the surface **nThrusterBase** and add it to the baseSurfaces layer.

11.   Select all of the curves, group them, and name the group **thrusterCurves**. Add them to the baseCurves layer.

12. Use the same processes you used to create the thruster engine to build the fuselage. The source curve will have eight CVs, making five spans. (See Figure 4-25.)

13. Use the Duplicate, Move, Rotate, and Scale tools to align the curves at different key points along the surface. The example shown in Figure 4-26 uses nine curves.

FIGURE 4-25   *Fuselage source curve displaying the CVs*

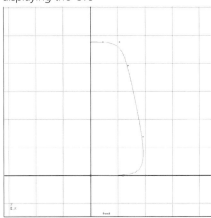

FIGURE 4-26   *Side view of the curves aligned*

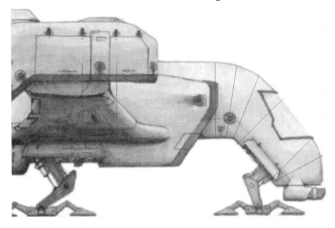

14. Loft the curves two at a time to create a total of eight surfaces. While you should use the default lofting settings of a single Section Span for most of the pieces, the two sections that make the sharpest turn should have two Section Spans so that they maintain their overall shape when attached.

15. Attach all of the surfaces together with the Attach tool at its default settings.

16. Select the single surface and click the Rebuild Surface button in the modeling Shelf.

17. Select the surface and choose Edit | Delete By Type | Delete History.

18. In the Attribute Editor, name the surface **nFuselageBase**. Add the surface to the baseSurfaces layer.

19. Select all of the curves, group them together, and name them **fuselageCurves**. Move this group into the baseCurves layer.

Modeling the Wing   Our spaceship is now really starting to take form. The only main piece remaining is the wing. Instead of drawing profile curves and lofting them as we did with the other pieces, we are going to start with a primitive NURBS cylinder, scale it, and then sculpt it into the shape we need.

1. Choose Create | NURBS Primitive | Cylinder ❐ to bring up the Cylinder Options window.

2. Choose Edit | Reset Settings to restore the Cylinder options to their default settings.

3. Set the Axis attribute to **X**. This will create a cylinder with the same orientation as our wing object.

4. Set the Number of Sections to **12**, and click the Create button to create the cylinder and close the Options window.

Now we'll shape the cylinder into a more rectangular shape. This will give us nice, round edges while saving time by starting with a cube and then attaching the surfaces together. We will then add some isoparms and move some more CVs around until we get the shape we need.

This process of moving the CVs around is known as *sculpting*. When sculpting, it is always important that you add geometry sparingly. Do as much as you can with the basic shape before you add isoparms. This way, you'll have a lot fewer CVs to worry about having to move. Your surfaces will also end up looking a lot smoother.

1. In the Side view, right-click the object and select Control Vertex from the marking menu.

2. Drag-select the first CVs above and below the equator along the Z axis. Scale these out along the Z axis until they almost match the CVs at the equator. The left image in Figure 4-27 shows the CVs (circled) after they have been moved.

3. Select the next four CVs and scale them up a bit in Y so that they almost align with the CVs at the equator along the Y axis.

4. Now scale the CVs out along the Z axis so that they almost line up with the CVs we scaled in the last step. (See the right image in Figure 4-27.)

FIGURE 4-27 *CVs scaled out from the center to align with the vertical axes on each side*

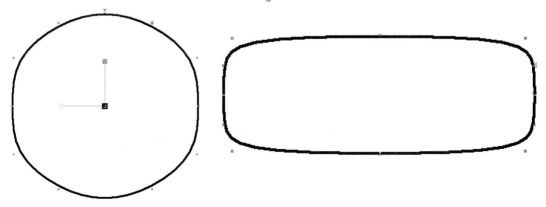

5. Select the entire cylinder and move it so that it lines up with the center of the point at which the wing meets the spaceship body.

6. Use the Scale tool to non-uniform scale the entire cylinder in Y and Z so that it almost matches the root of the wing object. (See Figure 4-28.)

7. Make any final adjustments to the CVs to create a nice, even edge.

8. Switch to a Top view and move the surface so that it sits at about the center of the wing. Scale it out in the X direction so that it extends just past the main engine and side thruster pieces in the drawing.

9. Select the last two rows of CVs along the right edge—the ones closest to the thruster.

10. Scale them down along the Z axis and move them back so that the front and back edges align to the front and rear edge of the wing in the drawing (Figure 4-29).

11. To add curvature to this piece so that its edges are shaped like they are in the drawing, we need to add a few isoparms. Right-click the object and choose Isoparm from the marking menu.

12. Click-drag one of the isoparms in the surface's V direction and drag it to one of the key points of change along the surface in the drawing.

13. Choose Edit Surfaces | Insert Isoparms ❑ to open the Insert Isoparms tool's Options window. Reset to the defaults.

FIGURE 4-28   *The scaled cylinder*

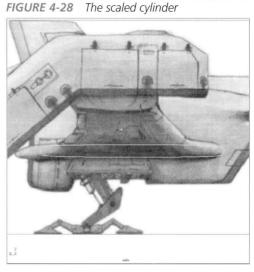

FIGURE 4-29   *Edge scaled down*

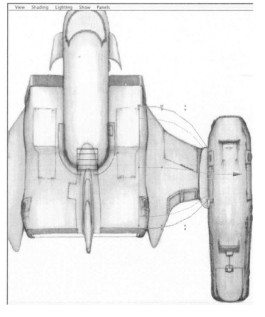

Note that inserting isoparms is similar to inserting edit points on curves. On curves, you select a curve point and then choose Edit Curves | Insert Knot (a *knot* is another word for *edit point*). The default setting for the Insert Isoparms tool will insert one isoparm at the place that we indicated on the surface. Using the Insert Location attribute in the Attribute Editor, you could choose two isoparms on the surface and set the tool to insert any number of isoparms between the selections. The number of isoparms inserted is based on the Multiplicity attribute.

14. Now add another isoparm at another key point in the surface.

15. Right-click and select Hull from the marking menu.

16. Choose the hull in the middle left, scale it, and move it along its Z axis until it matches the overall shape of the wing in the drawing. (Ignore the piece of the surface that extends out past the engine—we will deal with that detail later. For now, try to imagine the wing without that piece.)

17. Repeat this for the next hull over. By adjusting these two hulls together, you should be able to pretty well match the drawing, as shown in Figure 4-30.

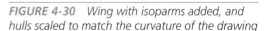

FIGURE 4-30   *Wing with isoparms added, and hulls scaled to match the curvature of the drawing*

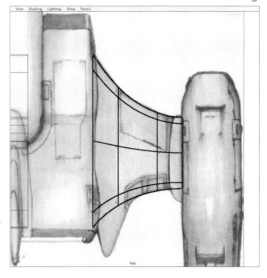

18. Now rebuild the surface and delete the history.

19. Now we need to shape the wing from the Front view. Since we don't have a front drawing to guide us, we'll have to make some guesses and use our eye. We at least know that the surface starts at the main engine piece and ends at the thruster. Therefore, that gives us a good place to start. The left side is already lined up, so we'll start with the right edge. Make the baseSurfaces layer visible. We'll use this layer to align the edge of the wing.

20. Select the two rows of CVs on the edge of the wing closest to the thruster.

21. Switch to the Front view and move the CVs up along the Y axis so that they are at about center with the height of the thruster's top leg.

22. It might help to switch to a wireframe display. Press the 4 key to display only the wireframe. You might also want to turn down the display smoothness by pressing the 1 key.

23. With all surfaces selected, press the 1 key. The result is shown here.

24. Now we need to rotate the next row of CVs (shown next) so that it "flows" toward the CVs on either side of it. Move this hull (the fourth hull along the V direction of this surface) up and rotate it along its Z axis so that the curvature of the surface passing though it looks even.

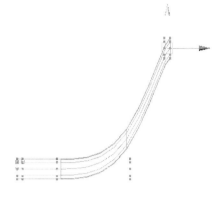

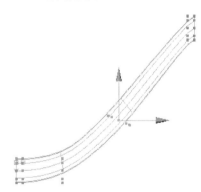

25. Add an isoparm about halfway between the one we just edited and the next one toward the right edge.

26. Select the new hull and move it up near the top edge. Rotate it again to match the flow of the surface.

27. Continue tweaking hulls by rotating and moving them until you end up with something that looks like Figure 4-31.

28. Select the surface and rebuild it using the Rebuild button in our modeling Shelf.

29. In the Attribute Editor, name this object **nRt_Wing**. Add it to the base surfaces layer.

The first pass of our model is now complete. At this point, you could mirror the geometry and hand it off to an animator. A model in this condition is perfect for animating because the geometry is not too complex. The animator would have no performance problems playing back the animation in real time.

FIGURE 4-31 *The surface with all of the hulls in position*

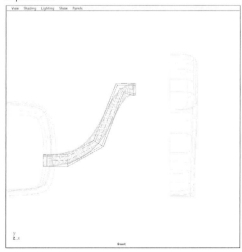

Second Pass: Breaking Up the Surfaces to Add Detail

This is the part where we really go to work. We have the basic forms down for each surface, but we haven't provided any detail. While the overall shape of the model might communicate what it is or represents, the details we add "sell" it as a real object—so that the people viewing it in the final render will believe that the object exists without thinking that it is some piece of NURBS geometry created on a computer. This is, after all, the goal of our modeling.

Knowing where to break up our spaceship model into separate surfaces requires a good deal of planning. Details such as the cockpit window and landing hatches in the drawing tell us where these objects are supposed to be. Once we know that information, we can start to see how the shapes of these details match with the flow of the surfaces in our existing base model. It would be nice if the edges of the cockpit window lined up exactly with the isoparms of the existing surface, but such great luck is rarely the case with most models. Our task then becomes apparent: we have to build new surfaces for the detailed objects and make them transition into the flow of the existing surface, while maintaining perfect continuity.

Based on the details, we next ask "What are the best places to break up our surfaces without creating overly complex geometry?" It is best to figure this out *before* you even begin inserting isoparms and detaching surfaces. Planning ahead will make the whole process easier and quicker. So grab a scrap of paper and sketch out the various surface patches and how they will flow together. Once you've made yourself think through it, you'll know exactly how to proceed and you'll be less likely to head down a dead-end road.

Figure 4-32 shows the plan for how the fuselage will be broken up into patches.

The tools we will use in this section are the Attach/Detach Surfaces tool, the Boundary tool, the Global Stitch tool, and the Align Surfaces tool.

Breaking Up the Fuselage Surface into Patches　First, we will examine the drawing and geometry to determine whether any details match the existing flow of the surface. Luckily, the landing gear hatch is a match. It also looks like a crease appears along that same edge. This tells us that two completely separate pieces are here, so we can detach them and not worry about them needing matching parameterization.

FIGURE 4-32　*Plan of the different surface patches*

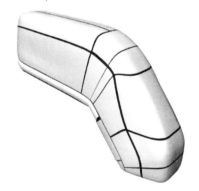

Before we touch anything, though, let's make a duplicate of our surface and assign it to a new layer. This way, we can always revert to the original surface if we need to. Select the fuselage and duplicate it by pressing CTRL-D (COMMAND-D).

> *N O T E*　*It's always a good idea to make a copy of your original surface, especially when doing patch modeling. You will often need to revert to the original if problems occur with the new patched surface.*

1. Create a new layer and name it **derivedSurfaces**.

2. Add the fuselage copy into the new layer and hide the base surfaces layer.

3. Change to wireframe mode, displaying the level 1 smoothness. Press the 4 key and then press the 1 key.

4. In the Side view, select the surface, right-click it, and choose Isoparm from the marking menu.

5. Click an existing isoparm and drag it so that it aligns with the landing gear hatch. Detach the surface and rebuild the resulting surfaces. (See Figure 4-33.)

FIGURE 4-33   Two surfaces after being detached

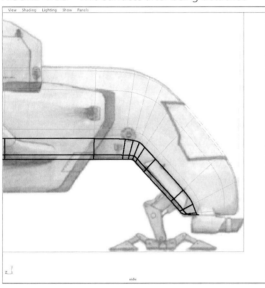

Writing a MEL Script Shortcut   Let's write a simple MEL script that will help us show and hide objects more quickly than using the Layer Editor or the Hide/Show command. Instead of actually changing the visibility of the object, we will execute a MEL script to move it far out of the way; then we'll execute another MEL script to move it back. The process we'll use is a great way to learn and modify MEL commands.

NOTE   *While the command that we deal with in this example is journaled in the Script Editor by default, many other commands, particularly those that deal with the user interface, are not journaled. In some cases, you might choose Script | Echo All Commands in the Script Editor. This will ensure that all script processes made in Maya are journaled.*

1. Open the Script Editor (choose Windows | General Editors | Script Editor) and choose Edit | Clear History.

2. In the view window, select any object and move it up along the Y axis, and then immediately undo.

3. Look in the Script Editor. Before the undo line, you'll see a line that looks something like this:
   move -r -os -wd 0 1.34937 0 ;
   Here, move is the *command*. The letters with dashes (such as -os) are *flags*, and the series of three numbers (0, 1.34937, and 0) are the values in X, Y, and Z. In this case, I moved the object in the Y axis to 1.34937 units. Now we'll replace that Y value with the number *10*.

4. Highlight the `move` line in the Script Editor, and press CTRL-C (COMMAND-C) to copy it. Paste it into the bottom window of the Script Editor, as shown in the following illustration.

5. Change the part that says 1.34937 to **10**.

6. Now highlight the entire line and LMB-drag it up to your modeling Shelf. Congratulations! You just wrote you first MEL script.

7. Back in the Script Editor, change that number *10* to **–10**. Again, highlight it and LMB-drag it into the modeling Shelf.

8. To test out what you've just done, zoom way out in your view window, select an object, and click the new button on the modeling Shelf that moves the selection up 10 units in Y. You should see the object pop up exactly 10 units away.

9. Click the other new button to reverse this and move the selection down 10 units. Now the object will be back where it started.

10. Select the bottom surface and use your new MEL script to get it out of the way for now.

Modeling the Cockpit Area   Let's attack the cockpit window first, since it presents the biggest challenge of any of the details in the model. We'll start by projecting a curve that matches the shape of the window onto the existing fuselage surface and detaching the surface around it. From that, we'll generate a new surface that matches the topology of the window object. Then we'll regenerate the surrounding surfaces so that they create a transition from the flow of the window to the flow of the fuselage.

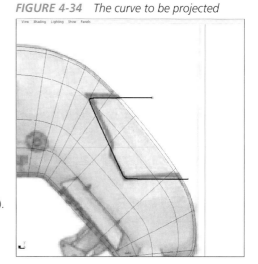

FIGURE 4-34   *The curve to be projected*

1. In the Side view, create a curve that matches the outline of the inside edge of the cockpit (Figure 4-34). This will be used to project onto the surface.

2. Select the curve, and then select the surface.

3. Choose Edit Surfaces | Project Curve On Surface ❏ to bring up the Project Curve On Surface tool Options window.

4. Reset the tool to its defaults, and click Project. This will create a curve on that surface.

5. To work with the curve freely, we need to duplicate it. Choose Edit Curves | Duplicate Surface Curves.

6. With the new curve selected, press the Move Up 10 MEL button we created earlier to move the curve out of the way. Delete the history on this duplicate curve.

Note that deleting the history will clear all dependencies on the selected object. This is important to do, because you might move or detach a curve that serves as an input to a surface. If that surface was still dependent on that curve, the surface would update to account for the change in its history. Consequently, that surface could be used as an input to an attach node and the objects attached to that would update as well. For these reasons, you want to *delete the history after every modeling operation*. If you don't, the model could completely fall apart when other operations are applied later.

7. Now select the curve on the surface and press the DELETE key to get rid of it. You can then zoom out, select the duplicate curve, and use the Move Back 10 MEL button to move it back down.

8. In the Layer Editor, create a new layer called **SourceCurves** and add the original curve that we drew into this layer and keep that layer turned off. Your model should look like Figure 4-35.

9. Right-click the curve and choose Edit Points from the marking menu.

10. Select the two edit points at the corners closest to the inner edge. Detach the curve at these points.

11. To derive the fourth edge, select the edge isoparm of the fuselage surface. With the edge isoparm selected, choose Curves | Duplicate Surface Curves.

12. Immediately delete the history on the new curve.

13. Move the fuselage surface out of the way using the MEL script button.

14. Select the top, bottom, and the new curves. Choose Edit Curves | Cut Curve ❑. Make sure you are using the default settings for this tool. Click the Cut button.

FIGURE 4-35 *Surface and projected curve*

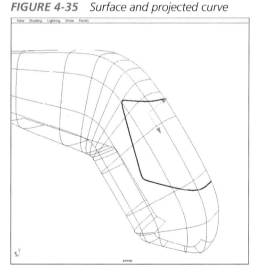

15. Now rebuild this curve to eight spans. You can delete any remaining curve ends.

16. Select all four curves and choose Surfaces | Boundary ☐ to bring up the Boundary tool's options.

The Boundary tool creates a surface from either three or four intersecting curves. When you use three curves, the tool actually inserts a fourth edge of 0 units in length. While common endpoints are not required to generate the surface, it is advised that your curves meet to produce predictable results. As always, the curves should be facing the same direction to have matching parameterization.

17. Reset the Boundary tool to its defaults and click the Boundary button in the Options window to create the boundary surface. Then close the Options window. The new surface matches the flow of the object it represents. (See Figure 4-36.)

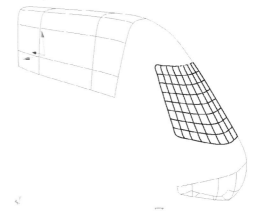

FIGURE 4-36   *Surface created with the Boundary tool*

18. With the border edges of the window defined, we can detach the surrounding surfaces. Select the isoparm in the V direction.

19. Detach the surface at three different existing isoparms so that four surfaces remain (not including the bottom piece that has already been detached). (See Figure 4-37).

FIGURE 4-37   *Surface detached into four pieces*

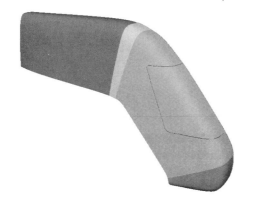

20. Rebuild the surfaces with our custom Rebuild Surface settings.

Be careful that you're selecting the existing isoparms instead of inserting a new one. Accidentally inserting new geometry will make it impossible to maintain para-meterization without re-attaching and rebuilding. A good technique for selecting isoparms efficiently is to click and drag over an isoparm.

21. Select all three curves for the window borders and rebuild them to eight spans. We now have three of the five curves we need to use the Boundary tool.

Note that depending on exactly how you drew your projection curve, the resulting curve may have many points. Rebuilding it to eight spans may reduce it so much that the shape of the curve changes. If this is the case, rebuild it with a higher number of spans. Just remember that any surface that the projecting curve must align with on the other side will need to have matching parameterization.

NOTE   If you are still having problems with the shape of the curve changing after you rebuild it, you may want to redraw it with one of the curve tools with the fuselage surface made live. In fact, this is probably the cleanest way to generate curves on surfaces rather than to use a curve that has been projected. However, in our case, the projected curve should work without any problems.

To generate the boundary curves for our patches, we'll derive curves from the existing surface. This involves using our base surface, selecting isoparms that intersect with the corners of the cockpit window, and duplicating them. We then use the Cut Curve tool and snap the endpoints to the corners to ensure that they are intersecting with the corners themselves and not some other point on the window curve. With these borders drawn out and parameterized to match neighboring surfaces, we'll use the Boundary tool to close them.

NOTE   You could also make the surface live and draw curves that snap to both ends. However, it is quicker and more precise to derive existing curves whenever possible.

FIGURE 4-38   Isoparms that intersect the corner of the window surface

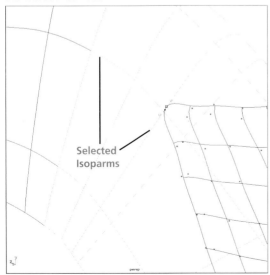

Selected Isoparms

1. Move the original surface back into place.

2. Right-click it to select its isoparms. First select one going in the U direction that intersects with the corner CV of the window surface.

3. Choose Edit Curves | Duplicate Surface Curves. Figure 4-38 shows the isoparms that intersect the corners of the window.

Make sure you select the window surface and turn on the display of the CVs so that you can see where the isoparms intersect. You'll need to have these CVs visible anyway so that you can snap to them later.

4. Right-click the curve and select Control Vertex from the marking menu.

5. With point snapping turned on, snap the end CVs of the curve to the corner CVs of the other surfaces. You should not have to move it too far—this just ensures that it is snapped.

6. Use the same process to draw the other boundary curves. Use your MEL script button to move that surface out of the way and have a look at what we have done so far. The resulting network of curves should look like the ones shown in Figure 4-39.

FIGURE 4-39   Boundary curves

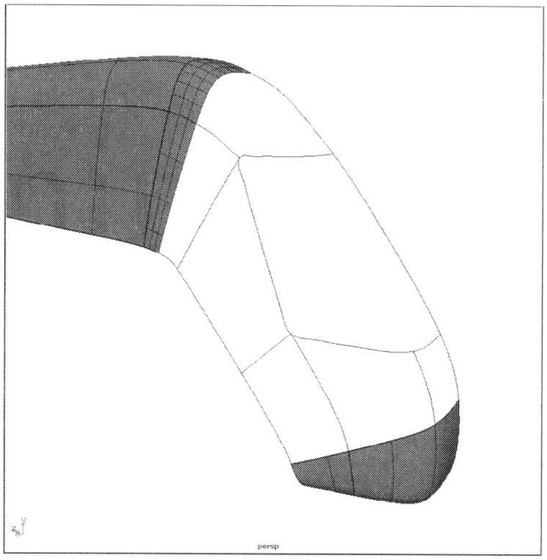

Creating Patches for the Surrounding Area   Now we can use the Boundary tool to generate surfaces between our curves and surfaces. We'll start at the top.

1. The window has eight spans in its U direction, and the surface on the other side has two spans. This means that we need to rebuild the other side's surface to have eight spans in the U direction. Choose the Rebuild Surface tool. Check the box next to U and set the U value to **4**.

2. Click Rebuild.

We are also going to rebuild the surface to have three spans in V. This will ensure that there is matching continuity to the surface on the other side of the surface we are generating. This way, we can reduce the spans in U of this next surface to four. Rebuilding this surface to three spans in V will ensure that the opposite edge will remain as is when we modify the window side edge to have better continuity with the new surface we are generating.

3. In the V direction, rebuild both of the curves to have four spans.

4. Now select the two curves and the two edge isoparms and choose Surfaces | Boundary. The new surface will be generated.

5. Continue this process to generate surfaces between the other curves and surfaces. Just remember to rebuild the objects so that the boundaries have the same parameterization in U and V. Use the example shown in Figure 4-40 to follow the correct parameterization.

At this time, it's a good idea to do a test render (as shown in Figure 4-40). We will need to set our anti-aliasing settings to the highest quality in the render globals. See Chapter 16 for more information about that.

FIGURE 4-40   *Patches (left) and rendered sample of the surface (right)*

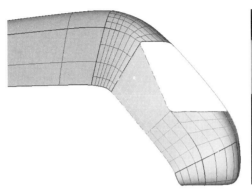
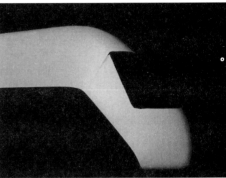

After you render this geometry, you will most likely see seams where the surfaces meet. One thing you can do is turn on Smooth Edge in the Tessellation attributes for each object. You can find the Tesselation attributes in the Attribute Editor for all NURBS surfaces, as shown here.

You can also use the following MEL script to turn on Smooth Edge for all selected surfaces:

```
string $sel[]=`ls -sl -l`;
for ($node in $sel)
{
setAttr ($node+".smoothEdge") on;
}
```

Fixing Continuity Between Patches   While turning on Smooth Edge may cause any gaps to disappear, the seams are still visible due to continuity problems. Although the surfaces are tangent in one direction, they aren't necessarily tangent in the other. You will notice, just by looking, that where the isoparms meet, the surfaces do not appear continuous. We can attack this problem in a few ways, the most obvious of which would be to use the Attach tool to attach all adjacent surfaces and then detach them. Doing so would ensure C2 continuity (see Chapter 3) between all of the surfaces. However, this would cause our carefully constructed surface to lose some of its shape. That is because using the Attach Surfaces command with the Blend option will create less complex geometry. (Two NURBS surfaces with one span each will have four rows of CVs in each direction. That's eight rows each. When attached with the Attach Surfaces command, the resulting surface will have five rows of CVs in the direction that the surfaces were attached.)

The Align Surfaces command is another option. This would fix the continuity between any two adjacent surfaces. However, once you align one surface to another, that surface then might lose continuity to a surface next to it. You would find that you needed to keep going around to all of the surfaces and realigning them until there weren't any more problems. This could get frustrating.

The Global Stitch command will do the trick in this case. The Global Stitch command will provide continuity between all of the surfaces that are selected when the command is executed. While this command is usually used in organic modeling to prevent a multi-patch NURBS model from splitting at the seams when it is animated, we will use it here to fix continuity problems, and then we'll delete the history. As long as the surfaces are left alone, they will maintain the continuity provided by the Global Stitch command.

1. Select all of the surfaces in the fuselage except for the window surface. Since the window is obviously a separate surface, we do not need to include it.

2. Choose Edit NURBS | Stitch | Global Stitch ❒. Set the options to match those in the following illustration. Click the Global Stitch button to execute the command and close the Options window.

3. Choose Edit | Delete By Type | History to delete all history on these surfaces.

4. With all of the surfaces still selected, turn on Smooth Edge and do another render. The multi-patch surface should appear as a single, continuous surface.

TIP   When evaluating the surfaces in the view windows or in a rendered image, any problems with the seams or continuity are better spotted if the surfaces have a shiny material applied to them. I recommend using a Blinn material with a small value for its Eccentricity attribute, a high value for its Specular Rolloff attribute, and the Specular Color turned all of the way up to white. For more information on materials and their attributes, see Chapter 13.

The entire process that was used to create the window can also be used to create the landing gear hatches. Use the following example as a guide for detaching and parameterizing the surfaces.

The only thing left to do for now is to round the rear part of the piece. Since the end is mostly hidden by the engine block, we really need to scale only the last row of CVs.

1. Select the last row of CVs of the upper and lower landing gear hatch pieces.

2. In the Top view, click the Scale tool.

3. Press the INSERT (HOME) key to change the pivot point.

4. Hold down the SHIFT key to constrain the movement to a right angle, and hold down the X key to snap to the grid.

5. Move the pivot left until it snaps to the origin line.

6. Press the INSERT (HOME) key again to return to the Scale tool. *Be careful not to click anything but the Scale tool*; otherwise, you will lose the pivot change that you just made.

TIP   *Notice the little circle at the top of the line that extends from the pivot point along the Y axis? Once you have repositioned the pivot point, you can click this circle to lock the pivot point for the components. As long as the pivot point remains locked to this position, any components in the object will use this as their pivot point.*

7. Scale this last row of CVs down uniformly just a bit. You can turn on the baseSurfaces layer to see the engine block. Tuck this row of CVs just below the engine block's surface.

8. Repeat step 7 for the next row. Scale the CVs out just a bit so that the surface does not round until the end.

Breaking Up the Engine Block into Patches   Now let's work on the engine block. To build the air intake in the front, we will detach the surface in a few places and connect the remaining pieces to build the inner wall. We'll then sculpt the inner wall to better conform to the fuselage.

FIGURE 4-41   *Engine block cut up into nine pieces*

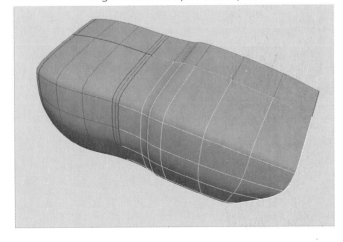

1. Insert two isoparms in the U direction on both the top and bottom.

2. Insert two more isoparms in the V direction, just behind where the fuselage meets the engine block.

3. Detach the surfaces at this point and rebuild. You will now have a total of nine pieces, as shown in Figure 4-41.

4. Rebuild the surfaces.

5. Insert an isoparm in the U direction for both of the front inner surfaces on the top and bottom of the engine block.

6. Detach these surfaces at the isoparm you placed in the last step and discard the pieces on the edge. (See the top-left image in Figure 4-42.)

7. Delete the history for all of the remaining surfaces of the engine block.

8. Select the isoparms on the outer edges, and loft them with six section spans. (See the top-right image in Figure 4-42.)

9. Choose Edit NURBS | Attach Surfaces with the default settings to attach and blend the surfaces together. (See the bottom-left image in Figure 4-42.)

10. Select the U hulls in this new piece, and move them out a bit, one by one, so that the surface rests right against the surface of the fuselage.

11. Then select the second and third CVs at the top, and fine-tune the alignment along that top edge.

12. For the last row of CVs, drag them all the way over in X so that they enclose the area around the rear of the fuselage. (See the bottom-right image in Figure 4-42.)

FIGURE 4-42   The process of building the inner wall of the engine block

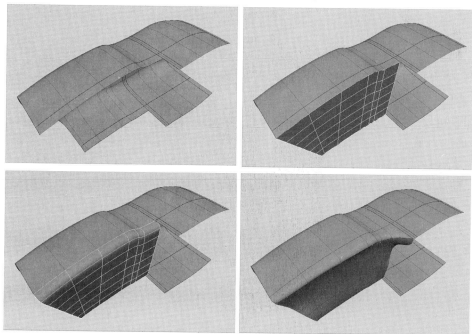

Blending the Tailpiece with Engine Block   To blend the tailpiece to the engine block, we will cut the tailpiece and the engine block into separate surfaces and then rebuild them so that they have matching parameterization. We'll use the Attach Surfaces command to blend the existing surfaces together and the Global Stitch command to close any gaps and fix the continuity between all of the surfaces.

1. Create the tailpiece using a cylinder with 12 sections. Scale the CVs and manipulate them into a rectangular shape, the same way the wing piece was created. The tailpiece is shown in Figure 4-43.

2. To shape the tailpiece vertically, it might be better to use a lattice than manipulate the CVs directly. This will let us use two rows of control points instead of the four rows that exist in the surface. To create a lattice, press F2 to display the animation menu sets.

3. Select the tailpiece, and choose Deform | Create Lattice. A control cage will appear around the cylinder.

4. With the lattice selected, look in the Channel Box. Change the number of divisions in S, T, and U to **2**. Right-click the lattice and choose Lattice Point from the marking menu. Select some of the lattice points and move them to shape the cylinder so that it matches the shape of the tailpiece.

5. When you are pleased with the shape, select the surface and delete its history.

NOTE   _Lattices will be covered in more depth in Chapters 8 and 10. For now, just realize that they are helpful when you're manipulating surfaces with many CVs._

6. To prepare the surface on the engine block, select the surface and duplicate it. Then hide it by choosing Display | Hide | Hide Selected, because we will need it again later.

7. Insert isoparms and detach the surface into six pieces (see Figure 4-44, left). You can delete the surface on the center edge that occupies the space where the tailpiece is.

8. Choose Modify | Transformation Tools | Move Normal Tool. Use this tool to move the CVs on the edges so that they better conform to the roundness in the tailpiece.

9. Rebuild the surfaces. Split the tailpiece in half by detaching the surface at the isoparms that sit on the YZ plane. Delete the half on the other side of our ship. Then detach the remaining half again into three separate surfaces and rebuild.

10. Now rebuild all adjacent surfaces so that they have matching parameterization. I chose to rebuild to five spans along the larger surface and two spans for the smaller surface (see Figure 4-43).

11. Rebuild the surfaces to three spans in the other direction. Again, refer to Figure 4-43 and note the parameterization of the surfaces shown.

12. Use the Attach tool with the default settings to attach all adjacent surfaces, and then rebuild them.

FIGURE 4-43 *Tailpiece created from a NURBS cylinder*

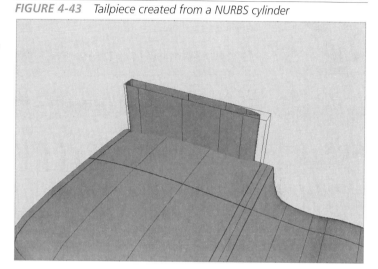

13. Detach these surfaces at the same isoparm where they were joined. The result should look something like Figure 4-44, right.

You will notice gaps between the surfaces at the corners. While we could select all of the surfaces in this area and use the Global Stitch command, Global Stitch will cause the boundaries of these surfaces to be averaged in order to close this gap. This might be okay for an organic model, but a hard-surface model is not very tolerant of the irregularities in the surface that might be caused by averaging. Therefore, it is best to close these gaps as best you can manually and then apply the Global Stitch command to make any last-minute adjustments to the continuity between the surfaces.

14. Select the corner CVs where the five surfaces come together.

15. Use the Scale tool to scale the CVs down to 0. You will need to use the Script Editor to make sure that they are scaled exactly to 0. To do this, non-uniform scale the corner CVs and then immediately undo (choose Edit | Undo).

FIGURE 4-44 *The engine block and tailpiece are detached and rebuilt with matching parameterization.*

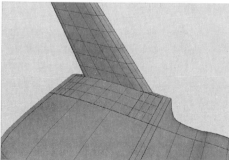
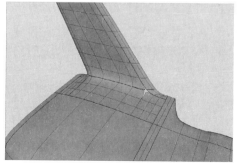

16. Open the Script Editor and scroll down so you can see the last few commands. Just before the undo line, you should see a line that looks like this:

```
scale -r -p 0.357318cm 2.566201cm 2.459544cm 1.283333 1.283333 1.283333 ;
```

17. Copy and paste this line into the input window at the bottom of the Script Editor. Change the last three numbers to *0* so that it reads like this:

```
scale -r -p 0.357318cm 2.566201cm 2.459544cm 0 0 0 ;
```

18. Press CTRL-ENTER (CONTROL-RETURN) to execute the command. The vertices will all be scaled to 0, making sure that they lie at the same point in space. It should look like the left image in Figure 4-45.

19. From here, use point snapping to snap each neighboring CV to its adjacent CV, and then use the Global Stitch command to fix the continuity between them (see the right image in Figure 4-45).

> TIP *While we aren't going to cover it in this book, those interested in this type of modeling will find some MEL scripts that are useful for manually achieving continuity between surfaces. One such script, called pointsAverage.mel, can be found at http://www.Highend3d.com.*

FIGURE 4-45 *Scale the CVs to 0 and then Global Stitch to fix the edges*

 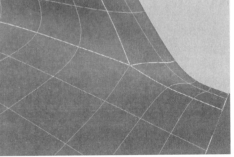

Detailing the Wing The only detail we need for the wing is the piece that extends out toward the rear of the spaceship. The technique will be similar to what we have used all along: we will detach the surface around the area of the wing, add geometry, and sculpt. The panel detail and creases will be added in the texture maps. Make sure you remember to duplicate the wing surface in the baseSurfaces layer and add it to the derivedSurfaces layer that we'll create in a minute.

1. Detach the wing at the points shown in Figure 4-46 to divide the wing into three pieces.

2. Rebuild everything.

3. Add an isoparm to the surface in the middle, select the rear CVs, and move them back to align with the drawing.

4. Using the Move and Scale tools, continue selecting CVs and sculpting them to create the object detailed in Figure 4-47.

Detailing the Thruster   The techniques for adding the detail to the thruster will be similar to those used on all of the other pieces so far. The hatches on the thruster can be modeled by detaching the area around the detail, projecting a curve, and then building patches in and around it. To blend the pieces sticking out, we will use the same techniques that we used to blend the tailpiece with the engine block. The result should look similar to Figure 4-48. Remember to open the MCR_Spaceship file on the CD and study the model.

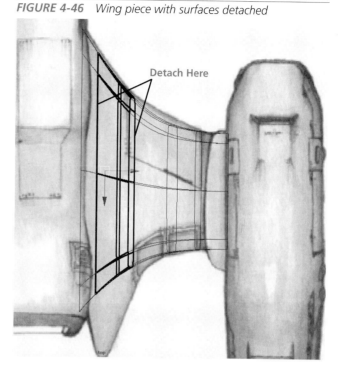

FIGURE 4-46   *Wing piece with surfaces detached*

Detach Here

FIGURE 4-47   *Sculpted wing*

FIGURE 4-48   *The completed thruster*

Final Pass: Adding the Secondary Surfaces

Our last pass consists mostly of adding secondary pieces that are derived from the existing surfaces placed in and around the model. The molding around the air intake on the engine block is an example of a derived surface, because we'll use the surface curves from the engine block to build it. The landing gear and all of the little parts extending from the thruster piece are built without any real relationship to the existing surfaces—that is, they are built as single elements and placed into position. Little details like this will give the model a sense of scale. For example, we can place a ladder on the engine block, and the viewer can relate that to the size of a person, which then indicates to the viewer the size of the entire ship.

Finally, the surfaces will be mirrored and attached. The end caps for the nose and thruster pieces are added, and the model is complete.

Modeling the Molding We'll begin with the molding around the air intake of the engine block.

1. Select the isoparms on the edges of the two intake surfaces and choose Edit Curves | Duplicate Surface Curves to derive them.

2. Move down the surface just a bit, select an isoparm, and choose Edit Curves | Duplicate Surface Curves to derive another curve (Figure 4-49).

3. Delete the history for the derived curves and move the surface out of the way with the MEL script button.

4. Use the Attach Curve tool, with the default settings, to connect instead of using the Blend tool to join the curve segment together, as shown in Figure 4-49.

5. Duplicate these curves and scale them up a tiny bit. Scale the originals down about the same amount.

FIGURE 4-49 *Curves derived from the surfaces (left) are lofted together (right)*

6. Select the Loft tool, and loft each curve with two section spans. You can loft these curves two at a time to generate surfaces between them.

7. Use the Attach tool with the default settings to blend the surfaces together.

8. Repeat this process for the rear of the engine block.

Modeling the Landing Gear   We will create the landing gear using the Revolve tool mostly. Although it creates very rigid objects with sharp edges, the Revolve tool can be useful for forming basic shapes. The key is to use 1-degree revolves with four sections. This will give us one continuous surface with four sides that have hard right angles. Extra geometry is then added and the object is sculpted. When the surfaces are rebuilt to a third-degree surface, we'll get nice, round edges.

1. Draw a profile curve for one of the landing gear segments.

2. Press the INSERT (HOME) key, and move the pivot point of the curve to a point in between the two sides of the landing gear (as shown at the left in Figure 4-50).

FIGURE 4-50   Process of modeling the landing gear

3. Choose Surfaces | Revolve ☐. In the Revolve Options window, set the Surface Degree attribute to Linear, and set Segments to **4**. The right image in Figure 4-50 shows the result.

4. Sculpt the surfaces so that they roughly match the landing gear in the drawing.

5. Insert two isoparms on either side of each edge (the left image in Figure 4-51). Make them as close to the edge as possible.

6. Rebuild the surface to a degree of 3. The surface remains rigid but has tiny, rounded edges.

7. Continue using this technique to build all the little pieces in the landing gear, as shown in the right image in Figure 4-51. You may also want to use some primitives, such as a cylinder, for some of the round pieces.

FIGURE 4-51   *Inserting the isoparms (left) and the finished landing gear (right)*

8. When you have assembled all of the pieces, group them together by selecting all of the surfaces and choosing Edit | Group. Then build the front landing gear in a similar way.

9. The seams at all of the hatches need to be better defined. Rolling in the edges will create nice detail in the surface and make them look like they have some thickness to them instead of the paper-thin appearance they currently have. This can be done pretty quickly by adding some isoparms at the edges and then scaling in the last row of hulls. See Figure 4-52.

FIGURE 4-52   *Front landing hatch after the edges have been rolled.*

Adding Extraneous Details   Now study the drawings once again and detect any details that are missing.

1. Notice that a bunch of little latches and hose sockets appear around the spaceship model. Create these separately and place them at the appropriate locations. (I added a little ladder on the engine block and vents that cap the air intake on the engine block. You can add any other details that you want.)

2. When you are happy with the way everything looks, select all the surfaces and open the Duplicate tool's Options window.

3. Set the Scale X value to **–1** and click Duplicate. This will mirror all of the surfaces you created along the X axis.

FIGURE 4-53 *Completed spaceship model*

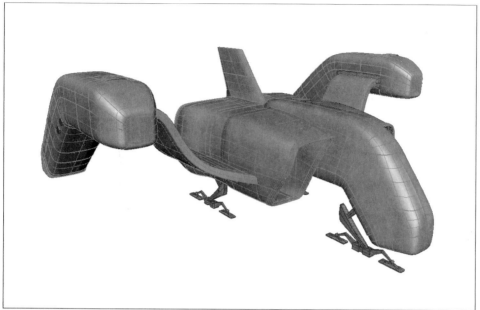

4. To complete the model, you can use the Attach Surfaces command to join each surface with its mirrored part along the X axis. the completed model is shown in Figure 4-53.

Summary

In each tutorial, we started with a large surface and then cut it up into smaller pieces to add details. This modeling process can be used to build just about anything. While the steps you use are going to be about the same and the process very repetitive, every model you build will present its own unique set of challenges. Good modeling requires a fair amount of experimentation and trial and error until the problem is solved.

Polygon Modeling

Like NURBS modeling, polygon

modeling can be used for creating characters,

objects, and environments. Traditionally,

polygonal modeling techniques were used

to create rigid, or hard-edged, models for

architecture and similar projects. But today's

game production companies utilize polygon

modeling techniques for both characters and

environments so that their games can maintain

real-time performance. Due to advancements

in polygonal and texturing toolsets, polygon

modeling is becoming the most popular way

to create organic characters in the film and game industries. This chapter will introduce the polygon modeling paradigm and discuss some of the tools used in a tutorial, where we will create a hard-surface model of a Humvee. Organic character modeling is discussed in the next chapter.

Basics of Polygon Modeling

You can model with polygons to produce some complex models with great amounts of detail. However, you'll find that you usually use the same handful of tools to build most of your models. You'll usually start building your model by creating a polygonal primitive, drawing primitive faces, or converting NURBS or subdivision models into polygons.

Let's start this chapter by learning some definitions of terms; then we'll discuss a few simple tools to help us create our first model in the tutorial.

Polygon Anatomy

A polygonal model is a group of points in 3D space that are connected to form squares or triangles called *faces*. These faces, not the vertices or edges, are used to calculate shading at render time. Figure 5-1 shows the components of a polygonal face, which are listed here:

- **Vertex** A point in space. Each vertex in a model has a unique identification number that will instruct the software of the location at which to begin connecting the vertices. The vertex is the most basic building block of a polygonal model. By editing the position of a vertex, you are changing the shape of the face that it creates.

- **Edge** The polygonal components that connect two vertices. The area between at least three connected vertices creates a face.

- **Face** A minimum of three vertices enclosed by three edges. Although you can create a face with any number of vertices, the faces will be broken up into squares or triangles at render time. A triangular face is called a *tri*, a four-sided face is called a *quad*, and a face with more than four sides is called an *n-gon*. The general rule for rendering faces is that they must be *planar*, or flat. The collection of connected faces in a model is called a *polygonal surface* or a *polygonal mesh*.

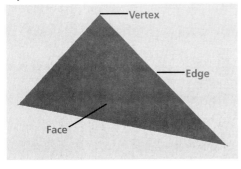

FIGURE 5-1   *Components of a polygon object*

NOTE   **UVs are the texture coordinates that relate to the vertices of a polygonal surface. Because UVs are not usually edited during the modeling process, they will not be covered in this chapter. See Chapters 13 and 14 for more information on UVs.**

Advantages of Polygon Modeling

Polygon modeling has several advantages over NURBS modeling.

Modeling Detailed or Branched Models Is Easy   Because polygon models are based on the connection of independent faces, you can introduce details anywhere on the surface without having to worry about parameterization. *Branching*, which occurs in areas such as fingers emerging from a hand, can be accomplished quickly and easily while maintaining a single surface.

In comparison, it is difficult or sometimes impossible to create localized details and branching structures using a single NURBS surface. You are forced to use a multi-patch modeling technique, and then you must manage continuity to make the structures appear to be a single surface. Good branching is especially difficult to accomplish when the object must be deformed for animation. The character shown in Figure 5-2 is a good example of branching, demonstrated in the arms that emerge from the body and the fingers that emerge from the hand.

FIGURE 5-2   *A polygonal character; branching of the arms and fingers would have been difficult using NURBS geometry.*

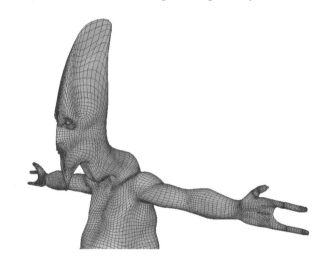

UV Texture Coordinates Are Assignable   With some extra work, you can have complete control over assigning UV texture coordinates to your polygonal model. You have full control over the layout of your UVs via the UV Texture Editor, which is discussed in Chapter 14.

FIGURE 5-3   *This camera has many hard edges that would have been difficult to model with NURBS.*

Hard Edges Are Easy to Create   It is easy to model objects with rigid surfaces and hard edges, such as the camera shown in Figure 5-3. If this object were created with NURBS, you'd have to add many CVs at the edges or use a surface of a lower degree. These kinds of details are of little concern when you're modeling with polygons.

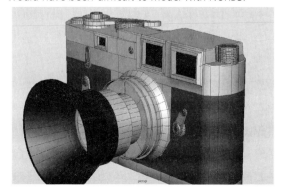

Simple Toolsets Are Available   While you might use several dozen commands and tools when modeling with NURBS, you can create detailed polygonal models using only two or three tools.

Models Are Transferable Between Different Software   Polygonal models are recognized by almost any 3D animation program, so, unlike NURBS models, you can transfer models between programs easily.

Disadvantages of Polygon Modeling

Following are some disadvantages of polygonal modeling.

It Takes Many Polygons to Represent a Smooth, Organic Object   To represent a smooth object, you will need to use a lot of polygon faces. This will result in slower interaction compared to that of NURBS models.

Data Size of a Smooth Polygon Object Is Comparably Large   Because of the number of vertices needed to create a smooth detailed object, the data size can be significantly larger than that of a similar NURBS model. Your computer may run into problems loading a scene if sufficient memory is not available.

Editing Smooth Objects Can Be Difficult   A smooth surface can be ruined by moving just one vertex. You can avoid this problem by making edits only to the low-resolution, presmoothed polygonal model and by using the Smooth tool as the final step. Using the smooth proxy modeling technique can circumvent the negative aspects of polygon modeling. In addition, a polygon model can be converted to a *subdivision surface* model. Both of these techniques allow you to edit a low-resolution polygonal cage and be able to see a smoothed version of the model at the same time. (You will learn more about this when we work on an organic character in Chapter 6.) In addition, you can convert a NURBS model to a polygon any time you want. Modeling in NURBS and converting to polygons at the end of the modeling process is a good technique as long as you organize you NURBS patches, as we did when we built the spaceship model in Chapter 4.

Tips for Polygon Modeling

To avoid any problems with your model, keep in mind the following tips as you work.

Keep Faces Planar   A *planar* face is completely flat. The following illustration shows how a triangular face is always a planar face (as shown in the objects on the left). Imagine selecting a vertex

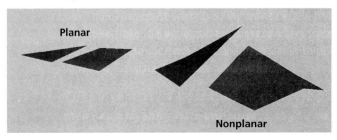

on a triangular face and moving it up; the result is still a planar face. But if a face has more than four points, pulling up one point can result in a nonplanar face (as shown in the objects on the right). You should avoid nonplanar faces because they can create problems when you try to deform or render them. You can avoid nonplanar faces by carefully manipulating the object's vertices. You can also choose Polygons | Cleanup ❑ and enable the Nonplanar Faces option in the Cleanup options. This will triangulate all nonplanar faces.

Manage Surface Normals As You Work   In Chapter 3, we talked about the normal direction for NURBS surfaces. Polygonal faces each have a normal as well, as shown in Figure 5-4. When merging multiple faces, it is important that the normals are all facing the same direction. Surfaces with mixed normals are called *non-manifold* geometry. You can check which way normals are facing by selecting a polygon object and choosing Display | Polygon Components | Normals. If you see that some normals are not facing the right way, use component mode to select those faces and then choose Edit Polygons | Normals | Reverse.

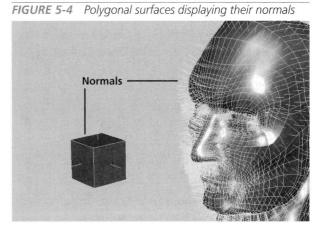

FIGURE 5-4   Polygonal surfaces displaying their normals

Normals

Keep Polygon Faces As Quads (Four-Sided)   First of all, it's much easier to view your models with one less edge through each face. If your aim is to create an organic, smooth surface later by using the Smooth command or by converting the surface into a subdivision surface, it's a good idea to use quad faces as much as possible from the beginning. Quad faces smooth and convert to subdivision surfaces without problems. Figure 5-5 shows both quad and tri faces being converted to subdivision surfaces. You should be aware that a polygonal model with non-manifold geometry won't convert to a sub-division surface model.

NOTE   Models built for integration into real-time game engines must often be constructed using triangular faces. A quad-faced model can be automatically turned into a tri-faced model by choosing Polygons | Triangulate.

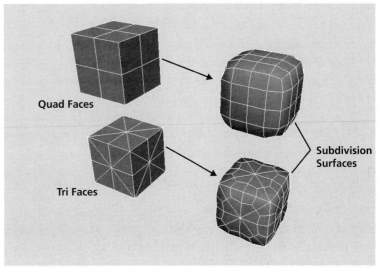

FIGURE 5-5   Quad and tri faces will be smoothed differently.

Quad Faces

Tri Faces

Subdivision Surfaces

Helpful Interfaces for Polygon Modeling

You will find that two interfaces are valuable assets as you work with polygons in Maya: the Heads Up Display (HUD) and the Custom Polygon Display.

Heads Up Display

The HUD for poly count, shown next, displays the number of polygonal vertices, edges, faces, and UVs for the entire scene (second column), a selected object (third column), and selected compo-

nents (fourth column). The HUD appears as an overlay in your view windows. The HUD is helpful in managing your polygonal models as you work. To turn it on, choose Display | Heads Up Display | Poly Count.

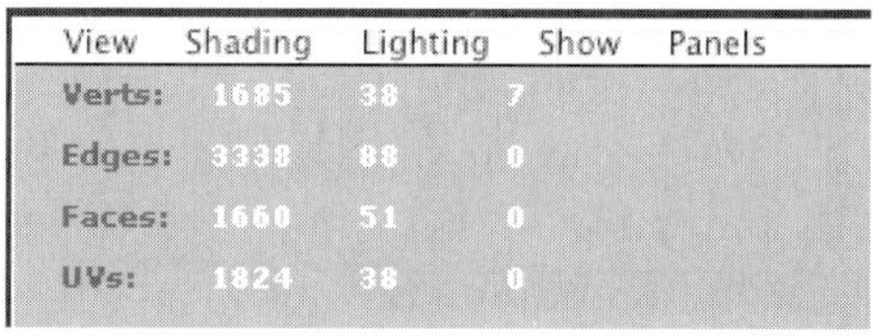

View	Shading	Lighting	Show	Panels
Verts:	1685	38	7	
Edges:	3338	88	0	
Faces:	1660	51	0	
UVs:	1824	38	0	

Custom Polygon Display

Choose Display | Custom Polygon Display ❑ from the main menu bar to open the Custom Polygon Display Options window, shown in Figure 5-6. This window lets you set how a selected polygo-nal object will be displayed in the view windows. While you can turn on the display of the normals and vertices just as you can by choosing Display | Polygon Components, this window gives you access to a whole lot more.

FIGURE 5-6   The Custom Polygon Display Options window

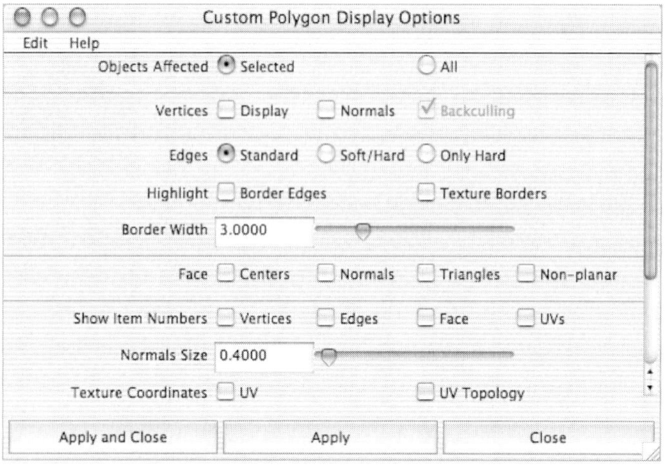

Some of the most useful options here control how various edges are displayed. When you are dealing with multiple polygonal surfaces, it can sometimes be difficult to determine where one surface ends and the other begins. Turning on the Highlight Border Edges option will thicken the edges along the borders of polygonal sur-faces. How thick they appear is controlled via the Border Width setting.

Backface culling (the Backculling option) is another useful setting that can be used as you work. By default, this is turned off. When you choose this option, the back of the polygonal faces will not render in the view window. This can speed up performance in the view window, because your computer's video hardware will not have to display the backs of any faces that it might otherwise render. For modeling, turning on Backculling can be helpful for selecting components. For example, if you drag-select several faces on a sphere, you might end up selecting many faces on the opposite side that you don't want. With Backculling selected, the faces on the opposite side will not be selected because they are not being rendered.

Creating Polygons

You can create polygonal objects in Maya in several ways. Polygonal surfaces can be generated directly from NURBS curves using any of the commands found in the Surfaces menu, or existing NURBS surfaces can be tessellated into polygonal surfaces. The processes for these two methods of generating surfaces are similar. If you'd rather not involve any NURBS at all, you can choose to begin with a polygonal primitive and sculpt it by splitting faces and transforming its components. You can even use the Create Polygon tool to draw each face one by one. Let's begin by looking at the options found in the surface-generating commands.

Generating Polygonal Surfaces from NURBS Curves

Throughout Chapters 3 and 4 we used the Revolve, Loft, and Boundary tools to generate many of the surfaces used in the examples and tutorials. With their default settings active, these commands generated third-degree NURBS surfaces from NURBS curves that were either drawn with the CV or EP Curve tools or duplicated from existing curves on surfaces.

Inside the Options window for any of these commands is an Output Geometry setting that lets you choose what type of geometry will be generated when the command is executed. Figure 5-7 shows the tessellation attributes in the Options window for the Revolve tool when the Output Geometry is set to Polygons. (You will have to scroll down the Options window to see all of these attributes.) Notice that many new options appear in the window once this is enabled.

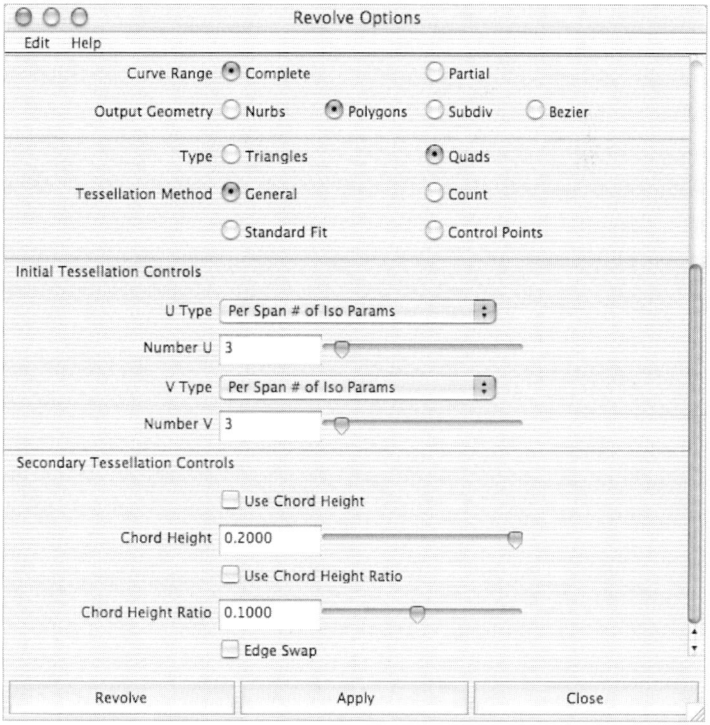

The first option in this new section, Type, will let you specify whether the faces on the resulting surface will be triangles or quads. The next attribute you can choose is the Tessellation Method. When one of these methods is selected, its options appear in the window section below.

FIGURE 5-7 *The Revolve Options window with the Output Geometry set to Polygons*

Figure 5-8 shows a NURBS curve and the polygonal surface that is generated with each Tessellation Method choice. From left to right is the NURBS curve, and then the surfaces generated by selecting General, Standard Fit, Count, and Control Points are shown. These methods are defined next.

FIGURE 5-8   *NURBS curve, General, Standard Fit, Count, and Control Points*

- **General**   This option gives the most control for tessellation based on the NURBS object. When the Revolve command was executed, the first tessellated surface shown in Figure 5-8 had the U Type and V Type attributes set to Per Span # Of Iso Params with a value of 2 in both directions. Since the isoparms in U were based on the spans of the source curve, the polygonal surface will have two segments for each span on the NURBS surface. Since the Revolve node's Segments attribute was set to 8 in the Channel Box, this means that the resulting polygonal surface will have 16 segments in the V direction.

- **Standard Fit**   This option will attempt to match the curvature along the surface as best it can based on the Chord Height ratio. This is the maximum distance from the curve that the face can appear. The result will always use more faces to define curvy areas and less faces for flatter areas. While you don't have precise control over the amount of segments, as you did with the General setting, the polygonal surface will still be pretty efficient in that polygons are created only where they are needed.

- **Count**   This method allows you to specify the total number of polygons on the surface without any regard for the curvature. The faces will be spread uniformly over the entire surface. While this may be the easiest method for obtaining a desired polygon count, it also leads to the most inefficient surfaces because a curved area will be defined exactly the same as a flat area.

- **Control Points**   This tessellation method simply facets the object by using the existing control vertices in the NURBS surface as polygonal vertices. No additional attributes control this setting. This can be a useful method for tessellating an object that you plan to smooth or to convert to a subdivision surface later on.

When the Output Geometry is set to Polygons, Maya will actually generate the surface as a NURBS object based on the surface command attributes and then convert it to polygons using one of these methods. Therefore, in the Channel Box, you will notice the appearance of a node called nurbsTessellate1 above the Revolve node. As you experiment with these methods, you can change the Tessellation Method and its attributes in the Channel Box instead of undoing the revolve and changing the settings in the Revolve Options window.

Converting NURBS Surfaces to Polygons

You can convert any existing NURBS surface to a polygonal surface by choosing Convert | NURBS To Polygons. This will give you the exact same options that you can find by using one of the surface-generating options discussed in the preceding section. In fact, when a surface is generated using one of the commands in the Surfaces menu, Maya internally generates a NURBS surface and then converts it using these same methods; so you end up with the same nurbsTessellate node in the surface's dependency graph.

Yet another way exists for accessing the same tessellation options. You can find the General, Standard Fit, Count, and Control Points tessellation options in the Rebuild Surfaces Options window (choose Edit NURBS | Rebuild ❐. This will result in the same nurbsTessellate node being placed above the NURBS surface to tessellate the object into polygons.

Converting a Multipatch NURBS Model to a Polygonal Model

Often, a NURBS model must be converted into a polygonal model so that it can be exported to another rendering application. Another reason for converting a NURBS model into polygons might be to have control over the UV (texture) coordinates in the UV Texture Editor (as demonstrated in Chapter 14).

When it comes to NURBS models that are created out of multiple patches, as we saw in Chapter 4, it may be desirable to convert the NURBS patches into polygons and then merge the resulting polygons into one complete surface. This is particularly the case when the model will be deformed during animation. Deforming a multipatch model can cause the seams between the surfaces to become visible during the animations. Combining these surfaces into one surface will keep this from being a problem.

A new feature in Maya 6 allows you to convert a multipatch NURBS model quickly into a single polygonal mesh. Previously, this process involved converting the NURBS patches to polygons, flipping surface normals so that they all conformed to one direction, combining the surfaces with the Polygons | Combine command, and then cleaning up and merging the overlapping vertices with the Edit Polygons | Merge Vertices command. If the NURBS model had quite a few patches, as our spaceship from Chapter 4 does, this could become a very time-consuming process. In Maya 6, this entire process can be achieved with a single click of the mouse button.

Let's take, for example, the hull piece from our spaceship model that we created in Chapter 4. This model was made up of 18 different NURBS patches. Choose Modify | Convert | NURBS To Polygons ❐ to open the Options window for this command, as shown here.

If the Attach Multiple Output Meshes check box is enabled, Maya will combine all of the selected NURBS surfaces into one mesh. The overlapping vertices along the edges of the original patches will be merged as long as they fall within a distance of the value set in the Merge Tolerance attribute. The Type attribute should be set to Quads so that the resulting tessellated faces will be converted to four-sided faces wherever possible.

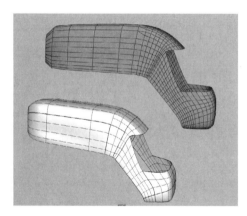

Setting the Tessellation Method to General will let you have precise control over how many faces are created from each NURBS patch, based on the conditions specified in the Initial Tessellation Controls section of this window. If the U Type and V Type attributes are set to Per Span # Of Iso Params, you can specify how many polygonal faces will be created for each span in the U and V directions. This illustration shows the NURBS model on the bottom and the converted polygonal mesh above it. Notice that Maya added edges to create triangles in the sections where there were two spans in one patch next to a patch with one in order to avoid creating a five-sided face.

Pure Polygonal Modeling

Another popular technique for creating polygonal models begins with a simple polygonal object, either a primitive or an n-gon. Details are added by dividing the faces and then extruding them to create a whole new set of surfaces. This is a popular modeling technique for games, because you as the modeler are conscious of every polygon that is created as you split and extrude faces. In conjunction with using the HUD, it lets you easily manage your polygon count for your models.

The three main tools used for this type of modeling are the Create Polygon tool, the Extrude Faces tool, and the Split Polygon tool. Use of each is demonstrated in the following tutorial.

Tutorial: Essential Tools for Polygon Modeling

This tutorial introduces several basic and essential tools for polygon modeling. You can create virtually any polygonal model using only these tools. Let's create a simple Humvee military vehicle model.

Set Up the Scene

Open the scene called Tutorial1HUMVEEstart from the Chapter 5 folder of the book CD. This will open a scene with top, front, and side references already applied to the respective image planes. Figure 5-9 shows reference planes with textures.

FIGURE 5-9   Reference planes with proper textures

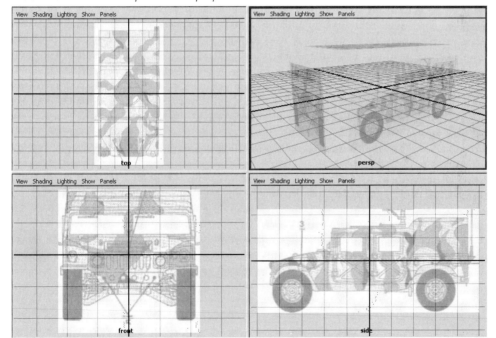

Start Modeling

You can draw faces with any number of edges using the Create Polygon tool (choose Polygons | Create Polygon Tool). The Create Polygon tool lets you create a polygonal face by clicking where you want the vertices to appear. This tool is often used to sketch out a face that roughly matches the profile of the object you are trying to model.

Start the model by choosing Polygons | Create Polygon Tool. In the Side view, LMB-click the bottom of the rear bumper to set the first point. Continue clicking in a clockwise direction around the entire shape of the Humvee at every point at which a change in an angle of the body surface occurs. See the illustration shown here for help. Press ENTER (RETURN) when you're finished.

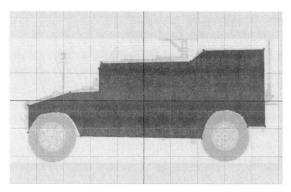

TIP **If you don't like where you clicked, you can press BACKSPACE (DELETE) to undo the last click. You can also use the middle-mouse-button (MMB) to edit the position of the last placed point.**

 Next, you will extrude the face of the polygon to give the polygon some thickness. The Extrude Faces tool will pull out the existing face while new faces are created to connect the existing face to the outer edges of the polygon. Select the face you created in the last step by RMB-clicking it and choosing Faces from the marking menu. The geometry will display a blue dot at the center of the face. LMB-click the dot to select the face.

You can also use a hot key to select a vertex, edge, or face, as shown here:

HOT KEY	SELECTION
F9	Vertex selection
F10	Edge selection
F11	Face selection
F12	UV selection

Choose Edit Polygons | Extrude Face. The face is duplicated, and a manipulator for the Extrude Faces tool will appear. You'll use this manipulator to move, rotate, and scale the new face by LMB-clicking and dragging on the respective part of the manipulator.

In the Top view, select the blue Z axis arrow and move it to the right, so that the edge of the extruded face will be set at the maximum width of the left side of the HUMVEE reference picture. The following illustration shows how the face is extruded.

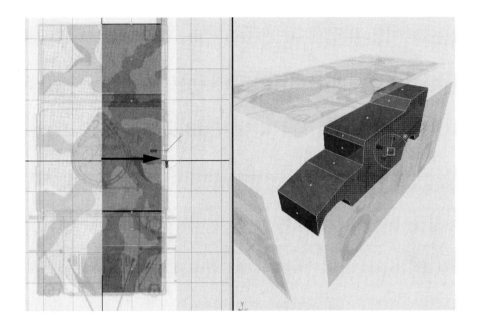

NOTE   *If you use the Extrude Face command, don't pull out the selected face and then use the Extrude command on that face again; if you do, you will have faces with a "zero length," which means that those extruded faces won't have any physical space. This can cause havoc when you start to split or smooth the polygons or render the object. If you see the blue dots on the middle of any edges when you are displaying faces, you know you have a problem. Try to fix this situation by selecting the model in object mode, choosing Polygons | Cleanup, and checking the Edges with zero length and Faces with zero geometry area. Then click the Cleanup button.*

Let's add more details using the second most important tool for polygonal modeling: the Split Polygon tool. The Split Polygon tool will create an edge between any points you click and divide existing faces into multiple faces. Thus, it lets you add more details to the model.

Select the model and choose Edit Polygons | Split Polygon Tool. The cursor will turn into a triangular arrow shape. In Perspective view, click the corner edges at the bottom of the window area, and then click the edge at the back of the vehicle to split that face. Then click the edge on the other side of the vehicle—a total of three clicks, as shown in the following illustration. Note that you can press the BACKSPACE key to undo any clicks. Press ENTER to finish. A new vertex will appear where you clicked, and the surface's face is now divided by edges.

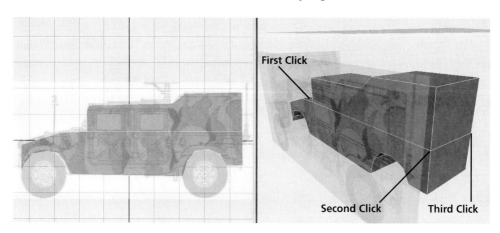

The two new vertices added at the rear of the vehicle may not be located at the same level as the vertices in the front window area. You can easily fix this by selecting the two vertices along the front of the object and the two in the back and then use the Scale tool to even them out. In the Side view, RMB-click the model and choose Vertex from the marking menu; then drag-select the two vertices in the front of the model, around the windshield area; then, holding down the SHIFT key, drag-select the two vertices in the back. Drag-selecting in the Side view like this will allow you to select the vertices that are directly behind each other. After selecting them, look in the Perspective view to make sure that all four vertices are selected. Choose the Scale tool and LMB-drag the Y scale manipulator to the center of the model. This will make all four vertices appear at the same level. You can adjust placement with the Move tool. See the following illustration for details.

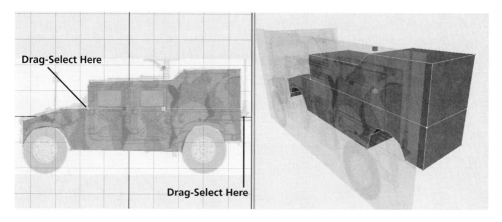

Useful options are available for the Split Polygon tool by choosing Edit Polygon | Split Polygon Tool ❑. Some of these options are explained next.

- **Subdivision**   Adds more vertices per edge that you create. A Subdivision of 1 will have no vertex between the edge you create, and a Subdivision of 2 will add one more vertex at the center of the edge you create.

- **Edge Snapping**   Extremely useful if you want to be more precise about splitting polygons. You can turn it on by checking the Edge Snapping check box in the Options window.

- **Snapping Magnets**   Sets how many magnets you want to have. A value of 1 will create a magnet at the center of the edge, so if you snap to the magnet, you can split the edge at the center. A value of 2 will create two snapping magnets, dividing the edge into thirds.

- **Snapping Tolerance**   Controls how "snappy" those snapping magnets are. If it's set to 0, it won't snap at all; if its value is 100, you will always snap at the snapping magnets or the existing vertex on the edge. So if you want always to snap at the center, set the Snapping Magnet to 1 and the Snapping Tolerance to 100.

 Another great tool you can use to create more details is the Cut Faces tool, which gives results similar to the Split Polygon tool; however, instead of clicking points, you create an edge by slicing through the model, just like cutting cake with a knife. While it's not as precise as the Split Polygon tool, Cut Faces is much faster to use. If you want to cut through only certain faces, for example, you can use the component mode to select those faces and then use the Cut Faces tool.

Now select the body of our Humvee model. Make sure you are in object selection mode, and choose Edit Polygons | Cut Faces Tool. In the Side view, create horizontal edges for the door area by holding down the left mouse button while choosing the angle and then releasing the mouse to cut the face. Holding the SHIFT key as you do this will let you choose the angle in 45-degree intervals. Create three vertical cuts for the side of the doors and one horizontal cut for the top of the door. The result should look like the illustration.

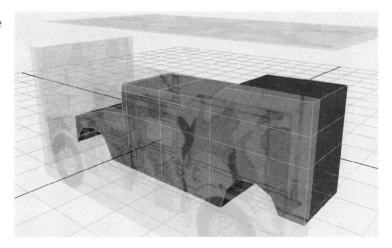

When you used the Cut Faces tool, you may have created edges that are extremely close to each other. We will use the Merge Vertices command to clean up this geometry.

1. To merge vertices, you first need to select the vertices to merge. RMB-click the geometry and choose Vertex from the marking menu.

2. Select the four vertices that belong to two edges at the top of the Front view.

3. Choose Edit Polygons | Merge Vertices ❑ to open the Options window.

4. Set the Distance value to 0.1, and click the Merge Vertex button. The vertices that are within 0.1 unit from one another will be merged into one edge. Note that the 0.1 value is the smallest distance between two or more selected points that will be merged together in Maya. You don't want to set this value too high, because many vertices will be merged at one spot.

5. Try this again on the middle roof edges. Figure 5-10 shows where vertices should be merged.

TIP   _**It's always a good idea to use Edit Polygons | Delete Edge to delete an edge. If you simply select an edge and click the Delete button, the edge will be deleted, but vertices of the edge will be left behind. Choosing the Delete Edge command, however, will also delete the vertices.**_

FIGURE 5-10   _Merge vertices around this area._

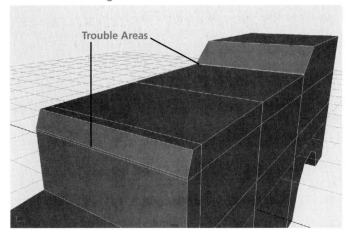

Add Detail

You can create almost anything in Maya by using the tools you just learned about. Adding detail to the model is a continuation of this process, where you extrude; adjust the placement of the vertices, edges, and faces; and then perform any cleanup necessary by merging vertices or edges.

Let's create window areas by extruding some more faces.

1. Select the face in the front windshield. Extrude the face and adjust scale and placement using the Front view. You may need to adjust vertices of the entire front area to accommodate the windshield's position.

2. Use the same technique for the side doors. You can actually extrude both side doors at the same time by selecting both window faces.

3. Choose Polygons | Tool ❑, and then make sure that Keep Faces Together is unchecked in the Options window. If this option is checked, extruded faces that share the same edges will be connected (that is, no new faces are created between those extruding faces).

4. You can add depth to the window area by extruding and not editing the position or scale and extruding again and moving the face inward. Figure 5-11 shows how extruding is used to create a side window.

FIGURE 5-11   Side windows can be made like this.

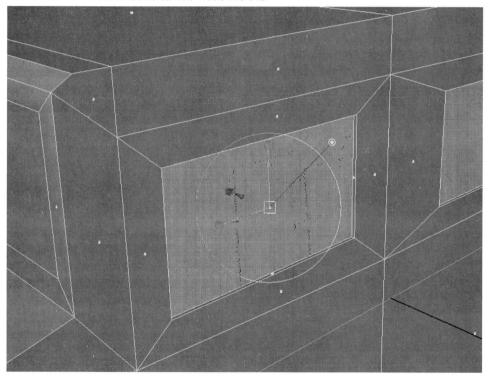

 5. Our Humvee currently has too many harsh 90-degree angles for the edges. The top edge of the Humvee is actually quite round. You can split those edges and break up the transition of a surface by using the Bevel command, which divides up the edge by a specified number of additional edges to make the surface rounder. Select the edges that belong to the right top of the Humvee and choose Edit Polygons | Bevel.

6. Once the Bevel command has been executed, you may want to adjust the Bevel settings. Since the Bevel operation has been added to the Humvee's history, we can edit this node and change the bevel settings. In the Inputs area of the Channel Box, click polyBevel1 and set the Offset to 0.1 and Roundness and Segments to 1. Figure 5-12 shows the process of selecting and then beveling an edge.

FIGURE 5-12 *Selecting (left) and beveling (right) the top edges of the Humvee*

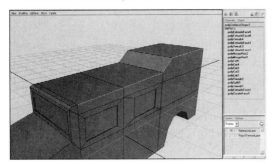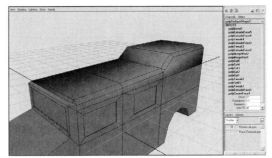

7. Now, if you look closely at top of the vehicle, you'll see strange shadow-like areas on the surface. These are caused by the Bevel command. Some of the edges created by Bevel are soft edges that simulate rounded edges. You can change the appearance of these edges by adjusting their normals.

8. Select the edges that surround this area and choose Edit Polygons | Normals | Soften/Harden ❏.

 9. In the Options window, click the All Hard option and then click Soft/Hard. This should get rid of the strange shadows on the faces. Figure 5-13 shows the softer edged model on the left and the harder edged model on the right.

TIP *If you are modeling an organic character using this technique, and you want to limit the number of faces, you can simulate smoothness by making all the edges soft.*

FIGURE 5-13 *Soften/Harden drastically changes how the model shades over the edges.*

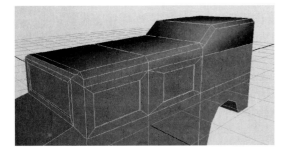

10. The Bevel command often creates an unorganized splitting of faces. Therefore, it's a good idea to clean up the beveled area by merging vertices and splitting polygons. Looking at the Front view, you can see that the right side of the Humvee needs a little tweaking. Select Vertex A and Vertex B (identified in Figure 5-14) and choose Edit Polygons | Merge Vertices.

11. Also, delete unwanted edges by selecting the edges shown and choosing Edit Polygons | Delete Edges. The geometry will now be cleaned up. Figure 5-14 show the vertices before and after being merged.

FIGURE 5-14   Vertices before (left) and after (right) being merged

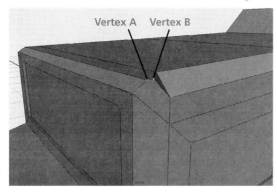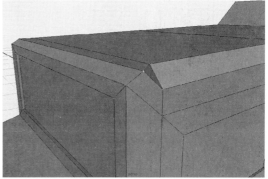

12. Use this same process of splitting, extruding, beveling, and merging to other parts of the model's detail and clean up the area in the vehicle's front.

13. Split three more polygons in the front bumper area on both sides. Delete the faces to remove these areas by selecting the faces and pressing the DELETE key. Also, delete any unwanted edges with the Delete Edge command. Figure 5-15 shows how these edges are split and deleted.

14. When you delete faces from a model, "holes" are created. You can fill these holes by selecting the model and then choosing Edit Polygons | Fill Hole. This will create faces between all of the gaps in the model. (The faces it creates may be n-gons.) After filling in the holes, inspect the new faces and use the Split Polygon tool to fix any faces that need it.

15. Continue using these tools and techniques to refine and detail the model. Use the Bevel tool to create transitions between hard-angled surfaces. Don't add more vertices and edges that lie along the Y-Z plane in the X axis. We need to mirror the model along that axis, and those points need to be located at the center of the mirroring axis. Figure 5-16 shows the model after more detail has been added.

FIGURE 5-15 *Edges in the bumper area are split (top) and then deleted (bottom)*

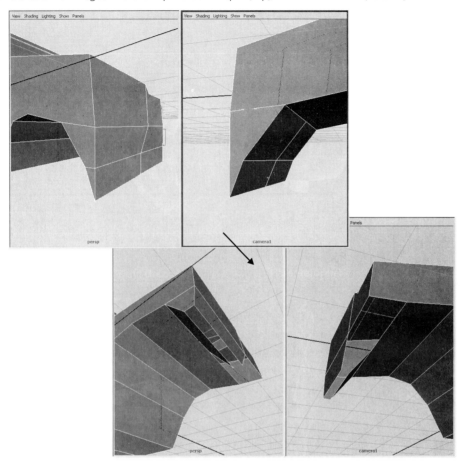

Booleans

Now let's punch a hole in the front of the model for the grill and lights using a Boolean operation. Booleans let you add two polygonal objects (a Boolean *union*), subtract one polygonal object from another (a Boolean *difference*), and extract the areas of two intersecting objects (a Boolean intersection). Figure 5-17 shows the results of all three Boolean operations in Maya.

FIGURE 5-16 *The model with more detail*

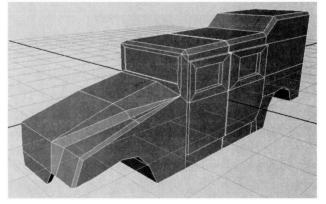

1. Create an object to use for subtracting holes for the grill and lights on the Humvee. Create a polygonal cylinder by choosing Create | Polygon Primitives | Cylinder.

2. Click the polyCylinder1 node under the Input section of the cylinder's Channel Box and make sure Subdivision Axis is set to 10 and Subdivision Height is set to 1.

3. In the Top view, use component mode to select three vertices that belong to the far-left side and scale them along the X axis toward the center of the manipulator, so that the three vertices will be straight vertically.

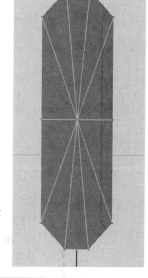

4. Do the same thing for the three far-right vertices. We do this because the grill hole has straight edges. You may need to elongate the shape more by manipulating points. Rotate the cylinder 90 degrees by typing **90** for the Rotate X-axis attribute in the Channel Box. Scale and orient it according to the front reference for the grill. Place it so that it intersects with the vehicle model. Duplicate it and move to where the other holes in the grill need to be. The illustration shows the shape's details.

5. Select the vehicle and then select polyCylinder1 (the first cylinder you created). Then choose Polygons | Boolean | Difference. This Boolean will initially result in the vehicle facing the direction opposite of what we want—that is, the normals will be facing in the wrong direction. To fix this, undo the Boolean operation and reverse the normals of the cylinder to get the expected result. Choose Edit Polygons | Normals | Reverse.

FIGURE 5-17   The results of Boolean operations

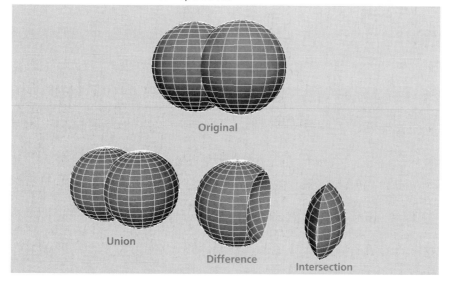

TIP   *Remember that we created a button earlier in this chapter for the Reverse command. You may find that clicking the button is faster than digging through the menus.*

NOTE   *Booleans sometime require some experimentation to achieve the results you want. If the geometry is facing the wrong direction, or if it disappears completely, the problem usually has to do with the normals of the faces involved in the operation. It is a good idea to evaluate the normals in a surface by turning on their display (choose Display | Polygon Components | Normals, or use the Shelf button you created earlier). Make sure that all of the polygons are facing in the same direction—but also in the correct direction.*

6.   Now create the hole for the light and lower bumper.

The result of these Booleans should look similar to those shown in Figure 5-18.

FIGURE 5-18   *Boolean operations are used to punch holes in the front bumper.*

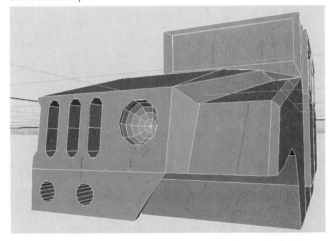

TIP   *A Boolean can mess up an object's faces by creating a lot of n-gons. For this reason, the Boolean operations should be used toward the end of the modeling process, when extrusions might become too complicated to set up. You should always clean up the polygonal faces as you work.*

Finish Up

You can continue to add as many details as necessary to this model by using these techniques and cleaning up the geometry as you go. When you are happy with the overall form of your model, you can proceed to the final phase, where we mirror the geometry and add secondary objects, such as tires.

In this section, you will learn how to use the Smooth operation. But before we move on, it is a good idea for you to delete the history on the existing model. It's always a good idea to keep history while you are working so you can go back and experiment with different values for the tools and commands that you used. The downside, however, is that the history can make the scene heavy and slow down your computer as you continue to make new edits and create new objects. Since we're finished with this part of our work, though, we can safely delete the history. Save the scene and we'll continue on to the final phase.

1. Select the Humvee body in object mode and choose Edit | Delete By Type | History. All the construction history is deleted.

2. Now we have created only the right half of our Humvee, so we need to mirror the model. Working in Front view, select the faces that sit along the Y-Z plane, as shown in the following illustration, and press the DELETE key.

3. Select the body and choose Polygons | Mirror Geometry ☐.

4. In the Options window, check the box next to –x to set the Mirror Direction, since you are mirroring in the negative X axis. Also check Merge With The Original. This will merge the two sides automatically.

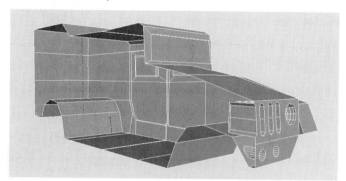

5. Click the Mirror button. Now you have created both sides of your Humvee, and the vertices have been merged at the center.

6. Now we'll add tires and a few other details to finish up the Humvee. Each tire can be made from a NURBS curve that is revolved. Choose Create | CV Curve Tool, and in the Front view, create a profile of the tire. Make sure you start the point from the top of the tire along the Y-Z plane and press ENTER (RETURN) to finish the curve with the CV Curve Tool.

7. Choose Surfaces | Revolve ☐. In the Options window, set the Axis attribute to X, and at the bottom of the window, set Output Geometry to Polygons. Tessellation Method should be set to Control Points.

8. Click the Revolve button. The other half of the tire should form to look similar to the illustration.

9. Now select the tire and choose Polygons | Mirror Geometry. Use the same options you used when you mirrored the vehicle to create the complete tire. Scale and move the tire to fit it into the wheel well. Delete the curve you used to create the tire.

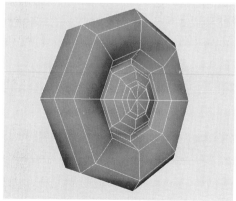

10. Before you duplicate and place the other three tires, let's make our newly created tire smooth. Select the tire and choose Polygons | Smooth ☐.

11. You don't want to smooth the tire too much, so change the Subdivision Level to 1. The higher this setting, the more polygons will be used to define the transition, and hence the smoother the object will be.

12. Click the Smooth button to create a smoother looking tire. Now you can duplicate the tire and place the other tires in their positions. Figure 5-19 shows the tires placed on a completed model.

You can add more and more details to make this model closer to the real thing.

FIGURE 5-19 *The completed model with the tires in place*

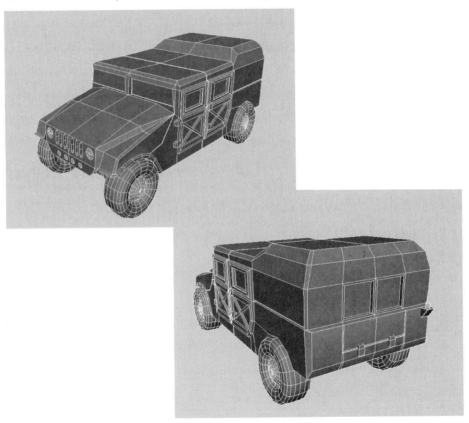

Summary

This tutorial should have been good practice to learn polygonal modeling methodology and get used to many useful polygon tools. In the next chapter, we'll cover how to create a smooth, organic character utilizing all NURBS, polygon, and subdivision surfaces.

Organic Modeling

So far, you have learned how to model

using various NURBS and polygonal modeling

techniques. The tutorials so far have covered

modeling hard surfaces, but in this chapter, we

will combine both the NURBS and polygonal

modeling toolsets and introduce subdivision

surfaces to create organic models. You will see

that the most efficient way to model characters

often makes use of the strengths of all three

toolsets.

Subdivision Surface Modeling

Recently, subdivision surface modeling techniques have become the standard modeling methods for modeling organic forms in both the game and film industries. These methods offer the control of NURBS modeling while maintaining the simplicity of polygonal modeling. Trims and complex patching are not needed because "branching," such as in the fingers in a hand or an arm from the torso, can easily be achieved by extruding a simple polygonal cage from an existing face. The vertices and edges of the polygonal object act as control objects that drive the smoothed, subdivided geometry underneath.

Definition   **cage**   *The low-resolution version of the model that controls the higher, smoothed version.*

Maya 6 offers two implementations of subdivision surface modeling: the *smooth proxy* and *hierarchical subdivision surfaces*.

Smooth Proxy

The smooth proxy method is common in many 3D software packages today. In Maya, any polygonal object can be converted into a smooth proxy by choosing Polygons | Smooth Proxy. A smooth proxy is a subdivided or smoothed copy of the model that is still connected to and controlled by the original, low-resolution model. Each polygonal face of the original object will be divided and smoothed according to the Divisions attribute of the polySmoothFace node that is created.

This polySmoothFace node is the same node that is added when you use the Smooth command (choose Polygons | Smooth). However, unlike the results of the Smooth command, when smooth proxy is used, the resulting smoothed shape is connected to the original polygonal object. The object is still visible so that you can select and edit its components while interactively seeing the resulting smooth mesh underneath. Detail is added by splitting, subdividing, or extruding the faces of the original object.

You can choose how the original object is displayed by setting the Smooth Proxy Shader attribute in the Smooth Proxy Options window before you execute the command. Choose Polygons | Smooth Proxy ❑ to open the Options window shown in the following illustration. The Smooth Proxy Shader attribute is set to Transparent by default; the Proxy Transparency setting lets you decide how transparent the control cage will be. You also have the option of keeping the display of the original object the way it was (by selecting Keep) or deleting the shader attributes altogether (by selecting Remove) so that just the edges of the low resolution object are visible.

One more thing to be aware of when you're working with smooth proxies is that Maya places the original and smoothed polygonal objects in *separate layers*. Look in the Layer Editor. By default, the layer that contains the smoothed object is set to Reference so that it cannot be chosen or changed while you're editing the original. This organization also lets you set the visibility of the objects. When you are finished modeling, you can turn

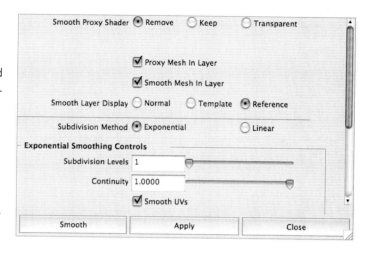

off the visibility of the original so that just the smoothed version will render.

Of course, you can always break the connection between the original object and the smoothed object by selecting the smoothed object and deleting its history or by deleting the original object. However, one of the great advantages of using the smooth proxy technique is that when it comes to *skinning*—binding the mesh to a skeleton—you can bind the low poly original to the joints and have that control the smooth mesh connected to it. This is much faster to set up than having to bind the smoothed geometry, because you are dealing with fewer vertices that need to be weighted to the joints.

Definition   **low poly**   *Short for low polygon; a low-resolution model.*

Hierarchical Subdivision Surfaces

In Maya, *hierarchical subdivision surface modeling* is called *subdivision surfaces*. Subdivision surfaces allow you to select certain areas and refine them through hierarchical levels. This lets you add finer details to the mesh without having to add more geometry to the original cage/polygon, ensuring a high level of detail in the resulting surface while maintaining a reasonably simple original (level 0) shape.

You can create a subdivision surface by choosing commands from the Create menu to create various subdivision surface primitives, as shown in the following illustration. You can also con-

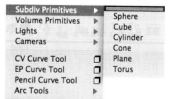

vert an existing polygonal or NURBS surface into a subdivision surface by choosing Modify | Convert and then choosing a conversion option. Let's examine some of the features of subdivision surfaces and learn how they work.

Subdivision Surface Modes and Refinement

Two modes can be used to add detail to a subdivision surface: standard mode and polygon proxy mode. Standard mode gives you access to multiple levels of hierarchical components within the subdivision surface. Polygon proxy mode is similar to the smooth proxy method discussed earlier in this chapter. In this mode, you can use polygonal editing tools to split or extrude the base polygonal object.

Standard Mode By default, a subdivision surface will be in standard mode when the surface is created or converted. This mode lets you access polygonal components at various levels of refinement at any area on the surface. If you use the marking menu to select a component (by right-clicking the object and choosing a component), Maya will display the selected component as a number. The sphere on the left in Figure 6-1 shows a subdivision sphere displaying its faces at the base level (level 0). The number 0 indicates the level of refinement with which you are currently interacting.

To start adding detail to the faces, you can switch to a higher level of refinement. The easiest way to do this is to right-click the component and choose Level | 1 from the marking menu. The selected components will *subdivide*. This means that for every one face, four faces will be created for you to work with, as shown in the sphere on the right in Figure 6-1. Notice that the faces are each displaying the number *1* to indicate the current level of refinement.

You can now edit any components at level 1 and then switch back to level 0 at any time by using the marking menu. You can also change levels by changing the Levels attribute in the Channel Box. If you've modeled as far as you can at level 1 and still need to add more detail, you can refine the display further by right-clicking the components of the region you wish to refine and choosing Refine from the marking menu. The components will be subdivided another level further.

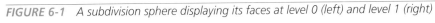

FIGURE 6-1   *A subdivision sphere displaying its faces at level 0 (left) and level 1 (right)*

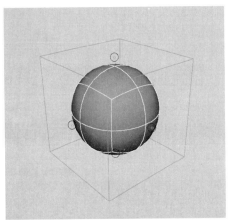
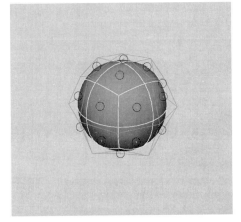

Polygonal editing tools such as Extrude Face and Split Polygon cannot be used on subdivision surfaces while in standard mode. To edit these kinds of tools, you must switch to polygon proxy mode.

Polygon Proxy Mode   You can switch from standard mode to polygon proxy mode at any time by right-clicking the surface and choosing Polygon from the marking menu. This creates a polygonal object that matches the base mesh (level 0) of the subdivision surface. You can use polygon proxy mode to finesse the main features of the model using any of the techniques discussed in Chapter 5.

> *NOTE* *When you convert back into standard mode after editing an object in polygon proxy mode, all of the construction history for the polygonal object will be deleted. Similarly, if you've added any deformers or added any other nodes to the construction history while in standard mode, you will have to delete the history manually when switching to polygon proxy mode.*

Additional Features and Tools for Subdivision Surface Modeling

As you can see, once you have an understanding of polygonal modeling, subdivision surface modeling will be easy. But the ability to smooth rigid polygonal faces is not the only thing this toolset has to offer.

For some modeled objects, you may not want the surface to be completely smooth. You may want to retain or introduce a hard edge or crease into your subdivision model. When using the smooth proxy method of subdivision surfaces, you may need to add a group of edges to your original cage model that are close to or even on top of one another. All this extra geometry can make editing the surface difficult.

 By using subdivision surfaces in Maya, you can add a *crease*. In standard mode, you can create creases to generate edges in the middle of a smooth surface without adding extra geometry. You can create a harsh edge called a *full crease* or a gentle bump called a *partial crease* simply by selecting edges or vertices of a subdivision model and selecting the appropriate command from the Subdivision Surfaces menu (Subdiv Surfaces | Full Crease Edge/Vertex, or Subdiv Surfaces | Partial Crease Edge/Vertex). The creases can always be removed by selecting the vertices or edges in the crease and choosing Subdiv Surfaces | Uncrease Edge/Vertex. Figure 6-2 demonstrates how a crease might look.

> *NOTE* *Adding a full crease also adds a higher level of refinement to the subdivision surface.*

Another similarity that subdivision surfaces share with NURBS is the ability to display the surfaces at different levels of smoothness while you're working in a view window. You can change

FIGURE 6-2   *Full creases or partial creases*
can be introduced anywhere on the surface
of an object.

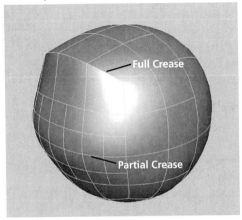

the display smoothness of a subdivision surface
by pressing the 1, 2, and 3 keys, just as you can
do with a NURBS model. This can make interaction
with subdivision surfaces much easier due to the
increased performance.

Disadvantages/Limitations of Subdivision Surfaces

While subdivison surfaces might sound like a "best of
both worlds" scenario, you should also consider the
following trade-offs.

Use Rules when Converting to Subdivision Surfaces

Conversion from polygons requires that you follow
certain rules:

- *Polygonal objects must be very clean and should be constructed of quad faces.* Triangles or n-gon faces may produce strange, flower-shaped artifacts when you convert to subdivision surfaces.

- *Non-manifold topology, such as faces that share the same edge, cannot have their normals pointing in the opposite direction.* It is always a good idea to clean up (choose Polygons | Cleanup) a polygonal surface to fix any of these problems.

- *Avoid converting geometry with poles.* A *pole* is the location where all the points meet in an infinitely small space. A pole will show up as a black dot in a subdivision surface.

Definition   ***non-manifold topology***   *Geometric configurations that, if unfolded, could
not lie flat on a plane without overlapping pieces.*

Limited Tools Are Available for the Subdivision Toolset   A limited amount of tools is
available in the subdivision surface toolset compared to what is available for polygonal surfaces.
You'll notice that the biggest shortcoming involves texturing a subdivision surface: a variety of
tools available for polygonal geometry for managing the layout of the UV (texture) coordinates
are not available in the subdivision surface toolset. (This will become more clear when we cover
UV layout in Chapter 14.)

A good workflow to use for texturing a subdivision surface is to convert the subdivision surface to
polygons at the base level and then texture the model. This will give you access to all of the tools
found in the Edit Polygons | Texture menu. You can use this technique to your advantage, because
you'll have to deal with much fewer UVs in the converted surface. When you are finished laying

out the UVs in the UV Texture window, you can then convert the surface back to a subdivision surface. Hopefully, this limitation will be insignificant with future releases of Maya, since these tools will continue to expand.

Problems Occur with Level Hierarchy   While using the hierarchical levels to refine a subdivision model may sound like a great option, it has its share of problems. If you refined the model to have a lot of levels, you will either have to lose those levels or you'll have a very complex model when you covert to polygons.

It's not wise to use levels greater than level 2 if you think you'll want to convert your subdivision model to polygons sometime later. In addition, smooth and rigid binding (*binding skin* is explained in Chapter 10) with joints works only for level 0 subdivision surfaces and ignores finer levels of hierarchy. Therefore, you must be diligent about inserting enough edges for the proper deformation.

Performance Issues Occur and Render Times Increase   While subdivision surfaces can be rendered to be infinitely smooth, rendering times are extremely slow. A smoothed polygon surface may render much faster because much less computation is involved in calculating the surface.

In addition, a detailed and complex subdivision model may experience problems with interactivity as it's being deformed. Because many dependencies need to be evaluated in a subdivision surface model, even though your skeleton might be bound to the base level, it can take a while for the actual surface to update when a joint is rotated.

Suggested Workflow for Subdivision Surface Modeling

The best feature of subdivision surfaces is that they allow you to add localized detail. Since it is always better to go as far as you can with the base level (level 0) polygonal model before jumping hierarchies, you'll find it best to model with polygons or with a smooth proxy until you take the basic shape as far as it can go. This will let you do your texture mapping on the polygonal model, and the performance of your computer will be faster as you model.

Ideally, the model should not be converted to a subdivision surface until the texturing is complete and the deformations have been added. At this time, the final pass of detail should be accomplished through hierarchical levels. Rendering is slow, but the smoothness you can get is worth the time. We will take a look at a detail of this workflow in the tutorial section of this chapter.

Conversion Among NURBS, Polygons, and Subdivision Surfaces

You can convert one of the three geometry types—polygons, NURBS, and subdivision surfaces—to another in various ways. NURBS surfaces are the most flexible geometry of the three. When modeled efficiently using the techniques shown in the spaceship tutorial (Chapter 4), a NURBS object can be converted to a polygon or subdivision surface with few problems. Polygons are the least flexible surfaces to convert. Polygons can be converted only to subdivision surfaces, and this sometimes doesn't work if a non-manifold geometry or other surface-related problems are encountered.

Subdivision surfaces can be converted to polygons or NURBS, but a NURBS model converted from subdivision surfaces requires serious cleanup. Therefore, the best tactics to use for creating a subdivision model is to create a rough proportion and parts with NURBS models first, and then convert them to polygons to connect the parts and model more details. Make sure you often check that your model can be converted to a subdivision surface. At the end of the project, you can convert the polygon model to a subdivision model.

Tutorial: Making a Head

Here, we'll create an organic polygon character using NURBS and polygonal modeling tools. We will first use a NURBS surface to create a head. In this case, the NURBS sphere is used because it offers enough existing components to block out a rough head shape. It will also give us a vague idea about how the model will look as a smooth surface. Next, we'll convert to polygons to add the details. We will edit this polygonal surface with the Smooth Proxy command applied so that we can continue to evaluate it in its smoothed form. The finished model is shown in Figure 6-3.

FIGURE 6-3   The finished head model

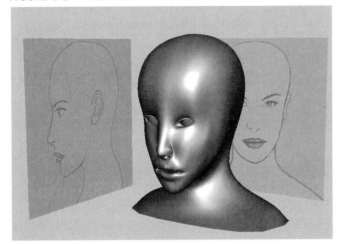

Creating a Head Model Using a NURBS Surface

First, let's create a simple head model using a NURBS surface. The main idea behind this phase is to construct the correct proportions and place some details. You don't need to be familiar with many NURBS tools to finish this section, but some new tools were included in this tutorial for learning purposes.

Setting the Scene

As usual, we start with our scene setup. Set the project and copy the two files that will be used as underlays, FrontFace.tga and SideFace.tga, from the CD onto your project's source images directory. Import each file onto its respective image plane and add the image planes to a new layer.

It's a good idea to set up a simple three-point lighting scheme for your scene. *Three-point lighting* is a term used in traditional film and photography to indicate one key light and two fill lights. The key light is generally brighter than the fill lights. Choose Create | Lights | Point Light. Use the Move tool to place the key light in the front upper-right area of the scene. You'll want to adjust the position after your model starts to develop, but this is a good place to start.

Create two more point lights to act as fills. Edit each light's intensity so that it is much lower than that of the key light. The intensity can be edited in the Attribute Editor or Channel Box. A value of 0.4 for each of the two fill lights is a good place to start. Move one light to the left-front side of the scene and the other one to the lower-right front of the scene. You can see the effect of the lights on the objects in the scene by pressing the 7 key. A setup like this can help you evaluate your surface as you model. (Lighting will be discussed in depth in Chapter 13.)

Modeling the NURBS Head

We will use a NURBS sphere to create a rough head. One pole of our NURBS sphere will be the mouth area. This is a great idea to accommodate any deformation of the mouth shape later on, because the area will have an isoparm/edge distribution that mimics our mouth muscles. Although we could use the mirror-modeling technique to model only one side and mirror it to the other side, we'll save that technique for polygonal modeling later in this chapter.

While you are modeling, keep the following in mind:

- If you want to choose several points at once, you'll find it handy to use orthographic view and select a group of points by drawing a marquee box around them; don't LMB-click each point. By using a marquee box, you can select the points on the left and right sides of the head. Lasso tools are also great to use for selecting CVs and vertices.

- You can "pickwalk" the selection of components by using the arrow keys on your keyboard. After you select a CV, press the right arrow key, and the next CV in the U direction will be selected. (This is another great benefit of using NURBS tools.)

- Don't worry about making both sides totally symmetrical, because you will delete the left side of the head later in the tutorial. Instead, focus on adding details to the right side of the head. You might even use the left side of the head to test ideas or practice, and then finalize them on the right side of the head.

- It's important not to move the points that sit on the YZ plane. This is because later on you will delete only half of the head, and you want the edge of the right half of the head to be placed against the *centerline*, or *axis of symmetry*. Keep the CVs straight in the Front view while you're modeling.

Now let's get started:

1. Choose Create | NURBS Primitives | Sphere. Click the makeNurbSphere1 node from the Inputs area of the Channel Box and change both the Sections and Spans attributes to **12**. This will add more resolution to the model.

2. We will mainly use Front and Side views for this part of the tutorial. In the Front and Side views, choose Shading | Shade Options | X-ray. This will let you see the underlay references on the image planes.

3. Let's start forming the mouth area. Enter component mode by pressing F8, and in the Side view, select the CVs from the bottom two rows. Draw a marquee by LMB-dragging to select points from both sides. Move the selection up to the middle of the sphere. This will create a hole for the mouth. Take a look at the following illustration to see which points to select.

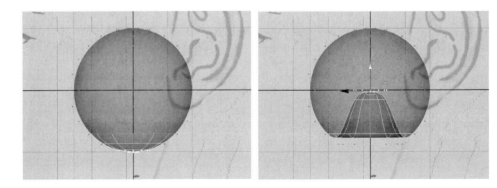

4. Now go back to object mode by pressing F8 again, and rotate the sphere in the X axis and scale it in all axes, so the newly created mouth area is located near the mouth in the reference drawing. Make sure you are rotating only in the X axis. You can double-check this in the Channel Box.

5. To correct the proportion of the sphere, apply the lattice deformer to the sphere and deform it. This way, the change in shape is much smoother than directly adjusting CVs.

(Remember that we did a similar move when we built the tail for the spaceship in Chapter 4.) Select the sphere, press F2 to open the animation menu set, and then choose Deform | Create Lattice ❑.

6. The Division attributes should be set to 2, 6, and 2, for S, T, and U, respectively (these represent the local special coordinates for lattices). Click the Create button. The lattice deformer appears around your object much the same way that scaffolding is placed around a building.

7. Right-click the lattice, and select the lattice components from the marking menu. In this case, only one component is available, Lattice Point. Choose it, and you can edit the surface that it is controlling in much the same way that CVs affect the surface. For this step, move the lattice points that belong to the three front rows so your head looks like the illustration shown here.

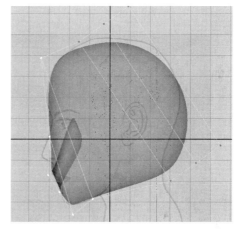

8. The back row of lattice points can be used to form the neck area. That way, you can use both poles of the sphere for starting the mouth and the bottom of the neck. Because, as mentioned earlier, poles will create problems when you eventually convert the object to a subdivision surface, place them in areas that are not visible. Select all the back points of the lattice, rotate them in the X axis, and scale the selection down.

9. Move the whole selection down to the neck area. Move the points at the top up, so they form the top of the head. Figure 6-4 illustrates the process of using a lattice to form the basic shape of the head and neck.

10. Switch to the Front view and repeat the process of editing the lattice so that the overall profile of the geometry matches the image planes. When you have finished with the lattice deformer, you can remove it by deleting the history for the NURBS object.

11. Now detach the bottom of the neck area, so you can get rid of the pole and create an opening in the surface. RMB-click the surface and choose Isoparms from the marking menu; then select the bottom-most isoparm and choose Edit NURBS | Detach Surfaces.

FIGURE 6-4   *Use a lattice deformer to form the basic shape for the head and neck.*

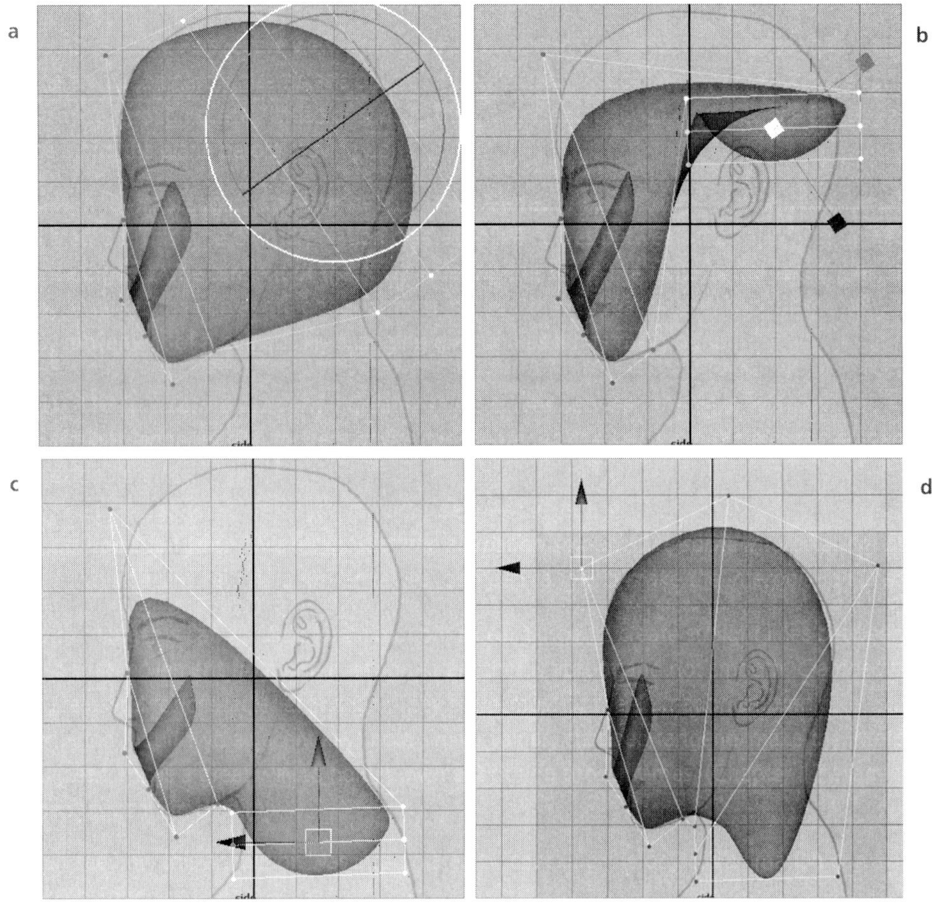

12.   Now choose the bottom two hulls and use the Move and Scale tools to open up this area to form the neck and shoulder areas. You can start editing individual CVs so that the head will better match the images plane in the Front and Side views. The result should look like the illustration shown in Figure 6-5.

13.   Now we can start to refine the mouth area. One of the biggest challenges with organic modeling is anticipating how moving certain CVs will affect the surface. Often, you will select and move a group of points to affect the surface, and at other times the position of just one CV makes all the difference. With practice, it will become easier for you to

make such changes and anticipate the results. In this step, use the Side view to select the points along the side of the mouth and move them back. See Figure 6-6 for details.

14. To resize the mouth area, select the hulls around the mouth and scale them at once. Select the first two hulls around the mouth. Be certain that you are selecting the hulls going around the mouth, not those moving toward the back of the head.

15. Note that you can use the arrow keys to "pickwalk" selected components in the U and V directions. In the case of our head, you may find it difficult to select the hulls inside the mouth because they are obstructed by the geometry on the outside. Instead of trying to select one hull inside, where it is surrounded by so much geometry, select a hull on the outside of the face that runs circular in the V direction. Now use the right or left arrow key to pickwalk selected hulls in the U direction until you reach the last hull inside the mouth.

FIGURE 6-5   *The result of opening up the area to form the neck and shoulder areas*

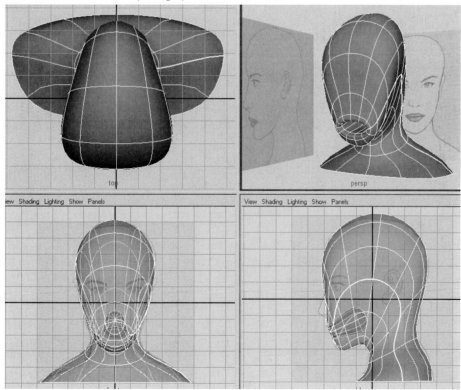

FIGURE 6-6   *Selecting the points along the mouth and moving them back*

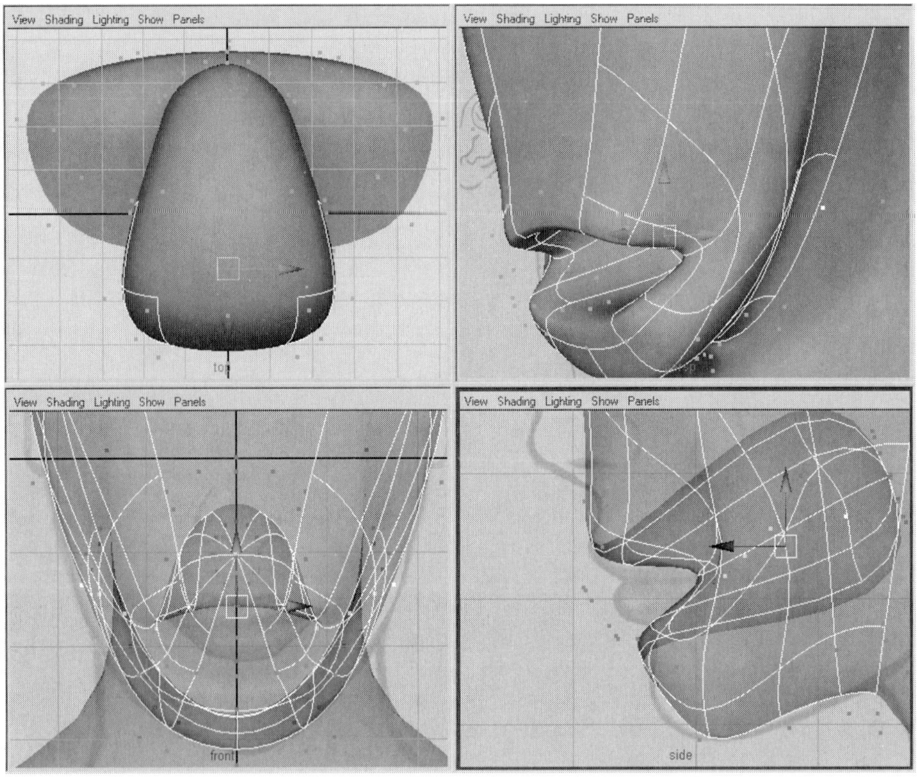

16. To select the second row as well, hold down the CTRL (CONTROL) key and right-click the model. Select Grow Selection from the marking menu. This will expand the currently selected components. With these hulls now selected, scale them along the X axis to make the mouth smaller horizontally. Scale along the Y axis to make the mouth area flat. Again, use the image underlay as a reference to judge the size and shape of the mouth.

17. When you've modeled as far as you can go with the existing NURBS components, you can begin adding more isoparms that will be used to define the details of the lips and the nose. Change the component selection mode to Isoparms, and then create five more isoparms. You will add three circular isoparms around the mouth and two vertical isoparms for the front-top-center for pulling out the nose. Don't worry about making them totally equal in both the left and right sides of the face. Before adding the isoparms, double-check the options for the Insert Isoparms command (choose Edit NURBS | Insert Isoparms ☐). In the Options window, make sure the Insert At Selection option is selected, Multiplicity is set to Increase By, Multiplicity is set to 1, and Keep Original is unchecked.

Using the Sculpt Surfaces Tool

The Sculpt Surfaces tool allows you to modify the model using a brush-based interface. As you will see, most of the toolsets in Maya offer this interface for performing various tasks. When it comes to modeling, the Sculpt Surfaces tool provides a great way to smooth, push, or pull the positions of the CVs on a surface without constantly having to make selections and use the transform tools for editing. This approach to surface editing will seem more intuitive to people who have sculpted in clay, as it works in a similar way. Let's take a look at some of the options available with the Sculpt Surface tool.

Select the NURBS surface in the view window and choose Edit NURBS | Sculpt Surfaces Tool ❑. The Sculpt Surfaces Tool Settings dialog box will open and the tool will become active. If you place the cursor over the head in a view window, you will notice that the cursor shows as a circular shape on the surface. This circular cursor is called a *stamp,* and painting on the surface using a stamp is called a *stroke*. You can use the stamp to push, pull, smooth, and erase operations on CVs within the bounds of the stamp. When you LMB-drag across a surface, the stamp will behave much like a paintbrush.

Let's take a look at the settings for this tool, shown in Figure 6-7.

- **Stamp Profile** Controls size, opacity, and shape of the stamp.

  - **Radius(U)** Controls the size of the stamp. You can change the radius size wile you work in the view windows by pressing the B key—hold down the B key and LMB-click and drag left and right in the view window. You will see the stamp size change.

FIGURE 6-7 *The Sculpt Surfaces tool's Settings dialog box*

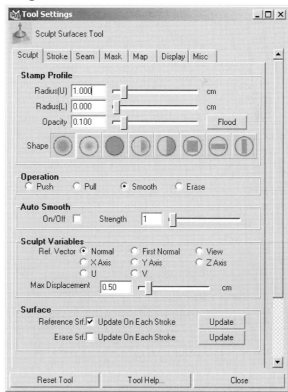

- **Radius(L)**   Controls the brush size if you are using a stylus tablet with your computer. It sets the minimum brush size when pressure on the stylus is low. The Radius(U) setting can't be smaller than the Radius(L) setting, so make sure Radius(L) is set to 0 if you are not using a stylus.

- **Opacity**   Controls the opacity of the operations you are painting. If it is set to 1, you are giving 100 percent *Max Displacement*—the amount of displacement, which is discussed in a minute.

- **Shape**   Controls the shape of the operation inside the stamp.

- **Operation**   Sets how the stamp will behave on the CVs. It will Push, Pull, Smooth, or Erase previous operations. Pull and Push move CVs in the direction you set in the Sculpt Variables area of the dialog box. The Smooth operation averages out placement of the CVs, so the surface gets smoother. Erase will erase any operations you have done to the surface. You can quickly change between these operations by holding down the U as you LMB-click and select an operation from the marking menu.

- **Auto Smooth**   Automatically smoothes the surface after the operation. You set the amount.

- **Sculpt Variables**   The following two settings change direction and depth applied to the tool:

  - **Ref. Vector**   Changes the direction of the tool. You can displace the surface's CVs in surface normal direction, according to the viewing angle, in the world space X, Y, and Z coordinates. The first normal will use the direction of the normal at the beginning of the stroke.

  - **Max Displacement**   A very important setting, which sets the amount of displacement each stroke applies to the surface. The value is measured in centimeters. Change this according to the size of your model. The displacement depth is indicated on the stamp by the arrow pointing out of the center, as shown in the illustration.

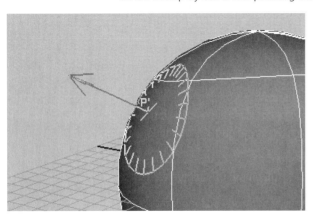

  - **Surface**   When using the Sculpt Surfaces tool, it is a good idea to understand how it works. When a surface is stroked, the vertices are displaced by the amount set in Max Displacement. This displacement calculation is based on the position of the vertices in the original, or *reference*, surface. The options in the Surface section of the Sculpt Tool's settings control when and if the current state of the object becomes the reference object while sculpting. The Reference Srf. Setting will create a new initial state for the sculpted surface either after every stroke or when the Update button is clicked. This option is enabled by default. This means that if the maximum displacement were set to 1, the CVs in the surface would be displaced by a value of 1 each time the surface was stroked. If this option were disabled, the reference surface would never update and the CVs would not be able to be displaced more than 1 unit total, no matter how many strokes were made.

Don't throw away your transform tools just yet. The Sculpt Surfaces tool works best when the existing geometry is already in place and needs just a bit of tweaking. Since the tool is used for modifying the positions of existing CVs, it will have no effect on areas of a surface in which no CVs appear. For this reason, we need to make sure that our head has enough existing geometry so that the Sculpt Surfaces tool will be more effective. Also, it is difficult to edit CVs precisely for fine-tuning. Small wrinkles in the face and areas around the eyes, for example, will always be better handled by selecting and editing the components manually.

With all that in mind, let's add some more isoparms to our head and tweak the existing CVs.

1. Scale, move, and rotate the CV points around the nose, eye, head, and neck areas to adjust their shapes. You may need to add a few more isoparms around the eye and neck areas to get the forms you like, but don't add too many isoparms at this point. Remember that most of the detail will be added after the surface has been converted to polygons.

2. While you are modeling, you may notice that the surface starts to get a bit bumpy. You could attempt to move around the CVs to try to fix this problem, but that may be tough. This is where the Sculpt Surfaces tool can prove very useful. But before using this tool, change the beginning/ending points of the surface. Notice that one of the isoparms on the surface is displayed thicker than the others. That thick line, or *seam*, signifies that the surface starts and ends here. Since we will be deleting one half of the head and mirroring it later, it's best to place this seam along the *axis of symmetry*—the axis along which the head will be mirrored.

3. Select the isoparm that runs along the YZ plane and choose Edit NURBS | Move Seam. An error may appear: "Knots are not uniform in (U or V) direction, cannot move seam." Don't be alarmed. We can rebuild the surface later to make it uniform in both directions.

4. In object selection mode, select the head, and then choose Edit NURBS | Rebuild Surfaces ❏. In the Options window, make sure Rebuild Type is set to Uniform, Direction is set to U and V, Keep Corners is checked, and change the U and V values to **18** and **20**. Then click the Rebuild button. This will rebuild, organize, and add resolution to the surface. Now when you select that isoparm again and try to move the seam, you will not get an error.

5. Select the NURBS surface in the view window and choose Edit NURBS | Sculpt Surfaces Tool ❏. Set the options as shown back in Figure 6-7 and try out the Sculpt Surfaces tool on the model to get a feel for it. Use the Perspective view. Try out all of the options available under the Operations section in the tool's settings to get a feel for how they work.

TIP   The most important thing to consider while using the Sculpt Surfaces tool successfully is to use the correct Max Displacement and Ref. Vector settings in the Settings dialog box. The exact Max Displacement value will depend on the scale of your model. Use a smaller Opacity setting (such as .1) to displace the CVs little by little. This way, you can edit the surface in passes instead of setting the Opacity high and editing it in one big stroke.

As you use the Sculpt Surfaces tool to sculpt the eye socket, for example, you will notice that it's cumbersome to paint only one side of the head. The Sculpt Surfaces tool offers the option of mirroring or reflecting any action you perform on one side of an object to the other side. This is perfect when you want to see the results of your sculpting on both sides of a symmetrical object.

6. Undo or erase all the sculpting you've done so far. In the Sculpt Surfaces tool's Options window, click the Stroke tab, check the Reflection On/Off option, and enable V Dir. Set the V Dir amount to **0.5**.

7. Bring your cursor to the surface, and you will see a stamp on both sides of the head. Now you can focus on one side, and the other side will automatically update to reflect the changes you make. Pull and smooth the jaw area and smooth out the mouth area. After a few minutes of experimenting, you should have a result similar to the one shown in Figure 6-8.

FIGURE 6-8   A basic sculpting should result in a head that looks similar to this.

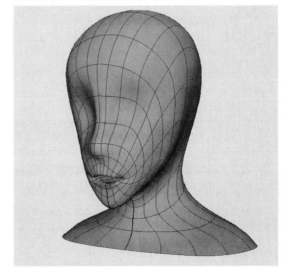

TIP *As you are finessing modeling of the face, remember that orthographic views such as Front and Side views do not have perspective correction. This means that the back of the head will not look proportional to the face if you are viewing the head "head on." If you rely on the Front view to adjust proportion, your head will look significantly thinner than it should when you're done. After you model the initial proportion using the orthographic view, you should do most of your modeling in the Perspective view. Orbit the view around the model and look at it from different angles after every edit you make to the surface to check the balance and form of the model.*

Converting NURBS to Polygons

It's time to convert our NURBS surface into polygons. Let's convert our NURBS head to polygons and use the smooth proxy modeling technique to model the details. We'll be able to work with a low-resolution polygonal cage while viewing the smooth object in the layer underneath.

Making the Conversion: NURBS to Polygons

Remember back in Chapter 5 how we covered the workflow concept and built a custom Shelf and Shelf buttons for converting multiple NURBS surfaces into polygonal meshes and then cleaning them up? This time we will use the Convert NURBS to Polygons command, but we'll add some different options.

1. Select the head model and choose Modify | Convert | NURBS to Polygons ❐. As discussed in Chapter 5, several options can be used to convert NURBS to polygons. This time, we want to convert to a polygonal model that is as simple as possible for use as a control cage. For this exercise, in the Options window set the Tessellation Method to Control Points. This option will convert the CVs of the NURBS model into polygonal vertices and build faces between them. If you smooth the resulting polygonal surface, it yields a shape similar to the original NURBS surface.

2. Check the Control Points option and click the Tessellate button. The converted polygon surface will appear on top of the NURBS surface. Hide the original NURBS head by selecting it in the Outliner (choose Window | Outliner) and pressing CTRL-H (CONTROL-H).

NOTE *The polygon surface might be slightly bigger and very rough compared to the reference picture, but don't worry about it. When you smooth this surface, it will fit exactly into the references loaded onto the image planes. However, if you smooth the surface every time you make an edit to the original shape, this could become a frustrating back-and-forth process. Instead, we'll use the Smooth Proxy command later to solve this problem.*

3. We want to work only with the right side of the head, so we should create a mirrored object that will update with the changes you make on the right side. To do this, first delete the faces belonging to the left side of the face, by selecting those faces and pressing the BACKSPACE (DELETE) key. (This is why you should have kept the vertical central points of the head on the YZ plane. If you did accidentally move one of these vertices along the X axis, you can correct the problem by switching to the Front view and using grid snap to snap the points to the Y axis.)

4. In object mode, select the polygonal head, and then choose Polygons | Smooth Proxy. This applies a transparent material to the rough polygon object and creates a smoothed polygon object inside the low poly surface. Because the shape nodes of these two polygonal objects are connected, if you edit the shape of the rough mode, the edits will also be applied to the smooth object. Smooth Proxy will also create two new layers, adding each object to the appropriate layer. The proxy mesh layer contains the low poly object that can be selected and its components edited. The smooth mesh layer contains the smoothed polygonal object; note that you cannot select this object because the layer is being referenced.

5. To create the other side of the head, we will create an instanced copy by duplicating and scaling the original half by –1 in the X axis (an *instanced copy* will update to maintain the shape of the original). Open the Outliner (choose Window | Outliner) and unfold the hierarchy underneath nurbsToPoly1SmoothProxyGroup by clicking the box with the + sign.

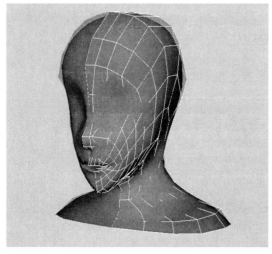

FIGURE 6-9 *The model after being converted to a smooth proxy and one half instanced*

6. Next select both nurbsToPoly1 and nurbsToPoly2 and choose Edit | Duplicate ☐. Change Geometry Types to Instance and click the Duplicate button.

7. After the instance is created, type **–1** in the Scale X field in the Channel Box. A mirror copy is produced.

8. Select each object in the Outliner (they should be named nurbsToPoly3 and nurbsToPoly4) and add nurbsToPoly3 to the proxy mesh layer and nurbsToPoly4 to the smooth mesh layer. Figure 6-9 shows the model after it has been converted to a smooth proxy; one half is deleted and it is replaced by an instance of the other side.

TIP An alternative way to use a smooth proxy technique is a plug-in called Connect Poly Shape (CPS), programmed by Dirk Bialluch. This plug-in makes smooth proxy modeling much more enjoyable by supplying myriads of custom windows and buttons. You can download this tool and instructions on how to use it in an HTML file from http://www.lightstorm3d.com/tools/freetools/html/ free_tools.html.

9. The parts of the head best suited for polygonal modeling are the areas around the eyes and nose. Let's start with the eyes. Create a NURBS sphere and change the scale to 0.8 for all axes. Using the reference images, move the sphere where the eyeball should be. Then start moving the vertices of the head model around the eye to close it. Create a layer for the eyeball and reference it, so you won't select it.

10. Use the Extrude Face tool (choose Edit Polygons | Extrude Face) to extrude the faces that define the eyeball area. Do this twice. Move the faces and vertices around the eye to achieve the shape you want. Figure 6-10 shows the process of selecting the faces and extruding them to fit around the eyeball.

11. After the faces have been moved into position, they can be split using the Split Polygon tool and then further edited to round the eyelids. When you use the Split Polygon tool, make sure that you create the edge all the way around the head so that all the faces remain as quad faces. The eye should look similar to the last stage (at right) shown in Figure 6-10.

TIP You may want to turn on x-ray shading mode for the Perspective view so you can better see the proxy object's component. In the view window's menu bar, choose Shading | Shade Options | X-Ray. You may also wish to display another instance of the Perspective view and leave that set to normal shading so you can compare it to the x-rayed view to see the changes and progress clearly.

FIGURE 6-10 *The process of building the eye*

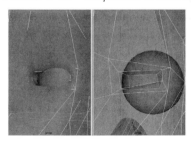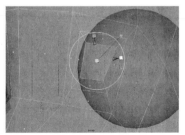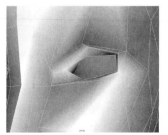

12. Make a nostril for the nose by first splitting the faces around the nose to give more details for modeling. Use the process of extruding, scaling, and moving faces to develop this area and move it up inside the nose. Shape the nostril by selecting and moving the vertices. Make the bottom of the nostril closer to the center of the face and the top of the nostril extend in the opposite direction.

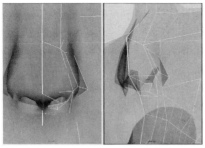

We could continue splitting and extruding faces to refine and detail this model further, but we will stop here for the sake of this tutorial. Next, we'll delete the instanced copies on the left side of the head and then mirror the original smooth proxy object so that we end up with one complete polygonal head whose vertices have been merged.

13. Using the Outliner, select the instanced proxy and the smooth objects on the left side of the head and delete them. In addition, you'll delete the original proxy object—but before you do this, make the smooth mesh match the proxy geometry's roughness. In the Outliner, select the right side smooth mesh and click the polySmoothFace1 Inputs node in the Channel Box. Change Divisions to **0**. This should make the smooth mesh match the shape of the proxy object.

14. Now select the proxy object and delete it. The smooth object's history gets deleted by deleting the proxy object.

15. Mirror the geometry by choosing Polygons | Mirror Geometry ❑. Select –X for the Mirror direction and check the Merge With The Original option. Merge Vertices should also be checked.

16. Click the Mirror button, and a mirrored copy will be generated. As long as the vertices along the center seam were on the center axis, they will be merged together. You can check to see if they are merged by choosing Display | Custom Polygon Display ❑; for the Highlight option, check Border Edges and then click the Apply button. The thick lines show unmerged edges.

NOTE   *It is always wise to keep a copy of the roughest polygonal shape, because it can be smoothed at any time. Conversely, it is not so easy to obtain a rougher polygonal model from one that has been smoothed.*

17. You can clean this up by selecting any vertices along those edges, choosing Edit Polygons | Merge Vertices, and changing to a larger threshold value. Figure 6-11 shows the mirrored and merged polygonal surface.

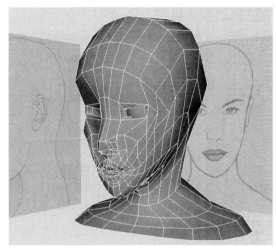

FIGURE 6-11   The head after it has been mirrored

Converting Polygons to Subdivision Surfaces

Finally, we've finished modeling most of the parts and merging both sides. We are now ready to enter into the final phase of this process. The workflow used so far has ensured that all of the polygonal faces are clean and are quads. The mesh can now be converted to subdivision surfaces to produce an infinitely smooth mesh to which we can add smaller levels of detail.

1. Select the polygon surface and choose Modify | Convert | Polygons To Subdiv ❏. The following options for conversion are available in the Options window:

- **Maximum Base Mesh Faces**   Sets the maximum number of faces the polygon surface can have for conversion. If the surface being converted has more faces than the amount specified here, the conversion will not work.

- **Maximum Edges Per Vertex**   Sets the number of edges a single vertex can have for conversion. If the surface being converted has more vertices than the amount specified here, the conversion will not work.

- **Standard**   Creates a standard mode subdivision surface. This will erase all the history of the polygon surface. By checking the Keep Original box, you can keep the original polygon surface. Otherwise, a subdivision surface will replace the polygon object. The proxy object will create a polygonal proxy subdivision surface. It's similar to using Polygon Proxy—the only difference is that the smoothed result is not made up of faces; instead, it's a real subdivision surface with infinite smoothness.

2. Set the Maximum Base Mesh Faces option to **1000**, the Maximum Edges Per Vertex option to **15**, the Subdivision Surface mode to Standard, and leave the Keep Original option unchecked.

3. Click the Convert button and see what happens. It is possible that the conversion may fail at this point. If so, you need to clean up the surface before converting it to a subdivision surface.

4. Select the head and choose Polygons | Cleanup ☐. In the Other section of the Options window, check the box next to Nonmanifold Geometry. In the Remove Geometry section, check the boxes next to Edges With Zero Length and Faces With Zero Geometry Area.

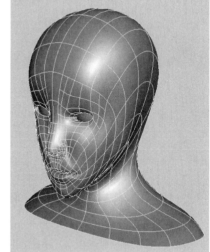

5. Click the Cleanup button. If the surface is shown in face selection component mode, you know the surface has been cleaned up. Try to convert the polygons to subdivision surfaces again. The result should look like the following illustration.

Now you have created a subdivision surface in standard mode. You can press the 1, 2, and 3 keys on the keyboard to change the display resolution. RMB-click and hold on the surface and choose Vertex from the marking menu. You'll notice that the vertex doesn't display only a point, but it shows number 0. This means you are looking at level 0 of the surface hierarchy. You can go to a higher level by RMB-clicking and holding again and choosing Finer from the marking menu. You will then see level 1 vertices. These components can be moved just like polygonal vertices.

As mentioned at the beginning of the chapter, it's best to do level 0 editing in polygon mode, because this mode lets you use many of the polygon tools, such as Extrude Face and the Split Polygon tool. The only reason we don't use polygon proxy mode as much as smooth proxy mode is because modeling subdivisions in polygon proxy mode is significantly slower than doing so in smooth proxy mode, especially if the model is complex.

However, since our head model is not very complex, let's try this:

RMB-click and hold on the surface and choose Polygon from the marking menu. A polygonal cage will appear over the subdivision surface. It looks much like smooth proxy mode. You can use this mode to add some more detail.

If you will be using this model for animation, you will most likely want to convert this back to polygons so you can set up deformers for animation (or for better texturing). Once again, Maya lets you convert from one geometry type to another. Choose Modify | Convert | Subdiv To Polygons ❑. In the Options window, you can choose what subdivision level you want to use to extract the polygons from. If you want to extract a base mesh, set the Tessellation Method to Vertices and set the Level to 0. You can replace, hide, or show the original object. As long as the polygon is clean, it's easy to go back and forth between polygon and subdivision surface.

Summary

This chapter has shown you the most efficient workflow to use for creating a subdivision surface. It also demonstrated the flexibility of using each geometry type as appropriate and then converting between them. Keep practicing, and you'll get used to using these tools. You could easily spend many more hours adding more details to our head model.

This will complete the modeling lessons in this book. In the next chapter, we will begin learning about animating in Maya.

III

Animation

Animation Basics

Animation can be defined as the process of "bringing art to life"; it is the point at which timing and motion come together to make artwork represent real life. The animation toolsets in Maya provide a wide range of control over timing and motion. But be warned, the realism part doesn't come with the installation alone—you as the artist must practice the art of animation before you'll be able to create realistic characters and objects.

Maya offers dozens of tools and features that let you create animation in many ways. Along with its basic keyframing and motion-editing abilities, Maya lets you animate using path animation, nonlinear animation, dynamics, motion capture, and procedural animation, which will be discussed in the following chapters. In addition, the nature of Maya's dependency graph allows for customization and control over large sets of animated objects.

Throughout the next six chapters, we will examine some of the features that will assist you in bringing your models to life. In Chapters 17 and 18, you will learn to use Maya's Dynamics toolset to create animation by running simulations of natural phenomenon. But let's start with the basics in this chapter. We will focus on learning keyframe animation and using the fundamental animation tools in Maya.

A Brief History of Animation

Animation has been around since the dawn of humankind—consider the ancient caves of southwestern Europe, which are decorated with paintings that contain not only detailed illustrations of animals from the region but also suggest how they moved. One could argue that even though these paintings are still, the artist has brought the creatures contained in them to life; hence, they have been animated, in a way.

However, suggesting motion is not enough. Over time, people have continued to utilize any technology available to make their still pictures move. Flipbook animations were produced by drawing frames along the edge or corner of a stack of paper or a book. As you flipped through the pages in the stack, your drawings would advance from one *frame* to the next. Another early animation technology was the turntable. A series of drawings, or frames, were placed along the inside walls of a cylindrical object that sat on a turntable. The cylinder had little slits between each frame. When a person looked into the cylinder through the slits from the outside while the turntable was spinning, she'd see the drawings advance from one frame to the next.

For both of these methods, animation time was limited and the characters had to be pretty small. In addition, few means were available to deliver such animations to an audience. In today's age of downloadable movies, it is easy for us to forget about all of the fantastic animations that must have been created by amateur artists all over the world. These small glimpses of animation rarely emerged outside someone's home or outside a carnival. For this reason, many of the great early animations have been lost.

What really enabled the assemblage and delivery of animation was the advancements made to the motion picture camera and film stocks in the late 1800s. By the early 1900s, stop-motion animation was accomplished by positioning objects on a set and capturing their positions, one frame at a time. As the film frames advanced, so did the objects. These same basic techniques are still being used today.

The ability to capture a sequence of drawings onto film and play them back through a projector was what eventually brought animation to the masses. However, for animation to be created efficiently for production—that is, for it to become a profitable industry—some procedures needed to be put into place. Disney was responsible for many of these developments in the industry.

The cycle, *repeat animation*, and *cross-over* techniques were developed by Disney to minimize the amount of manual labor it took to produce animation, by cutting down on the amount of drawings needed for the show. Many of these techniques have carried over into the digital realm and are used in Maya. One of the most basic techniques from the old days is the idea of keyframes and in-between frames. These form the basis for animating in Maya.

> NOTE *If you're interested in learning more about animation processes of the early days (or animation in general), be sure to read* **The Illusion of Life: Disney Animation (Hyperion Press, 1995) by Frank Thomas and Ollie Johnson. This book details many of the techniques developed by Disney that enabled the company to produce animated features within a reasonable budget. Later in this chapter, you'll find a list of other books that might be of interest.**

Keyframe Animation in Maya

In the old days of pencil-drawn animation, large-scale animation production would use a technique known as *keyframing*. Using this technique, a lead animator would draw a character at all of the key poses at different points in time throughout the animation. The key poses usually contained the more extreme positions and gestures for a character or poses that would be held and therefore visible for longer periods of time. An assistant animator would then be responsible for creating the drawings that filled in all of the poses that lie between those key poses. Let's take a moment to look at these processes and how they relate to and are executed in Maya.

Keyframe and Frame

Animation techniques in Maya are not so different from those developed by Disney some 80 years ago. Once an animator knows what he is going to animate, he will usually go though and *block* out the animation by posing the character at key points in time. (Remember the preproduction process discussed in Chapter 1? *Know* what you have to do *before* you try to do it.) For each of the poses, the animator sets a key for the position of all the different body parts that make up the entire pose at that frame. The values for the attributes being animated are stored at that frame. (Realize that any attribute can be animated in Maya, not just translation, rotation. and scale.) This stored data is called a *keyframe*. In order for any of the animated objects to "move," at least two keyframes are needed, each set at different points in time.

Along with the position of objects in an animation, time is an important variable. When dealing with animation, film, or video, the time variable is broken down into *frames*. How long is a frame, then? That depends on the *frame rate*. The frame rate is measured in frames per second (fps). Different technologies use different frame rates. In general, if you are making animation for NTSC (National Television System Committee standard) video, the rate is 30 fps—so three seconds of animation will need 90 frames. (You can also see it like this: one frame is 1/30th of a second.) For film, the rate is 1/24th of a second, or 24 fps.

Figure 7-1 shows a single ball animated over specified frames. An animation snapshot is created to show the motion.

> **NOTE**   *The terms keyframe and key are used interchangeably. In this book, the process of animating with keyframes will be called* **keyframing***. The terms* **keying** *or* **editing keys** *refer to setting and editing keyframes.*

In-Between and Interpolation

In 2D animation, humans must painstakingly create pictures to fit between keyframes to suggest motion. These frames are called *in-between* frames, and the process of creating them is called *tweening*. The in-between frames of a bouncing ball are shown in Figure 7-2.

FIGURE 7-1   *Examples of keyframes and frames*

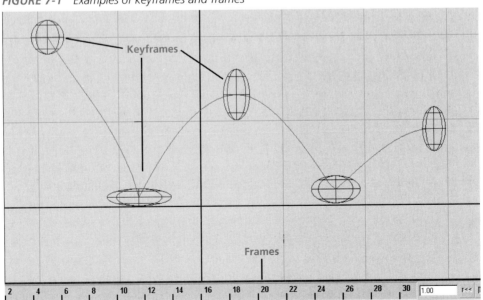

FIGURE 7-2 *In-between frames and keyframes of a bouncing ball animation*

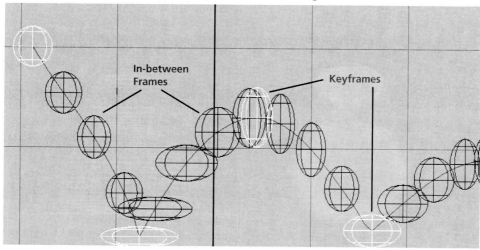

One of the many great advantages that 3D brings to animation production is that the software is able to calculate the positions for in-between frames for you. Since the objects have already been modeled with 3D geometry, the objects in the scene will accurately represent the object at any angle (something that 2D animation in applications such as Adobe After Effects or Macromedia Flash are not capable of doing). The calculation of these in-between frames is called *interpolation*.

The animator can control how the data is interpolated by editing the *animation curves*. An animation curve plots the change in value over a period of frames between two or more keyframes. You can change the interpolation by changing how the tangents behave as they enter and exit a keyframe. This means the curve is completely smooth as it enters and exits a keyframe. These tangents can also be broken and their direction edited independently of one another. The ball shown in Figure 7-2, for example, was animated by breaking the tangents of the keyframes where the ball hits the ground. The tangents were then edited so that they point upward in and out of the existing keyframe. The result is that the ball appears to bounce. In the bouncing ball tutorial later in this chapter, you will go through the steps of editing the curves to create the bouncing ball.

Definition   **tangent**   *A line or vector that indicates the slope of a curve at a given point.*

In the end, Maya is essentially creating a database, wherein a certain value has been assigned to a certain frame for a certain attribute that is being animated. Every time Maya advances to the next frame, it uses the animation curve to determine the value of the attribute at that frame. This occurs for every attribute that has a keyframe assigned at every frame.

How to Set Keys

Maya is all about control and flexibility; it offers a variety of ways to key attributes, but you'll usually key attributes through menu commands and windows in three ways, as shown in Table 7-1.

These methods will create a key at the current frame as set in the Time Slider. The illustration here shows the Channel Box displaying a NURBS sphere's transform node. When a key has been set on a channel, the value fields for that channel will be highlighted in orange.

Channels Object	
nurbsSphere1	▲
Translate X	-9.384
Translate Y	10.049
Translate Z	0
Rotate X	0
Rotate Y	0
Rotate Z	0
Scale X	1
Scale Y	1
Scale Z	1
Visibility	on

You can also key transformation quickly by pressing a hot key, as shown in Table 7-2. For example, if you want to key only movement of an object in the X, Y, and Z axes, you can press SHIFT-W.

> *NOTE   It's important that you are aware of what attributes you've keyed and limit keying only to necessary attributes to avoid confusion and save time. Maya will evaluate any attribute that has been keyed at every frame. This means that if you have an attribute that has keys set on it but the value is not changing, Maya is evaluating this attribute for no reason. This could slow down your computer's performance.*

The process of setting keys usually goes like this:

1. Set the current frame either by moving the Time Slider to the desired frame number or by typing the frame number into the Current Frame field.

2. Set the values for the animated attributes. If you are moving a piece of geometry into position, you will use the transform tools to edit the transform attributes.

3. After everything is in place, set keys on the desired attributes.

TABLE 7-1   Keying Methods

KEYING METHOD	FUNCTION
Select the object and choose Animate | Set Key.	Keyframes all the attributes in the Channel Box for the selected object.
Select the object, LMB-click attributes you want to key, RMB-click-and-hold, and choose Key Selected.	Keys only the desired attribute. You can also select and key multiple attributes.
Select the object; open the Attribute Editor by pressing CTRL-A (CONTROL-A); RMB-click-and-hold the attribute you want to key, and choose Set Key.	Keys only the specific attribute. The Attribute Editor has more attributes available to key than the Channel Box.

TABLE 7-2   *Transformation Hot Keys*

HOT KEYS	FUNCTIONS
S	Key all the attributes in Channel Box
SHIFT-W	Key Translation (move)
SHIFT-E	Key Rotation
SHIFT-R	Key Scale

It is important that you set the current frame *before* the object is moved (or before any attributes are changed). For example, if you had keyed a sphere's Translate X attribute at 0 and wanted to animate it to 5, but you set it to 5 without moving the Time Slider, the sphere would jump back to 0 as soon as you touched the Time Slider, because it is reverting to the position of its last key.

> NOTE   *If you do set the attributes before setting the Time Slider, you can advance the Time Slider without changing the attribute values for all objects by MMB-dragging the Time Slider.*

Viewing and Editing Keyframes

Once keys have been set on various attributes, you can view and edit them in a number of ways. As soon as you keyframe, three things will happen immediately to let you see that an object has been animated. First, when an object is selected, red lines, or tick marks, appear in the Time Slider. These indicate that keys are set at those frames. When attributes are viewed in the Channel Box, the fields containing the values will be highlighted in orange to signify that these channels have been keyed. In the Hypergraph, a keyed node will appear skewed instead of as a rectangular shape.

Once you begin to refine your animation, the keys set initially with the Set Key command are rarely used as is. You'll usually choose to edit the values for the attributes or change the frame at which the keys are set. Actually, you'll probably be doing a little of both. Maya offers four main interfaces to use for editing keyframes: the Time Slider, the Graph Editor, the Dope Sheet, and the Channel Box. Let's take a look at them one by one.

Time Slider

We have already talked about viewing keys in the Time Slider, but what about editing them? The Time Slider offers some basic, yet fast, ways of editing the position of keys over time. After setting the Time Slider to a frame that contains a key, RMB-click to view a marking menu that lets you Cut, Copy, Paste, and Delete keys as well as make other adjustments to the Time Slider.

If, for example, you want to copy a key on frame 1, you set the Time Slider to frame 1, RMB-click, and choose Copy from the marking menu. Then move the Time Slider to the frame where you want to paste it, RMB-click, and choose Paste | Paste.

If the animation is lengthy, editing keys in the Time Slider can be difficult, because the Time Slider may have to squish together all the frames to fit them in the display. You can use the Range Slider to limit how much of the Time Slider's range is displayed. Set the total frame range for your animation in the Playback Start Time and Playback End Time fields at the far left and right ends of the Range Slider (see Figure 7-3). You can slide the Range Slider by LMB-dragging to move through all the ranges. Figure 7-3 shows the Time Slider and Range Slider. The Range Slider has been set up so that the Time Slider displays only frames 1 through 60 in an animation that is 120 frames long.

You can also move and scale (shrink and enlarge) a group of keyframes using the Time Slider. This effectively shortens or lengthens animation. To do this, SHIFT-LMB-drag over the keys. A solid red color appears around your selection. The center arrows in the highlighted area will move the selected keys forward or backward in frames. Arrows at the opposite ends will scale the range of the key. If you scale the selected range down, actions inside the red area will occur in a smaller timeframe, creating a faster animation. If you scale the selected range up, the opposite will happen—animation will slow down. This is the easiest way to change timing of an entire animation. Figure 7-4 shows how timing is changed in the Time Slider.

Graph Editor

Using the Graph Editor is probably the most powerful way to edit keys. The art of animation involves many subtleties. Animators know that to add those subtleties can be a tedious process, and Maya's Graph Editor is intended to make that task easier. Not only does it let you edit the time and value for a key, but it also lets you edit the interpolation between the keys. By being able to edit the curve as it enters and exits a keyframe, the animator has more control over each keyframe, leading to more control over the entire animation and the realism of the shot.

You can display the Graph Editor by choosing Window | Animation Editors | Graph Editor. (You can also open it in as a panel in a view window.) As shown in Figure 7-5, the Graph Editor lists all selected objects and their keyable attributes in the Outliner section on the left side. The

FIGURE 7-3   *Time Slider and Range Slider*

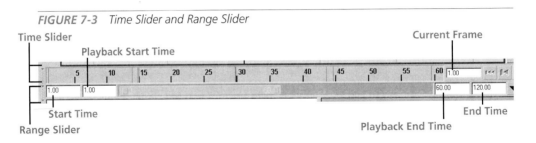

FIGURE 7-4   You can change timing quickly with the Time Slider.

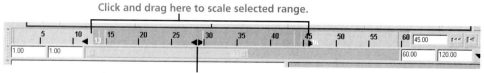

graph section on the right displays the *animation curves* for each selected attribute. Animation curves graphically represent changes in time (represented on the horizontal axis) and data values (represented on the vertical axis). They contain keys, represented by points, with tangents that control how the curve segments enter and exit a key.

 Many commands and tools available in the menus and Shelf of the Graph Editor let you control the interpolation of the curves by changing the behavior of their tangents. Keys can be inserted anywhere along the curve by using the Insert Key tool found in the Graph Editor's toolbar along the top. We will cover this editor in more depth in this chapter's tutorial.

FIGURE 7-5   The Graph Editor shows animation data as a series of curves.

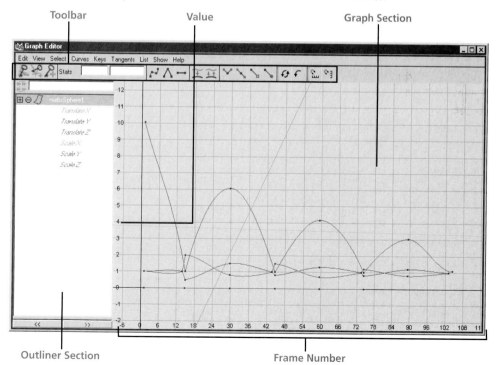

TIP   *Opening the Graph Editor in a panel is less cluttering than opening it in a separate window. You can also use Persp/Graph premade panel setup by clicking one of the saved Layout buttons below the tool box.*

Dope Sheet

The Dope Sheet can be accessed by choosing Window | Animation Editors | Dope Sheet. Instead of using a curve, the Dope Sheet represents keys as tick marks in frames. It resembles a database, similar to what you'd find in an Excel spreadsheet. Figure 7-6 shows a Dope Sheet.

This editor is most useful for making broad changes to animation to adjust basic timing. It won't let you view or edit the interpolation between the keys, but it does allow you to select and edit the position of keys for specific attributes. This is similar but more powerful than highlighting and moving keys in the Time Slider, because the Time Slider will not let you select specific attributes whose keys you need to edit.

With the Dope Sheet, you can edit all of the frames for multiple objects in a scene or selection or you can edit keys of specific attributes. You can even edit the placement of the keys for all Translate X attributes in the scene.

FIGURE 7-6   *The Dope Sheet provides a quick way to edit the timing.*

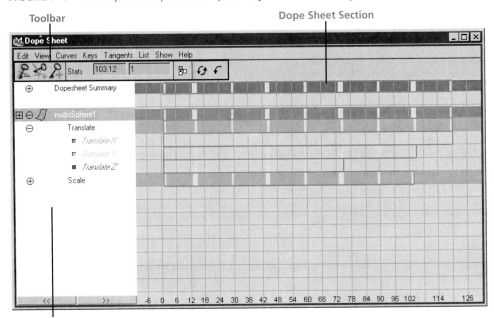

When you open the Dope Sheet, you see a list of selected objects on the left in the Outliner section. On the right side of the window is the dope sheet section that shows a green strip with black tick marks. These tick marks are the keys. If multiple attributes of an object were keyed at the same frame, clicking one of these ticks to select it and MMB-dragging with the Move tool will enable you to move all of the keys on that frame to another frame. If you unfold the object in the Outliner section, you can view individual attributes and see what frames have keys on them. From here, you can edit the attributes individually.

At the top of the Outliner is an item called Dopesheet Summary. Clicking this shows you where the keys are placed for all of the selected objects. The Summary is an easy way to edit the keys on all selected objects at the same time.

Channel Box and Attribute Editor

Keys can be set, cut, copied, and pasted in the Channel Box and Attribute Editor by RMB-clicking an attribute and choosing a command from the marking menu. You can delete all animation on any channel by first selecting an attribute in the Channel Box so that it is highlighted (the actual attribute, not the value), RMB-clicking, and choosing Delete Selected from the marking menu. You could also choose Break Connections from the marking menu, which will break the connection to the animation curve.

Playback Controls

To play the animation, use the playback controls at the bottom right of the Maya workspace. These controls should look familiar to you. Figure 7-7 shows the playback controls.

- **Go To Start Of Playback Range, Go To End Of Playback Range**   Moves the slider, respectively, to the beginning and end of the range of frames shown in the Time Slider.

- **Go To Last Frame, Go To Next Frame**   Moves the slider backward or forward, respectively, one frame every time you click.

- **Go To Last Key, Go To Next Key**   Moves the slider, respectively, to the last or next keyframe; this is a great way to hop around keyframes.

- **Play Backward, Play Forward**   Plays the animation backward and forward.

- **Auto Key**   Click this button, and it will turn red. As long as an object has a previous keyframe, you can simply move to a new frame and change an attribute's values and the channels will automatically be keyframed. This button is a quick way to keyframe many objects.

- **Animation Preferences**   Opens an Animation Preferences window to let you change settings, such as a time range in the Time Slider, height of the Time Slider, and speed of playback.

FIGURE 7-7   *The playback control buttons look similar to VCR controls.*

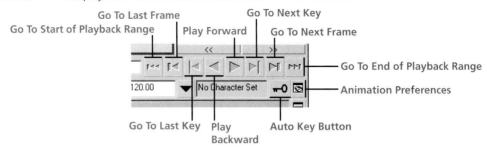

TIP   *In the Animation Preferences window, Maya's default Playback Speed is set to Play Every Frame. This will play every frame of the animation as fast as the computer is able to play it back. If the scene has many objects or is deforming complex geometry, the scene might play back slowly. If it is a simple animation, such as a bouncing ball, it will play back quickly. When you set the Playback Speed to Real Time, the animation will play back at a constant speed and drop frames to maintain real time if the animation is too complex.*

You can use the hot keys shown in Table 7-3 to move through the animation without touching a mouse. These are great for quickly reviewing an animation.

Let's work on a simple tutorial to learn how to keyframe and edit keys in Maya.

TABLE 7-3   *Playback Control Hot Keys*

HOT KEYS	FUNCTIONS
ALT-V (OPTION-V)	Play and stop animation
. (period)	Move slider to next keyframe
, (comma)	Move slider to previous keyframe
ALT-. (OPTION-.)	Move slider to next frame
ALT-, (OPTION-,)	Move slider to previous frame
K-LMB-drag, K-MMB-drag	Move slider left and right

Tutorial: Bouncing Ball

This tutorial will teach you how to keyframe and tweak animation by creating a simple animation of a bouncing ball. First, we will set up the scene for animation, and then we'll create objects, key the ball's animation, and edit and apply character animation techniques by adding more keyframes.

Set Up the Animation

Before we start animating, let's set up some preferences. First, we need to decide what the final output of this animation will be. If it's NTSC video, we need to set the frame rate to 30 fps.

If it's film, we'll use 24 fps. Although you can set the animation to a different frame rate later on, it's much easier to set it at the proper frame rate from the beginning.

> NOTE *If you set your animation to 24 fps and output to video, your animation will increase in speed. Therefore, it's important that you figure out your final output before you start.*

1. To change the frame rate, choose Window | Settings/Preferences | Preferences to open the Preferences window.

2. From the Categories list on the left side, select Settings, and change Time to NTSC (30 fps), as shown in Figure 7-8. Now Maya is set to use 30 fps.

3. Next, we change playback speed to be in real time. From the Categories list, select Timeline. The main Preferences window will update with new information. Under the Playback Speed box, choose Real-time [30 fps]. This way, when you click the Play button, the animation will play in real time.

FIGURE 7-8   *Setting preferences*

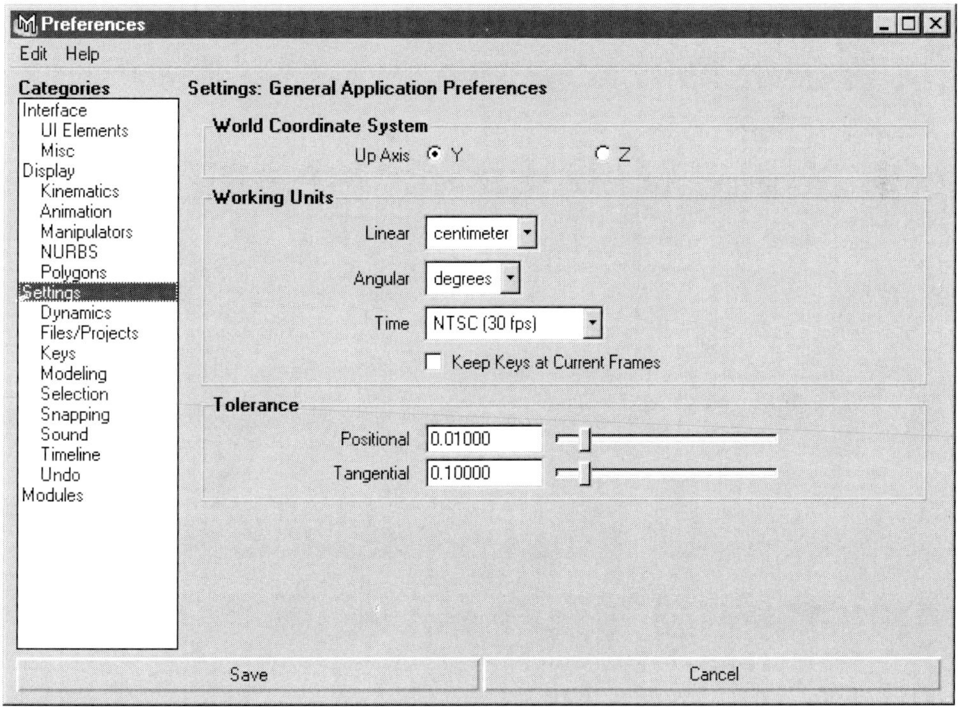

4. Now we set the range of frames for our animation. In the Range Slider, type **1** in the Playback Start Time field and type **120** in the Playback End Time field (see Figure 7-3). This indicates that you'll use frames 1–120 for your animation and limits the display in the Time Slider to those frames.

5. Choose Create | NURBS Primitives | Sphere, and then choose Create | NURBS Primitives | Plane. Now a NURBS sphere and a flat NURBS plane should appear in your scene.

6. Select the NURBS plane surface and scale it in all directions. In the Channel Box, set the Scale X, Scale Y, and Scale Z values to at least 80, so that you leave enough space for the ball to bounce around. The objects should resemble those shown in this illustration.

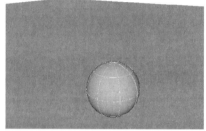

7. Before you start moving and keyframing the sphere, let's move the pivot of the sphere to its base. This will help squash and stretch the sphere's shape toward the bottom of the sphere. Select the sphere, select the Move tool, and press the INSERT (HOME) key on your keyboard. Move the green line down in Front or Side view, so the center of the pivot—the blue square—rests at the bottom of the sphere. Press the INSERT (HOME) key to close the pivot editing mode.

Setting Keys

Now we will begin positioning the ball and setting keys at different frames in time.

1. In the Front view, start animating the translation value of the sphere. Make sure you are working in frame 1—if you're not, move the Time Slider to frame 1. Start by moving the sphere about –10 units in the X axis and about 10 units in the Y axis. Press SHIFT-W to keyframe the translation only.

2. Move the Time Slider to frame 15.

3. Move the sphere so the bottom of it is at the NURBS plane just around the global axis (0,0,0). (See Figure 7-9.)

4. Press SHIFT-W to key translation again. Move the Time Slider back and forth between frame 1 and frame 15, and you will see the animation.

   This is how you keyframe animation in Maya. You move the Time Slider to the frame you want to keyframe, adjust values on attributes so it has the desirable values, and then set a key. If you move or scale the object before you change to a different time, the change you made will be discounted as soon as you change a frame. *You should always set the frame first.* Figure 7-9 shows the positions for the initial keyframing of the sphere.

FIGURE 7-9   *Initial keyframing positions*

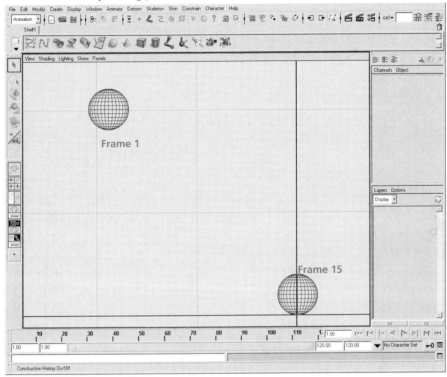

5. Continue keyframing. Move the Time Slider to frame 30 and move the sphere up and to the right side of the view. Since the ball's momentum should diminish a little with each bounce, the bounce lengths should get shorter in the X and Y directions as it progresses through the animation.

6. Move the sphere to around unit 6 in both the X and Y axes.

7. Move the Time Slider to frame 45, and then move the sphere so the bottom of it is at the NURBS plane.

FIGURE 7-10   *More keyframes are added every 15 frames*

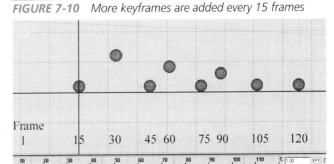

8. Keep keyframing every 15 frames, as shown in Figure 7-10, until you reach frame 120, where the sphere rolls to a stop. Figure 7-10 shows the positions of the ball at each frame to which it has been keyed.

Editing the Keys

Now change to the Perspective view. Click the Play button in the playback controls. You'll notice that the animation hardly resembles a bouncing ball. Instead, it looks odd—as though the sphere is swimming through space instead of striking the ground and bouncing. In fact, the ball appears to slide along the plane before moving up.

The reason for its dragging appearance is that we are using *spline* tangents, the default interpolation method. This type of interpolation creates spline curves between the keys, with unified, straight tangents. The tangent of the curve entering the key is the same as the tangent exiting the key. While spline curves are good for fluid motion, they're really not suited for showing the snappy movement of a ball quickly changing direction as it hits the ground.

Definition   **spline tangent**   *Creates spline curves between the keys, with unified, straight tangents. The tangent of the curve entering the key is the same as the tangent exiting the key.*
linear tangent   *Creates straight lines between keys.*
clamped tangent   *Makes most of the animation smooth, like spline interpolation, but if two adjacent keys hold similar values, clamped tangents make the interpolation linear.*

Two other tangents can be used for animation: *Linear* tangents create straight lines between keys, so that movement from one direction to another is abrupt and not smooth. *Clamped* tangents are useful for character animation. They make most of the animation smooth, like spline interpolation, but if two adjacent keys hold similar values, clamped tangents make the interpolation linear. This is a great way to hold movement during those frames. (Chapter 12 examines clamped tangents in detail.)

You can see how this animation was interpolated by checking the object's animation curve in the Graph Editor.

Select the sphere and open the Graph Editor by choosing Window | Animation Editors | Graph Editor. Figure 7-11 shows the Graph Editor displaying the animation curves for the sphere's translation attributes. These curves are color-coded to match the transform manipulator in the view windows: the X axis translation is in red, the Y axis translation is in green, and the Z axis translation is in blue.

The red animation curve that controls the translation in X is gradually increasing value from frames 1 to 120 because we moved the sphere in the positive X direction every time we keyed it. The green Y axis line appears like a wave, since we moved the sphere up and down every 15 frames. Because you can't translate an object in the Z axis in the Front view, the animation curve for the Translate Z attribute remains flat.

> _TIP_   **In general, it's a good idea to start keying a few attributes at a time and then begin layering more attributes in as you make another pass.**

FIGURE 7-11   *The Graph Editor displaying the curves for our ball*

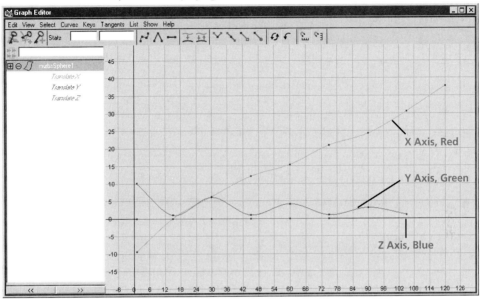

Now let's edit the animation of the sphere, starting with the Translate Y attribute.

1. In the Graph Editor, select Translate Y in the Outliner section and press the F key to fit the curve in the graph section of this window.

2. In the graph section, drag-select all of the points on the curve that have values of 1. These should be the points along the bottom of the arcing curve. These points correspond to the keys you set where the ball hits the ground.

3. Notice that keys are now displayed as yellow points with tangent bars. You need to break each tangent bar in half, so you can create a much sharper curve when the ball changes direction. In the Graph Editor, choose Keys | Break Tangent. This will break the tangent bar.

4. Select the Move tool (press the W key) and LMB-drag-select the tangent on the left side of the first key. The tangent should now be highlighted in blue.

5. Now MMB-drag the tangent upward. Notice that the tangent is no longer a straight line though the point; instead, it is broken. Try the same thing with the tangent on the right side of the first key.

6. Continue editing the other keys by selecting the tangents and pointing them upward. Use Figure 7-12 as a guide. Try previewing the animation in Perspective view. The motion of the ball should now look like it is bouncing after it hits the ground.

FIGURE 7-12 *Tangents on the animation curves are broken.*

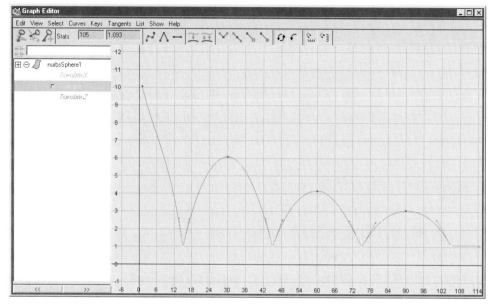

7. Now let's fix the animation on the Translate X channel. Click Translate X in the Outliner section of the Graph Editor.

8. Press the F key to fit the curve to the graph.

9. Delete all the keys except the first and last keys—LMB-drag-select a marquee box around those keys and press DELETE. This will create a straight line.

10. Click the Play button and watch the movement. You should notice that the movement is smoother, but it stops harshly at frame 120. Select the last key and then select its tangent.

11. In the Graph Editor, choose Tangents | Flat; the rate of change in the Translate X value around the time the curve enters this key is now very small. The effect is that the ball gradually slows down until it finally stops.

12. Now adjust the first key so that the tangent exiting the key points the curve so that it is straight or as constant as possible. The finished curve should look like Figure 7-13.

NOTE *If you are still not exactly clear on how this curve is affecting the animation, you should play around with this setup for a little while, moving the keys and tangents and seeing what effect the edits have on the motion.*

FIGURE 7-13   *The finished curve*

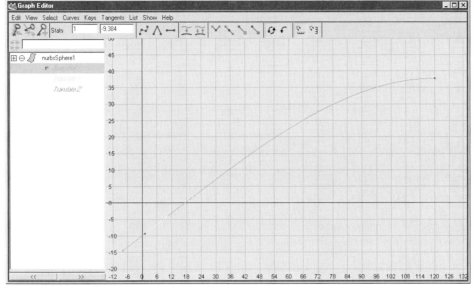

Adding Character

Now the ball has motion, but we still need to give it some character—some life! To do this, we will apply a fundamental principal of animation to the ball, which is known as "squash and stretch." Squash and stretch refers to object's natural flexibility that allows it to absorb inertia by squashing and stretching as it collides with other objects and moves through space. We can add squash and stretch to the ball simply by scaling the sphere. By including this technique, we can add some real character to the ball.

1. Select the sphere, and move the Time Slider to frame 1. Press SHIFT-R to keyframe the scale of the sphere.

2. Move the slider to frame 14 and press SHIFT-R to keyframe. Continue by placing another key at the frame just before the ball hits the ground, so that the ball maintains its spherical shape until it actually contacts the ground. Otherwise, it would gradually scale down as it approached the ground.

3. Click the Auto Key button in the playback controls.

4. Move the slider to frame 15, and scale the sphere up in the X and Z axes and scale it down in the Y axis. Better yet, in the Channel Box, type in numbers for the scale attributes. This will give you more precise control. Type in values of **2** for the X and Z axes and **0.5** for the Y axis. The sphere now appears "well squashed" when it hits the ground. If you scrub the slider, you will notice that the change in attributes is automatically recorded because we have selected the Auto Key.

5. Move the Time Slider to frame 30, and stretch the sphere. The scale values should be 0.8, 1.5, and 0.8 for Scale X, Scale Y, and Scale Z, respectively.

6. Key these values at frames 44, 45, 60, 74, 75, 90, 104, 105, and 110. You can gradually decrease the values to animate the loss in inertia as the ball comes to a stop. Squash and stretch should diminish as the ball moves forward. Figure 7-14 shows the result of the squash and stretch process.

FIGURE 7-14 *Squash and stretch will make the sphere appear to change shape as it bounces.*

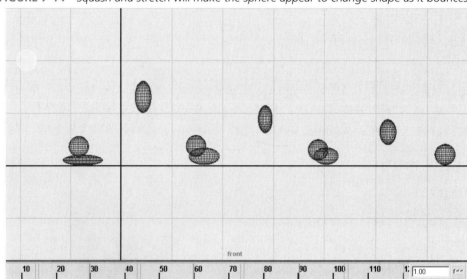

7. If you want to change the timing of the ball, the Dope Sheet is the best and quickest way to go. In the Dope Sheet, you can quickly change timing by grabbing keys and scaling them as groups. Open the Dope Sheet, shown in Figure 7-15, by choosing Window | Animation Editors | Dope Sheet. Now let's make the timing of the animation faster.

8. Select the Scale tool by pressing the R key.

9. Click nurbsSphere1 from the Outliner section in the Dope Sheet.

10. Drag-select all of the black tick marks (the keyframes) next to nurbsSphere1. These marks should now light up in yellow, and a white frame will surround all the keys.

11. Grab the right edge of the white frame and LMB-drag it to the left. Move it until the edge reaches number 30 (frame 30).

12. Play the animation, and you will notice that the animation is now twice as fast. You can move the right edge of the white box to the left to slow down the animation as well.

FIGURE 7-15   *The Dope Sheet provides a quick way to edit the timing of the entire animation.*

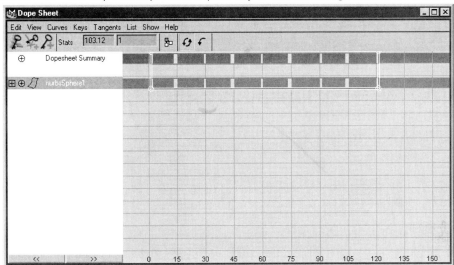

Using Playblast

Let's create a movie file directly from Maya to view our bouncing ball animation. Using Playblast is the best way to check the timing of an animation.

1. Make the Perspective view active by clicking in it.

2. Hold down the right mouse button over the Time Slider until the marking menu is displayed. Choose Playblast □.

3. In the Playblast Options window, make sure that View is checked and Show Ornaments is unchecked. This will create a movie from the selected view window, excluding stuff like a manipulator and an axis display. For the Viewer, you can select what player you would like to use to view this animation. For this example, we'll choose Windows Media Player. (Your exact options might be different depending on what platform you are using.)

4. Set Display Size to Custom and enter **320** and **240** in the boxes just below Display Size. Set Scale to **1.00**. Check the Save To File check box, and click the Playblast button.

5. A window will open asking you where you want to save the movie file. Save it to the best location—I often save it to the desktop for easy access.

6. You should see every frame of the animation played back in the view window, though not necessarily in real time. This is because Maya is rendering each frame on screen, and then capturing it and saving it. After all the frames have been captured, Media Player will show you the move file automatically. Figure 7-16 shows the Option window for Playblast and Playblast being played in Windows Media Player.

FIGURE 7-16 *Playblast is shown through Windows Media Player.*

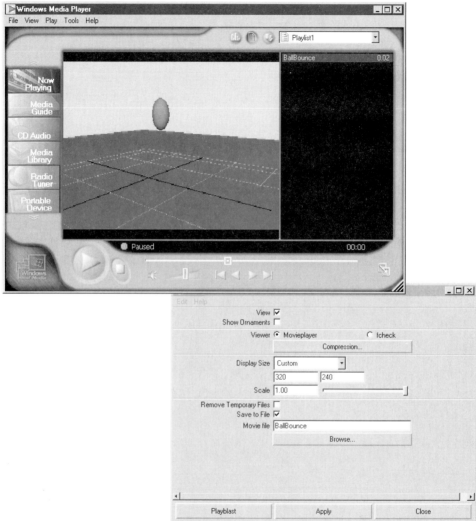

Play the animation and take a look at all the editing you've done to the sphere. This is basically the same workflow you'll use to edit any animation using the Graph Editor and Dope Sheet. No matter how complex your animation job may be, keyframing and editing animation are similar to the process discussed so far.

Basic Animation Principles

Last, but not least, when you are keyframing or editing keyframes in the Graph Editor, you should keep some of the fundamental principles of animation in mind as you work. The following information will help you create more realistic, visually stimulating animations.

Keep in mind that animation is *not* just *copying* natural movement; it's an *exaggeration* of it. In the beginning of this chapter, we talked about how traditional 2D cell animators developed well-established animation techniques to use while animating characters or natural phenomena. Let's take a look at these techniques so you can apply them to your own animations.

Squash and Stretch

Like a bouncing ball, we humans change shape as we move when we jump up and down: your knees, hip joints, and back are all bending straight while you are in the air and bending inward to absorb shock when you land on the ground. The basic theory of squash and stretch gives life to any character or object by adding the appearance of weight to them. Unless you are animating a rock, most things in this world (and some things not in this world) will have elasticity of some sort to absorb energy as it is applied to them.

> NOTE **When you add squash to stretch, be careful not to increase the object's size while at the peak of the squash and stretch. The volume of the object should be intact throughout the animation.**

Anticipation

Anticipation is act of holding energy that is about to be released. In our jumping analogy, you usually swing your arms backward and bend your knees and back inward to compress yourself before you jump. You can jump without this action, but jumping will be stiff and not very elegant. Animation is all about creating and releasing energy or interacting with an external energy source. Anticipation creates the energy in your scene. In addition, viewers can *expect* upcoming action by *feeling* anticipation.

Follow Through

Follow through is the opposite of anticipation. It's a technique used to absorb the shock of an energy by overshooting the action beyond. If we use our jumping analogy again, after a jump is over and you touch down on the ground, your body will not stay at the bending pose of squash. Your body should bend back to its natural posture. This act of continuing motion to reach the object's or character's most natural state is called follow through.

Secondary Action

Secondary action is the animation of extra parts or appendages of an object or a character used to exaggerate motion. To use the jumping analogy again, if you had large ears and a tail and you jumped, your ears and tail wouldn't move at the exact same rate that your body moved, and they wouldn't stop at the same time that your body stopped. Your ears and tail would swing their own ways, pivoting around where they are attached to your body. Adding such detail adds more complexity to your animation and creates believability and realistic qualities in your animations.

Further Reading and Practice

You might find the following 2D animation books helpful in understanding the finer points of creating realistic animations. Although these books cover 2D animation, the basic theory is the same for 3D animation.

- *The Illusion of Life: Disney Animation*, by Frank Thomas and Ollie Johnston (Hyperion Press, 1995). This book is the best animation resource around. It's fairly thick and expensive, but if you are serious about animation, it's a must-have.

- *Cartoon Animation*, by Preston Blair (Walter Foster Pub, 1995). This is another great book about 2D animation techniques. It has a lot of reference graphics, and it's fun to read.

- *The Animation Book: A Complete Guide to Animated Filmmaking—From Flip-Books to Sound Cartoons to 3-D Animation*, by Kit Laybourne (Three Rivers Press, 1998). This is a great reference book for 2D animators. It also has a lot of information applicable to 3D animation.

- *Animation from Script to Screen*, by Shamus Culhane (St. Martin's Press, 1990). Here's another good animation book from a master of animation. You can use many of the theories discussed in this book.

- *The Animator's Workbook*, by Tony White (Watson-Guptill Publications, 1988). This book offers many exercises for 2D animators.

Use daily exercises to sharpen your eye to get better at animating characters. Always be aware of how your body moves and how people and other characters move. It's a good idea to carry a sketchbook to write about and draw your discoveries, or you can videotape yourself or a friend to show a character's specific actions, and then review it carefully.

Summary

As you may have gathered from reading this chapter, the path to great animation is long and difficult, but it's also extremely rewarding to see your creation move and act like a real-life object or living being. Keyframing is an important part of animating, and like most other tasks, the more you use this feature, the better you'll get at creating realistic animations.

In the next chapter, we cover many of the deformers available in Maya to facilitate some animation, such as facial expression animation.

Deformers

In Chapter 7, we animated an object's

transformations by using translation, rotation, and

scale. But what would we do if we wanted to edit

and animate the *shape* of an object? True, scaling

an object will affect the overall shape, but what if

we needed more control over the vertices in the

object? One way we could accomplish this would

be to edit the positions of individual vertices on

the shape and key their locations at different

points in time. As you might imagine, though,

animating an object in this way could become

difficult to manage, especially if the object has a lot of geometry. Instead, you can use Maya's *deformers* to edit and animate the shape of an object.

Deformers give the animator simple control over large amounts of data. Instead of manipulating each vertex individually, you can apply a deformer to any piece of geometry or selection of vertices; you can then manipulate the entire shape by editing a few simple controls on the deformer. You might recall that we used a lattice deformer in Chapter 4 to model the tailpiece of our spaceship. By editing just a few of the control points on the lattice, we were quickly able to form the shape we needed for the tailpiece.

Maya offers a variety of deformers you can use to accomplish certain tasks. This chapter will cover many of these, including their best uses. In Chapter 11, we will look at how to use some of these deformers for character setup.

Types of Deformers

Maya currently offers eight types of deformers that can be accessed from the Deformers menu in the animation menu set (press F2 to access this menu set). Following are descriptions of each deformer.

Blend Shape Deformer

A blend shape deformer enables you to "morph" the shape of any object into the shape of another object. The original object is known as the *base object*, and the object into which it is being morphed or blended is known as the *target object*. Blend shape deformers are most commonly used for facial animation. We will practice facial animation with blend shape deformers in a tutorial later in this chapter.

To use blend shape deformers, first select one or several target shapes and then select the base object.

> *NOTE*   *Although it is not necessary for the target and base objects to have the same number of edit points, it can be helpful in achieving predictable results.*

Choose Deform | Create Blend Shape to create a blend shape node. Once this node is created, Maya assigns a weight attribute for each target object you selected. You can set the amount of influence that a target has on the base by editing the Weight attribute for that target in the Channel Box or in the Attribute Editor, which is shown in Figure 8-1.

Additional target objects can be added to a blend shape by selecting a target object and the base object and choosing Deform | Edit Blend Shape | Add. To remove a target object from

FIGURE 8-1   *Set the amount of influence by editing the Weight attribute.*

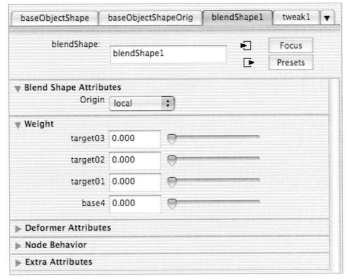

a blend shape, select the target object, select the base object, and then choose Deform | Edit Blend Shape | Remove.

Maya offers an additional window where you can edit blend shapes. Choose Window | Animation Editors | Blend Shape, and the Blend Shape window appears, listing all blend shape nodes that are contained in the scene. A slider interface for each target is available to give you better control over your blend shape animation. You'll also see a Key button you can click to set a keyframe for each target's weight attribute. Figure 8-2 shows the Blend Shape window in a scene that is set up for facial animation.

Lattice Deformer

A lattice deformer will deform an object through the use of a control cage (see Figure 8-3), similar to the way a low-level subdivision surface model can be used to control a higher-level model. However, the big plus with using the lattice deformer is that you get to choose the resolution of the lattice deformer's cage.

Suppose, for example, that you were working with a polygonal model of a head and had created 5000 faces, and you needed to make the jaw just a little narrower. You could use a lattice deformer and edit just a few of its control points instead of having to select the hundreds of vertices that would be necessary if you chose to edit the model directly. Figure 8-3 shows a head model surrounded by the control cage of a lattice deformer. The deformer has been used

FIGURE 8-2   *The Blend Shape window contains sliders to control the weight of the target objects on the base object.*

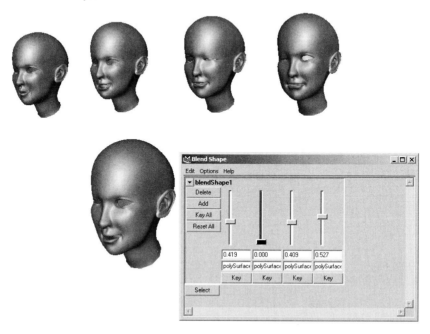

to make the top of the head larger and to elongate the nose. In this case, a single lattice point may influence 100 or more vertices on the model. This is why this deformer is great to use for both modeling and animation.

FIGURE 8-3   *Lattice deformer with the control cage surrounding the head model*

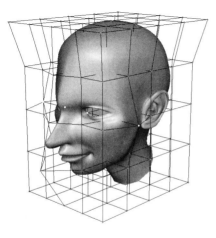

To create a lattice deformer, select an object or a group of vertices and choose Deform | Create Lattice. Once the lattice is created, you will notice that Maya created two lattice nodes in the Channel Box: a lattice and a base, named *ffd* and *ffdBase*, respectively (*ffd* stands for free-form deformation). The base lattice is invisible, but you can select it in the Outliner or the Hypergraph. The base is used as the zero point, or origin, for calculating the deform operation.

Lattices use their own local coordinate system, referred to as *STU*. The lattice can be subdivided along the S, T, and U axes by editing the S, T, and U Divisions attributes in the Channel Box or the Attribute Editor. Each point on the lattice can deform the surface it is controlling with an influence that is based on the number of divisions. In other words, if the lattice had four divisions in the S direction, and if the Local Mode box is unchecked in the Lattice Options window (Deform | Create Lattice ❑), as shown in the illustration, the vertices on the lattice have influence over the entire object.

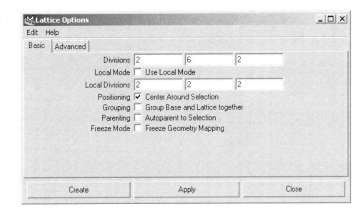

By default, when you create a lattice, its transform node is not connected to the object it surrounds. Therefore, if you move the object, the lattice will not move with it. To remedy this, you can choose options in the Lattice tool's Options window that allow you either to parent the lattice to the object or group the objects together (the Parenting check box and Grouping check box, respectively).

The lattice options can be reset or any tweaks can be removed by choosing Edit Lattice | Reset Lattice or Edit Lattice | Remove Lattice Tweaks, respectively.

Cluster Deformer

Clusters allow you to create a set of weighted vertices. When the cluster is transformed, the vertices of the affected object will follow, depending on their weight attributes. Clusters can be used by themselves or in tandem with other deformers. Often, clusters are created to deform a face to simulate various facial expressions. Once an expression has been created by moving around the clusters on the face, the model of the head can be used as a blend shape target. A cluster can also be used as a good modeling tool for making selection sets.

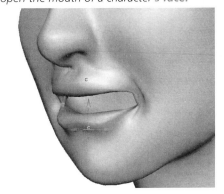

FIGURE 8-4   A cluster is transformed to open the mouth of a character's face.

Figure 8-4 shows a cluster containing vertices around the bottom of the mouth; the cluster is being transformed to open the mouth.

To create a cluster, select a group of vertices and choose Deform | Create Cluster. A small C icon will appear in the view windows. By selecting this C icon, you can use any of the transform tools to edit the cluster.

In the Channel Box, the default weight (the Envelope attribute) is set to 1. This means that the vertices will be transformed 100 percent with the cluster. If the Envelope is set to 0.5, the vertices would move half as much as the cluster (50 percent). An object can contain any number of clusters, and any vertex can be a member of multiple clusters.

The weight of each vertex can be edited using the Paint Cluster Weights tool. The Paint Cluster Weights tool uses Maya's Artisan brush-based interface to let you assign weight values to the vertices in a cluster by stroking them with a brush. To use the Paint Cluster Weights tool, select a surface that contains a cluster and choose Deform | Paint Cluster Weights Tool □ to view the tool's settings, as shown in Figure 8-5. If more than one cluster is used on the object, you can choose which cluster you want to modify by LMB-clicking the Cluster1.weights button in the Paint Attributes section. A pop-up menu will open, where you can select the cluster you want to modify.

> NOTE　**The other options available here are common to the Artisan interface covered in Chapter 6.**

In the Brush section, set the Opacity to a lower number, and choose the Smooth operation in the Paint Attributes section to smooth the weighting of the CVs. In the model, the color white represents CVs with a weight of 1, and the black color represents CVs with a weight of 0. You

FIGURE 8-5　*The weights of vertices in a cluster can be edited with the Paint Cluster Weights tool.*

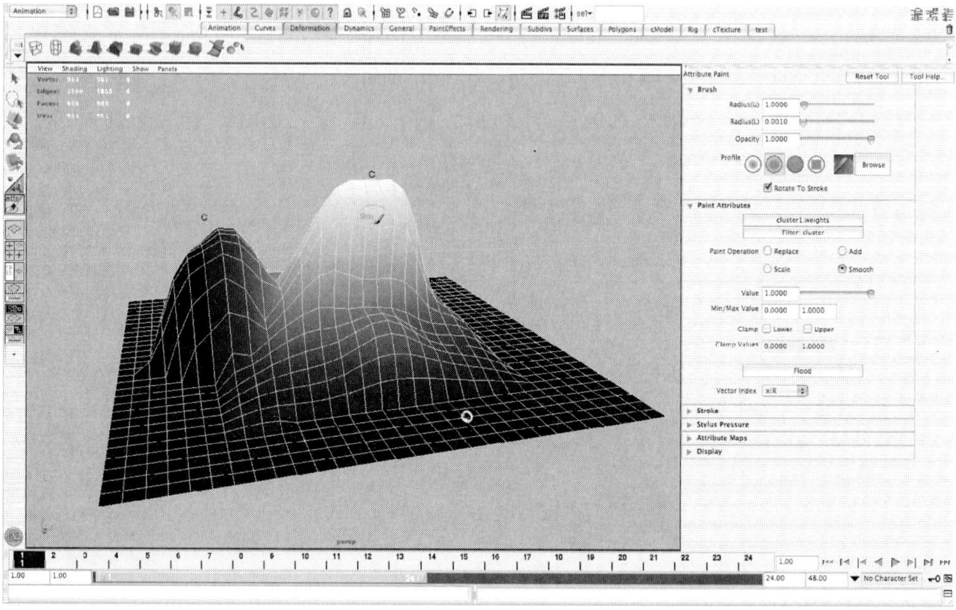

can choose the Replace option to replace the current weight with a value indicated in the Value attribute. Choosing the Add option will add to the current weight by a value indicated in the Value attribute.

> *NOTE If you want to edit the weight values of the CVs manually, you can use the Component Editor (choose Window | General Editors | Component Editor). With the Component Editor open, choose the Weighted Deformers tab. Then select a group of CVs in the view window, and click the Load Components button. The Component Editor is discussed in more detail in Chapter 10, when we bind a geometry to a skeleton.*

Use the Edit Membership tool (Deform | Edit Membership Tool) to add or remove points from the cluster. With the cluster selected, choose the tool and then SHIFT-drag to add points to the cluster or CTRL (CONTROL)-drag to remove them.

Nonlinear Deformers

The nonlinear deformers offer a set of simple nonlinear deformation functions. Several deformers can be used on one object or on a group of objects. You create these deformers by selecting an object, some vertices, or a group of objects, and then choosing Deform | Nonlinear and choosing a deformer from the submenu. Once the deformer is created, it can be moved, rotated, and scaled so that it is positioned as you want. The attributes can be controlled using the Show Manipulator tool by selecting the deformer in the Channel Box and then selecting the Show Manipulator tool from the tool box.

The following provides brief descriptions of each nonlinear deformer and how its specific attributes affect the object(s) being deformed. Figure 8-5 shows the effect that each deformer has on an object.

- **Bend deformer**   Bends an object. By default, the deformer will bend from the center of the object along the Y axis. You can change this by selecting the deformer and using the Rotate tool to rotate it so that it is deforming in the proper direction. The amount of bend is controlled by the Curvature attribute, which can be interactively edited in the view window by using the Show Manipulator tool and dragging the blue dot at the center of the deformer icon.

- **Flare deformer**   Lets you narrow or widen the ends of the object being deformed. The attributes for the start and end flares provide non-uniform scale controls for both ends of the deformer. These attributes can be controlled interactively by using the Show Manipulator tool and dragging the blue dots that appear on the circles at each

FIGURE 8-6   *Six nonlinear deformers and their effects on an object. Notice that each shows its specific manipulator.*

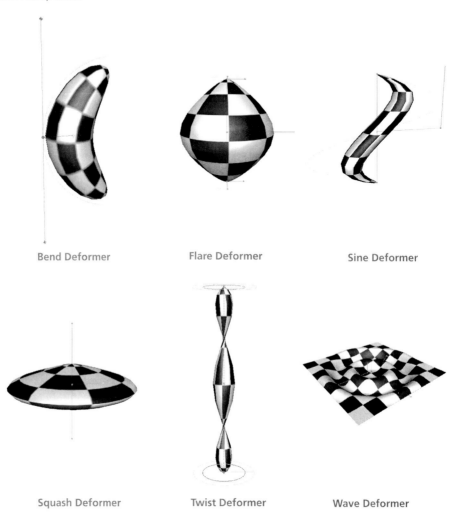

Bend Deformer   Flare Deformer   Sine Deformer

Squash Deformer   Twist Deformer   Wave Deformer

end of the manipulator. The Curve attribute will curve the surface between each end of the flare. The Curve attribute can be edited with the Show Manipulator tool by dragging the dot at the center of the manipulator.

- **Sine deformer**   Uses a sine function to create a curvy deformation. As in most sine functions, attributes are used to control the amplitude, wavelength, and offset of the sine wave. To control the frequency, select the deformer and use the Scale tool to scale it down. Then use the High Bound and Low Bound attributes to control the length of the deformer.

• **Squash deformer**   Squashes and stretches an object. While a similar effect can be achieved with the Scale tool, the squash deformer will keep the volume of an object intact using the Factor attribute. This attribute can be interactively controlled with the Show Manipulator tool by dragging the blue dot that extends from the center of the manipulator.

 • **Twist deformer**   Introduces a twist into the object to which it is applied. Two attributes control the twisting effect: Start Angle and End Angle. Essentially, these attributes control the rotation at both ends of the deformer.

 • **Wave deformer**   Simulates a ripple effect into the surface, similar to the way water forms a ripple when a rock is thrown into it. This deformer is similar to a sine deformer in that both share similar attributes, such as Amplitude, Wavelength, and Offset. However, the wave deformer is effective in a radial direction from its center, while the sine deformer works only in a single direction.

Sculpt Deformer

 You can use the sculpt deformer to sculpt the surface of a spherical object. Three modes are available for the sculpt deformer: flip, project, and stretch. In flip mode, the sphere will act as a force field that pushes points away from the center. Project mode is the opposite of flip—it pulls points toward the deformer.

Figure 8-7 shows a plane to which two sculpt deformers have been applied. The sculpt deformer on the left side of the plane is working in flip mode, pushing the surface down; the sculpt deformer on the right is set to project mode, which pulls the surface up.

Stretch mode will push points in the direction relative to the deformer's origin. This origin is based on the position of a locator object that can be transformed with any of the transform tools. A *locator* is nothing more than a transform node represented as a cross. Locators are used for all kinds of things in Maya—sometimes they are used to group other objects, and they can also be used as control objects for other objects in the scene. In the latter case, they represent the origin of the sculpt deformer. Figure 8-8 shows a sculpt deformer in stretch

FIGURE 8-7   *Sculpt deformers in flip and project modes*

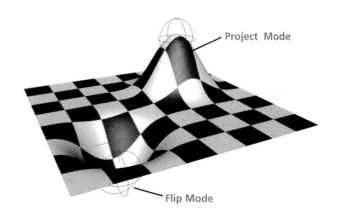

Project Mode

Flip Mode

FIGURE 8-8   *The sculpt deformer in stretch mode*

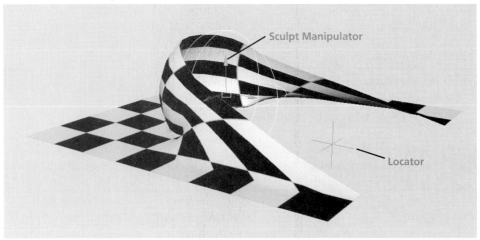

mode. Notice how the position of the locator and the sculpt manipulator are used to calculate which direction the vertices will be moved.

Jiggle Deformer

The jiggle deformer lets you add gelatin-like jiggling movement to your animating surface. When the jiggle deformer is added to a set of points on an object and the object is animated, the points on the surface keep moving while or after the movement of the object stops. This is a great deformer to use for secondary animation—think of a sumo wrestler's flabby stomach or a bulldog's dangling jowels as the characters move across a scene.

The Stiffness attribute controls how rigid the object is. You can choose a range between 0 to 1. A value of 1 makes the object stiffer, so it jiggles at a much higher frequency—almost like a vibration. A value of 0 makes the object very soft, so it will jiggle with a much slower, bigger motion. The Damping attribute controls how extreme the object will deform when it jiggles. This attribute also has a range from 0 to 1: A value of 0 will make the object highly elastic, and it will squash and stretch a lot. A value of 1 will make it stop jiggling immediately after the object's transforms halt. Basically, if you want an object to look very soft, keep both values close to 0. If you want to create a stiff and hard object, set values close to 1.

The Jiggle Weight value controls how much jiggle happens to an entire object. A value of 0 will remove all the jiggles, and a value of 1 gives the maximum jiggle. Usually, the 1 value gives too much jiggle and the resulting deformation is unpredictable.

Just as you can with a cluster deformer, you can change the weight of a vertex toward the deformer by using the Artisan brush interface. In this case, you can use the Paint Jiggle Weights tool by choosing Deform | Paint Jiggle Weights Tool. This tool works exactly like the Paint Cluster Weights tool that was discussed in the "Cluster Deformer" section earlier in the chapter.

FIGURE 8-9   A jiggle deformer is applied to a bouncing ball.

Figure 8-9 shows three different frames from a bouncing ball animation. The ball has a jiggle deformer with Stiffness value of 0.5.

Wire Deformer

The wire deformer uses a NURBS curve to deform an object. You can change the shape of an object by moving a curve or points on the curve. To create a wire deformer, first draw a curve that will be used as the deformer and another object that will be deformed. Choose Deform | Wire Tool. Select the object that will be deformed and press ENTER; then select the curve and press ENTER. The wire deformer will be created.

When the shape of the curve is changed, either by transforming the curve or editing its components, it will have a matching effect on the surface that it is controlling. Figure 8-10 shows a wire deformer that was drawn to match the shape of the mouth. This wire deformer can now be used to control and animate the mouth region.

FIGURE 8-10   A wire deformer can be used to control the mouth animation.

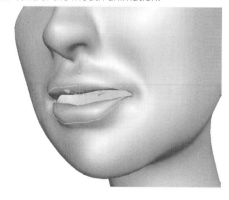

Wrap Deformer

The wrap deformer lets you use NURBS curves or surfaces and polygonal geometry to deform another object. This is a great option for deforming body parts that are built from heavy geometry. In Chapter 10, we will deal with the "skinning" process, when a geometry is binded to a skeleton. If the geometry is heavy, it can make this process more difficult because you'll need to manage many vertices. In such cases, then, a low-resolution version of the model can be created and binded to the skeleton. The low-resolution model can then be used as a wrap deformer that controls the high-resolution model. We will be covering this process in a tutorial in Chapter 11.

Figure 8-11 shows a wrap deformer applied to a head model. When a vertex on the deformer is moved, the deforming surface will follow.

FIGURE 8-11   *The wrap deformer*

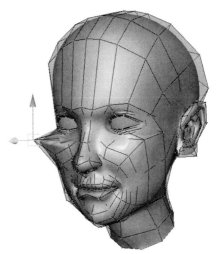

NOTE   *You can add these deformers to an entire object or to selected vertices only. However, make sure you don't add any vertices to an object after you apply the deformer, because the results will be unpredictable.*

Tutorial: The Jumping Slime

Here's a simple tutorial to practice using some of the deformers. In Chapter 7, we animated a bouncing ball using translation and scale. This time, we will build a slime character and use deformers to apply some of the principles of animation that we covered here and in Chapter 7. We will use lattice, bend, squash, and jiggle deformers for this tutorial for each specific task.

Creating a Model

First, let's create a model to use for the animation. To do this, we will draw and revolve a NURBS curve.

1. Start in the Front view. Choose Create | CV Curve Tool and draw a half profile of a snowman-like character at the right side of the Y axis, using about 12 CVs.

2. Press F3 to make sure you are viewing the modeling menu set. Choose Surface | Revolve to create a NURBS surface. Your object should look similar to what's shown in Figure 8-12.

3. In the Channel Box, rename the object.

FIGURE 8-12   *The NURBS curve is revolved to create our model.*

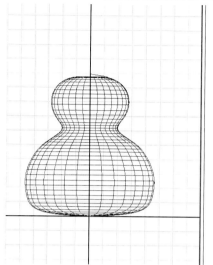

Using a Lattice Deformer to Modify the Proportion

You can use a lattice deformer to modify the shape and proportion of a model quickly, without having to edit any of the surface's CVs.

1. Select the slime object in a view window and choose Deform | Create Lattice ❏. Press the F2 key to change to the animation menu set.

2. The Divisions attributes determine details of the lattice in the S, T, and U directions. In the Lattice Options window, set these to **2**, **6**, and **2**, respectively. The options should match those shown in the illustration.

3. Check the Local Mode check box to turn on Local Division. This will further divide the influence of each lattice point on the deformed object. The default is set to 2, 2, and 2. This means that each lattice point will influence two lattice points away in all directions.

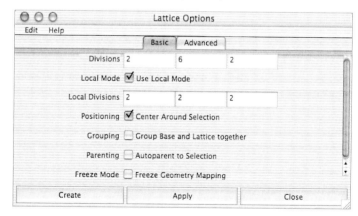

If the number is higher or Local Mode is unchecked, the lattice points will have a much wider influence over the deformed surface.

4. Keep Local Mode checked and leave Local Division set to 2, 2, and 2. The Positioning option should be checked so that the lattice will form around the deformed object. Click the Create button.

5. Right-click the lattice and choose Lattice Points from the marking menu.

6. Select some of the lattice points and edit them to sculpt and refine the model. Move the slime shape's "head" back and make his "stomach" much more prominent. Figure 8-13 shows the model as it is modified with a lattice.

FIGURE 8-13 *A lattice is used to modify the shape of the slime model.*

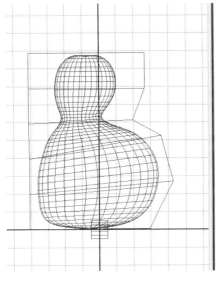 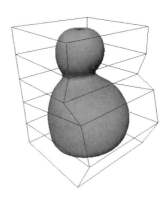

7. After you have finished modeling, choose Edit | Delete By Type | History. This will delete the lattice but leave the model in the shape in which it was deformed. This is known as *baking* the deformation. If the lattice were just selected and deleted, the model would revert back to the shape it was in before the lattice was applied.

TIP **A lattice deformer is great for modeling, because you can push and pull any number of points on a complex model using just a few points on the lattice. It is perfect for making slight modifications to the proportion of a model without interfering with the details.**

Keyframing Translation

Now let's begin keyframing the animation. First we will concentrate on the general movement of the slime object. We want the slime to start on the ground, stay there for about one second, and then jump upward. When it lands back on the ground it will bounce once.

1. Key the translation of slime at frame 0 by pressing SHIFT-W. In the Time Slider, set the Current Time to frame 30, and then press SHIFT-W once more.

2. Move the Current Time Indicator to frame 45. In the Front view, move the slime object up and over in the X axis. (Figure 8-14 shows the positions of the objects at each keyframe. Use this as a reference.) Once again, key the translation.

3. Now go to frame 60, move the slime to the ground level, and key it again. Move it up and over at frame 75 and touch down at frame 90.

FIGURE 8-14 *The keyframed positions of the slime*

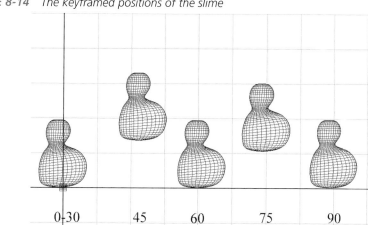

Editing Keys

Notice that our character is moving up and down at frames 0–30, even though we keyframed it to be stationary. This is because Maya is using spline tangents to interpolate between those keys. To fix this, we need to change the interpolation between these keys to linear and then break the tangents.

1. With the slime object selected, choose Window | Animation Editors | Graph Editor. Press the F key to frame the animation curves for this object.

2. Select the keys at frames 0 and 30, and choose Tangents | Linear In Graph Editor. This will flatten the animation curve between frames 0 and 30. It will have no movement.

3. Select the translate Y curve's bottom keys for the ground positions and choose Keys | Break Tangent.

4. Grab the tangents one by one and make them sharp, just as we did in the bouncing ball tutorial in Chapter 7. This will make the slime's movement much more sharp and bouncy. Figure 8-15 shows how the Graph Editor should look after you edit the animation curves.

FIGURE 8-15   *The animation curves are edited in the Graph Editor to create a bouncy motion.*

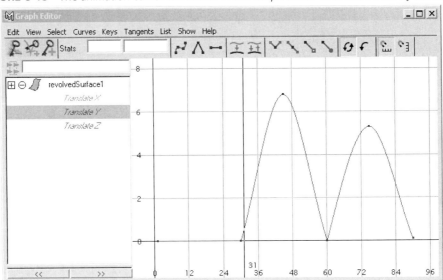

Adding a Squash Deformer

The character is now animated, but it is lacking some life. Let's add squash and stretch to it by applying a squash deformer.

1. Go to frame 0, and select the slime in a view window. Choose Deform | Create Nonlinear | Squash. You will see a green *I*-shaped deformer handle, and the slime turns magenta. Figure 8-16 shows the slime model with the squash deformer added.

2. Test the squashing effect by selecting the squash1 node from the Inputs section of the Channel Box (as shown in the illustration) and changing the Factor attribute by typing **1**. Then change the attribute to **−1**. Notice how the slime object changes with each attribute setting. The positive value will stretch the object, and the negative value will squash it.

INPUTS	
squash1	
Envelope	1
Factor	0
Expand	1
Max Expand Pos	0.5
Start Smoothness	0
End Smoothness	0
Low Bound	−1
High Bound	1

TIP   ***You can also click the Factor attribute in the Channel Box and MMB-drag it into in the Front view window to see how it will squash and stretch.***

3. You should notice that the way the slime is squashed and stretched toward the center of the character is a bit strange. In real life, it should be squashing and stretching from the bottom of the character, where it hits the ground. We need to move the deformer to fix this.

4. While the squash deformer is selected, select the Move tool in the tool box, or press the w key, and move the deformer down so the center of the deformer is at the bottom of the slime, as shown in Figure 8-17. Now use the Scale tool to scale the deformer in the Y axis, so the top of the deformer is at the top of the character. Try squashing and stretching the deformer now. It should squash and stretch from the base of the slime.

FIGURE 8-16 A squash deformer is applied to the model.

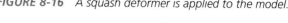

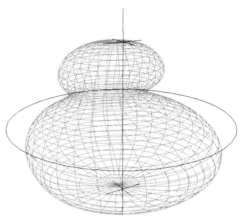

5. Select the squash deformer and SHIFT-select the slime; then press the P key, making the deformer a child of the character. Now the deformer should follow wherever the character is going.

FIGURE 8-17 Placing the squash deformer at the base of the model

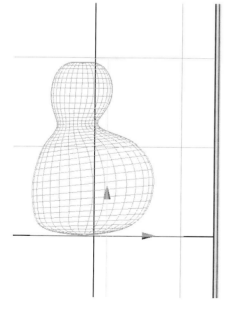

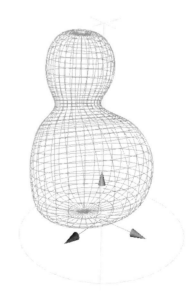

Keyframing the Squash Deformer

Now we will keyframe the Factor attribute on the squash deformer. This time, instead of adjusting the attribute in the Channel Box, we will use the Show Manipulator tool to edit the Factor attribute interactively in the view window.

1. Select the squash deformer in a view window.

2. In the Channel Box, select the squash1 node, and then click the Show Manipulator Tool in the tool box. The squash deformer will now show blue dots.

3. LMB-drag the blue dot at the right side of the squash deformer in the Front view to change the Factor attribute's value, as shown in Figure 8-18.

FIGURE 8-18   *Manipulating the squash deformer*

Drag this blue dot to edit the Factor attribute.

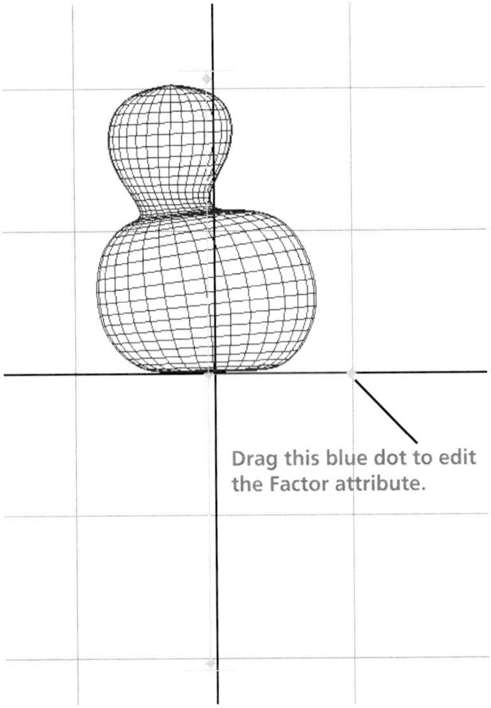

4. Go to frame 0 and change the Factor attribute to a value of 0 by choosing the Factor attribute in the Channel Box and then clicking the right mouse button. From the marking menu that appears, choose Key Selected. Move to frame 20 and key again.

5. Go to frame 30 and squash the slime. Key the Factor attribute for this new value. Go to frame 45 and stretch the character. Set another key.

6. Go to frame 59 and set the Factor attribute to 0. Set a key. This will prevent the character from squashing prematurely.

7. Squash again at frame 60. Continue stretching at frame 75, set the Factor attribute back to a value of 0 at frame 89, and then squash again at frame 90. Make the second bounce less of a squash stretch than the first bounce.

8. Then, for the next 20 frames after frame 90, you can squash and stretch slightly for every five frames or so. This will give jiggly follow-through movement to the slime character. Use Figure 8-19 as a reference for the squash deformer's keyframe.

FIGURE 8-19   *Squash deformer keyframes*

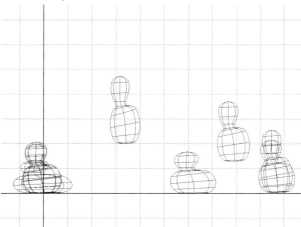

9. Play the animation and check your keyframes.

Adding a Jiggle Deformer

Let's give a gelatin-like jiggle to the entire character by adding a jiggle deformer.

1. Select the slime object and choose Deform | Create Jiggle Deformer. If you play the animation back, you will notice that the slime jiggles too much as it moves.

2. Select the jiggle1 node in the Channel Box. Change the Stiffness attribute to **0.5**, Damping to **0.3**, and Jiggle Weight to **0.8**. The values should match the settings shown in the illustration.

3. Play the animation and check the movement.

In this tutorial, you learned how to apply deformers for various modeling and animation applications. While we used only a few of the deformers here, they all work in a similar fashion, and the setup and controls are much the same for each one.

Tutorial: Facial Animation

As discussed earlier, the blend shape deformer is an easy deformation tool to use for morphing the shape of one object into the shape of another. In this tutorial, we will use a head shape supplied on the CD, or you can use the head you built in Chapter 6. We will duplicate the head and then shape each copy into a different expression. We'll then use these modified copies as blend shape targets in a blend shape deformer. Then we'll use the Blend Shape Editor to animate our faces.

To start, you'll need a model of a face. You can use the head you built in Chapter 6 or use the file entitled blendshape_start.ma from the CD.

Creating Facial Expressions

We first need to make a copy of the head and tweak the model to create various facial expressions. Later we can blend shape these heads with a base model.

1. Select the head you created (or the head from the CD) and choose Edit | Duplicate, or press CTRL-D (CONTROL-D). Use the Move tool to move the duplicate head up and over the original shape so that it is not overlapping. Continue this process until you create five duplicate heads. We will manipulate these five heads and use them as target shapes for the original—the base object—to morph into.

NOTE   You can move the head anywhere in the scene. As long as you use the default setting for the blend shape deformer, it remembers which control vertices are moved to where. Transformation of the target objects, such as move, rotate, and scale, has no effect on blend shape.

2. Tweak the shape of each head. Work with the mouth first. Make the first head have a smiling face. Look in the mirror and smile, and notice which parts of your face move. It isn't just your lips, but your entire cheek region. This means that you will have to move the vertices in the cheek region of the model as well as reshaping the mouth. You can either select each vertex in the face and move it or use the Sculpt Polygon tool and use Maya's Artisan interface to push and pull vertices around. When you are finished, the mouth area should look similar to the model shown in the illustration. In the Channel Box, name the model **happy**.

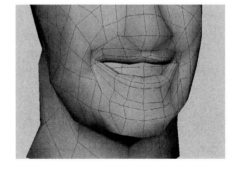

3. Now we'll make a version of the head with a closed mouth. Using another of the duplicates, move the vertices around the lips so that the lips are touching. It may be helpful to select all of the vertices in the lip region and scale them down along the Y axis. Once they have been scaled, you can use the Sculpt Surface tool in smooth mode to even out any abrupt changes in the vertices. This will give the face a relaxed look. But watch out! Don't smooth it too much, or you will lose the detail in the face. When you are finished, name this model **closed**.

4. Modify another head so that is makes a kissing expression. Use the techniques you used in steps 2 and 3 to shape the face. Name this one **kiss**.

Now we will make some expressions to modify the eyebrow region. Instead of just selecting the vertices in the eyebrow region and moving them one by one, we can make a cluster. If we then smooth the weight values in the cluster, the vertices in the center of our selection will move more than the vertices at the bounds of our selection and result in a much more natural shape when the cluster is translated.

5. Select the vertices around the top of the eyelid and upper brow region of the face. You can do this by selecting each vertex with the Selection tool, or you can use the Paint Selection tool (Edit | Paint Selection Tool) to paint over the surface and select vertices that are in range of the brush size.

6. With the vertices selected, choose Deform | Create Cluster. A cluster that contains the group of selected vertices will be created.

7. To smooth the weights of the vertices in the cluster, select the model and choose Deform | Paint Cluster Weights Tool ☐. The model will turn black, while the area containing the vertices in the cluster will be white. In the Paint Cluster Weights Tool setting window, set the Paint Operation attribute to Smooth. Now click the Flood button. This will smooth the weights from 0 to 1 over the entire selection. Click the Flood button a few times until the transition from black to white is gradual. Figure 8-20 shows the model after the cluster weights have been smoothed.

FIGURE 8-20   *The face model with the Paint Cluster Weights tool active*

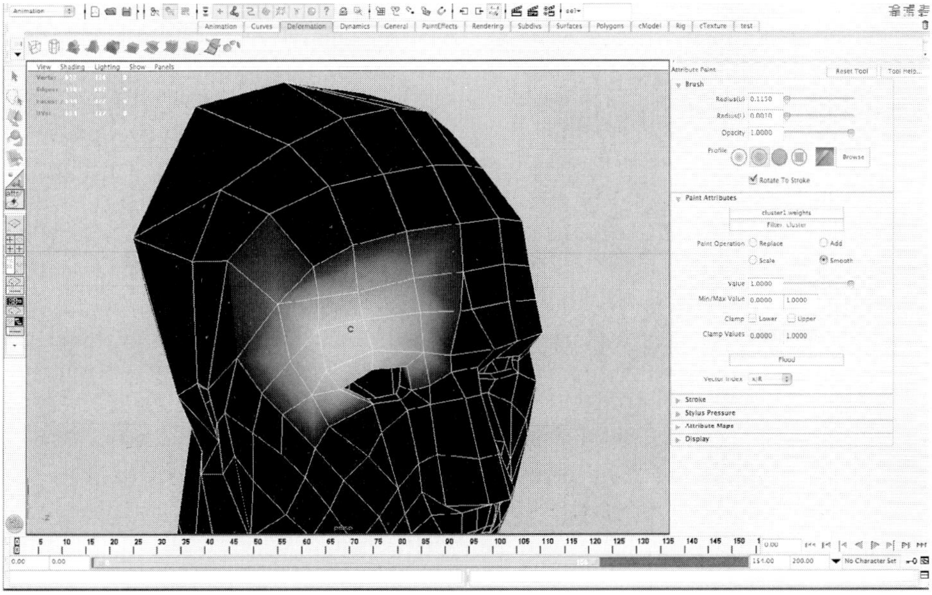

8. Now select the cluster with the Move tool by clicking the C icon in the view window. Move the cluster up along the Y axis. Name this head **R_browRidge**.

9. Repeat steps 5 though 8 for the other side of the face on another duplicate of the head. Name this one **L_browRidge**. The following illustration shows all of the heads that will be used as target shapes in the blend shape deformer:

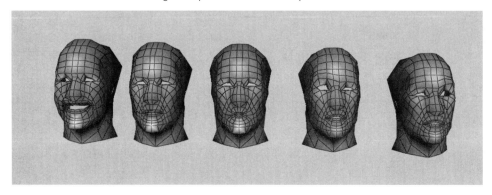

TIP *We created two heads with right and left brow ridges lifted up individually. This way, we can blend these shapes to create asymmetrical expressions to gain more interesting movement.*

Applying the Blend Shape Deformer

Now it's time to apply a blend shape deformer to the base object. Remember that to apply a blend shape deformer, you need to select the target objects first and then select a base object.

1. Select all the target shapes you created from left to right in the Front view. SHIFT-select the base object last. Choose Deform | Create Blend Shape ◻. Figure 8-21 shows the Create Blend Shape Options window.

FIGURE 8-21 *Create Blend Shape Options window*

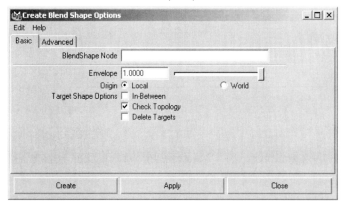

2. You can name the blend shape node by typing any name in the BlendShape Node box. Name your blend shape intuitively so you can later recall what it's for. Type **Expressions** in the box.

NOTE *Blend shape's calculation is just like any object node. You can select this node through the Blend Shape Editor, discussed later in the chapter in the section "Animating the Blend Shape."*

3. Envelope controls the amount of change of the blend shape. A value of 1 will change the base's shape to 100 percent of the target shape. If it's set to 0.5, the base object will change shape only to 50 percent of the target shape. Set this to **1**. You can change this later if necessary.

4. Origin determines whether the base object will use the target object's transformation (translation, rotation, and scale) for blending shape.

If it's set to Local, the base object will ignore the transformation of the target shape and consider only the changes you make in the target shape's placement of the control vertex. If it's set to World, the base will follow any transformation you make with the target shape. Generally, you'll want this set to Local, so that you can place and scale your target shape away from where the base object is. Set this to Local.

5. Three check boxes are available for the Target Shape Options:

- If the In-Between check box is enabled, the resulting blend shape node will have only one blend shape slider available. The slider will cycle through all of the target shapes in the order of the target shape selection, instead of showing a slider for each target shape. In-Between is useful if the change in shape is linear and you don't need to mix any shapes. Since we are creating a facial expression and want to mix different shapes, we want this box unchecked.

- Check Topology checks whether all the target shapes and the base shape have the same number of points. If this box is checked, Maya won't let you blend shapes with a different number of points. Because it's a good idea for the target and base objects to have the same number of points, the default is checked. Keep this box checked.

- Delete Targets automatically deletes target objects after you apply the blend shape. You may want to tweak the target shape later, so I would suggest just hiding target shapes or exporting them, so you can retrieve them later for further editing. Don't check this check box.

TIP *Remember that since construction history is turned on, if you change the topology of a target shape, it will apply to the base object as well.*

6. Finally, click the Create button to apply the blend shape. Now the base object will have the blend shape deformer added.

Animating the Blend Shape

Let's keyframe the blend shapes to animate the facial expressions. The blend
shape deformer provides a premade
and easy-to-use editor to help you
accomplish this task.

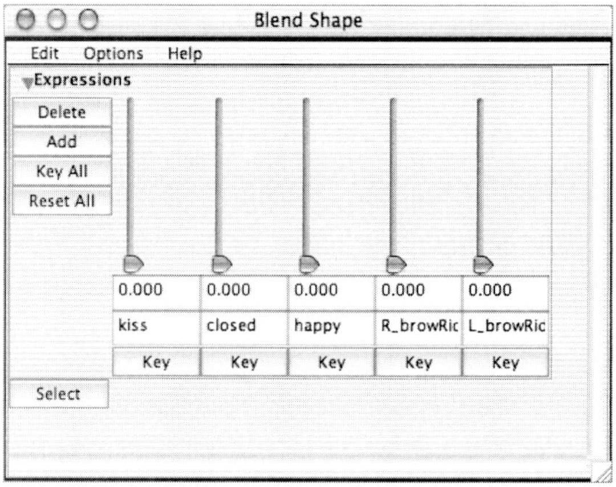

Open the Blend Shape Editor by choosing
Window | Animation Editors | Blend Shape.
A window with five sliders will appear.
Figure 8-22 shows the Blend Shape Editor
displaying the sliders for our Expressions
blend shape node.

The most prominent elements in the Blend
Shape Editor are the sliders. You can slide
these to change the shape of the base
object. Each slider represents the target shape. The name of each target shape is displayed at the
bottom of each slider. The field above displays the value of a target shape's weight. A value of 0 means
the target doesn't affect the shape of the base object at all. A value of 1 means 100 percent of the
target shape is applied to the base object. Move the slider and watch the base object in the view
windows to test the effect. You can use more than one slider to mix deformation. This way, you
can extract more subtle and complex shapes out of them.

FIGURE 8-22   Blend Shape Editor

> TIP   *While the range of the sliders defaults to 0–1, you can increase this range.*
> *You can directly type a number into these boxes—such as 2 or –1. This will move*
> *the surface points beyond or to the opposite of a target shape.*

The Delete button at the top left will delete this blend shape node. It's a quick way to get rid of
the blend shape deformer.

> NOTE   *Another way to delete a blend shape deformer is to delete the history*
> *of the base object.*

Clicking the Add button will add the current base object's shape to the blend shape node. This
is useful if you want to derive a target shape from a mixture on the current state of the base
object. Use the sliders to change the shape of the base object and select the base face. Then
click the Add button. The base object's current shape is now added to the list of sliders.

- The Key All button sets a keyframe for all of the values at the current frame.
- The Reset All button will set all of the sliders to a 0 value.
- The Select button will select the blend shape node.

Now let's keyframe these sliders.

1. Set the range of the animation to 120 frames by typing **120** in the leftmost box of the Range Slider. Move the Current Time Indicator to frame 0. If all the sliders in the Blend Shape Editor aren't set to 0, click the Reset All button. Then click the Key All button to key all the editor's sliders at frame 0.

2. Move the Current Time Indicator to frame 30, and click the Key All button again. This will keep the expression the same during the first second of the animation.

3. Move the Current Time Indicator to frame 50 and slide the closed and R_browRidge slider all way up to a value of 1. Click Key All.

4. Move the Current Time Indicator to frame 70, and set kiss, R_browRidge, and L_browRidge to a value of 1. Click Key All again.

5. Move to frame 80, and set the closed slider to 1, the kiss slider to around 0.5, and type **–1** into the fields for R_browRidge and L_browRidge. Click Key All again.

6. Move the Current Time Indicator to frame 100, and set the happy slider to 1. Change R_browRidge and L_browRidge to 1.5. Click Key All.

7. Move the Current Time Indicator to frame 120 and click Key All again.

NOTE   *If you are not using all of the target shapes, you can key them individually by clicking the Key button at the bottom of each slider.*

8. Play the animation and take a look at the expression animations.

The blend shape deformer is a great way to create facial animation. In Chapter 11, we will cover more advanced techniques with this deformer for character setup.

Advanced Deformer Tools

Before we move on to the next chapter, some additional concepts should be covered in regard to deformers. This information should help you better use the deformer tools.

Deformation Order

Deformation order is the order in which a deformer is applied to an object. This order is initially determined by the order in which the deformers are created on an object. When you add more than one deformer, the result of the deformation can be quite variable, depending on which deformer was added first. For example, if you apply a sculpt deformer to an object and then apply a cluster deformer, the cluster deformation will occur after the sculpt deformer and will override much of the sculpt deformer's effects.

Figure 8-23 shows a NURBS surface that has a sculpt deformer applied. Then a cluster deformer was applied to a group of vertices around the inner edge of the surface. This setup might be similar to something used for eyelids closing over an eyeball, where you would animate the cluster and the surface would deform over the spherical shape of the sculpt deformer. However, with the deformations applied in this order, the cluster overrides the influence of the sculpt deformer and the edge of the surface remains flush with the rest of the surface. We could delete the deformers and reapply them in a different order, but instead we will simply change the order.

 To fix this, we will use the List Of Input Operations window. Select the surface, click the Inputs To Selected Objects button in the Status Line, and then choose All Inputs from the drop-down menu.

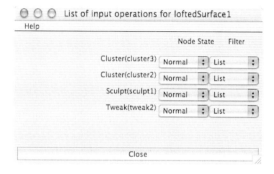

The List Of Input Operations window will appear, as shown next. This window shows the most recent input at the top. In our case, the cluster deformers are at the top and hence have precedence over the Inputs below them. If you wanted to turn off any one of the Inputs in this list, the Node State could be changed from Normal to Has No Effect from the drop-down menus in the Node State column.

By clicking the Sculpt(sculpt1) item in this list and dragging it to the top of the list, the order of the deformation will be changed. Now when the cluster is transformed, the vertices in its group slide over the sculpt deformer and give the desired results. Figure 8-24 shows the surface and deformers with the sculpt deformer on top. Compare this to Figure 8-23.

FIGURE 8-23 *This surface had a cluster deformer added after the sculpt deformer.*

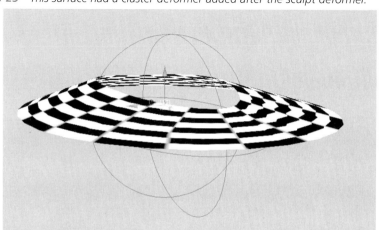

You can also insert a deformer into a specific level in the list of inputs at the time of the deformer's creation. In the Options window of each deformer is an Advanced tab, as shown in Figure 8-25. You can set any deformation order by choosing one in the Deformation Order box at the top. Six choices are available.

FIGURE 8-24   *The surface is deformed with the sculpt deformer at the top of the order*

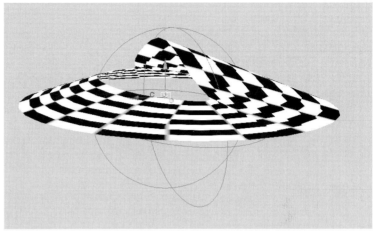

- **Default**   Adds a deformer on top of the existing one, so that the existing deformer will be applied after all the others have been applied.

- **Before**   Adds a deformer to the order just before the last deformer was applied. In this case, the last applied deformer may now override the deformer being created.

- **After**   Adds a deformer immediately after the deforming object.

- **Split**   Creates two objects with two deformations.

- **Parallel**   Creates a parallel blender node and blends all the deformer's effects on an object. You can control how much the weight of each deformer affects an object by adjusting the blend deformer's Weight attribute.

- **Front of Chain**   Works only for the blend shape deformer. A character with skeleton deformation benefits from this deformation order when a blend shape deformer is applied to it. This is discussed more in Chapter 11.

Intermediate Objects

You can view an object before it's being deformed by displaying intermediate objects. This is a good way to review how the deformers are acting on an object. To turn on intermediate objects, select the deforming object and choose Deform | Display Intermediate Objects. You can hide them again by selecting a deforming object and choosing Deform | Hide Intermediate Objects.

FIGURE 8-25   *Setting Deformation Order*

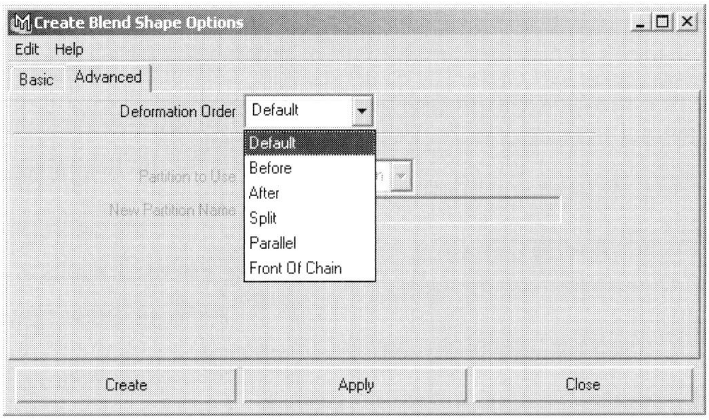

Create Blend Shape Options

Edit   Help

Basic   Advanced

Deformation Order   Default

Default
Before
After
Split
Parallel
Front Of Chain

Partition to Use

New Partition Name

Create   Apply   Close

Editing Membership

In editing membership, you add or subtract which objects or components will be evaluated in a deformation. You'll use three main tools to change membership: the Edit Membership tool, Prune Membership command, and Paint Set Membership tool.

Edit Membership Tool

The Edit Membership tool lets you quickly add and delete vertices from the membership. You must first create an object and add a deformer.

1. Choose Deform | Edit Membership Tool.

2. The cursor will turn into a selection arrow. Select a deformer whose members you wish to edit—this could be a lattice, bend deformer, or a blend shape target shape.

3. A deforming object will automatically go into a component mode, and all the vertices will turn yellow. Yellow means they are included in a membership with the selected deformer.

4. Draw a marquee box over vertices in the membership or SHIFT-LMB-click to add vertices to the membership; CTRL (CONTROL)-LMB-click to remove points from the membership.

Vertices that are not in the membership will turn brown. Figure 8-26 shows the Edit Membership tool in action.

Prune Membership Command

The Prune Membership command automatically removes vertices from membership if they have a weight below a certain amount. To use this command, select an object you want to prune and choose Deform | Prune Membership. Then select one of the deformers. We will use this tool in Chapter 10 when we skin a character.

FIGURE 8-26 *Edit Membership tool in action*

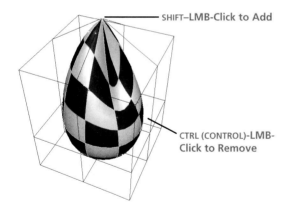

SHIFT-**LMB-Click to Add**

CTRL (CONTROL)-**LMB-
Click to Remove**

Paint Set Membership Tool

You can also paint memberships using the Artisan brush interface with the Paint Set Membership tool. To use this tool, select an object with a deformer and choose Deform | Paint Set Membership Tool □. Choose the deformer that you want to paint set membership from the Set Membership list in the tool's Options window. Paint on the object to remove or add vertices to the deformers membership.

Summary

Deformers are extremely useful for many applications. Each one of them can be utilized for modeling, character setup, and animation. We'll take a look at another type of deformer called a skeleton in the next chapter and learn how to set up a biped character.

Character Setup: Joints, Connections, and Kinematics

To animate a character effectively, you need a structure that will allow you to control the deformations of the geometry based on a real-life organism. In other words, if the leg needs to bend at the knee, you need to be able to select a deformer in the knee region, rotate it, and have the geometry follow. This type of deformer is of a special class called a *skeleton*. A skeleton in Maya serves the same function that a skeleton serves in real life—it forms the internal structure of the character and it serves as the framework for performing character movement and deformation.

Animating the skeleton involves rotating the joints and keying the poses. This type of animation is known as *forward kinematics* (FK). *Inverse kinematics* (IK), on the other hand, is an alternative method for controlling a skeleton. Figure 9-1 shows a completed biped skeleton with some IK and FK controls set up. In this chapter, you will learn about creating skeletons and controlling them with FK and IK.

FIGURE 9-1   *A character skeleton setup*

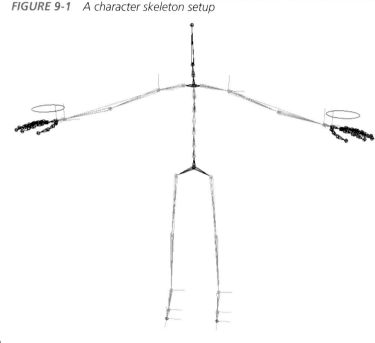

The Skeleton: Joints and Bones

In Maya, a skeleton is a hierarchy of a unique kind of transform nodes called *joints*. Maya skeletons behave like anatomical skeletons, also similar to the armature constructions inside a stop-motion puppet. They allow for easy posing and animating of a character by simply rotating joints.

Creating Skeletons

Skeletons are created using the Joint tool (choose Skeletons | Joint Tool).

Using the Joint tool, you can place a joint into the scene each time you click in a view window. The new joint is automatically parented to a previously drawn joint. This hierarchy of joints is visually indicated in the view window by lines, the *bones* that connect the joints. Bones point from a joint down the skeleton hierarchy to the next joint.

Here's how you draw a skeleton:

1.   Choose Skeleton | Joint Tool, and click in the view window to place the first joint. Click again somewhere else in the view window to create another joint. Notice that the joints are connected with a bone.

2. Place a few more joints in the scene and press ENTER (RETURN) to complete the skeleton.

TIP   **Hold down the X key to snap to the grid or the V key to snap to other joints.**

3. Now draw another skeleton, but this time, before you press ENTER (RETURN) to finish the skeleton, press the up arrow key. This will navigate the selection up the hierarchy to the _parent_ of the last joint you created. Click somewhere else in the scene and notice that you have now created a _branch_ in the skeleton. A branch occurs when a parent joint has more than one child.

4. You can continue to navigate through the hierarchy of the skeleton by using the up and down arrow keys.

Figure 9-2 shows a skeleton for a hand. Notice the branches that are created for the fingers and thumb.

FIGURE 9-2   _A skeleton is created for a hand._

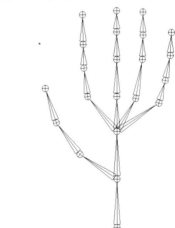

Selecting and Inserting Joints

After you have created the skeleton, you can select a joint by clicking it or by clicking the bone pointing at its child (which is usually easier than clicking the joint). You can then use the transform tools to move, scale, or rotate the selected joint. When you transform a joint with the Move tool, for example, all of the joint's children, or branches, will transform as well. This is the expected behavior for any hierarchy in Maya. If you want to edit the position of just one joint in a skeleton and you do not want to effect any of the child joints, select the joint and press the INSERT (HOME) key. This will isolate the selection to the single joint.

To insert a joint into a skeleton after it has been created, you can use the Insert Joint tool (choose Skeleton | Insert Joint). After choosing this tool, click the joint that will be the parent of the new joint you are creating and drag to place the new joint. To remove a joint in the hierarchy, select the joint to be removed and choose Skeleton | Remove Joint.

Suppose you created a skeleton and then decided that you needed to add additional joints— perhaps some joints for ears. You could simply select the Joint tool, click an existing joint in your skeleton's head (if that's where you want the ears to go) to select it, and then continue drawing more joints for the ears. Remember that the skeleton is just a _hierarchy_ of _joints_.

Another way to add joints to a hierarchy is to draw the new joints and then use the Edit | Parent command to add it as a branch to the skeleton. By selecting the root joint of the new skeleton and then SHIFT-selecting the joint that will be the parent, you can then choose Edit | Parent or simply press the P key, and the new joints will be branched from the parent joint.

Definition   **root joint**   *The topmost joint in the hierarchy.*

Joint Tool Options

Let's look at some of the Joint tool's options. Choose Skeleton | Joint Tool ☐. You'll see the tool's options, as shown in the following illustration.

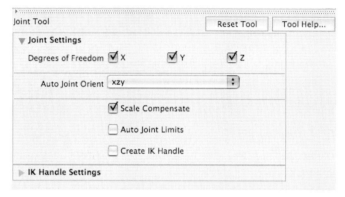

Here's a description of each option:

- **Degrees of Freedom**   This setting determines on which axes joints are allowed to bend. If all three axes are checked, you will create a *ball* joint that can rotate freely in any direction. If two axes are checked, you will create a *universal* joint that can rotate on two axes only. If only one axis is checked, you will create a *hinge* joint. These attributes can later be changed in the Attribute Editor.

- **Auto Joint Orient**   This controls the orientation of a chain of joints when the chain is first created. This is important if you want to twist the chain of joints on a particular axis. For example, if the X axis is the twisting axis, you would select xyz or xzy. The first axis in the Auto Joint Orient text box determines the orientation of twisting. You can also set Auto Joint Orient to None to set a global axis for the orientation of joints.

- **Scale Compensate**   Scale Compensate will allow you to scale each joint independently. Child joints won't be affected by scaling a parent joint.

- **Auto Joint Limits**   This function automatically limits the joint rotation. If the joint is created with a slight bend, for example, this function will prevent the joint from bending beyond 180 degrees. You can create much more detailed joint limitations by using the Attribute Editor.

- **Create IK Handle** This will automatically create an IK chain when the joint creation is complete, although it is recommended that you always set up the IK after the joints are created. (We will discuss IK later in this chapter in the section "Inverse Kinematics.")

Now that you have an idea of what joints are and how you can create them, let's build a skeleton for a character.

Tutorial: Drawing a Biped Skeleton

In this tutorial, we will create a skeleton for a biped character. We'll draw a separate skeleton structure for the leg, arm, hand, and spine. Once the joints are created, we'll edit and fine-tune their placement to match the features in the geometry. We'll then parent these separate skeletons together to create a single skeleton. Finally, we'll orient the joints and do some cleanup so that the skeleton will behave predictably when we set up the controls. But that all comes later. Let's concentrate on the skeleton for now.

The process demonstrated here is just one suggested workflow for setting up skeletons. Once you understand how Maya works, you can go about creating your skeletons any way you like. Even so, you should always make sure you do a few things:

- Always center your geometry so that its axis of symmetry is aligned with one of Maya's planes—the YZ plane, for example. This will let you mirror one half of the skeleton at the YZ plane's origin so that the mirror joints place themselves in the correct positions.

- Be sure that you name all of your joints. Even a simple biped character will have many joints. You want to be able to look at the joint names in the Outliner and know exactly what they are. Label arm and leg limbs with left and right.

 The Biped.ma file found on the CD contains a simple, low-resolution polygon model that you can use to set up your skeleton. Of course, you are encouraged to use the techniques found in Chapter 6 to build you own model.

Creating the Joints

Let's start by creating the joints for our skeleton for the left side of the body by using the Joint tool. The leg and spine skeletons will be drawn in the Side view window, while the arm and hand will be drawn in the Top view. By drawing the joints on a single plane like this, the joint orientations will be easier to fix later on. Also, we will make sure that joints that will be controlled by an IK chain (such as the arm, wrist, spine, and legs) will not be completely straight—that is, they will have at least some small degree of a bend.

1. Use the Layer Editor to create a new layer in the scene and add the character model to this layer. Name the layer **LowRez** and set that layer to be a template. The Layer Editor should look like the illustration.

2. In the Side view, draw the joints for the leg. This should include joints for the hip, knee, ankle, ball, and toe.

3. In the Outliner, name the joints **LT_Hip**, **LT_ Knee**, **LT_Ankle**, **LT_Ball**, and **LT_Toe**.

4. In the Side view, draw a skeleton that starts from the pelvis and goes to the top of the head. This should include a pelvis, six spine joints, a torso root (where the arms will attach), a neck, a head, and the top of the head. Figure 9-3 shows where the joints should be placed.

FIGURE 9-3   Joints are created for the leg and the spine.

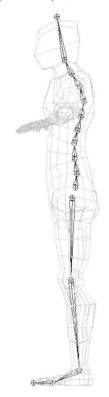

5. Give each of these joints a unique name that intuitively describes what it is. Name the six spine joints Spine_1, Spine_2, and so on. Alternatively, instead of selecting each joint and renaming it separately, you can use Maya's Quick Rename feature. Use the Outliner to select all of the joints in the spine. Select the topmost spine joint in the hierarchy and then, holding down the SHIFT key, select the last spine joint. All of the joints in the hierarchy between these two joints will now be selected, as shown in the following illustration:

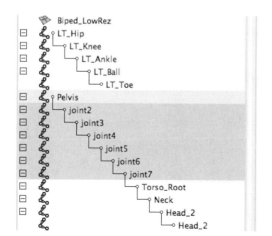

6. In the Status Line, click and hold the Selection option and chose Quick Rename from the resulting pop-up menu.

7. In the field next to Quick Rename, type **Spine_** as shown in the following illustration. Press ENTER (RETURN) and all of the selected joints will be named *Spine_* followed by a number (Spine_1, Spine_2, and so on).

8. In the Top view, draw a skeleton for the arm. Include a joint for the collar bone, shoulder, elbow, wrist, lower hand, and upper hand. Name these joints accordingly.

9. Now draw the joints for the fingers and thumb. To speed up the process, you can draw the joints for one finger and then duplicate that joint hierarchy and move it to position it with another finger. Figure 9-4 shows the joints that have been created for the hand and then named in the Outliner.

FIGURE 9-4 *The joints are created for the hand and the fingers, and then they're renamed in the Outliner.*

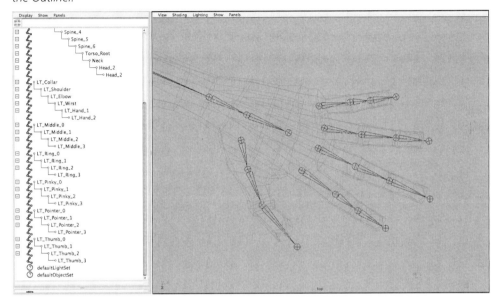

TIP *Sometimes, the size in which the joints are displayed can make their placement difficult. You can change their size by choosing Display | Joint Size | and selecting an option.*

This completes the joint creation for our character.

Selecting Joints

Always be careful when selecting joints. You need to be aware that when you select a single joint, all of the joint's children will highlight in green in the view window, even though only the parent joint is actually selected. This may seem obvious to some designers, but it can be confusing for beginners. For this reason, it is often best to select joints in the Outliner instead of in the view window. You can use the SHIFT key to select the first and last objects in the Outliner; everything in the list between your selections is selected as well, as described in step 5 of the previous exercise. To select multiple joints individually in the Outliner, hold down the CTRL (OPTION) key and select an object to add to the selection.

Aligning the Joints

We did a good job of drawing our joints so that they aligned with the geometry in a single view. However, the joints for the arms and legs will not be in the correct place when observed from another view window. The best way to fix this is to use the Move tool to translate the root of each limb into its correct position and then use the INSERT (HOME) key to move the child joints into position. Let's start with the leg.

1. In the Front view, select the LT_Hip joint and move it along the X axis until it lines up in the center of the left hip (the location of a hip joint in a real skeleton).

2. Select the LT_Knee and then press the INSERT (HOME) key and move the knee joint to about the center of the knee.

3. Continue this process for all of the joints in the leg. Always use the INSERT (HOME) key to move the joints into position. Do not rotate any of the joints, as rotating will make it more difficult to orient the joint later on.

4. Select the LT_Collar joint and use the Move tool to translate the arm up along the Y axis.

FIGURE 9-5 *The joints are placed for the left side of the body.*

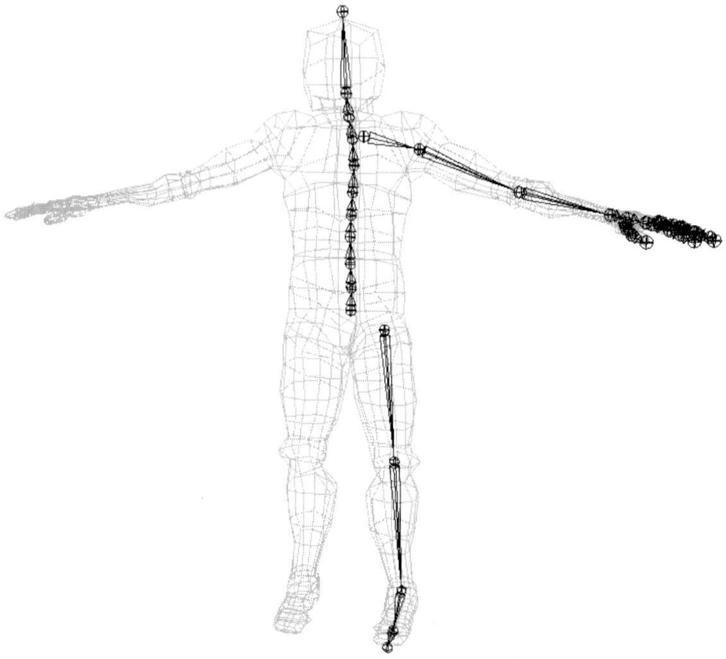

5. Select the LT_Shoulder joint and press the INSERT (HOME) key to move the shoulder joint into position. Continue this process for the rest of the joints in the arm. It is best to try and place the joints in the center of the volume of the geometry.

6. Repeat steps 1–3 for each of the fingers. Figure 9-5 shows the character with the joints placed for the spine and the left side of the body.

TIP   *When modeling an area where a joint will appear, it is best that the model have three edge rings around the joint area (an edge ring refers to a series of connected edges whose ends meet): one in the center of the joint and one on each side. The first and third edge ring will "pin" the geometry in place, and the middle ring will be used to maintain volume when the joint bends. When placing the joints, align each joint to the edge loop in the middle. This will allow for better deformations later on.*

Orienting Joints

Joint orientation is one of the most important aspects of setting up a skeleton that will behave predictably. Earlier in this chapter, we talked about the Auto Joint Orient attribute in the Joint tool's settings. This option sets the axis that the joint will be pointing down the bone. The default setting, XYZ, will point the X axis of the joint down the bone.

The Orient Joint tool can be used to change the orientation of any selected joint or hierarchy. Which axis you choose to orient down the bone is up to you. Choose whichever axis you feel comfortable with, but be consistent! Not only do you want to use the same joint orientations in a single character, but you should use the same joint orientations for *all* of the character rigs you build. If you want to drive yourself (and any animators you are working with) crazy, set up some characters to rotate joints on the X axis and other characters in the scene to rotate along the Y axis!

Let's change the orientation of these joints so that Y points down the bone.

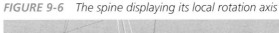

FIGURE 9-6   The spine displaying its local rotation axis

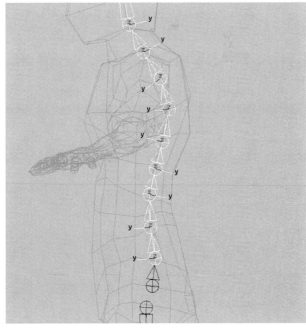

1. In the Outliner, select each joint in the spine, and choose Display | Component Display | Local Rotation Axis to view the local rotation axis for the selected joints.

2. Select the Pelvis joint and choose Skeleton | Orient Joint ☐. In the Joint tool's settings, set the Orientation axis to YZX and make sure the Hierarchy attribute is set to Orient child joints.

3. Click Orient and notice what happens to the local rotation axis of each joint. The Y axis is pointing down the bone. Figure 9-6 shows the spine displaying its local rotation axis.

The problem here is that, while this gives the Y axis a definite orientation, Maya does not have any way of determining which way the X or Z axis should point. The Z axis is either pointing one way or the other, depending on the angle between the joints. If you want the back to bend forward, you would need to rotate the joints along their X axes. However, depending on which way the X is pointing, you would either have to rotate it in the negative X or positive X. To get these joints behaving in a predictable manner that is easy to control, you need to rotate some of the local rotation axis 180 degrees on the Y axis so that all of the axes are pointing the same way.

4. Select the entire spine hierarchy and go into component selection mode (press the F8 key).

5. In the Status Line, enable the Miscellaneous selection type (the button with a question mark). This will allow you to select and rotate the local rotation axis.

    We will orient all of the local rotation axes in the same direction. The Z axis will point forward while the X will point to the left side of the body. However, no command is available in the interface to flip our local rotation axis. Instead, we will have to create one with a simple MEL script.

6. Choose Window | General Editors | Script Editor to open the Script Editor.

7. In the Script Editor, choose Edit | Clear History. This will remove all of the journaled commands in the history (upper) section of the Script Editor.

8. Now, back in the view window, select one of the local rotation axes, and with the Rotate tool, rotate it along the Y axis a bit and then immediately undo.

9. Look in the Script Editor. You should see that two commands have been journaled into the history window—one to rotate and the other to undo. Without knowing any MEL, you should be able to figure out how to reverse-engineer this command to rotate the local rotation axis 180 degrees in Y. The actual command is rotate. The –r flag stands for *relative*. This means that the rotation will happen relative to the current orientation (as opposed to an absolute rotation). The –os flag means that the rotation will occur in the object's own space. Then you'll see three numbers separated by spaces for values in X, Y, and Z.

10. Copy and paste this entire command from the history section into the input section.

11. Change the Y value to **180**. The command should now look like this:

```
rotate -r -os 0 180 0 ;
```

12. Highlight this command in the input window of the Script Editor and then LMB-drag to it the Shelf to make a Shelf button.

13. In the view window, select one of the local rotation axes and click the new Shelf button. The axis should now be facing the correct direction.

14. Use this command on each axis that is pointing in the wrong direction on the spine.

15. When you are finished with the spine, repeat this entire process for all of the joints in the entire body.

Completing the Skeleton

Now let's parent all the different hierarchies together and mirror the joints to make the skeleton for the other side.

1. In the view window, hold down the SHIFT key and select the root joint of each of the finger hierarchies.

2. Still holding down the SHIFT key, select the LT_hand_2 joint. Choose Edit | Parent (or press the P key) to parent the fingers to the hand joint.

3. Select the LT_Collar joint, and then SHIFT-select the Torso_Root joint in the spine hierarchy. Press the P key to parent the arm to the spine.

4. Select the LT_Hip joint, and then SHIFT-select the Pelvis joint. Press the P key to parent the leg to the spine.

5. To mirror the arms and legs to the other side, select the LT_Hip joint and then choose Skeleton | Mirror Joint □.

6. In the Mirror Joint Options window, set the Mirror Across attribute to YZ. Set the Mirror Function to Orientation. Finally, you can rename your mirrored joints by searching for *LT* and replacing it with *RT*. The options should look like the window shown in the following illustration. Click the Mirror button to mirror the leg.

7. Choose the LT_Collar joint, and then choose Skeleton | Mirror Joint. The arm will be mirrored using the settings we used in step 6.

8. Do a quick check on the joint orientation of the new mirrored joints. You may need to reorient some of the joints with the Orient Joint command and flip any local rotation axes with our custom MEL command. Figure 9-7 shows the entire skeleton with all of its joints correctly oriented. All of the joints have been named appropriately.

FIGURE 9-7   *The completed skeleton has been named and oriented correctly.*

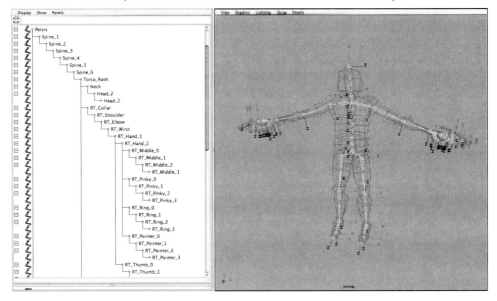

9. Now select the pelvis joint and choose Modify | Freeze Transformations. This will ensure that the skeleton can always return to this pose if we zero-out all of the rotation values.

10. Finally, we'll lock and make non-keyable all the joint attributes that will not be animated. Select all the joints in the skeleton, except for the Pelvis joint. In the Channel Box, select the Translate attributes (remember to select the names, not the fields with the values) and then right-click them. Choose Lock Selected from the marking menu.

11. Do the same thing for the Scale and Visibility attributes. These attributes will now be locked so that they cannot be edited accidentally.

Forward Kinematics

Forward kinematics (FK) allows you to animate a skeleton so that is behaves as a normal hierarchy. That is, when a parent joint is rotated, all of its children will follow. FK is useful for animating arcing movement, such as swinging or waving an arm or curling the fingers. Stop-motion puppets are animated through rotation inside an armature in a way that's similar to FK.

While animating with FK is pretty intuitive to anyone who has been doing basic animation in Maya, it does have some drawbacks for use in character animation. The biggest problem with animating with FK is that you can't anchor the end of a joint chain at a specific location while the parent joints are moved. For example, if you're animating a character's walk cycle, you want to be able to lock one of the feet to the floor while the body moves and the opposite foot moves forward. This is difficult to accomplish with FK. You would animate the pelvis to move the body forward, but since the feet are children of the pelvis, they will move forward with the body. This means you have to rotate the leg backward at every frame, just to make the foot stay put. To lock down this foot as you move the body, you must use inverse kinematics (IK)

Like FK, IK has its drawbacks. For many areas on a character, IK can make the simplest move-ments difficult to control. The movement of the fingers is a good example. In most cases, the motion of the fingers can be animated naturally simply by rotating the joints in the fingers. The problem, however, is that every time you need to open and close the fingers, you would have to select and rotate each joint into the desired pose—an extremely time-consuming process. It would be better to have just one attribute that you could use to open and close the fingers.

Fortunately, Maya offers several ways to connect the attributes of different objects together so that the attribute of one object can be controlled by the attribute of another. Remember from Chapter 1 that a Maya scene can be described as a collection of nodes with attributes that are connected. So far, we have been letting Maya make these connections when we create something with one of the menu commands, be it creating a NURBS sphere (a NURBS sphere has the makeNurbSphere node's outputSurface attribute connected to the nurbSphereShape's Create attribute) or extruding a polygonal face. In either case, Maya connects the attributes of different nodes to achieve an effect or shape.

One of the most powerful features in Maya is its ability to connect the attribute of any node to the attribute(s) of another node. You can make these connections in three ways: by making *direct connections* through the Connection Editor, by creating custom *expressions* with the Expression Editor, and by creating *keyed relationships* using Set Driven Key.

> **_NOTE_** **_While we are introducing this topic of connecting nodes in relation to controlling a skeleton, you should realize that these methods can be used to make connections for any purpose._**

Direct Connections

A *direct connection* occurs when the attribute of one node is equal to the attribute of the node connected to it. For example, if you had two cubes, cubeA and cubeB, and cubeB's attributes were directly connected to the corresponding transform attributes on cubeA, the Rotate X attribute of cubeB would be equal to the Rotate X value of cubeA. When cubeA is rotated on X, then cubeB will also rotate the same amount on X.

The real power of direct connections is that the attributes don't need to be connected to corre-sponding attributes of another object. In the cube example, we could connect the Rotate X of cubeB to the Translate Y attributes of cubeA, so that when cubeA is translated 30 units in Y, cubeB will rotate 30 degrees in X. Going a step further, we could even connect the Color attribute of the material that is applied to cubeA to the Scale Z attribute of cubeA. This way, when cubeA is scaled in down in Z, the color will change. As you can imagine, this can get pretty complicated.

The Connection Editor

An easy way to make direct connec-tions between attributes in Maya is to use the Connection Editor. The Con-nection Editor allows you to load the attributes of any two objects and con-nect them together by clicking and highlighting attributes in each column. Figure 9-8 shows the Connection Editor with the attributes of two cubes loaded. In this example, the output of cubeA's Translate Y attribute is connected to the input of cubeB's Rotate X attribute.

The left column displays the list of out-put attributes from the loaded node, and the right column displays the list of input attributes on the loaded node. Connections are made from left to

FIGURE 9-8 *The Connection Editor with the attributes of two objects loaded*

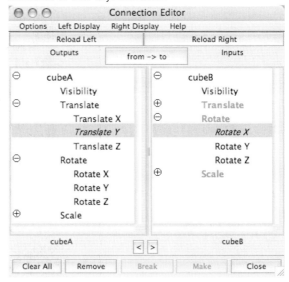

right—an attribute is selected from the list of outputs on the left, and then an attribute is selected from the list of inputs on the right. Selected attributes are highlighted. When a connection is made, the attribute's name will show in italic type, as shown in Figure 9-8 for the *Translate Y* output and *Rotate X* input. To break the connection, simply click the highlighted attribute from the list of inputs. The highlight will disappear and the text will return to a normal font, meaning that the connection is broken.

You should also notice that an attribute that has an incoming connection cannot be edited in the Channel Box. The Channel Box signifies this by highlighting the field in yellow. If you were to attempt to change the value of cubeB's Rotate X attribute, for example, Maya would return the following error: "The attribute 'cubeB.rotateX' is locked or connected and cannot be modified."

Practice Using the Connection Editor

Let's step through a quick exercise so that we can practice using the Connection Editor to set up some direct connections. In this example, we will use the direct connections to animate the curl-ing of a tail that contains six joints. Since our character does not have a tail, we will make one in a new scene.

1. Create a new scene and draw a skeleton that has six joints. Orient these joints so that the Y axis is pointing down the bone and the Z axis is pointing up, as shown in the illustration.

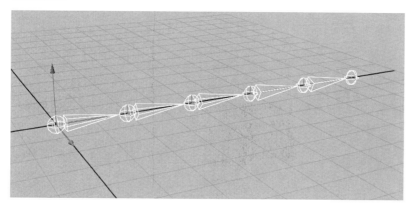

2. Name the joints **tail_1** through **tail_6**.

3. Choose Window | General Editors | Connection Editor to open the Connection Editor.

4. In the Outliner, select tail_1. With tail_1 selected, click the Reload Left button. The attributes for tail_1 will load into the left column.

5. Now select tail_2 and click the Reload Right button. The input attributes for tail_2 will load.

6. Find the Rotate attributes in each column. They will be in a folder called Rotate. Click the plus (+) symbol in front of the folder to see the individual attributes for Rotate X, Rotate Y, and Rotate Z.

7. To connect the Rotate X attribute of tail_1 to the Rotate X attribute of tail_2, click Rotate X in the left column, and then click Rotate X in the right column. The attributes will highlight when they are selected. Once the second attribute is selected, a connection will be made and the text will be italicized. The Connection Editor should look like the illustration.

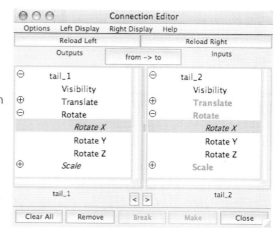

8. Now select tail_3 and click the Reload Right button in the Connection Editor. Once again, find the Rotate X attribute in the list of attributes in the right column and click it to make the connection.

9. Repeat the last step for the remaining joints. Tail_6 can be left alone because it does not have a child joint.

10. At this point, all of the Rotate X input attributes for joints tail_2 to tail_5 should be connected to the Rotate X output attributes of tail_1. To test this, select tail_1 and rotate it in X. All of the other joints in the skeleton should rotate the same amount.

11. You can verify that they are all rotating the same amount by observing the Rotate X attribute in the Channel Box or Attribute Editor.

Now that you have successfully connected these attributes, you can imagine the possibilities that the power of connections offers and the efficiency that it can provide to an animator. However, if we wanted each joint to rotate twice as much as its parent joint, we would need to use yet another tool. While we could use the Connection Editor in a combination with some other utility nodes, we will examine this problem by using expressions.

Expressions

Expressions are a powerful animation tool in Maya. Expressions are script-based instructions that let you control the attributes of objects. This control can be based on a mathematical function, a variable such as time, or the attributes of other objects. In this section, we will use expressions to connect the attributes of various objects together.

The Expression Editor

Choose Window | Animation Editors | Expression Editor to open the Expression Editor, shown in Figure 9-9. The Expression Name field at the top lets you name the expression that you are about to make. The Selection section will show you the name of the selected object and its selected attribute. This is a helpful way to look up or find the names of some attributes that might not be so obvious. In the bottom part of the Expression Editor, you can type in and create new expressions.

One of the simplest expressions you can write makes a direction connection between the attributes of two objects, thus duplicating the behavior of the Connection Editor. Using the tail that we created in the last section, the following expression could be used directly to connect the Rotate X attribute of tail_2 to the Rotate X attribute of tail_1:

```
tail_2.rotateX = tail_1.rotateX ;
```

If we wanted to mimic the tail's behavior that we set up in the Connection Editor, the expression would look like this:

```
tail_2.rotateX = tail_1.rotateX ;
tail_3.rotateX = tail_1.rotateX ;
tail_4.rotateX = tail_1.rotateX ;
tail_5.rotateX = tail_1.rotateX ;
```

FIGURE 9-9   *The Expression Editor*

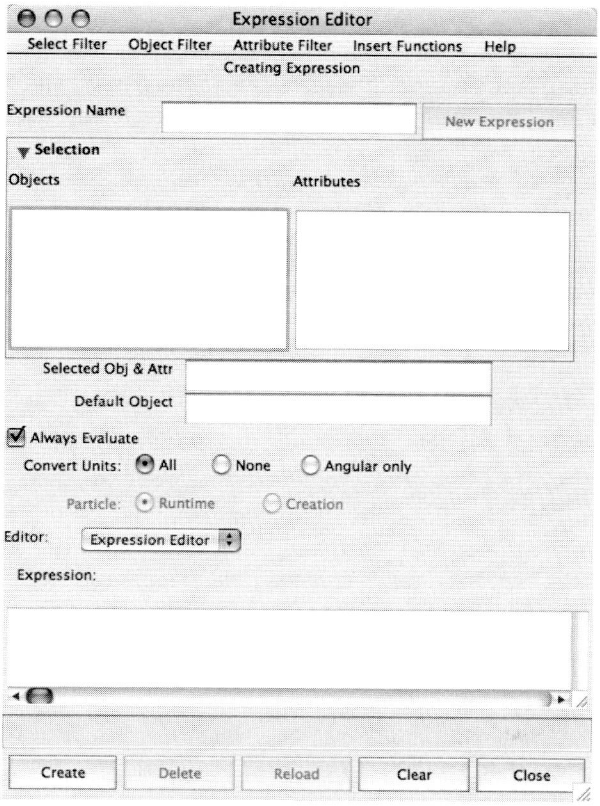

Here, we are connecting the Rotate X attribute of each child joint to the root joint, tail_1. The animation that results from rotating tail_1 in X is identical to what we did in the Connection Editor in the last example. However, in a case like this, the Connection Editor might be easier to use because the connections can be made through a series of clicks instead of typing script.

The real power of expressions comes into play when we need to specify exactly how the connections are made.

Creating Expressions

Let's say, for example, that we wanted to make each joint in our tail rotate twice as much as its parent joint. To do this, we can write expressions that use mathematical operations, in this case multiplying the rotation of each parent joint by 2.

1. Create another six joints, name them, and orient them just as you did in the preceding section.

2. Instead of using the main menu bar to open the Expression Editor, we will use the marking menu in the Channel Box. Select tail_2 in the Outliner or view window, and then highlight its Rotate X attribute in the Channel Box.

3. Right-click in the Channel Box and choose Expressions. The Expression Editor will open with the tail_2.rotateX object and attribute loaded into the Selected Obj & Attr field.

4. Copy and paste the tail_2.rotateX text from the Selected Obj & Attr field into the Expression area at the bottom of the Expression Editor window.

5. Now add the following script to complete this expression:

```
tail_2.rotateX = tail_1.rotateX * 2;
```

6. Click the Create button in the Expression Editor to create the expression that will connect these attributes in this manner. Once the expression is created, notice that the value field for the Rotate X attribute of tail_2 is purple. This indicates that the value is being controlled by an expression.

7. Test the expression by rotating tail_1 in X and verifying (in the Attribute Editor or Channel Box) that the X rotation value for tail_2 is twice as much.

8. Return to the Expression Editor and write the expressions for the rest of the joints. You do not need to create a new expression for each connection. All of the connections for each joint can be entered into this one expression. Figure 9-10 shows the completed expression in the Expression Editor.

You can use expressions to do a whole lot more. We will use expressions in Chapter 18 to control particle dynamics.

Keyed Relationship

A *keyed relationship* occurs when attributes are connected based on some custom input from the user. The user actually specifies, or *keys*, the attributes of an object based on the values of another object. The most common keyed relationship is the basic keyframed animation, in which the attributes of all animated objects are keyed at a certain frame. At another frame, they are keyed with different values. Every time a key is placed, a relationship is made between time and the animated attributes.

What if you wanted to key the attributes of certain objects based on something other than time? For example, if you wanted to pose the tail skeleton at different poses based on the rotation of the first joint instead of time, what would you do? If you were really great at math, you might be able to do this with expressions, but it would take way too long. To handle such a situation, Maya offers a tool called a *Set Driven Key*.

FIGURE 9-10   *The Expression Editor with an expression that is connecting each joint so that it rotates twice as much as its parent joint*

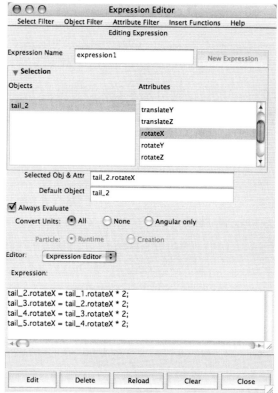

Set Driven Key

Maya's Set Driven Key creates a keyed relationship between the attribute of one object and one or many attributes of one or more objects. The output attribute—the attribute to which the other attributes will be keyed—is called the *driver.* In a normal keyframed animation, time is the driver. All of the input attributes that will be keyed based on the value of the driver are called the *driven attributes.* To create an animatable Set Driven Key, you must set at least two keys between the driver attribute and the driven attribute. Once this relationship has been established, all of the values between the keyed values are interpolated by an animation curve.

In this example, we will again use our six-jointed tail as the object for animation. The root joint's Rotate X attribute will be the driver for all of the rotation attributes of the other joints in the tail. Once again, start a project and create six joints. Orient them and name them.

1.   Choose Animate | Set Driven Key | Set ❑ to open the Set Driven Key window.

2.   Select the tail_1 joint in the Outliner or the view window.

3. In the Set Driven Key window, click the Load Driver button to load the tail_1 object and its attributes. The object will appear in the upper-left column, and the attributes will appear in a list in the upper-right column.

4. In the driver's attribute list on the right, find and select the rotateX attribute.

5. Use the Outliner to select the rest of the joints in the tail skeleton. Once again, that last joint, tail_6, can be disregarded.

6. In the Set Driven Key window, click the Load Driven button to load all of the objects into the list of driven objects in the lower-left Driven pane of the Set Driven Key window.

7. Select all of the objects in this list. Their attributes will appear in the lower-right column.

8. In the list of attributes, find the rotateX, rotateY, and rotateZ attributes and select all three of them by dragging the cursor over their names or by SHIFT-selecting them. Figure 9-11 shows the Set Driven Key window with all of these objects and attributes selected.

FIGURE 9-11 *The Set Driven Key window with the proper joints and attributes loaded and selected*

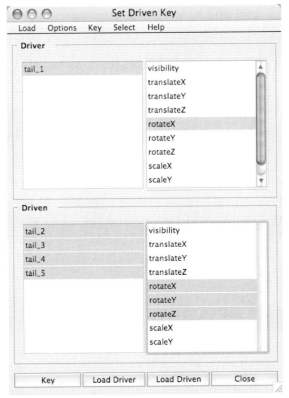

9. Click the Key button. A relationship is established between the values of the driven attributes based on the value of the driver attribute.

10. Now rotate the tail_1 joint to a value of 50 in X.

11. Select each of the joints and rotate them into a pose. They can be rotated in X, Y, and Z all at the same time. The illustration shows a tail in a suggested pose.

12. With the pose set, return to the Set Driven Key window and click the Key button again. This will create another relationship between the selected attributes at their current values.

13. Test the Set Driven Key by rotating the tail_1 joint in X. When it is rotated 50 degrees, the rest of the tail will rotate toward that pose.

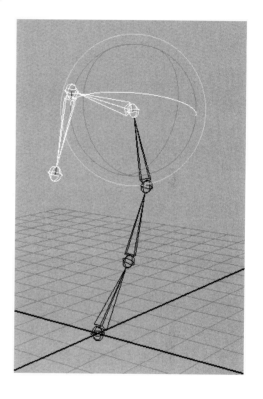

As you can see, keying the relationship instead of connecting it mathematically is an intuitive process. Set Driven Keys are often used to animate fingers, toes, tails, and even the spines of character. In the next tutorial, we will rig the fingers of our character using a Set Driven Key.

Tutorial: Set Driven Key for Finger Movement

Animating the finger movements on a hand would be a painstaking task if the animator had to rotate each individual joint in each finger of the hand every time the character had to move its fingers. Set Driven Keys make this task much less time consuming. By keying the position of each finger curl based on the attribute of a driving object, you need to animate only that single attribute to pose the finger. Furthermore, you could make another master control attribute that would animate the Set Driven Keys that control each finger so that one attribute could control all of the fingers at once.

Before we start, we must determine what object and attribute will act as the driver for all of these Set Driven Keys. Instead of using one of the joint's rotation attributes as a driver, we will create a new object, a NURBS curve, for the driver. The curve will be used as a *control object*. In most cases, this object will never be rendered. It simply provides a means to let you easily click something in the view window to access a list of keyable attributes in the Channel Box.

Definition   ***control object***   *Any object—a group node, a joint, or a piece of geometry—whose only purpose is to control other objects.*

For the attributes that will be used to drive the animation, we will create custom attributes on the NURBS curve. You can add a custom attribute to any node in Maya by selecting the node and choosing Modify | Add Attribute. We will practice adding custom attributes to the control object for the fingers in this tutorial. We will create a custom attribute for each finger that will curl the finger when the attribute is animated. Then we'll use these attributes as drivers to key the poses of the fingers straight and curled.

Create the Controls

We'll create a NURBS curve that will be used as the control object for the left hand. Custom attributes will be added to this object to control the fingers. Later, this control object will also be used to control the IK handle that will animate the arm. It is therefore important that you make sure that the circle is oriented so that the Y axis is perpendicular to the circle. The reasons why will be explained later when we set up the IK.

1. Choose Create | NURBS Primitives | Circle ❑. In the NURBS Circle Options window, choose Edit | Reset Settings. This will ensure that the circle has its Normal Axis attribute set to Y.

2. Rename the circle **LT_ArmCTRL** and move it so that it is close to the animation's left hand.

3. Select the LT_ArmCTRL object and choose Modify | Add Attribute to open the Add Attribute window shown in Figure 9-12.

4. Name this attribute by typing **PointCurl** into the Attribute Name field. The Data Type should be set to Float (the default), which will allow the data type to accept decimal numbers.

5. Use the Minimum and Maximum fields to set a range for the attribute's value. Enter **–5** for the Minimum, **10** for the Maximum, and **0** for the Default.

6. Click the Add button to add the PointCurl attribute to the LT_ArmCTRL object.

7. Repeat this process for the other three fingers and the thumb. Name the attributes **MiddleCurl**, **RingCurl**, **PinkyCurl**, and **ThumbCurl**. If you select the LT_ArmCTRL and look at the attributes in the Channel Box, you will see that the new attributes appear in this list.

8. At the moment, changing the values for these new attributes won't have any effect, because the attributes are not connected to anything. We will use a Set Driven Key to connect these attributes to the joint rotations of each finger. Choose Animate | Set Driven Key | Set ❑ to open the Set Driven Key window.

FIGURE 9-12   *The Add Attribute window*

Add Attribute: |nurbsCircle1

Help

New | Particle | Control

Attribute Name   PointCurl

☑ Make Attribute Keyable

Data Type

○ Vector   ○ Integer   ○ String
● Float   ○ Boolean   ○ Enum

Attribute Type

● Scalar   ○ Per Particle (Array)
             ☐ Add Initial State Attribute

Numeric Attribute Properties

Minimum   −5

Maximum   0

Default   10

Enum Names

OK | Add | Close

9. Set up the Driver first. Select LT_ArmCTRL in the view window and then, in the Set Driven Key window, click the Load Driver button. The list of keyable attributes will appear in the section on the right. Click the PointCurl attribute in this list.

10. Now set up the Driven. In the Outliner, select the joints called LT_Pointer_0, LT_Pointer_1, and LT_Pointer_2. Be sure to select each joint, not just the parent joint. You don't need to select the last joint in the finger because it has no child.

11. After you have selected these three joints, return to the Set Driven Key window and click the Load Driven button. All of the joints will appear in the list of driven objects.

12. Drag-select the joints in the Driven list to select them all, and their keyable attributes will be listed on the right.

13. Drag-select all of the rotate attributes. Figure 9-13 shows the Set Driven Key window as it should look when all of the attributes are ready to be keyed.

14. Verify that the rotation values for all of the finger joints are set at 0 by viewing them in the Channel Box. In the Set Driven Key window, click the Key button. This will set a key for the selected joints' current rotation values when the PointCurl attribute is set at 0.

15. In the view window, select the LT_ArmCTRL and set the PointCurl attribute to **−5**.

16. Use the Outliner to select the three joints of the left pointer finger again.

FIGURE 9-13   *The Set Driven Key window with the Driver and Driven attributes selected and ready to be keyed*

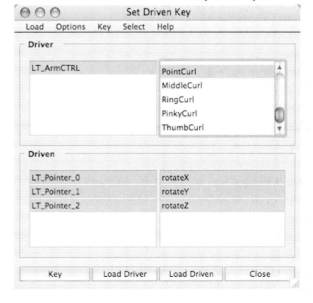

Set Driven Key

Load   Options   Key   Select   Help

Driver

LT_ArmCTRL	PointCurl
	MiddleCurl
	RingCurl
	PinkyCurl
	ThumbCurl

Driven

LT_Pointer_0	rotateX
LT_Pointer_1	rotateY
LT_Pointer_2	rotateZ

Key | Load Driver | Load Driven | Close

Use the Rotate tool to rotate the joints on their X axes so that the finger bends back just slightly. Because we took the time to orient the joints when we set up the skeleton, we are able to select multiple joints, rotate them at once, and have finger curl in one direction. However, the real power of using a Set Driven Key is that the driven objects do not have to have the same values. You may wish to grab each joint in the pointer finger and rotate it separately to achieve the desired pose.

17. When you are pleased with the pose of the finger bending backward, return to the Set Driven Key window and click the Key button.

18. Select the LT_ArmCTRL object and set the PointCurl attribute to **10**.

19. Once again, rotate the joints in the pointer finger. This time, rotate them so that the finger bends in the other direction, as if the finger were being curled in to make a fist. Figure 9-14 shows the left pointer finger in a curled pose. When you are pleased with the pose, return to the Set Driven Key window and click the Key button.

FIGURE 9-14 *The joints in the pointer finger are posed.*

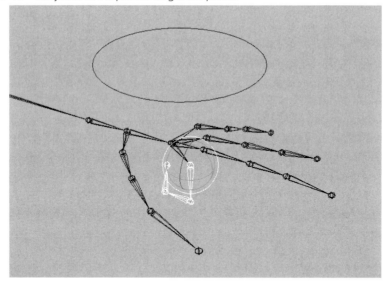

20. Test the PointCurl attribute by selecting it in the Channel Box and MMB-dragging in the view window to change the value interactively. The finger should curl when the PointCurl value nears 10, and it should bend backward at values from 0 to –5.

21. Repeat this entire process, steps 9–20, for the remaining three fingers and the thumb.

22. After you have set up all of the fingers to animate with a Set Driven Key, select all of the control attributes at once in the Channel Box, and use the middle mouse button to open and close the entire hand.

23. You can use another good control to spread the fingers. Use the Add Attribute command to add an attribute called Spread to the LT_ArmCTRL. Give it a minimum value of –5 and a maximum value of 5. Use a Set Driven Key to make this attribute drive the Z rotations of the knuckle joints of the pointer, ring, and pinky fingers.

24. Finally, duplicate the control object and name it **RT_ArmCTRL**. You will then need to go through the process of using Set Driven Key to connect all of the custom attributes to the finger joints on the right hand.

Inverse Kinematics

With inverse kinematics (IK), a series of joints are chosen to form an IK chain. Once the IK chain is created, two additional nodes are created. The *IK effector* is parented to the joint at the end of the IK chain. The *IK handle* is created and placed outside the joint hierarchy relative to the world space. The IK handle will act as a goal position for the effector. The IK *solver* then evaluates the position of the IK effector and makes the necessary calculations to rotate the joints in the chain so that the joint at the end of the chain will be in the same position as the end effector. This way, the hierarchy is animated by moving the object at the end of the joint hierarchy instead of at the top—hence the name, inverse kinematics; it's the inverse of FK.

Figure 9-15 shows a skeleton that is being driven with IK from joint_2 to joint_4. Notice the effector node in the Hypergraph that is a child of joint_4.

FIGURE 9-15 *A skeleton with IK set up to drive some of the joints*

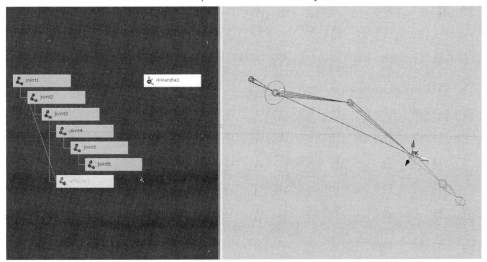

One of the drawbacks to animating with IK is that it can require the setup and use of additional controls to make the IK chain behave properly. Even with these controls, though, some animation that should be simple to do can take a lot of work to get right. A character swinging his arm as he walks, for instance, should be an easy thing to create. However, when the arm is moved back and forth with the IK handle that controls the skeleton from the shoulder to the wrist joints, it may be difficult to get the motion to look natural. To solve the problem, you must set up an additional control to affect the elbow in the middle of the IK chain. Then you would be dealing with two controls to make a simple motion. In the end, the animation might look a bit artificial because you are letting Maya decide how the arm is moving instead of rotating the joints yourself. In such a situation, the animation of the arm is better done with FK.

Some of the biggest computer animation studios in the world animate using only FK. Many of these studios' animators are traditionally trained, and the idea of letting the computer decide the movement of a character is hard to stomach. These animators would rather go through the pains-taking process of posing the character in place at each frame. For the rest of us, though, IK is a powerful tool and is necessary to help us animate quickly. We'll now look at how to set up IK.

IK Handle Tool

You can create an IK handle by choosing Skeleton | IK Handle Tool. Once the tool is invoked, click the parent joint that will be the start of the IK chain and then click the joint that will be at the end of the IK chain. You can create an IK chain for any amount of joints—but use caution, be-cause when more than three joints are included in a chain, it can be difficult to control.

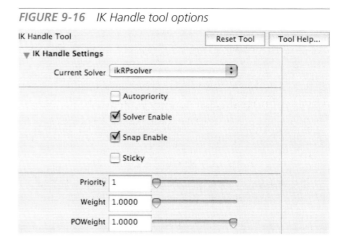

FIGURE 9-16 *IK Handle tool options*

To see the options available for the IK Handle tool, choose Skeleton | IK Handle Tool ❐. These options are shown in Figure 9-16 and are described next.

- **Current Solver** Two kinds of solvers are available here: ikRPsolver (IK Rotate Plane Solver) and ikSCsolver (IK Single Chain Solver). The ikRPsolver can have direct control over how the IK chain is oriented. For example, if you made an arm chain and you want to rotate a shoulder to point the elbow, the ikRPsolver contains an additional set of attributes to control the *pole vector*. This way, the IK chain can determine the orientation of the whole chain.

- **Autopriority**   Works only on ikSCsolver. It specifies which joint will be first affected by the IK handle.

- **Solver Enable**   Determines whether the IK solver will be on or off when the IK chain is created. It's on by default and can be turned off later by selecting the IK handle and choosing Skeleton | Disable Selected IK Handles.

- **Snap Enable**   Lets the IK handle be snapped onto the IK solver. It's on by default.

- **Sticky**   Locks the IK handle in place when the parent joint is moved. By default, this is turned off. This means that if an IK chain is connected from the shoulder to the wrist and then the pelvis is moved, the wrist will move with it just as if no IK were hooked up at all. If Sticky is turned on, the wrist will remain anchored to that position while the parent joints move. (Note that a similar effect can be achieved by parenting the IK handle to another object. We will discuss this setup in Chapter 10 when we discuss control rigs.)

Definition   ***pole vector***   *Part of an IK rotate plane handle that begins at the start joint, and along with the handle vector defines the IK handle's reference plane.*

Using the IK Handle Tool

After you've set up the options for the IK Handle tool, you are ready to use it on the joints. The default settings are fine for the purposes demonstrated in this book.

1. Draw a skeleton that contains five joints that can represent an arm that starts from the collar bone and goes to the hand. That leaves the shoulder, elbow, and wrist joints in between. As you draw these joints, it is important that you include a bend in the elbow so that the IK solver will have a preference as to which way the elbow will bend.

2. Select the parent joint and choose Skeleton | Set Preferred Angle. This will let the IK solver know that the small angle at the elbow joint has preference for animation so that the elbow will not bend backward.

3. Choose Skeleton | IK Handle Tool. Click the shoulder joint and then click the wrist joint. An IK chain will be created from the shoulder to the wrist.

4. After the IK chain has been created, the IK handle will be selected. Choose the Move tool and move the IK handle around. The IK solver will calculate how to rotate the shoulder and elbow joints so that the IK effectors at the wrist will try to match the position of the IK handle.

5. As you move the IK handle, you may find that you have no control over the position of the elbow. To control the elbow, choose the Show Manipulator tool from the tool box. A manipulator will appear that lets you control the pole vector. Move this manipulator to position the elbow. Figure 9-17 shows the pole vector being edited with the Show Manipulator tool.

FIGURE 9-17 *The pole vector is edited to position the elbow.*

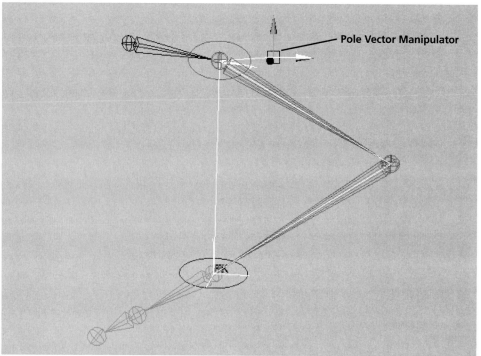

FIGURE 9-17 The pole vector is edited to position the elbow.

Tutorial: Creating IK Chains

Now we can use the IK Handle tool to set up IK chains for various parts of our skeleton. We will use the IK Handle tool to set up IK for the legs and the arms, and then introduce the IK Spline tool as a means of adding IK to the spine. To get the most functionality out of the IK chains, we will need to use quite a few control objects, which we'll deal with in Chapter 10. For now, we'll just concentrate on creating the IK.

> *NOTE* **Keep in mind that depending on what you are trying to animate, you may not need to set up all of these IK chains.**

The Legs

One of the biggest advantages of using IK is that it lets you anchor one of the limbs in place while the body moves. This is especially helpful for the legs during a walk cycle. Let's examine the actions of a foot during a walk cycle. As a character walks, the supporting foot on the ground needs to stay put, while the opposite traveling foot lifts into the air and the rest of the body moves forward. However, not just the supporting foot is on the ground. As the traveling foot lifts, the heel raises while the ball of the foot still contacts the ground. Just before the entire traveling foot leaves the ground, the ball lifts up as the foot pivots around the toe. When the traveling foot returns to the ground, the heel is planted first while the ball and toe pivot around until the foot is flat on the ground again.

From this study, we can deduce that our leg skeleton will need to have three IK chains: one will extend from the hip to the ankle (we did not draw a heel joint because the foot actually pivots around the ankle), the next from the ankle to the ball, and the third from the ball to the toe. Let's set this up for the left side of the body.

1. Load the Biped_02.ma file from the CD or use the skeleton that you created earlier in this chapter.

2. Before adding any IK, double check to make sure that all of the joint rotations are set at 0,0,0.

3. Select the pelvis joint and choose Skeleton | Set Preferred Angle. This will set the preferred angle for all of the joints in the skeleton.

4. Choose Skeleton | IK Handle Tool ❑. Reset the settings to their defaults.

5. In the view window, click the LT_Hip joint and then click the LT_Ankle joint. An IK chain will be created from the left hip to the left ankle. In the Outliner, name the new IK handle **LT_AnkleIK**.

6. Choose Skeleton | IK Handle Tool, or press the Y key, to select the last used tool. Click the LT_Ankle joint and then the LT_Ball joint. In the Outliner, rename this IK handle **LT_BallIK**.

7. Press the Y key again, click the LT_Ball joint, and then click the LT_Toe joint. In the Outliner, rename this IK handle **LT_ToeIK**. Figure 9-18 shows the left leg with all three IK chains added and named.

8. Repeat these steps for the right leg.

The Arms

IK is helpful in the arms when the hand needs to be locked down onto something—such as a table, a railing, or a door handle—while the body moves. You could get away with using an IK chain that controls only the joints from the shoulder to the elbow, but we'd have to use FK to

FIGURE 9-18   The IK chains are added to the left leg and named.

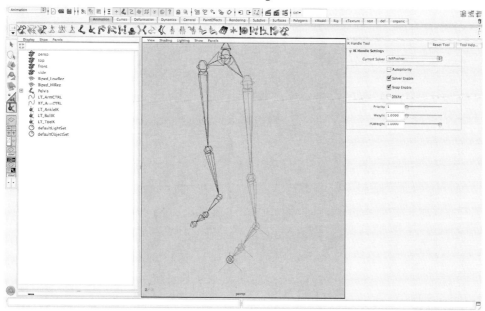

control the wrist if the hand were locked onto a table. Otherwise, the hand would go right through the table as the body moved and the joints of the arm rotated. Therefore, we need to create an IK chain that extends from the wrist to the hand (this is similar to the behavior of the foot). If you put your hand on your shoulder and move your shoulder back and forth and up and down, you'll notice a lot of movement in the collar bone. Therefore, we will also need a way to control that area. This means that we will use three IK chains for the arm.

1. Choose Skeleton | IK Handle Tool. Click the LT_Collar joint and then click the LT_Shoulder joint. In the Outliner, rename the IK handle **LT_CollarIK**.

2. Press the Y key to select the IK Handle tool again, click the LT_Shoulder joint, and then click the LT_Wrist. In the Outliner, rename this IK handle **LT_WristIK**.

3. Press the Y key to select the IK Handle tool. Click the LT_Wrist joint and then click the LT_Hand_1 joint. Rename this IK handle **LT_HandIK** in the Outliner. Figure 9-19 shows the left arm with the IK chains added and named.

4. Repeat this process for the right arm.

FIGURE 9-19   *The left arm with the IK set up and named*

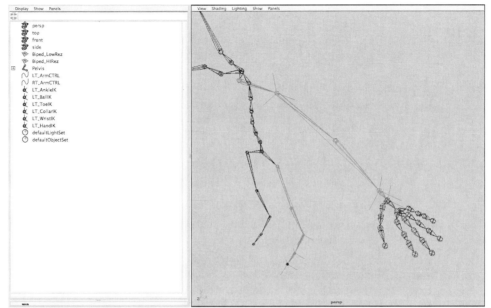

The Spine

The spine of our skeleton contains six joints plus the Torso_Root joint—seven joints all together, which is a lot of joints to control if you want the character to bend over or twist around. We could use a Set Driven Key and a control object to pose the joints of the spine as the character leans forward, backward, or side to side, or as it twists. Even though quite a few controls are included in this setup, it is impossible to key any of the joints individually if you want to pose the joints outside of what the Set Driven Key allows.

Using the IK Handle tool would make the back difficult to control, because too many joints are used. Therefore, we will use the IK Spline Handle tool, which bases the IK calculation on a NURBS curve. Instead of moving the IK handle itself, the control vertices of the curve are manipulated and the joints that the IK is controlling rotate to produce some very realistic motion.

The IK Spline Handle tool also provides some additional attributes to control the IK chain. Among them is the Twist attribute. By animating the Twist attribute, the IK chain will twist along the curve's direction based on a specified degree, linear or exponential. Let's set this up for our skeleton's spine.

1. Choose Skeleton | IK Spline Handle Tool ❑ to view the tool's options, shown in Figure 9-20.

FIGURE 9-20   IK Spline Handle tool options

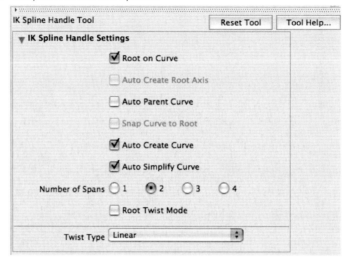

2. We want to change two options from their default settings. Uncheck the Auto Parent Curve option, which is on by default and will parent the NURBS curve to the skeleton. Since we will be setting up control objects for the IK chain later on and parent the curve to that, we don't need to parent it to the skeleton. The second option we need to edit is the Number Of Spans in the curve. You can set this based on how curvy the spine is or on how many joints are included. For a humanoid bipedal figure such as this one, using a two-span curve will give us a great amount of control over the spine of this character without getting too complicated. If you recall from the lesson on curve degree in Chapter 3, you will know that a two-span, third-degree curve will contain five CVs. By translating any of these five CVs on the resulting curve, we will easily be able to pose the spine. The options for the IK Spline Handle tool should look like those shown in Figure 9-20.

3. In the view window, click the Spine_1 joint and then click the Torso_Root joint. The IK chain will be created. In the Outliner, rename the IK handle **BackIK**. Name the curve **BackIKCurve**.

4. With the BackIKCurve selected, press the F8 key to go into component mode.

5. Choose one of the CVs on the curve and choose the Move tool. Move the CV around and notice how the joints in the spine are affected. Undo the movement so that the CV returns to its original position.

6. Select the BackIK handle and look at its attributes in the Channel Box. Find the attribute called Twist and select and highlight it.

7. MMB-drag the attribute in the view window to edit it interactively. Figure 9-21 shows the Twist attribute being tested on the spine joints of our skeleton.

You have now successfully set up all of the IK that will be needed to control the skeleton.

FIGURE 9-21 The Twist attribute is edited to test the twisting of the spine.

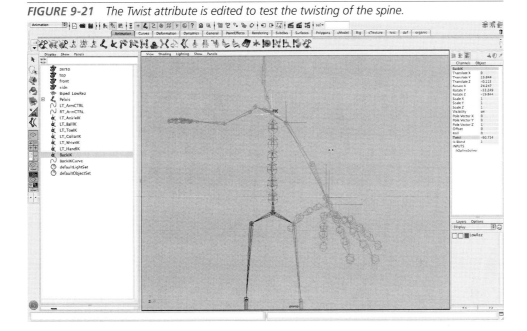

Summary

If you are really itching to start animating your character, the information covered in this chapter might be all you really need to know. However, we can take this setup further and make the rig even easier to control. In the next chapter, we will look at setting up additional controls that will minimize the amount of IK controls that we need to select and animate.

Character Setup: Character Controls

In Chapter 9, we created a skeleton.

We added Set Driven Key controls to animate

the fingers and inverse kinematics (IK) handles

to allow for control over the spine and limbs. At

this point, you *could* begin posing that skeleton

and setting keys directly on the joints, IK handles,

and Set Driven Key controls. However, deciding

what to select can be confusing, making the

FIGURE 10-1   *A completed control rig*

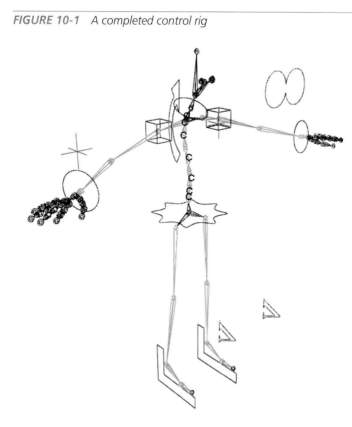

skeleton difficult to control. Instead of us deciding, we can build a rig in which the animator never has to select a joint or an IK handle—we can use a *control object* created from a NURBS curve or other piece of geometry to manipulate the joint rotations and IK handles for us. This lets us animators concentrate on animating, and not figuring out what bone or IK handle to select. Figure 10-1 shows a skeleton with a completed control rig.

This chapter will concentrate on creating controls that will operate, or *puppet,* the skeleton. In addition to the direct connections and Set Driven Key connections that were introduced in Chapter 9, here we will use constraints and demonstrate how they can aid in making connections between objects when you're building a character rig.

Constraints

Maya's constraints offer another way to connect the transform attributes of one object to the transform attributes of one or several other objects. For example, a point constraint could be used to connect the translations of one object to the other. The object that is being constrained is called the *constrained object,* while the object that it is being constrained *to* is called the *target object*.

Types of Constraints

Maya offers nine different types of constraints:

- **Point**   Causes the constrained object to follow the position of the target object(s).

- **Aim**   Orients a constrained object so that it points at the target object along a specified axis. We will use aim constraints later in this chapter to set up controls for eyeballs.

- **Orient**   Causes the constrained object to follow the rotations of the target object.

- **Scale**   Causes the constrained object to match the scale of the target object(s).

- **Parent**   Enables the constrained object to behave as if it were parented to the target object. For example, a parent constraint can be used for an animation in which a character picks up some object that then behaves as if it were a child of the hand.

- **Geometry**   Causes the constrained object to be restricted to a NURBS surface, curve, or polygonal surface.

- **Normal**   Causes the constrained object to orient itself along the surface normals of the target object. This is especially useful if you want an object to animate over a complex surface.

- **Tangent**   Causes the constrained object to orient itself to the tangent of a NURBS curve.

- **Pole vector**   Constrains the pole vector of an IK handle to a target object. By using this type of constraint, there is no need to control the pole vector of an IK handle with the Show Manipulator tool. A control object, such as a curve or surface, can be used as the target object instead.

Using Constraints

Creating constraints is a simple process; however, you must keep in mind the order in which the objects are selected. The target object is selected first, and the constrained objects are then selected. When every object has been selected, choose a constraint from the Constraint menu in the animation menu set.

The settings available for the constraints in the Options window are fairly similar for most of the constraints. The point, aim, orient, and parent constraints all have attributes called Maintain Offset, Offset, Constraint Axes, and Weight. The Orient Constraint Options window is shown in the following illustration.

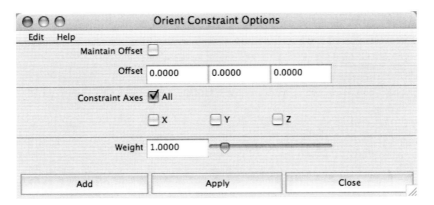

- **Maintain Offset attribute**   Preserves the original, relative value of the constrained object. For example, if an object positioned at 10,10,10 is point constrained to another object at 0,0,0 with the default settings (Maintain Offset is disabled), the constrained object will match the position of the target object once it is constrained. When the Maintain Offset attribute is enabled, the constrained object will maintain its relative distance.

- **Offset attribute**   Specifies an offset value relative to the target point. Note that the target point is the same as the object's pivot point. By default, these offset values are all set to 0.

- **Constraint Axes**   Specify which axes will be constrained. The default is set to constrain all three axes. However, an object can be constrained to just one or two axes of the target object.

- **Weight attribute**   Specifies how much the values of the constrained object are influenced by the target object. When an object is constrained only to one target, a value of *1* means that the object will follow the target constraint 100 percent. A value of *0* influence will completely disable the constraint. The Weight attribute can be edited or keyframed in the Channel Box or Attribute Editor after the constraint has been created.

An object can be constrained to more than one target. This can be done by selecting multiple target objects, then selecting the constrained object, and then choosing a constraint, or you can select the target and the constrained object and then the constraint can be repeated.

If an object was constrained to two different objects with two different positions, and both of the weight attributes are set to 1, the actual position of the constrained object will be equal to the average values of the constrained attributes.

While constraints are great tools for animation, as we will see in Chapter 12, they are also great for building control rigs. In this chapter, we will make use of the point, orient, aim, and pole vector constraints.

Building a Control Rig

The most important thing to do before rigging a character is to analyze the shots in which the character will act and figure out what it needs to do. No single character rig will work well in every situation. If a character will be acting in several shots in which its behavior is quite different, you may be better off building different rigs for the separate shots.

A recent trend in building control rigs has been to create control objects that describe their function instead of using locators. In his Siggraph master classes, Jason Schleifer demonstrated a technique called "iconic representation." Using this technique allows the animator to select a control object intuitively, because the object visually represents the function it is supposed to control. In contrast, using locators and selection handles will make it difficult for the animator to know exactly what he or she is selecting until he/she selects it and checks it. We will draw control objects using curves, use primitive shapes, and use the Text tool to create our icons.

> *NOTE* **The character rig shown in this chapter is a great setup to use for a skeleton that uses mostly IK to controls the arms, legs, and feet. Some more complicated rigs will be demonstrated later in this chapter; these allow the skeleton to switch between FK and IK. As you work through these tutorials, you should feel free to experiment with these techniques and perhaps devise your own rig. Remember that there is no right or wrong way to do this, only the way that works for the shot and for you.**

Leg Control

With the skeleton's joints drawn, placed, named, and oriented, it is time for you to create control objects for the IK handles that we created in Chapter 9. You may use the skeleton you built in Chapter 9 or use the BipedSkelComplete.ma file found on the CD.

In this example, we will create control objects for the leg. Remember that each leg should have three different IK chains: one from the hip to the ankle, one from the ankle to the ball of the foot, and a third from the ball to the toe.

So what will the control rig for the foot do? With the current setup, moving the entire foot would require that the animator select and key all three IK handles in the foot. Aside from it being a bit of a pain to see and select the IK handles, keying three different objects for one simple motion can make your animation data difficult to manage. Instead, it would be much easier to select a single object that controlled the entire foot and move or rotate that. For reasons such as this, we need to devise ways to better control our IK. This will be done by creating control objects that will in turn control the behavior of the leg.

More on Jason Schleifer

Many of the methods used here are based on the setup devised by Jason Schleifer and demonstrated during the Maya Master Classes in the summers of 2001 and 2002. These lectures are available on DVD from Alias (entitled "Integrating a Creature Rig into a Production Environment and Fast Animation Rigs") and include MEL scripts and documentation for automating many of these steps. You can download some of these scripts and other goodies from Jason's web site at *http://www.jonhandhisdog.com*. The authors wish to acknowledge and thank Jason for sharing this information.

We begin by creating a control object using the Text tool. Each IK handle will be grouped to it-self, and each group's pivot point will be snapped to match the IK handle. We'll then create a hierarchy between them so that when the parent group pivots, the children will pivot with it. This makes it possible to set up a leg that can point its toes and roll from the ball of the foot. Custom attributes will be added to the control object; these are connected to the rotation at-tributes of different group nodes. This way, all of the group nodes and IK handles in the leg can be hidden and exclusively controlled by the leg control. Finally, we'll create another control object to use as a pole vector constraint on the ankle IK. This will give the animator a visible object to choose and move to point the knee.

1. In the Side view, choose Create | EP Curve Tool ❐. In the Create Curve Options window, set the Degree to 1.

2. Draw an L-shaped curve that traces the area behind the foot. You may wish to make the geometry visible and align the curve to the base of the foot's geometry. This makes it easy to know when the foot is touching the ground, without having the geometry visible during animation.

FIGURE 10-2   *The foot control is aligned to the foot and its pivot is snapped to the LT_Ankle joint.*

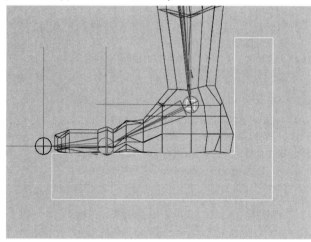

3. Hold down the V key and move/snap the pivot of the curve to the ankle joint. Now that the curve is aligned to the foot, you may have to move it along the Z axis to reposition it. Once in position, press the INSERT (HOME) key, hold down the V key, and move the pivot of the curve so that is snaps to the LT_Ankle joint (you may have to switch to the Perspective view to make sure it did not snap to the RT_Ankle joint). Press the INSERT (HOME) key again to exit pivot editing mode. The curve should look like the one shown in Figure 10-2.

4. Name the curve **LT_FootCTRL**.

5. Freeze Transforms on the LT_FootCTRL.

6. Test the LT_FootCTRL by parenting all of the IK handles to it. Then select the LT_FootCTRL and move and rotate it. The foot should move and rotate around its ankle, as shown next. Undo or zero the control back to its default position.

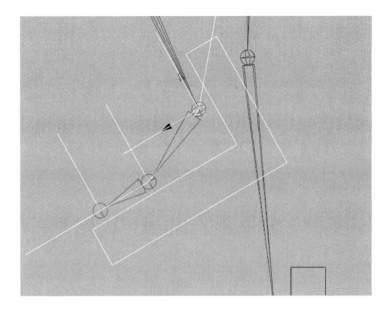

7. Create an empty group node by choosing Edit | Group, or by pressing CTRL-D (COMMAND-D). Name the group **LT_BallLift**.

8. Snap the LT_BallLift group to the LT_Ball joint.

9. Duplicate the LT_BallLift joint and rename it **LT_ToeLift**. Move/snap the LT_ToeLift group to the LT_Toe joint. You now have three transform nodes—the curve and the two group nodes.

10. Now create a hierarchy with the transform nodes and group the pivots appropriately. When the toe lifts or pivots, the entire foot should pivot around the leg. Therefore, we will make the LT_BallLift group, the LT_ToeIK, the LT_BallIK, and the LT_AnkleIK all children of the LT_ToeLift group. Select all of those objects in the Outliner, making sure that you select the LT_ToeLift last. Press the P key to parent the objects to the LT_ToeLift group.

11. When the ball of the foot rolls, as it would during a walk cycle, the toe remains planted as the ankle pivots around the ball. Therefore, if we parent the LT_BallIK and the LT_AnkleIK to the LT_BallLift group, the ankle will rotate around the ball when LT_BallLift is rotated. Since the LT_ToeIK is parented to the LT_ToeLift, the toe will remain planted as the ball of the foot rolls.

12. Now parent the LT_ToeLift to the LT_FootCTRL. The completed hierarchy is shown here.

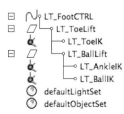

13. Now test it. If you select the LT_ToeLift group and rotate it, the entire foot will pivot around the toe. If you select the LT_BallLift and rotate it, the ball of the foot will roll. Meanwhile, these are all parented under the LT_FootCTRL to move the overall foot. Great!

NOTE *If the toe is not staying planted, make sure that the Enable IKFK Control option is disabled. Choose Skeleton | Enable IKFK Control to disable this. When disabled, no checkmark appears in front of the option in the Skeleton menu.*

One problem is that we still have too many objects to select to animate the foot. Therefore, we will create custom attributes on the LT_FootCTRL to pivot all of the transform nodes in all of the directions we need.

1. Select the LT_FootCTRL object and choose Modify | Add Attribute. In the Attribute Name field, type **ToeRoll**. Set the Data Type to Float and leave the Minimum and Maximum fields blank. Because we will be making direct connections, there's no reason to limit ourselves. The Add Attribute window should look like the illustration shown here. Click the Add button to add the attribute. Verify that the attribute has been added by looking in the Channel Box.

2. Repeat step 1 to add three more attributes: name them **ToeTwist**, **BallRoll**, and **FootLean**.

3. Now we will use the Connection Editor to hook up these attributes to the appropriate transform attributes of the LT_BallLift and LT_ToeLift nodes. Open the Connection Editor (choose Window | General Editors | Connection Editor). Choose the LT_FootCTRL and click the Reload Left button. Select the LT_ToeLift node and click the Reload Right button.

4. On the left, click the Toe Roll attribute. Connect this to the Rotate X attribute of the LT_ToeLift node on the right by clicking this attribute in the list on the right. (Remember that when the attribute names in the list are highlighted, it means that they are connected.) Connect the Toe Twist attribute to the Rotate Y attribute. Figure 10-3 shows the Connection Editor displaying the connections between the attributes of the LT_FootCTRL and the LT_ToeLift nodes.

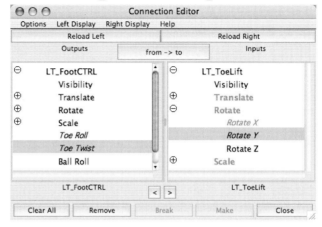

FIGURE 10-3   Connection Editor connections between the attributes of the LT_FootCTRL and the LT_ToeLift nodes

5. Select the LT_BallLift node and click the Reload Right button in the Connection Editor. Connect the Ball Roll attribute to the Rotate X attribute of the LT_BallLift node. Connect the Foot Lean attribute to the Rotate Z attribute. Figure 10-4 shows the Connection Editor once these connections have been made.

6. Test these connections by changing the values of these custom attributes on the LT_FootCTRL. For example, entering a value of **40** for the Ball Roll attribute will rotate the LT_BallLift node 40 degrees.

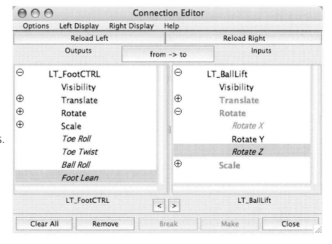

FIGURE 10-4   Connection Editor connections between the attributes of the LT_FootCTRL and the LT_BallLift nodes

7. At this point, we no longer need to have any of the group nodes or IK handles visible, since they are all controlled by the Foot control. Select the LT_ToeLift node and press CTRL-H (CONTROL-H) to hide all of the IK handles and transform nodes. Now you have a nice, clean leg to animate.

8. We're almost finished with the leg. The last thing we need is a control object to use as a pole vector constraint. Instead of drawing a curve, we will use the Text tool to create the control object. Choose Create | Text Tool ☐ and type in the letter **V**. Click the Create button to create the text as a NURBS curve.

9. Once the curve is created, you will notice that it is parented to a few extra group nodes. Ungroup it by selecting the curve and pressing SHIFT-P.

10. Name the curve **LT_KneeCTRL**.

11. Choose Modify | Center Pivot. Rotate the curve and snap it to the knee so that it is aligned. Then move it out so that it is placed in front of the knee. Name it **LT_KneeCTRL**. It is a good idea to freeze the transforms of the LT_KneeCTRL at this time. Figure 10-5 shows the knee control in place.

FIGURE 10-5 *The LT_KneeCTRL is created and placed in front of the knee.*

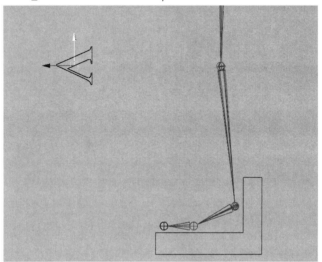

12. In the Outliner, select the LT_KneeCTRL and then select LT_AnkleIK. CTRL-click (COMMAND-click) to select these multiple objects. Choose Constrain | Pole Vector. Now the LT_KneeCTRL can be used to control the Pole Vector attributes on the LT_AnkleIK node.

13. Parent the LT_KneeCTRL to the LT_FootCTRL.

14. Test the LT_KneeCTRL by moving it around. You should also select the LT_FootCTRL object and move that around to make sure that the knee control does not go behind the knee, causing the leg to flip. If this is the case, move the knee control further in front of the knee.

15. At this time, the controls for the left leg are complete. You will now need to repeat this entire process for the right leg. One shortcut to use would be to duplicate the LT_FootCTRL. Not only does it save you from having to redraw it, but the custom attributes we created will also be duplicated.

Arm Control

The control rig for the arm is similar to that of the leg. In Chapter 9, we added three IK handles to each arm: one for the collar bone, one for the wrist, and one for the hand. With the arm, however, we are going to use three control objects: one will control the collarbone, the other will control the pole vector of the wrist IK to control the elbow, and the third will control the movement of the arm and the orientation of the wrist. This third control is the *arm control* we created back in Chapter 9. This is the NURBS circle that was used to add all of the custom attributes to control the fingers. We will also use it to control the arm and wrist.

When we created the arm controls in Chapter 9, we noted that the circles should be created with their normal axis pointing along the Y axis. This is so that the orientation of the circle will match the orientation of the joints. The reason for this is about to become obvious.

1. To orient the LT_ArmCTRL to the LT_Wrist joint, select the LT_ArmCTRL, and snap it to the LT_Wrist joint. Parent the circle to this joint and then zero out its rotations in the Channel Box.

2. Now unparent the LT_ArmCTRL from the LT_Wrist joint by selecting the LT_ArmCTRL and pressing SHIFT-P. The circle is now perfectly oriented with the wrist joint. Figure 10-6 shows the LT_ArmCTRL once it has been oriented to match the LT_Wrist joint.

FIGURE 10-6   *The LT_ArmCTRL once it has been oriented to match the LT_Wrist joint*

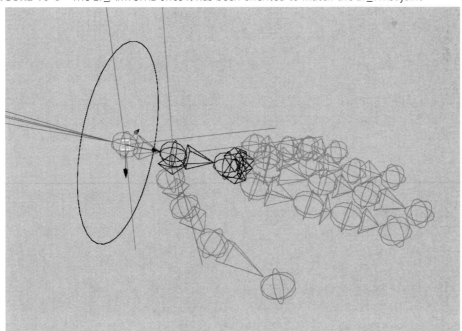

3. Parent the LT_HandIK handle to the LT_ArmCTRL.

4. Select the LT_ArmCTRL and then select the LT_WristIK. Choose Constrain | Orient. Then choose Constrain | Point. The LT_WristIK will now orient itself to the control object.

5. Test the LT_ArmCTRL. Since the wrist IK handle is constrained to it, the control object will now act as the goal for the IK solver. When the control is rotated, the wrist rotates with it. Another great thing about this setup is that when the wrist is locked down onto an object such as a table or railing, the hand will remain oriented as the body moves. Otherwise, you would have to counter-animate the hand so that it does not go through the table or railing.

6. To control the pole vector attributes of the wrist IK, we will create a locator and use it as a pole vector constraint (I know I said we would not use locators, but if we use them only for the arm's pole vector, it's OK). Choose Create | Locator.

7. Place the locator behind the LT_Elbow joint and choose Modify | Freeze Transformations.

8. Name the locator **LT_ElbowCTRL**.

9. Select LT_ElbowCTRL and then select LT_WristIK and choose Constrain | Pole Vector. Figure 10-7 shows the locator placed and used as a pole vector constraint.

FIGURE 10-7   A locator is placed and used as a pole vector constraint to control the elbow.

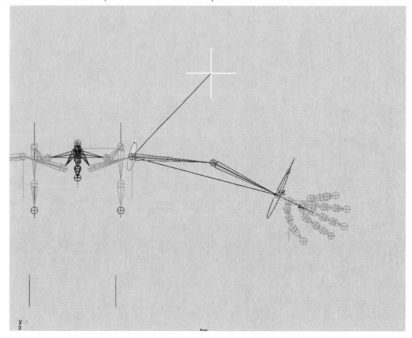

10. Now for the collar bone. The setup we will use lets the animator select a control object and move it to point the collar bone. Although much more advanced setups are possible, this one provides a good amount of control and is simple to set up. We will use a polygonal cube for the collar bone control. Choose Create | Polygonal Primitive | Cube. Name this object **LT_CollarCTRL**.

11. Move and snap the cube to the LT_Shoulder joint and freeze transformations.

12. With the LT_CollarCTRL still selected, select the LT_CollarIK handle and choose Constraint | Point.

13. Group the LT_CollarCTRL to itself (CTRL-G [COMMAND-G]) and name the group **LT_CollarCTRL_GRP**. Parent this group to the Torso_Root joint.

14. Choose Create | Null. This will create an empty group node. Name this group **LT_CollarCONST**.

15. Move and snap LT_CollarCONST to the shoulder joint.

16. With LT_CollarCONST still selected, select the LT_CollarIK handle and choose Constrain | Pole Vector. This will keep the arm from flipping when the body is turned. The complete arm setup is shown in Figure 10-8.

FIGURE 10-8 *The completed arm rig*

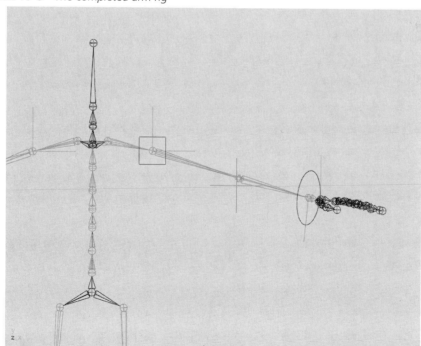

Back Control

Setting up the back is a little different from setting up the arms and legs. For the most part, this is because we used the IK Spline tool to create the IK for the back in Chapter 9. This type of IK system is based on a NURBS curve that is used to calculate the IK. The problem is that to modify the curve, you need to go into component mode and choose CVs on the curve every time you want the spine to bend a certain way. Often, you need to choose more than one CV to get the desired motion. Therefore, the back is in desperate need of a control rig that will simplify the animation.

We will begin by creating clusters for each CV in the BackIKCurve that was created when the IK Spline handle was added. These clusters will then be grouped to control objects for the upper and lower back.

1. In the view window, use the Show menu to hide joints and IK handles so that you can see the BackIKCurve curve easier.

2. Go into component mode and choose CVs. Choose Deform | Create Cluster ❑. In the Options window, make sure the Relative attribute is unchecked. This will keep us from getting any double transformations later on. Select the top CV and click Create in the Cluster Options window. Repeat this for all of the CVs. You will end up with seven different clusters.

3. Now for the control objects. We need to create one for the lower back, which will also control the hips. Then we need to create another that can control the upper back. For the hip control, create a NURBS circle. I scaled some of the CVs down to give the control a unique, identifiable look, as shown next.

4. Snap this circle to the pelvis joint. Parent the bottom two clusters to this circle. Name the circle **HipCTRL**.

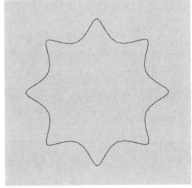

5. Point and orient constrain the pelvis joint to the HipCTRL. As long as your pelvis joint is oriented to the world— that is, the joint's local rotation axis matches the orientation of your Maya scene—there won't be any change in the rotations of the pelvis joint.

6. Create another control object for the upper back. (As shown in Figure 10-9, a Webdings font was used in the Text tool to create the circular arrows.) Place this curve in Side view and snap its pivot point to the Spine_3 joint.

7. Name this curve **UpperBackCTRL**.

8. Parent the first two clusters to the UpperBackCTRL. Now when you rotate the UpperBackCTRL, the spine will bend around the Spine_3 joint. Figure 10-9 shows the back being rotated with the UpperBackCTRL.

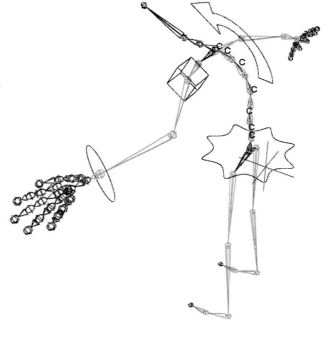

FIGURE 10-9 *The UpperBackCTRL is used to bend the upper part of the spine.*

9. We need the UpperBackCTRL to move with the HipCTRL, but we don't want it to rotate. Therefore, we will point constrain the UpperBackCTRL to the HipCTRL. To avoid the UpperBackCTRL snapping to the HipCTRL, we will first group the UpperBackCTRL to itself; then we'll modify the pivot point to match the HipCTRL and then point constrain this group to the HipCTRL. Select the UpperBackCTRL and press CTRL-G (COMMAND-G). This groups the UpperBackCTRL to a new group node.

10. Name this group **UpperBackCTRL_GRP**. Move and snap the pivot of this group to the pelvis joint.

11. Now select the HipCTRL, and then select the UpperBackCTRL_GRP and choose Constrain | Point.

12. The remaining cluster in the middle of the backIK curve will be set up to be always positioned between the UpperBackCTRL and the HipCTRL. We can do this by point constraining it to both controls. Select the UpperBackCTRL, the HipCTRL, and then the middle cluster.

13. Choose Constrain | Point □ to open the Options window. Click the Maintain Offset check box so that the cluster will maintain its current offset between the two control objects. Click the Apply button. The back controls are now complete.

Clean Up

If you look in the Outliner now, you will see that we've made quite a mess! While every object is easily identifiable by name, we still have a lot to look through if we are looking for something in particular. Also, in a production environment, it is quite possible that this character will be imported into a scene with other characters. Therefore, it is best to organize this character and all of its controls at this point.

We will create a master group that will contain the skeleton, controls, and miscellaneous IK handles. The skeleton is pretty straightforward and is already organized in its own hierarchy. The Controls group will contain all of the control objects that are outside of the skeleton hierarchy—this includes objects such as the foot and arm controls. A final category of objects is a miscellaneous category, which will contain objects such as the IK handles that are constrained to and being controlled by other objects. We will never need to choose these objects—in fact, if we built our rig correctly, we shouldn't ever choose any of these objects, because they are all constrained to various control objects. Therefore, we will place these objects in a group called Untouchables.

1. Select the pelvis joint and group it to itself (CTRL-G [COMMAND-G]). Name this group after your character. In this case, name the character and group **Biped**.

2. Move and snap the pivot of the Biped group to the pelvis.

3. Choose Create | Empty Group. Name this group **Controls** and move and snap it to the pelvis.

4. Parent the Controls group to the Biped group.

5. In the Outliner, hold down the CTRL (COMMAND) key and choose the LT_FootCTRL, RT_FootCTRL, LT_ArmCTRL, RT_ArmCTRL, LT_ElbowCTRL, RT_ElbowCTRL, UpperBackCTRL_GRP, and HipCTRL; then select the new Controls group. Press the P key to parent these objects to the Controls group.

6. Create one more empty group and name it **Untouchables**. Parent the LT_CollarIK, RT_CollarIK, LT_WristIK, RT_WristIK, BackIK, and BackIKCurve to the Untouchables group.

7. Select the Untouchables group and hide it by choosing Display | Hide | Hide Selection.

Rig the Eyes

If you've made it this far, rigging the eyes will be easy. To rig the eyes, we will first create a joint that will snap to each eye. These joints will then be parented to the head joint. The eyes will be point constrained to the joints. To orient the eyes, a target object will be created and used as an aim constraint.

1. Turn on the visibility for the layer named Eyes.

2. To create a joint that snaps to the pivot of the eyes, we need to give the Joint tool something to snap to. Select both eyes and choose Display | Component Display | Rotate Pivots. A little dot will appear at the center of each eye.

3. Choose Skeleton | Joint Tool. Hold down the v key to enable point snapping and then click the dot at the center of the nLeftEye object. Press ENTER (RETURN) to complete the skeleton. Figure 10-10 shows the joint after being placed at the left eye.

FIGURE 10-10 *A joint is placed at the pivot point of the left eye.*

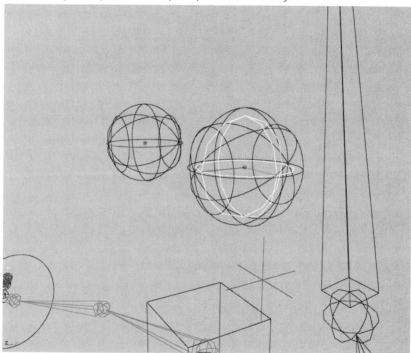

4. Name the new joint **LT_Eye**.

5. Repeat this process for the right eye.

6. Parent the two eye joints to the Head1 joint by selecting the eye joints and then the Head1 joint and pressing the P key.

7. Select the LT_Eye joint and then select the nLeftEye geometry. Choose Constrain | Point. Repeat this step for the right eye.

8. Choose Create | Locator and name the new locator **LT_EyeCONST**. Move and snap the locator to the LT_Eye joint. Move it out along the Z axis so that it sits in front of the eye.

9. With the locator still selected, select nLeftEye and choose Constrain | Aim. The nLeftEye object will now point at the LT_EyeCONST object along its X axis. However, in this example, the eye should be aiming along its Y axis. To fix this, we will have to edit the aim constraint's attributes.

10. Select the nLeftEye object and open the Attribute Editor. Find the folder in the Attribute Editor called Aim Constraint Attributes. Inside that folder, you should see an attribute called Aim Vector. Currently, it has a value of 1 for the X and 0 for the Y and Z. Change this so that the X is **0** and the Y is **1**. The nLeftEye will now aim toward the LT_EyeCONST.

11. Test the constraint by moving around the LT_EyeCONST. Repeat this process for the right eye.

12. Now create a control object. A number 8 turned on its side looks a lot like a pair of glasses. Use the Text tool to create a curve for the number 8. Orient it so that it is in front of the eyes. Name this **EyeCTRL**.

13. Parent both locators to the EyeCTRL. You may now hide both locators. When the EyeCTRL is moved, both eyes will orient themselves to point at it.

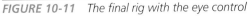

FIGURE 10-11   The final rig with the eye control

14. Finally, parent the EyeCTRL to the Controls group. Figure 10-11 shows the EyeCTRL in the final rig.

At this point, a control object is available to control each joint or IK handle. You no longer have to select a joint or multiple IK handles to animate the character. You may find that this is a bit too much for your shot, or perhaps it is not quite enough. Regardless, you can use these same techniques to simplify or refine your rig.

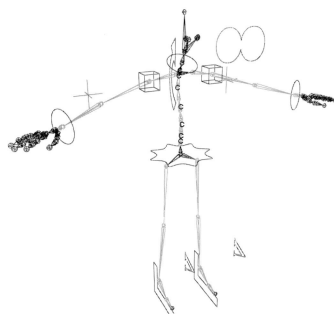

Switching Between IK and FK

It's often necessary to switch between IK and FK, especially in the arm's motion, so the best possible animation method is utilized for the animation.

FK is great for rotationally-based animation, such as a waving or swinging arm. It takes much less keyframing to create smooth-swinging animation of arms than does IK. IK is a must for goal-oriented movement of the joint. For example, if the character has to push the box using all its body movement, using FK for this animation requires rotating and keyframing the arm at almost every frame to try to keep the end of the arm planted on the box. It's almost impossible to do.

In some cases, the character must switch between these two types of behaviors over the course of one shot. In other situations, an animator may have a preference or want to experiment with both FK and IK. When necessary, you may need to build a rig that can do both. ·

Maya 6 provides a method for blending between FK and IK during animation. You can find several commands in the Animate | FK/IK Keys menu for enabling and disabling IK and setting keys on the IK handles and joints that are being animated. A nice feature of using this built-in system is that the animation curves for the FK/IK skeleton will appear dotted or solid in the Graph Editor depending on whether or not the IK is enabled. This makes it easy for the animator to know exactly where and when a selected joint is under the control of IK.

However, the system has some shortcomings when the IK handle is constrained to a control object. While a command called Move IK To FK (Animate | FK/IK Keys | Move IK To FK) will move an IK handle to its effector in the FK skeleton, the constraining control object will not be moved. Animating with this system then causes "popping" as the switch is made from FK to IK.

Traditionally, character riggers have relied on a custom three-skeleton system: one skeleton for IK, a second one for FK, and a third one for skinning. The skinning skeleton is orient-constrained to the other two skeletons and custom attributes use Set Driven Keys to blend between the weights on the constraints. Further controls can be set up to move the IK control objects to the FK rig, and vice versa, through the use of some simple MEL scripting.

The following tutorial describes how to set up an FK/IK arm using a three-skeleton system. After that, a short tutorial shows you how to animate using Maya's built-in FK/IK system. While you may decide that you like one method better than another, it is important that you know both so that your character rigs will remain as flexible as possible.

Tutorial: Creating an IK/FK Setup for the Skeletons

We will draw three skeletons and place each on its own layer, named appropriately.

1. Create the FK skeleton. Name the joints with an *FK* suffix (LT_Shoulder_FK, LT_Elbow_FK, LT_Wrist_FK).

2. Orient the joints using the Skeleton | Orient Joint command and set the Y axis to point down the bone. (See Chapter 9 for more information on joint orientation.)

3. In the Layer Editor, create a new layer and add the joints to this layer. Name the layer **FKArm**. Figure 10-12 shows the FK skeleton in the view window.

FIGURE 10-12   *The FK skeleton is created.*

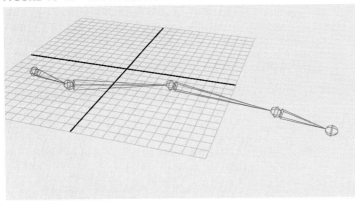

4. Duplicate the joints and name them with a *Bind* suffix (LT_Shoulder_Bind, LT_Shoulder_ Elbow_Bind, LT_Wrist_Bind).

5. Hide the FKArm layer by toggling off the visibility in the Layer Editor. Since this bind skeleton will be the one that you would use to bind, or skin the geometry to (we'll get there in Chapter 11), you may wish to add joints between the shoulder and elbow, and elbow and wrist. This will allow for a smoother deformation when the arm twists, because the twist can be distributed between multiple joints instead of just one. By unparenting joints, duplicating them, and then translating them along their aimed/oriented axis (the Y axis, in this case), these additional skinning joints are positioned exactly in between the existing ones. Figure 10-13 shows the skinning skeleton with two extra joints, the LT_bicept_Bind and the LT_forarm_Bind in the view window, and the binding skeleton and the joint hierarchy of the two skeletons is shown in the Outliner.

FIGURE 10-13   *The Maya interface showing the bind skeleton with extra joints*

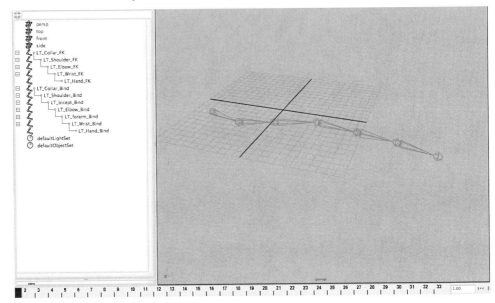

6. Now duplicate the FK skeleton from the shoulder down. Suffix the names with *IK*. You can actually unparent the LT_Shoulder_FK and LT_Shoulder_IK from the LT_Collar_Bind since the collar joint will not be involved in the FK/IK switching.

7. Place the IK Skeleton in a new layer named **IKArm**.

The skeletons have now all been created. It is time to set up the constraints.

Constrain the Bind Skeleton

Here we will orient-constrain the bind skeleton to the FK and IK skeletons.

1. To make things easier to see as we work, move the IK and FK shoulder joints up so that all three skeletons are visible. (Make sure all three layers are turned on.)

2. Orient-constrain the LT_Shoulder_Bind to the other two shoulder joints by selecting the LT_Shoulder_FK, the LT_Shoulder_IK, and then the LT_Shoulder_Bind, in that order. Choose Constrain | Orient.

3. Repeat step 2 for the elbow and wrist joints.

4. You can now move the IK and FK shoulder joints back down and snap them to the LT_Shoulder_Bind so that all of the joints are overlapping. You may also parent the shoulders to the LT_Collar_Bind. Figure 10-14 shows the joint hierarchy in the Outliner so far.

FIGURE 10-14 *The Outliner showing the joint hierarchy and constraint nodes.*

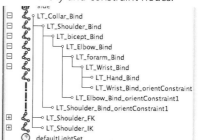

Set Up the IK

1. Use the IK Handle tool to add an IK handle from the LT_Shoulder_IK joint to the LT_Wrist_IK joint and then another IK handle from the LT_Wrist_IK to the LT_Hand_IK joint. Name these **LT_WristIK** and **LT_HandIK**.

2. Use the procedure shown in the "Arm Control" section earlier in this chapter to add a control object for this arm and name it **LT_WristCTRL**.

3. Don't forget to create a control to be used as a pole vector constraint. Again, use the procedure described in the "Arm Control" section for more information on how this is set up. Name the pole vector constraint **LT_ElbowCTRL**.

4. In addition to the pole vector constraint for the LT_WristIK, create a null (an empty group), by choosing Edit | Group, and name it **FKPole**.

5. Point-constrain the FKPole to the LT_Elbow_FK joint. We will use this null object as a target to move the elbow control to later on.

6. Add the LT_WristCTRL to the IKArm layer. Your scene should resemble Figure 10-15.

FIGURE 10-15 *The IK arm is set up with appropriate controls*

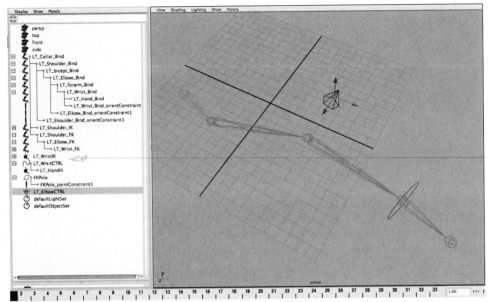

Make a Switch Control

Here we will create a control object that has an FK/IK switch attribute on it. At a value of 0, FK will be active. At a value of 1, IK will have control.

1. Make a new control object. Name it **FK_IKCTRL**.

2. Add an Attribute named **LT_Arm_FKIKSwitch**.

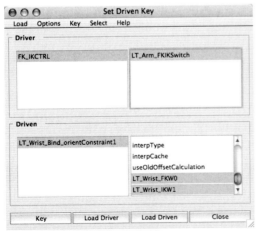

3. Use the Channel Control (Window | General Editors | Channel Control) to make all of the transform attributes on the FK_IKCTRL non-keyable.

4. In the Set Driven Key window, load this object and attribute as the driver.

5. Select LT_Wrist_Bind_orientConstraint1 and load it as the driven node. Select LT_Wrist_FKW0 and LT_Wrist_FKW1 as the driven attributes, as shown in the illustration.

6. In the Channel Box, set the LT_Wrist_FKW0 attribute to **1** and the LT_Wrist_FKW1 to **0**. Click the Key button in the Set Driven Key window.

7. Now set the LT_Arm_FKIKSwitch attribute to **1**, and then set the LT_Wrist_FKW0 attribute to **0** and the LT_Wrist_FKW1 to **1**. Click the Key button in the Set Driven Key window.

8. Repeat steps 6 and 7 for the elbow and shoulder constraints.

9. Finally, test it! When the LT_Arm_FKIKSwitch attribute is set to **0**, the bind skeleton should follow the FK skeleton. When it is set to **1**, the bind skeleton should follow the IK skeleton.

10. Use the Hypergraph to select the FK and IKArm layer nodes so that you can load their attributes into the Set Driven Key window and key their visibility to correspond to the correct mode.

Move IK to FK

Now everything should be switching fine. A problem that can arise when animating, however, is that when switching from one mode to the other, the different skeletons will be in different places. This can create jumps, or "swimming," of the joints during the transition. A good way to fix this is to move the IK to the FK skeleton after switching and then begin animating from that point.

To run through this manually, you would want to copy the position and rotation of the FK wrist joint and paste them into the *t* and *r* attributes of the LT_WristCTRL. In addition, you would also want the LT_ElbowCTRL to go to the position of the elbow. In this case, we created a null called FKPole that will be used as the target to match the ElbowCTRL.

However, doing this manually can be slow, annoying, and prone to error. The best solution would be to use MEL scripting to create a button that can move the FK skeleton to match the IK skeleton and another button that would move the IK skeleton to the FK skeleton. To do this, you must first understand some of the fundamental concepts behind scripting in MEL. We have included some information on writing MEL, as well as a tutorial and sample MEL scripts that will solve the problem of moving an IK skeleton to an FK skeleton, in the appendix of this book.

Tutorial: IK/FK Blending

IK/FK Blending is a built-in function in Maya for switching between IK and FK. Unlike the previous tutorial that utilizes constraints to switch between IK and FK, IK/FK Blending uses a built-in attribute called IK Blend, which is just like a switch: it can turn on and off IK solver and create a smooth transition between them. This simple tutorial will cover how to keyframe using IK Blend. Let's create a pushing box animation using IK Blend. The arm swinging toward the box is animated by FK, and the pushing box movement is animated with IK.

1. In the Front view, create a polygon cube and create three joints for the arm. Name each joint: shoulder, elbow, and wrist. Choose the IK Handle tool (Skeleton | IK Handle

Tool) and create an IK chain from shoulder to wrist. You can also open a scene called IkBlendStart.mb from the CD and work with it here.

2. Let's begin with the FK animation to create the swinging motion of the arm. If you take a look at ikHandle1's IK Blend attribute, you'll see it has a value of 1 right now. For FK animation, this should be set to 0. Simply type **0** in the IK Blend attribute's box in the Channel Box. Press the s key to keyframe all of the animatable attributes on the IK handle. This arm can now be animated using FK.

3. Select the shoulder joint and rotate it back at frame 0. Press SHIFT-E to keyframe the rotation. Move the Time Slider to 30 and rotate the shoulder forward to just before it touches the box. Key it again.

4. Go to frame 1, select the elbow, and rotate it so the arm will be bent and in position to push the box from the front, as shown in the illustration.

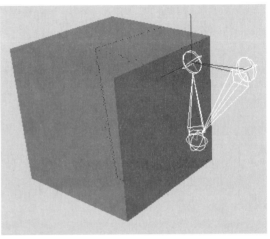

5. At frame 30, key the IK Blend attribute again at a value of 0. Go to frame 60 and change the IK Blend attribute to 1, and move the ikHandle1 against the box.

6. Press the s key to keyframe. This will turn on the IK fully at frame 60, and it blends the IK and FK motion between frames 30 and 60. Maya gives you visual feedback by displaying three skeletons—one labeled *FK*, the other *IK*, and the third showing the actual blended version.

7. Now it's time to key ikHandle1 for IK animation. Go to frame 80 and press the s key again, preventing the arm from moving for 20 frames. Go to frame 100 and extend the arm so that it begins the motion of pushing the box. Press the s key.

8. Now animate the box from frames 80 to 100, so it matches with the movement of the arm. You can open the IkBlendFinish.mb file from the CD to see the resulting movement.

Summary

This chapter has demonstrated various techniques for character rigging a skeleton for different types of animation. Although every techniques has its advantages and disadvantages, there is no right or wrong way to rig. It is up to you as the character rigger to decide what is best. In the next chapter, you'll explore various ways to skin a character so it is ready for animation.

Character Setup: Binding Skin

Now that we have created a skeleton

that is easy to control, the next step is to make

that skeleton control the geometry. This is done

through a process known as *skinning*. Skinning

assigns how the vertices of the geometry (or lattice)

are influenced, or weighted, to a joint. Skinning,

or *binding skin*, is the process of assigning how

the vertices (control vertices, polygonal vertices,

lattice points, and so on) are influenced by the

position of a joint. Figure 11-1 shows a character

that has been bound to a skeleton, which is then

posed by moving the control rig. This chapter will explore various ways to skin the character so it is ready for animation.

When talking about vertices that have been bound to a skeleton, we refer to them as *skin points*. The influences of the skin points to the joints are called *weights*. A vertex with a weight of 1 toward a joint will be 100 percent influenced by the joint when it is transformed. A value of 0.5 would mean that the vertex is 50 percent influenced by transformation of that joint. While Maya offers two different options, Smooth Bind and Rigid Bind, for determining how the skinning is calculated; these options can be used in combination with deformers to ease the process of skinning complex geometry. Let's explore these two methods of binding skin and walk through some simple examples of setting them up.

FIGURE 11-1   *Binding skin*

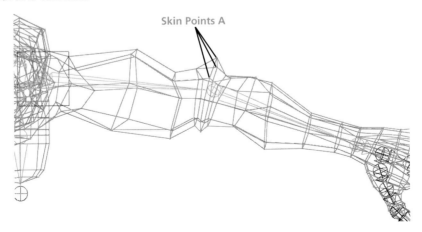

Smooth Bind

You access smooth binding by choosing Skin | Bind Skin | Smooth Bind in the Animation menu set. Smooth binding is the preferred method of achieving realistic deformation of the geometry. Smooth Bind allows for each skin point to be influenced by multiple joints. For example, examine the elbow region shown in Figure 11-2.

FIGURE 11-2   *The elbow region of the arm that will be deformed by the skeleton using the Smooth Bind command*

Skin Points A

Skin points A is a group of three skin points that align with the elbow joint. We need to figure out how those skin points should be weighted to the joints around them to achieve the most realistic deformation when the elbow joint is rotated. Let's think about it: if skin points A was assigned a weight value of 1 to the elbow joint, it would then rotate around the elbow joint by an influence of 100 percent, as shown in Figure 11-3.

However, such a rotation is not natural, and we really want those skin points to stay in line with the elbow joint. To achieve this, the vertices will have to share their influences between multiple joints. In this case, they will be weighted with a value of 0.5 to the elbow joint and 0.5 to the shoulder joint. This will result in a nice, even deformation, as shown in Figure 11-4.

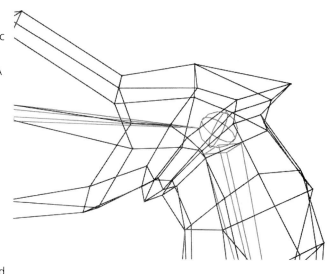

FIGURE 11-3   *Skin points A assigned a weight value of 1, rotating around the elbow joint by an influence of 100 percent*

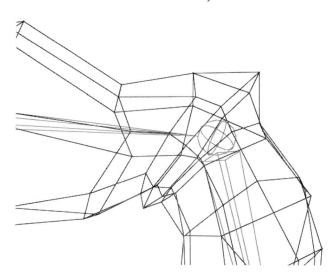

FIGURE 11-4   *An even deformation, with skin points weighted to 0.5 to the elbow and 0.5 to the shoulder joint*

In this situation, the default settings for the Smooth Bind command will assign weight values that are pretty close to 0.5 to the shoulder and 0.5 to the elbow joint. However, most of the time, weight values must be edited and adjusted manually to perfect the deformation. In regions such as the shoulders and hips, a default Smooth Bind will almost always require some more extreme adjustments to be made to the weighting. Maya offers the Paint Skin Weights tool that allows you to use Maya's brush-based Artisan interface to assign weight values quickly to skin points toward a specific joint. Figure 11-5 shows the weights in the arm being edited with the Paint Skin Weights tool.

FIGURE 11-5   *Assigning weights with the Paint Skin Weights tool*

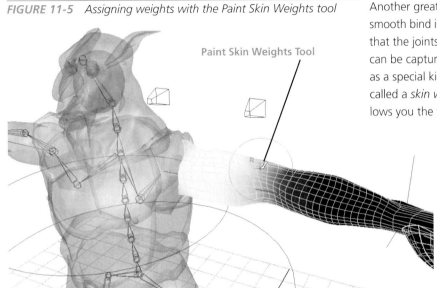

Paint Skin Weights Tool

Another great advantage to using smooth bind is that the influences that the joints have over vertices can be captured and saved out as a special kind of texture map, called a *skin weight map*. The allows you the flexibility to detach the skin, disable any influence the skeleton has over the vertices, and make changes to the geometry. When the new edits are complete, the mesh can be smooth bound again and the skin weight maps imported back onto the geometry. This way, you will never lose what could be hours' or days' worth of work just because a small change had to be made to the geometry. Using skin weight maps can also provide you with a decent starting point when weighting characters with similar skeleton structures. If you work on weighting one biped character, you can easily transfer the weights to a different biped character. This is a huge time-saver for any character-based production.

Let's walk though a short example that demonstrates how to use the Smooth Bind command and edit smooth skin weights.

Tutorial: Using Smooth Binding

We'll take a look at how smooth binding works and what options are available before you work on your character.

Scene Setup and Skinning

1. Create a NURBS cylinder by choosing Create | NURBS Primitives | Cylinder. View the attributes for the makeNurbsCylinder1 input node by clicking it in the Channel Box. Change the Spans attribute to **6** and the Height Ratio to **4**.

2. In the Front view, create three joints by choosing Skeleton | Joint Tool and clicking in the window from bottom to top, as if you were drawing the skeleton for an arm. Offset the middle joint so all the bones are not exactly in a straight line. Rename joints 1, 2, and 3 to **shoulder**, **elbow**, and **wrist**. Figure 11-6 shows how this initial setup should look.

FIGURE 11-6   *Surface and joints*

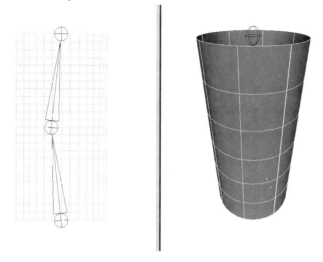

> **NOTE**   *You can select the surfaces and the joints in any order when you bind.*

3. Select the shoulder joint and SHIFT-select the NURBS cylinder. Choose Skin | Bind Skin | Smooth Bind ❐. The Smooth Bind Options window is shown here.

This window contains the following options:

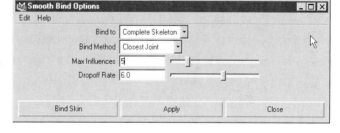

- **Bind To**   When set to Complete Skeleton, you need to choose only one joint from the skeleton hierarchy and Smooth Bind will use the entire hierarchy for smooth binding. The Selected Joints option uses only selected joints for binding. When skinning to a large skeleton, it is best to use the Selected Joints option here and manually select the joints in a skeleton to exclude the "tip" joints—the joints at the end of each branch. Since the tip joints should usually never influence any skin points, you don't need to add them as influences.

- **Bind Method**   Determines how joints influence skin points. If this is set to Closest Joint, Smooth Bind will consider the hierarchy of the joints for influence. For example, if the left ankle joint is the closest joint to skin point A, the next closest joint to influence the point would be the left heel and the ball of the left foot. Because those joints are hierarchically closest to the left ankle joint, the Closest Distance option will use the joints' distance from points for binding. In the last example, if the right foot joint is close to the left foot surface, the right ankle joint may influence skin point A.

- **Max Influences**   Controls how many joints or influence objects each skin point can use. You can change this setting by choosing Skin | Edit Smooth Skin | Set Max Influence. A value from 3 to 5 works well for this attribute in medium- to high-resolution geometry.

- **Dropoff Rate**   Determines how rapidly the influence of each joint will diminish in relation to its distance from each joint. If this is set to a high value, the influence will decrease faster than if set to a low value.

4.   For now, leave the options set at the defaults and click the Bind Skin button. The skin is bound. Select the elbow joint and rotate it to see how the NURBS cylinder deforms.

TIP   *When dealing with low rez geometry, the best results can be obtained by setting the Max Influences to 1 and then gradually adding weight to points with the Paint Skin Weights tool.*

NOTE   *When you bind the surface, the transformation attributes of the surface will be locked. You will now move, rotate, and scale the surface with the joint only. To disconnect the binding, you will need to use the Detach Skin command, which is discussed later in this chapter in the section "Detach Skin."*

Editing Skin Point Weights

The Smooth Bind method gives the skin a good crease in the elbow, even with the default binding. However, the skin around the elbow might be compressing too much when the elbow joint is rotated, as shown in Figure 11-7. You can edit skin points' weights to correct this in two ways: via the Component Editor and by using the Paint Skin Weights tool.

FIGURE 11-7   *The elbow joint is rotated and the skin is deformed.*

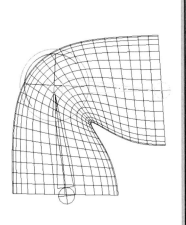
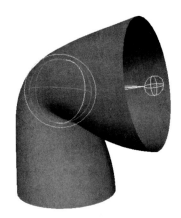

Here's how to edit the weights of the skin points using the Component Editor:

1. In the view window, select the row of CVs below the points that belong to the center of the cylinder. Open the Component Editor by choosing Window | General Editors | Component Editor.

TIP *Joints have selection priority. That is, when you drag-select over the skeleton, it is selected instead of the CVs that were intended. To fix this, disable joints from the object selection mask in the Status Line so that joints are no longer selectable in the view windows.*

2. In the Component Editor, locate and select the Smooth Skin. You will see the name of each joint along the top and the name of each selected CV at the left. These decimal numbers indicate the weight of each skin point to a joint. All the weights for each joint should add up to a total of 1. Figure 11-8 shows the Component Editor with the Smooth Skins tab loaded and displaying the weight values for the selected vertices.

3. Drag-select down the row for the elbow joint to select all of the fields in that row. One of the selected fields will prompt you to enter a number. Type **0** and press ENTER (RETURN). You'll notice that the weight from the elbow joint becomes 0 for all the selected vertices. Maya then redistributes the weighting to the other joints so that the total adds up to 1.

4. Now rotate the elbow joint and see what it does. The outer arm surface around the elbow joint doesn't compress as much and has more creases.

While the Component Editor allows you to edit weights through numerical input, you can also use the Paint Skin Weights tool.

NOTE *You must be working in shaded mode to paint skin weights.*

FIGURE 11-8 *Component Editor displaying the weights for the selected vertices*

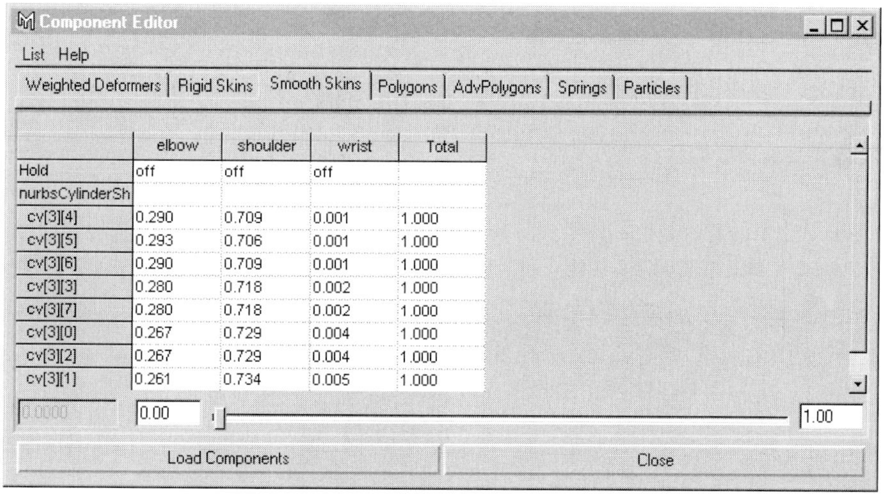

1. Select the NURBS cylinder and choose Skin | Edit Smooth Skin | Paint Skin Weights Tool
   ▢. The surface turns black and white, and the red paintbrush icon and Tool Settings
   window will appear. Figure 11-9 shows the geometry and the Paint Skin Weights tool
   settings.

2. In the Brush area of the Tool Settings window, you can change brush size, opacity, and
   brush shape just as with other Artisan tools such as the Sculpt Surface tool discussed
   in Chapter 6. The black and white colors signify weights from the joint selected in the
   Influence area's Transform list of the Tool Settings window. Currently, the shoulder joint
   is selected and the white area on the surface indicates that the weight to that joint is
   set to 1, black represents a weight value of 0, and the gray values cover all weight
   values in between. Select the elbow, and then select the wrist joint, and you will see
   the color changes on the surface.

3. Let's decrease the influence of the shoulder joint around the wrist side of the elbow by
   painting a value of 0. First, select Wrist from the Transform list in the Tool Settings window
   and click the Toggle Hold Weights On Selected button. This will hold the weight of the
   wrist joint, so that no weight is added or decreased from the wrist joint. The painting job
   will now affect only the shoulder and elbow joints.

FIGURE 11-9   *Paint Skin Weights Tool Settings window*

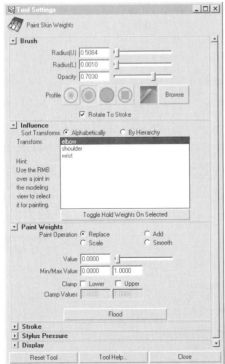

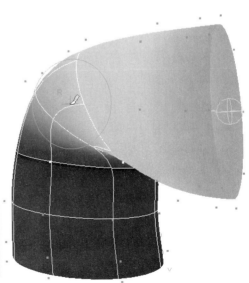

4. Select Shoulder from the Transform list, and in the Paint Weights area, change
the Paint Operation to Replace, setting the Value to **0.0000**. The Paint Operation
determines how the painting will edit weight. Choosing the Replace radio button will
completely replace the value (given that the Opacity attribute is set to 1), choosing Add
will add the value, choosing Scale will multiply the existing value by the new value, and
choosing Smooth will average weights between skin points in the painted region.

5. Paint above the center of the NURBS cylinder area. The gray area of the cylinder should
turn black, meaning that these vertices will have zero weight to the shoulder joint. Continue
painting until that center region is entirely black. Keep in mind that the brush works only
when it contacts the vertices; painting on the surface between the vertices has no effect.

6. Rotate the elbow joint to see what it does. The creasing effect should be severe now.
Figure 11-10 shows the elbow cylinder after the skin weights have been edited.

7. Next, you can remove all of the weight from the wrist joint with a simple step. Select Wrist
from the Transform list and click the Toggle Hold Weights On Selected button again. In the
Paint Weights area, make sure Paint Operation is set to Replace and the Value is set to 0, and
then click the Flood button. The Flood button will flood a value of 0 to an entire surface,
thus taking off all the weight from the surface. The cylinder should now look all black.

FIGURE 11-10   The new elbow and settings

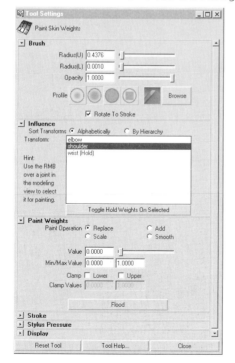
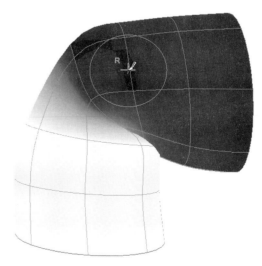

Adding an Influence Object

Editing influences of joints over skin points can get you only so far. Even after spending hours tweaking the weights in the Component Editor, the deformation can still appear "rubbery." Animating the compression and expansion of muscle and fat regions cannot be done through skin weighting alone. When this type of anatomical accuracy is required in the deformation of a character's limbs, it is necessary to use an *influence object*.

Influence objects are additional objects, other than joints, to which vertices can be weighted. Influence objects can be used to fix areas of your geometry that should lose or gain volume when deformed with the joints. Any piece of geometry can be used as an influence object. In this example, we will use a polygonal sphere to influence the elbow region of our arm. A Set Driven Key will be used to control the position of the sphere in correlation to the bending of the joint.

1. Before you add an influence object, you'll need to go back to the *bind pose,* which is the original joints' rotation when the skin was bound. Any time you add new joints to the skin or add an influence object, you'll need to revert back to the bind pose. Select the shoulder joint and choose Skin | Go To Bind Pose. This command will automatically rotate the joints back to their original states when the skin was bound.

2. Create a polygon sphere by choosing Create | Polygon Primitives | Sphere. Open the polySphere1 node in the Channel Box and change the Subdivision Axis and the Height attributes to **10**. Move and scale the sphere around the elbow bone area. Parent the sphere to the shoulder joint. Figure 11-11 shows the position of the sphere.

FIGURE 11-11   Placing a sphere to use as an influence object

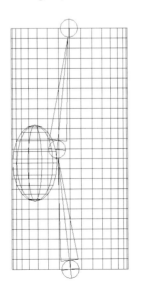
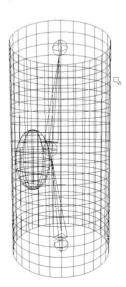

3. Select the NURBS Cylinder and SHIFT-select the polygon sphere. Unlike with the skinning process, the order of selection is very important. Choose Skin | Edit Smooth Skin | Add Influence.

4. If you try to move or scale the polygon sphere, it will change the shape of the elbow area. Select the polygon sphere and SHIFT-select the shoulder joint; press the P key to parent, so the influence object can now move with the joints. Move and scale the influence object to create the desired shape when the elbow joint is bent. Figure 11-12 shows the effect of the influence object on the arm when the elbow is bent.

5. Select the sphere and choose Animate | Set Driven Key | Set ❏ to open the Set Driven Key window. The sphere will be the driven object and the elbow joint will be the driver.

6. In the Set Driven Key window, click the Load Driven button to load the sphere as the driven object. Now select all of the transform attributes listed in the right-hand column.

7. In the view window (or in the Outliner), select the elbow joint. Click the Load Driver button in the Set Driven Key window, and then select all of the rotate attributes in the right-hand column.

8. Click the Key button in the Set Driven Key window to key the relationship between the selected attributes.

9. Rotate the elbow joint to its original rotation (0,0,0). Move the sphere around so that it is in a good position for the arm with the elbow rotated this way. In the Set Driven Key window, click the Key button to key the relationship between the selected attributes.

FIGURE 11-12   Elbow influence object

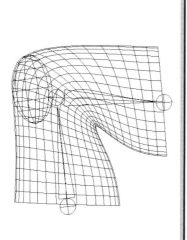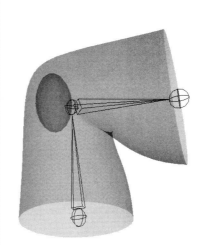

10. Finally, test the Set Driven Key. Rotate the elbow joint. As it bends, the position of the sphere should change toward that first keyed position.

You should now have an idea of what the workflow for smooth binding is like. Later in this chapter, we will apply and refine these techniques to rig an actual character.

Rigid Bind

Unlike the smooth binding technique, rigid binding (choose Skin | Bind Skin | Rigid Bind) enables only one joint to influence a skin point. This results in a harsh, stiff deformation of the surface surrounding the joints. Many real-time video games use rigid binding for its simplicity and speed, as the deformations can be calculated much faster when weights are not shared between joints.

However, when used alone, rigid binding does not produce very natural-looking deformations. Therefore, you need to use rigid binding in conjunction with deformers to obtain smooth deformations. To make the joint area's deformation smooth, you can first apply a lattice deformer to the surface and then Rigid Bind that lattice deformer with skeleton joints. While the lattice points will be rigidly deformed, the lattice's attributes can be edited to distribute the influence smoothly over the geometry. A premade lattice deformer called a *flexor* is specifically intended for this type of use. While similar to a lattice, the flexor has many built-in attributes that can control a variety of creasing effects. Figure 11-13 shows a flexor and lattice that are rigid bound to a skeleton and used to deform an arm.

FIGURE 11-13 An arm is deformed using a Rigid Bind rig.

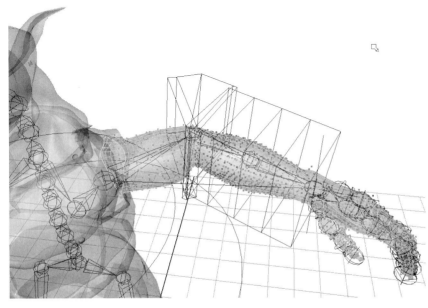

The process of skinning with deformers that are used between the skeleton and geometry is known as *indirect skinning*—that is, the skin is not directly bound to the joints. Instead, the deformer is used as an in-between object. In this section, we will practice using Rigid Bind with both direct and indirect skinning techniques. Following that, we will look at another indirect skinning technique that uses Smooth Bind with a wrap deformer to create a skinning rig that can be used on characters with heavy, complex geometry.

Tutorial: Using Rigid Bind

This tutorial illustrates how to use rigid binding for both direct and indirect skinning workflows. The options for the Rigid Bind command are discussed and the flexor deformer will be introduced.

Scene Setup and Skinning

1. Create a NURBS cylinder by choosing Create | NURBS Primitives | Cylinder. View the attributes for the makeNurbsCylinder1 input node by clicking it in the Channel Box. Change the Spans attribute to **6** and the Height Ratio to **4**.

2. In the Front view, create three joints by choosing Skeleton | Joint Tool and clicking in the window from bottom to top, as if you were drawing the skeleton for an arm. Offset the middle joint so all the bones are not exactly in a straight line. Rename joints 1, 2, and 3 to **shoulder**, **elbow**, and **wrist**.

3. Select the shoulder joint and SHIFT-select the NURBS cylinder. Choose Skin | Bind Skin | Rigid Bind ❐. The Rigid Bind Skin Options window will open.

Options for rigid binding are shown in the following illustration and are discussed next.

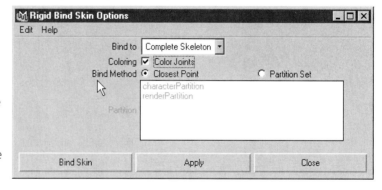

- **Bind To** The same as the Smooth Bind option of the same name. The Complete Skeleton option will allow you to bind an entire skeleton hierarchy while selecting only one of the joints from that hierarchy. The Selected Joints option binds only selected joints to the skin.

- **Coloring** Allows you to color code the joints as well as the skin points with corresponding colors. For example, if the elbow joint is red, all the points that are bound to the elbow joint will also be red. This is a useful option for quickly editing weights.

- **Bind Method** Determines how points are bound to the joints. The Closest Point option binds points to the nearest joint automatically. The Partition Set option uses premade partitions that you can create before binding. When Partition Set is active, a list of all available partitions will be included in the Partition list.

FIGURE 11-14   A stiff elbow

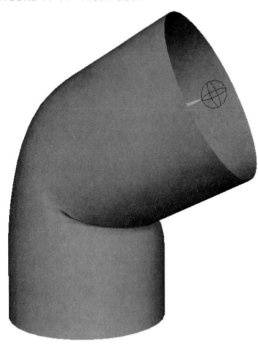

4. Set the Bind To option to Complete Skeleton, check Color Joints, and set the Bind Method to Closest Point.

5. Select the NURBS cylinder, and you now see the joints are colored individually. Rotate the elbow and you will see that deformation around the elbow is pretty stiff and collapsing on the inside of the bend. Figure 11-14 shows the result of this rigid deformation.

6. Right-click the geometry and choose CVs from the marking menu. You will see that CVs are also color coded to the corresponding joints. Select a few CVs and open the Component Editor (Window | General Editors | Component Editor). You will notice a new tab called Rigid Skins, which shows which joint is controlling the selected CVs, as shown in the illustration. The weight value for all of these CVs will be 1.000 toward a single joint, since only one joint can influence each skin point. However, this does not mean that the weight values cannot be edited. Indeed, they can.

7. In the Component Editor, choose some of the weight values for the CVs that are weighted to joint2Cluster2 (the elbow joint) and change their values to **0.5**. In the view window, select the elbow joint, rotate it, and note the behavior of the vertices that were just edited. They are now only half-way influenced by the transformation of the elbow joint. However, the remainder of their weight is not redistributed to be shared among other joints as when using Smooth Bind. Instead, the result is more straightforward. These skin points are simply affected by this one joint only by a factor of their weight. So you can see that it is possible to obtain a smooth deformation using Rigid Bind alone.

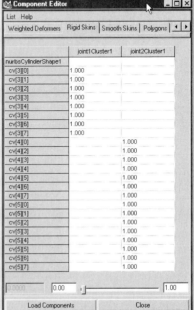

	joint1Cluster1	joint2Cluster1
nurbsCylinderShape1		
cv[3][0]	1.000	
cv[3][1]	1.000	
cv[3][2]	1.000	
cv[3][3]	1.000	
cv[3][4]	1.000	
cv[3][5]	1.000	
cv[3][6]	1.000	
cv[3][7]	1.000	
cv[4][0]		1.000
cv[4][2]		1.000
cv[4][3]		1.000
cv[4][4]		1.000
cv[4][5]		1.000
cv[4][6]		1.000
cv[4][7]		1.000
cv[5][0]		1.000
cv[5][1]		1.000
cv[5][2]		1.000
cv[5][3]		1.000
cv[5][4]		1.000
cv[5][5]		1.000
cv[5][6]		1.000
cv[5][7]		1.000

The grouping of points for the particular joint is called *set membership*. All the skin points of the rigid skinned surface should belong to at least one of the set membership. You can edit skin points' membership in two ways: by using the Edit Membership tool or the Paint Set Membership tool.

The Edit Membership tool works like this:

1. Select the tool by choosing Deform | Edit Membership Tool.

2. LMB-click the elbow joint, and all of the skin points that are members of the elbow joint become highlighted in yellow.

3. To add more skin points for this membership, you can hold down the SHIFT key and LMB-click the point. To remove the points from the membership, hold down the CTRL (CONTROL) key and LMB-click the point. This way, you can quickly add and remove skin points to any joints. Try changing membership and undo back to the original set membership.

TIP   *Removing skin points can lead to "orphaned" points (points that are not members of any joint cluster) and therefore this is better avoided. It is better to select the joint that will be added to and use the Add (SHIFT key) function to "yank" the point from the previously defined membership so points will not be left behind when the skeleton is moved.*

The Paint Set Membership tool works in a similar way, but it uses Artisan tools to edit the membership by a painting method.

1. Select the NURBS cylinder and choose Deform | Paint Set Membership Tool ❑.

2. Select a set from the Set Membership area of the Tool Settings window (Figure 11-15).

3. LMB-click or drag on the surface to add, transfer, or remove the skin points from the set membership. Try painting with these different operations and undo back to the original set membership.

Creating a Flexor

A *flexor* is a lattice-like object that enhances the deformation around a joint. Turn the page to see how it's used.

FIGURE 11-15 *Using the Paint Set Membership tool*

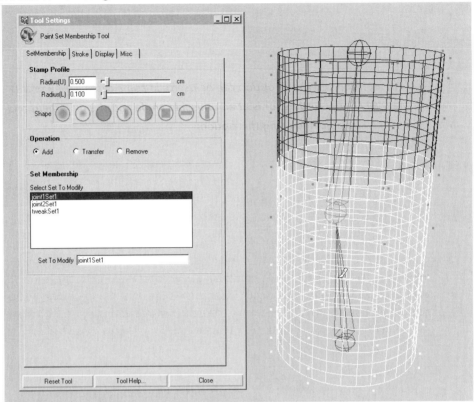

1. Making sure the elbow is in the original straight position, select the elbow joint and choose Skin | Edit Rigid Skin | Create Flexor. The Create Flexor window will open.

2. Make sure the Joints section has At Selected Joint(s) checked. This will create a flexor only at the selected joint. You can also create flexors on the entire length of bones by checking the At All Bone(s) option in the Bones section.

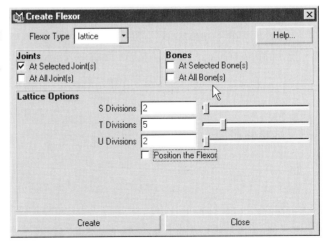

3. The Lattice Options determine the number of divisions in the flexor (see Chapter 8 for details on divisions). Let's keep these set at the default: 2, 5, 2. If Position The Flexor is checked, you can change the placement of the flexor. Leave that option unchecked. Click the Create button.

NOTE   *The Position the Flexor option can be useful in some cases. Many times the automatically generated flexor is at an unusable angle and the placement and dimensions must be adjusted using this option.*

4. The flexor appears over the elbow joint. Select the elbow joint and rotate it to bend the NURBS cylinder. You see that, currently, too much collapsing is happening around the inner side of the elbow and too much rounding/expansion happens along the outer part of the elbow joint.

5. Select the flexor you just created and look in the Channel Box. Click the jointFlexor1 node to view its attributes. To make the elbow stick out more, change the Rounding attribute to **10**. To make the inner side of the elbow not collapse on itself, change the Creasing attribute to **–5**, and then change the Length In and Out attributes to **20**. You can see how the flexor allows you to create better creasing around the joint by easy-to-use preset attributes. Figure 11-16 shows the geometry before and after the flexor attributes are edited.

FIGURE 11-16   *The geometry before (left) and after (right) editing the flexor's attributes*

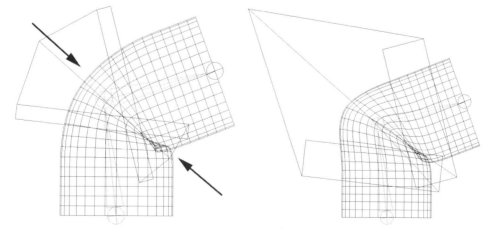

Indirect Skinning Using a Wrap Deformer

When you're dealing with a heavy, complex model, the process of skinning and editing weights can become tedious because of so many vertices to manage. Even with great tools such as the Paint Skin Weights tool, perfecting the skin weights in a character is a difficult task.

One way to simplify the skinning process is not to bind complex smoothed surfaces directly to joints. Instead, you can bind (smooth or rigid) a rough cage object to a skeleton that will in turn control a smoothed version of the geometry through the use of a wrap deformer (Deform | Create Wrap). This is similar to using the Smooth Proxy command that was covered back in Chapter 6. Because much fewer points on the rough object exist, the process of weighting skin points becomes much more manageable. You can also make the rough object visible and the smoothed object invisible while you are animating to speed up display and increase productivity. When you are finished, simply turn off the visibility of the cage object and turn on the visibility of the smoothed object. At that point, you are ready to render. Figure 11-17 shows a smooth surface with a low-polygonal model used as a wrap deformer.

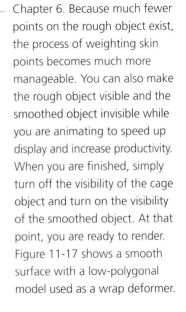

FIGURE 11-17   *A smooth surface with a low polygonal model used as a wrap deformer*

Tutorial: Using Indirect Skinning

The indirect skinning workflow is actually quite easy and gives you the best control over the surface. This simple tutorial shows you how to use it.

1. Create a polygon cylinder by choosing Create | Polygon Primitives | Cylinder.

2. In the Channel Box, select the polyCylinder1 node and change the Height attribute to 6, the Subdivision Axis attribute to **10**, the Subdivision Height attribute to **6**, and the Subdivision Caps attribute to **0**.

3. Delete the history by choosing Edit | Delete by Type | History and duplicate the cylinder.

4. Create two new layers, and put each cylinder in separate layers. Smooth the duplicate cylinder by choosing Polygon | Smooth. Delete the history again.

5. Select pCylinder2 (smooth cylinder) and then SHIFT-select pCylinder1 and choose Deform | Create Wrap. A wrap deformer is now created and applied to the smooth cylinder. When the geometry of this rough wrap deformer is edited, it will deform the smoothed version of the model.

6. Create a skeleton in the Front view window. Draw three joints from bottom to top. Select a joint and pCylinder1 and choose Skin | Bind Skin | Smooth Bind.

7. Now you can rotate the second joint (elbow joint) and you will see the smooth version is following the rough version. Because the rough version has much fewer vertices, it will be much easier to manage the weighting.

While this simple example shows how this works, it is important that you realize some of the applications for this workflow. At times, you may want your character model used in three different geometry types—polygons, NURBS, and subdivision surfaces. A low polygonal cage could be extracted from these models through the use of options available in the Modify | Convert menu and some of the polygonal editing tools. These low-resolution objects can be combined and then reapplied to the multiple surfaces that make up your model. So in this case, not only would you be dealing with a simplified version of the model that is easy to skin and fast to animate, but you are also dealing with only one geometry type for the entire model.

More Skin Commands

A couple other commands are found in the Skin menu that need to be discussed—particularly, Detach Skin and Go to Bind Pose.

Detach Skin

To disconnect, or unbind, a bound surface from a skeleton, you can use the Detach Skin command. To use this command, select the skinned surface and choose Skin | Detach Skin.

If you look at the options for this tool, you'll see two attributes: History and Coloring. If you choose Delete History for the History attribute, the Detach Skin command will disconnect the binding and delete all of the history on the geometry. The surface will snap back to its original position before it was being transformed by binding joints. Keep History is similar to the Delete History option, but it will keep skin cluster nodes in the object's history. This is particularly useful if you need to detach the skin and edit the joints, for instance, but you want to retain the existing smooth skin weights after you detach the smooth skin and bind the skin again. The Bake History option will delete all the history and keep the transformation of the object the same as when skin is detached. You can also select the surface and choose Edit | Delete By Type | History. This will have the same effect as Bake History.

Go to Bind Pose

When you want to add another joint or an influence object to the skin, your model needs to be in a *bind pose*. Bind pose is the state that the surface was in when it was skinned. It's easy to reach bind pose if no IK or other controlling objects are on joints. You can simply select the root joint and choose Skin | Go to Bind Pose. If the character setup has IK or constraints, this command will return an error. To work around this, you need to disable the IK and constraints. Choose Modify | Evaluate Nodes | Ignore All to turn off all the IK and constraints. Then select the root joint and choose Skin | Go to Bind Pose.

Tutorial: Smooth Skinning a Character

Now that you understand the basics of skinning, it is time to practice on a model. You should always do the following before you begin the skinning process:

- *Finish all the modeling.*   You can tweak the surface by moving CVs after you bind the character, but adding and deleting points will really mess up your geometry. Make sure you finish modeling before you bind.

- *Freeze transforms and delete the history.*   Strange things will start to happen if you don't begin with a clean geometry. When possible, it is always best to delete all history and freeze the transformations on the geometry. If for some reason your model has dependencies that are needed, consider deleting the history and reapplying or reconnecting the nodes that are needed.

- *Disable IK and zero out joints.*   When the IK and controls were added in Chapters 9 and 10, it is likely that some of the joints' rotations were shifted, particularly when the pole vector constraint was added. For this reason, it is best to return the skeleton to the position it was in when the joints were carefully placed and the transformations were frozen. If you were careful to do this back at that stage of the game, you can type in **0** for all of the rotation attributes for all of the joints in the skeleton (this can double for manually setting the bind pose). If the IK is currently enabled, you may not be able to edit the rotation values for the joints being controlled by the IK. For this reason, you can choose Modify | Evaluate Nodes | Ignore All.

- *Don't bind overly complex models.*   The more complex the model, the more time and effort you will spend tweaking weights. Evaluate your model and determine whether it will be best to use a direct or indirect skinning approach.

- *Know your shot.* This goes for any part of the production pipeline. If parts of the model will not be seen deforming, don't spend a lot of time adjusting the skin weights for those regions. Also, add influence objects only where they're needed. Unless the camera will shoot a close-up of a hand, for example, nobody will see or appreciate the hours of work you put into setting up anatomically precise influence objects.

Skinning a Character

Let's apply the smooth skinning to the character.

Binding with Smooth Skin

We'll start by binding with smooth skin:

1. Open the scene from the CD called ReadytoSkin. You should see a NURBS character model with a complete character rig, like the one we built in Chapter 9.

2. So far in these examples, we have been binding our geometry to the entire skeleton. While this is fine for smaller skeletons, in this case it will leave us with too many joints that will end up being edited not to influence any geometry. The joints in question are the tip joints, or the joints that are found at the end of every branch in the skeleton. Realize that the tip of the finger will be deformed by the second to last joint, not the last joint. Because this joint exists only for visual reference (or it could be used as a pivot for some kind of animation), it does not need to be included as a joint that will have any influence over the geometry. Select the pelvis joint and choose Edit | Select Hierarchy to select all of the children of the Pelvis joint.

3. In the Outliner, unfold the Pelvis hierarchy so that all of the children are visible. Starting from the top of the list and working your way to the bottom, deselect any of the tip joints by holding down the CTRL (COMMAND) key and clicking the joint in the Outliner. It is also a good idea to remove any object in this hierarchy that is not a joint. This could be a piece of geometry, an IK effector, or some other object.

4. Still holding down the CTRL (COMMAND) key, select the top group node for the surface called Monster01. Choose Skin | Bind Skin | Smooth Bind ❐. Set the Bind To attribute to Selected Joints, the Bind Method attribute to Closest Joint, Max Influence to **3**, and Dropoff Rate to **5.0**. Click the Bind Skin button. You may need to wait a bit to finish all the binding calculation.

5. The character is now bound. Try moving a footControl or an armIK to see how it looks. Make sure you undo back to when you skinned the character.

Saving the Bind Pose

Right after the skinning is done, you should keyframe all the control object's animating attributes, so you can save the bind pose. The bind pose is very important, because if you want to add joints or influence objects, you have to be in the bind pose.

1. In the Range Slider, type **–30** in the second white box from the left. This will make the animation start from frame –30.

2. You will save the bind pose at frame –30. Move the Time Slider to the –30 frame and keyframe the following object's attributes.

- Left and Right footControl: key everything.

- PelvisControl: key Translate and Rotate XYZ.

- SpineControl: key Rotate XYZ.

- Left and Right armIKs: key Translate XYZ, and Rotate XYZ, Middle, Index, Pinky, Thumb Roll, and handSpread.

- Left and Right armPoleVectors: key Translate XYZ.

- neck_a: rotate XYZ.

3. By keying all these attributes, you can pose the character any way you want while painting weights and just by moving the Time Slider to –30 to revert back to the bind pose any time you like.

Alternative   As an alternative, if you did the binding with all of the joints' rotation values set to 0, there isn't much of a need to key anything here. Instead, you might wish to create a Shelf button for the bind pose. To do this, open the Script Editor and choose Edit | Clear History to clear the history part of the window. In the Outliner, select the Pelvis joint and then SHIFT-select the last joint in the hierarchy so that all of the joints between these two selected objects will become selected. If you look in the Script Editor, you should see a command that says:

```
Select -r
```

This command is followed by a list of everything in the hierarchy. Copy and paste this command and the list into the Input window. Read through the list of items selected and delete any objects that are not joints. On the following line, type this:

```
Rotate 0 0 0;
```

Now highlight the entire contents of this window and drag it into the Shelf. A button will appear for this command. Test it by rotating some of the joints and then clicking this button. The skeleton should return to its joints all having 0 for their rotation values.

Editing Skin Weights

Let's evaluate the job that the Smooth Bind command did on our model. Once the problem areas are identified, we can edit the weights accordingly.

1. Bend the left arm by selecting L_armIK and moving it toward the body. The smooth skinning calculation should have done a pretty good job with initial skinning. However, if you try to bend beyond a certain point, the elbow surface will compress and crunch in on itself, as shown in Figure 11-18.

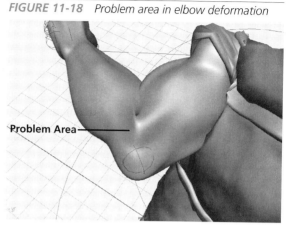

FIGURE 11-18   Problem area in elbow deformation

2. You need to edit the skin weights around the elbow surface to make the deformation smooth. You can achieve this by using the Paint Skin Weights tool. Select the left arm surface and choose Skin | Edit Smooth Skin | Paint Skin Weights Tool □.

3. In the Paint Skin Weights Tool's setting window, select L_elbow from the Transform list and change Paint Operation to Replace, set the Value to **1**, and set the opacity to **0.2**. Then paint around the gray to black area of the top elbow surface. It should turn whiter.

FIGURE 11-19   The elbow region after editing the weights with the Paint Skin Weights tool

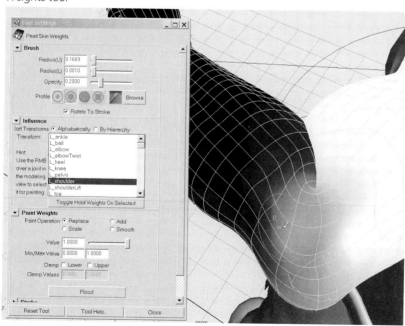

4. Select the L_shoulder joint from the Transform list in the Paint Skin Weights Tool's setting window and paint using the same operation and value at the oppose side of the elbow area. These edits to the skin should improve the look of the deformation. Figure 11-19 shows the elbow region after editing the weights.

5. Now finish off this area by painting with the smooth operation. With the L_shoulder still selected, choose Smooth as the Paint Operation. Paint around the area where the surface intersects with itself. Select the L_elbow again and do the same. It should smooth out the skin weights around this area.

FIGURE 11-20 Stomach area

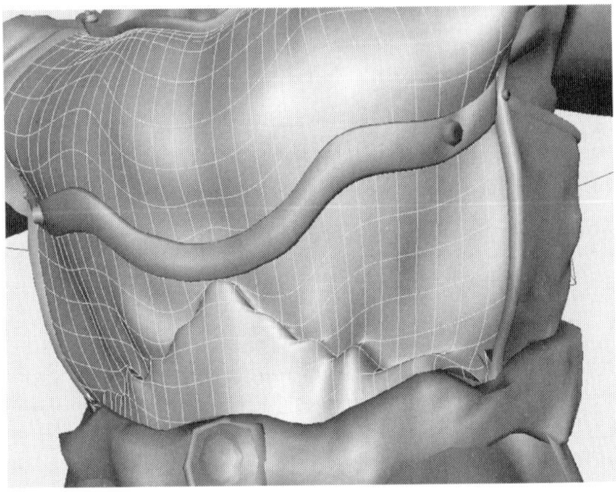

6. Let's edit the skin weight around the stomach area. Grab the spineControl and rotate it forward so the monster is slightly bowing. You will notice that the geometry in the stomach area crunches into a triangular shape (Figure 11-20). Select the Shirt surface (stomach area surface) and choose the Paint Skin Weights tool. You can see the reason for the triangle shape by selecting spine_shoulder, spine_e, spine_d, spine_c, spine_b, spine_a, and root in the Influence window. Most of the weight is on the spine_shoulder joint area, while the center portion is mainly influenced by the spine_a and spine_b joints.

FIGURE 11-21 The cleaned surface

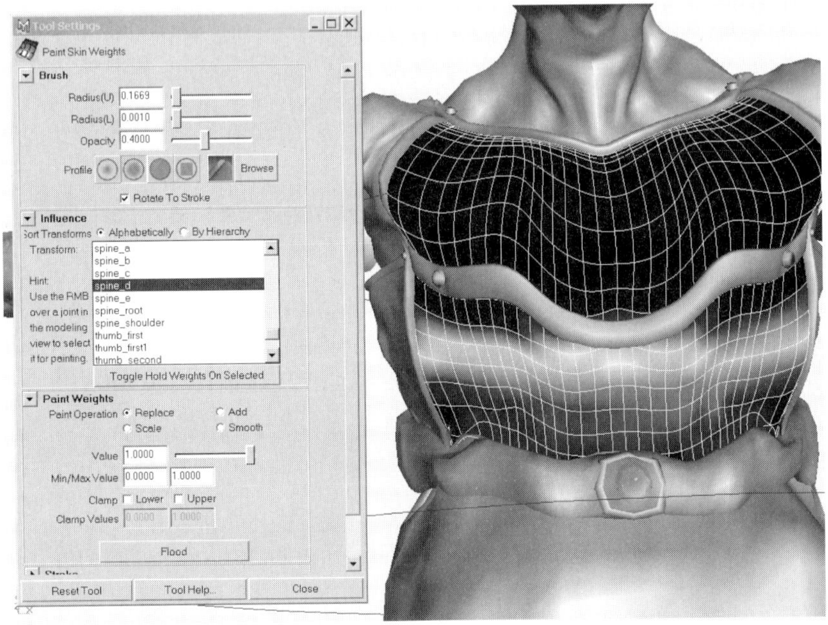

7. In the Paint Skin Weights tool's Settings window (Figure 11-21), set the Opacity to **0.4**, set Replace as the Paint Operation, and set the Value to **1**. Choose spine_e and paint around the top part of the triangle area horizontally. It should untangle the triangular mass. Continue to do the same painting for spine_d, spine_c, spine_b, and spine_a. This should smooth out the triangle area.

8. Once you have finished painting the weights for a joint, you should "hold" them so that the weighting is not affected when you start painting weights for another joint. Remember that the total weight must add up to 1. This means that if you are adding weight or reducing the weight of a skin point toward a joint, that extra weight will be pulled from other joints or redistributed. Holding the weights keeps the held joint from being added to or subtracted from. To hold the joint, select the joint in the Transform list in the Paint Skin Weights tool's Settings window for the Paint Skin Weight Map tool and click Toggle Hold Weights On Selected. The word *Hold* should appear next to the joint's name.

9. A problem with painting skin weights is that some of the joints might get only a minuscule amount of the weight, which can make the scene file large and make the scene heavy. To counter this, you can delete small influences from skin weights. Select the Shirt surface and choose Skin | Edit Smooth Skin | Prune Small Weights □. The Prune Weights Options window is shown next. Any influences' skin weight values with the Prune Below value will be automatically deleted. The default is 0.01, but change it to **0.05**. Click the Prune button. The skin weight should be simplified.

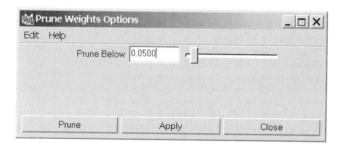

10. These grayscale skin weight maps can be exported for later use. If for some reason you have to unbind the character, you can save all of the skin weights as a texture map for each joint. Select the surface for which you want to save the skin weight maps, and choose Skin | Edit Smooth Skin | Export Skin Weight Maps. By default, Maya will save the skin weight maps in the Sourceimages folder in the current project's directory. Later you can reapply the weight maps by first selecting the surface and choosing Skin | Edit Smooth Skin | Import Skin Weight Maps. Select the shirt's surface again and choose Export Skin Weight Maps, name the file **shirtWeightMaps**, and click the Write button.

Adding an Influence Object

Now let's add an influence object:

1. Select the neck_a joint and rotate it. The neck rotates fine, but the head begins to lose its volume. This is because the skin points in this area are being influenced by the shoulder joints.

2. This can be easily fixed by creating a skull-like object and changing it into an influence object. Create a polygonal sphere. In the Channel Box, change the Subdivision Height and Axis attributes to **10**, and translate and scale it inside the head, so it becomes roughly the size of a skull. Name this object **headInfluence**. Figure 11-22 shows the approximate placement of the sphere inside the head.

3. Go back to the bind pose by moving the Time Slider to frame –30; then select the head surface, and SHIFT-select headInfluence. Choose Skin | Edit Smooth Skin | Add Influence. If you get an error, you are not in the bind pose or you made selections in the wrong order.

4. Make the headInfluence a child of neck_b; that way, when neck_a is rotated, headInfluence also rotates together with it. Try rotating neck_a again; it should look much better.

FIGURE 11-22   *A sphere is placed in the head and used as an influence object.*

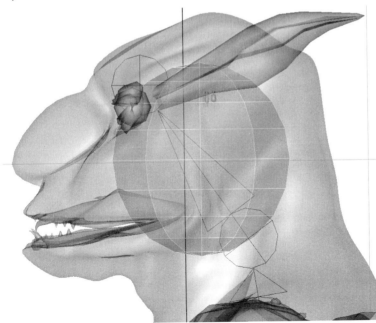

Another great trick with an influence object is using it to simulate muscles and lungs. Let's create an influence object to simulate breathing.

1. Create a polygonal sphere, change both the Height and Axis Subdivisions to **10**, and translate and scale, so it will fit in the upper chest area. Name it **breathInfluence**.

2. Select all of the surfaces around the chest, SHIFT-select breathInfluence, and choose Add Influence.

3. Make breathInfluence a child of back_shoulder. By scaling breathInfluence, you can simulate the expanding chest while the model is breathing. Figure 11-23 shows the placement and scale of the sphere used as an influence object for breathing.

FIGURE 11-23 *A sphere is placed in the chest area and used as an influence object to simulate breathing.*

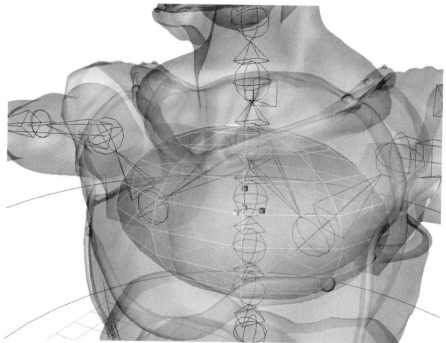

Summary

Smooth skinning is a great way to achieve realistic muscle deformations in your characters. However, many influence objects are needed to maintain anatomical accuracy during animation. It is therefore always important to know your shot and what parts of the character will be visible in the final animation. Also, while smooth skinning can be considered more advanced than rigid skinning, rigid skinning can be much faster to set up and is therefore a very useful and valid skinning method.

▲ This spaceship was constructed using a network of rectangular NURBS patches. Learn to build this step-by-step in Chapter 4.

Careful study of the real world helps you create realistic surfaces.

▲ The surfaces in this scene were shaded by utilizing several material attributes to give them a metallic finish. Lights and fog were added for atmospheric effects. Create this scene in Chapter 14.

▲ The green color of this teapot spills onto the yellow walls around it when Global Illumination is used to render the image. See Chapter 16 for how to achieve this effect.

Global Illumination and caustics affect light and color diffusion.

▲ Caustic reflections from the teapot are cast onto the wall. Learn how to create caustics in Chapter 16.

▲ The three spheres in
this image were lit
using a High Dynamic
Range (HDR) image.
Learn how to use HDR
and other rendering
functions in Chapter 16.

An infinite number of effects can be created with the Dynamics toolset.

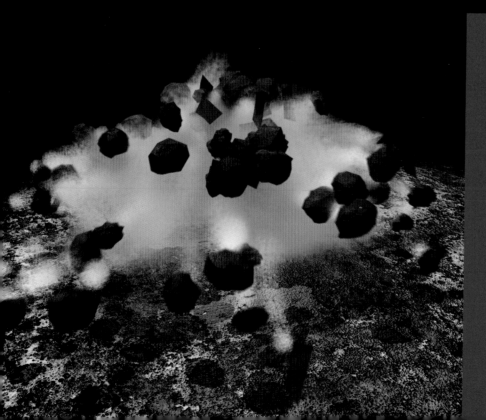

▲ Using Maya's Dynamics
toolset, you can create
many different effects.
Learn how to build this
explosion in Chapter 17.

By rendering a scene in different render passes and compositing them in post-production, you are free to experiment with different surface characteristics without having to re-render anything. Learn to render and composite this image in Chapters 20 and 21.

Rendering in layers and passes gives you precise control over an image.

This is the result of a rendering experiment where each bead is created from a different material and lit with an HDR image.

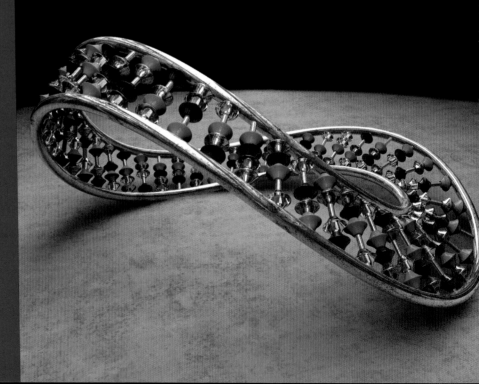

▲ *Moria Orc* by Lisette
Titre. *Moria Orc* and
Rastafarian (below)
were both created
using NURBS patches
to model the shapes.
The models were then
converted to polygons
and the patches
combined to produce
a single surface.

Push your images to look like they were captured in the real world.

▲ *Rastafarian* by Lisette
Titre. In both *Moria
Orc* and *Rastafarian*,
the UV (texture)
coordinates were
created in the UV
Texture Editor and the
texture was painted in
Photoshop. This
texturing technique is
demonstrated in
Chapter 14.

▲ *Blue Claw and Sword Handle* by Aaraty Mehta. This was modeled with polygons and textured using extensive bump maps to give it a weathered look.

Good texture mapping can add amazing details to a rendered scene.

▲ *Branches* by Libia Maria Arbeláez. The artist created NURBS extrusions and animated the curves, keeping their own history for the animation. She then created a procedural shader and composited the image in Apple Shake and Adobe After Effects.

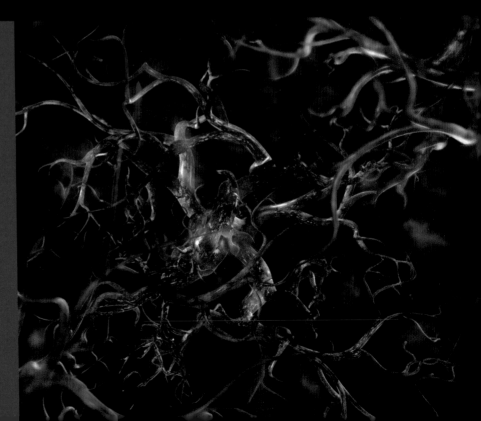

▲ *NSX2* by David Mershon. This car was modeled from a network of NURBS patches. The same approach is demonstrated in the spaceship tutorial in Chapter 4.

Using NURBS patches helps in creating well-formed surfaces.

▲ *Domes Scene* by Ping Xie. All shapes on the models were created entirely in NURBS, mostly by revolving complex profile curves. Textures and bump maps were then projected onto the surfaces. The image was then rendered with Mental Ray.

▲ *Chung Kuei* by
Jacky Wu.

鍾 馗
Chung - Kuei

Combine NURBS and polygonal modeling to create organic models.

▲ *Ghosts* by Jacky Wu.
Jacky Wu's characters
were modeled in
polygons using the
techniques
demonstrated in
Chapter 6.

頑皮鬼
Naughty Ghost

貪吃鬼
Greedy Ghost

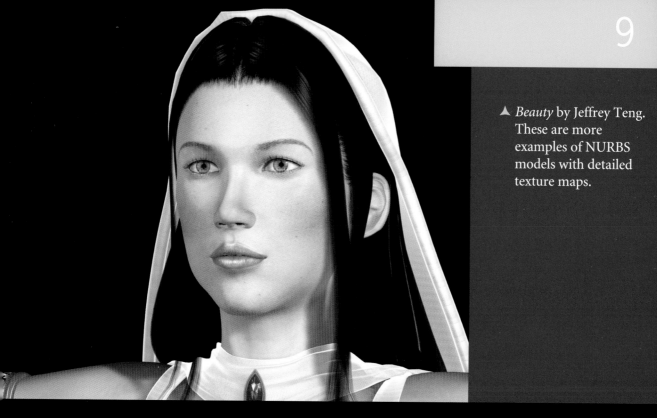

▲ *Beauty* by Jeffrey Teng. These are more examples of NURBS models with detailed texture maps.

Use multiple texture maps to control a single material attribute.

▲ *Eagleman* by Jeffrey Teng.

▲ *Robot 12* by Shau-Ren, Chiou. The following four images were modeled with polygons. The diffused shadows on the objects were created by rendering with Global Illumination in Mental Ray. See Chapter 16 to learn to use Global Illumination.

Global Illumination affects absorption, reflectivity, and refractivity.

▲ *Robot 13* by Shau-Ren, Chiou.

▲ *Tina Face* by
Shau-Ren, Chiou.

A photon map controls distribution of light in the scene.

▲ *Door Sample* by
Shau-Ren, Chiou.

▲ *ZorgYZR* by Theerapol Srisuphan. *ZorgYZR* and *Tanya* (below) were both built using a combination of NURBS and polygons. Many of these same techniques are demonstrated in Chapters 3, 4, 5, and 6.

Polygon modeling is the most popular way to create organic characters.

▲ *Tanya* by Theerapol Srisuphan.

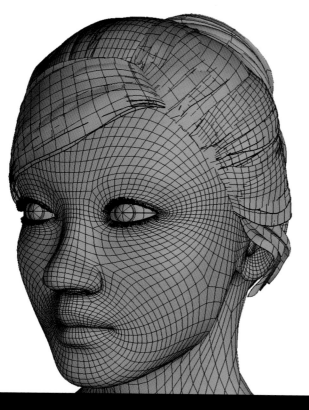

▲ *Young Woman-Wireframe* by Tsun-Hui "Andrea" Pun. This wireframe render is an example of a very well-structured polygonal mesh suitable for complex animation.

The Hypershade is an artist-friendly interface for creating textures.

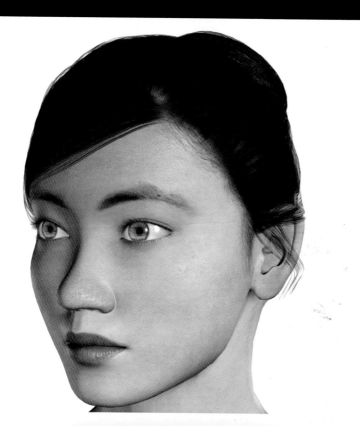

▲ *Young Woman* by Tsun-Hui "Andrea" Pun. Realistic skin can be achieved by using the Hypershade to combine texture files, materials, and utilities. This is the same geometry used in the image above, which is rendered with a complex skin shader. Learn how to create shaders such as these in Chapter 14.

▲ *World War II Boeing B-17F* by Timothy Odell. Maya and Photoshop were both used to create, render, and composite Timothy Odell's animations. These rendering and compositing techniques are discussed in Chapters 20 and 21.

Compositing gathers all of a scene's elements into one cohesive piece.

▲ *World War II Pilot* by Timothy Odell.

▲ *Mega Jaw* by Tinnakan Lohsisupacahi. Extensive use of bump maps add the wrinkles and other details to the skin of this creature.

Subdivision modeling offers artists control and simplicity.

▲ *Hover Tank* by Shinsaku Arima. Shinsaku built this humanoid tank to teach his students how to use subdivision modeling techniques to model machines. Learn more about this in Chapter 5.

▲ *Rim Pully* by Dario Lopez, Jr. Grunge maps can be applied to surfaces to create very realistic weathering and aging. See Chapters 14 and 20 to learn to use grunge maps.

Grunge maps provide precise control over surface details.

▲ *Attack* by Tom Meade. This image uses the spaceship that we modeled in Chapter 4. The image was rendered in separate passes, as demonstrated in Chapter 20, and composited in After Effects, as described in Chapter 21.

Character
Animation

In the previous three chapters, we built

a character rig that can be controlled easily. This

chapter covers some techniques that will make

the art of character animation fast and efficient.

After some additional setup techniques, we'll

practice setting keys on various control objects to

produce our first character animation. We will also

look at ways to make a character interact with other

objects. At the end of the chapter, you will learn

how nonlinear animation is done in Maya through

the Trax Editor.

Tutorial: Walking and Pushing a Box

This tutorial covers how to operate our 3D puppet to make a convincing walking animation. We'll create a fairly complicated setup to ease this animation process. After we make the character walk, we can try layering more interesting animation. Then we'll use Maya's IK blending function to blend between IK and FK to make the character push a box.

Setting Up the Character for Animation

We'll do four things in this section: First, we'll create a low-resolution version of the character that is to be animated. This will free us from any computationally intensive operations that can occur when animating and deforming high-resolution geometry. Second, we will simplify the list of all keyable attributes for each object that will be animated. This will eliminate the possibility of creating keyframes on attributes that are not animated, thus simplifying the amount of data that Maya needs to evaluate. Finally, we will create some Shelf buttons that will further ease the selection of certain objects in the scene.

Setting Up the Low-Resolution Geometry

The art of animation is all about timing and motion. To animate successfully, you need to be able to work and view your animation in real time without dropping any frames during playback. While Maya can handle the display and interaction of heavy scenes, at some point, the scene will become too much for your computer hardware to handle.

Creating a low-resolution version of your character animation is one of the best ways to sidestep any possible performance problems that might occur. When making a low-resolution model for animation, two performance problems need to be solved: The first problem is that of the video card's limitation to display a certain number of polygons per frame. Even the newest, most powerful graphics cards will get bogged down when the scene gets complex. This is best avoided by creating a version of the model that has a small number of polygons. The model should contain only enough information to define the overall volume of the character. Being able to view the space occupied by the character will allow you to achieve more accurate placement in the scene and will avoid the character moving through floors, walls, or other characters. There's no specific technique to use when creating a low-resolution version of a character. The technique you use depends on what type of geometry the high-resolution is made of (polygons, NURBS, or subdivision surfaces). For a model created in NURBS, it might be best to convert the model to polygons using one of the tessellation methods discussed in Chapter 6. The same is true for subdivision surfaces. If you have a polygonal model, you might try the Reduce command (Polygons | Reduce). In some cases, it might be just as easy to create a new model quickly from scratch. In any case, the model should have as few polygons as necessary.

The second performance problem to overcome is the one placed on the computer's processor during a deformation. Remember that a deformer, such as the skin cluster used for skeletal deformations, creates a node in the geometry's dependency graph that needs to be evaluated every time the skeleton is transformed. When an indirect skinning technique is used, several nodes may need to be evaluated to result in the final deformation. Even on low-resolution geometry, this could slow down you computer. To remedy this, the low-resolution version of the model needs to be broken up into different pieces and then parented to the corresponding joint. For instance, the face in the thigh region of the model can be extracted (Polygons | Extract) and then parented to the hip joint. The region from the knee to the ankle is extracted and parented to the knee joint. This process continues until each piece of the model is parented to a joint. When the skeleton moves, the geometry parented to it will move as well. Although gaps will exist in the joint regions and the geometry may overlap in other areas, that is not important. The real gain is in removing any need to evaluate a deformation.

Open AnimationStart.mb from the book CD. This scene contains a model that has been rigged and skinned using the techniques demonstrated in Chapters 9, 10, and 11. We have already created a low-resolution version for the character used in this scene. Notice that a layer for a low-resolution character is included; you will use this later to animate. Turn off the visibility for the layer named HiRezCharacter, and turn on the visibility for the layer named LowRezCharacter to see the low-resolution character. Figure 12-1 shows the low-resolution version of the character.

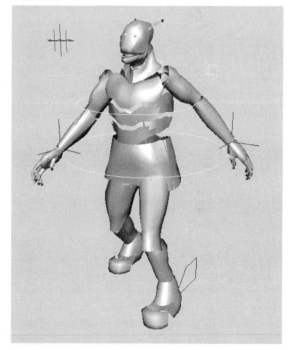

FIGURE 12-1   *Low-resolution model to use for animation*

Making Shelf Buttons for Animation Controls

The iconic character animation controls, such as the pelvisControl and the foot controls, were created so that they are highly visible and easy to select in a view window. However, when the scene has many objects obscuring the control, it can still be difficult to select. Therefore, we will create a UI for selecting certain objects by making Shelf buttons.

1. Create a new Shelf by clicking the down arrow button labeled Menu Of Items To Modify The Shelf, at the left side of the Shelf. Select New Shelf. The New Shelf window will open. Type **Character_Control** for the Shelf name and click OK.

2. Now you are ready to add Shelf buttons. Open the Hypergraph (choose Window | Hypergraph) and the Script Editor (choose Window | General Editors | Script Editor).

3. Select pelvisControl from the Hypergraph. Now look in the Script Editor. In the top section of the Script Editor (the History window), you should see this command:

```
select -r pelvisControl ;
```

4. Highlight this by LMB-dragging over it. Then MMB-drag it to the Shelf to create a new Shelf button. That's it! You made a Shelf button to select a pelvisControl.

5. Select L_footControl and drag the command to the Shelf in the same way. Create Shelf buttons for R_footControl, L_armIK, R_armIK, spineControl, L_armPoleVector, R_armPoleVector, neck_a, and eyeControl. The order in which you create the buttons is the order in which they'll appear on the Shelf. If you create the buttons in the order listed here, the buttons will cover the objects in the character from its foot to its head in a well-organized arrangement. Test the Shelf buttons to make sure that each object is selected when its button is clicked.

6. It's a good idea to label these buttons to make it obvious which button selects what object. Again, click the down arrow button on the left end of the Shelf to view the menu of items that modify the Shelf. Choose Shelf Editor, and the Shelf Editor window will open.

7. Click the Shelf Contents tab, and then select −r pelvisControl from the list. You'll see an Icon Name box at the bottom; type **Pelvis**. Now select the −r L_footControl, and you'll see that *Pelvis* appears on the bottom of the Shelf button.

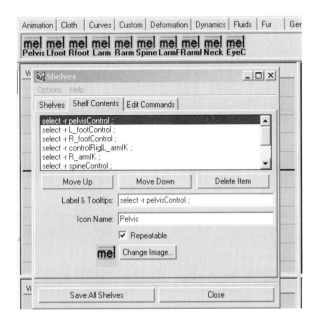

8. Name the rest of the buttons—**Lfoot, Rfoot, Larm, Rarm, Spine, LarmP, RarmP, Neck,** and **EyeC.** Click the Save All Shelves button. The illustration shows the window and the buttons with their new names. This Shelf is probably saved at the default location at C:\ Documents and Settings*Name of your login accounts*\My Documents\maya*x.x*\prefs\shelves. Look inside the folder and you'll find a script named shelf_Character_Control.

NOTE   If you want to use this Shelf on another computer, you can paste it into the same folder on another PC. For this reason, it is helpful to copy this file into your project directory so that it will always be available to use, no matter where you may be.

Simplifying Attributes in the Channel Control

The next step is to simplify the list of keyable attributes for all of the animatable objects. For example, if you select the pelvisControl and look in the Channel Box, you will notice that it currently displays all of the default transform attributes for this object. Not all of these are needed for this animation, however. You can use the Channel Control window to make attributes non-keyable. In addition, attributes can be locked so that they cannot be accidentally edited.

1. On the Shelf, click the Pelvis button to select the pelvisControl object.

2. Choose Window | General Editors | Channel Control to open the Channel Control window. The attributes that will not be keyframed are the scaleX, scaleY, scaleZ, and visibility attributes. Select these attributes from the Keyable list on the left side of the window, as shown in the illustration. You can use the CTRL (COMMAND) key to select multiple items.

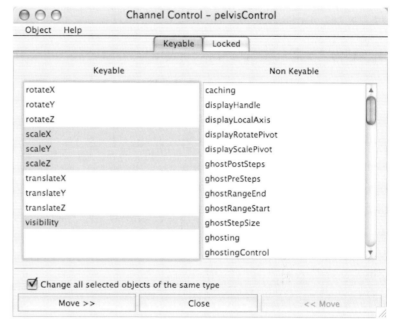

3. Click the Move>> button. Those attributes are moved into the Non Keyable list of attributes and are no longer visible in the Channel Box. When the object is selected and the S key is used to set keyframes, only the attributes that are keyable will be keyed—that is, those listed in the Channel Box.

4. Even though the scale and visibility attributes are no longer keyable, you can still edit them. For instance, the pelvisControl object can still be selected and scaled with the Scale tool. To prevent any changes from happening, the attributes can be locked. In the Channel Control window, select the Locked tab at the top of the window. Find and select the scaleX, scaleY, scaleZ, and visibility attributes in the list of Non Locked attributes in the right column. Click the <<Move button to lock the attributes. Now when the pelvisControl is selected and the Scale tool in invoked, the pelvisControl cannot be edited.

5. The foot controls can both be selected and edited at the same time. Remember that we added some custom attributes to the foot controls to control the behavior of the foot. Lock the scale and visibility attributes for these objects and make them non-keyable. As long as the check box next to Change All Selected Objects Of The Same Type is checked, attributes with the same name will be moved for the different objects.

6. Click the Larm and Rarm Shelf buttons. Use the Channel Control to make the scaleX, scaleY, scaleZ, offset, roll, twist, and visibility attributes locked and non-keyable.

7. The spine control needs only to rotate, so make the scaleX, scaleY, scaleZ translateX, translateY, translateZ, and the visibility attributes locked and non-keyable.

8. The left and right arm pole vectors need only the translateX, translateY, and translateZ attributes, so make sure everything else is locked and non-keyable.

9. The neck needs only to rotate. Make the scaleX, scaleY, scaleZ, translateX, translateY, translateZ, and visibility attributes locked and non-keyable.

10. For the eyeControl object, make the rotate, scaleX, scaleY, scaleZ, and visibility attributes non-keyable and locked.

The attributes of the control objects are now simplified, and we can start animating the character.

Setting the Animation Preferences

Let's set up the scene so we can animate it correctly. First, make sure you are animating for the proper output. If you are animating for video output, you should be using 30fps (that is, if you are in the United States).

1. To set the frames per second, choose Window | Settings/Preferences | Preferences. Select Settings from the left side of the Preferences window. Set the Time attribute to NTSC [30fps].

2. Now change the types of tangents that will be used to interpolate the animation data in and out of every keyframe that is set. Select Keys from the list on the left and change the Default In Tangent and Default Out Tangent to Clamped. The Default tangent is set to Spline, which always makes a smooth curve between the keys to simulate smooth acceleration and deceleration. Using Spline as an animation type can cause the object to slide or continue moving after it should have stopped. Using clamped tangents helps this situation by making the animation curve straight, meaning there is no movement, when two adjacent keys have the same value. Figure 12-2 shows how each tangent affects animation.

FIGURE 12-2   How spline and clamped tangents affect animation

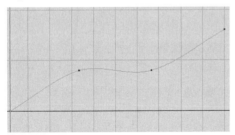

Spline Tangent

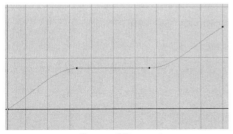

Clamped Tangent

It's always a good idea to set keys for the bind pose at the beginning of the animation. You can key the bind pose by keyframing all the attributes of all the controls at the bind pose. This is important, because you may want to change skin weight, create blend shapes, or texture the character afterward. It's easy to create a bind pose.

1. Make sure the character is at the bind pose. Choose Modify | Evaluate Nodes | Ignore All. This will temporarily turn off the IK, constraints, and dynamics.

2. Select the spine_root joint and choose Skin | Go To Bind Pose. If you don't see any movements in the joints, you're ready to go. Otherwise, you have to snap each control to the appropriate position, such as spine_control to spine_root joint, L_footControl to L_heel joint, L_armIK to L_wrist joint, and so on. Then choose Modify | Evaluate Nodes | Evaluate All.

3. Finally, keyframe all of the control objects at frame –1, so by just scrubbing the Current Time Indicator to –1, you will achieve a bind pose. In the Range Slider, type **–1** in the Playback Start Time field.

4. Move the Current Time Indicator to –1 and use the Outliner to select each control object. Press the S key to keyframe all the attributes.

5. Try posing a character at frame 1 and then move the Current Time Indicator to –1 to see if the character goes to a proper bind pose.

Now you are ready to animate!

Creating Walking Animation

We will first attempt to create a walk cycle.

1. In the Range Slider, set the Playback Start Time to 1 and the Playback End Time to 100. Frames 1 through 100 should appear in the Time Slider.

 2. In the tool box, click Persp/Graph/Hypergraph.

3. Choose Panels | Orthographic | Side from the Hypergraph window. Since the character is walking parallel to the Z axis, we can mainly use the Side view to see the progress. Figure 12-3 shows how the workspace is laid out.

4. It's best to keyframe the main body movement first and then layer the detail of other body parts' animation later. For a walking animation, the first objects to animate are pelvisControl, L_footControl, and R_footControl. At this point, be sure that only the low-resolution version of the character is visible.

5. Set the Current Time Indicator to frame 1. Select the pelvisControl (either in the view window or using the Shelf button) and in the Side view, move it about 2 units forward and 1 unit down.

FIGURE 12-3 *Window setup for the walking animation*

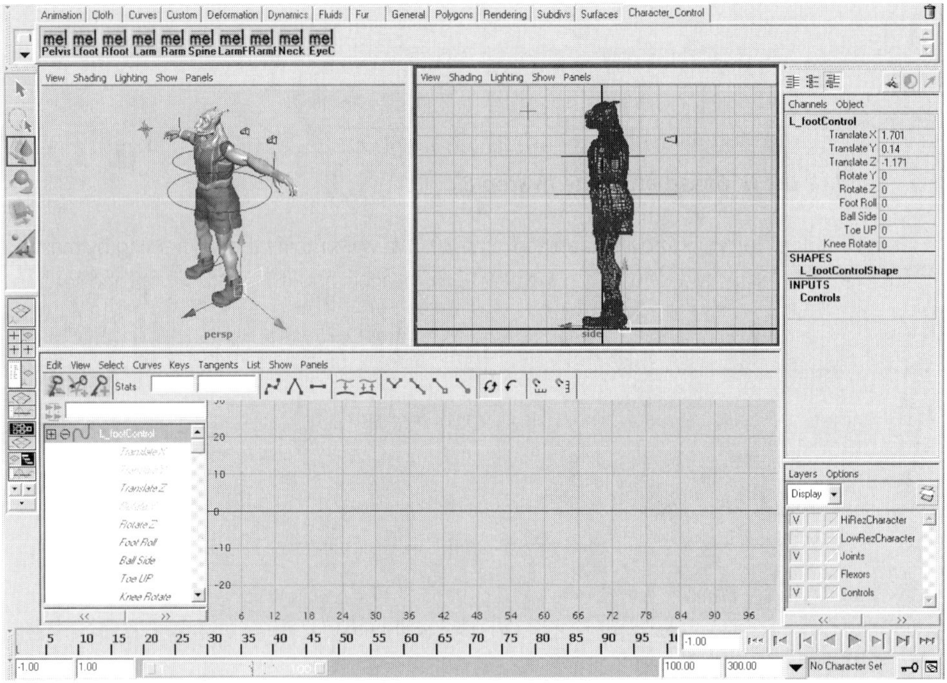

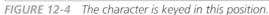

6. Select the L_footControl and move it forward, so the pelvis of the character is in the middle of both feet.

7. Key the pelvisControl, L_footControl, and R_footControl by selecting all three objects and pressing the S key. It's important to key the R_footControl even though it hasn't moved. Figure 12-4 shows the position of the controls as they are keyed at frame 1.

FIGURE 12-4 *The character is keyed in this position.*

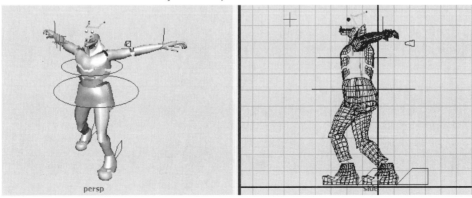

8. Notice that the arms are not following the body. This is because the IK handles for the arms are not children of the hierarchy or constrained to any of the objects in the hierarchy. Select both arm IK handles and change the IK Blend attribute to 0; then press the S key. This turns off the IK solver for arms; they should follow the body movement from now on.

NOTE *For Maya 4.5 or earlier versions, change the Solver Enable attribute instead of the IK Blend attribute in step 8.*

9. Drag the Current Time Indicator to frame 30. We will simplify the keyframing by making each step 1 second long. Move the pelvisControl again about 2 units forward and set a key.

10. Move the R_footControl, so the pelvisControl is at about the middle of both feet. Key both the right and left foot controls.

11. Scrub the Current Time Indicator back and forth from frames 1 to 30 to see the first step of the walk cycle.

12. Set the Current Time Indicator to 60 and move the pelvisControl forward. Move L_footControl forward, and key all three controls. Repeat this step for frame 90.

13. Activate the Perspective view and click the Play button (or press ALT-V [OPTION-V]) to check the animation. Figure 12-5 shows how the pelvisControl and foot controls are placed every 15 frames.

TIP *If you want to see something similar to Figure 12-5, which shows a snapshot of objects at particular frames, choose Animate | Create Animation Snapshot. Specify from which frame to which frame you want to view and how many frame increments you want to include in the snapshot. You can also show a trail of motion by choosing Animate | Create Motion Trail.*

FIGURE 12-5 *Placement of the pelvisControl and the foot controls every 15 frames*

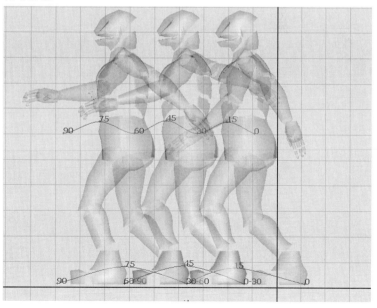

Now we need to take another pass at this animation to make the feet lift off the ground and the pelvis bob up and down as the character walks. To do this, we'll need to keyframe the Y translation of the pelvisControl and foot controls. At frames 15, 45, and 75, the pelvisControl should be lifted up a bit to compensate for the foot coming forward that is also lifting up.

1. Go to frame 15 and move the pelvisControl and the R_footControl slightly upward. Key them by pressing the S key. Go to frame 45, and this time move pelvisControl and L_footControl up and key them. Key the same pattern at frame 75, with pelvisControl and R_footControl.

2. Play the animation. It should look more convincing now that the feet are lifting off the ground.

3. Let's take another pass and add another layer of animation. The next important keyframe will control the shifting of the center of gravity. Because the character is lifting its foot up, it should shift the center of gravity to the left and right. The center of gravity can be controlled by translating the pelvisControl in the X axis and rotating pelvisControl's Z axis. Change from Side view to Front view. If you go to frame 15, you see that the character is doing something impossible: his center of gravity is at the middle of both feet, even though his right foot isn't holding his weight.

4. Move the pelvis control about half a unit toward the left foot and rotate it slightly in the Z axis, about –5 degrees. Key the position for the pelvisControl at this frame.

5. Go to frame 45 and move the pelvisControl about half a unit toward the right foot and change the Rotate Z to 5, and set a key. Repeat this step for frame 75. This frame should be similar to frame 15.

6. Play the animation, and you can see that the character's movement is much more convincing.

7. A big monster like this guy should rotate its pelvis side to side while walking. Go to frame 15 and rotate the pelvisControl about –10 degrees in Y. Set a key. In frame 45, change the Rotate Y attribute to 10 and set a key. In frame 75, change the Rotate Y attribute back to –10 and set a key.

8. Play the animation in the Perspective view. His lower body now has much more realistic motion.

9. Let's finish up the lower body motion by adding some roll to the foot. Select the R_footControl and go to frame 15. Set the footRoll attribute to 3 and key it by pressing the S key. In frame 25, change the Foot Roll attribute to –3 and key it again. In frame 30, change the value to 0, and this time key the Foot Roll attribute individually. You can do this by highlighting the Foot Roll attribute in the Channel Box, holding down the right mouse button, and choosing Key Selected. Because this frame doesn't correspond to

any other attribute's animation, it's a good idea to key it separately. Again, go to frame 75 and repeat the same process. After finishing with the right foot, select L_footControl and do the same keyframing for frames 45, 55, and 60. The lower body animation should be complete.

10. The monster's upper body needs to be animated to correspond to the lower body for its motion to look natural. Also, the arms need to swing to counteract the movement of the pelvis. Start with the spineControl. The spine should rotate slightly in the opposite direction of the pelvis to counteract the movement. Select it and go to frame 1; then key it by pressing S. At frame 20, rotate in Z about 4.5 degrees and set a key. This will counteract the excessive weight shifting of the bottom of the body. In frame 30, key the Rotate Z attribute at 0. At frame 50, key it at –4.5, change it to 0 at frame 60, and key it again. Key it to 4.5 at frame 80 and 0 at frame 90.

11. Next we'll work on the spineControl's Y axis rotation. This rotation drives the swinging of the arms. Go to frame 15 and change the Y axis rotation to –10, so that the left shoulder is forward. At frame 45, change it to 10, and then at frame 75 change it back to –10. Make sure to key each time. This movement gives a more animated feel to the upper body, but it can look too exaggerated.

12. Making the neck animation counteract to the spine will compensate for this problem. We will add animation for the neck joint in the Rotate X and Rotate Y attributes. Select the neck_a joint and key at frame 1 by pressing the S key. Go to frame 15, and in the Front view, try to make the head point straight ahead by rotating it in the X and Y axes. Key this by pressing the s key. Do the same thing for the neck joint at frames 45 and 75. Set all the rotation to 0 at frame 90 and key. This should make the head face forward throughout the animation.

13. The next big step is animation of the arms. We turned off the IK solver earlier on, but since this arm movement will be swinging, the arms are best keyframed using FK animation. We will animate shoulders, elbows, and arm IKs (for wrist and elbowTwist joint's rotation). Before starting the animation of the arms, create Shelf buttons that will select each shoulder and elbow joint.

14. Start at frame 1. Rotate the shoulders and elbows so the arms are closer to the body on the side. Make sure to rotate one axis at a time by highlighting the axis you want to rotate in the Channel Box and MMB-dragging in the view window. If the manipulator is used, you may end up rotating on all three axes. Also remember that the elbow joint is a hinge joint, so make sure that it rotates only in the Z axis. Key all four joints.

15. Move to frame 30 and switch the arm rotation, so that the left arm is in front and right arm is in back. Set a key. You need to highlight only the Y axis and rotate it to swing. Use the same process to swing the arm at frames 60 and 90. Play the animation to check your progress.

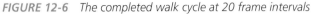

FIGURE 12-6 *The completed walk cycle at 20 frame intervals*

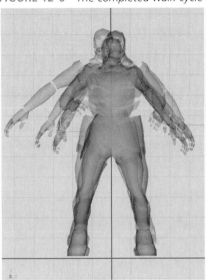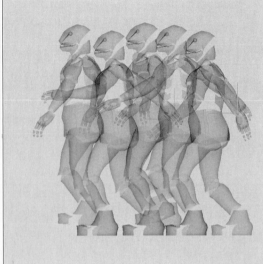

16. You can make the animation more interesting by slowing the elbow rotation slightly. Make the elbow rotate more, but make it happen about five frames after the shoulders' rotation is at their peak. Key the elbow rotation at frames 35, 65, and 95.

17. Delete keys at frames 30, 60, and 90 for the elbow rotation. The easiest way to do this is in the Graph Editor. Select the keys and press DELETE. Figure 12-6 shows the completed animation at intervals of 20 frames.

Animation Techniques

It's a good idea to study up on traditional animation techniques. You can learn more about this by checking out these great animation books:

- ***The Illusion of Life: Disney Animation*** by Ollie Johnston and Frank Thomas (Hyperion Press, 1995). This book is a bible for the animator. It contains many descriptions about Disney's animation techniques.

- ***The Animator's Survival Kit*** by Richard Williams (Faber & Faber, 2002). This book contains a treasure chest full of animation techniques. If you want to buy only one book for animation, this is it.

- ***Cartoon Animation*** by Preston Blair (Walter Foster Pub., 1995). Many nice 2D cartoon drawings appear in this book, and they are all in motion, too. This book shows principles and methods of animation in a fun way.

The basic walking animation is complete. Of course, you should continue to add more secondary movement by continuing to make more passes. Ears can be rotated to simulate swinging motion. Keys can be offset so that corresponding motions are not so mechanical. Any little things that give this monster more character will make it look more realistic.

Pushing a Box Using IK Blending

Now we will make the character push a box. This will utilize the IK blending function in Maya, which was briefly explained in Chapter 10. IK blending allows you to switch between FK and IK by keying the state of the IK solver so both of the monster's arms can swing freely while walking, and then lock onto the box by switching to IK.

1. Open the scene called pushingBoxStart.ma on the CD. Play the animation and you will see the character walking and then standing in front of a box. At frame 110, set a key on the IK Blend attribute with its value set to 0. Make sure you create this key by keying just this selected attribute.

2. In the Side view, move the IK handles in front of the body. Key the translation.

3. In frame 140, select both arm IK handles and turn on IK by setting the IK Blend attribute to 1. Highlight this attribute in the Channel Box, right-click it, and choose Key Selected.

4. Scrub the Current Time Indicator between frames 110 and 140, and you should see the arm moving between them smoothly. Adjust the placement of the IK handles and animate pole vectors from frames 110 to 140 to add elbow animation, so the elbows are pointing down more. Also, rotate the IK handles so the character has both hands against the box at frame 140.

5. Now animate the pelvis control, foot controls, arm IKs, and box to make the box move forward. Try using different timing, so the box appears to be heavy or light.

As you can see, the IK blending function allows you to switch between IK and FK easily.

Nonlinear Animation

Nonlinear animation, an industry buzzword for a quite a while, is similar to nonlinear film or video editing. Before digitization of film or video footage became widely available, all the footage had to be recorded on tapes. A tape is linear; you can't easily cut and insert footage because all the other sequences have to be pushed back, too. But nonlinear editing allows you to cut and paste footage anywhere in the recording of time, because you are arranging clips, and entire sequences will conform to your operation. Nonlinear animation works on the same principle. Nonlinear animation can treat each animation as a clip of footage, and you can insert that clip anywhere in the timeline. You can create a library of motions and simply drop them in wherever they belong.

For long sequences with many repetitive motions, you and your team members can pull out motion clips and add, mix, and blend them together, resulting in a shorter and more efficient animation workflow. Nonlinear animation is used often in games and TV series, where many team members can access a bank of animation clips and poses to aid in creating a lenqthy animation quickly.

Creating Character Sets

Before you start converting animation into clips, you should group objects' keyable attributes into sets to make clip handling more efficient. You can group keyable attributes into special groups called *character sets.* Character sets can hold keyable attributes from any objects. When a character set is selected, you can view the list of all animatable attributes in one list in either the Outliner or the Channel Box.

Tutorial: Creating Character Sets

Making a character set is easy.

1. Open the scene called TraxWalkCycle.mb from the CD. This scene contains a walk cycle animation of a character. The character is walking in place. The values for all of the animated attributes are the same at frame 1 and frame 120, making the animation seamlessly cycled.

2. Let's organize this animation's character sets into upper body and lower body sets, so we can add more motion to these two sets separately. Open the Hypergraph and select pelvisControl, L_footControl, and R_footControl.

3. Choose Character | Create Character Set □ to open the Create Character Set Options window shown in Figure 12-7. Type **LowerBody** in the Name field at the top. Several options appear here:

FIGURE 12-7   *Create Character Set Options window*

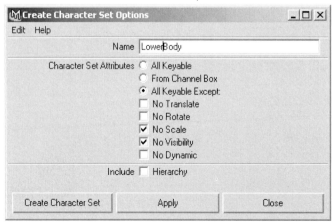

- **All Keyable**   Makes all keyable attributes of the selected object part of the character sets.

- **From Channel Box**   Lets you select specific attributes in the Channel Box, and creates character sets only for those selected attributes.

- **All Keyable Except**   Lets you check a number of boxes below to be part of the character set. Because it says *except,* any box with a checkmark *won't* be a part of the character set. The default is a checkmark for No Scale and No Visibility. These attributes won't be a part of character sets.

- **Include Hierarchy check box**   If this is turned on, all the children below the selected object's attributes will be a part of the character sets.

4. Leave these options at their default settings and click Apply. The LowerBody character set is created.

5. Take a look at the Channel Box. All of the attributes in this set are listed here. Also at the bottom-right side of the interface, just to the left of the Auto Key button, "LowerBody" appears as the active character set in the Character Set Selector, as shown in the illustration. While this is active, every time the Key All command is used (the s key), all attributes in this set will be keyed. This keeps you from accidentally not keying something because it was not selected.

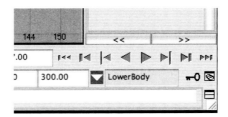

6. In the Hypergraph (or Outliner), select L_armIK, R_armIK, L_armPoleVector, R_armPoleVector, SpineControl, neck_a, L_shoulder, L_elbow, R_shoulder, and R_elbow. Choose Character | Create Character Sets ❑ and name this set **UpperBody**.

7. Click the Create Character Set button. The UpperBody character set is created.

Editing Character Sets
Because we used the Channel Control window earlier to clean up keyable attributes in the Channel Box, all of the attributes in the character sets should now be pretty well organized. No unneeded attributes should appear in the list. If you do want to delete or add attributes to any particular character set, it is best to use the Relationship Editor:

1. Choose Window | Relationship Editors | Character Sets. Click a character set you want to edit at the left side of the Relationship Editor window.

2. Click the plus mark next to the character set in the right side to see all of the attributes for the character set.

3. To remove an attribute from the Relationship Editor, select it and choose Edit | Remove Highlighted Attributes.

FIGURE 12-8 *Relationship Editor for character sets*

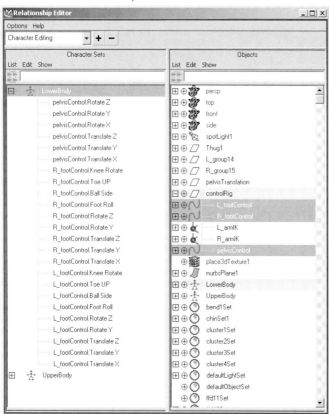

4. To add attributes, select the character set to which you want to add attributes from the left side of the window, and then find an object whose attributes you want to add from the right side of the Relationship Editor. Click the attribute and it is automatically added to the selected character set.

Figure 12-8 shows the Relationship Editor for character sets.

Using the Trax Editor

The Trax Editor lets you mix animation clips in much the same way that you might assemble a movie in video editing software. You can use the Trax Editor to arrange a bunch of clips in any order and blend between them. Each clip can be mixed, sped up, slowed down, cycled, and split so that you can quickly assemble a complex animation.

Tutorial: Creating the Clips

Before you can begin editing the clips, you need to convert an animation or pose into clips so that it can be used in the Trax Editor. A *clip* is just a chunk, or block, of animation data for a specific set of attributes. Let's make some clips from the walk cycle animation.

1. Use the Character Set selector drop-down menu to make the LowerBody character set active. Choose Create | Clip ❏ to open the Create Clip Options window shown in Figure 12-9. The following options appear in this window:

- **Name** Type in a name for your clip.

- **Keys __ Leave Keys In Timeline** If this box is checked, the animation data will remain in the Graph Editor and Time Slider. Usually, since you are trying to create a nonlinear editing environment, you wan to leave this unchecked.

- **Clip __ Put Clip In Visor Only** Checking this option will remove the keyed animation and create a clip, but the new clip will be stored only in the Visor (another window used for selecting nodes in Maya).

- **Clip __ Put Clip In Trax Editor And Visor**   This option creates a clip and immediately adds the clip to the Trax Editor and the Visor. It's the default option and the most logical one if you want to use the Trax Editor right away.

- **Time Range**   This determines the range of frames from which the clip is generated.

  - **Selected**   Uses the selected time range. To select a time range, SHIFT-drag in the Time Slider. A range will be highlighted in red; this is the selected range.

  - **Time Slider**   Uses the active range in the Time Slider.

  - **Animation Curve**   Uses the start and end of the animation curve of animating attributes.

  - **Start/End**   Lets you specify the clip's time range by typing in the Start Time and End Time of the range.

- **Subcharacters**   A subset of a character set. By keying the character set, the subcharacter set under it will be automatically keyed as well. But the subcharacter set can also be independently adjusted. By checking this box, the clip will contain subcharacter sets.

- **Time Warp**   Lets you adjust the speed of the clip with a curve without changing the animation curve of the original clip. This slows down the workflow, so it should be used carefully.

- **Include Hierarchy**   All the objects under the selected object's hierarchy will also be included in the clip. If it's unchecked, only the selected object will be included in the clip.

FIGURE 12-9   *Create Clip Options window*

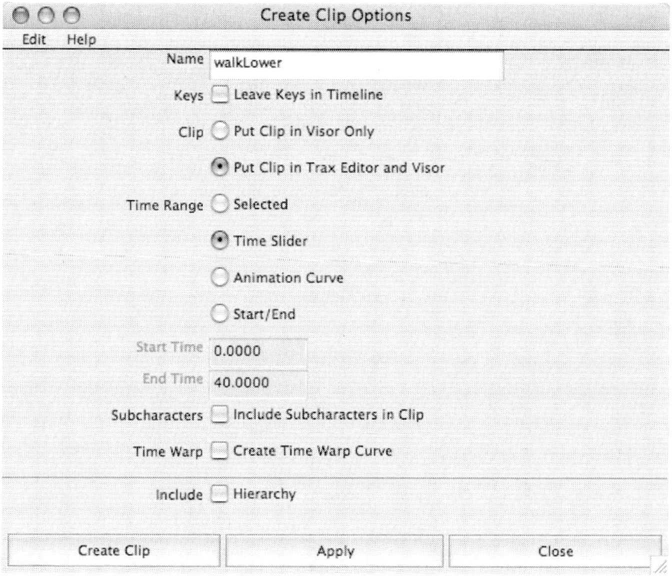

2. Set the options to match those shown in Figure 12-9. Click the Apply button.

3. Choose Window | Animation Editors | Trax Editor.

4. Load the clip into the Trax Editor by choosing List | Load Selected Characters from the Trax Editor's menu bar. The Trax Editor is shown in Figure 12-10 with the walkLower clip loaded.

5. You'll see that a clip called walkLower is generated and placed in the Trax Editor. If you click the Play button, it doesn't look like it has changed. But select the pelvisControl and open the Graph Editor. There is no animation in the Graph Editor, because the animation of the pelvisControl is now totally controlled by a clip in the Trax Editor instead of in keyframes.

6. Let's try making a clip for the UpperBody. This time we'll create the clip from the Trax Editor. Select the UpperBody in the Outliner, and then in the Trax Editor choose Create | Clip □.

7. Name the clip **walkUpper** and check the Put Clip In Visor Only check box. Click the Create Clip button.

8. Play the animation. Since no clip appears in the Trax Editor and keyframes have been removed, there is no animation on UpperBody.

FIGURE 12-10   The walkLower clip is loaded in the Trax Editor.

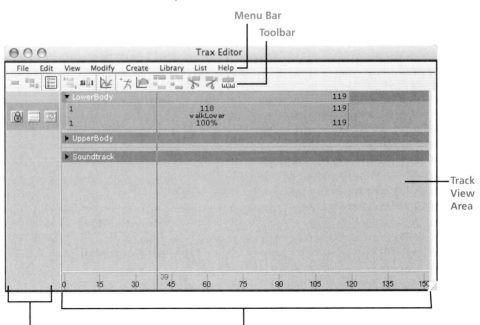

9. You can insert the generated walking clip easily by choosing Library | Insert Clip | walkUpperSource. You should see that the walkUpper clip is now loaded into the Trax Editor, and the body is properly animating.

Animating in the Trax Editor

By simply editing the clips in the Trax Editor, we can change the timing and cycle the clips so that the clip can be repeated. Let's change the timing of the animation by manipulating the clip. It's easy to do this in the Trax Editor:

1. Move your cursor to the lower-right corner of the walkLower clip in the Track View area, where it says "119." The cursor should turn into a slider. Click and drag it to shrink the clip to frame 60. Do the same thing for the walkUpper clip.

2. Play the animation, and the character is now walking twice as fast as before and stops at frame 60. To slow down the animation, simply lengthen the clips. For now, keep the clips at 1 to 60 frames.

3. You can cycle this walk easily using the Trax Editor. Hold down the SHIFT key and move the cursor to the bottom-right corner of the walkLower clip. When you see the cursor change to an arrow in a circle, LMB-drag it to frame 119.

4. Do the same for the walkUpper clip. Now the character is walking twice as fast for 120 frames. That's how you can cycle the clips. Figure 12-11 shows the shortened and cycled clips.

FIGURE 12-11   The clips have been scaled to 60 frames and then cycled to 120 frames.

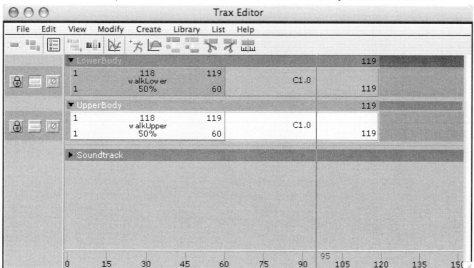

5. Double-click the walkLower clip in the Trax Editor, and look at the attributes for the clip in the Channel Box.

- **Weight**   The power of the clips affecting the character set. A setting of 1 is full power, and if this attribute's value is 0, no animation appears in a clip.
- **Enable**   Turns on/off the clip.
- **Offset**   Lets you offset the animation:
  - **Absolute**   Uses exact values from the clip—for example, if the character is walking forward and you made a clip out of it, the Absolute value will play the animation until the end of the clip, and the character will move back to its original position at the first frame of the clip when it's cycled.
  - **Relative**   Makes the character move forward and keeps it moving.
- **Start Frame**   Lets you manually assign when the clip starts.
- **Cycle**   Lets you numerically input how many times the clip should cycle.
- **Scale**   Lets you shorten and lengthen the clip. This controls the speed of the animation. The smaller the number, the faster the animation will become.
- **Start And Duration**   Shows the current starting frame and length of the clip.

6. If you are happy with the results in the Trax Editor, you can merge the walkLower and its cycle into a new combined clip. This lets you treat it as a totally new single clip. In the Trax Editor, select walkLower and choose Edit | Merge ❏.

7. Type **fastWalkLower** in the Name field and check Add To Trax. This will immediately replace walkLower with a newly merged clip. Checking the Add To Visor option will not replace the original clip, and the merged clip will be added to the Visor.

8. You can export these clips to their own folder so you can reuse them later for other projects. In the Trax Editor, select fastWalkLower and choose File | Export Clip.

9. Name the clip **fastWalkLower** and click the Export button. It should be exported to the clips folder of your current project.

10. To import a clip, select a character set to import and choose Edit | Import Clip. Use the same procedure to create and export a fastWalkUpper clip.

Combining and Blending Clips

Now we will create a new clip and blend it with the clips we just exported.

1. Change the Range Slider's range from frame 1 to frame 90. Go to frame 1 and delete both clips from the Trax Editor. There should be no more animation.

2. At frame 1, pose the character so it is in a neutral pose, before jumping. Select the LowerBody character set using the Character Set Selector and press the S key to key the pose for the lower body.

3. Select the UpperBody character set from the Character Set Selector and key by pressing s. Keying various poses using character sets is easy to do in this way.

4. Go to frame 30 and move the character down, so it is anticipating a jump. You can move the character down by translating the pelvisControl.

5. Change the knee rotate attributes for both foot controls, so the legs are spread apart. Put his arm behind the body.

6. Rotate both the pelvisControl and the spineControl, so that the body is curled forward a little. Key both character sets.

7. In the Time Slider, MMB-drag from frame 30 to frame 40. This will move the Current Time Indicator but leave all animation channels constant. Key both character sets. The purpose of this key is to hold the anticipation pose for 10 frames.

8. Go to frame 50 and make him jump up by translating the pelvisControl and both foot controls upward. Rotate the pelvisControl and the spineControl so the spine appears to be bent backward. Rotate the shoulder and elbow so that they're moving forward. Key both character sets.

9. Now create an extreme pose for the mid-air jump. Go to frame 60 and extend the back a bit more. Rotate the arm a bit more forward. Move the pelvisControl up just a bit more as well. Key the character sets.

10. MMB-drag from frame 40 to frame 70 in the Time Slider, and set keys for both character sets to hold this pose. MMB-drag from frame 1 to frame 90 and key both character sets. This key will set the character back to the default position so that the animation is now cycled.

FIGURE 12-12   Poses for the jumping animation

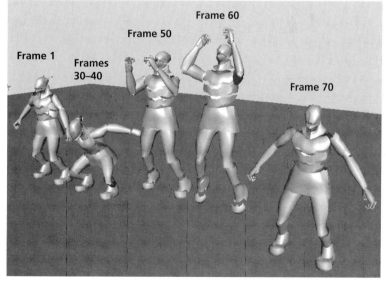

The jumping animation is done! Keying using character sets is a great way to make animation based on specific poses. Look at Figure 12-12 for the four poses you want to make for the jumping move.

Now let's create a clip out of the animation you just made.

1. Select the LowerBody character set from the Character Set Selector and choose Create | Clip ❏ in the Trax Editor.

2. In the Create Clip Options window, name the clip **jumpLower** and enable the Put Clip in Trax Editor and Visor option.

3. Choose the Time Slider for the Time Range setting. Do the same procedure you did for the UpperBody character set, but name the clip **jumpUpper**. Set the Range Slider's range from 1 to 300.

4. Move the jumpLower clip to frame 120 by LMB-dragging so the jump starts at frame 120. Also, move the jumpUpper clip to frame 125. Now a little delay occurs in the arm motion, which makes the jump looks more natural.

5. Add the merged fast walk clips to both character sets. Choose File | Import Clip, and then select fastWalkLower and click the Import button. Do the same for fastWalkUpper.

6. LMB-drag to move both clips to run from frames 2 to 120. Figure 12-13 shows how the clips should be laid out.

FIGURE 12-13   *The clips are laid out in the Trax Editor.*

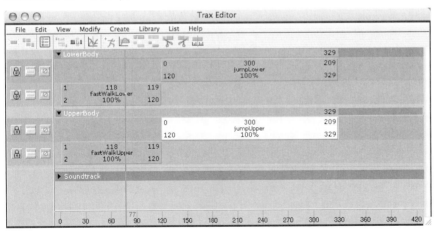

7. Play the animation. The motion is abrupt between the two clips, causing them to snap. You can fix this problem by creating a blend between the clips. In the Trax Editor, select fastWalkLower and SHIFT-select the jumpLower clip.

8. Choose Create | Blend. A blend is created between the two clips in the Trax Editor. Apply a blend to the UpperBody clips, too. Move jumpLower and jumpUpper about 20 frames to the left. Play the animation again. The transition between the clips should look much smoother now.

At some point, you may wish to edit the keys in an individual clip. As mentioned, the keyframe data was removed when the clips were created. However, you can edit the keys by selecting a clip and choosing View | Graph Anim Curves. This will show the animation curves in the Graph Editor for the selected clip. Edit this Graph Editor to fine-tune the motion. Figure 12-14 shows the Graph Editor displaying the animation curves for the clip selected in the Trax Editor.

Animating in the Trax Editor takes a little more work to set up and get used to, but the benefits of using it are incredible for any production environment. The ability to have several people working simultaneously on a motion library for a character is an invaluable asset. You can even use clips on different characters, as long as the rigs are similar.

FIGURE 12-14   *The Graph Editor displaying the animation curves for the clip selected in the Trax Editor*

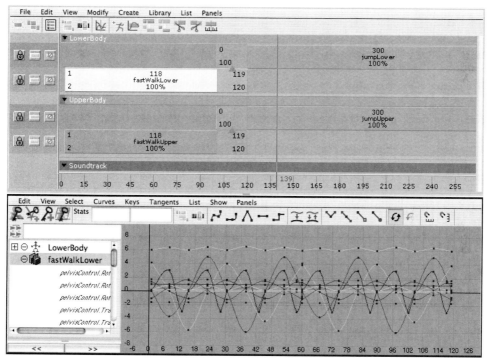

Animation Retargeting

Animation retargeting, one of the most exciting new features in Maya 6, lets you transfer the animation data from one skeleton to another, even if the skeletons are proportioned differently. This means that once you have spent time building a rig for a character, as we did in Chapter 10, the rig can be included in a motion library, from where the animation can be transferred to other skeletons in all of your future projects.

Retargeting Workflow

The workflow involves setting a neutral pose for both the source (the animated) skeleton and the target skeleton. The skeleton is usually in the neutral pose when the joints are placed to match the model. Any animation will be transferred using this neutral pose as the base reference.

Once the neutral pose is set, the joints in both the source and target skeletons must be labeled. Joint labeling is different from just naming joints—to label joints, you choose Skeleton | Retargeting | Joint Labeling to label each joint in a hierarchy. This process tells Maya where similar joints are located in different skeletons. For example, the right elbow joint must be labeled the same for both the source and target skeletons, even though the actual names of each of the joints might be something more specific.

Once the joints in both skeletons are labeled, the retargeting options are set and the retargeting of the animation is performed. Once completed, the target skeleton will animate to match the source skeleton, but at the same time the target will retain all of its unique proportions and characteristics.

Retargeting Tutorial

In this section, we will practice retargeting the animation between a fully rigged and animated biped skeleton and a smaller target skeleton. This example uses the rig that we built in Chapters 9 and 10 as the source skeleton. The target skeleton, named char2, is much smaller and has slightly different proportions. This scene is called mcr_retarget.ma and can be found on the CD. Figure 12-15 shows the two skeletons in the Front View window.

FIGURE 12-15   The source skeleton (left) and the target skeleton (right)

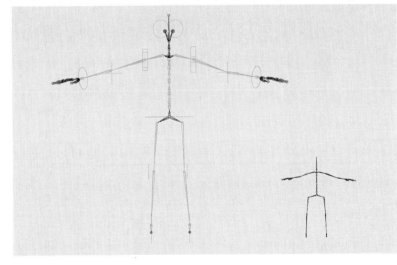

1. Select the root joint on the *source* skeleton. In this case, the root joint is named pelvis.

2. Choose Skeleton | Retargeting | Set Neutral Pose.

3. Select the root joint on the *target* skeleton. This joint is named char2_ pelvis. Choose Skeleton | Retargeting | Set Neutral Pose to set the neutral pose for this skeleton.

4. Select both skeletons, and choose Skeleton | Retargeting | Show All Labels. This will show the labels for all of the joints. By default, they are all labeled None.

5. Because the names of the joints in both skeletons differ only in their prefix, we can quickly label the joints by using the Label Based On Joint Names command. Select the root joint of the source skeleton, and then choose Skeleton | Retargeting | Label Based On Joint Names. The joints will be labeled. Repeat this process for the target skeleton.

6. Inspect the labels. Because the target skeleton did not have any prefixes specifying whether the joints were on the left or right side of the body, you must use the Joint Labeling menu to specify this. Select one of the joints on the left side of the target skeleton and choose Skeleton | Retargeting | Joint Labeling | Right Side. Choose a joint on the left side and choose Skeleton | Retargeting | Joint Labeling | Left Side.

7. You must set a custom label for some joints, such as the ball joints in the foot. Select the left ball joint on the source skeleton and look in the object's Attribute Editor. In the Joint Labeling section, set the Type to Other and label the joint in the otherType field as shown in the illustration.

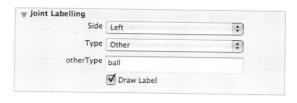

8. Continue using these techniques until all of the joints are labeled and each joint in the source skeleton has a matching joint in the target skeleton. Figure 12-16 shows both skeletons with joint labeling turned on.

FIGURE 12-16   Two skeletons with joint labeling turned on

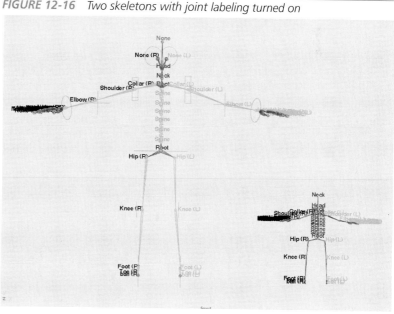

9. Select the root joint on the source skeleton (the pelvis joint). Hold down the SHIFT key and select the root joint on the target skeleton.

10. Choose Skeleton | Retarget ❑. Set the Time Range to Start/End and set the End Time to **40**. Click the Retarget button. Maya will transfer the animation data from the source skeleton to the target skeleton.

Object Interaction

How would you animate objects that are being "picked up" and "put down"? Animating the visibility of several duplicates in different locations might be one solution. Counter animation, or keying the carried object at every frame so it remains in the same place, might be another. However, both of these options require lengthy setups, and making changes to either of these setups could require hours of work. In other words, neither is a good option in a fast-paced production environment.

Constraints

In Chapter 10, we used constraints to help rig our skeleton, but constraints are also a valuable animation tool. Constraints offer an excellent method for solving the "pick up/put down" scenario. Constraints can be keyed on and off, making the relationship between the constrained object and the target object temporary. While point and orient constraints may be used together for object interaction, Maya's parent constraint allows for constrained objects to behave as if they were temporarily parented into the hierarchy. The constrained object will move and rotate around its target object.

Using the Parent Constraint

In this example, an arm will pick up a ball and put it down on top of a cube. For this to work properly, the ball must be parent constrained to both its original position and the hand. However, the constraint to the hand should be added with the hand in position to pick up the ball. This will enable us to take advantage of the Maintain Offset option in the parent constraint's settings. The constraint weight attribute to the original position is keyed at 0 (off) and the hand lifts the ball to the cube. Then the ball is put down and set to its resting position on the top of the cube. The weight to the hand can now be keyed at 0 (off) and the hand can move away.

1. Create a new scene and draw three joints to create an arm.

2. Use the IK Handle tool to create an IK chain that controls the joint hierarchy. Either parent or point constrain the IK handle to a control object. For this example, create a cube to use as a control object.

3. Now create a sphere and another cube to use as props in the scene. Scale and position them so that they look similar to Figure 12-17.

4. Create a locator (choose Create | Locator) and parent constrain the ball to this locator. Select the locator, SHIFT-select the sphere, and then choose Constrain | Parent ❑.

5. In the Parent Constraint Options window, make sure that Maintain Offset is checked.

6. Select the constraint in the Outliner, and then set a key on the constraint weight at a value of 1 by clicking the Locator1 W1 attribute in the Channel Box; then right-click and choose Key Selected from the marking menu.

7. Key the arm's IK in its original position. Then, at frame 30, key the IK so that it is in position to pick up the ball.

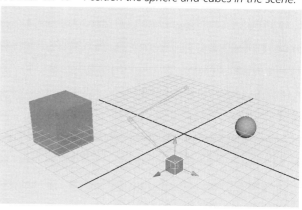

FIGURE 12-17   Position the sphere and cubes in the scene.

8. Select the hand (the control cube), then select the ball, and choose Constrain | Parent ☐. Make sure that Maintain Offset is checked. Also, you can set the Weight attribute to **0** before constraining the object. Key the weight at this frame.

9. Advance one frame, set the Locator1 W1 attribute to **0**, and set the P Cube1 W0 attribute to **1**. Key these values. Your scene should look like Figure 12-18.

NOTE   *You may have to set your tangents to stepped so that no interpolation occurs between the keys set on the constraint's weight attributes. You can quickly do this by selecting the constraint and then holding down the SHIFT key and drag-selecting all the keys in the Time Slider. Then right-click and choose Tangents | Stepped from the marking menu.*

FIGURE 12-18   *The scene so far*

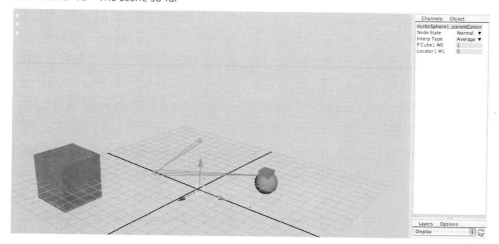

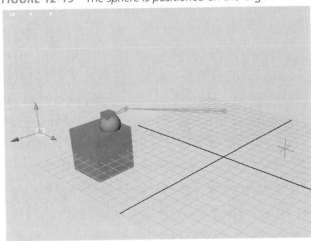

FIGURE 12-19   *The sphere is positioned on the large cube.*

10. Thirty frames later, the IK handle should be placed and keyed in position to set the sphere on the large cube, as shown in Figure 12-19.

11. Select the sphere, and then choose Constrain | Set Rest Position. This will keep the ball from snapping back to its origin when all constraints are set to 0.

12. Select the constraint and key the P Cube1 W0 attribute to 0.

13. Finally, move and key the position of the control cube so that the arm is away from the ball.

14. Play back the animation to see the result.

Summary

Character animation can take a lifetime to master. To create good animation in a reasonable timeframe, the most successful approach will be a combination of your technical and creative abilities. We hope that the information provided over the last four chapters will help lay a foundation for your future animations.

Next, we will switch gears and explore the world of surfaces and textures.

Texturing, Lighting, and Rendering

Texturing and Lighting Basics

One of the fundamental concepts in

color theory is that color cannot exist without light,

nor can light exist without color. In this chapter, we

will explore Maya's tools for adding light and color

to your scene. *Texturing* generally refers to the

process of building a surface's detail and indicating

how that surface will react to light. In the real

world, all surfaces can be described by their color,

shininess, smoothness, and opacity. In Maya, a

surface's material contains attributes to control

all of these characteristics. By assigning different

values to these attributes, you can make a surface appear to be made out of a variety of materials, including plastic, metal, glass, or wood. These values can be controlled by a texture—either a bitmap file or a procedural texture—giving the material attributes some detail, irregularities, or pattern.

As is usually the case in any visual art, your greatest asset in the texturing process is your own eyes—use them to study the world around you. Being able to recognize and break down a surface and how it reacts to light is the first step in this process. Learning about the different materials and how to control their attributes in Maya is the next. Therefore, it is always important to do research. Find photographs of surfaces similar to the ones you are trying to emulate. If possible, keep something made of this material at your desk so you can play with it and move it around in the light.

Hypershade: Maya's Texturing Interface

The Hypershade window (Window | Rendering Editors | Hypershade) is shown in Figure 13-1. This is where you will build and edit materials for all the objects in your scene. Like the Hypergraph, the Hypershade displays a dependency graph of the different materials in your scene. In fact, these materials display the exact same nodes and you could do all the same editing and connecting by using the Hypergraph and other menu commands. The main difference between the two is that, when dealing with material-related nodes (also known as *rendering nodes*), the Hypershade displays its node icons, known as *swatches* in Maya, in more detail. This means that a file texture node's icon displays a thumbnail version of the actual texture. A material node will display everything from the falloff of the specularity to the peaks and troughs of its bumps. This, in addition to all the material-related menu sets readily available with a right-click, makes the Hypershade a much more artist-friendly interface than the Hypergraph.

 TIP **When working with Hypershade, it can be helpful to use one of the saved panel layouts. A button that changes the layout to the Hypershade/Perspective layout is available in the toolbar.**

The basic workflow of building a material is to start with a rendering node, such as a basic material, and edit its attributes. Other nodes, such as textures, can be connected to these attributes by dragging and dropping them onto a material and choosing the desired connection. Placement nodes are then edited to direct how a texture is positioned on a surface. For more advanced materials, additional *utility nodes* are connected to tweak the attributes of the other nodes in the network. As you'll see, even a relatively simple exercise in the Material Editor can lead to a few dozen separate nodes and connections. The network of connected nodes that feed into a material is called a *shading network*. Therefore, a completed material is often called a *shader*.

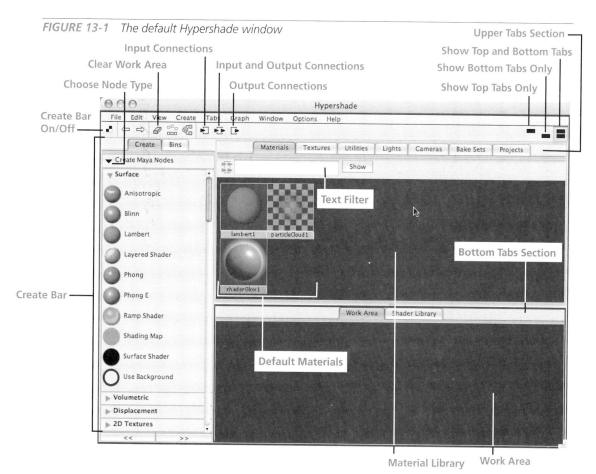

FIGURE 13-1 *The default Hypershade window*

Hypershade Sections

The Hypershade is divided into three main sections: the Create Bar, the top tabs section, and the bottom tabs section. In the Create Bar, you can create any of the rendering nodes by clicking them. Click and hold the Choose Node Type arrow to view the different types of rendering nodes. You may choose the Create Maya Node (the default), Create Mental Ray Nodes, or Create All Nodes. Once a selection is made, the relevant nodes will appear in the Create Bar. Items in the Create Bar are also available by right-clicking in the other sections of the Hypershade window, so to create more space to work, you may want to hide the Create Bar. To do so, click the Create Bar On/Off button in the toolbar, shown in Figure 13-1. The top tabs section contains all of the rendering nodes in the current scene; they are organized by category: Materials, Textures, Utilities, Lights, Cameras, Bake Sets, and Projects. Here's how this works. If, for example, you click a Blinn material in the Create Bar, a new Blinn material icon will appear in the Materials tab. Likewise, any texture that is created will be displayed in the Textures tab. This feature organizes the different kinds of nodes in your scene.

The third section of the Hypershade, the bottom tabs section, is where you can view, select, and edit the connections of the rendering nodes. To view a node in the work area, you can MMB-drag the node's icon from one of the top tabs down into the work area. To view its connections, you can use one of the three connection buttons in the Hypershade toolbar. This will expand that node to show its input connections, output connections, or both, in the work area. To clear this space, use the Clear Work Area button in the toolbar. Selecting one of the rendering nodes from the scene library tabs and clicking one of the display connections buttons will automatically clear the work area and display the connections for the selected node.

These two sections of the Hypershade can be hidden by using the three buttons in the upper-right corner of the Hypershade toolbar. Clicking the first button hides the lower tabs and expands the space for the upper tabs. Clicking the second button hides the upper tabs and shows only the lower section, and clicking the third (the default view) displays both tab sections.

To move around in the Hypershade window, you use the same pan and zoom controls used in most of the other windows in Maya. To zoom in and out, hold down ALT (OPTION) and then RMB-MMB-drag. To pan, hold down ALT (OPTION) and the MMB-button and drag. Pressing the F key fits all the swatches in the active window. All the items available from the Hypershade menu bar are available with a right-click. When you start a new project, Maya loads three materials by default, as shown in Figure 13-1. These are the Lambert, a particle cloud, and a shader glow. Every time you create a new piece of geometry in the scene, it will use this Lambert material. Any particle cloud or glow will use the other defaults, respectively.

Working with the Hypershade

Let's practice working with the Hypershade by creating a Blinn material and connecting a texture to the color attribute.

1. The Create Bar should be turned on and displaying its Create Maya Nodes option; click the Choose Node Type arrow and select Create Maya Nodes from the resulting menu, if necessary.

2. Click the sphere icon labeled Blinn. A Blinn material will be added to your scene and will appear in both the Materials tab and in the Work Area tab. If this is the first Blinn material you have created in the scene, it will be named blinn1. The next time you create a Blinn material, it will be named blinn2.

3. Scroll down in the Create Bar and find the Textures section. Unfold this section to see the texture nodes. Click the Checker icon (see Figure 13-2). A checker texture node is added to the scene and appears on the Textures tab and the Work Area tab. Depending on where your Blinn material was positioned in the Workspace, your checker texture node might overlap it. If this is the case, simply select one of the nodes in the work area and drag it out of the way so that all the nodes are visible. The work area should like that shown in Figure 13-2. In addition, notice that a 2D placement node has also

FIGURE 13-2   *2D placement node, checker texture, and Blinn material in the work area*

been created and connected to the checker texture node. This controls how that texture fits into the texture space. We'll look at this feature in more depth in the "Placement Nodes" section later in the chapter.

4. We want to have this checker texture control the color attribute of the Blinn material. We can make this connection directly in the Hypershade by dragging and dropping the checker node's icon onto the material node's icon. In the work area, select the checker texture node and MMB-drag it onto the Blinn material node. When you release the mouse button, a marking menu appears with a list of attributes that the checker texture can be mapped to by default. Since we want to map this to the Color attribute, choose Color from the list. A connection is made, and the material node icon is updated to display the checker texture on the material. Your work area should look like the illustration.

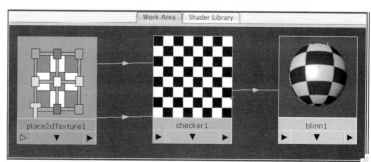

5. Lastly, we assign the material to an object in the scene. Create a NURBS sphere (Create | NURBS Primitives | Sphere). You can assign the material to the object simply by MMB-dragging the material swatch onto the object in the view window or the Outliner. Another way would be to select the object, right-click a material in the Hypergraph, and choose Assign Material To Selection from the marking menu. To view the texture on the object in a view window, make sure you turn on hardware texturing by pressing the 6 key.

TIP *You can quickly assign a texture to a group of objects by first selecting them all and then using the marking menu option to assign materials.*

Using the Attribute Editor for Editing Materials

The Attribute Editor (shown in Figure 13-3) also plays an important role when you are working with materials. While connections can easily be made in the Hypershade window alone, the actual editing of attribute values is done in the Attribute Editor. Connections to other textures can also be made in the Attribute Editor. In fact, this tool offers access to more of the possible connections than the marking menu that is displayed when a node is dragged onto a material in the Hypershade.

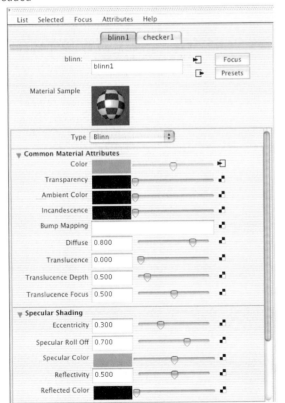

FIGURE 13-3 *The Attribute Editor with a material node loaded*

To get the most out of material editing, it is best to use the Hypershade and Attribute Editor together. Generally, you use the Hypershade to view connections and select particular nodes. Once selected, that node's attributes are displayed in the Attribute Editor, where they can be edited. Connections to textures are probably best made through the Attribute Editor, and then additional utilities and optimizations can be made back in the Hypershade.

NOTE *When connecting nodes in the Hypershade, you might also use the Connection Editor. You will see examples of this workflow in Chapter 14.*

Let's try using the Attribute Editor to make connections to textures. We are going to continue working with the material we created earlier. If you no longer have that scene available, follow steps 1–5 in the preceding section to create a Blinn material with a checker texture connected to the color attribute.

1. Open the Attribute Editor, either by pressing CTRL-A (CONTROL-A), clicking the Show Attribute Editor button in the Status Line, or double-clicking a material node in the Hypershade.

2. Click the different nodes in the Workspace and notice how the Attribute Editor loads the specific attributes for the selected node. The Blinn material node attributes describe the basic surface characteristics, the checker texture attributes contain values that edit the colors in that checker pattern, and the placement node attributes have values for translations, rotation, and other spatial attributes.

3. Let's change the color of the checker pattern. Select the checker texture node in the Hypershade. In the Attribute Editor, click the color swatch in the Color1 attribute. The Color Chooser, shown here, will open. Use the chooser to change the white to red. Click the Accept button to close the Color Chooser.

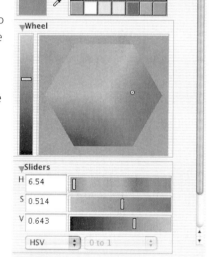

4. In the Attribute Editor, you can use the slider to the right of the color swatch to change the brightness value of the red. Change the Color2 attribute to blue.

FIGURE 13-4   Changing values in the Attribute Editor

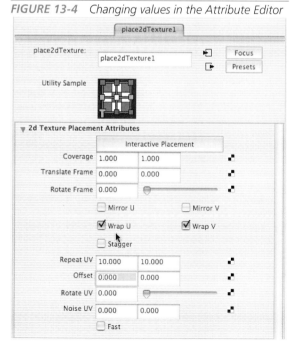

5. Now we'll change the tiling of the checker pattern. Select the 2D placement node (named place2dTexture1) in the Hypershade to view its attributes in the Attribute Editor. Change the value of Repeat UV to **10** for both U and V, as shown in Figure 13-4. The checker pattern on the checker node icon in the Hypershade window will change to show more tiles. Moving downstream, the Blinn material node also updates to show the new checker pattern mapped to it.

6. Next, we'll edit the bump attribute of the Blinn material node by connecting a texture to it. Select the blinn1 material in the Hypershade window to display its attributes in the Attribute Editor, as shown in Figure 13-3. Find Bump Mapping in the Attribute Editor (under Common Material Attributes). Click the checker button at the right to add a connection to this attribute. This will bring up the Create Render Node window shown here.

7. The Create Render Node window is really the same as the Create Render Node menu in the Hypershade window. Make sure that projection type is set to Normal at the top of this window. Then select the Checker texture. You'll notice that in the Hypershade, a new checker texture node is connected to a bump2d node, which is in turn connected to the bump attribute of the Blinn material node. A bump map creates raised and indented areas in a surface when it is rendered. Lighter grayscale values raise the surface, while darker values create indentations. (We'll talk more about this attribute in the "Material Nodes" section, later in this chapter.) Of course, this can be reversed by assigning a negative value to the bump depth attribute or by using a reverse utility node.

TIP *As you continue to add nodes, the work area in the Hypershade will start to become cluttered and difficult to read. For this reason, it is a good idea to select the material node, in this case the Blinn1 material, and click the Input Connections button in the Hypershade window's toolbar (see Figure 13-1). This will regraph the entire connection network and clean up the work area.*

We want the new checker pattern to control the bump value of the surface, but we also want it to align with the checker pattern connected to the color attribute. We could go in and make sure that the Repeat UV values of the placement node of the color map match the values of the bump map, but this would be time-consuming and would likely result in errors if more attributes in that node needed to be duplicated.

Instead, we'll connect the entire placement node that is controlling the checker pattern on the color attribute it to the new checker pattern that is connected to the bump map.

8. Select the 2D placement node that is connected to the checker texture node controlling the color channel. Then MMB-drag it onto the checker texture we created in step 7. Choose Default from the resulting marking menu to complete the connections. Now if you roll over the new connection lines, you'll see that the OutUV and the OutUVFilterSize output attributes are connected to the UVCoord and UVFilterSize input attributes, respectively. The old placement node is no longer connected and can be deleted by selecting it and pressing the DELETE key. The work area should look like the example shown in Figure 13-5.

9. Lastly, we can edit the amount of effect that the bump map has on the surface by editing the bump depth attribute in the bump2d node. Select the bump2d node in the Hypershade window to view its attributes in the Attribute Editor. You will see two attributes displayed: Bump Value and Bump Depth. The Bump Depth is the attribute that the checker texture is controlling. The Bump Depth controls the amount of the effect that the map will have in creating the bumps on the surface.

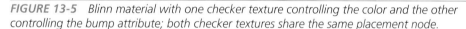

FIGURE 13-5 *Blinn material with one checker texture controlling the color and the other controlling the bump attribute; both checker textures share the same placement node.*

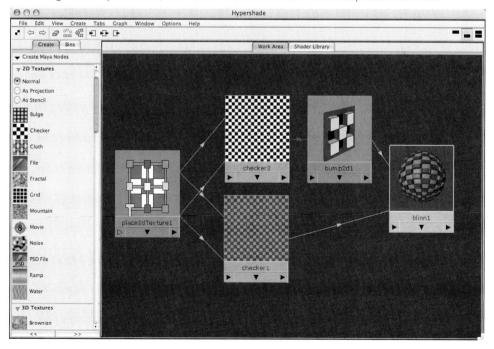

10. Change the Bump Depth value with the slider or by entering a value numerically. Watch the effect this has by viewing the material node in the Hypershade window. The illustration shows the some material applied to a sphere. The material on the right uses a positive Bump Depth value, while the material on the left uses a negative value. The effect is that the bumps are inverted.

Rendering Nodes and Their Attributes

In the last section, you saw some of the basic rendering nodes. Rendering nodes can be divided into five basic categories: materials, textures, utilities, lights, and cameras. The Blinn and Lambert materials are examples of material nodes, the checker node is an example of a texture node, and the placement node is a type of utility node. While we have already used these nodes, connected them, and edited their attributes, we have only touched the surface (so to speak). In the next few sections we will dig deeper and examine some of the individual attributes of the material, texture, and utility nodes. Then, in Chapter 14, two tutorials will allow you to put these basics to use in building several materials to texture map surfaces of different shapes.

Material Nodes

Material nodes are responsible for controlling the characteristics of a surface. The main material nodes in Maya are Anisotropic, Blinn, Lambert, Phong, Phong E, and Ramp Shader. While the texture nodes might display a pattern hinting at the material that a surface could be made of, the material node is primarily responsible for communicating this effect. Even without a texture containing pictorial details, the type of material node and the settings of its attributes will largely tell you the material is made of plastic, metal, glass, rock, or other material. The way material interacts with its environment—the objects, colors, and lights that surround it—provides most of the visual clues about its substance.

Look at the candle pictured here. What is it about its surface that tells us it is made of wax? The reflection of the light source on the object is very soft, because the light is being absorbed into all the little pores on the surface instead of reflecting back. This characteristic is controlled by the *specularity attributes* of the material. Notice that the top of the candle is illuminated from the flame inside it. You can see the light coming through the wax. This is controlled by the *translucency attribute* of the material.

Take a moment to analyze the surface characteristics of a mirror. What color is a mirror? It is actually black, but it does not give off any of its own color. Instead, its surface is almost completely reflective, so it just reflects what is around it. To create a material attribute for a mirror surface, you would turn down the *diffuse value* all the way, so that the color of the object is not reflected back into the camera.

All the materials in Maya share the same set of attributes. These are known as the *common material attributes*. Where these materials differ is in the way they calculate their specular and reflection attributes, if they have any. The Lambert material does not have any specular attributes. It is best used for matte surfaces, such as chalk or certain types of paper or fabric.

Common Material Attributes
The common material attributes for all of Maya's materials are as follows:

- **Color**   The color of the material. Assigning an RGB or HSV (Hue, Saturation, Value) value using the Color Chooser sets this attribute. Its brightness value can be controlled with the slider.

- **Transparency**   Controls the transparency/opacity of the surface. A value of 0 (black) renders the image 100 percent opaque. A value of 1 (white) renders the object totally transparent. A color value can also be used; it will act as a color filter over objects behind it.

- **Ambient Color**   Sets the color of the darkened or black areas. Think of it as bringing up the black contrast levels of an image in Photoshop. When used together with ambient lights, the color and brightness of the lights control the amount of ambient color specified in this attribute, which will contribute to the final render.

- **Incandescence**   Controls the self-illumination, or luminance, of the object. This attribute creates the illusion that the object is emitting light. The material will illuminate the color set using the Color Chooser with the brightness amount set with the slider. Note, however, that this will not cause the object to illuminate any objects around it.

- **Bump Mapping**   Alters the surface normals to create the illusion of raised areas and indentations on a surface. This attribute uses an 8-bit grayscale image to assign transparency values: 0 (black) is the lowest or deepest, while 1 (white) appears to be raised or highest.

- **Diffuse**   Sometimes called falloff, this attribute controls the amount of light reflected back from the surface. At a value of 1, the surface will reflect back 100 percent of the color specified in the color channel. The default value is 0.8.

- **Translucence**   Controls the amount of light that can pass through an object. Think of the way light travels through wax, leaves, and certain plastics and rubbers. At a setting of 0.0 (the default), no light shows through. At 1.0, all light shows through.

- **Translucence Depth**   Controls the amount of decay that will occur as the light moves through the object. When the value is set to 0, no decay occurs and the light emitted through the other side will be just as bright. In most cases, the light will lose some of its brightness and decay before it reaches the other side of the object.

- **Translucence Focus**   Sets the amount of blurring on the surface of backlit objects. The light scattering on a thin surface, such as a leaf or skin, will cause this effect. At 0.0, light is scattered in all directions.

Specular Shading Attributes

As mentioned, specularity controls the reflectivity of a surface. Even a surface that doesn't necessarily reflect objects around it will reflect the light sources that illuminate it. This is known as the *specular reflection*. The specular attributes differ slightly depending on the material you are using. Usually some type of control can be used for the size of the highlight and another control for how it falls off; this is illustrated in Figure 13-6. Some materials, such as the Phong material, use composite algorithms to calculate the specular shading; others, such as Phong E, Blinn, and Anisotropic, break up the specular attributes into a several attributes for finer control. The Anisotropic material even lets you control the shape of the specular reflections.

The reflectivity of an object determines how much of the environment or other objects will be reflected from the surface. The color of the reflection is determined by the reflected color attribute. For a surface to reflect objects around it, raytracing must be turned on in the Render Global Settings window. (Render Global Settings will be discussed in detail in Chapter 16.) Because raytracing is very processor-intensive, it can take a long time to render. So reflections are sometimes faked by applying an environmental reflection map to the reflected color attribute. We will play with this in the next exercise.

Texture Nodes

Texture nodes contain the picture or pattern that will be mapped onto a material. In Maya, you can use a procedural texture or a file texture.

Procedural Textures

Procedural textures are completely computer generated from mathematical equations. Checker, bulge, fractal noise, and cloth are all examples of procedural textures. Each has its own specific parameters to achieve its unique results. One of the biggest advantages of using procedural texture maps is that they are resolution-independent. Whereas bitmapped file textures will start to soften and break apart as you zoom closer, procedural textures will remain infinitely sharp no matter how close you get.

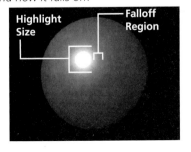

FIGURE 13-6   You can control a highlight and how it falls off.

A subset of procedural textures is called *3D textures*. Because a procedural texture is not limited to 2D pixel information, the computer is able to calculate the depth of a texture. Marble or any kind of rock is a good example from the real world. The patterns in marble are continuous through its mineral layers, changing slightly from slice to slice. A 3D texture in Maya behaves the same way. This texture is especially useful if the surface is semitransparent.

The placement of 3D textures also has some advantages. Because you are not limited to a 2D projection method, distortions and discontinuities are less of an issue with 3D textures. We'll discuss this further in the next section, "Placement Nodes."

File Textures

File texture nodes contain a bitmapped image that is imported into the scene. This image can be loaded through the Image Name attribute in the file texture node's Attribute Editor. Further adjustments can be made to this image in the Color Balance section of the file texture's Attribute Editor. Color Gain and Color Offset control the brightness and contrast of the texture's RGB channels, and Alpha Gain and Offset control the levels of the file texture's alpha channel.

Placement Nodes

A placement node is a type of utility node. These nodes are automatically created with and connected to a texture node. They can also be created through the Create Utility menu. Placement nodes control how a texture is mapped to a surface. Two basic kinds of placement nodes can be used: 2D and 3D. To understand the difference between these nodes and how to use them, we first need to talk about how a texture is mapped to a surface.

Implicit UVs and Projection Nodes

Maya uses one of two methods of mapping textures: normal and as a projection. The normal method uses the existing UV coordinates in a surface (known as *implicit UVs*) to decide how the texture is mapped across it. The projection method uses a primitive shape—such as a plane, sphere, cube, or cylinder—and projects the texture from that shape onto a surface. Whenever you create a texture node from the Create Render menu, you specify whether it will be mapped normally (as in implicitly) or as a projection. Normal and projection modes can be used on both NURBS and polygonal objects. However, while NURBS surfaces already have UVs due to their nature, polygonal objects might require a fair bit of work to assign them properly.

Recall the discussion from Chapter 4 about surface parameterization. Any point on a NURBS surface can be described by a parameter with values for U and V between 0 and 1. The surface origin is at 0,0 and the opposite corner could have a parameter value of 1,1; 2,2; 5,5; or 6.3,8.9. A 2D texture has a coordinate system as well. Think of a texture, a bitmapped file created in Photoshop, laid out on a grid. Texture coordinates have U and V coordinates from 0 to 1, with 0,0 at the origin (bottom-left corner) and 1,1 at the end (upper-right corner). When the texture is applied to a surface, Maya internally parameterizes the surface from 0 to 1 if it isn't already done, and then it can easily match the corresponding coordinate from the texture. No matter how curvy or twisted the surface, the texture borders of the texture map will match all edges of the surface, as shown in the NURBS surface here. The 2D texture node can then be used to manipulate the position of this texture on the surface, control how much of the surface it will cover, or control how many times it will repeat.

A polygonal object, however, does not have these implicit UVs. UV sets can be created and assigned to any polygonal object by using one of the texturing tools found by choosing Edit Polygons | Texture. With these texture tools, the UVs can be assigned planarly, cylindrically, or spherically. Individual faces, or groups of faces, can be selected and assigned with a different type. If the surface is irregular or has areas obstructed by other polygonal faces, such as a humanoid face, the UV texture tools can be used to unwrap the UVs and lay them out flat so the UVs can moved around to coincide with specific points on the texture. Once an object has a UV set assigned to it, a texture can be mapped to it in normal mode.

Whenever a texture is projected, Maya creates a projection node (a type of utility node) to specify how this texture will be projected. The texture's output is fed into the projection node, and then the projection node is fed into the desired attribute of the material. This projection node is capable of projecting that texture in a number of different ways: planarly, cubically, cylindrically, or spherically. These types of projections can all be set in the projection node's Attribute Editor by changing the Proj Type attribute.

The projection node actually maps the texture onto an imaginary surface with implicit UVs and then projects it onto the object from that position, regardless of the surface's UVs. The result is an even distribution of the texture on the faces or parameters that are perpendicular to the projection plane. However, as the angle of the projection to surface increases, the texture will begin to stretch, as shown here.

The 3D placement node determines the position of this projection node in world space. The exact position of the texture map on the surface can be edited by grabbing this placement node, moving it, and rotating it in the view window to achieve the desired placement. The Scale tool can be used to change the tiling.

Projections are most useful for mapping a singe texture across multiple surfaces. (A great example of this can be found in Chapter 20. It could also be useful to apply textures to the multi-patch NURBS spaceship model that we built in Chapter 4.) Another good use for projections is when you want to map a texture to a surface so that it specifically does not use the surface's implicit UVs. Sometimes, the parameterization or the layout of the UVs flows in an undesirable direction for texture mapping, or it is uneven. The next illustration shows two identical NURBS surfaces

with checker textures applied to them. The poles of these surfaces (the point where all of the isoparms intersect) are at their centers. The surface on the left has the map applied in normal mode so that it follows the surface's parameterization. The surface on the right has the texture projected from a planar projection type.

2D Placement Node

Whenever you are dealing with a 2D texture—whether it's a procedural or a bitmap image—you will use at least the 2D placement node. This node controls how the texture map is placed within the UV space from 0 to 1. Let's take a look at some of the attributes of the 2D placement node and the ways they affect how the texture is mapped. The first three attributes listed in the Attribute Editor deal with how the texture frame is laid out. The rest of the attributes deal with how the texture behaves within that frame.

- **Coverage** Controls the amount of surface the texture will cover. A value of 0.5 for the U value will cover 50 percent of the surface in the U direction. This value can be interactively changed in the view window by clicking the Interactive Placement button in the 2D placement node's Attribute Editor and MMB-dragging the edge of the 2D placement frame on the surface in the view window (see Figure 13-7).

FIGURE 13-7 *Interactively changing the coverage attribute with the Texture Placement tool*

- **Translate Frame** Sets the position of the covered area. This value can be interactively edited in the view window using the placement tool: MMB-drag in the middle of the frame and position the texture in the desired position.

- **Rotate Frame** Orients the covered area. To rotate the frame interactively with the placement tool, MMB-drag one of the corners of the frame.

- **Mirror** Mirrors the tiles next to one another to hide possible tiling artifacts, such as seams. This attribute requires that the Repeat values be set to more than 1. Figure 13-8 shows an example.

FIGURE 13-8 *Two surfaces with the same texture repeated, but the texture on the right has Mirroring turned on*

- **Wrap U and V** Sets whether a map is repeated in U and V over the entire surface.

- **Repeat UV** Specifies how many copies of the texture map are mapped within the coverage area along either the U or V directions. This is sometimes called *tiling*.

- **Offset**   Offsets the pattern of the texture map.
- **Rotate UV**   Rotates the texture itself. Realize that this differs from Rotate Frame in that the actual transforms of the frame remain. It is just the texture map within that frame that rotates.

> *TIP   All of the attributes in this second set can also be edited interactively with the Interactive Placement tool. When you select this tool, it is set to label mapping mode by default. This mode lets you edit the coverage/frame attributes as we did previously. If you double-click the Interactive Placement tool icon in the toolbar and change its setting to Surface Placement, you can edit the other tile-based attributes. MMB-drag the UV frame and place it on the surface. Select the edges and MMB-drag to change the coverage. If a point on the corner is selected and MMB-dragged, the rotation of the frame can be edited.*

3D Textures and 3D Placement Nodes

As mentioned, the 3D placement node is used mainly to position a texture or projection node in 3D space. While you have already seen how it is used to position a projection node that is projecting a 2D texture, you've not yet seen it used for a 3D texture. A 3D texture is a special kind of procedural texture map. Instead of being a flat surface, the 3D texture has depth to it. This means that you could map a 3D texture to a sphere and not worry about it stretching anywhere. All points in the surface in 3D space are evenly mapped. The place 3D texture node positions the 3D texture. The next illustration shows a 3D marble texture applied to a head. The box around the head is the placement node used to position the texture.

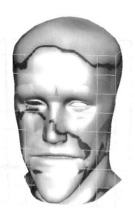

The 3D placement node is really not much more than a basic transform node. In this situation, the placement node is positioned in world space. The transform tools are used to move, rotate, and scale the texture. Since the placement of a 3D texture is based on the place 3D texture node's world space coordinates, realize that any object with a projection or texture that is mapped with a 3D placement node will "move through" the 3D texture space when the object is transformed in any way. One way to avoid this would be to group the place 3D texture node to the object to which it is being mapped. However, while this will work fine for rigid objects such as spaceships or cars, you'll have problems if the mapped geometry deforms. Therefore, when using 3D textures that need to stay put, it is a good idea to

"bake" them onto a material. This can be done by selecting the material node and the surface it is mapped onto and choosing Edit | Convert To File Texture in the Hypershade. This will save a texture map corresponding to how the material is mapped to the surface and will create a duplicate of the material with the texture nodes mapped as normal textures.

Light Nodes

Maya's light nodes are designed to work just like lighting in the real world. This allows a traditional lighting designer to begin using Maya quickly, because the tools have familiar names and behaviors.

Traditionally, lights serve two main purposes in film and still photography: The first is, obviously, to illuminate the scene being photographed. Without light there would be no color—the printed film would be nothing but black. The other purpose for lighting is to add a dramatic effect or mood to a scene. In fact, lighting may be one of the first visual effects ever used. Heroic characters are traditionally well lit, even shining, whereas villains lurk in shadows or are backlit. Just as it is important to do research and collect references on your models and textures, it is important to take notice of lighting, both in the natural world and in the movies.

Types of Lights

Maya has six different types of lights: ambient, directional, point, spot, area light, and volume. All these lights can be created from the main Create | Lights menu or in the Create Lights menu in the Hypershade. The different types of lights (shown in Figure 13-9) create the following effects:

- Ambient light simulates diffused lighting in all directions. Use this light as a fill light to brighten the dark areas of the scene or even out the lighting entirely.

- Directional light shines evenly in one direction only, such that the rays are emitted parallel to each other from an infinitely large plane. Use this light to simulate a light source such as the sun. Maya uses a directional light as the default light in the scene.

FIGURE 13-9   Different types of lights and how they illuminate

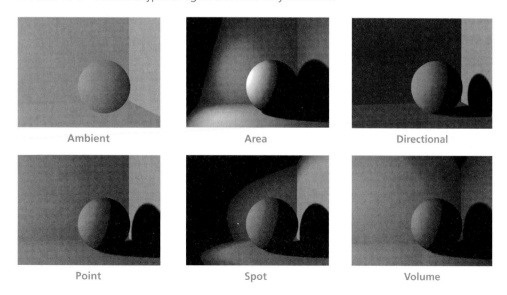

Ambient   Area   Directional

Point   Spot   Volume

- A point light shines evenly in all directions from the location of the light. Use a point light to simulate an incandescent light bulb.

- A spot light shines evenly within a narrow range of directions (defined by a cone) from the location of the light. Use a spot light to create a beam of light that gradually becomes wider—for example, a flashlight or car headlight.

- An area light is a 2D rectangular light source. The size of the light, which can be determined using the standard scale tools, has a direct effect on the distribution of the light in the scene. Sunlight coming through a window is a common example: the light can be scaled to fit the window shape while the reflection of the light on, say, the floor is brightest closest to the window and falls off farther away from the window.

- A volume light illuminates objects within a finite region defined by a primitive shape: sphere, box, cylinder, or cone. The direction of the light can be set to outward, inward, or down, making a volume light capable of simulating many of the other light types in Maya. Another advantages of using a volume light is that its total decay distance is indicated by its icon in the view window, so precise placement is easily achieved without having to do numerous test renders. The color range is also controllable through a ramp interface. This allows you to control the color of the light at any point along its volume decay. It can also be used to control the falloff.

Light Attributes

Lights in Maya can be translated, rotated, and scaled just like any other piece of geometry in the scene. After adding a light to a scene, the best way to place it is to select it and choose the Show Manipulator tool from the toolbar. This will let you position the light as well as its reference or target. Another way to place a light is to look through it and use the standard camera tools— track, dolly, and zoom—to place and point the light precisely. Just select the light and choose Panels | Look Through Selected.

FIGURE 13-10   The Intensity Sample swatch in the Attribute Editor shows the general effect of a light intensity value.

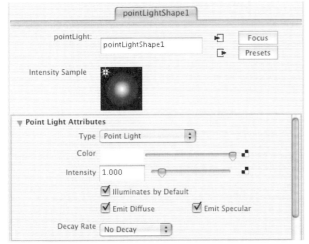

You can edit a light's attributes in the Attribute Editor, shown in Figure 13-10. Attributes common to all lights are color and intensity, which are pretty straightforward. The color of the light is used to set the color the objects in the scene will receive from their illumination. It is even possible to map a texture to this attribute. The intensity of the light controls its brightness. You can get a rough approximation of the general effect a certain intensity value will produce by monitoring the Intensity Sample swatch (shown in the figure) in the light's Attribute Editor.

It is important that you realize that lighting is an additive/subtractive process. If you have two lights with exactly the same attributes and positions in space and both have an intensity value of 1, they will produce the same amount of light that one light with an intensity value of 2 would produce. It is also possible to use a negative intensity value to subtract or dim light that is emitted from other lights in the scene.

Area, point, and spot lights all have an attribute called *decay rate*. The decay rate controls how quickly the light's intensity decreases over distance. The default is set to No Decay. This means that the light's intensity is continuous, and therefore it can reach every object in the scene regardless of how far the object may be from the light. To make the decay falloff faster, use Linear (slowest), Quadratic, or Cubic (fastest). The falloff of a spotlight with the four different decay settings is shown in Figure 13-11.

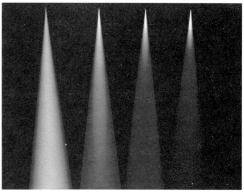

FIGURE 13-11 *From left to right, a spotlight with No Decay, Linear, Quadratic, and Cubic decay settings*

Spot Light Attributes

A spot light contains three main attributes for controlling its beam. The *cone angle* is simple. It is the angle in degrees from one edge of the light's beam to the opposite edge. The *penumbra angle* controls the falloff, in degrees, of the edges of the beam. This can be a positive or negative value. If it's positive, the falloff will occur from the edge of the light, determined by the cone angle, outward by the penumbra angle. Therefore, if the cone angle was set to 30 and the penumbra angle was set to 5, the light would have a total angle of 40 (30 + 5 + 5—that is 5 degrees on each side). The beam's falloff would begin at 30 degrees and would fall off to an intensity of 0 at 40 degrees.

The overall shape can be previewed and edited in real time by monitoring the Light Shape swatch found in the spot light's Attribute Editor. Figure 13-12 shows a spot light's beam projected onto a surface. The spot light has a cone angle value of 40 (the default), but the left half has a penumbra angle value of –5 and the right side has a penumbra value of +5.

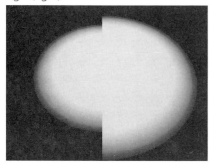

FIGURE 13-12 *Spot light beam with a negative (left) and positive penumbra angle (right)*

The *dropoff attribute* is also unique to the spot light. It is similar to a penumbra with a negative value, in that it controls the falloff from the beam's cone angle inward. But it behaves more like the decay rate, in that it is based on the distance from the center of the beam instead of from the edges. The Light Shape swatch in the Attribute Editor should give a good indication of what effect the Dropoff setting will produce.

FIGURE 13-13   *A rendered image of a glow effect with a lens flare*

Light Effects

The point, spot, area, and volume lights are all capable of producing various lighting effects, such as Light Fog, Light Glow, or both. These effect settings are located in the Light Effects folder of the Attribute Editor. To apply these light effects, click the map button next to the desired attribute. This creates the respective node in the scene and connects it to the attribute. For example, if you click the Light Fog map button, a lightfog node is created, which contains the attributes for editing the color and density of the fog. The material editing tutorial in the next chapter gives more detail on the use of Light Fog.

When Light Glow is activated (by pressing its map button), an opticalFX node is created in the scene and connected to the light. This node contains all the attributes used to edit any property of an optical glow effect. For a light to be visible to the camera, Light Glow must be enabled. This produces a sort of star-shaped glowing region that simulates the effect of a light viewed through a lens (see Figure 13-13).

FIGURE 13-14   *Attributes and folders in an opticalFX node's Attribute Editor*

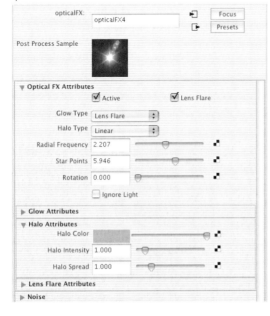

Five different glow types are available, and their specific attributes can be edited on the Glow Attributes folder of the opticalFX node's Attribute Editor. You can also add a halo around the glow. Its attributes are then edited in the Halo Attributes folder shown in Figure 13-14. Finally, a lens flare effect can be added by selecting the Lens Flare check box and editing the respective attributes.

Shadows

Lights not only illuminate objects in a scene, but they also produce shadows. Maya offers two different methods for calculating shadows: depth map and raytraced. In this section, we focus on depth map shadows. Raytraced shadows are discussed in Chapter 16, when we deal with rendering.

Before you can create shadows, the light must be capable of casting shadows. All light types except for ambient lights are capable of producing depth map shadows. These shadows are calculated using an image map that is rendered from the light's perspective relative to the surface it illuminates. The renderer then uses this depth map to determine which objects are lit and which ones fall into shadow.

To turn on shadows, select the light and find the Shadows folder in the light's Attribute Editor. Then check the box next to Use Depth Map Shadows. If you render your image with the default shadow settings, chances are that the shadows produced will have somewhat jagged edges (see the leftmost image in Figure 13-15). To fine-tune the shadows, you can use some of the depth map shadow attributes.

First, edit the Dmap Resolution setting. This sets the resolution of the depth map that Maya uses to calculate which objects are illuminated. It is best to use the same resolution as the output resolution of the image. (For more information on rendering and output resolution, see Chapter 16.) If your output resolution is set to 640×480, set Dmap Resolution to 640. From there, you can begin increasing the Dmap Filter Size setting in small increments until the edge of the shadow is smooth enough (see the rightmost image in Figure 13-15).

> _NOTE_   _**Be very careful with these attribute settings, because increasing them too much can increase render times.**_

Camera Nodes

Though you might not have been aware of it, we have been using cameras throughout this book. All the view windows are seen though cameras, and additional cameras can be created with the Create | Cameras command from the main menu bar. Cameras can be transformed and animated just like any other object in the scene. While they can be selected in the Outliner or Hypershade, probably the easiest way to select a camera is to choose View | Select Camera from the View window's menu bar. At that moment, you could press the S key to key its transforms or view its attributes in the Attribute Editor or Channel Box.

Many camera attributes simulate the workings of a real-world camera, so it is important that you understand how they work and how these attributes relate to and affect one another. Take, for example, a common 35mm camera; the 35mm is a measurement of the width of the film. The piece of film ready

FIGURE 13-15   _Two images lit by a directional light with Use Depth Map Shadows turned on: the image at the left uses the default shadow attributes, and the image at the right has increased Dmap resolution and Dmap Filter Size settings._

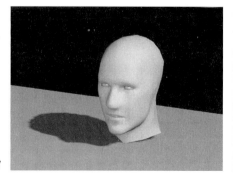

for exposure is held in place by the *film gate*. While the film gate is 35mm wide in this case, it could have various heights and as a result produce images with different *aspect ratios*. If you wanted to choose a lens for a 35mm camera that would most closely approximate normal vision, you would need a 50mm lens—50mm is the distance between the lens and the piece of film in the film gate, which is known as the *focal length*.

With this in mind, look at the camera attributes in Maya. You will find the Film Gate Aspect Ratio attributes in the Film Back folder and the Focal Length attribute in the Camera Attributes folder. Now suppose that we want to do a close-up of a character's face. In the real world, you have two options: move the camera closer or change the focal length. Changing the focal length would require a lens change or the use of a zoom lens. In Maya, you can simply change the Focal Length setting. A higher value will zoom in closer to the scene, simulating a telephoto lens; a lower value will give you a wide view. Notice as you change the focal length that the angle of view also changes. These attributes are inversely proportional to one another—that is, as the focal length gets longer, the angle of view becomes narrower, and vice versa.

Another way you could zoom in for your close-up is by changing the Film Gate setting. In the real world, this would require a change of cameras. But in Maya, if you change to a 16mm film gate, the 50mm lens that gave you a normal view with the 35mm film gate will behave like a telephoto lens—the 100mm lens with the 35mm film gate.

Note that switching the film gate is not really a great option, like switching to a different camera. For continuity's sake, it is best to use the same camera all the time. Switching the film gate can change your aspect ratio—the width and height ratio of the frame—which is not desirable. Usually, the aspect ratio of your view window does not reflect the aspect ratio of your film gate. This could make it difficult for you to frame your shot. Luckily, you can view the film gate's aspect ratio in the Cameras view window either by turning on Display Film Gate in the Display Options folder in the Attribute Editor or by choosing View | Camera Settings | Film Gate. You should see a frame in your window. To set how much space is around that gate, find the Overscan attribute in the camera's Attribute Editor and change its value. Your view should look something like Figure 13-16.

FIGURE 13-16   *The view window with the film gate on*

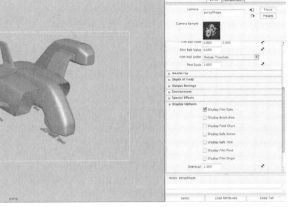

These are only a couple of the important camera attributes. We discussed a camera's image plane attributes in Chapter 4, when you set up underlay images on image planes in the camera views. We will discuss other camera attributes throughout the book. Of particular interest is the tutorial in Chapter 20, which deals with setting up a camera projection.

Workspace Setup for Efficient Material Editing

We have been working in quite a few windows as we've edited our material. The three sections of the Hypershade window are used in combination to create different render nodes; view all the render nodes in the current scene; and select, map, and edit connections on a specific node. Meanwhile, the Attribute Editor is loading the attributes for any node that is selected in the scene.

Aside from the Perspective, or Camera, view window that will most likely be visible, one more window is a vital asset to material editing. The *interactive photorealistic rendering* or *IPR* tool is one of the many great examples of Maya's ingenuity. This tool is part of the Render view window, and it provides a great way to fine-tune material attributes, because it lets you see the results of any attribute change on the object in your scene almost immediately. IPR does, however, have some limitations. It is not capable of some of the more advanced rendering features, such as raytracing, motion blur, and particle rendering.

To set up and use this tool, you first need to have created a primitive object in the current scene, created and applied a material to it, and opened the Attribute Editor. At that point, you can follow these steps to experiment with IPR:

1. From the Hotbox menu, choose Panels | Saved Layouts | Hypershade/Render/Persp. This will arrange panels so that you have all the windows necessary for building materials and accurately mapping them onto surfaces in the scene.

2. To better optimize your windows, hide the Create Render Node menu that sits along the left side of the Hypershade window: click the checkered button in the upper-left corner of the Hypershade toolbar. Render nodes can all be created by right-clicking in the Hypershade and choosing the desired node from the Create marking menu or by clicking the Texture Map button in the Attribute Editor and choosing the node from the pop-up menu.

3. Drag-and-drop the material to be applied to the object in the scene from the Materials tab in the Scene Library section into the Workspace. Then display its input connections by clicking the Input Connections button in the Hypershade toolbar. In the upper-right corner of the Hypershade, click the button to display just the bottom tab section. This will hide the top panel and Scene Library tabs and leave more room for you to zoom in and frame all the nodes and connections on the selected material (Figure 13-17).

4. Use the camera orbit, zoom, and pan hotkeys to frame the object in the center of the view window, or select the window and press the F key.

FIGURE 13-17   Panels set up for optimal material editing

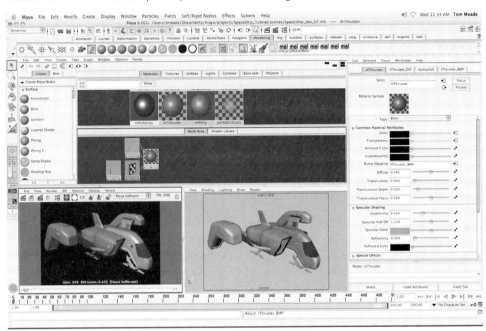

5. In Render view, click the IPR clapper button. This displays a rendered image of the scene that is framed in the view window. Drag a box around an area of the scene or object that displays most or all of the rendering characteristics. The smaller the selection area, the faster the update will happen, but try to include the specular highlight, the overall falloff from the diffuse, any reflections, and any opaque and transparent parts of the surface. If no one area has all of these characteristics displayed, choose an area with some of them and then select another to work on.

6. In the Attribute Editor, start to adjust some of the material attributes of the material applied to the object. Notice what happens in the Render view window. The area defined by the selected region updates to match the new values set in the Attribute Editor.

Summary

By now, you should have a pretty good idea of how to create and edit materials, lights, and cameras and be somewhat comfortable with using the Hypershade to make connections between nodes. We will practice using all of this information in the tutorials in the next chapter.

Texturing in Practice

To gain a full understanding of all the

nodes you learned about in the last chapter, you

will need to practice the process of applying

materials to a surface in a scene and building it

to resemble some element in the real world. In this

chapter, we set up and work through two projects.

The first project focuses on building materials. It

covers basic material creation with the rendering

nodes covered in Chapter 13. Additional utilities

and Set Driven Keys will be used to attenuate

certain material attributes further. The second

tutorial is geared toward mapping the materials to objects using projection mapping and layout UVs. We will also look at some texture map creation techniques in Photoshop that will help you push your rendered images to look even more like they were captured in the real world.

Before you go on, make sure that you have carefully studied the information in Chapter 13. You should have a good understanding of how to make connections in both the Hypershade and the Attribute Editor using the techniques demonstrated in the chapter. The instructions in this chapter assume that you know what to do when we say "connect a 2D placement node to the texture," as steps such as these will not be defined in great detail.

Tutorial: Basic Scene Texturing

This tutorial involves texturing two NURBS objects. We'll use both imported bitmapped files and Maya's procedural textures. The geometry is made of simple primitives, which will further accentuate what good texture mapping can add to a rendered scene. The scene consists of a cylinder and a plane, with the plane representing the floor and made of a material that resembles ceramic tiles. The cylinder is made of metal tiles with a glass window placed on either side of it. We will add rivets and other details until we have created a scene that is fairly complex. Last, we'll add some lights to the scene and do some final tweaking to the material attributes.

Create the Objects and Assign a Basic Material

Let's get started.

1. Create a NURBS cylinder and a NURBS plane. Set up the Workspace. Use the Hypershade/Render/Perspective layout, which can be found under the saved layouts section of the Panels menu.

2. In the Hypershade window, create a material for the floor. Use a Blinn material. Select the new material, and rename it **mTileFloor** in the Attribute Editor.

3. In the Attribute Editor, connect a procedural checker texture to the color channel by clicking the little checkered button to the right of the color channel's slider. Before you select the checker texture from the Create Render Node window, make sure that the projection type is set to Normal, as shown here. Because the floor is a NURBS object with even parameterization, the texture will be applied evenly to the plane.

    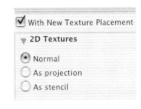

4. Select the floor in the view window and right-click the mTileFloor node in the Hypershade. Choose Assign Material To Selection from the marking menu to assign this material to the floor. MMB-click in the view window to make it active, and then press the 6 key to turn on hardware texturing. Now you should see the checker pattern mapped to the floor.

5. In the Hypershade window, select the mTileFloor material and click the Input Connections button in the toolbar. This will display the input connections to the material and clean up the organization of the workspace. You may also wish to hide the upper tabs section of the Hypershade window so that you have more room to work with this material.

6. Because we'll be creating quite a few nodes in this material, it is essential that you keep the project organized by naming the nodes as you create them. Select the checker pattern and rename it **tFloorColor**. Then select the 2D placement node connected to that, and name it **placeFloorChecker**.

7. With the placeFloorChecker node still selected, change its Repeat attributes in U and V to a value of **20**.

Note that sometimes the texture maps appear blurry in hardware shaded mode. You can increase the quality by selecting the material and editing its Texture Resolution attribute in the material's Attribute Editor under the Hardware Texturing folder, as shown in the illustration. Use the pull-down menu to change the display resolution from Default to Highest [256×256].

▼ **Hardware Texturing**	
Textured channel	Combined Textures
Texture resolution	Highest [256x256]

Create a Layered Texture

In many situations, you'll want to use multiple texture maps to control a single material attribute. In the case of the material for our floor, we will add another texture that will add white borders around the tiles to simulate the grout that exists between tiles.

Look through the various procedural textures available in the Create Render Node window, and you'll notice that the Grid texture will work well. But if you connect the grid texture to the color attribute, the connection to the checker texture will get broken. It is important that you realize that an input attribute can have only one incoming connection. You can feed an output attribute to many different inputs, but it never works the other way around. To compensate for this, we will use a layered texture node.

A *layered* texture node is a type of rendering node that allows multiple texture files to be combined together in a singe node. This is similar to compositing an image using Photoshop layers. The textures can be arranged in any order, their opacity edited, and the blend type chosen to control how each layer will affect the layer underneath. Masks can also be applied to any layer by connecting other textures to the alpha channel of the layer you want masked. This is exactly what we are going to do now.

1. Right-click in the Workspace area and choose Create | Layered Texture from the marking menu. The new node will appear in the Workspace. Name it **layeredTextureColor**.

You will notice that the node is green. This is because the layered texture has a default green layer already in it.

2. Now create a grid texture node and call it **tTileGrid**. Click the layeredTextureColor node to select it and look in the Attribute Editor. You should see a big, white space with a green block inside it. This is where you can arrange your textures into layers. The leftmost texture will be the one on top.

3. MMB-drag the tTileGrid texture from the Workspace window into this white space in the Attribute Editor. Do the same thing with the tCheckerTexture node. You should now have three blocks in the Layer Editor: two textures and the default green layer.

4. Click the check box under the green block to delete that layer. Arrange the remaining two layers so that the grid texture is on top or to the left of the checker texture in the Attribute Editor. When you are finished with these steps, the layered texture's Attribute Editor should look like the illustration.

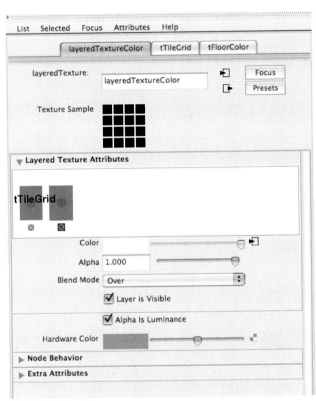

5. In the Hypershade, connect the layeredTextureColor node to the color attribute of the mTileFloor node. The original connection will automatically disconnect.

Masking One of the Layers

Notice that the layered texture's icon in the Hypershade is showing only the grid texture. This is because the grid texture is on top and the blend mode is set to Over in the Attribute Editor. You could change the blend mode by first clicking the layer in the Attribute Editor and then use the pull-down menu in the Blend Mode attribute channels. But we don't want to blend the layers together; we just want the white lines of the grid to sit on top of the checker pattern and have the black part masked out.

> _NOTE_ *A manual in the reference section of Maya's online documentation called "Nodes and Attributes" contains all of Maya's nodes with a description of their related attributes. This can be a helpful guide when working with the Connection Editor.*

We are going to use the alpha value of the grid texture's output to mask the grid texture's color channel in the layered textured node.

> _NOTE_ *You can connect nodes in the Hypershade in various ways, and we will be using most of them in this tutorial. You'll find that some ways are faster than others, and some of the lengthy processes are necessary in some situations. Be aware of these methods and use the ones that suit your tastes, per situation.*

1. Roll over the existing connection between the tTileGrid node and the layeredTextureColor node and look at its connections. It should be connected to a node called layeredTextureColor.Inputs[1]color. Figure 14-1 shows these connections in the work area. Take notice of what number that is (in this case, it is input 1). MMB-drag and drop the tTileGrid texture node onto the layeredTextureColor node and choose Other from the marking menu. This will bring up the Connection Editor.

FIGURE 14-1 *Showing connections in the work area*

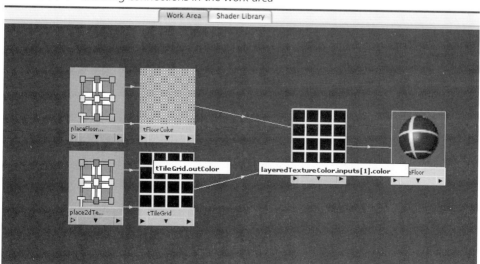

TIP   *Oftentimes, when you drag-and-drop nodes onto one another to make connections, the default list from the resulting marking menu does not include the connection you need. In such cases, you must open the Connection Editor. It tends to be a bit more complex, because you'll usually have to scroll through a lot of attributes to find the one you want. This is why it is important to use your existing scene and roll over connections to check the names of connections. You can reverse-engineer connections this way and then have some idea of what name to look for in the Connection Editor.*

2. Choose Out Alpha from the Outputs list in the left column of the Connection Editor window. Look for the corresponding input number in the Inputs list in the right column. Since the grid texture was the first one added, look for Inputs[1].

3. Click the + icon to expand this list. Select Inputs[1].Alpha from that list to make the connection. It should look like Figure 14-2. Close the Connection Editor and look at the layeredTextureColor icon in the Hypershade. You should now be able to see the checker pattern underneath the grid.

FIGURE 14-2   *Making the connection in the Connection Editor*

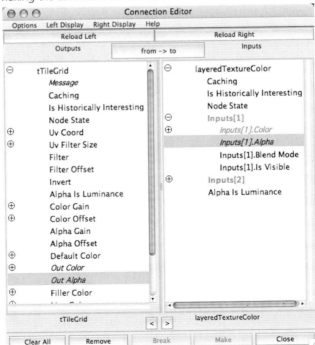

4. Zoom on the floor in the view window and do a test render. In the Render view window, choose Options | Render Globals. Unfold the Anti-Aliasing Quality Attributes tab and choose Intermediate Quality from the Presets pull-down menu. This will increase the render quality enough so that you should be able to see your grid line over the checker tiles.

NOTE *The Render Globals window is covered in more depth in Chapter 16.*

Set the Placement of the Tiles

Now let's move on to adjusting the tiling of the grid so that it matches the checkers.

If you set the repeat values to match, you can see that the checkers are at a 2:1 ratio to the grid. Therefore, double the Repeat values for the grid in U and V so that they have Repeat values of **40**. Also, select the tTileGrid node and edit its line width attributes in the Attribute Editor. A value of **0.1** for U and V looks good, as shown in the illustration. You could continue to add as many layers as you like. You might want to add some stains or dirt to the floor—it's up to you.

Create the Bump Map

The tiles should be raised slightly above the grout that is holding them in place. Fortunately, we have already included a grid that defines this region in the tTileGrid texture, so we can use this for the bump map. However, we want the white lines to appear lower than, not raised above, the tiles. This is what would result if we directly connected the tTileGrid node to the Bump Value attribute, because white raises the surface and black, or darker values, lowers it. We therefore need to invert the grid before we connect it to the bump channel. We will do this with a reverse node.

NOTE *While we are using the reverse node here as an example of this commonly used utility, the Bump Value attribute can actually be inverted by using a negative value. Most of the other material attributes require a positive value.*

1. Right-click in the Workspace and choose Create | General Utility | Reverse. Hold down the SHIFT key and MMB-drag and drop the tTileGrid node onto the reverse node. (Holding down the SHIFT key will bypass the marking menu and launch the Connection Editor.)

2. In the Connection Editor, connect the OutAlpha attribute of the tTileGrid node to the Input X attribute on the reverse node.

3. Then connect the Output X attribute of the reverse node to the Bump Value attribute on the material to complete the connection. If you make this connection by MMB-

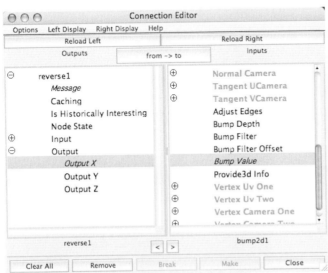

dragging the reverse node onto the mFloorTile material node and choose Bump Mapping from the marking menu, a bump2d node will be created and the Connection Editor will open. If you look in the Hypershade, the bump2d node will be connected to the Bump Mapping attribute on the mFloorTile node. To complete this connection, we need to connect the Output X attribute from the reverse node to the Bump Value attribute on the bump2d node. This illustration shows the Connection Editor once this connection has been made.

4. Do another test render. Now you'll see a small gap between the tiles. You can adjust the amount of this gap by adjusting the Bump Depth attribute in the Attribute Editor.

Create the Specular and Reflectivity Maps

We need something to break up the specular highlights and reflections over the entire surface. Ceramic tiles are often sprayed with a coating that provides a slightly rough surface. We are going to use a Noise procedural texture to control the eccentricity and the reflectivity attributes of the mTileFloor material. We also want the grout between the tiles to be less specular than the tiles. This means that we'll have to create another layered texture, combine the Noise texture and the tTileGrid node, and blend them to get the desired look.

1. Right-click in the Workspace and choose Create | 2D Texture | Noise. Name the texture **tTileNoise**.

2. Right-click again and choose Create | Layered Texture. Name this **layeredTileSpec**. Connect the tTileNoise and the tTileGrid nodes to the layeredTileSpec node and arrange them so that the grid is on top.

3. The layered texture node allows for the blending of textures on the texture below it. These options in the Blend Mode attribute specify how the pixel values are combined through a mathematical operation. For this step, we will use the Multiply option, which will darken the texture. Set the Blend Mode attribute on the tTileGrid node to Multiply.

4. Set the repeat values for the noise texture's 2D placement node high, so that the noise is very tight. A value of 200 will do for both the U and V directions.

5. Connect the layeredTileSpec to the Specular Color attribute and the reflectivity attribute of the mTileFloor material. Here's another way to connect these attributes—with the material attributes visible in the Attribute Editor, MMB-drag the layeredTileSpec node onto the Specular Color attribute line in the Attribute Editor. The connection will be made. Repeat this process for the reflectivity channel.

NOTE *The position of the light or lights that emit the specular highlight and the position of the camera viewing the object will affect the visibility of the specular highlight. You may have to orbit the camera to reposition it while you tune the specular highlight.*

Create a Reflection Map

The last thing we'll do to the floor material is add an environment reflection map to it. This will help us evaluate the reflectivity of the surface without having to wait for a raytrace calculation. Any image can be used as a reflection map, but ideally you want to use some 360-degree panorama. This way, you can move your object through the scene and have it reflect back an entire environment. If you were to use a regular photograph, you might notice the seams where the environment textures wrap around.

A variety of special cameras and software let you create perfect 360-degree environment maps. The dvGarage, a company dedicated to providing tools and training for digital artists, offers a product called the Reflection Toolkit (*http://www.dvgarage.com/*), which contains a collection of 30 reflection maps that have all been shot and corrected for seamless projections. We have included one of these images as a sample on the CD, which is shown in Figure 14-3.

Even though your actual environment might not look anything like the one photographed in the reflection, any reflection map that is seamless will work for most situations. It really helps to integrate all of the objects in a scene when they are all using the same reflection map. For objects that are close together and need more accurate reflections, raytracing can be added. You can make additional render passes with raytracing and composite these with the reflection

FIGURE 14-3   *Environment reflection map*

pass in post-production. We will look at ways to handle this in Chapters 20 and 21. For now, let's take a look at the effect that adding a reflection map has on the scene.

1. Use the Attribute Editor to connect a texture to the Reflected Color channel of the mTileFloor material. When the Create Render Node window appears, scroll down and reveal the Environment Textures section. Choose Environment Sphere from the list. This will add the envSphere1 node to the scene.

2. Connect a file texture to the Image attribute of the envSphere1. That will create a file texture node called File1. Name this node **envReflect**.

3. With the envReflect node selected, click the File Browser button next to the image name attribute. This will bring up the file browser, where you can navigate to the location of the MCR_reflection_lobby.tga file and open it. This will load into that envReflect node.

4. Do another test render. Our floor looks good—as you can see in the illustration. Now let's move onto the cylinder.

Create Material Based on a File Texture

We'll use the cylinder to represent some kind of tank or chamber in the scene. It should look like it is made of sheet metal, with rivets joining the sheets of metal together. It will include a window. Instead of creating patterns and textures with Maya's procedural-based textures, we will use some generic textures prepared in Photoshop. This will save us some time and let us focus on building the material itself and learning about some other utility nodes. The illustration shows a texture map that was prepared in Photoshop. The dirt and grime on the map were added using the dvGarage's Surface Toolkit, and the files used here are from the book CD.

1. Create a new material. Again, use a Blinn material since the specular attributes of the Blinn work well for accurately describing metallic surfaces. Name the material **mTank**.

2. Start with the color channel. Connect a file texture to the color channel. Name the file texture node **tTankColor**. Add the MCR_textTut_mtl_Color.tga file to the node through the image attribute in the Attribute Editor.

3. Set the Hardware Texturing attribute for this material to Highest. Apply the material to the cylinder and view its connections in the Workspace. With the color texture now visible in the view window, select the 2D placement node and set the repeat values. Use **6** in U and **6** in V. Also, rotate the frame 90 degrees with the slider in the Rotate Frame attribute.

4. Select the tTankDiff node and choose Duplicate | With Connection To Network. This will duplicate this node and keep it connected to the 2D placement node. Rename the node **tTankSpc**, and then replace the current image file with MCR_textTut_mtl_SPC.tga. This process of duplicating the network will save you the steps of building each node from scratch and making the appropriate connections. Repeat this one more time and name the third file texture node **tTankBMP**; load the file called MCR_textTut_mtl_BMP.tga into this texture node.

FIGURE 14-4   *The Hypershade showing all connections up to this point*

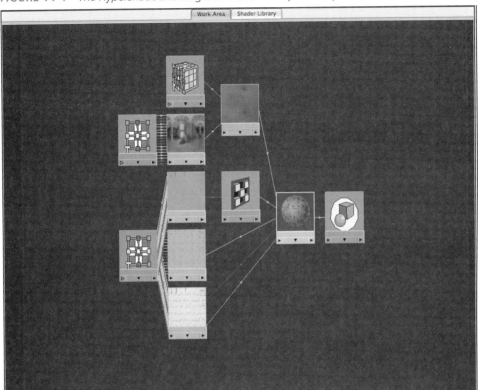

5. Connect the specular map to the material's specular color attribute. Connect the bump texture to the bump-mapping channel. Then connect the outAlpha attribute of the tTankSpc node to the reflectivity of the material. Figure 14-4 shows the connections in the Hypershade.

6. In the upper tabs section of the Hypershade window, open the Textures tab. Find the envSphere1 node that we created for the floor. MMB-drag it over to the Reflection Color attribute in the material's Attribute Editor. Now both the floor and the tank share the same reflection map. Do a test render to make sure everything is in place.

Use IPR to Fine-Tune the Material Attributes

The texture maps we've added so far control the basic attributes for this material. From here on, we will be making some adjustments to these textures to fine-tune the rendered image. In this process, you can determine whether the material needs to be more or less reflective, or whether the bump map shows up fine or is too deep. To adjust the strength of the texture maps, we will be adjusting the file textures' Color Balance attributes. These essentially control the color levels and contrast of the bitmap images within Maya. If the reflection is too bright on the surface, you know that the file texture is too light and needs to be darkened. This tweaking process is best handled with IPR (interactive photorealistic rendering).

1. Frame your cylinder in the view window and click the IPR button in the Render view's toolbar. Drag a box to define the region that you want to see updated with the changes you make. It is best to find an area of the surface that contains the specular highlight.

2. In the Hypershade, select the mTank material and view its attributes in the Attribute Editor. First, we'll adjust the specular attributes so that the material appears to be more metallic. Set the Eccentricity to about **0.6**, and set the Specular Rolloff attribute to about **0.4**. Bring the Diffuse attribute down to about **0.3**. Each time an adjustment is made to one of these attributes, the image in the Render View image will update. Figure 14-5 shows an IPR of the image in the Render View window.

FIGURE 14-5   *IPR render in the Render View window with important details captured*

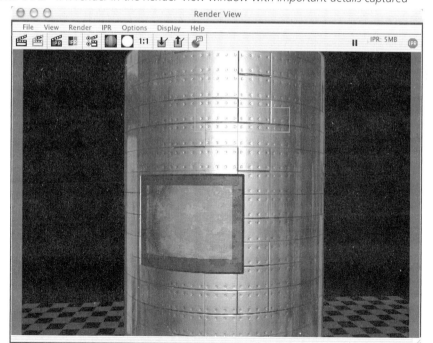

3. To adjust the reflectivity of the object, select the tTankSpc node in the Hypershade. Scroll down through its attributes and reveal the Color Balance section. Reflectivity attributes use the alpha value of the texture map to control reflectivity. This is convenient because the reflectivity maps are often the same as the specular maps. However, you usually want to be able to control the reflectivity and specular maps separately. This means that you can use the Alpha Gain and Alpha Offset attributes to control the levels of the texture, and control the overall reflectivity as a result. The Color Gain and Color Offset attributes can be used to control another attribute, such as Specular Color. Use the Alpha Gain to turn the reflection down with a value of about **0.4**. Turn the specularity up just a bit by increasing the value of the Color Offset attribute. You'll have plenty of time to tweak this further in a later step—we're just looking for a ballpark figure now.

4. Select the tTankDif node and find its Color Balance settings. Turn the Color Gain down to about a third of the total so that the texture is mostly a dark gray.

5. Before adjusting the tTankBmp node, select the bump node and adjust its Bump Depth attribute—set it to **0.2**. With that node taken care of, you can now adjust any of the Color Balance attributes.

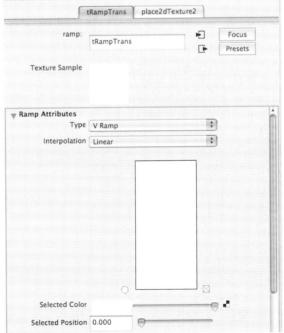

FIGURE 14-6   Editing a ramp texture

Create the Window

By now, the material you've created should start to resemble a metal tiled structure. Now we are going to explore some more rendering nodes that will help us add some detail and final tweaks. We will create a glass window on the surface of the cylinder by using a transparency map controlled by a procedural ramp texture. We can then use that ramp texture node to mask or modify the other textures and attributes.

1. Connect a texture to the Transparency node of the mTankTile material. Choose a Ramp texture from the Create Render Node window. Name this new node **tRampTrans**.

2. Use the Ramp Editor in the Attribute Editor to make the entire ramp white. You can delete a color from the ramp by clicking the box on the right side of the color. Figure 14-6 shows the ramp once it has been edited in the Attribute Editor.

3. Select the 2D texture node that is controlling the placement of this new ramp node. Use the Interactive Texture Placement tool to edit the coverage and translation of the texture, as shown in Figure 14-7. Size and place it in the proportions of a window.

4. Go to the color balance settings and set the Default Color attribute to Black. The Default Color attribute controls the color of the surface that is not being covered by the selected map. By setting this to Black, you now have a perfect mask, or transparency map.

5. If you do a quick test render, you should see a hole in the surface where we placed the Ramp texture. However, even though this area is now transparent, the material's specular, reflectivity, and bump attributes are still visible. We need to mask them.

We could use the tRampTrans node as a mask, but that would mask the textures right along the edge of the transparent window. It will look much better if we add a border around the window. Therefore, we'll duplicate the existing ramp node and its placement node and modify its scale just a little. We will then use this new ramp to mask out the specularity, diffuse, and bump textures so that the tile pattern does not continue over the window or its borders.

Stencil nodes are introduced in the next steps. A stencil node masks out parts of a texture that is connected to the stencil node's Image attribute. Another texture is connected

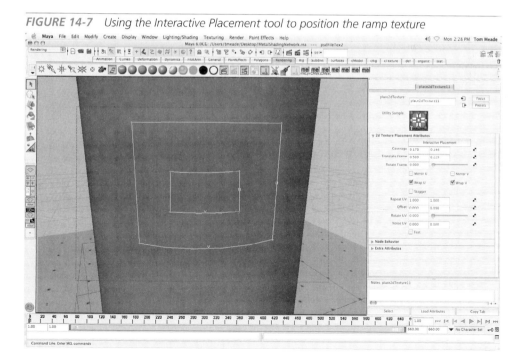

FIGURE 14-7   Using the Interactive Placement tool to position the ramp texture

to the Mask attribute and is used to mask, or cut away, whatever falls in the black or darker regions.

1. Turn on the hardware texturing for the transparency channel and set it to highest quality. Using the white block on the black background provides a good visual reference for placing the new texture.

2. Select the tRampTrans node and choose Duplicate | Shading Network. This will duplicate the selected node and any upstream connections. Name the duplicate **tWinMaskRamp**. Use the Texture tool to scale up interactively the coverage of the new map, so that it creates a border around the transparent region.

3. Right-click in the Workspace and choose Create | Utility Node | Stencil to create a stencil node. Name it **StencilSpec**. Use the Connection Editor to connect the outColor attribute of tTankSpc to the Image attribute of the stencil node. Then connect the tWinMaskRamp to the Mask attribute of the stencil node.

4. To complete the connections, connect the outColor attribute of the stencil node to the Specular Color attribute of the mTankTile material. If you do a test render, you'll see that the specular texture no longer covers the area around the window. Figure 14-8 shows the surface before and after the mask is added.

TIP *Sometimes it can be difficult to make out what texture is doing what to the rendered image. If you right-click the attributes in the Attribute Editor, you'll see an option to Ignore When Rendering. Set all of the attributes except for the one you are working on to Ignore. When you are ready to move on to the next attribute, choose Don't Ignore When Rendering for that attribute.*

5. Repeat step 4 for the Color attribute.

FIGURE 14-8   *The surface before (left) and after adding the mask*

6. The bump and the reflectivity textures will be handled a bit differently. Both of these attributes use the outAlpha attribute of an incoming node to control the attribute. Instead of masking a texture output, the mask can be used as an input to control the file texture nodes' alphaGain or alphaOffset attributes.

7. Duplicate the tWinMaskRamp node with connections to the network and name it **tWinAttenRamp**. We want a separate copy of this node so we can adjust it independently of the other channels later on.

8. Connect the outAlpha attribute of the tWinMaskRamp node to the alphaOffset attribute of the tTankSpc node. Figure 14-9 shows this connection in the Hypershade. This connection will add the pixel values of the mask to the pixel values in the texture. Any black values in the ramp will leave the original Reflectivity values alone. The white values in the ramp will make that region 100 percent reflective. Do a test render to see that the window area is now completely reflective.

FIGURE 14-9   Connection in the Hypershade

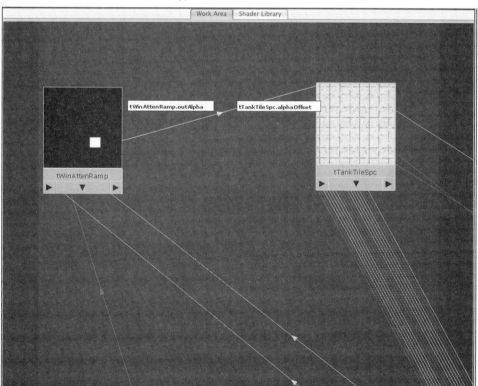

9. The reflection can be attenuated by selecting tWinAttenRamp and changing the value of the white ramp. You could even apply another texture map to that Selected Color attribute and then edit its color balance attributes. You can see how powerful this can be.

10. Setting up the bump is similar to the reflectivity, but one more step is involved. For the bumps to face the correct direction, the mask will have to be inverted. Right-click in the Workspace and choose Create | General Utility | Reverse. A reverse node is created. Reverse nodes are capable of inverting pixel values, so what is black will be output as white.

11. Use the Connection Editor to connect tWinMaskRamp to the Input X attribute of the stencil node. Connect the Output X attribute of the stencil node to the alphaGain attribute of the tTileBmp node. The edge of the window border can be manipulated by editing the ramp colors. The faster the transition from black to white, the tighter the edge will be.

The Fresnel Effect

The last thing we need to add before making the final tweaks is to set up some controls for attenuating the reflectivity and transparency based on the view angle. As you walk down the street, notice how light bounces off the glass windows of buildings. The windows are always highly reflective as you approach them and view them at an angle, but when you stand and look straight into them you can almost see through them. This is known as the Fresnel Effect, and it is crucial for creating realistic-looking materials.

To set this up in Maya, we will need to use yet another utility node and a Set Driven Key. Even though the Set Driven Key is mostly used for animation, it can be useful for other operations where nodes are connected whose relationships will be determined by a curve. Both reflectivity and transparency should be set up for this behavior—except the curves will be reversed. This is because at a facing angle value of 1, looking straight at the surface, you want a low reflective value but a high transparent value. Keep this in mind as we set and edit the curves.

1. Right-click in the Workspace and choose Create | General Utility | Sampler Info. A samplerInfo node will be created.

2. In thinking about what you need, it is always a good idea to edit the values of different attributes to find the one that will do what you're looking for. For reflectivity, the brightness of the texture has to change. In this case, changing the value of the alphaGain attribute has the effect we need.

3. Right-click the alphaGain attribute for the mTankTile material and choose Set Driven Key. The Set Driven key window will open.

4. alphaGain should be loaded as Driven. If it is not, select the material in the Hypershade and click the Load Driver button in the Set Driven Key window. Select the Alpha Gain attribute from the attributes list.

5. Select the samplerInfo node in the Hypershade and click the Load Driver button in the Set Driven Key window. Scroll to the bottom of the list of attributes and select facingRatio. Your Set Driven Key window should look like Figure 14-10. Click the Key button to make the connection and set the key. Then close the Set Driven Key window.

6. It is a good idea to update the Workspace window manually and frequently. This is especially important after connecting with a Set Driven Key, because the nodes will rarely show that they are connected. Do this by selecting the material and clicking the Input Connections button in the Hypershade toolbar.

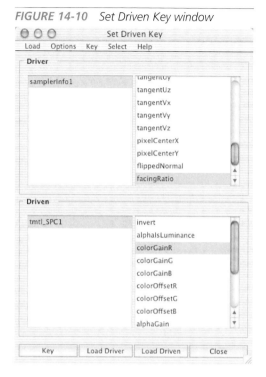

FIGURE 14-10   *Set Driven Key window*

7. Select the animation curve node in the Workspace that is now connected between the samplerInfo node and the texture. From the main menu bar, choose Windows | Animation Editors | Graph Editor.

8. Frame the Graph Editor so that values 1,1 are clearly visible. A facingRatio value of 1 is the point where the camera or view is perpendicular to the surface—that is, looking straight at it. A value of 0 means that the camera or view is parallel to the surface. For this attribute, insert a keyframe at 1,0. This sets a key for the reflection value of 0 when the facing ratio is equal to 1, or facing straight at the surface.

9. Move the first key to 0,1. Select both points and set their curves to Continuous. Open an IPR window, render a region, and start tweaking this curve until it looks good.

10. The same process can be followed for the transparency channel. The only difference is, as mentioned earlier, that the curve will be in the reverse direction, starting at 0,0 and ending at 1,1. Figure 14-11 shows a render of the cylinder. Notice how the surface is more reflective around the edges due to the Fresnel Effect.

FIGURE 14-11 *Final textured cylinder*

NOTE *A common alternative to using a Set Driven Key for these effects is to use a Ramp texture. The facingRatio attribute is connected to the V Coord attribute on the Ramp texture, and the outColor attribute from the ramp is then connected to the alphaGain attribute.*

Set Up Lighting

The final part of this tutorial deals with lighting. Before you begin, it is best to establish a "mood." What sort of feelings should this scene convey to viewers? What colors define those feelings? What exists in the scene to work with? In our case, the answers to all of these questions is "not a whole lot," so let's use that as the basis for determining the mood. To compensate for not having any walls or any sort of definable boundaries, we will rely on fog effects generated from the lights—we'll go for a sort of eerie feeling. Cool colors, such as blue and green, should be abundant. We'll even use lights to hint that something is happening inside the tank.

With that concept in mind, we'll determine what we can use in Maya. The key lights, the lights in the scene that are the primary source of illumination, will be based around three spotlights that are hanging above the scene. We will place these and look at some of the effects they can be used to create. Then we'll add some fog lights to fill in the empty space in the background. We'll do some test renders to check shadows and materials and then render the final image.

1. To make our scene a little more interesting, we'll duplicate the cylinder and place the copies in different parts of the frame. This will also be a good test to see how our material holds up from different angles. Make five duplicates of the cylinder object and position them around the floor.

2. Choose Create | Lights | Spot Light. The spot light will appear at the scene origin. Use the Manipulator tool to position the light so that it is high above the scene and pointing down at one of the cylinders. To better align the light, select it and choose Panels | Look Through Selected. You can now use the camera positioning tools (Dolly, Track, and Orbit) to position the light exactly how you'd like it.

3. Turn on hardware lighting by pressing the 7 key so that you can see the light's effects in real time. Play with the Intensity setting. Since this is our key light, it should be the brightest light in the scene.

NOTE *Depending on the hardware capabilities of your graphics card, the hardware lighting may or may not be similar to the final rendered look. It is always best to use IPR to fine-tune and adjust the lights.*

4. In the spot light's Attribute Editor, click the Add Node button in the Light Fog channel. The color node will appear, where you can set a color for the fog. Change it to a whitish blue.

5. Back in the view window, you will notice that a cone shape extends from the light (see Figure 14-12). This is the cone angle and indicates the area of the fog, the angle of the light cone, and the total dropoff range. Adjust the Cone angle attribute so that it encompasses just the cylinder.

6. With the light selected, uses the Scale tool to change the length of the dropoff.

FIGURE 14-12 Render showing a spot light and its corresponding manipulator

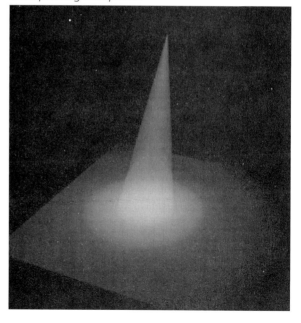

7. Turn on the depth map shadows in the Attribute Editor. Test render. When you are happy with the light, add another two spot lights, hang them from the top, and point them in varying directions. These lights should be just slightly less intense than the key light. Figure 14-13 shows the placement of all three lights.

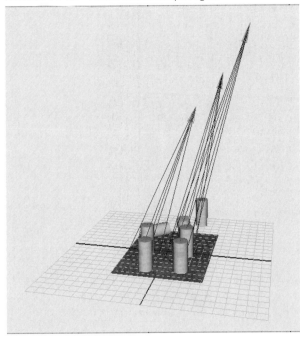

FIGURE 14-13   Placement of all spot lights

8. Create a directional light (Create | Light | Directional Light). These lights are great at simulating natural sunlight, because the light rays are projected in parallel. This also makes them useful as fill lights because you can get nice, even fills throughout the scene without having to set up too many lights. Position this light high above the others. Use the Manipulator tool to point it at the center of the scene. Change the intensity to about **0.4**. Create another light and place it closer to the ground and pointing sideways. Set its intensity to **0.2**.

9. To add fog, create a point light and place it in the scene on the other side of the camera. In the light's Attribute Editor, turn on the Light Fog option by clicking the Connect Node button in the Light Fog channel. Change the Light Fog color node to a bluish color. Set the fog Radius to **15**.

10. Add another point light and position it inside of one of the tanks. Enable the light fog and set it to a greenish color. Make sure the radius is small enough to fit within the bounds of the tank, as we want it to be contained within the tank.

11. Continue to tweak the lights until the scene is evenly lit. Before rendering the image, it is a good idea to go back into the material attributes and make final tweaks. Just when you think you nailed your material, adding a light can blow it all out.

The final rendered scene is shown in Figure 14-14.

FIGURE 14-14   *Final rendered scene*

Advanced Texture Mapping

So far, all the texturing we have done has been mapped onto the geometry in normal mode. Normal mode uses the existing UV coordinates of a surface to fit the texture. A NURBS surface, by its nature, already contains this information. Polygonal geometry, on the other hand, does not contain any UV information. How, then, would we map a texture to a polygonal surface?

One solution is to use a projection node. (See Chapter 13 for more information on 2D and 3D projection nodes.) Projections are a quick way to apply a texture to any surface that does not have any UV coordinates assigned—or, in some cases, where the existing UV information is undesirable for texture mapping. A problem with projections is that severe stretching or warping can occur when the surface being mapped has curvy or overlapping regions. In these situations, it might be best to assign UV coordinates to the surface and then apply the texture normally.

UVs can be assigned to any polygonal surface by using one of the four methods available by choosing Edit Polygons | Texture: Planar Mapping, Cylindrical Mapping, Spherical Mapping, and Automatic Mapping. Once the UVs are assigned, they can be manually edited in the UV Texture Editor (Window | UV Texture Editor). The goal is to have the UVs evenly laid out, without any overlapping pieces, to fit within the UV coordinates of 0 and 1.

The process begins by a careful evaluation of the geometry. Does the shape of the model conform to any UV mapping modes in the submenu after choosing Edit Polygons | Texture? Can it be broken down into separate segments that are then individually assigned UV coordinates? What about this creature's head? How will I overcome all of these overlapping regions from the nose? These are the types of questions you must ask yourself and problems you need to solve.

Tutorial: Assigning UVs

This tutorial will go through the steps of assigning UVs to a polygonal model of a human head. However, this same procedure can be used to map any object.

 Open the MCR_polyhead_mdl.ma file on the CD. This model does not have any UVs assigned to it. If you were to create a material with a texture map, it could not be mapped on the surface and therefore would not show up when the surface is rendered. Study the head and try to find a UV mapping method that can be used. Cylindrical mapping works well for objects such as this, so that is what we will use to assign UVs to it.

1. Select the head in a view window and choose Edit Polygons | Texture | Cylindrical Mapping. A cylindrical shaped manipulator will appear around the head in the view window.

FIGURE 14-15   *The head is cylindrically mapped*

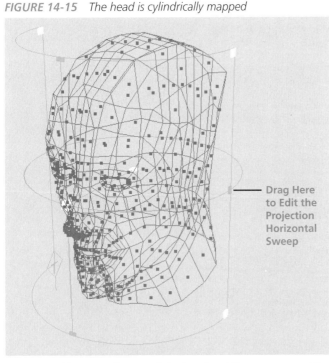

Drag Here to Edit the Projection Horizontal Sweep

2. The default settings for the Cylindrical Mapping command show the Projection Horizontal Sweep attribute set to 180. This means that the cylinder will wrap around the head only 180 degrees, and therefore the UVs that are not within that cylinder will fall outside the 0 to 1 range. The Projection Horizontal Sweep attribute can be interactively edited in the view window by clicking and dragging the red square on the edge of the cylinder. Drag it around until the cylinder wraps a complete 360 degrees around the head. Figure 14-15 shows the head being cylindrically mapped.

If a texture map were assigned to the model at this point, it would appear to wrap around the head as if it were being cylindrically projected. However, the top of the head and the area around the nose would display texture stretching. To fix this, we will manually edit the UVs in the UV Texture Editor.

Editing UVs in the UV Texture Editor

Figure 14-16 shows the UV Texture Editor displaying the UVs from the head model. This is where all of the UV editing will be done. Look at the grid in the UV Texture Editor, and you will notice that it is marked to show the coordinates in the U and V directions, both positive and negative. The texture map will occupy the region that falls within positive 0 to 1 space. Any UVs outside this area will either not be covered by the texture or will get the repeated texture (if the Repeat attributes are enabled in the Place 2D texture node). Therefore, it is desirable that all UVs are assigned to this region.

FIGURE 14-16   *UV Texture Editor showing the planar projection the face*

By setting the cylindrical mapping's Projection Horizontal Sweep attribute to 360 degrees, Maya was able to keep most of the UVs within the 0 to 1 space. What we need to do now is look for areas that are overlapping. The chin is a good example. If you look at this region in the UV Texture Editor (shown in Figure 14-16) you will notice that some of the UVs are overlapping the UVs in the neck. This means that if you want to texture the chin so that it has a pimple, for example, that same pimple will appear on the neck. Let's fix this.

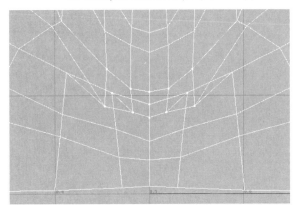

1. Select the head in the view window and choose Window | UV Texture Editor. The UV Texture Editor will open and show the current layout of UVs for the head model.

2. In the UV Texture Editor, right-click the UVs and choose UVs from the marking menu. Drag-select the chin area with overlapping UVs. The selected UVs will highlight in green, as shown in the illustration.

NOTE   Once the UVs have been selected, you can use the transform tools to move, rotate, or scale them in the UV Texture Editor. Realize that while the UVs will be highlighted in the view window, they cannot be transformed there. That is because the view windows let us work in 3D space while the UV Texture Editor considers only two dimensions (U and V).

3. An easy way to fix these UVs is to use the Relax UVs command. In the UV Texture Editor, choose Polygons | Relax UVs ❐. We can leave all of the options set at their defaults except for the Pin Unselected UVs option. Make sure this option is enabled. This will hold all of the unselected UVs so that they are not affected by the Relax UVs command. Click the Relax button. Notice that the UVs in the chin are no longer overlapping.

4. You can continue selecting UVs and using the Relax UVs command for other areas that have overlapping UVs—such as the nose and the eye areas. If the Relax UVs command is unable to fix the problems, select individual UVs and use the Move tool to lay them out manually.

Creating a UV Template

Once the UVs have been assigned and laid out so that no pieces overlap, you can move on to texture mapping the object. This might include importing pre-made texture maps or using Maya's 3D Paint tool, discussed in Chapter 15. One of the best ways to create an accurate texture for this object is to use the UV layout as a template that you can paint on in a paint package such as Adobe Photoshop. A great new feature in Maya 6 lets you create a layered Photoshop document (PSD) from right within the Maya UI. The layers in this PSD file can be connected to any material attribute desired, plus, you have the option of including the UV layout in a layer, so you know exactly what part of the geometry you are painting on in Photoshop. Using the PSD file for your textures can also help you better organize your files since you will not need a separate file for each attribute.

Let's create the Photoshop document and connect it to a material that is assigned to the model.

1. Right-click the head geometry and choose Material | Assign New Material | Blinn.

2. Select the head geometry in the view window, and then choose Texturing | Create PSD File. This will open the Create PSD Texture Options window, shown in Figure 14-17. Here we can create and connect a unique layer from the Photoshop document to a specific attribute on the current material.

3. In the Image Name field, set the path and filename for the new PSD file that is about to be created.

FIGURE 14-17   Create PSD Texture Options window

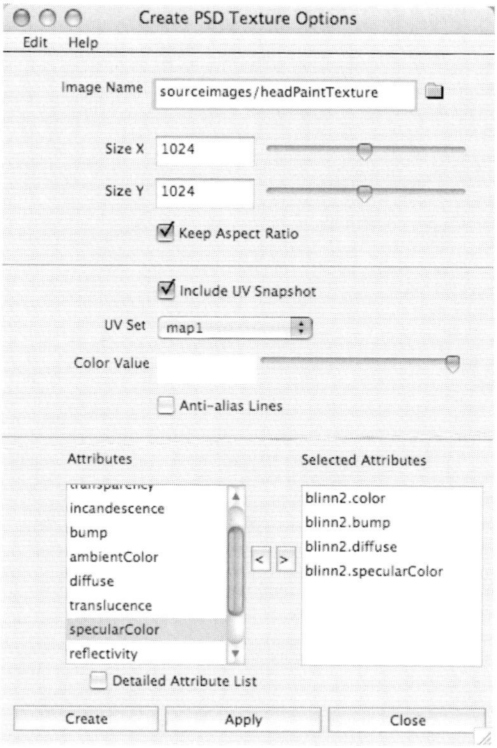

4. Set the resolution of the file using the Size X and Size Y attributes. It isn't so important that you set the correct resolution here, as the PSD file can easily be resized in Photoshop before you begin painting. However, the texture should be created large enough with enough resolution to draw the UV template.

5. In this window, we need to make a selection of attributes that we want to create and to which a layer will be connected. Select the Color attribute from the Attributes list and click the right arrow (>) button to move the attribute into the list of Selected Attributes. Do this for the bump, diffuse, and specularColor attributes as well.

6. Click the Create button. A Photoshop file will be created and written to the location specified in the Image Name field. This PSD file will contain five layers—four layers for the attributes and one layer that contains the UV snapshot.

7. In the Hypershade, graph the input connections to the Blinn material and check that four file textures are connected to the material, all mapped to the appropriate channels.

8. Now you can open the PSD file in Photoshop. You will see that a separate layer has been created for each material attribute specified in the Create PSD Texture Options window.

With everything now set up, you can begin painting in the different layers. As soon as you save the PSD file, you can immediately see the results in Maya by selecting the PSD file texture node in the Hypershade and clicking the Reload File Texture button in the Attribute Editor.

Advanced Shading Networks and Utilities

As you have probably noticed, dozens of other shading nodes and utilities are available in the Create Render Node menu in the Hypershade window. Many of these nodes contain compositing functions and data conversion utilities for building complex shading networks. We have already discussed some of these nodes, such as the Sampler Info, the Reverse node, and the Stencil node, but many other functions are available that will let you composite or layer separate materials together to achieve some very complicated shading effects with a great amount of control over how the material will interact with different lighting conditions and viewing angles.

In this section, we will study how some of these utilities can be used to create custom shaders. To get an idea of how some of these utility nodes work, we will first discuss how we can build up a reflective material, similar to a Phong or a Blinn, by compositing several surface shaders materials together. After that, we'll look at a similar technique that can be used to create a realistic skin shader.

Custom Reflective Shader

In some situations, you may not have quite enough control over certain attributes in some of Maya's default materials. For example, perhaps the specular attributes in the Blinn, Phong, or anisotropic materials are not able to produce the precise falloff from the specular highlight that you need. Or perhaps you need to create a custom cartoon shader that has more control over certain material characteristics than Maya's Ramp material will give you. Whatever the case may be, at times you will need to create custom shading networks that will work for your project. If you can't think of any reasons for this right now, if nothing more, this study will help you realize how Maya actually breaks down, calculates, and composites individual material attributes when it renders images.

Figure 14-18 shows the Hypershade window displaying all of the connections for a custom reflective material that would be similar to a Blinn or Phong material. Take a moment to study the figure and try to understand the basic flow of connected nodes.

This network utilizes a separate surface shader material node to represent each main material attribute: Color, Specular Color, and Reflectivity. The falloff of each of these attributes is controlled by a ramp texture whose V coordinate (vertical ramp color) is driven by the Light Info node (for the color and specular) and a Sampler info node to control the falloff of the reflections, to create the Fresnell Effect, discussed earlier in this chapter. The surface shader materials are composited together using either MultiplyDivide nodes or PlusMinusAverage nodes. These nodes allow you to apply a mathematical operation to the color values in the inputs. Let's take a close look at the surface shader that is controlling the color of this shading network.

FIGURE 14-18   *Shading network for a custom reflective material*

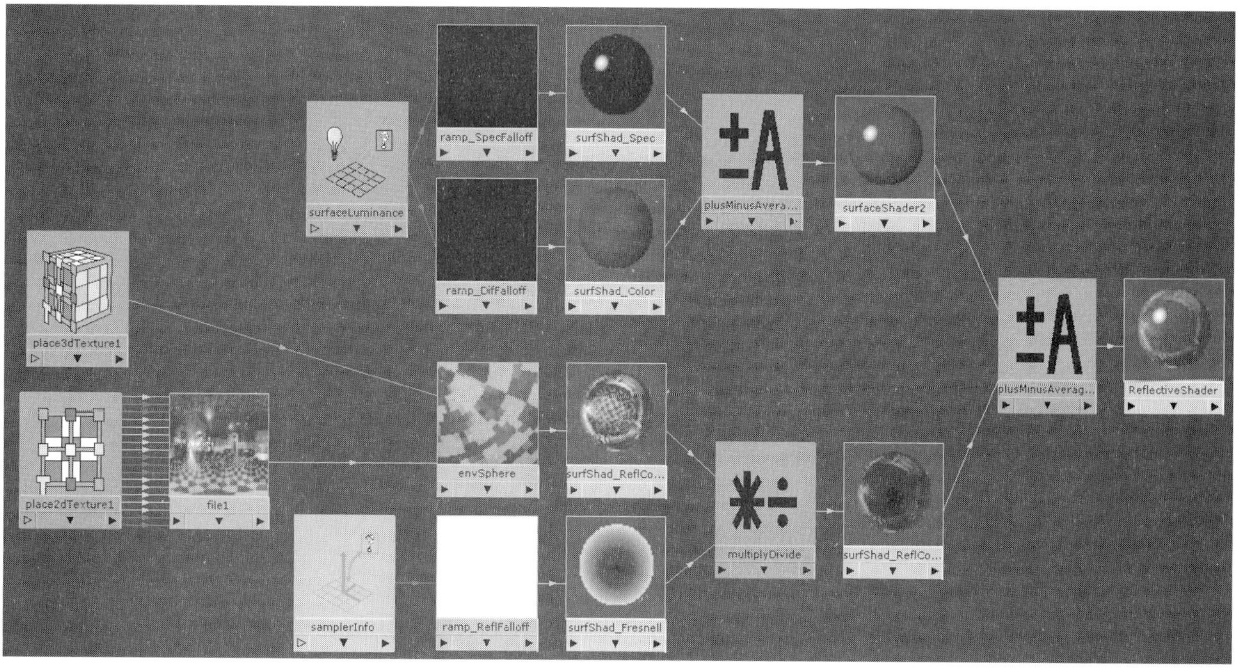

Representing Color

Look at the surfShad_Color node and its inputs, shown in Figure 14-18. Understanding these connections will give you a good idea of how this entire network operates. The surfShad_Color node is a material node type called a *surface shader*. Surface shaders are the most basic of all of the material types available in Maya. They do not interact with the lights in the scene at all. Therefore, any surface shader with its default settings that is applied to a surface will render completely matte black. You won't find any kinds of shading effects in many of the other material nodes discussed so far.

A surface shader has only four shading attributes available: Out Color, Out Transparency, Out Glow Color, and Out Matte Opacity. One particularly great use for a surface shader is when you want to use a matte painting or photograph in a scene and you want Maya to render the material using the luminance values from the image. In this case, you would connect your texture to the Out Color attribute of the surface shader. When the scene is rendered, the objects that are using that surface shader will not be affected by any lights or shadows in the scene. We will use this technique in Chapter 20 when we set up the camera-mapped scene.

In the case of the shading network shown in Figure 14-18, the Out Color attribute has a ramp texture named ramp_DifFalloff connected to its input. To get the surface shader to interact with any light source in the scene, the ramp's V Coord attribute is driven by a surface luminance node. A surface luminance node performs a similar function to the sampler info's Facing Ratio attribute. Instead of returning a value based on the viewing angle, however, the surface luminance returns the value based on the light in the scene. These connections will produce an effect that is almost identical to a Lambert material.

The color of the material is controlled by the Hue and Saturation of the color at the top of this ramp. The diffuse value of the material would be controlled by the Value of that color. With this setup, you also have some additional control over the shading that you would not find by editing any of the attributes in a Lambert material. For instance, you can adjust how quickly the light falls off over the surface by adjusting the position of the bottom, black color on the ramp. This type of effect is useful when creating a cartoon type shader.

FIGURE 14-19   *A ramp is edited to control the shading on the sphere*

Additional colors can be added to the ramp for other kinds of effects. Look at Figure 14-19 to see the effect that adding a color to the ramp would have on the shading of a sphere. This material resembles how the sphere might shade if it were made out of velvet. As you can see, setting up material this way opens up many possibilities.

The Specular Highlight

The setup for the specular highlight in Figure 14-18 is almost identical to the way that the color is controlled. The main difference is that the ramp that controls the Out Color on the surfShad_Spec material falls off much faster. The size of the highlight is determined by how quickly the ramp transitions from white to black. By changing the interpolation of this ramp, different effects can be achieved.

A cartoon shader, for example, might have the Interpolation set to None. In this case, there would be no transition from white to black. Figure 14-20 shows a rendered sphere whose color and specular highlight is controlled by ramps that have their Interpolation set to None.

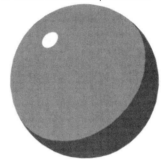

FIGURE 14-20   A cartoon shader is achieved by turning off the Interpolation of the colors on the ramp textures.

Add and Multiply Materials Together

To combine the color and specular materials, we will add the two surface shaders, the surfShad_Color and surfShad_Spec. This is achieved by sending the Out Color attributes from each shader into the 3D inputs on the plusMinusAverage node. The 3D inputs are used because they can handle all three values, HSV, that control color. Since the black in the surfShad_Spec has a value of 0, the black area has no effect when the materials are added together. The result of this operation is output to the Out Color attribute on the surfaceShader2 node.

To create the Fresnell Effect for the reflections, the surfShad_ReflComp node had to be darkened. To do this, a multiplyDivide node was used to multiply the surfShad_ReflComp and the surfShad_Fresnell materials together. In a multiply operation, a white value, or 1, will not have any effect on the color it is multiplied by (1 × Y = Y). Any color multiplied by 0 will return 0, or black. Any color between white and black will cause the result to be darker.

Finally, the surfShad_ReflComp and the surfaceShader2 are added together to give us the final result at the ReflectiveShader node. Amazing shaders can be created by experimenting in the Hypershade like this.

Skin Shader

Finding a solution to rendering realistic skin has been the holy grail of the world of shader development. You need to deal with many different factors when shading the skin. Take a moment to analyze how skin interacts with light in the real world. What color is it? Well, that really depends on a few things: the skin pigment, the amount of fat, and the angle that the light is interacting with it, for example. Our skin is a thin, semitransparent layer that covers a layer of translucent fat. That fat contains tiny blood vessels. Underneath that is a layer of muscle that is very red due to the amount of blood present.

Developing a shader that would allow light to interact properly with all of these layers of trans lucency is currently outside the realm of possibilities with any of Maya's material nodes. Currently many plug-in shaders are available on the Web and in development that use a process called *subsurface scattering* that more accurately simulates the ways in which translucent objects are shaded. However, many of these techniques rely on raytracing and/or Global Illumination algorithms, which can cause render times to be rather long.

We can somewhat fake this subsurface scattering effect by layering several materials together inside of a Layer Shader node. A Layered Shader node works similarly to the Layer Texture node that we used earlier in this chapter. It allows you to layer, or stack, several materials on top of one another and control the transparency of each layer. In this particular example, we will layer a surface shader that represents the skin on top of a solid red material that represents the blood. The transparency of the skin layer and the Specular Color will be attenuated depending on the facing ratio of the surface to our viewing angle.

Figure 14-21 shows the shading network for a basic skin shader. We'll begin by looking at the Lambert_BaseColor node. This node is used to represent the skin pigment and it is where you would connect any textures that control the Color, Diffuse, and Bump attributes. The specularity is handled in a separate material. The specular material in this case is a Phong E type with a black-and-white ramp controlling the Specular Color attribute. The ramp's V Coord attribute is then controlled by the samplerInfo node's Facing Ratio attribute. (While this particular example uses only one material for specularity, ideally, you might choose to add another specular material with a different ramp that controls the Highlight Size and Roughness attributes along with the Specular Color attribute. Experiment with these ideas until you achieve the look you want.)

The lambert_BaseColor node and the phongE_Spec materials are added together using the plusMinusAverage node, and the result is output to the surface shader named surfShad_comp. The surfShad_comp node is then placed on the top layer of the layeredShader node. Below that is the lambert_Blood node. This node is simply a Lambert material with a red color and slightly red Incandescence color set to a very subtle luminance.

Finally, the ramp_transCTRL is used to control the transparency of the surfShad_comp layer in the layeredShader. The ramp-transCTRL's V Coord attribute is controlled by the Facing Ratio attribute on the samplerInfo node's Facing Ratio attribute. When the material is applied to a surface, the result will be that the fleshy skin color appears to have a translucent quality, letting the color of the blood that is underneath show through. For examples of this type of skin shader, please see the color inserts in this book. Also, a Maya scene file called skinShader.ma that contains this shading network can be found on the book CD.

FIGURE 14-21   *The shading network for a basic skin shader*

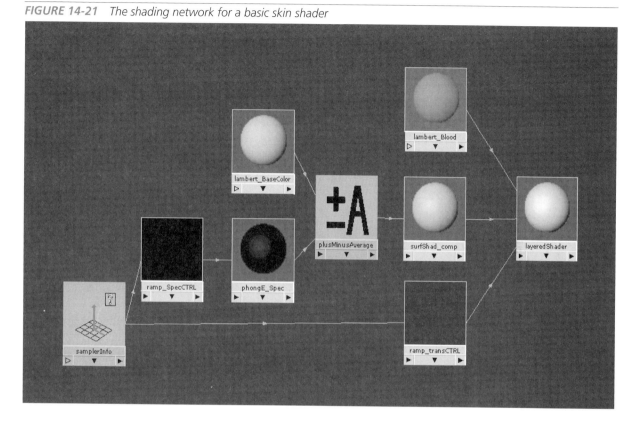

Summary

In this chapter, we experimented with several different material attributes and learned how the textures can be accurately mapped onto a surface. While the tutorials had different focuses, the lessons learned can be combined to create high-quality rendered images. Remember, though, the real strength to creating good surfaces comes from careful study in the real world.

In the next chapter, we will look at the Paint Effects toolset in Maya and learn about ways to paint directly on objects in the view window.

Painting in Maya

The paint tools in Maya offer some of

the most unique and innovative features and

solutions in the program. You can use these tools

to paint onto a standard 2D canvas, paint directly

onto 3D models, or even create 3D objects such

as plants and hair with the stroke of a brush. This

chapter will show you how to use the paint tools

for all of these applications.

Maya's paint tools are divided into three main categories: the Artisan tools, the Paint Effects tools, and the 3D Paint tools. We have already used the Artisan tools, such as the Sculpt Surfaces tool and the Paint Skin Weights tool, to manipulate geometry and manage our smooth skinning data (Chapters 4 and 11). In this chapter we will focus on the Paint Effects tools and the 3D Paint tools.

Paint Effects

You can use Paint Effects to create entire objects just by dragging on a canvas or in one of the view windows. Paint Effects is more like a particle-based technology than a geometry- or pixel-based one. This means that instead of being made up of polygons or pixels, objects created with Paint Effects are made up of tiny particle-like matter. Maya 6 ships with hundreds of Paint Effects brushes that let you paint all kinds of objects. Brush strokes can be as simple as a pastel or oil paint, or as complex as trees, flowers, or rain. Once they are created, objects made with Paint Effects can be animated to appear to grow over time or be affected by forces such as the wind.

Strokes, Brushes, and Tubes

Paint Effects works by applying paint, or a pattern that is defined by a brush, to a stroke that is created when you click and drag your cursor in a canvas or view window with the Paint Effects tool (Paint Effects | Paint Effects Tool). A *stroke* is a curve attached to a hidden NURBS curve that instructs brushes on how the paint should be applied. In the case of an airbrush, for example, the paint is applied to the curve and rendered as a simple airbrush stroke. However, some of the bushes available will "grow" *tubes* as the stroke is created.

Take a look at Figure 15-1. The image on the left shows a stroke that was created with the birchMedium.mel brush. The tubes—branches and leaves—are extending from the stroke. The image on the right shows what the stroke looks like when rendered.

Tubes are used to simulate organic growth or branching. As you drag the cursor in a canvas or view window, tubes will extend from the curve. The tubes are created by Maya sampling the curve made by the stroke. If the points on the curve are far apart, meaning that the stroke was made quickly, fewer tubes are created. If a tree brush was selected, for example, the resulting branch may not have as many little branches or leaves as a branch that was created from a stroke that was denser or drawn over a longer period of time. At some point, the maximum number of tubes for each brush will be reached and the object will stop growing. In Paint Effects terms, this object will have reached its *lifespan*.

You can select a brush from the brush library in the Paint Effects tab of the Visor window. Open the Visor window either by choosing Window | General Editors | Visor or by choosing

FIGURE 15-1 *The view window at left shows a Paint Effects stroke and tubes; the image is rendered at right.*

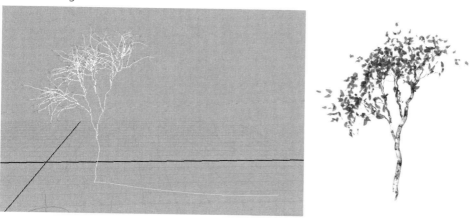

Paint Effects | Get Brush. The Visor window is shown in Figure 15-2 with the Paint Effects tab selected and displaying the available brushes. The Paint Effects brushes are organized into separate folders on the left side of the window. Clicking a folder will display its contents on the right. Clicking a brush will make the Paint Effects tool active with the selected brush loaded.

FIGURE 15-2 *The Paint Effects brush library shown in the Visor*

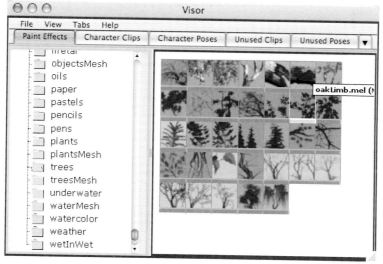

The brush that you select from the library is known as a *template brush*. The idea is that you use a brush's settings as a starting point to enhance and customize the look of the Paint Effects objects that are created. We will get into editing the template brushes in the tutorials in this chapter.

Paint Effects Limitations

Because Paint Effects is such a unique technology, it does has some limitations when used with other parts of Maya. The most significant limitations have to do with rendering. Paint Effects is supported only in the Maya software renderer. Mental Ray will not render objects created in Paint Effects. Even when you're using the Maya software renderer, render times can be quite long—almost unmanageable—if the scene contains a lot of strokes that contain many segments. Be mindful of this as you use the Paint Effects tool. Using fewer strokes to cover an area will render much faster than using many strokes to cover the area.

Paint Effects does not work well with raytracing. Objects created with Paint Effects won't reflect or refract. (See Chapter 16 for more information on raytracing reflections and refractions.) To make the Paint Effects reflect and refract, you must convert the Paint Effects into a 2D image and apply it as a texture or choose Modify | Convert | Polygon Model (more on this step later in the chapter). Also, since it does not work with raytracing, Paint Effects can't cast raytraced shadows; use Depth Map Shadows instead. You can also render Paint Effects objects separately and composite them with the rest of the image in a compositing application.

One of the most amazing aspects of Paint Effects is its ability to add animation. Turbulence can be added to simulate objects blowing in the wind. However, you cannot directly apply Maya's dynamic fields to the Paint Effects objects. All animation done to the Paint Effects object must be created by editing attributes on the Paint Effects' *tube node*. This may make it difficult to match any dynamic simulation on other objects in the scene that use fields or have the Paint Effects objects collide with other objects in the scene. While converting the Paint Effects objects to polygons and using soft and rigid body dynamics (explained in Chapter 19) is a workaround, you should be aware of these limitations if you plan to use Paint Effects in your productions.

Paint Effects on a 2D Canvas

While Maya is generally considered a 3D application, it can be used as a traditional 2D paint application to paint on a 2D canvas. However, the brushes available in the Paint Effects toolset let you go beyond just painting color, as you would with a brush in Photoshop or Painter. Simply by clicking and dragging across the canvas, you can use Paint Effects to draw tree branches, clouds, hair, or even flesh.

Using Paint Effects on a 2D canvas is great for painting texture maps or creating matte paintings that you will eventually reuse in your Maya scenes. However, it is also a fast way to spice up a web page or page layout for print design.

Let's get started by learning some of the basic interface options and terminology used in Paint Effects.

1. Create a new scene.

2. Choose Panel | Paint Effects or press the 8 key in the Perspective view. This will open the Paint Effects window. The default for the window is the 2D mode panel. Within this panel, you can paint as you would with any 2D paint program. Figure 15-3 shows the Paint Effects window's toolbar.

NOTE   *While you may use the Paint Effects tool in 3D by painting in the view windows, you can also paint in the Paint Effects window by choosing Paint | Scene. This will load one of the existing camera views in the scene. You can then use the Camera menu to select a specific view. The advantage to painting in this window is that some of the brushes do not display details while working with them in the regular view windows. The Paint Effects window was designed to allow you to see the results of your brushes without having to do test renders.*

3. Now load template brush settings by selecting a brush from the Visor. Open the Visor by choosing Window | General Editors | Visor, and click the Paint Effects tab.

4. When loaded, the left side of the Visor shows folders containing Paint Effects brushes. Select any brush and paint in the Paint Effects window to experiment. Some of the brushes, such as oil paint and pastels, behave like more common 2D paint brushes, while others, such as the flower and tree brushes, create branching structures.

FIGURE 15-3   The Paint Effects window's toolbar

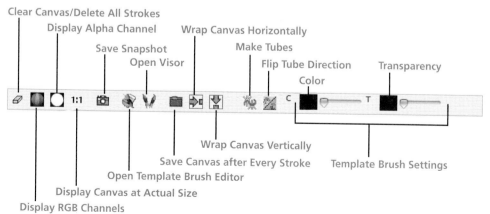

5. Click the Clear Canvas/Delete All Strokes button on the toolbar. This will erase whatever you have done so far. Now let's create a leaf texture to apply to a plane geometry.

6. Choose Canvas | Set Size. Set the X and Y sizes to **512** and click the Set Size button.

7. To make the texture tileable, you can use the Wrap Canvas functions by clicking the Wrap Canvas Horizontally and Wrap Canvas Vertically buttons. This will make the Paint Effects texture wrap around vertically and horizontally so seams will be invisible when the texture is repeated over a surface.

8. Open the Visor and select the mapleCluster.mel brush from the trees folder.

9. Paint two or three strokes from bottom to top in the Paint Effects window. LMB-click and drag only very little to make the stroke fill the top of the panel. You should see several limbs with a lot of leaf details. It may take a several tries to get the look you want. The illustration shows the result of the strokes so far.

NOTE *When you use the Paint Effects tools here in 2D, Maya will immediately apply the paint to the stroke and then delete the stroked curve, leaving just the paint. Therefore, you cannot go back and manipulate that curve or edit the brush attributes once the object has been painted, as you would be able to do in 3D.*

10. You can now export this image into a tileable, seamless texture by first saving the image. Choose Canvas | Save.

11. In the Save dialog box, name the file and click Save.

NOTE *You can save the image in a variety of formats. If you choose Save As □, you can also check or uncheck the option to Save Alpha. Having an alpha channel will allow you to composite your Paint Effects creations easily in other applications.*

The texture you have created can now be applied as a texture map to a square plane to simulate the leaves and branches on a tree or cast shadow for light passing through the leaves and branches. Paint Effects is perfect for helping you quickly create organic textures.

Paint Effects in a 3D Environment

The most exciting aspect of Paint Effects is its ability to create 3D objects. A Paint Effects stroke can be created simply by painting in the view window or directly onto geometry. In this section, we will use Paint Effects to create an underwater scene with seaweed, coral, sea anemones, and bubbles. To create the initial geometry, we will use one of the Artisan brush tools—the Sculpt Surfaces tool. Let's get started.

We'll start by creating the ocean floor geometry:

1. Open a new scene and choose Create | NURBS Primitives | Plane.

2. In the Channel Box, set the Scale X, Y, and Z attributes to **30** and change Patches U and V to **15**.

3. Use the Sculpt Surfaces tool (Edit NURBS | Sculpt Surfaces Tool) to add bumps to the surface to resemble the ocean floor. Save and name this plane **oceanFloor**.

4. You can deform a surface like this grid by using the Map function of the Sculpt Surfaces tool, which uses the luminance values or alpha channel of a texture map to push or pull the CVs on the surface. To use this function, open the Sculpt Surfaces Tool Settings window. Choose Push as the Operation, and change Opacity and Max Displacement to **1**.

5. Click the Map tab at the top of the Tool Settings window, and then click the Browse button and find the OceanFloor.iff file in Sourceimages folder of the Chapter 15 project folder on the CD. This texture map is used to displace the oceanFloor surface. Look in the view window to verify that this has happened.

6. Click the Reload button to add more displacement. Figure 15-4 shows the Map tab and the deformed surface.

7. Open the Hypershade and create a Lambert material. Apply it to the oceanFloor surface.

8. Map OceanFloor.iff to the Color attribute of the material. Using this map to displace the surface as well as using it as a color map will make the sunken areas darker.

FIGURE 15-4   *The Map tab and deformed ocean floor*

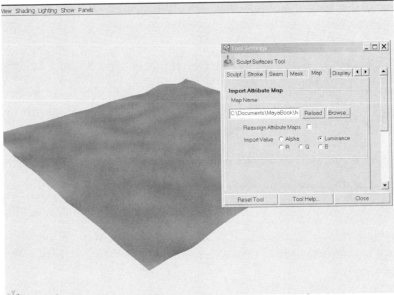

Next we'll create Paint Effects strokes in 3D. If we were to start painting in the view window right now, the strokes would actually be created on the view panel's grid, not the geometry. To paint directly onto geometry, we need to make the surface paintable.

1. Select the oceanFloor surface, and choose Paint Effects | Make Paintable. Now this surface is a paintable surface and the Paint Effects' strokes will be created on the surface.

2. Choose Window | General Editors | Visor to open the Visor. Find the underwater folder on the left side and open it.

3. Click kelp.mel and LMB-drag to start painting on the oceanFloor surface. You should see the curve generated on the surface and green kelp tubes growing out of the surface.

TIP   *The speed at which you drag a brush over the surface affects the complexity of the tubes that grow out of the strokes. A slower stroke will create more sample points and hence create more tubes that grow. Experiment with creating strokes to get the results you want.*

4. Try using other brushes, such as fanCorals.mel and seaUrchins.mel, to populate the ocean floor. You can control the size of the objects you are creating by adjusting the size of the brush. To change the size of the brush, hold down the B key and drag left to right in the view window. The brush cursor gets larger and smaller, depending on which direction you drag.

5. Render the scene by clicking the Render The Current Frame button in the Status Line. Figure 15-5 shows the rendered image. It looks pretty good, but each element is still too uniform looking, and we may want to make the kelps a bit taller.

NOTE   You can paint in either the view windows or the Paint Effects window by choosing Paint | Paint Scene (instead of Paint | Paint Canvas). Painting in the Paint Effects window will let you view your strokes in greater detail than you can in the view windows. However, viewing all of these details can put a strain on your computer. It's more efficient to paint in the view windows and do test renders to see detail.

FIGURE 15-5   *Rendered ocean floor image*

FIGURE 15-6 *The Attribute Editor displaying the attributes for the kelp stroke's shape*

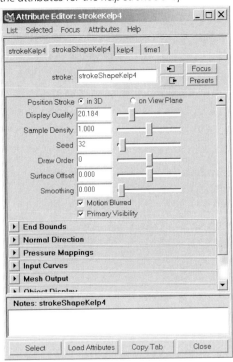

Now let's edit the attributes for the strokes and brushes. If you want to change the size and other aspects of the kelp, you can open the Attribute Editor to access a stroke and edit the brush's attributes for individual strokes. You can also change how complex the tubes are displayed or the number of seaweeds emerging from the strokes.

Select one of the strokes and open the Attribute Editor. Click the strokeShapeKelp tab that contains the stroke's attributes. Figure 15-6 shows the attributes for the stroke.

TIP **You'll find it easier to choose strokes by using the Outliner window rather than clicking in the view window.**

A few sliders here are very important:

- **Display Quality** Changes the complexity of how tubes are displayed. A higher number displays more accurate tube shapes, but will slow down the interactivity.

- **Sample Density** Determines how many sample points the stroke has. The more sample points, the more places tubes will grow.

- **Seed** Sets how each tube is randomized. Set various Seed values on strokes so that the objects look different from one another.

By manipulating these three values in particular, you should be able to see tubes more clearly, have more tubes grow, and add or decrease randomization.

The Kelp tab contains attributes for the kelp brush. Here, you can edit the actual appearance of the tubes that will in turn render the brushes differently. You can control such aspects as color (texture) of the brush and the number and complexity of the tubes, turn on shadow casting, and apply animation. In fact, so many attributes are available here that it can be daunting. By experimenting with all of the attributes that are discussed in the following section, changing values, and viewing the results of those changes, you will gain a good understanding of how Paint Effects works.

NOTE *While this example explores brush attributes by editing attributes of a brush after it has been applied to a stroke, you can edit the brush settings before creating a stroke by choosing Paint Effects | Edit Template Brush Settings. A window will open that contains all of the brush attributes discussed here.*

Figure 15-7 shows the kelp's brush attributes in the Attribute Editor.

- **Brush Type**   Determines what kind of brush this is. This is the most defining attribute in any brush, as it determines its general function: Paint, Smear, Blur, or Erase. Any time you need to create a Paint Effects object, you'll set this to Paint.

- **Global Scale**   A very important attribute that sets how large the Paint Effects object will be. By adjusting this attribute, you can make the kelp bigger or smaller per stroke. Realize that this attribute is controlled by the brush size at the time of creating the stroke.

- **Tubes**   This section contains many important attributes for controlling the behavior of the tubes. Remember that the tubes control the general shape and complexity of the Paint Effects brush. A lot of these attributes are related to how the tubes will branch out from other tubes as the object grows. Following are the two most important attributes:

  - **Tubes**   The Tubes check box enables tubes on the stroke. If this is not selected, no branching will occur. Brushes such as the airbrush do not use any tubes. If you were to disable this check box now, the kelp plant would disappear, because without any tubes, the brush will be able to apply only a texture to the stroke.

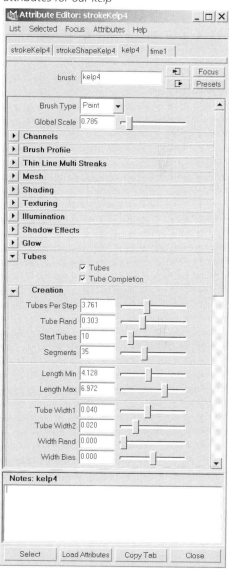

FIGURE 15-7   *The long list of brush attributes for our kelp*

- **Tube Completion** As you paint a stroke, a tube is "planted" at the various sample points. As you continue the stroke, the tubes grow until they reach the end of their lifespan. This means that the tubes from the last sample point may not be as fully grown or complex as the tubes from the first sample point of the stroke. When Tube Completion is disabled, the tubes will remain at their current growth when you release the mouse button. However, if Tube Completion is checked, all of the tubes will grow to reach their maximum lifespan.

- **Creation: Tubes Per Step** Number of tubes planted per the number of sample points in the stroke.

- **Creation: Start Tubes** Number of tubes created from the first sample point of the stroke. Many of the Paint Effects brushes, such as the kelp brush in this example, have this attribute set to 0. This means that only a single object will be created from this stroke.

- **Creation: Segments** Changes the length of each segment. As the value increases, the kelp becomes smoother and straighter.

- **Creation: Length Min/Max** Sets the minimum and maximum length of the tubes. Paint Effects creates tubes with random lengths within the Length Min and Length Max values.

- **Creation: Tube Width 1 and Tube Width 2** Sets the width of the tubes as they grow from the base (Width 1) to the tip (Width 2).

- **Growth** Other elements, such as branches and flowers, can be added by checking the appropriate box here (shown in the illustration) and tweaking the attributes relating to each growth. Checking one of the boxes will activate the corresponding controls for branches, twigs, leaves, flowers, and buds.

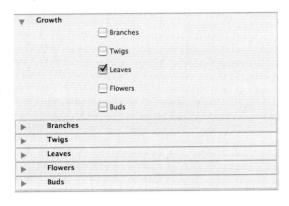

Adjust attributes for each stroke curve to create a variety of different Paint Effects objects. Slightly altering each one will allow you to create a more natural, less uniform scene.

Animate the Brushes

Another powerful feature of Paint Effects is its ability to add animation to the tubes. You can, of course, set keys on any of the attributes available in the Attribute Editor and animate them over time. On the kelp, for example, you can also keyframe Azimuth Min and Azimuth Max attributes found in the Width Scale section of the brush's Attribute Editor. This will adjust the tilting of the tubes and simulate them drifting in water.

However, Paint Effects brushes were designed with specific attributes that let you animate Paint Effects objects so that they can appear to grow over time, react to forces or turbulence, spiral, bend, or twist. Many of the brush presets—such as those for kelp, for instance—have some of these animation attributes already enabled. If you click the Play button next to the Time Slider, you will notice that some animation has already been applied to the kelp—it sways and bends a bit to simulate being affected by underwater currents. This is due to the kelp having Turbulence applied to it. Turbulence applies noise to the motion of the tubes.

Let's adjust this animation to make the current appear rougher.

1. Use the Outliner to select one of the kelp plants in your scene. In the Attribute Editor, select the brush node and expand the Tubes | Behavior | Turbulence section so that you can see the attributes shown in the illustration.

2. Notice the that Turbulence Type is set to World Force. This means that the turbulence is added in "world" space. This setting is more useful than the Local Force option, because the World Force will appear more uniform when applied to different strokes. If you wanted to disable the turbulence from the kelp, you would set the Turbulence Type to None.

3. To make the kelp animate faster, increase the Turbulence Speed attribute. Click the Play button to see the result.

TIP **You don't have to stop the animation to see the results of editing the animation attributes. You can adjust the attributes while the animation is playing.**

4. Now let's add some bubbles to the scene that animate flowing upward. In the Visor, select the bubbles.mel brush in the underwater folder.

5. In the view window, draw a few strokes on the oceanFloor object. The bubbles will be created. If you open the Attribute Editor and look at the Turbulence settings (Tubes | Behavior | Turbulence), you'll notice that Turbulence has already been enabled.

6. Do a test render of a few frames to see how the bubbles look. The bubbles flow upward because a negative gravity force has been applied to them. To slow down the animation a bit, we can adjust this gravity to lessen its effect on the bubbles. Make sure that the bubbles stroke is selected, and look in the Attribute Editor. Find the Forces section (Tubes | Behavior | Forces). In this section, you'll see an attribute called Gravity. Change it to **-.8** to slow down the effect.

Render the Scene

When you are finished adding Paint Effects objects to the scene, you can begin to set up the scene for the final render. To make this scene look believable, we need to add lights, a background, and shadows. First we'll add the lights.

1. Create a directional light (Create | Light | Directional Light) and aim it at the ground. Set the color of this light to light blue.

2. Add another light. This time, create a spot light. Position this light above the scene. This light will be used to cast the shadows and water caustic pattern.

3. Map a file texture to the Color attribute of the spot light. Import the caustic.jpg file found on the CD.

4. Enable Depth Map Shadows on the spot light. Do a test render.

5. While the caustics are visible on the ground, the Paint Effects objects are not casting any shadows. For Paint Effect objects to cast shadows onto other objects, you must turn on the Cast Shadow attribute for each brush in the scene. Select all of the Paint Effect brushes in the scene from the Outliner, and then find the Cast Shadow attribute in the Channel Box. Set this attribute to **1** (on).

TIP *You can set attribute values for an entire selection of objects by editing the attribute in the Channel Box or the Attribute Spreadsheet Editor (Window | General Editor | Attribute Spreadsheet Editor). This will not work, however, in the Attribute Editor.*

6. Add a background. To do this, create a NURBS sphere and scale it up so that the entire scene, including the perspective camera, is inside the sphere.

FIGURE 15-8   *The final render of the underwater scene*

7. In the Hypershade, create a Surface Shader material and set the Out Color attribute to a dark-blue color. Apply this material to the NURBS sphere.

8. We need to make sure that this background object will not cast or receive any shadows from the spot light. Select the NURBS sphere, and in the Attribute Editor, select the nurbsSphereShape1 node. In the Render Stats section, disable the check boxes next to Cast Shadows and Receive Shadows.

Figure 15-8 shows the final render of this underwater scene.

By this point, you should have a good understanding of how to use Paint Effects to create organic forms, edit brushes, and add animation to the brushes. These same techniques can be applied to create a variety of objects quickly and populate your scene to create forests, hair, or outer space starfields and gases.

3D Paint Tool

The 3D Paint tool in Maya allows you to paint textures directly onto a 3D model in the view windows. This feature has quite a few applications in Maya. You could use the 3D Paint tool to create textures that control any attribute on the material of the target surface. This means that you would not have to leave Maya and revert to a painting application such as Photoshop to create texture maps for your models. Instead, all of the painting could be done in Maya, directly on the model. Furthermore, you can use 2D Paint Effects brushes to paint on the models, giving you access to and control over hundreds of patterns that are not available in other paint programs.

Unfortunately, painting directly on a model does not offer the precision or speed that you might find in a dedicated painting package. The ability to apply filters and work with an unlimited amount of layers is also lacking. (Although a layering system *could* be set up using Maya 6's new PSD texture node and layered texture nodes, it would behave slowly.) If you want to be able to 3D paint with all of these features, you are better off using Maxon's BodyPaint 3D or Right Hemisphere's Deep Paint 3D.

If the final output for your objects will not require precise texturing, such as .swf images for the web rendered with the Maya vector renderer, using the 3D Paint tool may be all that you need. However, by using the techniques demonstrated here in combination with the UV layout techniques shown in Chapter 14, you will be able to create great texture work.

This section describes a general workflow for setting up the 3D Paint tool for painting a model and discusses some other applications for using this tool to mark sections of a model or clean up and fix areas of an existing texture.

3D Paint Workflow

This section will demonstrate a step-by-step approach to using the 3D Paint tool to paint a model. We will cover laying out the UVs on a model before painting, setting up a material that is paintable, and then using some of the 3D Paint tool's main functions to paint the texture. This tutorial should provide all you need to get started painting with the 3D Paint tool. The rest is just practicing the art of painting.

Prepare the Surface for Painting

When you paint on a surface, Maya samples the UV coordinates of your brush stroke and writes the stroke to a bitmap texture file. Therefore, before you can paint on a surface, you must ensure that no UVs overlap on the model. If any overlapping UVs exist, for example, a brush stroke on the lip of the model may also end up on its ear.

If you will be importing the file that we are about to paint into another paint program, you would probably want to spend some time laying out the UVs using the techniques you learned in Chapter 14. However, if you are going to use only the 3D Paint tool and you do not require a organized UV layout, you can use the Automatic Mapping command to lay out the UVs automatically so that they do not overlap.

Here's how it's done:

1. Open the paintHead.ma file found on the CD. (This is the same head that we modeled in Chapter 6.)

2. Select the head and choose Window | UV Texture Editor. The UV Texture Editor displays the current layout of the UVs for this model. As you can see, it is a mess right now!

3. To paint cleanly on this surface, we need to organize these UVs. Choose Edit Polygons | Texture | Automatic Mapping. This will lay out the UVs based on the projection of six planes. Figure 15-9 shows the UVs in the UV Texture Editor before and after the UVs have been laid out. While the UVs at the right may not be as organized as, say, the UVs shown in Chapter 14 in Figure 14-17, we can rest assured that there are no overlapping UVs. The model is now ready to paint.

Create a File Texture

Neither the geometry nor the material is capable of storing texture information. As you should know by now, texture information is stored in a texture node, such as a file texture. If we tried to use the 3D Paint tool on the model at this time, an error would result, telling us that no file texture has been assigned to the current attribute on the selected model.

FIGURE 15-9 *The UVs displayed in the UV Texture Editor before (left) and after (right) the Automatic Mapping command is applied*

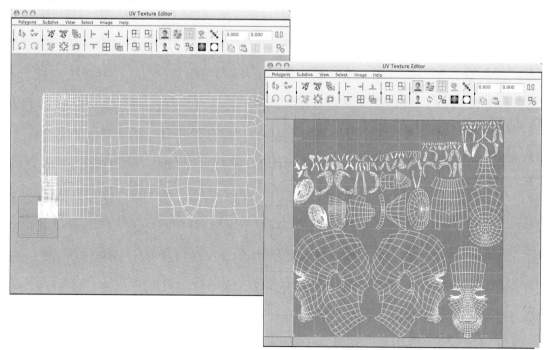

Remember that when you paint on a model, you are actually just painting onto a texture map that is connected to the material that has been applied to the model. Therefore, you must assign a file texture to the attribute of the area on which you want to paint. To make things easy, Maya lets you assign a file texture to a specific material attribute right in the 3D Paint tool's settings panel. Here's how its done:

1. Right-click the head geometry and choose Material | Assign New Material | Blinn.

2. Select the head geometry and then open the 3D Paint tool's settings window by choosing Texturing | 3D Paint Tool ❏. Scroll down to the File Textures section. The options for this section are shown in Figure 15-10.

FIGURE 15-10 *The File Textures settings in the 3D Paint tool's settings window*

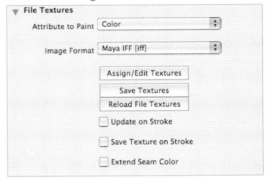

3. Choose an image format from the Image Format pull-down menu. It is recommended that you use the Maya IFF [iff] selection.

NOTE To open a file in this format from within Photoshop, you will need to install the iff plug-in that comes with the Photoshop install CD. If you do not have this CD, it is best to choose another file format, such as Targa (tga).

4. Click the Assign/Edit Textures button. A window will open that allows you to specify the resolution for the file that is about to be created. Set the resolution of the file using the Size X and Size Y attributes. When setting the size, you must be concerned about using textures that are too big or too small. A texture that is too large will hinder performance, while a texture that is too small will break up and look "jaggy" in the renders. For now, set both of these attributes to **1024**; note that it is always a good idea to do a few tests before committing to a resolution. Click the Assign/Edit Textures button. A file texture will be created and connected to the Color attribute of the Blinn material.

5. Now change the paintable attribute to Bump by choosing Bump from the Attribute To Paint pull-down menu. Once again, click the Assign/Edit Textures button to set the resolution size and create a file texture connected to the Bump attribute of the Blinn material.

6. Continue assigning a file texture to the Specular Color and Diffuse attributes of this Blinn material.

7. In the Hypershade, graph the input connections to the Blinn material and see that four file textures are connected to the material, all mapped to the appropriate channels, as shown in the illustration.

Painting on Surfaces

Now we are ready to begin painting. For this part, we will use many of the other settings found in the 3D Paint Tools settings panel,

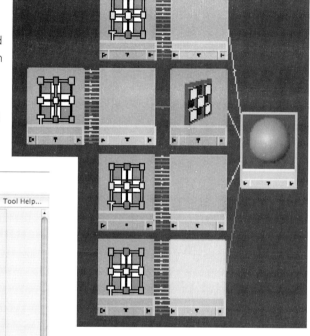

FIGURE 15-11   The 3D Paint tool settings

which is shown in Figure 15-11. We'll begin by painting in the color channel.

1. In the 3D Paint Tools settings panel, set the Attribute to Paint back to Color. This will allow us to paint onto the file texture that is connected to the Color attribute.

2. At this point, the default color of the texture is gray. We want to change this to a flesh color. We can fill the entire texture to one color by using the Flood option. In the Flood section, click the color swatch next to the Color attribute. Find a color that works well for skin in the Color Chooser and click Accept. Click the Flood Paint button and the entire model will fill in that color.

3. Let's paint the lip area a reddish color. In the Brush section, select an Artisan brush with a soft edge (the first one on the left).

4. In the Color section of the Attribute Editor, set the Color attribute to a reddish color.

5. In the Perspective window, click and drag over the lips to paint that area red. Remember that you can hold down the B key to change the brush size interactively.

6. Continue painting any other detail that you want—perhaps redden the cheeks and darken the areas around the eyes. When attempting to paint subtle colors, use a low Opacity setting on the brush, such as 0.2, and stroke the geometry a few times until the paint becomes visible, to produce the best results.

7. When you are happy with the paint, save the strokes to the connected PSD file. In the 3D Paint tool's settings window, scroll down to the File Textures section and click the Save Textures button. You can use the Save The Texture On Stroke and Update On Stroke options to write the data directly to the PSD file and save that file as soon as you are finished painting a stroke. However, while this may seem convenient, it can slow things down if you are painting to a large texture. Therefore, it is better to manually save the strokes when you are ready.

8. Another important option in the File Textures section is the Extend Seam Color check box. This is especially helpful when the UVs were laid out with the Automatic Mapping command, as was used here. Because you may be painting across multiple UV shells, it is possible that you will start to see seams in your strokes, where one UV shell ends and another begins. This option will extend the stroke a bit past the actual seam in the UV shell, making your seams invisible.

9. You can also use Paint Effects brushes to paint on your textures. Because these are actual file textures that you are painting on, the resulting Paint Effects brushes will be in 2D. If you wanted to add 3D Paint Effects objects, such as hair, you would need to make the surface paintable by choosing Paint Effects | Make Paintable, selecting a brush from the Visor, and then painting. For now, though, we will add some eyebrows with the Paint Effects brush. To select a brush from the 3D Paint tool settings, click the Get Brush button. This will open the Visor.

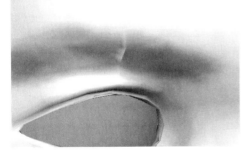

10. In the Visor, look for the hair folder; inside is an eyebrow.mel brush. Select this brush and drag over the eyebrow area on the geometry. An eyebrow will appear. Unfortunately, because of the way that paint is applied to the tubes in a Paint Effects brush, Maya is unable to extend the seam color, resulting in visible seams, as shown here.

11. We'll just have to touch it up. Select the soft-edged Artisan brush that we used to paint the lips. Click the Eyedropper button next to the Color attribute to activate the sample color function.

12. Click over the eyebrow where the Paint Effects stroke is visible and sample its color. Make the brush size very small, and paint the areas where the seam is visible. This should clean up the area pretty well.

13. Once you are pleased with the color map, you can select another attribute to paint onto. In the 3D Paint tool settings, scroll down to the File Textures section and select another attribute from the Attribute To Paint pull-down menu.

14. If you would rather continue working on the other channels in Photoshop, just make sure that you click the Save Texture button. You may then open the file in Photoshop. Once you make any changes in the Photoshop file, you can go back to Maya and click the Reload Texture button in the 3D Paint tool settings to see the updated texture.

Other Applications

If you've gone through the previous tutorial and don't find that the 3D Paint tool will be useful for your production needs, perhaps you'll find it useful in other ways.

Marking Areas on a Surface

One of the most useful applications for Maya's 3D Paint tool is to use it simply as a marking tool to direct painters where to paint in a 2D paint program. Even when the UVs have been laid out in an orderly and recognizable fashion, the scale of the UV layout may not be proportional to the actual texture that you need to paint. In other words, if you paint a circle on a texture map in Photoshop and then apply it to a material in Maya, the circle might appear stretched due to the layout of the UVs. In such a case, you can use the 3D Paint tool to mark areas that need to be painted on the model.

Another excellent use for this tool is for use with dynamics. This topic is covered heavily in Chapters 17, 18, and 19, where you will learn that many particle attributes can be controlled with a texture—Surface Emissions are one example. You could easily paint onto a area of a model that will control the point at which the particles are emitted.

Cleaning Up Existing Textures

Earlier, we used the Color Sample and Brush tool to clean up a seam that resulted from painting over multiple UV shells. While that was a simple example, you may find that at times the detail in the texture map is too heavy to use the color sampler. In such cases, the Clone feature of the 3D Paint tool is just the solution.

Figure 15-12, left, shows a surface whose two sides do not have corresponding UVs, and an obvious seam exists in the texture. By setting the Paint Operation to Clone and then sampling an

FIGURE 15-2   *The clone operation is used to fix visible seams in a texture map.*

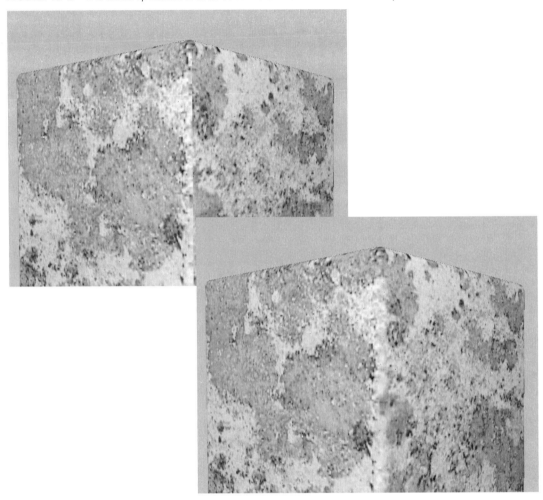

area with the Set Clone Source button, the brush will clone the sampled area when a stroke is painted. The image on the right shows what the surface looks like after being touched up with the clone operation.

Summary

This chapter explored some of the features available to you with Maya's paint tools. You can see that no shortage of options exists when it comes to painting in Maya. The trick is finding out which tools are right for your particular job.

In the next chapter, we will explore rendering methods that will give your images extra shine.

16

Rendering

Maya's software renderer uses your
computer's CPU and Maya's software rendering code
to convert all of the 3D elements of your scene—
geometry, textures, lighting, and effects—into a
pixel-based image that can be opened in an image-
editing application, a video-editing application, or
in an Internet browser. In this rendered image, none
of these elements can be transformed in 3D space
or have their materials edited. They are fixed, and
any changes that need to be made will require that
the image be re-rendered or the pixel information
modified in an image-editing program.

The software renderer is also capable of making many additional calculations that are not possible in real time and, hence, not displayed in your view window. In software, rendered image anti-aliasing and texture filtering can be calculated to give your image smooth edges and textures. Fog from lights can be rendered. Reflections can be raytraced and refracted. Motion blur can be added. With the new addition of Maya's Mental Ray renderer, some of these features are enhanced to add caustic effects, global illumination, and HDRI (high dynamic range imagery, discussed later in the chapter in the section "HDR Images with Final Gather"). This chapter examines all of these cases and shows examples of each. We will start by looking at some rendering options in the Render Global Settings window. Then we'll talk about some techniques for improving smoothness and eliminating seams in NURBS geometry. After these basic concepts are explained, we'll move through a tutorial that shows some additional rendering effects and introduces a workflow for working with the Mental Ray renderer.

Rendering in Maya

Maya offers both software and hardware renderers. The hardware renderer uses the real-time, OpenGL (Open Graphics Library) enabled rendering engine of your computer's video processing unit. This type of rendering is used to view geometry, textures, particles, lights, and shadows in the view windows. All of these can be viewed in real time, or near real time, depending on the power of your video card. While this type of rendering is great for fast interaction, the image quality and limited display of certain effects prohibit it from being used as a final image for television or film production. Hardware renderers similar to Maya's are sufficient for real-time games that you might find on a video game console such as a PlayStation or Xbox. Some elements in Maya, such as several of the particle types, can be rendered only in hardware. For these, you can use the hardware renderer to render each frame of an animation as a file or sequence of files to be composited together with the software renderer to create the final image or animation. We will discuss the hardware renderer in detail in Chapter 17.

The remainder of this chapter covers Maya's software renderer. In this kind of rendering, all elements in the scene for a given frame are gathered. Each object in the scene is positioned according to its keyframed translation values at a given frame. If the object is being driven by inverse kinematics (IK), a dynamic simulation, or expression, these are calculated first and the object is translated to match. If the object is a piece of NURBS geometry, it is tessellated into polygonal facets. Every object is combined with its material into a shading group node. This shading group is then calculated along with the light to produce shadows, bumps (from the bump map attributes), reflections, highlights, and any other effects such as fog.

With all of this information gathered, the renderer divides the image into chunks based on the amount of RAM available and begins calculating each pixel, one at a time, for the final image. All of the chunks are combined and written into a file as one frame of the animation. Before they are written, the renderer does some additional work. Anti-aliasing and texture filtering can be performed to eliminate the jagged edges between objects and any noise that might arise from the detail in the texture map. Other effects, such as motion blur, are also added to moving objects.

This intense process can take minutes, hours, or even days, depending on the complexity of the scene. Understanding the different attributes and their settings can help you minimize these render times and give you precise control over the final look of the image.

Preparing to Render

The process of rendering usually involves these steps:

1. The scene is set up (modeling, texturing, animation, lighting, and so on).

2. A rendering engine is selected.

3. Render globals are set up.

4. The scene is rendered by clicking the Render Current Frame button in the Status Line, or the entire range of frames specified in the Render Global Settings window is rendered by choosing Render | Batch Render.

Render Global Settings Window

The Render Global Settings window (shown in Figure 16-1) is the main interface for editing the resolution, quality, and complexity of an image or animation. It can be accessed by choosing Window | Rendering Editors | Render Globals or by clicking the Display Render Globals Window button in the Status Line.

> *NOTE Keep in mind that Render Globals does what its name implies: it controls the render attributes of the scene globally. In some cases, the settings in the Render Global Settings window will override a setting found elsewhere for an attribute on a specific object. Shadows, raytraced reflections, and NURBS tessellation are good examples of this. While they can be turned on or set on a per-object basis, these individual settings can either be limited or ignored by modifying the respective setting in the Render Global Settings window. In other cases, it will set the value for everything in the scene that it relates to and can be overridden only elsewhere in the Maya user interface. Edge anti-aliasing and pixel sampling are good examples of this.*

In this section, we look at some of the most commonly used attributes in the Render Global Settings window. These attributes, such as File Format and Resolution, are native to this window and do not require any tweaking on a per-object basis. Attributes that merit a lengthier discussion and examples will be discussed in their own sections later in the chapter. Finally, we will

FIGURE 16-1   The Render Global Settings window

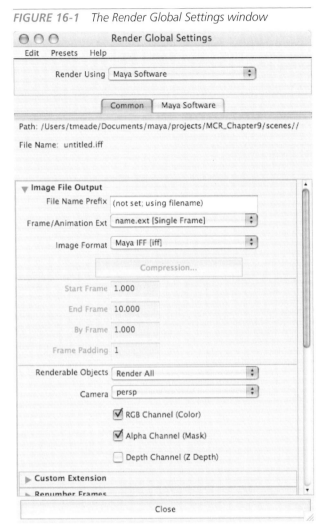

review this information when we set up the rendering of our final scene in Chapter 20. For now, we'll concentrate on the basics.

Select a Rendering Engine

Currently, Maya ships with four different rendering engines: the Maya software renderer, the Maya hardware renderer, the Mental Ray renderer, and the vector renderer. In many situations, you may need to render different elements of your scene using different rendering engines. To make this more manageable, the Render Global Settings window has been organized into two main sections, each grouped under a specific tab. Figure 16-1 shows the Render Global Settings window with the Maya software renderer loaded.

The Common tab displays the attributes that are common to all four rendering engines. These settings control such things as output resolution and range of frames—things that are not so specific to the "look" of the render.

The other tab will display attributes that are specific to the rendering engine that is selected from the Render Using pull-down menu at the top of the window. These attributes are specific to the rendering software and contain settings for quality (anti-aliasing and texture filtering) and specific rendering algorithms (raytracing and global illumination).

Common Rendering Attributes

The Common tab contains all of the basic settings for the renderer. It includes mainly the Image File Output section and Resolution settings.

The Image File Output section controls the range of frames output from Maya and what file format and channel information they will use. The two first attributes, the File Name Prefix and the

Frame/Animation Ext, let you specify a name for the rendered files and choose how you would like that name displayed along with its frame number and file extension. This helps make the rendered files output from Maya compatible with different compositing programs.

The Image Format attribute lets you specify the file type to which the images are rendered. While you have the option of outputting the entire range of frames (specified in the Start Frame, End Frame, By Frame, and Frame Padding attributes) as a QuickTime movie, most of the Image Format options are single image formats. Rendering an animation as a sequence of frames is highly recommended. Then, if anything goes wrong—the software crashes or a power loss occurs—you can output a single file for each frame rendered. The objects rendered and the camera from which they are rendered is selected from the Renderable Objects and Camera attributes. Finally, the Channel attributes let you select from what channel information will be used in the rendered image. We will use these settings later in the chapter.

The resolution attributes specify the resolution of the rendered image(s). The Presets pull-down menu contains many industry-standard resolutions for television, film, and computer screens. Custom resolutions can be set in the Height and Width attributes and the Pixel Aspect Ratio (the ratio of the width to the height of the image) can be set in this section as well.

Renderer-Specific Attributes

The second tab in the Render Global Settings window will load settings that control specific attributes for the selected renderer. In general, all of these attributes let you control the quality of the output data through some kind of anti-aliasing controls. In the case of the Maya vector renderer, the quality is mainly controlled by three attributes in the Appearance Options section. The Maya Vector tab is shown here. Since the Maya vector renderer renders vector data that can be exported to Macromedia Flash or Adobe Illustrator, the concept of anti-aliasing does not really apply. Instead, the renderer uses the Curve Tolerance and Detail Level attributes to control how smooth the edges of the objects are rendered.

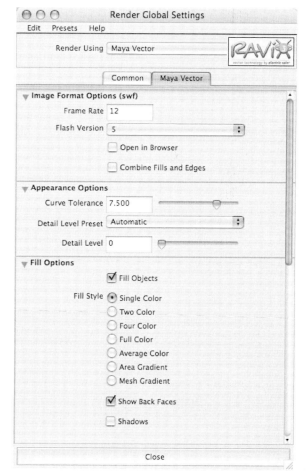

For the other three renderers, anti-aliasing is controlled through a number of attributes specific to each renderer. These will be discussed next. Without getting into the specifics, you can use preset anti-aliasing settings for both the Maya software renderer and the Mental Ray renderer through the Quality pull-down menu in this tab.

Most of the other attributes in the renderer-specific tab control the unique rendering algorithms of each renderer. Raytracing, Global Illumination, and Final Gather each use different rendering algorithms to determine how the final image is rendered. The specifics of these algorithms are discussed in the sections that follow.

Anti-aliasing

The Anti-aliasing settings available in the Render Global Settings window control the overall quality of the image. Specifically, anti-aliasing handles how the edges of objects in the scene are softened, or blurred, so that they blend with any objects behind them. It is a rare chance that the edges of objects in your scene will directly coincide with the square edges of the pixels in the rendered image. Therefore, it is necessary for the renderer to anti-alias the edges so that they blend; otherwise, the edges of objects will appear rough or "jaggy."

Figure 16-2 illustrates how the rendering engine will render a white object against a black background without any anti-aliasing. The image on the left represents how the objects are laid out in your scene, and the image on the right shows how that image was rendered without using anti-aliasing. The grid represents the pixel borders. In this process, the renderer will take one sample for each pixel, and whatever color has the majority within that pixel will be the color that is rendered for that pixel in the rendered image. The result, shown in the right image, has very rough edges.

The Maya software renderer and the Mental Ray renderer anti-alias edges by supersampling pixels that have a high degree of contrast. In *supersampling,* the renderer takes multiple samples from each pixel region and then blends them together to assign a value to the final, rendered pixel. Figure 16-3 shows the image from the previous example after it has been supersampled so that the renderer is taking four samples per pixel instead of just one, as shown in Figure 16-2. If a pixel contains two white samples and two black samples, the resulting pixel will be 50 percent gray.

The more samples that are taken, the slower your render times can become.

FIGURE 16-2   *A white object against a black background is rendered without any anti-aliasing, resulting in the image shown at the right.*

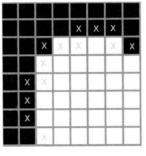

FIGURE 16-3 *Gray values
are determined for each
pixel based on four samples
taken from each pixel.*

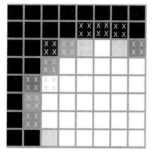

Therefore, you should use high anti-aliasing settings only for
your final render and use no, or low, anti-aliasing settings as
you preview your renders. Fortunately, quality presets are available in the Render Global Settings window.

Anti-aliasing Quality Settings

When using the Maya software renderer, the first section in the
Render Global Settings window is called Anti-aliasing Quality
and contains all of the attributes for controlling the anti-aliasing
in the current scene. The Anti-aliasing Quality settings in the
Render Global Settings window are shown here.

The Quality preset lets you choose between
six different options that set all of the
attributes in this section. These options
range from Preview Quality, the lowest
setting, to 3D Motion Blur Production at
the highest, and slowest, setting. For the
most part, these quality presets are all that
you need to deal with when rendering most
scenes. However, additional tweaking may
be necessary at times.

The attributes found in the Number Of
Samples section control the anti-aliasing for
the scene. The Shading and Max Shading
attributes deal with how many samples are
taken for each pixel, as discussed previously.
The Shading attribute sets the minimum
number of samples used for each pixel for
the entire scene. It is most ideal to keep this
setting as low as possible. A value of 2 is
probably high enough unless artifacts appear.

To make anti-aliasing more efficient, the renderer uses an adaptive algorithm that will
supersample only the areas of the image that
need it. This adaptive algorithm is based on
the contrast between the pixels in the image.

Max Shading sets the amount of samples taken when the contrast between edges exceeds the values set in the Contrast Threshold settings. Therefore, if the Shading attribute is set to 2, the renderer will take one pass at the image by sampling each pixel twice. If the contrast between these samples exceeds the amount set in the Contrast Threshold settings, the renderer will supersample those pixels by the amount set in the Max Shading attribute.

Once the anti-aliasing process is complete, the image can be blurred slightly to get rid of any problems that the anti-aliasing process missed. You can select a filter type in the Pixel Filter Type pull-down menu. The Box filter is the softest, while the Gaussian filter is a bit sharper.

Anti-aliasing in Mental Ray

When the Mental Ray renderer is selected in the Render Global Settings window, the anti-alias quality settings can be accessed in the Sampling Quality section, shown next. Mental Ray's anti-

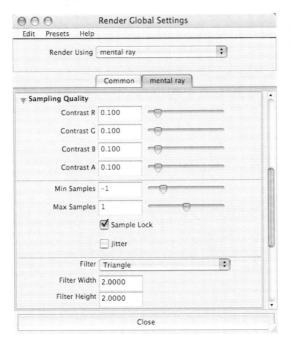

aliasing algorithm works similar to the Maya software renderer but it provides an additional optimization. On the low side, Mental Ray has the ability to sample not just one sample for every pixel, but it can do, for example, one sample for every four pixels. This is great when creating previews or even images that have a lot of solid colors.

Instead of setting the number of samples directly, as in the Maya software renderer, you set the Min and Max Samples based on an exponent. A value of 0 is equal to one sample per pixel. A value of 1 means that four samples will be taken for each pixel. A value of 2 will take sixteen samples. A value of −1 will take one sample for every four pixels.

The Min and Max Samples attributes are analogous to the Shading and Max Shading attributes in the Maya software renderer. Min Samples controls how many samples are taken during the first pass of the render. If the contrast values of these samples exceed that of the Contrast RGBA attributes, additional samples are taken. The maximum number of samples taken is determined by the Max Samples value.

Raytracing

A rendering engine can use many different methods to calculate the shading of a 3D scene. The renderer can consider all of the surface, material, and lighting attributes and calculate the final image in many ways. The default renderer in Maya uses what is called "normal vector interpolation" shading. This shading occurs by interpolating the vertex normals and shading every point on the surface by computing the relationship between the angle of its normal and the angle of its light. While this works well for rendering objects that get all of their color information from the material's color and/or light, it does little to solve the issue of rendering a reflective surface, where points on the surface must also reflect the colors of the objects that surround it. Raytracing offers a very accurate solution to this problem.

How Raytracing Works

Raytracing is a rendering algorithm that provides a very accurate method of calculating reflections and shadows. In the real world, rays of light, or photons, are emitted from a light source until they hit an object and then bounce off and possibly hit another object. They continue to bounce around until they are reflected back up into space. If a computer were to calculate all of this behavior, a very long time would pass before you saw your rendered image. But we are not concerned with all the rays that bounce up into space or travel in the opposite direction from our point of view—only the rays that end up in our eye or, in Maya, in our camera have any significance to our rendered image. To speed rendering, then, raytracing traces the rays of light from the camera out into the 3D scene.

Figure 16-4 demonstrates how raytracing works. For each pixel in the rendered image, a ray is shot straight away from the camera. The ray will travel until it hits an object in the scene. The surface value at this specific point is calculated. Next, another ray is shot from this point on the surface toward the point in space that is emitting the light. If it encounters another object in its path, the renderer knows that that point is not absorbing any light and therefore will return a value of 0, or black. Obviously, if more than one light is in the scene, more than one calculation will have to be made from this point.

If the shadow calculation returns and tells the renderer that it was able to reach the light's source without intersecting anything, and this point has a reflectivity value of more than 0, the ray is reflected from that point. The angle at which this reflected ray is projected is equal to the angle between the ray from the camera and the surface normal (sometimes called the *angle of incidence*). The reflected ray then continues in a straight line until it intersects another object. At this point, the process repeats. The value of this new surface is determined. This value is then multiplied with the first value by a factor of the reflectivity and the result is added to the original surface value. Ideally, this process continues until the reflective ray does not intersect any more

FIGURE 16-4   *Diagram of the raytracing process*

objects. Figure 16-4 illustrates the process of a ray being shot from the camera and bouncing off the objects in the scene.

If the surface that intersects with the reflected ray intersects with a transparent surface, a *refracted* ray is generated. The angle of this ray is determined by the thickness of the surface. This refracted ray simulates the way that light rays are bent as they travel through transparent solids. For this reason, to get an accurate refraction, the object must have two surfaces to determine the thickness.

Using Raytracing in Maya

To use raytracing in Maya, at least two objects must be present in a scene, since the first object must have something to reflect; at least one light source must also be present. If reflections are to be calculated, the reflectivity of one of the materials must have a reflectivity value greater than 0.

> *NOTE*   *Both the Maya software renderer and the Mental Ray renderer support raytracing. This example uses the default Maya software renderer. By default, raytracing is turned off in the Maya software renderer, but it is turned on in the Mental Ray renderer.*

To practice using raytracing, we will use a simple scene containing four walls, a floor, a ceiling, a teapot, and a directional light. To follow along, use the raytrace.mb scene included on the CD. It meets all of the minimum requirements for raytracing, as mentioned earlier. It is a simple setup. The room has a different colored wall so that you can see exactly how the raytracing is evaluating the reflections.

1. With the objects, materials, and light set up, do a quick test render by clicking the Render Current Frame button in the Status Line. This should give you a good idea of what the scene looks like without raytracing enabled. Figure 16-5 shows a test render of the scene without raytracing. Notice that the teapot is really dark. This is because its material has a low diffuse value. We'll assume that the teapot should have a chrome-like surface so that most of its color will come from reflecting the objects around it.

FIGURE 16-5   *Scene without any raytracing*

2. Turn on Raytracing by checking the Raytracing check box under the Raytracing Quality section in the Render Global Settings window, shown next. With these default settings, do another test render of your scene. It takes a lot longer to render than it did before you turned on raytracing.

▼ Raytracing Quality		
	☑ Raytracing	
Reflections	1	
Refractions	6	
Shadows	2	
Bias	0.000	

3. In the image shown in Figure 16-6, the teapot is reflecting all of the objects around it, but although the floor has a small reflectivity value and is reflecting the teapot, something does not look quite right. This is because we are raytracing only one reflection. For the floor to reflect the reflection of itself on the teapot, we need to increase the number of reflections that the raytracing is creating.

FIGURE 16-6   *The scene is raytraced with the default reflectivity setting of 1.*

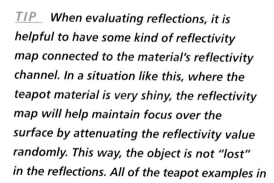

TIP   *When evaluating reflections, it is helpful to have some kind of reflectivity map connected to the material's reflectivity channel. In a situation like this, where the teapot material is very shiny, the reflectivity map will help maintain focus over the surface by attenuating the reflectivity value randomly. This way, the object is not "lost" in the reflections. All of the teapot examples in this chapter use grunge maps from the dvGarage's Surface Toolkit. Samples are available on the CD that comes with this book, but because this toolkit is one of the most valuable tools for anyone doing texture mapping, you should get it for yourself. Go to* http://www.dvgarage.com *for more information.*

4. In the Hypershade, select the mTeapot material node and look in the Attribute Editor. Scroll down to the section called Raytrace Options and change the Reflection Limit to **2**. If you were to go ahead and render the scene right now, you would not see a difference, because the Reflections attribute in the Render Global Settings window is still set to 1. The attributes in this section control the maximum amount that the renderer will calculate per attribute, regardless of what the settings are for each individual material.

FIGURE 16-7 *Scene is raytraced with a reflection setting of 2 on the teapot material.*

5. Change this attribute to **2** and render the image again. Figure 16-7 shows the result of this adjustment. Notice that you can now see that the reflection of the reflection is visible on the floor.

You can begin to see how adjusting these attributes on a per-object basis is so efficient. If we had to turn up the reflections to 2 for all objects in the scene, the render times could become intolerable. In most cases, a setting of 1 reflection will be sufficient, especially in animation, where the image might be moving so fast that the viewer would never notice that the reflections were not completely accurate.

Because of this, it is sometimes necessary to raytrace only the closest object to the reflective object and then use an environment map for the rest of the scene.

6. To remove an object from the raytracing calculation, select the object. In this case, select the red and green walls. In each of these object's Attribute Editors, find the Render Stats folder and uncheck the Visible In Reflections check box. Do a test render and you'll see that the walls are no longer reflected.

You can use the Environment Ball or Environment Sphere methods discussed in Chapter 13 to set up the environment map and connect it to the Reflected Color attribute of the teapot material. This way, the accuracy of the reflection of the floor leads the viewer's eye away from any inaccuracies in the environment. If this were an animated shot, you could save hours by calculating only the floor in this rendering pass.

The dvGarage reflection maps work perfectly in situation like this. In Figure 16-8, a map from the Reflection Toolkit shows its reflection on the objects.

Set Up Shadows

With the reflections covered, the last thing we need to do is add the shadow. Until this point in this book, we have been using only the depth map shadows. Raytraced shadows are much more accurate than Depth Map Shadows. While we are going to practice turning them on here,

FIGURE 16-8   *The scene is rendered again with an environment map mapped to the Reflected Color attribute of the teapot material.*

their usefulness will become more evident when we make the teapot transparent later on in the chapter.

1.   Select the directionalLight1 node from the Outliner or the Hypershade window. In the light's Attribute Editor, find the Shadows folder; then find the Raytrace Shadow attributes. Check the Use Raytrace Shadows check box. Render the image to see the effect. This will produce a sharp shadow on the floor and red wall.

2.   To soften the shadow edges a bit, increase the Light Angle attribute in the light's Attribute Editor under the Raytrace Shadow attributes. This simulates a larger light source, which produces softer edges on the shadows. The default setting of 0 is producing laser-perfect edges, which are not really desirable for most scenes. If you increase this value to 20 and render again, you'll see a more diffused shadow around the inner, sharper one. However, this diffused shadow is very grainy. To soften the grain, we'll increase the Shadow Rays value. Try a value of **10**. Figure 16-9 shows the scene rendered with raytraced shadows.

Set Up Refractions

As the Light Angle and Shadow Rays attribute values are increased, the rendering time starts to become pretty lengthy—too long for use in many production environments. In situations like these, it is best to use the Depth Map Shadows because they are much faster. As you study transparent objects next, it will become more obvious when raytraced shadows are necessary.

FIGURE 16-9   *The scene is rendered with a raytraced shadow that has been softened with the Light Angle and Shadow Rays light attributes.*

As light passes through a transparent surface, the light rays are bent. Consider a glass window—the thicker the glass, the larger the angle that the light rays are bent. This effect is known as *refraction*. Because raytraced rendering methods use a ray-emitting method, it is easy for them to calculate refractions as well as reflections accurately. We will use an object that's similar to our existing teapot with a few differences. For one, the teapot will be mostly transparent, as if it were made out of glass. The walls will use a checker texture, because the effects of the reflection will be more obvious with a pattern behind the teapot.

1. Find the scene called teapot_RaytraceRefractions.mb on the CD, and open it in Maya.

2. Render the scene with the default settings. In this case, raytracing has not been turned on in the Render Global Settings window. The result is a transparent teapot without any reflections or refractions, as shown in the first image in Figure 16-10.

3. Select the teapot material and turn on Refractions under the Raytrace Options folder in the material's Attribute Editor. Then turn on Raytracing in the Render Global Settings window. To evaluate the refractions, turn off all reflections by setting the Reflection attribute to **0**.

FIGURE 16-10 *Close-up of the teapot without raytracing, and then with a value of 2, 4, and 6 refractions*

No Raytracing

Two Refractions

Four Refractions

Six Refractions

4. When using refractions, it is a good idea to find out exactly how many refractions you will need. The default is 6, which is the minimum number you need to refract all of the overlapping surfaces in the teapot at this angle. Just to see what happens when there are not enough refractions, turn down the Refraction setting to **2** in the Render Global Settings window and do a test render. The teapot renders in black (see Figure 16-10), which tells us that not enough refractions are used in the calculation to render all of these overlapping transparent surfaces.

5. A value of 4 (see Figure 16-10) is enough to refract the main areas around the pot, because the light needs to pass through only four of the surfaces, but the areas where we can see the handle through the teapot and some of the edges at the top are still problematic, as more overlapping surfaces are in these areas. With that understood, set the Refractions value back to **6** and render it (again see Figure 16-10).

6. Now we know we have enough refractions, but we aren't seeing any of the distortion effects of the background caused by the bending of light rays through the transparent surface. This is determined by the Refractive Index attribute in the material attributes. A value of 1 is the default and simulates the refractive index of air. The refractive index for glass is about 1.6. Set this value for the refractive index on the teapot material and render the scene to see the effect.

7. Now for the shadow. Because refractions cast their own shadows, we don't need to turn on Raytraced shadows for the light. Instead, turn up the Shadows attribute, found in the Raytracing Quality section of the Render Global Settings window, to 2 (the default). Render the image again. You can see that the shadow has more transparent areas where the light is passing through less dense areas of the teapot. The overall lightness of this shadow can be attenuated with the Shadow Attenuation attribute in the Raytrace Options section of the teapot's material node. A higher value will create a denser, darker shadow.

8. To finalize this scene, turn up the raytraced reflections and use our environment map to reflect areas not covered by geometry in the scene. The final raytraced scene with refractions is shown in Figure 16-11.

TIP **To achieve even a higher degree of realism, you can add the Fresnel Effect to attenuate the reflections and transparency. This technique is covered in Chapter 14.**

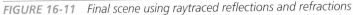

FIGURE 16-11 *Final scene using raytraced reflections and refractions*

Masking Techniques

In large productions, you will usually render your scenes in different layers and passes. A scene render can be broken up and organized from something simple, such as background and foreground elements, to rendering every object separately. Issues will occur in compositing when any of the rendered layers obstructs a layer underneath it. While you could swap the layers during the middle of the shot in your compositing package, a better solution is to render a mask.

Rendering a mask into the alpha channel of the output image gives the compositor something to work with. The compositor does not have to guess which object is obstructing another. Instead, when an object from the top layer of the composite is supposed to pass underneath, the mask will hide it so that it does not show up on top.

Here we will use an example of a moon rotating around a planet. You will create three different materials for this example: one for the planet, another for the moon, and the third as a mask channel, and set it up so that the rotating moon will be the layer on top.

1. Start a new scene. Create two spheres and scale one of them up so that it is about five times larger than the smaller one. Move the small sphere out into an orbiting position. If you scale the first sphere up 5 units, then moving the small sphere out 10 units along its X or Z axis will work fine.

2. Instead of keyframing this animation, we will set it up procedurally by writing an expression. First, we'll move the pivot point of the moon to the center of the scene. Select the moon and press INSERT (HOME) and turn on grid snapping.

3. Drag the pivot to the 0,0,0 origin of the world, and press INSERT (HOME) again. In the Channel Box, right-click the moon's Rotate Y attribute and choose Expressions from the marking menu.

4. In the Expression field, type this:

```
nurbsSphere1.rotateY= 30*time
```

5. Apply the moon material to the moon. Add any material attributes that you wish. Apply the matte material to the planet. Since no specularity is needed for the mask object, a Lambert material will work best. Set the Color attribute to black and turn the Diffuse value all the way down.

6. In the material's attributes, find the Opacity Gain slider in the Matte Opacity folder. Turn this all the way down to 0, as shown next.

7. In the Render Global Settings window, set the Channels attribute called Alpha Mask to on. Set the range of frames, resolution, and quality settings and render out the animation. You can play back the animation in Fcheck or your compositing program. For this example, though, we'll just look at a single frame rendered in the Render View window.

8. Play the animation until the moon is partially occluded by the planet. Render the view window using the Render Current Frame button in the Status Line. In the Render View window, click the Display Alpha Channel button in the toolbar. You can see that the alpha channel does not include a transparency, or white, pixel value for the mask object. In a compositing program, this alpha channel could be used as the mask for the moon layer. (We will discuss how to composite this in Chapter 21.)

Motion Blur

To understand motion blur, it is important that you understand how a camera in the real world works. (See Chapter 13 for information on lighting, texturing, and cameras.) Motion blur is an artifact of exposure time. It is noticeable as a blurry trail left behind a moving object. In general, the faster an object moves by the camera, or the greater the change in distance of an object from frame to frame, the longer the blurred trail will be.

Maya offers two kinds of motion blur: 2D and 3D. The 2D motion blur is a post-rendering effect and is calculated only in two dimensions. It is faster to render, but it may not produce a realistic effect if the objects in the scene move toward the camera. The 3D motion blur option works similar to a real camera, and at the default setting it depends on the shutter angle for the amount of blur. You can increase the amount of motion blur by increasing the Blur By Frame attribute. A setting of 1, as shown in Figure 16-12, will blur the image over one frame based on a 180-degree shutter. A Blur By Frame value of 4, also shown in Figure 16-12, looks at the motion of objects over four frames and applies the blur.

If the motion blur appears too grainy, additional samples can be calculated in the Anti-aliasing Quality section of the Maya Software tab in the Render Global Settings window. Two attributes here can be used to improve the quality of the motion blur: the 3D Blur Visibility and the Max 3D Blur Visibility. Since these settings are adaptive, increasing the Max 3D Blur Visibility will render additional samples only where needed.

FIGURE 16-12   *3D motion blur with a Blur By Frame setting of 1 (left) and 4 (right)*

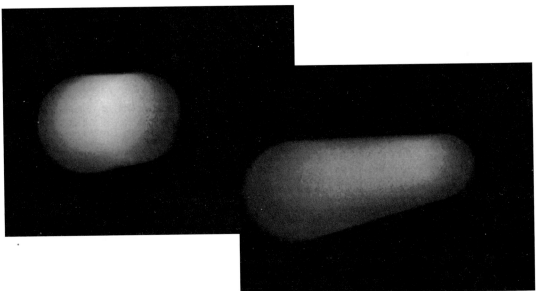

Environment Fog

Environment fog is used to simulate atmospheric effects. Since you don't have precise control over the way the fog is distributed in Maya, it simulates the haze or moisture in the air rather than producing patchy fog or clouds—such effects are handled much better with light fog and particles. However, when using Maya for realistic rendering, environment fog is a must-have, since some bit of atmosphere is always visible, even on the clearest of days.

 We will use the example that we created in Chapter 14—the scene with the cylinders with the windows and all of the fog lights. If you don't still have the scene, you can use the MaterialSceneFinish.mb file on the CD.

1. Open the Render Global Settings window. Make sure that the resolution is set low and the Quality attribute is set to Preview or Intermediate at the most. This will let you preview the effect without having to wait. Scroll down in this window and find the Render Options section. Click the connection button next to the Environment Fog attribute field to add an Environment Fog node to the scene.

2. Open the Hypershade, and you'll notice that a new envFog material appears. This is a *volumetric* material, which means that it does not need to be connected to an object to render. If you graph its output connections, you'll see a Light Linking node connected to it. Connected to the Light Linking node is a point light called envFogLight. Since this light is linked only to the envFog node, it has no effect on the other objects.

3. Render the scene. Figure 16-13 shows the effects of the environment fog so far. In this case, the fog appears behind the objects in the scene. While this might be fine for some effects, we want the fog to cover the objects that appear directly in front of us.

4. To fix this, we will use the Saturation Distance in the envFogMaterial node's Attribute Editor. This represents the value, in units, from the camera from which the fog will begin to be visible. The default is 100. Set the Saturation Distance to **5** and render a preview. The result should match Figure 16-14.

5. To adjust the height of the fog, check the box labeled Use Height in the Attribute Editor. The default settings here will do the job. However, if you want to make the fog extend higher, adjust the Max Height attribute.

6. The Blend Range attribute can also be used to adjust the density of the fog as it nears the Max Height.

FIGURE 16-13 *Fog is visible in the background of the scene.*

FIGURE 16-14 *The scene is rendered with the fog material's Saturation Distance attribute set to 5.*

Mental Ray

Maya ships with another software-based renderer in addition to its own. At this time, the Mental Ray renderer is not capable of handling everything in Maya, but it does have some features not available in the Maya software renderer. While it does an exceptional job at raytracing and anti-aliasing, the Mental Ray renderer also offers Global Illumination, caustic effects, and an area lighting method called Final Gather.

The normal vector interpolation and the raytracing methods used so far do an excellent job of rendering the shading on surfaces and accurate reflections. However, they fall short of being able to account for the light spill, diffusion, or color bleeding that is evident in the real world. For the rest of this chapter, we will examine some of the features in Mental Ray that change the way lighting in a scene is calculated. The Global Illumination and caustics rendering methods use light-emitting photons that diffuse and spill colors, shadows, and reflections. The Final Gather method does not use any lights at all. Instead, it uses the area around each object to create even, realistic lighting.

Global Illumination

Global Illumination works by shooting photons from lights and creates a photon map according to their distribution in the scene. The way that these photons are distributed is based on the absorption, reflectivity, and refractivity of an object. The effects of this type of rendering are most noticeable in the color bleeding between objects and soft diffusion of light across a scene.

For this tutorial, we will use the teapot_GI.ma scene included on the CD. It is similar to the rendering example that we have used so far, except the teapot is now a solid green color and the room colors are fairly plain. We will use this color scheme to make the effects of Global Illumination obvious.

1. Render the image with the Maya software renderer. The result is shown in Figure 16-15. You can save this image and use it for comparison with the Global Illumination rendering we are about to perform.

FIGURE 16-15   *Scene rendered with the Maya software renderer*

2. Now to enable Mental Ray. In the Render Global Settings window, choose Mental Ray from the Render Using pull-down menu. Select the Mental Ray tab. You should now be able to view the settings for Mental Ray, shown here.

3. Set the Quality attribute in the Quality folder to Previewgloballllum. This turns on Global Illumination and sets the Sampling Quality attributes to a medium setting for faster renders. You can verify that Global Illumination is turned on by scrolling down to the Caustics and Global Illumination folder in the Render Global Settings window and making sure the box next to Global Illumination is checked.

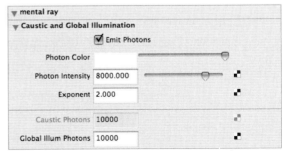

If you rendered the scene right now, it would not look different from the last image we rendered with the Maya software renderer. This is because the lights in the scene have to be set up to emit photons in order for the Global Illumination to be calculated.

4. Select the point light in the scene (this is the only light used). In the Attribute Editor, scroll down and find the section named Mental Ray. In this section, click the box next to Emit Photons, as shown here.

- The Photon Intensity attribute here controls the brightness of the emitted photons. If you click the Render button and don't see any Global Illumination effect, try increasing the Photon Intensity attribute value.

- The Global Illum Photons attribute sets the number of photons that will be emitted from the light so that Mental Ray can render the Global Illumination effect. Because the number of emitted photons will have an impact on render times, it is best to keep this as low as possible. Remember that the number of photons needed to create a quality render will depend on the scale, in Maya units, of the scene being rendered. If the scene is small, it may not take too many photons to fill the area being rendered. Therefore, the correct amount of photons will vary greatly from scene to scene.

TIP   _**While setting up Global Illumination in a scene, it can be helpful to work with large Energy values so that you can closely monitor what is going on. The Energy attributes can then be reduced for the final output.**_

5. Set the Global Illum Photons attribute to **1000**. This will be enough to cover the scene with photons, but they will not be so finely distributed that they can't be recognized.

At this point, you have enabled enough controls for the renderer to make a Global Illumination calculation. Do a test render and view the results.

FIGURE 16-16 _Scene rendered with Global Illumination enabled but with a low emitted photon value_

Figure 16-16 shows the teapot rendered with these settings. Notice the big, circular-shaped spots of color all over the scene. By setting the Global Illum Photons value low, the photons are easy to see and should give you some idea of what they are doing to bleed the color throughout the scene.

6. To blend these photons in the rendered image, we will go back to the Render Global Settings window and adjust some more settings. The two attributes we will concentrate on in this step are the Global Illum Accuracy and the Global Illum Radius, shown here.

	☑ Global Illumination	
Global Illum Accuracy	64	
Global Illum Radius	0.000	

- The Global Illum Accuracy setting represents the number of photons that the Mental Ray looks for within the area represented by the Global Illum Radius. It then composites what it finds, and the result is the Global Illumination effect. Low Global Illum Accuracy values will yield grainy images, and high values will give you smoother, more precise results but will take more time to render. If you set the Accuracy value higher than the number of photons emitted by all the lights in the scene, your image will never render because the photon calculation won't finish.

- The Global Illum Radius attribute is the size (in Maya units) of the effect that the photon produces when it hits an object. Larger numbers produce bigger effects but usually less accurate results. High Radius values combined with low Accuracy values can give you a good approximation of what your scene will look like and are great for test renders. Low Radius values combined with high Accuracy values will provide the most accurate representation of the final image but will take much longer to render.

A value of 0 for either of these attributes will tell the renderer to make its best guess.

7. In the Render Global Settings window, begin adjusting the Global Illum Accuracy attribute. Set it to **1** and you see the effect. The photons are not sharing any space at all. You want to increase this value until it has little or no effect—this means that no more photons fall within that radius. For the accuracy to have any more effect, the number of photons emitted form the light must be increased. A value of around 60 works well for Global Illum Accuracy in this scene.

8. Now adjust the Global Illum Radius attribute. Increase it until the photons are big enough to cover the areas evenly but are not so spotty. A value of 4.5 is good.

9. Now return to the light's Attribute Editor and adjust the values for the Photon Intensity, Exponent, and the number of emitted photons. Increase the number of photons until they blend enough so that you can no longer make them out. Increase the Global Illum Photons attribute to **4500**.

10. To determine how bright the overall effect will be, use the Photon Intensity attribute. A value of **7000** gives the walls a nice bleed from the green teapot.

11. The scene was set up to use regular Depth Map Shadows, but we need to turn shadows on in the Mental Ray Render Global Settings windows for them to render. Set the Shadow Maps to on. Figure 16-17 shows the final rendered image for this scene.

FIGURE 16-17   Final scene rendered with Global illumination and shadows

Caustics

Caustics are light patterns that are created when light from a light source illuminates a diffuse surface via one or more specular reflections or transmissions. Caustics use the same method of emitting photons from light sources as Global Illumination. Therefore, the process for optimally rendering caustics is similar to what we did in the previous section.

 Find the scene on the CD called teapot_ caustics.ma. This scene shows the transparent teapot, and the light has been moved down just a bit so that it is casting a shadow on the wall.

FIGURE 16-18   Teapot rendered with Maya's default renderer using raytracing

1. Render the scene with the Maya software renderer. It is all set up for the right amount of reflections and refractions in the Raytrace settings for the teapot material. The rendered image is shown in Figure 16-18.

2. In the Render Global Settings window, choose Render Using Mental Ray. You should now be able to view the Mental Ray Render Globals tab in the Render Global Settings window.

3. Set the Quality attribute to PreviewCaustics.

4. Now increase some of the raytracing values. Because of the angle at which we are looking at the teapot, maximize the number of refractions calculated. Set Max Refraction Rays to **10**. If you did a test render, you would see that the dense area around the handle and spout of the teapot are dark. You can make these areas more transparent by increasing the Max Ray Depth. Set this to a value of **6**.

5. Select the point light in the scene (the only light). In the Attribute Editor, scroll down to the section named Mental Ray. Click the box next to Emit Photons. Because the number of emitted photons will dramatically increase render time, set the Caustic Photons attribute to **1000**. This will be enough to cover the scene, but they will not be so finely distributed that they can't be recognized.

6. At this point, you have enabled enough controls for the renderer to make a calculation for the caustics. Do a test render. Figure 16-19 shows the scene rendered with caustics. You should notice two things: the caustic effects are very spotty and the shadow is no longer transparent.

FIGURE 16-19 Scene rendered with a Caustic Photons value of 1000

7. First we'll fix the shadow. If you scroll down to the bottom of the Caustics and Global Illumination section of in the Render Global Settings window, you will see a Direct Illumination Shadow Effects check box. Enabling this check box will allow the shadow to maintain its transparency.

8. Now adjust the Caustic Radius value. In the Render Global Settings window, begin increasing the Caustic Radius attribute and doing test renders until increasing this number no longer has an effect. Try a value of **5**.

9. Now adjust the Caustic Accuracy in the same manner. Increase this value until it has little or no effect—**200** looks good. Figure 16-20 shows the result of the render after these settings are adjusted.

10. We need to get rid of the strong highlight that the caustic is making on the wall with the shadow. We can do this by editing the wall material's Diffuse value. A value of 0.6 minimizes this bloom. You might also try turning down the Photon Intensity value of the photon-emitting light. The result should resemble Figure 16-21.

FIGURE 16-20 *Scene rendered with the Caustic Accuracy and Caustic Radius increased*

Once you have found a Photon Intensity attribute that works, you may wish to try adjusting the overall quality of the image by increasing the number of photons that are emitted from the light, lowering the Global Illumination Radius, and increasing the Global Illumination Accuracy. But be prepared to wait. Remember that if you are rendering for animation purposes, some of the artifacts caused by the photon emission may not be so noticeable.

FIGURE 16-21 *Fine-tuning is done to the diffusion of the walls and the energy of the emitting photons for the final image.*

Final Gather

Setting up lighting in Maya to simulate the way light behaves in the real world is difficult, to say the least. To achieve even lighting across a scene, you will almost always use multiple lights. As we have seen so far with Global Illumination, we can set up fewer lights since Global Illumination gives us much of the even diffusion that we get when using multiple lights. It is from these lights that Global Illumination emits photons, which bounce off objects in the scene and record their color data so that it can be transferred to the surface shading of other objects. Final Gather goes one step further toward simulating the way light works in the real world.

Take, for example, the inside of your house during the day. You can turn off all the lights, but if the house has windows and the doors between the rooms are open, light will make its way through from the outside by bouncing around off every surface it hits inside. This generally diffuses the light and produces some even lighting throughout your house.

Final Gather works similarly. The light used to illuminate objects is generated by the other objects in the scene. The light rays just keep bouncing off objects, spilling the colors and creating very diffuse, soft shadows as it heads toward places in the scene where it cannot so easily bounce. All that is really needed, of course, is a surface with some sort of luminosity to emit the initial rays. This is usually done in Final Gather by placing an object, usually a dome-shaped object, with a material that has its incandescence turned up. This incandescent object is what begins the lighting reaction, which is then transferred to the rest of the scene.

While Final Gather will produce the highest quality lighting in a scene in most cases, it is also the slowest to render. Therefore, it is helpful to use Final Gather in conjunction with Global Illumination to achieve the desired results with acceptable render times.

 In this example, we will again be using our teapot scene. Find the teapot_FinalGather.ma file on the CD.

1. In the Render Global Settings window, choose Render Using Mental Ray. You should now be able to view the Mental Ray Render Globals tab.

2. Set the Quality attribute to PreviewFinalGather.

3. Scroll down the list of attributes and turn off Global Illumination. Then, in the Final Gather section, make sure that Final Gather is enabled.

4. Select the light in the scene and turn its intensity all of the way down to **0**. With Final Gather, we do not need to use any lights. Turning this down will keep Mental Ray from using the default lighting in the absence of any other lights. If you rendered the image right now, it would be all black. This is because we need an illuminating surface to use as the main source of light.

5. Create a sphere. Edit the makeNurbSphere1's attributes so that it is only a half sphere, and scale it up so that it acts as a dome that surrounds the entire scene. Figure 16-22 shows the scene in the view window with the half sphere used as a source of illumination.

6. Create a new Lambert material. Turn the Incandescence attribute up 100 percent and apply it to the dome-shaped geometry.

7. Before we render, find the Final Gather Rays attribute in the Final Gather section of the Render Global Settings window and set it to **300**. Render the image to see the results. You will immediately notice the nice, even lighting and smooth, soft, and diffused shadows in the scene. Figure 16-23 shows how the scene looks rendered with Final Gather. Hard to believe that we didn't need to set up one light!

8. To adjust the color of the lighting, change the Incandescence value of the Lambert material on the dome object to a bluish color and see the results.

9. To adjust the overall effect on the teapot, we can adjust the material's Irradiance Color. Select the teapot material and scroll down in its Attribute Editor to find the Mental Ray folder. In that folder is an attribute called Irradiance Color. Turn this down to change the brightness of the Final Gather effect.

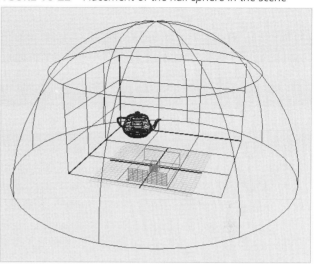

FIGURE 16-22   *Placement of the half sphere in the scene*

FIGURE 16-23   *The scene rendered with Final Gather*

HDR Images with Final Gather

The term "image-based rendering" has become popular recently. It describes a type of rendering that uses images from the real world to calculate lighting. Image-based rendering includes camera mapping, described in Chapter 20, which occurs when images from the real world are projected onto simple geometry that roughly resembles their shape from a specific camera angle. In these kinds of scenes, it is not necessary to add light because all of the lighting information is already inside the photograph.

When we start thinking about these concepts in terms of Final Gather, image-based rendering can mean that we use photographs from the real world to control the Incandescence attribute of our dome or irradiating surface's material for the Final Gather render. The problem is, however, that a regular photograph does not have all of the information we need. We would need a file format that does not just record colors that are dark and bright, but one that understands overexposure as well. Thanks to the work and research of Paul Debevec, we have an image format that encompasses all of this information into a single file. This file format is called the *HDR file format*.

Paul Debevec's web site, at *http://www.debevec.org/,* offers a program called HDR Shop that allows you to create images in this file format. Images are also available on the site for download that can be used in Final Gather. This is what we will be working with in this section.

HDRI stands for *high dynamic range imagery*: a normal 24-bit image can represent brightness as only one of 256 levels—this means that a pixel with a brightness value of 256 (that is, white) is exactly twice as bright as mid-gray (brightness of 128). While color space represents a printed image fine, it bears no relation to reality, where the bright sky outside your window is, in fact, many thousands of times brighter than the mid-gray page in front of you, and the spot where the sun shines is probably millions of times brighter. By using a 32-bit floating point number (floating point numbers are capable of representing enormous ranges by moving their decimal points around) to represent each pixel brightness for R, G, and B instead of a limited 8-bit integer (a whole number limited to a range from 1 to 256), HDR images can truly represent the range of brightness found in real life. This is important if you want to re-create realistic lighting accurately using a rendering technique such as Final Gather.

 Once again, and for the last time, we will use our teapot scene as the test scene for the study of HDR rendering. You can use the scene from the last section or start with the teapot_HDR.ma scene on the CD.

1. In the Render Global Settings window, choose Render Using Mental Ray. You should now see the Mental Ray Render Globals tab.

2. Set the Quality attribute to PreviewFinalGather.

3. Scroll down the list of attributes and turn off Global Illumination. Then, in the Final Gather section, check to make sure that Final Gather is enabled.

4. Select the light in the scene and turn its intensity all of the way down to **0**. With Final Gather, we do not need to use any lights. Turning this down will keep Mental Ray from using the default lighting in the absence of any other lights.

5. We could create a sphere, as we did in the previous tutorial, and then map the HDRI image to it, but instead we will use an image-based lighting node. This will create a spherical environment similar to an environment sphere that we have used in past tutorials, except the image-based lighting node has specific attributes that let you control the lighting in the scene when using Final Gather. To create the image-based lighting node, find the Image Based Lighting section and click the Create button. The image-based lighting attributes are shown in Figure 16-24.

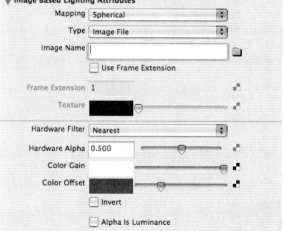

FIGURE 16-24   The attributes for the image-based lighting node

6. Open the Attribute Editor to view the attributes for the image-based lighting node. You'll see an attribute call Image Name. Click the file browser button to browse to the CD and open the HDR_sample.hdr image, shown here.

7. In the Render Global Settings window, find the Final Gather Rays attribute in the Final Gather section and set this to **200**. This should provide you with a low-quality render that is reasonably fast.

8. You can adjust the brightness levels of the HDR image in the Attribute Editor by editing the Color Gain and Color Offset attributes.

9. You can make any adjustments to the object's materials to control how they interact with the Final Gather rendering by going into each material's attributes and adjusting the Irradiance Color in the Mental Ray section.

FIGURE 16-25   *The final image rendered with Final Gather*

10. Once you are happy with the way the scene looks, increase the number of emitted rays in the Final Gather section of the Mental Ray Render Globals tab. You might also try adjusting the Min and Max Radius values and see how far you can get with those before having to increase the number of emitted rays. Render your final image. Figure 16-25 shows the scene rendered using Final Gather with an HDR image.

In production situations, you might find that using both Global Illumination and Final Gather is the optimal way of working. In a situation like this, go through the process of setting up each render type individually. You will want to concentrate on using Global Illumination for the lights and shadow casting and use Final Gather to fill in the scene with even light across it. By adjusting the Energy values of the light-emitting photons in the Global Illumination calculation and Irradiance Color attribute in each material's Attribute Editor, you can fine-tune the balance between the two effects. Using both rendering algorithms together with midrange quality settings will produce great images with manageable render times.

Summary

This chapter provided an overview of the major rendering features and work flows available to you in Maya. Raytracing, Global Illumination, and Final Gather can help you produce realistic imagery when needed. As you've seen here, most of these options can be enabled and controlled in the Render Global Settings window. While the software-based renderers have been covered here, Chapters 17 and 18 will make use of the Maya hardware renderer to render particles.

V

Particles, Emitters, and Fields

Particles
and Fields

Particles are points that can be

displayed or rendered as dots, spheres, clouds,

blobs, fog, smoke, and a whole lot more. Once

the particles have been created in a scene, their

behavior and appearance can be controlled

through the use of fields, ramps, goals, and

expressions. An infinite number of effects can

be created this way, ranging from running

water to fire and explosions.

Creating Particles

You can create particles in three ways in Maya: with the Particle tool, with an emitter, or by using the `emit` MEL command. In this section, we will concentrate on the first two methods and discuss some of the most commonly used attributes.

Particle Tool

Maya's Particle tool (Particles | Particle Tool) can be used to place individual particles or groups of particles into a scene. This tool offers three ways to add particles: the first is the default point-and-click method, the second is through the Sketch Particles option that allows you to sketch or paint particles, and the third lets you define the bounds and place a 2D or 3D grid of particles.

To create particles with the Particle tool:

1. Make sure the Dynamics menu set is showing in the toolbar (press F4). In a new scene, choose Particles | Particle Tool ❑ to open the Particle Tool Settings window on the right side of the screen. Click the Reset Tool button to make sure you are at the default settings. In this mode, you can click in the view windows and place particles one at a time. The particles will be drawn as tiny crosses.

2. You can set the number of particles created each time you click by setting the value of the slider in the Particle Tool Settings window. The Radius slider controls the distance that the new particles will be created from the point at which you click. Try increasing these values and experiment.

3. Continue placing particles in the scene, and when you are finished, press ENTER (RETURN) to finish and close the tool. A single particle node is created in the scene (Figure 17-1).

NOTE   *When shading mode is activated in the view window, a bounding box will appear around the entire group of particles.*

By turning on Sketch Particles in the Particle Tool Settings window, you can LMB-hold and paint the particles.

Delete that particle group and go back to the Particle Tool Settings window. Check the Sketch Particles box. Click and drag in the view window and notice the results. You can paint the particles in the scene according to the Number of Particles and Maximum Radius attributes in the Particle Tool Settings window. The Sketch Interval attributes controls how far apart each little cluster of particles will be as you drag (much the same way the brush spacing control works on Photoshop brushes).

FIGURE 17-1   Particles are sketched.

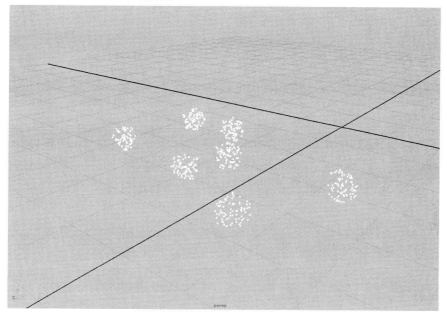

You will often want the placed or sketched particles to adhere to some shape instead of just lying flat. Recall our NURBS modeling lesson back in Chapter 3, when we drew a curve on a surface by making the surface live. The same process can be used to place particles. In this example, we will create a terrain and sketch the particles onto it to create a sort of mist or ground fog (shown in Figure 17-2).

1. Create a NURBS surface, and use the Sculpt Surfaces tool to push and pull the CVs to give the surface an irregular shape.

2. Select the surface, and choose Modify | Make Live (or click the Make Live button in the toolbar). You can now sketch particles directly on the NURBS object.

3. When you are finished sketching, press ENTER (RETURN) to close the tool and create the node. The result should look something like the example shown in Figure 17-2.

NOTE   *While these particles are placed as fog might fall on the ground, they will not render to resemble fog—nor will they render at all when using Maya's software renderer. We will discuss particle display attributes and rendering particles in depth later in this chapter. For now, concentrate on creating and placing the particles with the Particle tool.*

FIGURE 17-2   *Particles are sketched onto a live surface.*

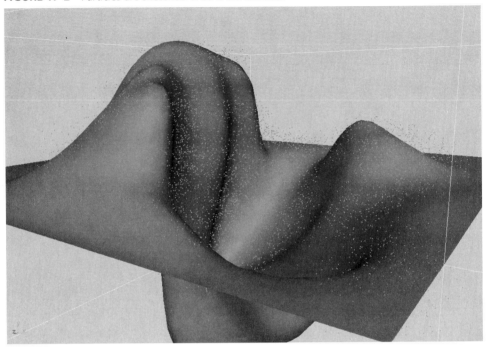

The third way to create a particles with this tool is to use the particle grid. This does just what you might imagine—it creates a 2D or 3D grid of evenly spaced particles. Basically, the grid is created by placing the points that define opposite corners in each direction. This can be done interactively by clicking in the view window or by choosing the With Text Fields option and entering the grid dimensions in the Particle Tool Settings window. A particle grid is a fast way to create a large body of particles into one node. Here's how it's done:

1. Clear the scene or start a new scene, and this time check Create Particle Grid in the Particle Tool Settings window.

2. To create a 2D particle grid, click once in the view window to place one corner and click again at another spot to define the opposite corner. Press ENTER (RETURN) to close the tool and complete the grid.

3. The Particle Spacing attribute in the Particle Tool Settings window controls the density of the grid. Increase this value just a bit, and create another grid to see how it looks. *But be careful!* Creating a grid that is too dense can really slow down your computer. It is best to increase the Particle Spacing attribute in small increments.

4. Delete any particle nodes in the scene to make way for a 3D particle grid. To define all of the corners interactively, you'll need to work between multiple view windows that display different view planes. Use the default Four View view.

5. In the Perspective view, click to place the corners that define the base of the grid.

6. Switch to the Side view or Front view. Press the HOME (INSERT) key and drag one of the points up or down. Press ENTER (RETURN) and a grid will be created. Figure 17-3 shows a particle grid.

FIGURE 17-3   *The base of a 3D particle grid is defined in the Perspective view (left), and the height of the grid is defined in the Side view (right).*

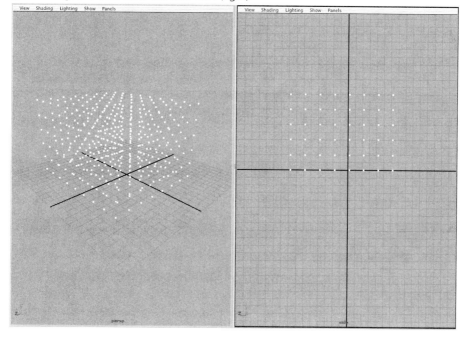

Emitters

You can also create particles through emitters, which "shoot" particles away from the emitting point. Without any fields to control their behavior (see the "Fields" section later in this chapter for more information), these particles will continue along their path at the speed at which they were emitted. The way that these particles are emitted is determined by the emitter's emission Type attribute. The rate at which they are emitted is controlled by the emitter's Rate attribute. A whole slew of other attributes can be set for emitters. We will address the basic attributes in this section and introduce others throughout this chapter as we work through some more complex examples.

To create an emitter, choose Particles | Create Emitter. By default, an *omni* emitter is created. When you create an emitter, a particle node is also created with connections to the emitter. It is important to distinguish which nodes control which attributes for the desired behavior. If you wish to edit the way particles are being emitted, such as the emission rate or speed, you'll edit the emitter attributes in the Attribute Editor or the Channel Box. If you want to edit the actual behavior of the particles after they've been emitted, such as their color or lifespan, edit the particle node's attributes.

If you examine the connections to this emitter network in the Hypergraph, you will also notice that both of these nodes are connected to a time node. As you might imagine, this is due to the fact that the emitter creates particles at a rate based on time. If you click the Play button in the Time Slider, the particles will emit over the period of time specified by the range. At the end of the range, playback will return to the beginning and the emission will return to its initial state. As you experiment with particles and emitters, it might be best to set the time range to 500 frames. This will give you time to study the behavior of the emitters and particles as you adjust attributes.

Another important thing to mention when dealing with any type of dynamic simulation in Maya is that the playback speed in the Timeline preferences (Window | Settings/Preferences | Timeline) needs to be set to Play Every Frame. This is because Maya calculates the position of the particles based on their position in the previous frame. If any frames are dropped to maintain the real-time performance, the position of the particles will be inaccurate. If you'd like to get an idea of how the particles are animating in real time, using Playblast can be very helpful.

Emitter Type

The type of emitter will determine how the particles will emit from the emission point and, in the case of the *volume emitter*, how large and in what shape the emission points will be. Three emitter types are available when using the Create Emitter command: the *omni* emitter, a *directional* emitter, and a *volume* emitter. (Note that particles can also be emitted from surfaces and curves by using the Emit From Object tool covered later in this chapter in "Create the Particle Trails.") Figure 17-4 shows particles emitting from the three types of emitters.

FIGURE 17-4 *From left to right, omni, directional, and volume emitters*

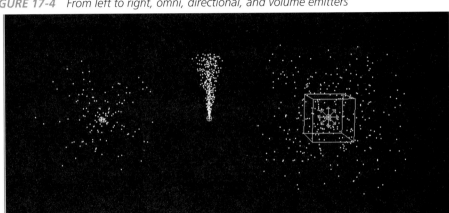

- **Omni (default) emitter** Emits particles in all directions; works really well for explosions.
- **Directional emitter** Emits the particles in a specified direction. We will use the directional emitter later to emit laser blasts from a cannon.
- **Volume emitter** Emits particles from a volumetric space. Volumetric shapes include a cube, sphere, cylinder, torus, and cone.

Emission Attributes

Once you have created an emitter, you can begin editing its attributes. While all of the attributes can be set in the Create Emitter tool's Options window, it is usually easier to create an emitter with the default settings and then tweak them in the Channel Box or Attribute Editor. Some of the basic emitter attributes are listed here:

- **Rate** Controls particles emitted per second. The default is 100.
- **Cycle Emission** By default, particles will be emitted randomly from an emitter. When this option is set to Frame [Time Random On], the emission cycle will be looped over the number of frames specified in the Cycle Interval.
- **Min/Max Distance** Controls the distance from the emitter point that particles will be created. All particles will be created randomly between these two distance settings. The Max distance must be greater than or equal to the Min distance.
- **Speed** Units per second that the particles travel as they are emitted. Randomness in particle speed is introduced by entering a value in the Speed Random attribute.
- **Volume attributes** If Volume is selected as the Emitter Type, the Volume Shape will let you choose between a cube, sphere, cylinder, torus, and cone. The size and position can be edited with the remaining Volume Speed attributes.

Particle Attributes

To this point, we have been using the default particle attributes. While some uses for particles and emitters have been suggested, it might be difficult for you to imagine how these effects are created with these little points. By editing the particle node's attributes, we can control the color of the particles, how long they live, how they are displayed, and much more.

Lifespan

The Lifespan attribute controls the amount of time, in seconds, that a particle will live. To begin playing with particle attributes, create an emitter with the default settings and select the particle node. Press CTRL-A (CONTROL-A) or open the Attribute Editor from the Status Line to display the particle node's attributes. Scroll down to the Lifespan Attributes folder.

A lifespan mode can be selected from the Lifespan Mode attribute's pull-down menu. To see how these lifespan attributes affect the behavior of the particles, you should make sure your time range is set to about 500 frames and click the Play button. As you select different lifespan modes from the pull-down menu, the results will show in the view window.

The following lists the modes from the pull-down menu:

- **Live Forever**   The default setting. In this mode, the particles will never die in the scene.
- **Constant**   This mode allows you to specify the precise length of time that a particle will live. This amount of time is set in the Lifespan attribute.
- **Random Range**   Introduces a random lifespan for the particles. The target lifespan is determined by the Lifespan attribute. Random variations will be plus or minus the amount of time specified in the Lifespan Random attribute.
- **LifespanPP Only**   Controls the lifespan of individual particles. With this mode active, you can select individual particles and then use an expression to control the lifespan in the Per Particle Attributes section of the Attribute Editor.

Render Attributes

The Render Attributes section in the Attribute Editor contains the attributes that control how particles are displayed. The default is set to Points, and this is what we have been using so far. To change this type of display, select another option from the Particle Render Type pull-down menu. You can choose from among 10 different types. We are not going to go through all of them here, as they are all well defined in Maya's documentation. Instead, we'll cover the overall process of changing the rendering type and adding attributes for the specific type.

Notice that when you view all of the display options in the Particle Render Type pull-down menu, each of the last three types, Blobby, Cloud, and Tube, has *[s/w]* after its name in the list. This signifies that these particle render types need to be rendered in Maya's *software renderer*. The other seven rendering types will render only in the OpenGL-based hardware renderer, which is discussed later in this chapter in the section "Hardware Renderer." For now, just be aware of what this [s/w] means.

Each of these rendering types, as shown in Figure 17-5, has specific attributes to control the way it appears. Once a rendering type has been selected in the Particle Render Type attribute pull-down menu, click the Current Render Type button. Active fields will appear in the section below the button that are specific only to that rendering type. In the case of the Spheres rendering type, an attribute will appear that controls the Radius. The Streak rendering type will have attributes that control the Line Width of the streaks and attributes that control the Tail Size and Tail Fade. These types of attributes are called *dynamic* attributes. Dynamic attributes are loaded for specific tasks instead of loading all available attributes. Not only does this make scrolling through an already long list of attributes easier, but it also cuts down on general memory usage since Maya does not have to load all of this information every time a particle group is created.

FIGURE 17-5   Examples of all 10 rendering types

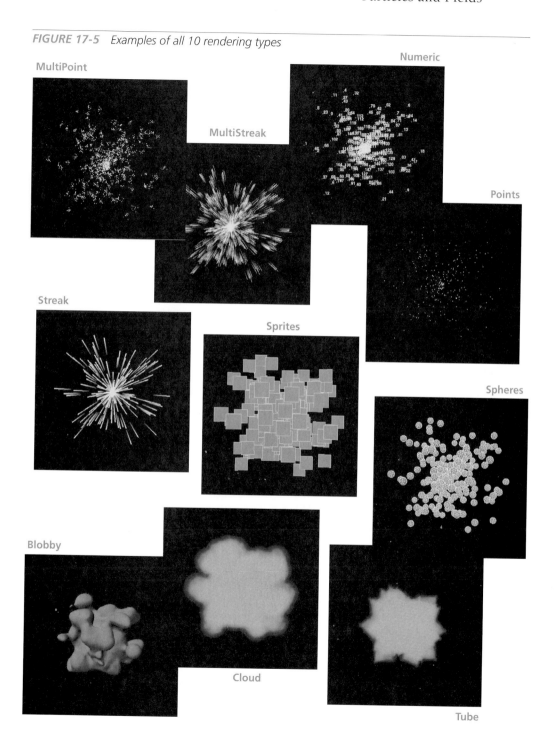

Per Particle Attributes

Another section in the particle shape node's Attribute Editor is called the Per Particle (Array) Attributes. While the other attributes in the other folders contain attributes that control the appearance or behavior of the particle group as a whole, per particle attributes are capable of controlling the appearance or behavior of individual particles. Depending on the attribute chosen, per particle attributes can be controlled either by an expression, a ramp texture, through the Component Editor, or by all three. To determine what kind of controls can be used for one of the per particle attributes, right-click in one of the pink fields in the Per Particle (Array) Attributes section of the Attribute Editor. The marking menu will display which control technique can be used.

> NOTE *Much of the information on particle expressions is beyond the scope of this book. It is important that you read Maya's* **Using Expressions** *manual, specifically the section on particle expressions, to get a complete foundation for using this technique.*

Using Expressions

Let's edit one of these attributes with an expression. Here, we will look at some examples in which using an expression will be relatively simple. For instance, we can write a simple expression to control the lifespan of the particles instead of using the attributes in the Lifespan Attributes section of the particleShape1 node.

1. Create an emitter with the default settings. Use the Outliner to select the particle node (particle1), not the emitter.

2. In the Attribute Editor, set the Lifespan Mode attribute in the Lifespan Attributes section of the particleShape1 node to LifespanPP Only. This will force the particles to derive their lifespan value from the Per Particle (Array) Attributes section.

3. Scroll down in the Attribute Editor to the Per Particle (Array) Attributes area, as shown in the illustration. Right-click in the pink field next to lifespanPP and choose Creation Expression. This will open the Expression Editor.

4. In the Expression Editor, the name of the particle node and attribute that is selected appears in the Selected Obj and Attr fields. Either retype or cut and paste this name into the Expression field in the white space at the bottom of the Expression Editor. Then continue writing the expression control with a random function. Your expression should look like this:

```
particleShape1.lifespanPP=rand(5,8);
```

5. Click the Create button in the Expression Editor to create the expression. Click Play to see the result. The particles are created with a random lifespan between values of 5 and 8 seconds.

Using Ramp Textures to Control Particle Behaviors

Another technique used to control per particle attributes is the use of a Ramp texture. For this example, we'll use a Ramp texture to control the color of particles over their lifespan. If you look down the list of available per particle attributes, you won't see any attribute to control color. This is because color is another one of those dynamic attributes that needs to be loaded.

1. Click the Color button in the particle node's Attribute Editor. A window will appear that allows you to specify whether this dynamic attribute will control the entire particle group or on a per particle basis. Choose Per Particle Attribute and click the Add Attribute button. A new attribute will be created in the Per Particle (Array) Attributes section called rgbPP.

2. Right-click in the pink field next to rgbPP in the Per Particle (Array) Attributes section and choose Create Ramp. The rgbPP field will now show `<-arrayMapper1.outColor`.

3. Choose <-arrayMapper1.outColor | Edit Ramp from the marking menu. The ramp Node Editor appears in the Attribute Editor. This will allow you to control the color of the particles over the course of their lifespan. The color at the bottom of the ramp indicates what color the particles will be at the beginning of their lifespan, and the color at the top shows what color they will be at the end of their lifespan.

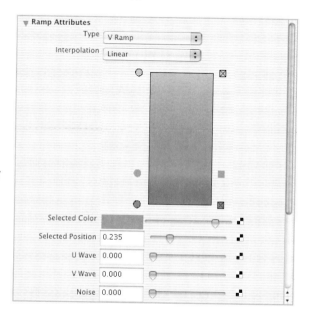

4. Add another color to the ramp by clicking inside the ramp display. Another color marker will be added to the left of the ramp, as shown in the following illustration. You can change the color of any of the markers by clicking one of the color markers to the left of the ramp and then editing its value in the Selected Color attribute. Remember that clicking the color chip will bring up the Color Chooser. If you decide that you don't want a color that has already been inserted, click in the box on the right side of the ramp.

5. Move the colors to position their keys at different points on the ramp by clicking its color marker and dragging it up or down.

6. Click the Play button in the Time Slider to see the results. Make sure to press the 6 key to turn on the display of colors in the view window. You can continue to fine-tune the ramp until you are pleased with the results in the view window.

Using the Component Editor

The third way to set per particle attributes is through the Component Editor. This technique involves selecting certain particles and then keying in numeric values for any of the attributes in the Component Editor. For this example, we will add a per particle opacity attribute to the particle node and set the opacity levels on a certain few of the particle groups.

1. Create a particle group with the Particle tool. (Alternatively, you could choose to use an emitter, but you would let the animation play for a few seconds so that you can select some of the particles.) For this example, create a 3D particle grid.

2. In the view window, right-click the particles and choose Particle from the marking menu. Select the top few rows of particles by clicking or drag-selecting them.

3. In the particle shape node's Attribute Editor, scroll down to the Per Particle (Array) Attributes section and add an opacity attribute by clicking the Opacity button below the list of per particle attributes. An attribute named opacityPP will be created and available in the list of per particle attributes.

4. Right-click in the pink field next to opacityPP and choose Component Editor from the marking menu. The Component Editor will open.

5. Find the opacityPP attribute list along the top of the Component Editor. All of the selected particles' fields will be highlighted. Change the opacity value to **0.3**. Now the top few rows of particles will be much more transparent than the bottom rows.

Fields

Fields simulate the forces of nature, such as gravity, air, turbulence, and vortex. They are normally applied to objects to create fluid, natural motion. The behaviors of fields can be fine-tuned by editing their attributes in the Channel Box or Attribute Editor. To gain a full understanding of what all of these fields do and how their attributes affect their behaviors, you need to spend time experimenting. For now, we'll introduce the different fields and show you how they affect objects in the scene by demonstrating them on a particle group. We will then look at some of the common attributes shared among the different fields.

Applying Fields

Fields can be applied to any object or group of objects in a scene. When applied to a particle group, the outputForce attribute of the field is connected to the inputForce attribute of the particle's shape node. The particle shape node's fieldData is then connected to the field's inputData attribute. These connections can be viewed in the Hypergraph, as shown in Figure 17-6.

When a force is applied to a piece of geometry, however, Maya will create a rigidBody node that contains these same inputForce and fieldData attributes. That rigidBody node is then connected to other nodes that will control the geometry under the effects of the field. (We will cover rigid bodies in depth in Chapter 19.) At this time, let's concentrate on connecting fields to particle groups to study their effects.

As you might guess from everything you've learned in this book so far, a field could be created from the Fields menu and then connected using the Hypergraph and Connection Editor. However, scrolling through a list of attributes and trying to figure out which ones make the desired connection when you are unfamiliar with them can be somewhat cumbersome. For this reason, Maya offers several ways of connecting fields to objects in the UI.

FIGURE 17-6 *The Hypergraph shows connections between a particle group and a turbulence field.*

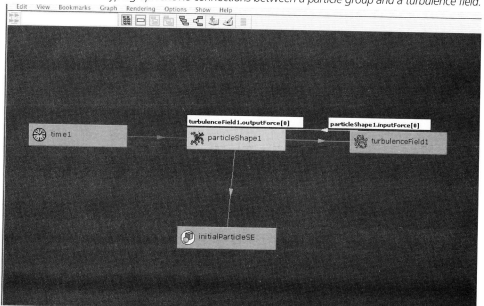

Selecting Objects when Creating Fields

Probably the simplest and quickest way to create a field with connections to an object is to select the object, in this case a particle group, and create a field though the Fields menu. For example, create a particle grid, and with it selected, choose Fields | Turbulence Field. In the Hypergraph, select the particle group, and click the Input And Output Connections button in the Hypergraph's toolbar; you can see that they are connected.

But perhaps the most intuitive way to check the connections is simply to click the Play button in the playback controls. If the particles start moving around, you know that they are connected.

Affect Selected Object(s) Command

Often, a field will be created in the scene with none or only some of the objects selected that need a field. To select one or many fields and the objects that need to be affected by those fields and connect them quickly, you can use a menu command. To see this work, create a particle group or two and then create a turbulence and a gravity field. Select all of these objects (in any order) and choose Fields | Affect Selected Object(s). Look in the Hypergraph or click the Play button to see whether all of the connections were made.

Making Connections with the Dynamic Relationships Editor

The Dynamic Relationships Editor, shown in Figure 17-7, can be used to make or break any type of dynamic connections. It could be used to connect fields to objects, particles to emitters, and collisions between objects. It can also be a quick way to view dynamic connections without having to play the animations or pan through the Hypergraph.

1. Create a particle grid and a turbulence field. They should not have any connections.

2. Choose Windows | Relationship Editors | Dynamic Relationships. This will bring up the Dynamic Relationships Editor.

3. Make sure that the Fields radio button is selected in the Selection Modes section. Select the particle group node from the list of objects on the left side of the window. The particle node will appear in the section on the right with a list of all fields in the scene.

FIGURE 17-7   *Dynamic Relationships Editor*

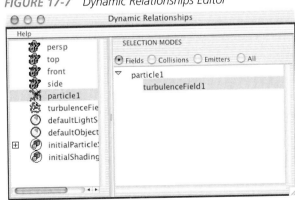

4. To connect the particle group to the turbulence field, select it from the list under the particle group in the right side. It will highlight to indicate that it is now connected and will affect the particle group.

5. Create another field in the scene—make it a uniform field. Notice that it will appear in the list under the particle group. You can click that field to highlight it and add it to the fields that affect the particle group. Click either one or both fields to disconnect them from the particle group.

Types of Fields

Nine types of fields are capable of simulating natural motion found in the real world. Each of these fields can be created by selecting it from the Fields menu. The best way to experiment with fields and learn what they do is to create a particle grid, add a field to it, and play back the animation. Because particle grids create the particles with uniform spacing throughout, it is easy to see exactly how the field is affecting it.

> _NOTE_ *Once again, the Maya documentation describes each field and its specific attributes at length. You should review and study this information.*

This section will give a brief description of each field and point out some of the attributes that are specific to each one. In addition to the examples shown in Figure 17-8, QuickTime movies on the accompanying CD show animated examples of each field. The common field attributes will be discussed in the following section.

- **Air**   Objects connected to an air field will move or float through the scene, depending on their mass. A feather will generally float, while something heavier will be less affected by this field. Some presets are available in the Creation options for this field for Wind, Wake, and Fan. Using these presets will set up the attributes for the field to simulate these types of occurrences in nature. The figure shows an air field being animated through a particle grid and displacing the particles in its range.

- **Drag**   Slows or dampens moving objects by applying a braking force that is controlled by the Magnitude attribute. If the Use Direction attribute is turned on, the braking force will be applied in the directions specified in the Direction attribute fields. The figure shows a directional emitter emitting particles in the Y direction. The Drag field is causing them to break so that they appear to collect above the emitter.

FIGURE 17-8 *Examples of fields*

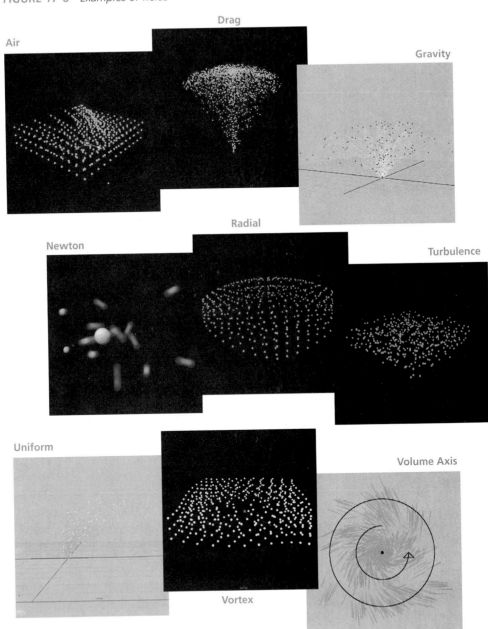

- **Gravity**   Simulates the earth's gravitational force by accelerating objects in the negative Y direction by default. However, the direction can be changed in the Attribute Editor by setting one of the Direction attributes. Also, the Magnitude attribute (the strength of the effect) is set to 9.8. (Remember that the law of gravity accelerates objects at a rate of 9.8 meters per second, regardless of their mass. Therefore, if you wish to simulate objects behaving under the law of gravity, you'll need to set your units to work in meters or set the magnitude to 980 if you are working in centimeters.)

- **Newton**   Simulates an attractive force between any two objects proportional to the product of their mass. Editing the mass of any object will change the effect of the Newton field. When applied to a particle group, the particles will be attracted toward the center of the field according to the Magnitude attribute setting. A similar effect can be achieved by changing the Dynamic Weight attribute of the particle group. A use for this type of field is exemplified by a planet orbiting around the sun or electrons orbiting around a nucleus. The figure shows a NURBS sphere that owns a Newton field. (Note that objects emitting fields will be covered in Chapter 18.) The particles have a velocity of 1 in their X direction while they are attracted to the sphere; the result is that they appear to orbit the sphere.

- **Radial**   Pushes or pulls objects toward the field depending on whether the Magnitude attribute value is positive or negative. Debris being thrown by a point explosion would be a good use for the Radial field.

- **Turbulence**   Introduces irregular motion, or noise, into the object's motion. While the Magnitude attribute controls the strength of the effect, the Frequency controls how often the disruption occurs. If you need more disruption over the area being affected, increase the Frequency. A common thing to do with a Turbulence field is to animate the Phase attributes. This will give the turbulent effect some direction useful for creating such effects as waves in the ocean.

- **Uniform**   Similar to gravity in that it accelerates objects in a given direction, but a Uniform field takes the mass of the objects it is affecting into the calculation. Whereas Gravity accelerates object at the same rate, no matter what their mass, Uniform will accelerate heavier objects faster. The figure shows particles being emitted from a directional emitter. The particles have been assigned a random mass between 0.2 and 2. The Uniform field has been applied to push the particles in the X direction. The heavier particles are less affected by the Uniform field, and the lighter particles are more affected.

- **Vortex**   Pulls objects in a circular, whirlpool-like behavior. The Axis attribute controls which axis the affected objects will swirl around. This field would work well for tornadoes, fires, and black holes.

- **Volume Axis**   Creates a volume shape and controls how objects move around in it. Several attributes are used for setting the volume shape.

Common Field Attributes

All of the fields in Maya have attributes that are specific to their type. Some of these attributes will be covered as we use these fields in tutorials. However, other attributes are common to all of the fields. By understanding what these attributes do, you will gain a better understanding of how fields work.

Before we begin demonstrating these attributes, create a particle grid that covers the entire default grid in the Perspective view. For the sake of performance, keep the particle count reasonable for real-time interaction. Use a Particle Spacing setting of 2 units. To see how these attributes affect the motion of these particles, change the Particle Render Type attribute to Spheres. Also, make sure you set your time range long—500 frames will do.

- **Magnitude** Controls the amount, or strength, of the field. A higher value will increase the strength of the effect. Entering a negative value will reverse the direction of the effect. For a Gravity field, the objects will accelerate upward instead of downward; a Radial field will pull objects toward it instead of away.

- **Max Distance** Controls the maximum distance, in units, that objects will be affected by the field. To use the Max Distance attribute, the Use Max Distance attribute must be set to On. The default value of most fields will create the field with the Use Max Distance set to Off. (Both the Radial and the Air fields have their default set to On.) In these cases, the field will affect everything in the scene that is connected to it no matter how far an object is from the field's origin (see Figure 17-9). Also, neither the Max Distance attribute nor the Attenuation attribute will have any effect. When Use Max Distance is turned on, any object connected to the field and within the distance specified in the Max Distance attribute will be affected by the field (see Figure 17-9).

FIGURE 17-9 *Left to right: a particle grid has Use Max Distance set to Off, Use Max Distance set to On with a Max Distance value set to 10, and the same Use Max Distance setting but with the Attenuation value set to 4*

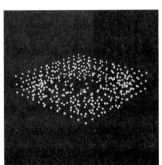
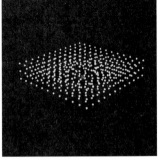

- **Attenuation**   Exponentially controls the falloff of the field's effect from its origin. With a value of 0, the effect will remain constant. Any larger number will increase the attenuation so that the objects closer to the field's origin will be more affected than those close to the Max Distance (Figure 17-9).

TIP   **You can use the Show Manipulator tool to edit the attributes of any selected field in the view window.**

Hardware Renderer

Maya's hardware renderer uses your computer's real-time OpenGL-based video processor to render images, instead of the software renderer that we have used so far. The hardware renderer is faster than the software render, but the quality, especially in terms of anti-aliasing, is not as good. While the renderer is capable of rendering geometry, most of the particle render types can be rendered only in the hardware renderer.

As of version 5, Maya offers a completely rewritten hardware renderer to take advantage of the newest hardware rendering technologies found in the latest video cards. Using the hardware renderer is similar to using the software renderer. It can be enabled in the Render Global Settings window or from the Render menu.

In this section, we will look at some of the basic features of the hardware renderer. As an example, we'll create an omni emitter that emits red particle streaks. If you were to render this in the regular software renderer. it would appear as a black screen.

1. Open the Render Global Settings window. Choose Maya Hardware from the Render Using menu. A new tab appears that contains attributes specific to the hardware renderer (Figure 17-10).

2. To Render the current frame, click the Render Current Frame button in the Status Line, just as you would if you were rendering with the software renderer.

3. In many cases, you will be compositing the particle effects with geometry that has been rendered in a separate software render pass. Render layers can be created in the Layer window and objects assigned to the layers. When Enable Render Layers is turned on in the Render Global Settings window, you can quickly hide the geometry and render just the particles.

4. Some nice blurring or smoothing effects can be achieved by using motion blur. The attributes for controlling motion blur are shown in Figure 17-10. With the Enable Motion Blur option checked, the renderer will render several frames and composite them together to create one frame for an accurate motion blur. The Motion Blur By

FIGURE 17-10   *Render Global Settings window with the hardware renderer selected*

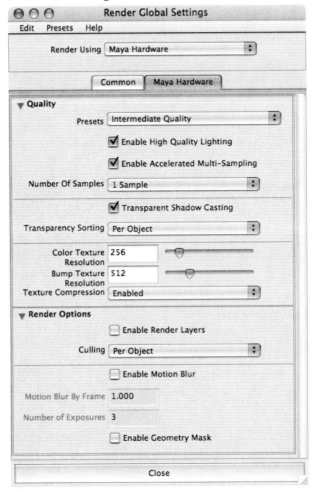

Frame attribute sets how many frames will be used in the calculation. The Number Of Exposures attribute sets how many frames are rendered between the current frame and the number of frames before it as specified in the Motion Blur By Frame attribute. A good rule of thumb is to set the number of exposures to one less than the number of frames. This will produce the best quality motion blur. Figure 17-11 shows the effects of motion blur on streak rendered particles.

This should give you a good reference to using the hardware renderer. While the remainder of this chapter will focus on the software renderer, we will be using the hardware rendering engine to create some fire effects in Chapter 18 and some heat ripples in Chapter 20.

FIGURE 17-11   *The streaks are rendered with (left) and without (right) Enable Motion Blur turned on with a Motion Blur By Frame value of 10.*

Tutorial: Build an Explosion

With some of the basics of working with particles, emitters, and fields now covered, we are ready to put them to work and create something. This tutorial will take you through the process of building an explosion. To accomplish this task, we will use some of the basics covered so far in this chapter and introduce some additional tools and concepts that show Maya's power in creating effects of this type.

For this shot, we want to create a cannon shooting a laser blast at a group of objects. When the laser blast hits the objects, an explosion will occur. In some cases, you might want to render the laser blast and explosion separately and composite them together later in a compositing package. While this is optimal for high-end post-production, let's say that in this case we are just trying to previsualize a concept and don't have time to go back in and match and composite an explosion at every laser blast collision. We do, however, want to impress our client and give him a sense of how dramatic a good explosion would be in the scene.

We will begin by creating the explosion. This will entail creating an emitter that emits the initial stage of the explosion. Once this is in place, these particles will emit a second particle group to represent fire and smoke trails. Fields will be added and their attributes fine-tuned until we have the look and behavior we want. Then we will model some simple geometry and use the Instancer to link them to the particle object. This will replace the particles from the initial explosion with actual modeled geometry. Then we'll set up the cannon and use particle collision events to emit the explosion particles when the laser blast collides with the objects.

NOTE   *For each of the illustrations used in this section, animated examples can be found on the accompanying CD. It is a good idea to have these available as you go through the tutorial, if possible.*

Create the Explosion

Before we set up the cannon and laser blast that will cause the explosion, we will create the explosion itself. We'll start with an emitter and rough out the overall size and span of the explosion.

Set Up the Emitter

1. Choose Particles | Create Emitter ❒ and reset the options to their default settings (Edit | Reset Settings). Click the Create button to create the emitter. This will create two nodes—an emitter node and a particle node. Name the emitter node **Emitter_Explosion** and the particle node **particle_debris**.

2. Edit some of the emitter's attributes. With the emitter selected, press CTRL-A (CONTROL-A) or click the Show Attribute Editor button in the Status Line to bring up the Attribute Editor. Change the Emitter Type attribute to Directional. Then scroll down to the next folder in the Attribute Editor, Distance/Direction Attributes. Change the Direction X attribute to **0** and set the Direction Y attribute to **1**. You may also wish to use the Show Manipulator tool to edit some of these attributes in the view window. Play back the animation to see the results.

3. Now that the emitter is pointing in the right direction, we need to adjust the Spread attribute. This will widen the angle of the particles that are emitted from the emitter. The last attribute in that Distance/Direction Attributes folder is called Spread. A value of 1 would emit in a full 180-degree spread. We want it just less than that, so change this to a value of **0.8**. The view should look similar to the illustration.

NOTE   *Some of the particle display attributes have been modified for some of these illustrations. Since these will all be modified later to resemble fire and smoke, it is not necessary for you to change these attributes now.*

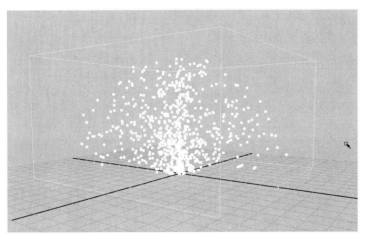

4. As this explosion occurs, the emitter should emit for one frame only. To specify this, we can key the Emission Rate. Make sure that the Time Slider is at frame 1. Set the Rate (Particles/Sec) attribute to **0**. Right-click this attribute in the Attribute Editor and choose Set Key to set a key for that value at frame 1. Move the Time Slider out to frame 3 and set another key for a Rate attribute to **0**. Go back to frame 2, change the Rate to **2000**, and set a key. Now when you play back the animation, the emitter will emit a short burst of particles.

Create the Particle Trails

As the debris breaks away from the center of the explosion, we want to create trails of fire and smoke. To do this, we will use the existing particles, the particle_debris, as an emitter by using the Emit From Object command. By selecting an object and choosing Particles | Emit From Object, an emitter will be attached to the object and particles will be emitted from it.

1. Select the particle_debris node. Choose Particles | Emit From Object. An emitter will be grouped underneath the particle_debris node. Rename this node **emitter_trail** and name the new particle group **particle_trail**.

2. Set the Rate attribute of the emitter_trail node to **50** and set the Speed attribute to **0.1**. We are setting the Speed to 0.1 because we want the particles to trail behind the object from which they are being emitted, not shoot off. A low value here is enough to make them spread but keep them from moving too fast.

3. Click the Play button to see the result. It should look similar to the illustration.

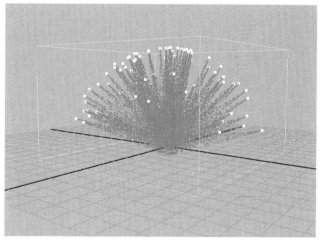

NOTE As you work, you might notice that your computer is slowing down and frames are being dropped. This is not good when you're working with dynamics. Because most dynamic calculations are made on a frame-to-frame basis, dropping a frame can lead to an inaccurate simulation. For this reason, it is best to work with the animation Timeline preferences set to Play Every Frame. Make sure this is enabled once you start running dynamic simulations. If you want to preview the animation in real time, it is best to use the Playblast engine.

Add Fields

Now the particles shoot out upward from the emitter and continue along their paths. Although this might be fine for an explosion that takes place in outer space, the explosion in this example takes place on or near the ground on a planet with a gravitational force. For this reason, a Gravity field will be applied to the particle_debris node to pull the particles down after they are emitted. For the smoke trails, an Air field will be used to make the smoke rise up into the air as it dissipates.

1. Select the particle_debris node. Choose Fields | Gravity. This will create a Gravity field that is affecting the particle_debris particles once they are emitted from the emitter. If you play back the animation, however, the gravity appears to be pulling the particles down a little too much.

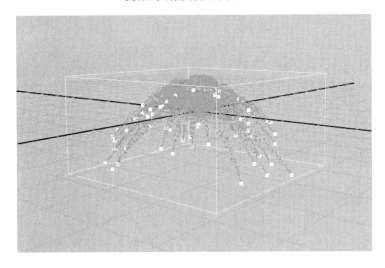

2. Select the gravityField1 node and view its attributes in the Attribute Editor. In the Gravity Field Attributes folder, change the Magnitude attribute to **0.5**. This will lessen the strength that this field exerts on the affected objects. Click the Play button to see the result. It should look similar to the illustration.

3. As the trailing particles are emitted, they should rise up in the air a bit. This effect is due to the fact that smoke particles are hot and therefore less dense than air, so they rise. Select the particle_trail node and choose Fields | Air Field. This will create the Air field at the origin and attached to the particle_trail node.

4. If you click Play, you will see the trails quickly shoot upward from the center. This is the result of a few things. The most affected particles are those near the center of the scene, because the Air field is created with its Use Max Distance set to On. If you recall from the discussion on field attributes earlier in this chapter, turning this setting on will have the field affect only the particles closest to the field's origin by a range set in the Max Distance attribute. However, in this case, we want the Air field to affect everything connected to it in this scene. In the Attribute Editor, with the airField1 node selected, scroll down to the Distance folder and uncheck the Use Max Distance box. Play back the animation to view the result.

5. Now the effect of the Air field is even, but the particles rise up a little too fast. This can be fixed by editing the Air field's Magnitude and Speed attributes. Set the Magnitude to **0.4** and the Speed to **0.4**. The illustration shows the trails with the Air field applied.

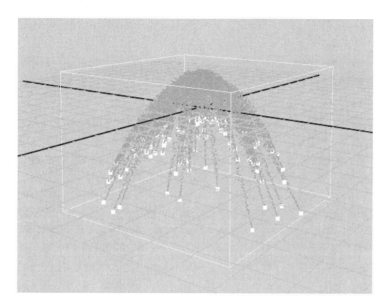

6. Add a Turbulence field to the trails so that they break up irregularly as they are emitted and rise. Select the particle_trail object and then choose Fields | Turbulence Field. The default settings are a little too strong, so you'll need to turn down the Turbulence field's Magnitude attribute to **5**.

7. If you play back the animation, you'll notice that the Turbulence field is affecting the particles in large chunks. To make this area a bit finer, you'll need to turn up the Frequency attribute. A higher frequency will make the turbulence occur more times over the given space and therefore create very fine irregularities for the particles to travel through. A value of about **8** works well in this setup.

8. Animate the Turbulence field's Phase Y attribute with a simple expression that will create 10 cycles over the time range with an amplitude of 20 units. In the Attribute Editor, right-click the Phase Y attribute and choose Create New Expression from the marking menu. In the Expressions Editor, enter the following into the text field and click the Create button.

```
turbulenceField1.phaseY=20*sin(10*time);
```

The result is shown in the illustration.

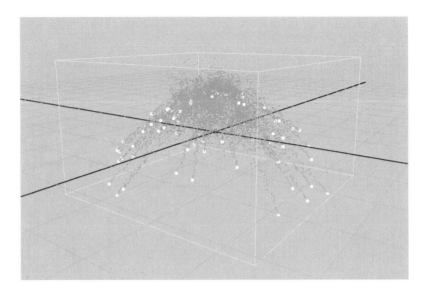

Edit the Particle Attributes

Everything we have done so far in this exercise has used the default particle rendering type, *points*. Points are a great way to begin setting up a particle system because they don't require too much power from your video processing unit. For the sake of performance, it is always good to start with this type, set up any particle interaction, and then go on to change the particle display type.

In this section, we will edit the particle attributes for the smoke trails. This is where we'll replace the particle point display with something that resembles smoke. We'll leave the actual particle debris node alone for now, as we are going to use a different process to change its display type. This will be addressed in the next section.

1. Select the particle_trail node object and view its attributes in the Attribute Editor. We'll begin by editing the Lifespan attributes. Scroll down the Attribute Editor to the Lifespan Attributes folder. Set the Lifespan Mode attribute to Random Range. The two fields below this will become active. Set Lifespan to **1.2** and Lifespan Random to **0.7**. When you play back the animation, the newly emitted particles will "die" between 1.9 and 0.5 seconds.

2. To change the particle display type, scroll down to the Render Attributes folder and set the Particle Render Type attribute to Cloud [s/w]. This will change the render type to clouds. (The [s/w] indicates that this rendering type will need to use the Maya software renderer instead of the hardware render buffer that most of the other display types require.)

3. Click the Current Render Type button to add the dynamic attributes for this rendering type. Three fields will appear in the space below this button. If you click Play now, the particles will be much too big. Set the Radius to a small value—**0.02** is a good place to start. If you play it back now, the radius is much closer to where it should be. However, the radius should increase as the smoke dissipates. To take care of that, we will edit some Per Particle attributes.

4. Scroll down to the Per Particle (Array) Attributes folder in the Attribute Editor. By default, no attribute controls the per particle radius. Therefore, you'll need to add a dynamic attribute. In the Add Dynamic Attribute folder, click the General button. This will open the Add Attribute window. Select the Particle tab, scroll down the list, and find the radiusPP attribute, shown in the illustration. Select it and click the OK button. The radiusPP attribute will now appear in the list of Per Particle attributes.

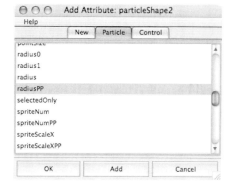

5. We will use a ramp to control the radius per particle. This ramp is based on the lifespan of the particles. This means that the radius will have a value set by the ramp value at the bottom of the ramp when a particle is born and will end with the value at the top of the ramp. To add the ramp, right-click in the radiusPP field and choose Create Ramp from the marking menu. To edit the ramp, right-click again in that field and choose <-arrayMapper1.outValuePP | Edit Ramp from the marking menu. The Attribute Editor will load the Ramp Editor.

6. The default ramp is created, white at the bottom and black at the top. Because we want the radius to be small when it is born and largest when it dies, we want black, the small value, to be at the bottom and white, the larger value, to be at the top. Make this happen by clicking the black circle at the top on the left side of the ramp and pull it down to the bottom. Then grab the white circle and move it to the top. Delete the gray color in the middle by clicking the box on the right side. The ramp should look like the illustration.

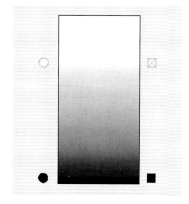

7. If you play back the animation, you will notice that the radius is being scaled from 0 to 1. As we determined in step 3, a value of 1 is much too large and this range is too wide. We can edit this range by editing the Array Mapper node. Select the particle_trail object, and look at the Attribute Editor. Right-click in the radiusPP attribute field and select Edit Array Mapper. This will display the ramp's array mapper node in the Attribute Editor. Here you can set the minimum and maximum values for the ramp. Enter **0.02** as the Min Value. For the Max Value, type in **0.2**. Play back the animation to see the result. The particles should get bigger as they near the end of their lifespan so that they look like the illustration.

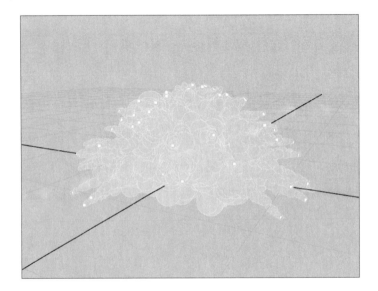

Create the Particle Material

When using the regular hardware rendered particles, attributes such as Color and Opacity can be set in the particle attributes on a per object or per particle basis. This means that you could create an opacityPP attribute and then control it with an expression or a ramp. However, when dealing with software rendered particles, these attributes will not have any direct effect on the rendered particles. While these attributes can be connected to a material through the use of a particle sampler info node, it is much simpler to control these attributes—Color, Transparency, and Incandescence—with a ramp through the particle cloud's Life attributes.

Whenever a particle group is created, it is connected to two of Maya's default materials—the Lambert and the particle cloud. Depending on the Particle Render Type attribute, Maya will use the hardware render attributes as specified in the particle shape node's attributes, the Lambert material for blobby particles, or the particle cloud for the cloud rendering type. In this section, we will create a new particle cloud material, assign it to the particle group, and then edit some of its attributes to make it look like fire and smoke.

1. Open the Hypershade window (Windows | Rendering Editors | Hypershade) or use the Hypershade/Perspective layout, accessible by choosing Panels | Saved Layouts | Hypershade/Perspective or by clicking the Hypershade button in the toolbar. Create a new particle cloud material. This can be found in the Create Materials menu under the Volumetric folder. Name this material **mSmoke**. Apply it to the particle_trail node.

2. With the mSmoke material selected and its attributes shown in the Attribute Editor, notice the attributes called Life Color, Life Transparency, and Life Incandescence, as well as the regular Color, Transparency, and Incandescence attributes. Using these Life attributes will allow for the control of these particular attributes over the lifespan of the particles. This workflow is similar to editing the per particle attributes for the color, opacity, and incandescence in the particle node's attributes. Begin by editing the Life Color attribute. Click the Map button next to the Life Color attribute and select Ramp Texture from the Create Rendering Node window.

3. Edit the ramp so that it cycles through four different colors. The color at the bottom of the ramp is the color that the particles will be at birth. Make this white by clicking the color chip next to Selected Color and editing the color in the Color Chooser. Click Apply. Move the next color key down so that only a hair of the white shows through.

It should be at a position of about 0.015. Make this second color a bright orange. The third color should be a bright yellow. Set its position to about 0.215. Finally, add one more color by clicking in the ramp somewhere. Position this color at around 0.500. This fourth color should be a medium gray to represent the color as it turns into smoke. The ramp should look like the illustration (except in color).

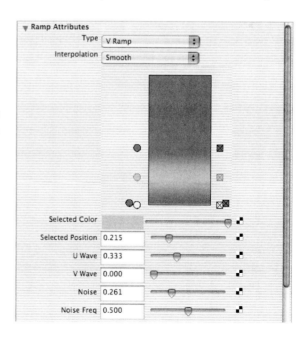

4. In the Hypershade, select the mSmoke node to view its attributes. Map a Ramp texture to the Life Transparency attribute. Set it so that the ramp is black at the bottom (opaque) until a position of 0.07 and fades to gray at about 0.165 and then to white at the top. It should look like the illustration.

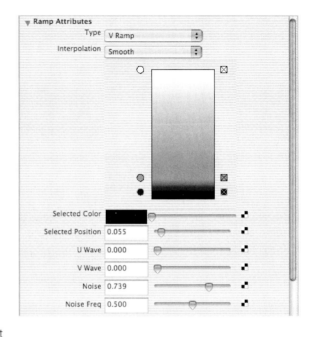

5. Add another ramp to the Life Incandescence attribute. This ramp should be two colors. The bottom color should be a bright orange and be positioned at about 0.165 to match the point where the yellow flame fades into a gray smoke. The second color, a black, non-incandescent value, should be positioned at about 0.450 to correspond with the bright-yellow flame into the gray smoke. The ramp should look like the illustration.

6. Play back the animation and stop it right as the explosion is at its largest, around frame 30. Click in the Perspective view and use Maya's software renderer to do a test render. It should look similar to Figure 17-12. A color plate in the color section of this book shows the explosion in color.

Use the Instancer to Insert the Debris

In the case of the debris flying away from the explosion point, we are not going to use any of the 10 particle render types. Instead, we are going to introduce the particle Instancer. The particle Instancer lets you replace a particle with an actual object in the scene. The object could even be animated and then inserted as a particle instance. This would be a great way to create a swarm of bees, spiders, ants, or even a large crowd of people. For this exercise, though, we are going to create some simple debris with some sculpted spheres and poly faces. We will create three types of debris—two of them will be based on a poly sphere and the other on a poly face.

FIGURE 17-12   A test render of the explosion

1. Create a polygonal sphere. Change its attributes so that it has 8 by 8 subdivisions. Use the non-uniform scale tools in the Y and Z to make the object less spherical.

2. Use the Sculpt Polygons tool (Polygons | Sculpt Polygons) to push and pull the vertices on the object so that it quickly takes on an irregular form. It can be very rough since the pieces will be small and flying by fast. Name this object **pDebris**. Figure 17-13 shows an example of the pDebris model.

FIGURE 17-13   The poly object will be used as the source objects for the debris.

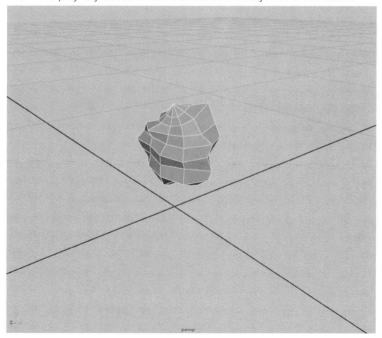

3. In the Hypershade window, create a new Lambert material and call it **mDebris**. Create a rock-like texture for the color channel. You may create your own or use the MCR_debris_CLR.tga texture map that is included on the CD. Apply it to pDebris.

4. Select pDebris and hide it by pressing CTRL-H (CONTROL-H).

5. With pDebris still selected, add the particle_debris object to the selection and choose Particles | Instancer (Replacement). A new object is created called **instancer1**. Select this object in the Outliner and view its attributes in the Attribute Editor. You will see that pDebris has been added to the Instanced Objects list. You could remove or add objects to this list by selecting them and choosing Add Selection or Remove Items.

6. When the animation plays back, notice the objects are emitted from the emitter (see Figure 17-14). However, they are not spinning as they move. We can set the instances to rotate based on some of the other particle attributes. Find the Rotation options in the Instancer (Geometry Replacement) folder of the particle_debris shape node's attributes. Set the Rotation attribute to Velocity, so that the instances will rotate according to the velocity of the particles

FIGURE 17-14   Objects are emitted from the emitter.

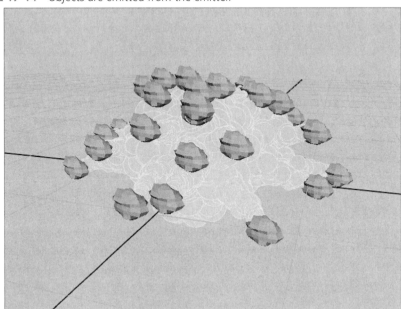

Set Up the Laser Cannon Emitter and Scene Objects

At this point, the explosion is pretty much set. It is emitting the debris, which then emit the smoke and fire trails, and the fields are set up with Turbulence, Gravity, and Air. Now we are going to put that aside for a moment and set up another emitter along with some objects. We'll build a simple object that represents a cannon and attach the emitter to it. The rest of the scene can be simple—a plane for the floor and three cubes that are sitting on top of it. The cannon will rotate on its Y axis as it fires laser blasts at the cubes. See Figure 17-15 to get an idea of how this setup will look.

1. Select the Emitter_Explosion node and delete it. We will be using particle collision events to emit particles from here on. Select the particle_debris object and the particle_trail object and press CTRL-H (CONTROL-H) to hide them. We want to get these out of our way while we set up the rest of the scene and not have all of these particle systems hinder the performance.

FIGURE 17-15 The scene is set up with the cannon rotated at frame 1.

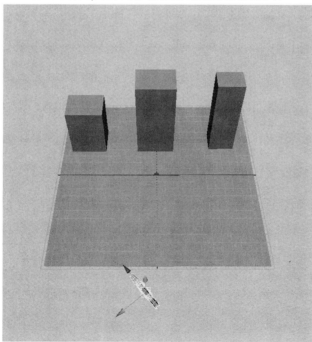

2. To create the set, first create a poly plane for the floor. Scale it up 25 units in all directions. Create a cube and scale it up in the Y and Z axes. Duplicate it two more times and scale each duplicate so that they are all a little different. Place them near the edge of the poly plane. See Figure 17-15 for details.

3. Create a cylinder that will be used for the cannon (or quickly model one, as shown in the example). Rotate it so that its end is pointing toward the cubes. Figure 17-15 shows the approximate scale and placement.

4. Create an emitter. Make it a directional emitter and name the emitter **emitter_laser**. With the emitter selected, SHIFT-select the cylinder. From the animation menu set (F2), choose Constrain | Point Constraint. The emitter is now constrained to the cylinder object. But it needs to rotate with it as well. With both of the objects still selected, choose Constrain | Orient Constraint.

NOTE   *Instead of using constraints, you could just parent the emitter to the cannon. However, using constraints makes it easier to choose the emitter in the Outliner because it is not necessary to unfold hierarchies.*

5. Set the emitter's attributes so that it is emitting 1 particle per second. Edit the Direction so that the particles are shooting toward the cubes. Direction Y can be set to **–1**, but the setting depends on how the cylinder was rotated, so you might have to play with it. Change the Speed to **50**.

6. Select the particle object that was created with the emitter. Name this **particle_laser**. Edit the Particle Render Type attribute to Streak. Add attributes for this render type and set the Line Width to **6**, the tail Fade to **0.4** and the tail Size to **2.7**. Add a color attribute per object. Set the red value to **240**.

7. Animate the rotation of the cannon. At frame 1 it should be aimed off to the left side of the leftmost cube at about 40 degrees. At frame 150 it should be rotated about –40 degrees so that it is aiming off to the left (Figure 17-15).

Set Up Particle Collisions

Instead of tracking where these shots hit the cubes and compositing in the explosion, or keying the position of the emitter, a particle collision event will be created that will emit our explosion whenever a laser blast collides with the cubes. The debris will then be set up to collide with the floor when it lands.

1. Select the particle_laser object and then select the three cubes. Choose Particles | Make Collide. Double-check that the connection was made by looking in the Dynamic

Relationships Editor. Play back the animation to see if any collisions occur. Chances are that a collision will happen at least once. If not, you may have to change the starting or ending keyframed position of the cannon.

2. With the particle_laser object selected, choose Particle | Particle Collision Event. This will open the Particle Collision Event Editor. Particle_laser should be highlighted in the Objects list at the upper left of the window. This indicates that this particle will trigger the event. Make sure the All Collisions check box is checked. In the Event Type section, set the Type to Emit. Have it emit 80 particles with a spread of 0.8 (just as our original test emitter did).

3. The Target Particle attribute is the particle group that will be emitted during this event. In this case, we want the event to trigger the particle_debris group. Therefore, in this field, type **particle_debris**. Set the Inherit Velocity to **0.02**. This means that the speed of the emission will be based on 0.02 times the speed of the laser particle, which will equal 1, about the same speed that our original emitter was set to. These settings will cause this event to produce similar results to what we had in the test emitter. Finally, check the Original Particle Dies box. This will eliminate the laser blast as soon as it collides with one of the cubes. The Particle Collision Events window should look similar to Figure 17-16.

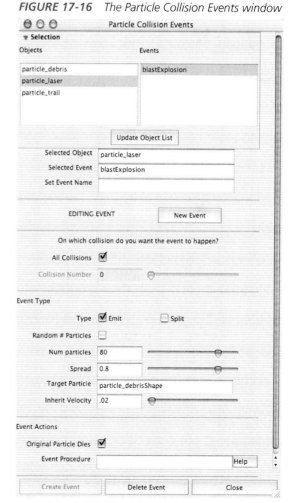

FIGURE 17-16 *The Particle Collision Events window*

4. Unhide the particle_debris object. You can display the instanced geometry in a bounding box to improve performance. To do this, select the instancer1 object and set the Level Of Detail attribute to Bounding Boxes. Play back the animation to test everything. You may have to change the Inherit Velocity attribute in the Particle Collision Events window to get the desired result.

5. The particle_debris and the particle_trail objects need to collide with the floor when they land. Select both of these objects and then select the floor. Choose Particles | Make Collide. If you play back the animation to test the collisions, you'll notice that the debris objects are bouncing on the ground like crazy.

6. The bounciness can be controlled by an attribute called Resilience, which exists on a node called a geoConnector node. This node is connected between any two colliding objects. To select this node, select the floor object and then flip through the connections in the Attribute Editor until you find the geoConnector node. Once it's selected, you can set the Resilience (bounciness) to about **0.2**. Then set the Friction (stickiness) to about **0.2**. Play back the animation and continue to adjust this until you're satisfied. You should have something similar to Figure 17-17.

FIGURE 17-17   *The animation up to this point*

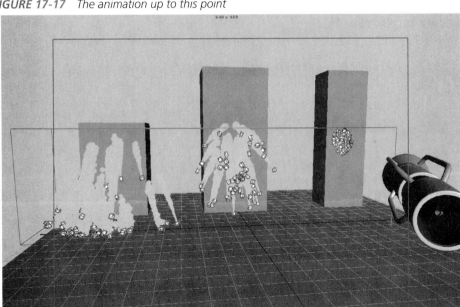

Render

In this situation, we are using particle effects with two different renderers. The explosion uses Maya's software renderer, while the laser blast uses the hardware render buffer. In this situation, you will have to render the animations separately. One will contain the geometry and the explosion, and the other will contain the laser blast alone. You may even wish to render the geometry and explosion separately so that you can make tweaks to the set and you won't have to wait for the computationally intense rendering of the particle explosion. Figure 17-18 shows the final composite.

FIGURE 17-18   *Explosion composited with the laser*

Summary

In this chapter, you learned about the basics of creating particles and controlling them in the scene using fields. These lessons will lay the groundwork for the next two chapters, where you will learn about additional ways to control particles to create more sophisticated effects. Once you understand the basics of dynamics, you can apply them to various applications and purposes.

Advanced Particle Systems and Effects

In Chapter 17, you learned about the
basics of creating particles and controlling their
behavior with fields. In this chapter, we will dig
a little deeper into the Dynamics toolset to create
some more complex effects.

In addition to being emitted from points and volumes, particles can also be emitted from vertices, surfaces, and curves, as well as from each other. Texture maps can be used to control emitter and particle attributes on a particle-emitting surface. The particles' behavior can be further controlled though the use of scripts, called *expressions*. Furthermore, particle *goals* are used to attract particles to other objects for another level of control. In this chapter, we will look at examples involving each of these techniques and then practice using them in a tutorial.

Emit From Object

Recall from Chapter 17 that when we created the explosion, we used the Emit From Object command to emit particles from the existing particles. Here, we'll take a closer look at this command and the options available when used in conjunction with a curve or a surface. Depending on the object used as the emitter, various effects can be achieved by using different emitter types.

Curve Emissions

Curves offer a large degree of control as particle-emitting objects. Emitting from a curve essentially lets you *draw* where particles need to be emitted from in your scene. This section explores two different ways that curves can be used as emitters.

Using Omni and Directions Types from Curves

With its default settings, choosing the Emit From Object command with any object selected will produce omni emissions from the CVs or vertices of that object. In the case of a NURBS curve, the particles will be emitted from the CVs. An obvious use for this would be in placing multiple emitters at different points in the scene without having to create each emitter separately.

To set up a curve emitter, create a curve and select it. Choose Particles | Emit From Object ❏ and reset the options to the defaults. Click the Create button and play the animation. You will see that the CVs of that curve are acting as omni type emitters. Figure 18-1 shows the behavior of particles being emitted from a curve with the default settings.

> NOTE   *This type of behavior will be created any time the Emit From Object command is applied to any objects containing vertices—this applies to NURBS surfaces and curves, polygonal objects, and even lattices.*

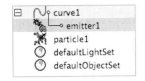

If you look in the Outliner, notice that the emitter1 object has been parented under the curve (as shown in the illustration).

Any time particles are set to emit from an object, the emitter will be hierarchically linked in this way. If you select the emitter, its attributes will be displayed

FIGURE 18-1   *Curve with particles being emitted from its CVs*

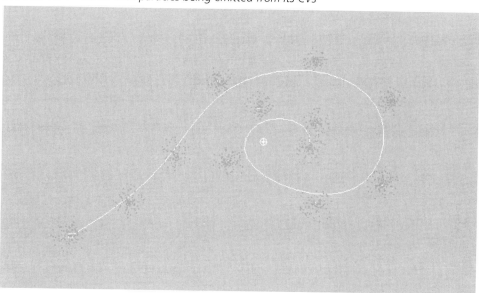

in the Channel Box or Attribute Editor and can be edited just as we edited the emitters in the previous lessons. Changing the emitter's Emitter Type attribute to Directional will allow you to control the direction of the emission with the Direction X, Y, Z, and Spread attributes. As mentioned, this might be useful if you needed to place a bunch of emitters in a scene quickly. For example, say you were creating a rooftop scene and you needed to create smoke emitting from all of the smokestacks on houses in the background. Creating an emitter for each one could be tedious.

However, in such a situation, you might also want to be able to control the attributes of the individual emitters so that they are all using different rates. This can be done by selecting the curve and choosing Particles | Per Point Emission Rates. This will add extra attributes to the curve shape node to control the rate of emission from each point, as illustrated in Figure 18-2. If you are looking at the attributes in the Attribute Editor, look in the Extra Attributes folder and you will see a folder called Emitter1 Rate PP. In that folder, you will find an emission rate attribute for each vertex in the curve.

While this smokestack example is a rather obvious suggestion, some interesting effects can be created just by drawing a simple curve with some CVs and rotating the curve. Figure 18-3 shows a render made from a straight curve emitting particles at the CVs that was animated along its X and Y axes. To set up something like this, draw a curve and rebuild it so that it has the desired amount of CVs to act as emitters. Leave the Emitter Type set to Omni. Set the emitter's

FIGURE 18-2   *Curve with per point emissions using a directional emitter*

FIGURE 18-3   *Rendered MultiStreak particles emitted from a rotated curve*

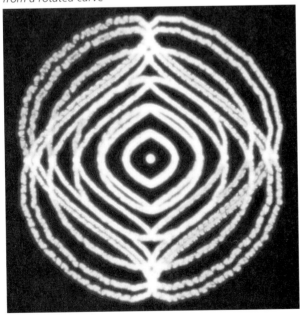

Rate attribute low. Add the per point emission attributes to the curve. Higher values here will create thicker looking lines in the rendered image. On the particle's shape node, set the Render Type to Multipoint and use a ramp to control the rgbPP and opacityPP attributes. Start animating the curve's transforms. Experiment, experiment, experiment. Have fun with it. When you are happy with the way the results look in the view window, render a frame in the hardware renderer with sampling turned up to about 16 or 32. Use motion blur and multiple exposures to soften the look further.

Using Curve Emitter Types

In this section, we continue working with a curve and the Emit From Object command, but instead of using either the Omni or Directional type of emitter that is available in the emitter's Attribute Editor, we will be using the Curve emit type. This will enable particles to be emitted continuously along the curve. This option will allow you to create quite a library of effects. The precise placement of fire sources, shock-wave explosions, and water wakes—to name a few—can be achieved by having these effects continuously emit along a curve.

To set this up, follow these steps.

1. Start a new scene, and create a NURBS circle or curve. With the circle selected, choose Particles | Emit From Object, and use the command's default settings.

2. If you were to play back the animation now, you would get a similar result to what is shown in Figure 18-1, with the particles emitting from the circle's CVs. But this time, a different type of emission will be used. In the Outliner, select the emitter, and in the Channel Box or Attribute Editor, change the Emitter Type attribute to Curve. Then click Play to see a very different effect.

The particles are now emitting from all of the points along the curve. Depending on the size of your curve, the default emission rate of 100 particles per second might not be quite enough to see exactly what is going on. You can increase the emitter's Rate attribute to get a better indication of what is happening. In fact, if you scale the circle, you'll see that you might need to increase the rate so that the overall emission density remains constant. Fortunately, Maya provides an attribute to do just this without your having to change the rate. If you are going to be animating the scale of your circle, you can use an attribute called Scale Rate By. If you have this attribute turned on in the Attribute Editor, Maya will modulate the emission rate to keep the emission density constant.

Figure 18-4 shows particles emitting from the NURBS circle, whose Scale attributes are being animated to increase over time. The result is a shock-wave type effect similar to those used in popular science fiction/ fantasy films.

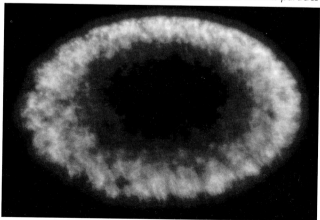

FIGURE 18-4 *The scale of a circle is animated as it emits particles*

Another great use for an effect with this type of emission would be to create the small, foamy wakes created when rippling seawater collides with a boat or a piling in the water. At the points of intersection between the water and the object, particles need to be emitted. This can be quickly set up by using NURBS surfaces for the two intersecting objects and the Create Intersection command to create a curve on surface where the two objects intersect. This curve is then used as the emitter. Whenever the surface of the water changes its height, the intersection curve is deformed to match the intersection. Therefore, the wake always occurs at the intersection between the two surfaces.

NOTE   ***To enhance this example, read the "Creating the Waves in the Ocean" section in Chapter 19 so that you can deform the water surface with soft body dynamics.***

Let's set up a simple simulation for this effect. For this example, we'll use a plane and a sphere.

1. Create a NURBS plane and sphere.

2. Select both surfaces and choose Edit NURBS | Intersect Surfaces. A curve on surface will be created.

3. Select the curve on the sphere's surface. Use your pick masks to turn off surface selection so that you can more easily choose the curve on the surface.

4. With that curve on the surface selected, choose Edit Curves | Duplicate Surface Curves. This will create an actual curve whose shape is dependent on the intersection between the two surfaces.

5. To use this new curve as an emitter, select the curve and choose Particles | Emit From Object.

6. Use the Attribute Editor to edit some of the emitter's attributes. First, change the Emitter Type to Curve. You'll also want to set the Speed attribute very low, probably less than 0.1. Also, change the direction so that it is emitting only in the positive Y. Change the Rate attribute to about 200 particles/second.

7. For the particle's shape node, change the Lifespan Mode to Random Range with a Lifespan of **1** and Lifespan Random of **0.2**. Change the rendering type to Multipoint and turn the Multi Count down to about **6**.

8. With the particles selected, add a Gravity field so that they fall after they are emitted.

NOTE *The exact settings you use will depend on the scale of the objects you started with. These are just suggested settings that will yield something close to the water wake.*

9. Key the position of the sphere so that it begins almost entirely underneath the surface at frame 1 and then is about halfway revealed at frame 60. Click Play to see the effect. The particles are emitted wherever the two surfaces meet. Figure 18-5 shows the particles being emitted along the intersection of the sphere and the plane.

10. You can further enhance this image by selecting the particles and then the surface and choosing Particles | Make Collide. Now when you play back the animation, the particles will emit and fall with gravity until they collide with the plane before they die off. You may also wish to add an rgbPP and an opacityPP attribute so that the particles are white and they completely fade out by the end of their lifespan.

NOTE *In this situation, there appears to be a "bug" in the Maya software, where the particles will emit in the negative Y direction once they have been made to collide. To compensate for this, change the emission direction to –1. This will cause the particles to emit in the positive Y direction.*

FIGURE 18-5 *Particles emitted at the line of intersection*

Surface Emissions

Just as we saw with the curve emissions, a surface can be selected and the Emit From Object command used. With the default settings, this command will create an Omni emitter at each of the vertices. The Per-Point Emission Rates command could be used to add control of the individual emission rates at each vertex. Far more interesting effects are possible when the emitter's Emitter Type attribute is set to Surface. This will create a random emission of particles from all points on the surface. A texture can then be assigned to the emitter to control the particle colors and the rate of emission from the various points on the surface.

Using Textures with Emitters

In this section, we will create the effect of a surface that is burning. A surface will be chosen as an object from which particles will be emitted. To create realistic-looking flames, an animated noise texture will be used to control the emission rate to keep the particles from being emitted uniformly across the surface. Finally, the effect will be rendered using the hardware renderer.

Set Up the Surface   Before we begin experimenting with texture emissions, make sure that the emission surface has been properly configured.

1. Create a NURBS plane. Scale the plane up to 5 units in X, Y, and Z.

2. Select the surface, and choose Particles | Emit From Object, keeping the default settings.

3. In the Attribute Editor, set the Emitter Type attribute to Surface. Set the Rate attribute to **500**.

4. Select the particleShape1 node and set the Lifespan Mode to Random Range, with a Lifespan value of **1** and a Lifespan Random value of **0.5**.

5. In the Range Slider, set the range of frames from 1 to 300. Click Play to see the particles emitting from the surface.

Add Fields to Control Particles   As soon as the particles are emitted from the surface, we want to be able to control their behavior with fields. We will use two fields—the Gravity and Turbulence fields.

1. Since we will be strictly using fields to control the particle behavior, we can turn the emitter's speed all the way down. With the emitter selected, find the Speed attribute in the Attribute Editor and set it to **0**.

2. Select the particle group and add a Gravity field by choosing Fields | Gravity. But wait—the Gravity field, with its default settings, will pull the particles downward, but we want them to rise into the air. To fix this, select the Gravity field and change its Direction Y attribute from −1 to **1**. The particles should now flow in the correct direction. Change the Magnitude attribute to **20** so that they move faster.

TIP   Remember that you should have your Playback Speed set to Play Every Frame in the Preferences window. However, depending on your computer's processing and display power, you will not be seeing real-time performance in the view windows. It is therefore recommended that you use Playblast (Window | Playblast) to render a few seconds of the animation so that you can get an idea of how fast the particles are moving.

3. Now we'll add a Turbulence field to give the particles some random motion as they rise upward. Again, make sure the particle group is selected and choose Fields | Turbulence. In the Attribute Editor, set the Magnitude to **20** and the Frequency to **5**.

Control the Emission Rate with a Texture

Now let's set up the emitter so that it uses a Noise texture to control the emission rate. We can then animate the Noise texture's Time attribute so that the emissions are always changing over the surface.

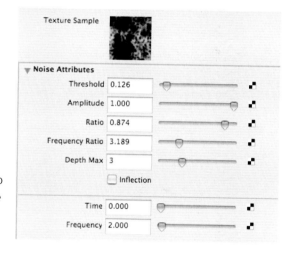

1. In the Hypershade, choose Create | 2D Texture | Noise to create a procedural-based Noise texture.

2. Use the Attribute Editor, shown here, to change the Frequency to 2.000. Set the Threshold at around 1.25. Animate the Time attribute by keying it to a value of **0** at frame 1 and **5** at frame 300. Now the pattern in the texture map will change over time.

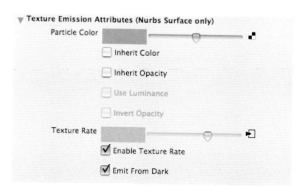

3. Select the emitter and scroll down near the bottom of the Attribute Editor to find the Texture Emission Attributes folder, shown in the illustration. Inside, you'll see an attribute called Texture Rate. Any easy way to connect the Noise texture to this attribute is to MMB-drag it from the Hypershade and drop it onto this attribute in the Attribute Editor.

4. If you were to play back the animation now, you would see no difference in the behavior of the particles' emission rates. To make our example work, we need to do two things. First, the Enable Texture Rate check box must be enabled here. Next, we must enable the Need Parent UVs option, which allows Maya to get the values from the texture and find what UV coordinate a specific value is at. Scroll back up to the top of the emitter's Attribute Editor and find the Need Parent UVs check box and enable it. Now play back the animation to view the result.

Rendering the Particles   Finally, we can set up some of the particles' rendering attributes to give them a fire-like appearance. We will use MultiStreak particles and edit their color and opacity until the scene looks similar to fire. Then we'll use the Maya hardware renderer to render the animation.

> *NOTE To perfect the look of the fire, you should import it into a compositing program and fine-tune the animation to get the precise appearance.*

1. Select the particleShape1 node and look in the Attribute Editor. Set the Particle Render Type attribute to MultiStreak.

2. Just below that, click the Current Render Type button to add dynamic attributes for the MultiStreak type.

3. Set the render attributes to match the values shown in the illustration.

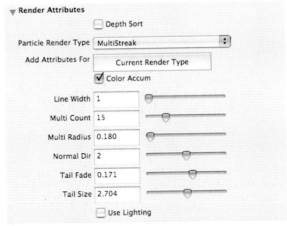

4. In the Per Particle (Array) Attributes folder, add Per Particle attributes for color and opacity by clicking the Color And Opacity button below the list of current Per Particle Attributes. When the Add Attribute window opens, enable the Add Per Particle Attribute check box (shown) and click the Add Attribute button. Attributes named rgbPP and opacityPP will now be available in the list of Per Particle Attributes.

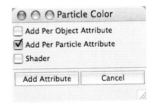

5. Right-click in the pink field next to rgbPP and choose Create Ramp from the marking menu. The field will now say *<- arrayMapper1.outColorPP*. Right-click again in this field and choose Edit Ramp. This will load the attribute for our color ramp.

6. In the Attribute Editor, change the ramp colors to cycle from yellow to a deep orange to red.

7. Create a ramp for the opacityPP attribute and edit the ramp so that it goes from transparent (black) to semitransparent (gray) and back to transparent (black).

8. Select the emitter and increase the Rate attribute to **2500**. The idea is that we are trying to create enough particle streaks to make them dense enough so that the individual clusters don't stand out. You can adjust the Rate attribute here and the Multi Count and Multi Radius attributes on the particle shape node. If you can achieve the correct balance, any visible streaking can be fixed with motion blur in the renderer or by blurring and layering it in post-production.

9. Open the Render Global Settings window (Window | Rendering Editors | Render Globals). Choose Maya Hardware from the Render Using pull-down menu. Select the Maya Hardware tab and set the Quality to Production Quality.

10. Check the box next to Enable Motion Blur and set Motion Blur By Frame to **3**. Set the number of Exposures to **16**. This means that the renderer will take 16 renders of each frame. When using the MultiStreak and Multipoint rendering types, the renderer will randomize the positions of each streak in one cluster each time it renders that frame and then composite them. This will soften the streaks. Then the renderer blurs the composite with the renders from the previous three frames. The end result is the fire shown in Figure 18-6. While some of the streaking is still visible, it can be easily corrected in Photoshop or After Effects.

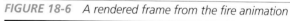

FIGURE 18-6   A rendered frame from the fire animation

11. After doing a few test renders, select the Common tab in the Render Global Settings window, name the file, choose the name.#.ext option from the Frame/Animation Ext pull-down menu, and then set the End Frame attribute to **300**.

12. Choose Render | Batch Render to render the entire animation. Since the hardware renderer is actually rendering each frame 16 times, this will take a long time to complete.

Particle Expressions

Particle expressions use MEL to control particle behavior and create relationships between particle and object attributes over time. Expressions typically yield the greatest amount of control of the behavior of particles on a per particle basis. With particle expressions, mathematical functions can be assigned to any per particle attribute and will dynamically drive that channel. Dependencies between existing attributes can be defined and custom attributes created. In this section, you will learn how to create some simple expressions through some of the most commonly used functions.

Data Types and Syntax

Several types of attributes are used in Maya: vector, integer, float, Boolean, and enum. When dealing with particle expressions, the most common types are vectors and floats. A *float* is known as a *real number* in mathematics. It can be any number, positive or negative, and may include a decimal. A translate Y attribute is an example of an attribute that uses floats. It contains a single value that may be a decimal number. A *vector*, on the other hand, is an array of three floats. Color attributes are vectors in which the value is given for red, green, and blue. The colorPP attribute could be assigned a vector for green, which would be written in MEL as <<0,1,0>> (color channel values are specified in a range from 0 to 1, not 0 to 255, as in some programs). Position is another example of a vector in which the value describes a position in X, Y, and Z.

When writing any kind of MEL script, it is important that you use the correct syntax. To define or assign a value to an attribute, the object must be defined first, and then the attribute appears, and the two are separated by a dot (.). For example, if we needed to set the value for the lifespanPP attribute to 1, it would be written like this:

```
particleShape1.lifespanPP = 1;
```

> NOTE *When using expressions to control the lifespanPP attribute, the Lifespan mode attribute must be set to lifespanPP in the particle shape's Attribute Editor only. Otherwise, your particles will continue to get their lifespan values from the Lifespan mode setting.*

Another important piece of syntax is the semicolon (;) used to mark the end of a statement. When writing expressions (as opposed to writing a regular MEL script), a statement must assign a value to one or more attributes. It can be helpful in reading and editing existing expressions if a carriage return is used to separate values. As long as the statement has not been closed by a semicolon, the expression can continue to be read. For example, instead of assigning a vector like this

```
particleShape1.velocityPP = <<1,.5,2>>;
```

it could be written like this

```
particleShape1.velocityPP = <<
1,
.5,
2
>>;
```

Creating Particle Expressions

The Expression Editor is used to write and create expressions. One way to create an expression for a per particle attribute would be to right-click in one of the per particle attribute fields in the Attribute Editor and choose either Creation Expression or Runtime Expression. A creation expression is executed only one time during a particle's life—at its birth. A runtime expression executes on every frame. Particle attributes driven by runtime expressions are capable of changing at any frame, as defined by the expressions. Because this is happening on every frame, runtime expressions can cause the scene to run very slowly.

When the Expression Editor is opened by right-clicking one of the attribute fields, the object name and selected attribute appear in their respective fields. The expression can be typed into the Expression text field at the bottom of the window and created by clicking the Create button. Because all names are case-sensitive, syntax errors can be avoided by copying and pasting the name of objects and attributes from the Selected Obj & Attr field into the Expression field and then completing the expression by assigning a value. Assigning a creation expression to a particle group that controls lifespan and velocity would look like Figure 18-7 in the Expression Editor.

Functions

A *function* in Maya is a built-in operation that can be used to generate values that control object or particle attributes. Many different types of functions can be used. We are going to look at only some mathematical functions such as `sin` (sine) and `cosin` (cosine) and random number functions such as the `rand` function. A list of all available functions is available in the Insert Functions menu in the Expression Editor. When a function is chosen from this menu, it is inserted at the cursor in the Expression field at the bottom of the Editor window.

FIGURE 18-7 *Assigning a creation expression to a particle group that controls lifespan and velocity in the Expression Editor*

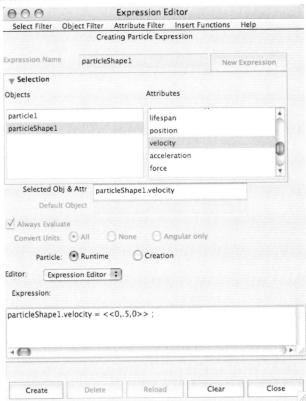

We will use the rand function to control the lifespanPP attribute as an example. The following expression would generate a random value between 0 and 5 and assign it to the lifespanPP attribute of a particle group:

```
particleShape1.lifespanPP = rand(5);
```

The number inside the parentheses is called the *argument*. We could add another value to this function:

```
particleShape1.lifespanPP = rand(3,5);
```

This expression would generate a float value between 3 and 5 and assign it to the lifespanPP of the particleShape1 object. It is even possible to insert functions into vectors. If we add an rgbPP attribute to the particle group, we can use the rand function in one or all of the vector values.

This example uses the `rand` function to determine the value of the green channel between 0.4 and 1:

```
particleShape1.rgbPP = <<.8,rand(.4,1),.5>>;
```

If this expression is created as a runtime expression, the function will be generated and assigned for each particle at every frame.

`linstep` is another commonly used function in Maya. `linstep` (and the closely related `smoothstep`) provide functionality that is similar to that of the Ramp texture. This function returns a value between 0 and 1 that is linearly proportional to a specified range. To use `linstep` you must specify a minimum value, a maximum value, and a parameter that is used to generate the proportional number.

Take, for example, controlling the opacity of a particle group. Once the opacity attribute has been added to the particle group as a dynamic attribute, an expression can be used to control its opacity over time. The following could be used:

```
particleShape1.opacity = linstep (0,10,age);
```

At the first frame, the opacity will have a value of 0 (transparent), and at 10 seconds, it will have a value of 1 (opaque). Because this is a linear function, the opacity value at 5 seconds would be 0.5, and at 2 seconds, 0.2. Here, `age` is a *predefined variable* (explained in the next section), acting as the parameter used to generate the opacity value.

Variables

Variables are containers that store information while a script is executing. Variables can be constant or changing. Two kinds of variables are used in Maya: predefined and custom. We have already seen some examples of using a predefined variable—`age`, `time`, and `frame` are all examples of predefined variables. If an expression assigns the frame variable to a particle's Y velocity as a runtime expression, the particle's velocity attribute will be assigned whatever the frame number is for that frame. If it is at frame 1, the Y velocity will equal 1; at frame 2, the Y velocity will be 2; and so forth.

Custom variables let you declare a value based on what you define and store it. Custom variables must always start with a dollar sign ($). You must first define the variable before using it in your expression.

Suppose we wanted to control the color of a particle based on its speed. Unfortunately, no attribute is available for speed, so we will need to declare it by basing its value on the magnitude of its velocity. First, we must understand that speed is a *float* value, a magnitude of how fast we are going. Velocity is a *vector*. It not only tells us how fast we are going, but it also tells us what direction. A velocity of <<0,2,1>> tells us that this object is moving 2 units per second in Y and 1 unit per second in Z. The mag function will return a floating-point number from a vector based on a mathematical formula. Therefore, we can use the mag function to define our custom variable. We can then use this variable as a value within any expression. It might look something like this:

```
float $speed = mag(particleShape1.velocity);
particleShape1.rgbPP = <<.2,$speed,.5>>;
```

Custom Attributes

Just as custom attributes can be added to any node in Maya, custom per particle attributes can be added to a particle node. You can create a custom attribute and define it with an expression. This new attribute can then be accessed by any other expression on any other object in the scene. Take our speed exercise from earlier. If the speed was necessary to calculate a number of attribute values, you would have to define it each time it was used. Therefore, it might be faster to create a custom attribute called *speed* and define that variable using the preceding expression.

To add a per particle attribute to a particle shape, click the General button in the Add Dynamic Attributes section of the Attribute Editor. This will open the Add Attribute window. With the New tab selected, name the new attribute **speed**. Make sure the Data Type is set to Float and set the Attribute Type to Per Particle. Click the OK button, and the speed attribute is created and appears in the list of Per Particle (Array) Attributes. That attribute can now be defined by creating a runtime expression and typing this:

```
particleShape1.speed = mag(particleShape1.velocity);
```

Once it has been defined, a variable is no longer needed in any expression when referring to the speed of particle shape 1.

Particle Goals

Another method for controlling the motion of particles is through the use of *goals*. Using this method, a particle's position or motion can be influenced by any object. By assigning goals to a particle group, the individual particle will be attracted to an object's vertices, pivots, or the UV coordinates of a NURBS surface. This can be useful for creating all types of effects. For example, beads of mud or water can be made to run along the surface of an object. By adding fields and controlling the goal weights of the particles, effects such as dust being blown off the surface of an object can be achieved.

Using a Surface as a Goal

To use an object as a goal for a particle, first create an emitter with the default settings and then create a surface. Select the particle group, and then select the surface and choose Particles | Goal (make sure the tool is set to its default settings). Play back the animation, and as the particles are emitted from their emitter, they are attracted to the vertices on the surface. The first particle emitted will be attracted to the first point, or CV, of the surface. The second particle will be attracted to the second point, and so on. When the emitter has emitted more particles than there are vertices on the surface, it will return to the first point.

In the example shown in Figure 18-8, a NURBS sphere is used as the particle goal for a particle group. When the animation is played back, the particles are attracted to the CVs of the sphere. Notice that an oscillation occurs as the particles are emitted. They overshoot their target and return before they settle at the CVs, instead of locking onto them by default. This is related to the Goal Weight attribute. The Goal command sets the Goal Weight attribute for the particles attracting to the nurbsSphereShape1 to 0.5 by default (as shown in Figure 18-8).

FIGURE 18-8 *Particles are attracted to a sphere with a goal weight of 0.5.*

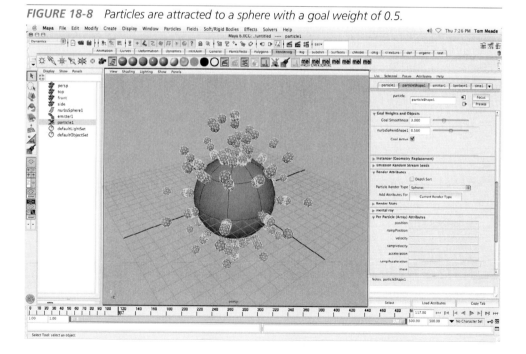

For every object added as a particle goal, a Goal Weight and a Goal Active attribute are added to the particle group (as shown in the illustration). A particle with a Goal Weight of 1 will be completely attracted to its target. No oscillation of the particles will occur as they settle. A particle with a Goal Weight of 0 will not be attracted to the object at all, and the particles will emit and disperse into the world.

Additional objects may be added to the list of goals to which the particles can be attracted. The goal weights can then be animated between the objects. If a particle group had two target goals, for example, each with a Goal Weight of 0.5, the particles would converge midway between the two targets. By animating these goal weights, the particles could transition from one object to another.

goalU, goalV, and goalPP

While using the vertices of objects as particle goals can be useful, far more interesting is when the goalU and goalV attributes are added to the particle group as dynamic attributes. When this is done, particles can be attracted to any point on a NURBS surface and therefore can cover an entire object or move along it. By adding the goalPP attribute, the goal weight of individual particles can also be controlled. In this section, we will demonstrate how these attributes can be used by stepping through a small project, in which beads of goo will emit from a NURBS surface and run down it. When the goo beads reach the base of the object, we will use an expression to set its Goal Weight to 0 so that the particles will fall off the surface and be taken over by dynamic forces. Any surface can be used, or you can open the goohead.mb file available on the CD.

1. Open the goohead.mb file. Create an emitter with the default settings.

2. Select the particle object and the head surface, and choose Particles | Goal. The particles will now be attracted to the surface.

3. Change the Goal Weight attribute on the particle shape node to a value of **1**. This will cause the particles immediately to lock onto the vertices of the surface without any oscillations.

4. Change the particle Render Type attribute to Blobby Surface, and add attributes for that render type. Set the Radius to **0.2** and the Threshold to **1**. When rendered, these particles will "melt" together to form a blob. Set the particle's Lifespan Mode to Random Range with a Lifespan of **5** with a Lifespan Random of **1**.

   If you were to play the animation now, the particles would be attracted to the CVs of the NURBS head. But we want them to be able to be attracted to any point on this surface. To do this, we will add the dynamic attributes for goalU and goalV.

5. In the particle shape node's Attribute Editor, scroll down and find Add Dynamic Attributes. Click the General button and the Add Attribute window will open.

6. In the Add Attribute window, select the Particle tab. SHIFT-select the goalU and goalV attributes (as shown in the illustration) from the list and click Add. These two new attributes will be added to the list of Per Particle Attributes in the particle shape node's Attribute Editor.

When the animation is played back, the particles are immediately attract to the surface origin, at parameter 0,0.

> *TIP   When dealing with goals, it is important that you know how your surface is parameterized, where the origin is, and which direction the surface is going. When using expressions to control any of these attributes, it can be helpful to use a parameterization value of 0 to 1. This way, you don't have to worry about finding the specific number of spans in a surface to get the placement or control you need. By knowing where the surface begins and which way it flows, you can easily predict what values should be used to control the direction that the particles will move across the surface.*

For this next part, we will use a creation expression to define an initial position along V. This will attract the particles to random parameters along the surface's V direction. A ramp will be used to control the goalU attributes. The color at the base of the ramp will determine the U parameter value where the particles are initially attracted. As the lifespan of the particles increase, their goalU value is determined along the ramp until the color at the top determines their final position in U at the end of their lifespan.

1. Right-click in the goalV field in the particle shape node's Per Particle Attributes folder. Choose Creation Expression from the marking menu. This will open the Expression Editor.

2. In the Expression field, type the following expression and then click the Create button:

```
particleShape1.goalV=rand(0,1);
```

3. Right-click in the goalU field in the particle shape node's Per Particle Attributes folder. Choose Create Ramp from the marking menu. Then right-click the array mapper in that field and choose Edit Ramp. The Ramp Editor appears in the Attribute Editor.

4. By default, the ramp uses white, a value of 1, at its base. With these default settings, the particles would initially be attracted to the base of the surface and flow upward. The quickest way to fix this would be to drag the positions of the colors on the ramp to reverse them. Also, the white color should be placed about a quarter of the way down, so that the particles have a goalU value of about one and three-quarters the way through their lifespan. The ramp's attributes should look like the illustration.

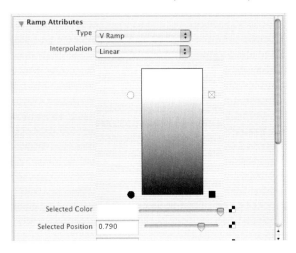

At this point, the particles are attracted randomly to a goal in V and begin flowing from a U value of 0 (black, at birth) to 1 (white, three-quarter lifespan). When they reach the bottom, however, we want them to lose their goal weight and fall with gravity. To do this, we'll need to add a goalPP attribute. We will then use a simple runtime expression to control this attribute so that whenever a particle has a goalU value of 1, it will have a goal weight of 0 and fall off the surface. Any fields that are connected to it would then take over the motion of the particles.

5. In the particle shape node's Attribute Editor, scroll down and find the Add Dynamic Attributes area. Click the General button and the Add Attribute window will open. In the Add Attribute window, find the goalPP attribute from the list on the Particle tab.

6. Right-click in the goalV field in the particle shape node's Per Particle Attributes folder. Choose Runtime Expression from the marking menu to open the Expression Editor.

7. In the Expression Editor, type the following and then press the Create button:

```
if (particleShape1.goalU == 1)
particleShape1.goalPP=0;
```

The particles will no longer be attracted to the surface when they reach the bottom and will continue with their velocity. At this point, you could fine-tune the animation so that a Gravity field will take over the animation once the goalPP reaches 0. Also, a radiusPP attribute could be added and controlled so that the particles would be small and grow as they continue along the surface. When rendered, the result should look similar to Figure 18-9. Make sure you look at the gooHead_final.mov file on the CD for the completed animation.

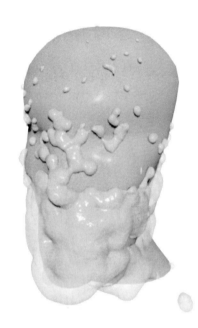

FIGURE 18-9   The goo runs down along the surface and falls off at the bottom.

Crowd Simulation Using Particle Goals

The visual effects and games industries always need to be able to produce a mass of animated characters quickly—be it soldiers, birds, bees, bugs, rats, or even orcs. These masses of animated characters are often referred to as *crowd simulations*. While some companies spend millions of dollars developing crowd simulators where each agent, or individual character, is almost capable of "thinking" or responding to its environment, you can actually set up a simple crowd simulation in Maya using particle goals.

The setup for a crowd simulation is not much different from the goo head exercise. Once the ground plane is set up to act as a goal object, the Instancer (see Chapter 17) can be used to replace the particles with a character that has a walk cycle animation. You'll find a Maya file called marchingSoldier.ma on the CD. When this character is used as the instance object, you will get an army of marching soldiers walking across the ground. While it might not stand up to a close-up camera angle, the army would work fine as a background element in almost any scene. Figure 18-10 shows a marching army of soldiers.

FIGURE 18-10   Particle goals and the Instancer are used to set up this crowd simulation of marching soldiers.

Effects

Maya includes a small library of built-in effects that are accessible from the Effects menu in the Dynamics menu set. Most of these effects have been programmed using complex expressions and custom attributes on particle systems to enable the user to control specific types of effects and particle behavior. This can be a time-saver for the user who needs to use some of the more common effects but who does not have the time or knowledge of expressions to set this up.

Fire

The Fire effect adds a particle group, fields, ramps, expressions, and textures to the scene when it is created. It uses the cloud rendering type; therefore you must use the software renderer to render the image. By default, fire is set to emit from a surface, so a surface needs to be selected as well. This setting can be changed by opening the command's options and editing the Emitter Type before creating the fire. All of the attributes to control the look of the fire can be edited in the Extra Attributes folder of the particle shape node's Attribute Editor.

Smoke

The Smoke effect uses a sequence of animated particle sprites to give the effect of smoke. Sprites are image planes that always face the camera. Textures are applied to these image planes and can be cycled through during the animation. Maya includes a 50-frame smoke sequence in the Gifts directory in the same directory as the Maya application. When you create smoke, you first need to go into the Smoke Options window (Effects | Smoke ❑) and specify the path to the image sequence in the Sprite Image Name. You can use your own sequence of images here as well. After you've set up the path, an object must be chosen as an emitter. The rest of the smoke's attributes can be edited in the particle shape node's Extra Attributes section. This type of rendering requires the Maya hardware renderer.

Fireworks

The Fireworks effect uses several custom attributes to control particles emitting from other particles to simulate a rocket, a rocket trail, and the fireworks explosion. Fireworks create their own emitters and three different particle groups for the rocket, the burst, and the trail. Because fireworks use the points and streak rendering types, they must be rendered with the Maya hard-ware renderer.

Lightning

The Lightning effect creates a lightning bolt between any two transform nodes. It uses a series of expression-driven joints to deform a soft body curve used as the input to the path of an extruded surface. To create lightning, you must first select two objects. Once the lightning has been created, all of the attributes used to control the behavior and color can be edited in the lightning group node's Extra Attributes folder. To get the full effect of the glow, the lightning must be rendered in the software renderer.

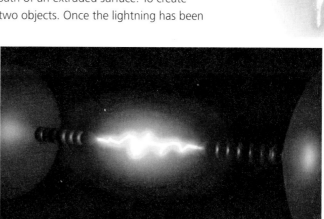

Shatter

Shatter will duplicate and break up any type of geometry into polygonal pieces called *shards*. These shards can be set up to any thickness or be completely solid. This effect provides a quick way to break up an object into many pieces with a random, jagged edge. The illustration shows a shattered sphere set to solid shatter after the pieces have been affected by gravity.

Curve/Surface Flow

Curve/Surface Flow will create an emitter and use a picked curve or surface as a path along which the particles flow. By default, the Curve Flow command will place six locators along the curve. The desired number of locators must be set in the command's Options window before the curve flow is created. By scaling the circle at each locator, the Goal Offset value at that point is increased and the particle flow widens or narrows. The position of the locators can be edited by selecting the parent Flow group and editing its locator position attributes. The particle's Lifespan, Goal Weight, and the emitter's Emission Rate are controlled under this group as well.

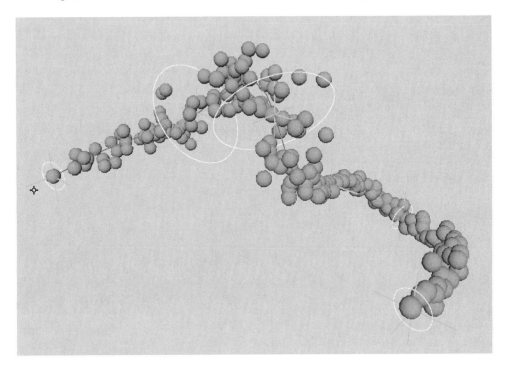

Summary

At this point, you should have an idea of how to create particles and control them using fields, goals, and some simple expressions. If fiddling with several dozen attributes to achieve a stock effect such as fire or lightning does not appeal to you, you can use the preset effects found in the Effects menu. Either way, you'll agree that Maya's Dynamics toolset offers a high degree of flexibility.

One aspect not covered is how to apply these kinds of dynamic controls directly to geometry. In the next chapter, we discuss rigid and soft bodies, or the application of dynamic forces to control geometry.

Rigid and Soft Body Dynamics

As you saw in the previous

two chapters, Maya's dynamics engine

can greatly improve productivity by

speeding up the animation process and

creating more accurate motion. While

we so far have used particles affected

by dynamic forces, we will now turn to

using actual modeled geometry in a scene.

Rigid Body Basics

A *rigid body* is a NURBS or polygonal surface that can react to the dynamic forces of fields and collisions. Thus, any object or group can be turned into a rigid body, can react to a field such as air or gravity, and can collide with other rigid body objects. In this section, you will learn how to create rigid bodies for dynamic simulations. Some of the basic attributes of a rigid body node will be explained through examples. Finally, you'll put this knowledge to use by setting up a simple bowling simulation. Most of the examples shown in the illustrations and figures have accompanying animated movies on the CD included with this book. Make sure that you view these movies as you follow along.

Active/Passive Rigid Bodies

Two types of rigid bodies are used in Maya: *active* and *passive*. An active rigid body can be animated with fields and collisions. A passive rigid body can have active rigid bodies collide with it but will not react or be animated with fields. To demonstrate, let's work with a polygonal box and a plane, with the box located several units above the plane, as shown in Figure 19-1.

Let's see what happens when we turn both of the objects into active rigid bodies. Select the objects in the view window and choose Soft/Rigid Bodies | Create Active Rigid Body from the main menu. Select the box and choose Fields | Gravity. The right image of Figure 19-1 shows the results when the animation is played back. The box falls down as it reacts with gravity, colliding with the plane. The plane will then react to that collision and continue in the direction in which the box pushed it.

FIGURE 19-1   *When the box is dropped onto a plane, the plane falls with the box.*

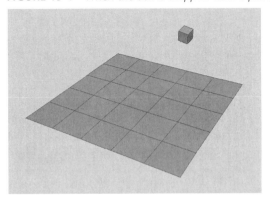 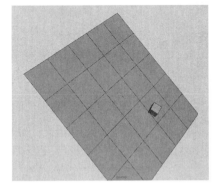

NOTE   *Make sure that the Playback Speed attribute in the Timeline Preferences window (Window | Settings/Preferences | Preferences) is set to Play Every Frame. This will ensure that the simulation runs accurately. (See Chapter 17 for an explanation.)*

While we still want to have the box collide with the plane as it falls, let's make the plane remain stationary. To accommodate this, the plane needs to be turned into a *passive* rigid body so that it will not move when the box collides with it. Delete the rigidBody node by selecting the plane and choosing Edit | Delete By Type | Rigid Bodies. Then choose Soft/Rigid Bodies | Create Passive Rigid Body to turn the plane into a passive rigid body.

> *NOTE   Active and passive rigid bodies create identical connections to an object when they are created. The rigidBody node that is created is the same regardless of what type—active or passive—you selected from the Soft/Rigid Bodies menu. However, in the Channel Box, the Active attribute for the rigidBody node is set to on for active rigid bodies and off for passive rigid bodies. Instead of deleting the rigid body and creating a new one, as mentioned, it is quicker to select the rigidBody node and change this attribute from on to off in the Channel Box. This attribute can also be keyed so that, for example, a passive rigid body's transformations can be manually keyframed, and then at some point this value could be set to on, at which point the dynamic forces connected to it would take over.*

Now that you've changed the plane to a passive rigid body, when the animation plays back and the box falls and collides with the plane, the plane does not move with the box. Instead, the plane remains static and the box bounces up and down until it settles, as shown in Figure 19-2. The way that it bounces and settles, as well as many other of its properties, can be controlled by editing the rigidBody node's attributes.

FIGURE 19-2   The box bounces off the floor while the floor remains stationary due to the object's active settings.

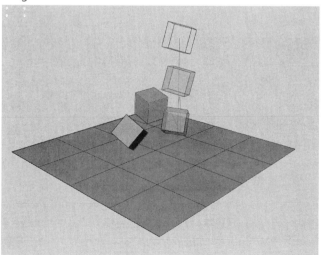

Rigid Body Attributes

A rigidBody node's default list of keyable attributes in the Attribute Editor is long and can be a bit intimidating. But most of the attributes in the list are pretty straightforward and are easy to understand with a little experimentation. We'll define most of these attributes in this section and show examples when necessary. In the next section, we'll use most of these attributes to control the behaviors of a bowling ball and pins.

Initial Velocity and Initial Spin

These attributes provide a velocity for the translations and rotations at the first frame of the simulation. The values for these attributes are numbers in Maya units, or degrees, that the object will move during 1 second. Assigning our box an initial velocity in X will make it move in the X direction. After the first frame of the animation, any dynamic fields will take over and control the remainder of the simulation. The box, in this case, will not continue to accelerate on its X axis.

Center of Mass

The Center of Mass attribute controls an object's center of gravity. By default, the center of mass is at the center of the rigid body object's bounding box. This simulates where the heaviest spot on the object is located, so that any forces or interactions will occur around this point.

For example, imagine two rigid body cylinders that are being affected by gravity and are colliding with a plane. One cylinder has its Center of Mass attribute set at the default and the other has its Center of Mass in Y attribute placed at the base of the cylinder object. Also, both cylinders have some initial spin in X. The first thing you will notice when you click the Play button is that the cylinder objects spin around their centers of mass as they fall. After they collide with the plane, bounce, and begin to settle, they will behave quite differently. While the cylinder with the default Center of Mass settles down to lie on its side, the cylinder with the Center of Mass at the base will eventually settle on its base.

Impulse, Impulse Position, and Spin Impulse

These attributes apply a constant acceleration to the rigid body for every frame in which they are active. For this reason, these values are usually keyframed to a value for a short period and then keyframed to 0. If the values were left constant or not keyframed to be 0, the object would continue to accelerate at the set value for every frame in the entire animation, which is usually not the desired effect. In fact, in most cases, it is suggested that you try to use fields to introduce motion to an object during the animation instead of using impulses.

Mass

This attribute sets the weight, or mass, of an object. It is particularly important to define the mass among all objects that collide so that they produce realistic results. For example, a little baseball won't knock over a stack of heavy crates when it rolls into and collides with them. Instead, the crates might not even budge, and the ball's motion would be stopped. On the other hand, if the ball were made out of lead and the crates were empty, the ball could roll straight into the crates, knock them out of the way, and not even be slowed down much. This relationship between objects is defined by the Mass attribute.

Bounciness

This attribute controls the resilience of the object. Use a value between 0 (not bouncy) and 1 (very bouncy) for realistic effects. A value greater than 1 will invoke bounces into rigid bodies without any initial activity to begin with. In other words, an object at rest on a plane could begin bouncing when this value is set higher than 1.

Static and Dynamic Friction

The Static Friction attribute controls the amount of friction, or "stickiness," applied to an object at rest. The Dynamic Friction attribute controls the amount of stickiness applied to a moving object. Since these two attributes are usually set to the same values, it is recommended that you set them both at the same time to avoid possible confusion later.

Collision Layer

Collision layers group the collisions between objects as a way to improve performance during simulations. The Collision Layer attribute assigns the rigid body object to the specified layer. In other words, if two groups of objects are reacting to separate collisions in a scene and will not be interacting at all, collision layers might greatly speed up the playback of the animation.

By default, when all of the collisions reside on the same layer, Maya must check for collisions among all of the objects multiple times per frame. This might be fine if only a few objects are included in a scene, but when several objects appear, it might be optimal to set the objects on different collision layers. For example, suppose a scene has two sets of boxes—one on either side of the scene—and two separate balls each collide with one of the sets. The best way to set up such a scene would be to set the Collision Layer attribute to 1 for the ball that collides with set 1, and assign the second ball and box set a Collision Layer value of 2. Now, even if one of those balls were to roll over to the opposite set of boxes, it would not collide with them. However, if you still need both of the groups to collide with the floor, you can set the floor's Collision Layer attribute to –1, which will cause it to collide with all objects.

Stand In

The Stand In attribute specifies what type of geometric primitive, cube or sphere, will be used in place of the actual piece of geometry. Using the Stand In attribute can be a tremendous performance booster, especially when you're working with complex geometry. We will talk more about how Maya tessellates the geometry in the next section, but for now, realize that every face of an object must be evaluated when calculating a collision. By using a stand-in object, the simulation uses only a small number of faces that define the primitive object's shape. In the case of a sphere, however, the accuracy of the simulation will actually be improved by the use of a stand-in object, because it will be infinitely smooth instead of possibly being affected by each face being calculated one at a time.

Tips for Setting Up a Rigid Body Simulation

When using rigid body dynamics, much could go wrong that would produce unwanted results or errors that could affect the performance or accuracy of the simulation. This is especially true for an animation dealing with collisions. Following is a short list of items to check on or set up prior to running the simulation.

Make sure surface normals are facing in the correct direction.   Collisions occur only between normals that are facing each other. You will get unpredictable results and even interpenetration errors if the geometry has not been set up correctly.

Set proper tessellation or use stand-in objects.   Because Maya uses polygonal facets to calculate collisions, it is important that you make sure that the correct tessellation occurs while using NURBS geometry. While rigid body tessellation attributes are available, it is recommended that you use polygonal geometry when performing rigid body simulations. This gives you precise control over the position of the faces, and you can build more efficient geometry for better performance. Primitive stand-in objects can be chosen from the rigid body attributes or higher resolution geometry, including NURBS, can be constrained to the rigid bodies during simulation and used at render time.

Play every frame.   In the animation preferences, make sure that the Playback Speed is set to Play Every Frame. When running a dynamic simulation, the positions and orientations of any dynamic object are calculated based on the position and orientation values from the previous frame. It is therefore very important that each frame be calculated; otherwise, the resulting simulation that is output at render time may be very different from the simulation previewed in the view windows. Use the hardware render buffer or Playblast to test the animations in real time.

 Create a run-up.   Objects that sit on top of one another or touch at the beginning of an animation should be allowed to settle before the first actual needed frame of the animation. In other words, if the rigid body objects in a scene need to be still at frame 1, you may need to start the simulation 20 frames before that. This concept is known as a *run-up*. If, for example, you had a stack of rigid body boxes with gravity pulling them down, the boxes should be set up so that they are not touching at the first frame. Leave extra frames at the beginning of the animation so that the boxes have time to settle. Alternatively, you can set up the scene, play the animation until the objects settle, and then choose Solvers | Initial State | Set For Selected. When the animation is reset to the first frame, the objects will remain in this settled position.

Use the rigid solver to fine-tune rigid body simulations.   Once a rigid body is created in a scene, a rigid solver is also created. This provides a global method of controlling certain attributes related to the rigid bodies in the scene. (See Figure 19-3 for the rigidSolver node's attributes.) In addition to being able to turn off the calculation states, such as collisions, friction, bounciness, and other states, you can also specify the number of times that Maya checks for collisions per frame. In many cases, an object might be moving so fast that the actual collision with another object happens between a frame. By default, Maya checks for collisions about three times per frame, but that may not be often enough for some animations. Decreasing the Step Size attribute in the rigidSolver node will fix this.

Cache data before time scrubbing.
Since dynamics are calculated based on the previous frame, scrubbing through the timeline will produce unpredictable results and even errors. If you need to scrub through the animation, you can use the Cache Data option in the rigidSolver node attributes to cache the data. When turned on, the animation is played through with every frame and cached as it goes. Any of the cached frames can then be scrubbed through. If changes are made to the simulation, however, the cache must be

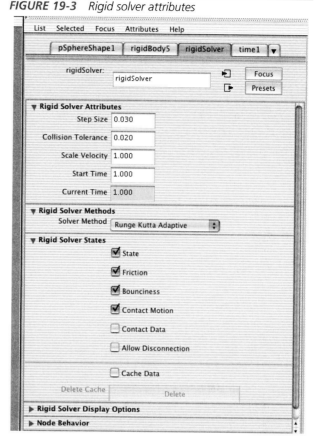

FIGURE 19-3   Rigid solver attributes

deleted before the results can be viewed. This is done by clicking the Delete button under the check box to turn on the cache data in the Attribute Editor.

Tutorial: Create a Bowling Simulation

In this tutorial we will use rigid bodies to set up a simple dynamic simulation of a bowling ball knocking over some pins. The ball and the pins will be active rigid bodies with a Gravity field, and the floor will be a passive rigid body. Throughout the tutorial, we will experiment with changing certain attributes and watching the effect they have on the simulation.

Start with the Bowling_Start.mb scene on the CD. This scene has been set up to include all of the geometry needed for the example. You will notice that each of the pRigidPin objects has a NURBS object constrained to it. The NURBS objects have all been placed in the display layer called *NURBS pins*. The visibility of this layer has been turned off. This setup lets you use these polygonal, low-resolution pins as the rigid bodies and then hide them at render time, giving you precise control over the collisions and saving calculation time since the NURBS objects do not have to be tessellated at runtime.

After we set up the ball and floor to be rigid bodies, we'll add gravity to the ball and the rigid solver's attributes are adjusted so that the motion of the ball looks pretty realistic. Next, we'll turn our attention to the pins, which will also be turned into rigid bodies and connected to the Gravity field in the scene. Their mass and center of gravity will be adjusted until the simulation appears accurate. When finished, the animation on all of the objects is baked and can be rendered. While this is probably one of the simplest simulations we can run, this same basic process can be used to set up any simulation.

1. Open the scene file named Bowling_Start.mb on the CD.

2. Select the floor, and choose Soft/Rigid Bodies | Make Passive Rigid Body. Use the default settings.

3. Select the ball and choose Soft/Rigid Bodies | Make Active Rigid Body.

4. With the ball still selected, add a Gravity field by choosing Fields | Gravity. Set the time range to **500**, and click the Play button to view the animation so far.

*TIP   **You can save a step by selecting the ball and adding the Gravity field directly. The object will automatically be turned into an active rigid body.***

5. Because the default Magnitude attribute of the Gravity field is set to 9.8 meters per second and we are not working to scale, we need to increase the gravity so that it better suits our scene. Select the Gravity field, and in the Channel Box, set the Magnitude to **30**, as shown in the illustration. Use Playblast to render the animation and check the animation in real time.

Channels	Object
gravityField2	
Translate X	0
Translate Y	0
Translate Z	0
Rotate X	0
Rotate Y	0
Rotate Z	0
Scale X	1
Scale Y	1
Scale Z	1
Visibility	on
Magnitude	30
Attenuation	0

6. The bowling ball is bouncing too much. Select the ball and choose its rigidBody1 node in the Channel Box to view all of the node's attributes. Find the attribute called Bounciness and set it to **0.2**.

7. Now set the Initial Velocity X attribute to **40** so that the ball will have some velocity in the X direction at the beginning of the simulation. After the first frame, the ball will be controlled by fields and the rigid body attributes.

8. Now that the ball has an initial velocity, you can move it back in its –X direction so that it rolls across more of the floor.

9. The ball appears to slow down a bit more than it should. This is due mainly to the friction, or the stickiness, setting between the two objects. Since the ball is already

moving when it colides with the floor—that is, it does not need to start from a resting position—we want to edit the Dynamic Friction attribute, not the Static Friction attribute, to change this value. Set the ball's Dynamic Friction attribute to **0.05**. Do another Playblast render to view the animation in real time. See Figure 19-4 to get an idea of the ball's motion path.

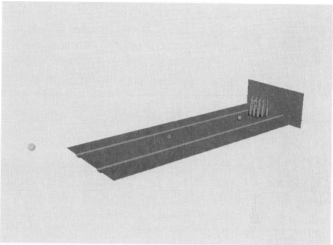

FIGURE 19-4 After editing the ball's rigid body attributes, the ball's motion should be smoother.

10. You might notice that some degree of noise exists in the ball's motion as it rolls on the floor. This is because the ball is made up of flat faces and therefore is not perfectly smooth. We could increase the tessellation of the ball object, but since the ball is a perfect sphere, we can use a sphere as a stand-in object. This can be set in the rigid body's attributes, where you'll see an attribute called Stand In. Use the pull-down menu to select Sphere. After you replace the ball with a sphere, Playblast the animation and notice that the ball's roll is much smoother and therefore more realistic.

11. Select all of the pins. Choose Soft/Rigid Bodies | Make Active Rigid Body. Play back the animation.

12. Notice that as the ball collides with the pins, it slows down and almost stops. This is because each pin has a Mass of 1—the same mass as the ball. We need to decrease the Mass attribute value of the pins so that the ball can cut through them without slowing down much from the collision. Changing the Mass will also make the pins appear to fly out when they are hit by the ball. Select all of the pins, and set their Mass attribute to **0.1**.

13. To make the pins appear more top-heavy, we'll edit the Center of Mass attribute. In wireframe mode, you should be able to see a small *x* near the center of each pin. Select the Center of Mass Y attribute in the Channel Box.

14. MMB-drag in the view window to edit the value interactively. Set the attribute so that it is just higher than the height of the ball. This will cause the pins to spin more when the ball collides. A value of **2.5** should do it. Play back the animation.

15. Select all of the pins, and then select the Gravity field. Choose Fields | Affect Selected Objects. The pins will now fall with gravity after the ball collides with them.

16. To keep the ball and pins from flying off the platform, we will make the plane behind them a passive rigid body. Select the plane and choose Soft/Rigid Bodies | Make Passive Rigid Body.

17. With the plane still selected, change its Damping attribute to **1**. This will absorb the energy from any colliding object and cause it to settle. Figure 19-5 shows the positions of the pins during and after the collisions.

FIGURE 19-5   *The pins during and after the collision*

 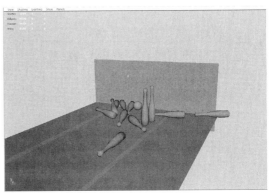

18. When you are happy with the simulation, you can bake the animation data onto the transforms' animation channels as keyframes. Baking a simulation will sample the objects' transforms at specified increments of the simulation and set keyframes on them. Once this is done, the rigid solvers can be deleted and the animation can be played back and scrubbed through. Since Maya no longer has to calculate motion or collisions, the scene will play back much faster. Select all the pins and the ball. Drag-select all the translate and rotate channels in the Channel Box.

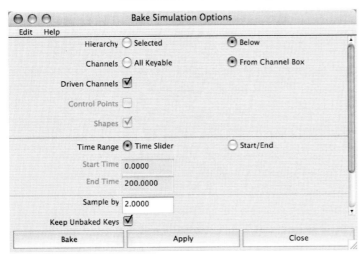

19. Choose Edit | Keys | Bake Animation ❐ to see the tool's settings. Make the settings match those shown in the illustration. Click Bake. The animation will play back and set a key on every other frame.

20. We can now remove all the rigid bodies in the scene by choosing Edit | Delete All By Type | Rigid Bodies. This will erase all of the rigid bodies and thus stop the computer from having to calculate any collisions. Click the Play button in the Time Slider, and you'll notice that the performance is much faster. You can also delete the Gravity field.

21. To render the scene, turn off the visibility of the layer named PolyPins and turn on the visibility of the layer called NurbsPins. Render the animation.

Rigid Body Constraints

So far, we have examined and produced animations in which the objects interacting to collisions and fields are not attached to any other objects. When the bowling ball collides with the pins, the pins fly away until they are stopped by another collision or brought down by gravity. In many situations, you may want an object to be connected to another object that limits the object's motion in some way. This is where rigid body constraints come in handy.

Types of Rigid Body Constraints

Maya offers five different types of rigid body constraints: nail, pin, hinge, spring, and barrier. You create them by selecting any rigid body or two (depending on the type) and choosing Soft/ Rigid Bodies | Create Constraint ❑. You can then select the type of constraint in the Create Constraint Options window or change it in the Attribute Editor or Channel Box after the constraint has been created.

- **Nail** Constrains one rigid body to any point in the scene. The object being constrained is then free to move in all directions, but it remains equidistant from the constraint during the simulation. To limit the motion of an object, a second nail constraint can be added and placed elsewhere. Consider a ball in a pendulum. To construct this in Maya, a sphere should have two nail constraints mounted to different positions in the world, thus constraining their movement in one direction.

- **Pin** Connects two rigid bodies with a ball joint. The chain used in the next example shows how a pin constraint can be used.

- **Hinge** Locks the translation of the rigid body while constraining the rotation to one direction. The mechanisms in a door and a gear are good examples.

- **Spring** Provides an elastic connection between any two rigid bodies or any one rigid body and any point in the scene. The constraint will always try to return to the length set for the Rest Length attribute. The Stiffness and Dampening attributes of this constraint can also be edited.

- **Barrier** Provides a plane with an infinite height and width that will limit any rigid body by not letting it move past.

Simulating a Chain with Rigid Body Constraints

Imagine, for example, that a chain is bolted to a wall. As gravity pulls down the chain, the individual links are each constrained to one another, while the top link is constrained to the wall. To set up such an animation, we need to use two types of constraints—nail and pin constraints. Each link will be constrained to another with a pin constraint, while the top link will be constrained to a point in the scene. Gravity will be applied to the links and the animation played back.

1. To create the chain, create six simple cubes: create one polygonal cube, scale it a bit, make five duplicates of it, and then place the cubes to look something like Figure 19-6.

FIGURE 19-6   *The chain is modeled from duplicated cubes.*

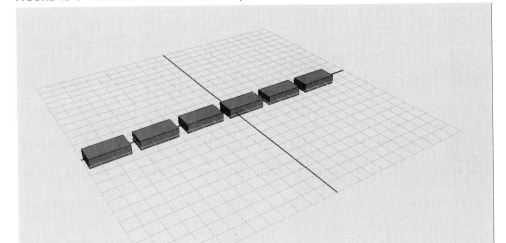

2. Select the first two links and choose Soft/Rigid Bodies | Create Constraint ❏ to open the Options window. Select Pin from the Constraint Type attribute and click the Create button.

3. Select the second and third links and press the G key to repeat the last operation. Continue adding a pin constraint between each of the remaining links.

4. Select the last link and choose Soft/Rigid Bodies | Create Constraint ❏ to open the Options window. Select Nail from the Constraint Type attribute and click the Create button.

5. Use the Move tool to move the constraint out to the end of the link at the end of the chain. By default, the constraint was placed at the link's center of mass when it was created.

6. Select all the links, and then choose Fields | Gravity Field to add gravity to the links.

7. Click the Play button, and the chain will fall with gravity and remained linked together by the pin constraints, while the top link holds them all at the point specified by the nail constraint. The chain "hangs" from the top link. You may wish to select all of the rigid body nodes in the scene and change their Damping to **0.3** and the Bounciness to **0.1** so that the chain settles faster.

Tutorial: Setting Up Rigid Body Interaction with Particles

In this short tutorial, we will practice setting up a water wheel using a hinge constraint. The water wheel will be powered by a flow of particles that collide with and collect on the paddles of the wheel. As the particles collect, they build enough mass to set the wheel into motion as it rotates around its hinge constraint.

1. Open the file called waterwheel.ma on the CD. This file contains a model of a water wheel and a volumetric emitter that emits multipoint particles.

2. Select the particle group, and then SHIFT-select to select all the paddles on the wheel. Choose Particles | Make Collide. Playback the animation and make sure that the particles are colliding with the paddles.

3. Select the particle group again and add a Gravity field to it (choose Fields | Gravity Field). Leave it set at its default Magnitude for now.

4. To fix the bounciness, select the particle group and then select the geoConnector1 node in the Inputs section of the Channel Box. Set the Resilience attribute to **0**. This will turn off the bounciness between the particles and the paddles. Play back the animation to make sure it is working correctly. It should look similar to Figure 19-7.

5. With the particles and collisions pretty much set up, we can convert the paddles to active rigid bodies. Select the paddle objects and choose Soft/Rigid Bodies | Create Active Rigid Body.

FIGURE 19-7 *The particles collide with the paddles, run off, and continue falling with gravity.*

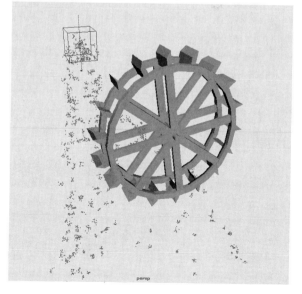

6. When the animation is played back, you'll notice that nothing has changed. Even though the particles are colliding with the geometry, the water wheel is not turning. This is because we need to set the rigid body node, not just the geometry, to react to the collisions. Select the rigidBody node that is connected to the paddle object. In the Channel Box, in the list of attributes for the rigidBody node, you'll see an attribute called Particle Collision. Set this to On.

TIP   You can select rigid body nodes and many other kinds of nodes in the Outliner by choosing Display | Shapes from the Outliner menu. When the object is unfolded, the transform and shape nodes, as well as the rigid body node, are displayed as separate objects.

7. When the animation is played back, the particles collide with the paddles and knock the paddle objects away. While we need the paddles to remain in place on the wheel, we also need them to rotate around the center of the water wheel. A hinge constraint is the answer.

8. Select the paddles and then choose Soft/Rigid Bodies | Create Constraint ❏ to open the Options window. Set the Constraint Type to Hinge and click the Create button. We won't worry about setting the Initial Position in this window, as this is easier to do interactively in the view window.

9. With the hinge constraint still selected, rotate it 90 degrees on its Y axis. When the animation is played back, the paddles now rotate around the hinge constraint as they are powered by the flowing particles.

10. To fine-tune this interaction a bit, increase the Mass attribute on the rigid bodies to **1000**. This is important because each particle in the group has a Dynamic Weight value of 1. If the Mass on the rigid bodies were left at 1, the water wheel would be completely outweighed by the possible thousands of particles that bombard it. Therefore, we need to make the rigid body objects "heavier" by increasing their Mass attribute. Another way to achieve the same result would be to lower the particle group's Dynamic Weight attribute. Select the particle group and change the Dynamic Weight value to **0.5**. Also, set the Conserve attribute of the particles to **0.9** so that they settle on the paddles instead of continuing with their momentum from the emitter.

11. Finally, increase the Magnitude of the gravity until the water is flowing at a speed of 60. You may also want to set the Static Friction attribute on the rigidBody node to **5** so that the wheel starts up slowly before it gets moving.

Figure 19-8 shows the completed water wheel simulation. You can view the rendered QuickTime movie on the CD.

Soft Body Basics

In Maya, a soft body is an object whose vertices—be they CVs, polygonal vertices, or lattice points—are each constrained to a corresponding particle within a single particle group. These particles can be animated through any of the techniques discussed so far: collisions, fields, expressions, goals, and springs (which we are about to cover). The result is an object that can deform based on any of these dynamic animation techniques. An infinite number of effects can be produced this way—cloth, flesh, hair, and water surfaces are the most obvious examples.

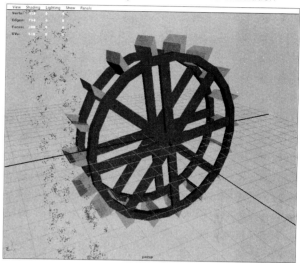

FIGURE 19-8 *The completed water wheel simulation*

Creating Soft Bodies and Soft Body Goals

In this section, we cover the basics of creating a soft body and animating it with a field. We will use a NURBS plane to represent a flag that will be animated by a field to make it appear as if it were being blown in the wind.

Start by creating a plane with 10 spans in U and V. With the surface selected, choose Soft/Rigid Bodies | Create Soft Body ❏ to bring up the Options window.

By default, the Create Soft Body's Creation Options attribute is set to Make Soft. This setting creates a soft body object out of the surface by locking each CV of the surface to a particle. Any field applied to the soft body or any collision that is calculated will cause the surface to react accordingly. While this might be useful to add some irregularities into a surface, it can be difficult to animate because no controls can be used to retain the original shape of the surface. If a Turbulence field is applied, for example, the particles and therefore the surface would continue in their own directions, as derived from the Turbulence field. After a few seconds, the surface might be scattered all over the scene—looking something like Figure 19-9.

FIGURE 19-9 *A Turbulence field is applied to a soft body object that has the default creation options.*

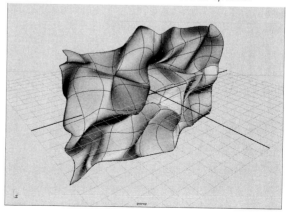

To help you better retain the shape of the original surface, the Create Soft Body command will let you make a duplicate of the surface and use the non-soft surface as a *goal* object. Goal objects behave the same way that the particle goals behave (as covered in Chapter 18). However, each particle's goal is mapped to the corresponding CV on the non-soft surface.

Let's continue with the flag example.

1. Delete the particle group that is attached to the surface, or create a new one to start fresh.

2. Select the surface and choose Soft/Rigid Bodies | Create Soft Body ❑ to open the Options window.

3. Create the soft body by duplicating the original surface and making the copy the soft body. Then set the tool to hide the original, non-soft object and make that original surface the goal object.

4. Make sure that the Turbulence field is affecting the soft body object, and click the Play button to view the animation. Notice that the surface is deforming a bit, but it is still retaining its overall shape. In fact, the deformation may be so subtle that you might be tempted to increase the Magnitude attribute on the Turbulence field. While this will work, you could also edit the Goal Weight attribute of the soft body object.

5. Select the soft body particle group and look at its attributes in the Channel Box. Notice that the attributes are much the same as the default attributes for a particle group created with the Particle tool or an emitter. They are indeed the same nodes, with just a few attributes added to control soft body goals.

6. If you change the Goal Weight [0] from its default value of 0.5 to **0.1** and play back the animation, you will notice that the surface deforms as it is directed by the Turbulence field, but eventually it returns to its original goal position.

Goal weights can also be edited on a per-particle basis by using either the Component Editor or the Paint Goal Weights tool. To set them using the Component Editor, use the pick masks to select individual particles and then choose Windows | General Editors | Component Editor. Scroll all of the way to the right, and you'll see a Goal PP column. Drag-select all of the fields under that attribute so that you can enter a value once and they will all update.

The other goal weight editing option is to use the Paint Goal Weights tool. Select the soft body surface and choose Soft/Rigid Bodies | Paint Soft Body Weights Tool ❑ to bring up the tool's settings. You'll see the Artisan interface in the Attribute Editor, and you can paint the weights directly on the surface, where white has a Goal Weight value of 1 (does not deform) and black has a Goal Weight value of 0.

Using Springs

Springs improve the amount of deformation control by creating a relationship between the vertices themselves. Therefore, when one vertex is affected by a field or collision, it is capable of pulling another vertex or group of vertices that are connected to it by a spring. Exactly how this relationship affects the connected particle can be controlled through the spring's attributes. The resilience, or bounciness, and dampening are the two basic controls provided by the spring attributes.

If we connect springs to our flag object, we can achieve an added level of structure and control. As is the case with any cloth type of object, any manipulation of any point on the surface will affect other points as well. We want to make sure that as the turbulence affects certain points on the surface of the flag, other points on that surface are also affected.

With the surface selected, choose Soft/Rigid Bodies | Create Springs ❏ to open the tool's Settings window. Springs can be added to any particle object—they are not exclusive to soft bodies. When dealing with a soft body, however, the default settings need to be edited to suit the situation. In this example, we will set the Creation method to Wireframe so that it creates springs between particles within a distance set in the Wire Walk Length. In this case, set the Wire Walk Length to **2**. Click the Play button and view the animation. We will be examining springs and their attributes further in the following tutorial, where we will create a water surface with rain causing ripples on the surface.

Tutorial: Creating a Soft Body Ocean

In this tutorial, we will use soft body dynamics to create an ocean surface. We will apply a Turbulence field to a soft body NURBS plane to produce an overall rippling motion. The Turbulence field's frequency and phase attributes are used to control the overall behavior, while the soft body object's Goal Weight is modified to control the viscosity. Once we are happy with the ocean's behavior, we will drop particles on the surface to simulate raindrops. Springs will be added to the soft body so that a rippling effect will occur. A material can then be applied to give the surface some extra detail.

While this example attempts to re-create the behavior of a large body of water, similar techniques can be used to create movement on small puddles of water, or even mud. As we edit attributes, we will suggest settings to achieve the effects resulting from different liquids and volume sizes.

Creating the Waves in the Ocean

We'll start by making waves.

> *TIP* **Set up the Workspace so that it is displaying the Outliner in addition to the other windows. When working with dynamics, you'll find that objects can be selected easily in the Outliner.**

1. Create a new scene in Maya and set up a new project. Name it **Ocean.mb**.

2. Create a NURBS plane with 40 spans in U and V, and scale it up to be 25 units in X and Z.

3. Convert the plane into a soft body object by choosing Soft/Rigid Bodies | Create Soft Body ❑. Set the options so that they match the illustration and click the Create button.

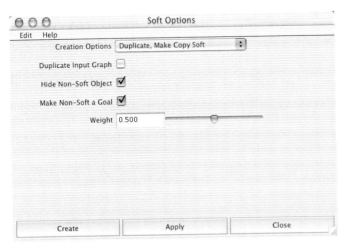

4. Rename the soft body plane **waterSoft**.

5. With the soft body object selected, add a Turbulence field by choosing Fields | Turbulence. Make sure the tool is reset to its default settings. The Turbulence field will be created and connected to the waterSoft soft body plane.

6. Now if you click the Play button, you might notice a little movement on the surface, but not much. Increasing the Magnitude attribute will increase movement, but the dynamic animation will still be too subtle. Since a large, wavering body of water will rarely return to its equilibrium, we know that we need to set this attribute low for on ocean-like behavior. Decrease the Goal Weight attribute on the soft body particle node to **0.2**. This will loosen the surface and make the waves deeper. The result should look similar to Figure 19-10.

FIGURE 19-10 *The soft body is animated by a Turbulence field with a Magnitude of 5 and a Goal Weight of 0.2.*

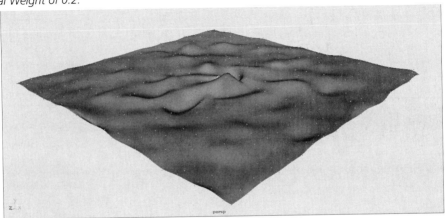

7. We need to give the waves in the ocean a direction, because now they are just moving up and down. This can be achieved by animating the Turbulence field's Phase attribute. Instead of keying it, we will animate it procedurally through an expression. Right-click the Phase X attribute and choose Expressions from the marking menu. This will open the Expression Editor. In the Expression field, type the following line, and then click Create:

```
turbulenceField1.phaseX=2*time;
```

TIP *When you right-click an attribute, the selected object name and attribute show up in the Selected Obj & Attr field in the Expression Editor. You can copy and paste that line into the Expression field and continue to type the expression. This will save time and lessen the chances of typing in the wrong words.*

8. The Frequency attribute of the field must also be reduced. The Frequency controls the length of the waves, and since we would like large, rolling waves as opposed to short, bumpy ones, we need to set this attribute lower. A value of 0.5 will work well. Playblast the animation to see the animation in real time.

Set Up the Rain Particles

Now we will create a volume emitter that will emit the particle raindrops. Gravity will then be added to these particles to control their fall toward the ocean surface. If an object, such as a ball, vehicle, or character, was falling from the sky instead of particles, we could set up collisions to create the displacement in the ocean. But because the raindrop particles are so small, the collision impact is not that great. We will create an Air field that will emit from each particle to displace the soft body surface around each particle. By itself, the interaction will cause the soft body particles to bob up and down. To create ripples in the water around where the raindrop particles collide, we will add springs between each soft body particle.

1. Create an emitter and set it as a Volume type. Scale it up so that is about the same size as the ocean in X and Z but only about 1 unit high. Move it up in the scene so that it sits far above the ocean.

2. Edit the emitter's attributes in the Attribute Editor. Set the Emitter Type to Surface and the Rate (Particles/Sec) attribute to **20**. Click the Create button. Click the Play button and you should see the particles being emitted from the surface.

3. Select the particle object and then choose Fields | Gravity to add a Gravity field and connect it to the rain particles. Set the gravity's Magnitude attribute to **50** so that the particles fall at the correct rate.

4. Select the new particle group and name it **particle_Rain**. In the Attribute Editor for this group, set the Particle Render Type to Streak. Add attributes for this current render type and add a Per Object color attribute so that it matches the settings shown here.

5. To use each particle as a source of an Air field, first create the Air field (choose Fields | Air Field). Select the

particle_Rain group and then choose Fields | Use Selected As Source Of Field.

6. Edit the Air field's attributes. Set the Magnitude to **0** and the Max Distance to **1**. You will need to make sure that Use Max Distance is enabled so that you can edit the value in the Attribute Editor. Also, make sure the Apply Per Vertex check box in the Special Effects Folder is checked so that each particle, instead of the entire group as a whole, can be used as the source of the field.

NOTE If you are editing these attributes in the Channel Box instead of the Attribute Editor, you will be able to see and edit values for attributes that may be inactive and grayed out in the Attribute Editor. Editing these attributes in the Channel Box will have no effect. For this reason, you should work in the Attribute Editor until you have a better understanding of how these attribute settings work.

7. For these Air fields to affect the soft body particles, they need to be connected. Use the Dynamic Relationship Editor (Windows | Relationship Editors | Dynamic Relationship Editor). In this window, select the waterSoft object. With the fields selection mode enabled, choose airField1 from the list on the right. The window should look like the illustration.

8. When you click the Play button, you should see the rain particles make little indentations in the soft body surface.

9. Because the turbulenceField1 is also affecting the surface, it might be best to disable it while we fine-tune the interaction with the falling rain particles. In the Dynamic Relationship Editor, select the waterSoft object if it isn't already still selected, and then click turbulenceField1 in the right column to deselect it. Now when you play back the animation, only the Air field from the rain particles should affect the soft body water surface.

NOTE   *If the surface were mud instead of water, the indentations made by the raindrops would refill much slower, if at all. This behavior can be created by editing the Conserve attribute on the soft body particle group that is parented to the waterSoft object. By default, it is set to 1, but you can try a lower value to see the effect.*

10. Select the waterSoft object and choose Soft/Rigid Bodies | Create Springs ❏ to bring up the tool's Options window. Set the Creation Method to Wireframe and set the Wire Walk Length value to **2**. This will create springs between all of the particles.

11. Select the spring group and change its Stiffening attribute to a value of **100**. Now when you play back the animation, the springs connecting the particles that are affected by the Air field pull the other particles and create a rippling effect. You may wish to lower the Goal Weight on the soft body particles to make the drops have more of an effect. A Goal Weight of 0.15 works well. The result should look similar to Figure 19-11.

FIGURE 19-11   *The soft body water is affected by the particle rain drops.*

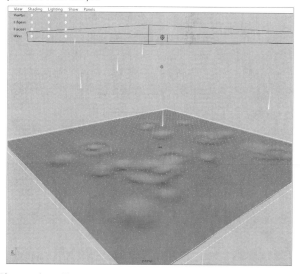

12. Now enable the turbulenceField in the Dynamic Relationship Editor so that the water has waves again. However, now that the Goal Weight of the soft body has been lowered, the magnitude that we were originally using on the turbulenceField is too great. Change it to **5**.

TIP *You may want the water surface to have some waves already present at frame 1 of the animation. You can disconnect the Air field from the water surface in the Dynamic Attribute Editor and let the animation play for a few seconds. Then select the water surface in the view window and choose Solvers | Initial State | Set For Selected. Reconnect the Air field to the surface. Now, at frame 1, the surface will already be deformed.*

Create a Water Material

While we don't want to wander too far from the topic of this chapter, it is important that you realize that small rippling effects such as those in water can be more efficiently achieved through the use of materials. To create the tiny ripples in the ocean, we can use a bump map generated from a *3D fractal texture*. The 3D fractal texture will produce the desired pattern, and because it is a 3D texture, it will change as the surface moves through it as it is affected by the dynamic forces in the scene. As an added touch, we will create and adjust environment fog before rendering the final animation.

1. In the Hypershade, create a new Blinn material. Name it **mOcean**.

2. Click the Map button in the Bump Mapping channel, and the Create Render Node window will open. In the 3D Textures section, choose the Solid Fractal texture.

3. Graph the connections to the material in the Hypershade and edit the solid fractal texture so that Frequency Ratio is set to **2.5**.

4. Select the bump 3D node and change its Bump Value attribute to **0.5**.

5. Select the material node and set its Color attribute to a deep, ocean blue. Adjust the Eccentricity to about **0.1**, the Specular Roll Off to **1.7**, and the Reflectivity to **0.7**.

6. In the Raytrace Options section of the Attribute Editor, turn the Reflection Limit up to **3** and make sure that Raytracing is turned on in the Render Global Settings window. Also in this window, add an Environment Fog node and change its color to a bluish white.

7. Set the Resolution and Anti Aliasing quality and range of frames, and then use the Batch Render command to render the animation.

 8. To render the particles, you will need to use the Maya hardware renderer and then composite the pieces in a compositing program. The result should look something like Figure 19-12. Also, be sure to look at the final animation included on the CD.

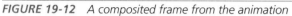

FIGURE 19-12   *A composited frame from the animation*

Summary

Maya's dynamics open up a whole new realm of possibilities for creating just about any type of effect. Having the ability to apply fields to geometry and having them react to other pieces in the scene are very powerful animation tools. While keyframed animation will always be best suited for precise character animation, dynamics are a great solution for letting the chaotic forces of nature take over your scene.

Post-Production

Rendering for Post-Production

In the next two chapters, we'll examine a technique for rendering a scene in separate passes that can be composited in an application such as Adobe After Effects. We'll put together a small visual effects shot of a landing spacecraft. But before we render anything, of course, we need to create all of the elements. We'll handle this in four parts. In the first part, we will create the environment or background element using a photograph that is supplied on the book CD.

Using a technique called *camera mapping*, we'll introduce *parallax* (explained in a bit) and enable the camera to be slightly animated. Next, we'll prepare a reflection map based on the background image and some other photos taken from the site. This will help us create a color-based relationship between the spaceship and the background. Then we'll deal with the spaceship and its texture maps. We will use the ship that we modeled in Chapter 4, converted to polygons and texture mapped. We'll also add some simple animation to the spaceship and camera. With the textures assigned to their respective attributes, we'll use a MEL script to isolate certain attributes on the ship's materials. For each separate pass, a scene file will be saved. Finally, we'll create a batch render script and use the command line to render all of the scene files.

This chapter will serve as a good review of the information covered so far in the book. If you find yourself struggling through some of these sections, you might find it helpful to go back and reread the section(s) relative to the step(s).

Camera Mapping

A *camera map*—also called a camera projection, digital backlot, or digital matte—is a texture that is projected from a camera onto an object or group of objects that are aligned with the objects in the image. The projection works like a virtual backlot to help a scene look as though it were being shot at an actual location. Figure 20-1 shows a camera mapping example from the dvGarage Camera Mapping Lab (*http://www.dvgarage.com*), a training product designed to help you master this technique. Notice the simple geometry that has been placed in the scene to match the objects in the photograph. When the camera pushes in, the scene appears to be in full 3D.

The camera mapping technique is used in almost every big-budget film today. In fact, camera mapping is an economical production technique that can be used in just about any film, no matter how small the budget. *Establishing* shots, the shots in a film or show that begin a scene by establishing a location, are often completed using a camera mapping technique.

For example, suppose you were producing a feature film and you needed to include a scene of a secret meeting between members of the British Parliament. All of the film's interior scenes may have been shot on a sound stage or on location inside a building in Los Angeles. However, the director needs to establish the Parliament scene to communicate that it is taking place in the Parliament Building in London, and he wants to include a shot of Big Ben. One option would be to hire a camera crew and have them get a shooting permit, travel to London, set up the gear in front of Big Ben, and roll the film—a very expensive and complicated situation, even for something as simple as this. Another option would be to build a miniature model of Big Ben or model it from scratch in Maya. However, this, too, is an expensive option, especially since it will be needed for only this single shot.

Camera mapping can save the day (and a lot of money). Because only a single photograph is needed, it could even be purchased and downloaded from a stock photo library on the Internet (such as at *http://www.artbeats.com*). The image is brought into Maya, where it is set up to be

FIGURE 20-1   A camera map of the Bangkok skyline (courtesy of dvGarage)

projected from a virtual camera that's positioned relative to the objects in the photograph. Simple geometry, such as planes and cubes, are placed in the scene to match the ground and the buildings—as shown in Figure 20-2 in the next section. Once the camera is set up to project the image onto this geometry, another camera is added in the same position, where it can be animated to a certain degree. When the camera is moved—say, zoomed in just a bit—the objects in the foreground will move more quickly toward the camera than the objects in the background. This effect, known as *parallax,* tricks the viewer into thinking that the shot was taken with a motion picture camera rather than a still camera.

Big-budget, special-effects movies make huge use of camera mapping. Films such as *Star Wars Episode 1: The Phantom Menace* and *Episode 2: Attack of the Clones* used camera mapping extensively. Often, miniature sets were built for effects scenes that use motion control cameras to film sequences. But again, in the case of establishing shots, these models could be photographed, and then, in the hands of the computer graphics artists, used as camera maps. Several articles on computer graphics have mentioned one particular shot in *Star Wars: Episode 1,* in which the artist used several photographs of a model taken from different positions and projected them from several different cameras onto very rough geometry. The render camera, the one actually rendering the scene, flew through these very simple objects that were being texture mapped from the different cameras to create a fly-through of the entire model.

One last example of camera mapping is the *digital matte painting*. The matte painting has been in use since the early days of film. Before there was a such thing as compositing in post-production, all special effects were done in camera, meaning that the matte paintings were hung behind the set and the scene was shot. After basic compositing techniques were available, sets could be painted on glass, which was then combined with the live elements in post-production. However, in most of these cases, the camera had to be still because it was not possible to create parallax with these techniques.

Using camera mapping techniques, an artist can now create a painting—traditionally or digitally—which can be used as a camera mapped image. It must, however, obey the laws of physics with respect to perspective and camera lenses. It can therefore be helpful to the painter to begin with a photograph, where the distortion caused by perspective is already established. Some artists might even set up some simple objects in a 3D scene, render them, and use the rendered image as a template, on top of which paint is applied.

How Camera Mapping Works

In camera mapping, an image is projected from a camera that is set up to use the same focal length and aspect ratio used by the camera that took the original photo. A simple grid or cube is aligned to some object that lies along or extends from the ground plane. When all of the sides of this object match the perspective lines in the photograph, you know that the ground plane and camera position have been established. At this point, the projection camera is locked down and any other objects in the photo have some basic geometry placed and aligned to them.

A material is created that uses a projection to map a texture to it. The projection mode is set to use the perspective of the projection camera to project the texture. This is similar to regular planar projections, but instead of being projected orthographically, or in parallel, the image is projected with the converging perspective lines unique to a specific camera lens. This texture is then applied to all objects in the scene that will use this map.

Finally, the projection camera is duplicated and the duplicate is used as the animated render camera. When this camera is moved, its relationship to the objects in the scene changes as it would in the real world, because the parallax has been simulated.

Tutorial: Camera Mapping a Junkyard Scene

In this section, we cover the process of setting up a simple camera map step by step. The photograph we'll use was chosen for its simplicity. Most of the objects in the scene are box shaped, which will make matching the placement of simple polygonal cubes relatively easy.

Prepare the Photograph

The first part of the process involves a little preprocessing of the photograph. The image used for the final render should be a high-resolution image. The higher the resolution in the image, the further in you can zoom with your render camera. It is safe to suggest that the camera projected image should be at least twice the size of the intended final output resolution. However, if you plan to zoom way in, you will need an image with very high resolution.

Working with such a large image in Maya can be cumbersome, and in fact some video cards cannot display images that are more than 2048×2048. For this reason, it is a good idea to make a low-resolution version of the photo. In addition, you should draw some straight lines along any pairs of parallel edges on this same low-resolution version. This will help you see the edges while you are trying to line up the cubes in the view window. Also, drawing edges that run horizontally across the photo at the base of the objects will help you align the objects relative to one another. Figure 20-2 shows the junkyard photograph with the perspective lines drawn in. Save a version of this file and name it **MCR_c20_junkyard_ref.iff**. This version should be about 900 pixels wide. (You may also find this reference image with the perspective lines on the CD.)

FIGURE 20-2   *The low-resolution reference image with lines drawn over parallel edges*

Set Up the Projection Camera

The most important part of this entire process is making sure that the camera that projects the texture is set up as accurately as possible. The camera projecting the image should use the same focal length and aspect ratio as the camera that took the original photograph. For this reason, it is helpful to know the focal length of the lens that was used to take the photograph.

When you have the focal length data, you can be sure that once you have aligned one object between the camera and the photo, the rest of the geometry will fall into place. Without this information, you could guess the focal length, but it would take much trial and error to set up the scene properly. Without establishing how the lens distorts parallel lines, you might find that after you place one object, matching the next one is more of a challenge—it may need to be moved farther away or scaled bigger or smaller than it should be in relation to the objects in the scene. If this is the case, you know that you need to try a different focal length. Even if you can line up the object with the photograph by scaling or moving it away, once you begin animating the camera, the image will quickly fall apart.

> *TIP*   *When I shot the photo for this exercise, I made sure to align the center cross hairs in my camera at the point where the brick wall meets the ground. This ensured that the camera was pointed at an object on the ground. When I orbit my camera later on, it will rotate around that point, and since I know that the X axis lies on the ground, I can place my other objects relative to it. This is information you may not have if you are using a stock photo, but take note of these things if you are shooting your own photograph. It will make alignment in Maya much easier.*

Let's begin the setup:

1. Set up a new Maya project and start a new scene. You may wish to copy the MCR_c20_junkyard_ref.iff and MCR_c20_junkyard_HR.iff images to the source images directory of the new project.

2. Create a new camera (Create | Cameras | Camera) and name it **projectionCam**. Move it back along the Z axis and use the Show Manipulator tool to snap the camera's reference point to the world origin. When viewing the scene through this camera, having the camera pointing at this world origin will put the X axis along the centerline of the photograph.

3. In the projectionCam's attributes, set the focal length to **52**, since the photograph was taken with a 52mm lens.

4. In the Render Global Settings window, set the resolution to match the resolution of the photo. In this case, it is 1079×719.

5. Look through the projectionCam and create an image plane for that camera by choosing View | Image Plane | Image Plane Attributes. In the Attribute Editor, load MCR_c20_ junkyard_ref.iff in the Image attribute. Click the Fit To Resolution Gate button.

TIP *You may need to adjust the camera's Overscan attribute so that the entire image plane is visible.*

Our image is now set to project from a camera with the same focal length and aspect ratio as the original photograph. We now need to position this camera so that its height and orientation with respect to the ground matches the position and orientation of the original camera. We will use the large bin on the left side of the photo to calibrate this.

6. Switch to a Side view and create a polygonal cube that is 2×2×2. Edit its pivot point to the base of the object, and then move the cube so that it sits on the XZ plane. Turn on snapping to make sure that it is sitting on the axis.

7. Switch the view though the projectionCam. Orbit the camera up and try to align the grid lines with the base line of the left bin. As long as you don't move the camera with the pan control, that center X axis will always be on the ground. Once the grid lines are aligned with the base of the bin, we can use the cube to determine the distance, or how far back the camera needs to be from the center.

8. Zoom out so that the edge of the grid is visible in the foreground. Use the Move tool to move the cube over in X about −5 units and in Z about 5 units until the lower corner lines up with the photograph. The cube should actually sit right below the bottom edges of the bin, since the bin seems to be sitting a few inches off the ground. You may need to tweak the camera by orbiting or nudging the cube in the X or Z axis. Just be sure not to pan the camera or move the cube in the Y axis.

9. Scale the cube in Y until the top edge aligns with the top edge of the left bin in the photograph. Do any final bits of tweaking to get both the upper edge and the lower edge in alignment. When those edges are matched, the cube can be scaled along its Z axis and translated in Z until the front and rear edges are aligned.

TIP *It may be best to select the attribute in the Channel Box and MMB-drag in the view to manipulate the scale and position of the cube.*

10. The cube may seem a bit crooked. It is possible that the ground is not entirely flat where the bin is sitting. If you have done everything possible to align it using the steps so far, you can rotate the cube on the Z axis just a little until all of the edges line up. Figure 20-3 shows the cube placed in its final position.

FIGURE 20-3 *The Maya scene showing the placement of the first cube*

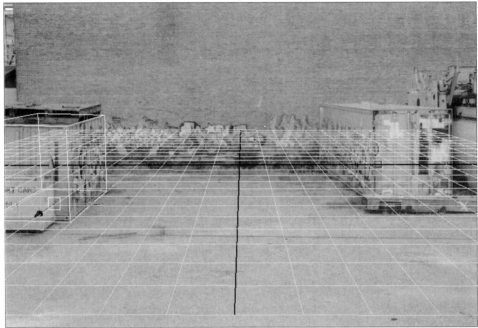

11. Now that the projection camera is placed, lock it down so that it can't be moved by accident. Select all of the attributes in the Channel Box, right-click them, and choose Lock Selected from the marking menu.

Place the Other Objects

Now that the camera's position is established, the rest of this process can go rather quickly. Create more polygonal cubes and align them with objects in the scene. You may be tempted to go a bit overboard—just remember that this is just one shot that will go by very quickly to the viewing audience, and plan your details accordingly. We will be adding a ship landing in the middle of the scene, so most of the viewers' attention will be directed on the ship. For this reason, it is best to place geometry only for the main objects in the scene. If something still stands out as wrong when the shot is composited, you can add more geometry and quickly re-render the background.

The quickest way to continue placing the objects would be to duplicate the cube you created for the left bin. Set all of the duplicate's rotation values to 0, and move it into position on the large bin on the right side. Use the horizontal grid lines to determine the point where the front edge should align, and then go about scaling, moving, and rotating the cube until it fits. It usually takes a few rounds of small adjustments to get it right.

With these two objects now placed, the boundaries of the scene are established. Switching to the Perspective view will allow you to duplicate and move the other objects roughly into position based entirely on their spatial relationships. Then switch back to view the scene through the perspective camera to fine-tune the placement so that all of the objects are in alignment with the photograph. Eight cubes total should be enough to cover all of the main objects.

Finally, add a plane for the ground and scale it up to cover the entire scene. Then add another plane for the rear wall. It should extend directly up from the X axis origin. The completed placement should resemble that shown in Figure 20-4.

FIGURE 20-4   The scene with all of the objects placed

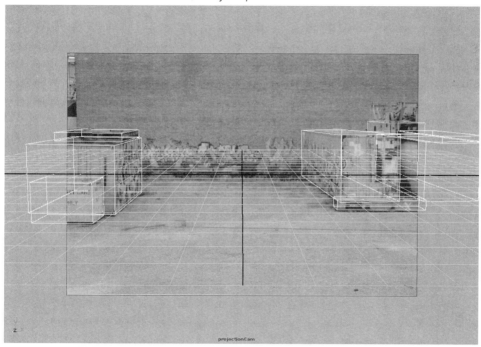

Create the Projection Material

Now let's create the material and map it onto the geometry. Essentially, we will create a material and add the high-resolution map as a projection. The projection type will then be set to a special type called Perspective.

1.   In the Hypershade window, create a new Surface Shader material. The Surface Shader is great for this sort of application because it uses a texture's brightness values so that there's no need to light the objects or adjust any material attributes to make this work.

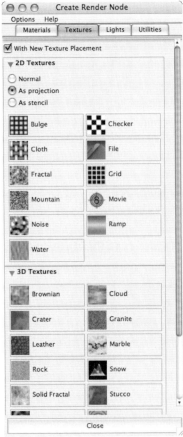

2. Connect a File texture to the color attribute of the Surface Shader material. In the Create Render Node window, select the As Projection type instead of Normal, as shown.

3. Load MCR_c20_junkyard_HR.iff into the file texture node.

4. Select the 2D projection node connected to the file texture in the Hypershade window and view its attributes in the Attribute Editor. Set the Proj Type attribute to Perspective.

5. Underneath that, open the Camera Projection Attributes folder and set the Link To Camera attribute to projectionCamShape and the Fit Type to Match Camera Resolution. This will set the projection to use the projectionCam to project the texture with the aspect ratio set by the resolution. The Attribute Editor settings should look like the illustration.

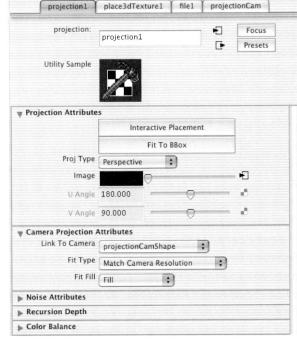

6. Turn the incandescence value of the Lambert material all the way up. This ensures that the texture will render at full brightness, without any lights.

7. Select all of the geometry in the scene, and then in the Hypershade, right-click the material and choose Assign Material To Selection from the marking menu. The map will be applied to all of the objects.

Set Up the Render Camera

A minimum of three perspective cameras should be used in a camera mapping scene. We have already dealt with the first two. One camera is used as the working camera, as it would be in any other 3D scene. You use this camera to navigate around your scene and place and edit objects. The second camera, the projection camera, is used to project the image. You'll create a third camera as the render camera. This camera will be animated and used to render the scene. It is best to duplicate the projection camera once it has been established and locked. This way, the render camera is in its default position.

1. Select the projectionCam, duplicate it, and set the view window to look through it. Rename this duplicate camera **renderCam**.

2. Set the animation frame range to something small—in this case, 90 frames.

3. Select the renderCam and set a key at this position.

4. Go to frame 90. Zoom-in the camera a bit and move it down. Set a key for this position.

5. Set up the Render Global Settings to render all 90 frames of the animation. In the Resolution section of the Render Global Settings window, check the box next to Maintain Width/Height Ratio and set the Width to **600**. Set the Frame Padding to **4**. This will number the frames so they have four digits, starting with frame 0001. When numbered like this, After Effects can properly import a sequence of frames.

6. In the Anti-Aliasing Quality folder, set the Quality to Production. This will create nice, anti-aliased edges.

7. Do some test renders of various frames from the animation. Pay particular attention to the frames from the end of the animation. You'll notice that the texture on some of the foreground items spills over onto objects behind them. This is most obvious with the orange beam in front of the bin on the right side of the frame. To fix this area, you need to make a duplicate of the MCR_c20_junkyard_HR.iff file and then, in Photoshop, paint out the area (using the Clone tool) on the bin where this overlap occurs. Return to Maya, duplicate the surface shader's entire network (choose Edit | Duplicate | Shading Network from the Hypershade's menu bar), and then replace the current file texture with the one that has the beam painted out from the bin. Apply this material onto the bin. Now the obstructed area on the bin will be revealed as the camera moves in.

TIP *You may notice that the texture is blurry on some of the faces. This is caused by the default filter setting on the file texture node. If you select the file texture node that contains the camera mapped texture, you'll see a Filter attribute in the Effects folder of the node's Attribute Editor. Maya's default is set to 1; in most cases, you will find that this is too much. Start with a setting of 0.1 and do a test render. You can increase the value, but you'll rarely need to go much higher than that.*

8. When the test render looks OK, render all 20 frames and view them in Fcheck. It should appear that the scene was actually modeled in 3D. If not, take careful notice of the problems, and make the adjustments in the scene by moving some of the cubes. If you are still stuck, open the MRC_c20_cameraMap_finish.mb file on the CD and study that. Also, look at the MCR_c20_cameraMap_Finish.mov to see a render of the scene so far.

Creating a Reflection Map

In Chapter 14, you used a reflection map from dvGarage's Reflection Toolkit. In most cases, one of those reflection maps will do a fine job, even if the map does not contain any of the objects from your scene. The primary use of the reflection map is simply to give reflective objects something to reflect—it helps to "sell" the object as something that is made from a reflective material. To this end, the maps included in the Reflection Toolkit are sufficient.

In Chapter 16, you learned about raytraced reflections. These might be necessary when an object that will be given much attention in the scene needs to reflect the objects surrounding it. For example, in a scene with a highly reflective glass sitting next to a soda can, with these objects at the center of attention, you could pretty easily pick out that something is wrong if that soda can is not reflected in the glass. It is easier to get away with not using raytraced reflections, even in these types of situations, when the objects are moving. In such cases, you have much more freedom to decide whether to use a reflection map, raytracing, or both. Just remember that raytracing is a processor-intensive operation and can tie up your computer for hours or even days if the scene is complex.

So what do you do when you need semi-accurate reflections in the scene but you don't want to spend the time raytracing?

FIGURE 20-5   The EnvBall map of the junkyard scene

Environment Ball

A Maya rendering node called an EnvBall (Environment Ball) allows you to add reflection maps that were taken by photographing a chrome ball (see Figure 20-5). EnvBall is an excellent choice for situations in which only one side of the reflected object is visible. To obtain the reflection map that will be used on the EnvBall, you can either bring along a chrome ball and photograph it on site or place a highly reflective chrome sphere in the middle of a Maya scene and photograph it with the renderer. By using raytraced reflections to calculate the reflections on the sphere, the sphere will reflect the surrounding objects pretty accurately. But since the ball will be used as a map, you will need to use raytracing only once.

Set Up an Environment Ball

With our junkyard environment, the ball can be set up between two camera-mapped objects. Capturing reflections between these objects from a still photo might have otherwise been impossible. However, images still need to be provided for the area behind the camera. Therefore, it is necessary to use some other photos. These other images don't need to represent the rest of the scene accurately, because our camera will never turn that much, so any images will do. In this case, we will use an image that was taken near the site of the camera-mapped image. Once these images are mapped to a dome and covering the part of the environment not already covered by existing geometry, the reflective sphere is rendered. This render is then imported back into the scene and used as an EnvBall texture.

1. Open the completed camera map scene on the CD, or use your own scene.

2. Create a sphere and place it between the two bins. Scale the sphere so that it is roughly the same size as the spaceship.

3. Create a new Blinn material. Set the following attributes to the specified values. The rest of the material attributes can remain at their defaults.

   - Diffuse: 0

   - Eccentricity: 0

   - Specular Roll Off: 1

   - Specular Color: 1

   - Reflectivity: 1

4. To create the rest of the environment for the sphere to reflect, create another sphere. Detach it on its horizontal and vertical equators so that it is in four equal pieces. Scale a quarter piece so that its boundaries touch or overlap all of the boundaries of the existing

FIGURE 20-6   *Piece of the sphere scaled to the boundaries of existing scene*

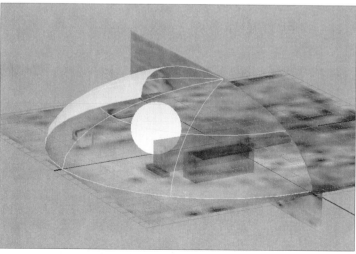

ground plane and wall. Figure 20-6 shows how the scene should now look.

5. Create a new Surface Shader material. Map a file texture to its Out Color attribute and import the MCR_c20_BackBuildings.iff file to it. Make sure this is mapped to the material as Normal, not Projection.

6. Now we need to set each object so that it will be visible only in the reflection, not in the rest of the scene. We can do this by turning off each object's Primary Visibility attribute. The fastest way to do this for all of the objects at once is to choose Windows | Rendering Editors | Rendering Flags. Select all of the shape nodes (except the sphere being reflected) and set the Primary Visibility to Off. The Rendering Flags window should look like Figure 20-7.

FIGURE 20-7   Rendering Flags window settings

7. Create a new camera. In the Render Global Settings window, set the Output Resolution to 2K. Also, while you have that window open, turn on Raytracing. View the scene through the new camera and turn on the resolution gate (View | Camera Tools | Resolution Gate).

8. Frame the reflecting ball so that its edges just touch the resolution gate. Render the ball. The final render should look something like Figure 20-5, shown earlier.

9. Save this render in your project directory as **MCR_junkyard_Reflection.iff**.

10. In the Hypershade, create an EnvBall node. In the Hypershade window, choose Create | Environment Textures | Env Ball. Map a file texture to the image attribute of this node and then import the MCR_junkyard_Reflection.iff that we just created.

11. Select all of the geometry and the projection camera, and then create a new layer and add all of the selected pieces. Now the environment can be turned on and off by toggling the visibility of the layer.

You have now successfully created a good environment map for our scene. Save this scene and keep that EnvBall node handy. We will be connecting that to the reflection color attributes for the surfaces on the spaceship when we do our reflective render pass.

The Ship

The spaceship that we modeled in Chapter 4 will be the hero of this shot. The ship will descend and land in between the two bins in the camera-mapped scene. Instead of just hitting the render button and saying the shot is finished, we will set up and save a scene file for each individual render pass.

> _NOTE_   _We won't cover the actual texture mapping of the ship here. The completed ship on the CD has already been converted to polygons to create a single piece of geometry for each part to make texture mapping easier. UV coordinates have been assigned and texture maps have been created. The focus in this lesson will be on learning how to turn off certain material attributes to create a specific render pass. However, you are encouraged to study the geometry, textures, and UV layout. The techniques used have all been covered in other chapters in this book._

Tutorial: Animating the Ship

Now it is time to animate. Keep in mind that the camera movement is limited due to the camera map we're using. We won't go through the animation step by step here, but we will point out a few things that will help get you going. When in doubt, you can view the final shot on the CD or study the Maya scene files.

1. In the Preferences window, set the Time to 24 frames per second (fps). (This is the framerate for film, unless you are going to video, which would be 30 fps.) Set the Range Slider to 72 (3 seconds). Again, you could make it longer, but we want to keep render times as small as possible.

2. Add the ship to the project by choosing File | Import and navigating to the mcr_c20_ spaceship.ma file. Now you can begin animating.

3. Its easiest to set the first key for all of the channels on the frame where the ship is in its final position—which is on the ground. Set that key around frame 60.

4. Go to frame 1 and move the ship up in Y so that it is just above the brick wall in the background, about 3 units high. Set a key for that position on the Translate Y channel.

5. From here, you can set keys for each of the other channels individually. In the example, the ship is moving toward the camera and drifting to the right just a little. It is also rotating on its X and Z axes as it comes down and flattens out. Use the Graph Editor to edit these curves. In most cases, you won't really need to add many keyframes between the first and last.

6. Next, animate the camera. If you have not already done so, duplicate the projectionCam and name it **RenderCam**. Move the RenderCam up just a bit and rotate it so that it is pointing at the ship.

7. Set a key for the first frame. Move to frame 60, where the ship has landed, and frame it. You'll want to zoom in just a bit. Set a key for that frame. Flatten the end tangents on the camera's animation curves so that it gently comes to rest.

8. Finally, add some secondary motion. Animate the side thrusters so that they rotate to help the ship level out and land. You'll notice that when you import the ship, the parent group node, PolyShip_XFORM, includes some custom attributes for the landing gears. These have been set up using Set Driven Keys; you might wish to animate the landing gears extending for the landing.

9. You'll also see a group node underneath the PolyShip_XFORM called PolyShip_Noise. On this node, add some subtle oscillations by using expressions. Select the PolyShip_Noise group and right-click its Rotate X attribute in the Channel Box. Choose Expressions from the marking menu. Use a math function to have the ship oscillate on a sin wave. In the Expressions field, type the following:

```
polyShip_Noise.rotateX = sin(4*time);
```

10. A value of 4 will work fine here, but it is always good practice to put values used in scripts and expressions into a variable, and make that variable editable inside the Channel Box. To set this up, we will add a custom attribute to the polyShip_Noise node called noiseRate. This attribute name will then be substituted for the 4 in the expression. When the value is changed in the Channel Box, the expression will use the new data without you having to edit the expression. Once you've added the new custom attribute, edit the expression so that it reads as follows:

```
polyShip_Noise.rotateX = sin(polyShip_Noise.noiseRate*time);
```

This will rotate the ship back and forth on its X axis 1 unit four times (or by any value used in the noiseRate attribute) during the animation.

11. Do the same thing for the Rotate Z attribute. These expressions can then be baked into editable keys by selecting the group and choosing Edit | Keys | Bake Simulation. Set the Sample Rate to **10**. You can then edit the curves in the Graph Editor. Modify the last keys so that they are at 0 when the ship lands. The Graph Editor should look similar to the illustration.

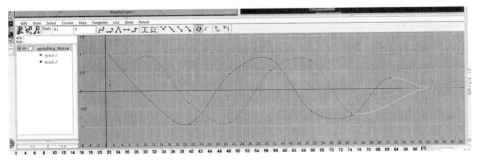

Tutorial: Rendering Separate Passes

In any production environment, a finished image rarely comes directly from your 3D application's rendered output. It is almost always tweaked further in a compositing program. At the very least, some color correction may be needed or some hardware-rendered particle effects composited together with the software renders. But using a compositing package with Maya can take your images to a higher level.

By rendering the 3D assets in separate layers and passes, you can get precise control over many attributes of the final image. Rendering in layers is a good way to separate the background and foreground elements or isolate individual objects. Then, each of these objects can be rendered in separate passes. One pass could contain just the color attributes of the object, and another might contain only the reflections. These can then be brought into a compositing package and combined.

Working in this way has many advantages, the most obvious of which is that you can make changes to certain elements of the scene without having to re-render the entire thing. You could swap an existing environment for a new one. By rendering in passes, you could change the color of a model from red to blue just by re-rendering a color pass for that object. You could make the object look more or less reflective just by adjusting the opacity of the reflection pass within the compositing program itself. You would not even need to go back to Maya and re-render anything.

You will often use the compositing program to integrate 3D elements with live-action footage shots on film or video. In such cases, you will need to color correct the 3D images to match the light and dark values of the live-action plates. Once again, you could just adjust the shadow pass to match the value of the shadows in the background image. Or you could tone down or color tint the specular highlights to match the bright areas or lighting in the background.

In this section, we will render 14 separate passes. While this might seem like a lot, the amount of work you need to do to set it up is far less than performing test render after test render to get the surfaces looking correct in Maya. This setup will mostly involve turning off all but one material attribute on the objects and saving a scene file for that pass. In the next section, we will use the command line to batch render all of the scenes.

Load tmRenderPass

While Maya's user interface has some controls for rendering passes (found in the Render Global Settings window) it is not sufficient for the work we are about to do. For one thing, this process makes extensive use of the Incandescence material attribute to render various masks. Maya's render pass controls do not provide any control over this attribute. Another issue is that there is no way to isolate the specular highlights from the overall reflections.

On the included CD is a MEL script that will allow you to turn on and off these attributes separately. So before we begin, find the scripts called tmRenderOn.mel, tmRenderOff.mel, and tmRenderUI.mel and copy them into your Maya Scripts directory. The exact location of this directory will vary depending on your operating system. An example for Windows is C:\\ Documents and Settings\<*your user name*>\My Documents\Maya\6.0\Scripts\. On the Macintosh that would be in /Users/<*your user name*>/Library/Preferences/Alias/maya/6.0/Scripts/.

Open Maya, and on the command line, type the following:

```
TmRenderUI;
```

This will open the Options interface for using these scripts, which is shown in the illustration. Create a Shelf button for this script so that you have easy access to it.

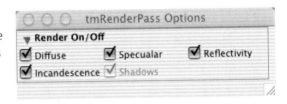

Hard Color Pass

This pass will create that harder light on the surface, which will represent the direct light from the sun. Even though the photo was taken on a very cloudy day, it is helpful to render this pass in case you want to manipulate the entire scene to look like it was taken in bright sun.

1. Set up a directional light pointing down, a little to the left of camera.

2. Set the Diffuse attribute on all of the ship's materials to **0.1**. An easy way to do this at one time is to SHIFT-select all of the materials you need to edit and then change the value in the Channel Box.

3. For the mDetails material, set the Diffuse a bit higher, at **0.2**. If you set the light's intensity higher than the default, the result will be a heavy contrast between the light and dark areas. Try setting the light's Intensity value to **4**.

4. Open the tmRenderPass options and uncheck everything but the Diffuse check box.

5. Do a test render, and when you are happy with the scene, go to the Render Global Settings window and set the Quality to Production Quality and set the desired output resolution. Also, make sure the frame range is set to start at 1 and end at 120.

6. If the background is still visible, turn off its display layer. We want only the ship to be rendered in these passes.

7. When everything is all set, save the file with a new name in the render scenes directory in the project directory. The file on the CD is called MCR_JYL_RP_Dif_hard. The result should look like the image shown in Figure 20-8.

NOTE *It is always a good idea to use a naming convention that you stick to throughout a project. That way, you can identify any file without having to open it. In our case, "MCR" tells us that the file is part of the Maya Complete Reference projects, specifically, the junkyard landing ("JYL"). The "RP" stands for Render Pass and then identifies it as a diffuse, hard light pass. See Figure 20-8 for a rendered sample of this pass.*

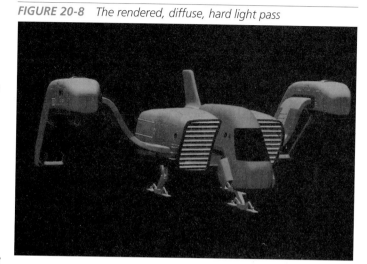

FIGURE 20-8 *The rendered, diffuse, hard light pass*

Diffused Color Pass

For the most part, the light in this scene is even, but this is often difficult to achieve using conventional rendering techniques. For this pass, we are going to use Mental Ray's Final Gather renderer. This will give us nice, even, diffused light over the scene.

NOTE *You may choose to use the Mental Ray renderer for all of these passes. With the exception of this pass, we will stick to the Maya software and hardware renderers. As of version 6, you cannot render a scene on multiple processors with Mental Ray, so it still may be beneficial to use the Maya software renderer when you can.*

NOTE *You may need to review Chapter 16 for Final Gather basics.*

1. Create a half sphere that covers the ship positions from start to finish. Create a new Lambert material, apply it to the dome, and set the Incandescence on this material to about **0.75**.

2. Select the dome object, and in its Render Stats folder in the Attribute Editor, turn off the Primary Visibility.

3. In the Render Global Settings window, enable Mental Ray and choose PreviewFinalGather for the Quality. If you are doing test renders, set the Final Gather Rays to **200**. Set the Max Radius to **1.2** and the Min Radius to **0.12**.

FIGURE 20-9 The diffused color pass

4. When you are ready to do the final render, change the Final Gather Rays value to **800**. In the Sampling Quality section, set the Min Samples to **–2** and the Max Samples to **2**, and change the Filter type to Gaussian.

5. Save the scene, shown in Figure 20-9, in the render scenes directory with a new name— **MCR_JYL_RP_Dif_soft**.

Hard Reflection Pass

We want a sharp reflection for all of the shiny pieces on the ship. The reflection should be as clean and sharp as possible. Take the EnvBall containing our reflection map and connect it to the Reflected Color attribute on all of the materials on the ship. Make certain that the Reflectivity attribute on all of the ship's materials is set to 1.

1. In the tmRenderPass Options window, uncheck every option except the Reflectivity option.

2. Once again, save the scene file. Name it **MCR_JYL_RP_REF_ Hard.mb**. Figure 20-10 shows an example of how it should look.

Soft Reflection Pass

This one is easy—we need to create another reflection pass for the duller materials. You can sometimes get away with using the texture's Pre Filter attribute, but this can be set only to 10.

FIGURE 20-10 The hard reflection pass

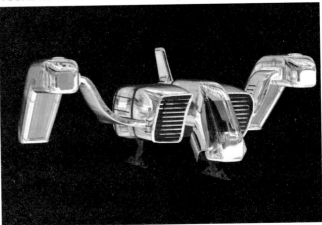

For our project, we need to go higher. Therefore, select the file texture being used as a reflection map, and change its Filter attribute to a setting of **50**. The Filter attribute can be found in the

Effects folder of the file texture's Attribute Editor. Render a test and save the scene as **MCR_JYL_RP_REF_soft.mb**. Figure 20-11 shows how it should look.

Hard Specular Pass

The specular attributes often communicate what a material is made out of. This hard specular pass will be used for the shinier, less porous parts of the metal.

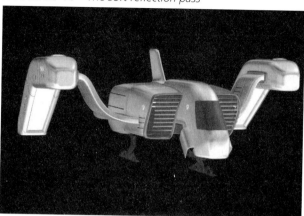

FIGURE 20-11 *The soft reflection pass*

1. The Specular Roll Off needs to be set high. By default, the slider for this attribute goes to a value of 1, but this can be overridden. A Specular Roll Off value of **2.5** for the metal on the ship should do it. This can be a bit lower for the details and landing gear, perhaps a value of **1.5**. Remember that one of the benefits of rendering in passes is that you don't have to be precise when setting these material attributes. They can all be adjusted in real time in your compositing application.

2. The eccentricity should be set very low. A value of **0.2** or less will work for the main parts. For the window, it can be even less, like **0.1**.

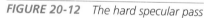

3. With these set up, turn on the Specular option in the tmRenderPass Options window and turn everything else off.

FIGURE 20-12 *The hard specular pass*

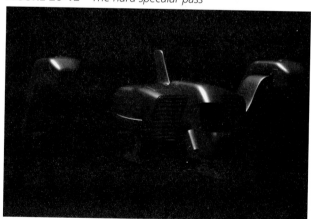

4. Test render, and save the scene as **MCR_JYL_RP_SPC_hard.mb**. Your render should look similar to Figure 20-12.

Soft Specular Pass

Here we will do the opposite of the hard specular pass.

1. Set the Eccentricity attribute to **0.5** and **0.3** for the Specular Roll Off. The Eccentricity on some of the other smaller pieces can be even higher, to a value of **0.7**.

FIGURE 20-13   The soft specular pass

2. Do some test renders, and when it looks similar to what is shown in Figure 20-13, save the scene file in the render scenes directory as **MCR_JYL_ RP_SPC_soft.mb.**

Noise/Grunge Pass

Noise can be used to break up specular highlights and reflections. In a single-pass rendering method, you would add a Noise texture to control the specularity and the reflectivity of the texture. You might even add it to the Color or Diffuse attribute so that these noise patterns show through. However, making all these adjustments on every channel can take a long time. A huge advantage of the multipass rendering technique is that you can render the grunge pass once and then use it to affect any other render pass when you composite later on. You can achieve very precise control over surface detail in this way.

Instead of rendering this in a color channel, the Noise texture will be placed in the incandescence channel. This is the best way to create a flat render with a very high contrast. All of the ship's materials had a noise map already applied to them when you imported the project. In most cases, these maps were created based on the basic detail from the bump and color maps and then the noise patterns were added. You can use the procedural textures in Maya to this same effect. In fact, the landing gears use procedural textures. However, in the areas of greater visibility, you should use something with a bit more randomness if you are going for a realistic look. The dvGarage's Surface Toolkit contains hundreds of images. While they are based on photographs taken of concrete and metal, their natural randomness means they'll work for just about anything.

FIGURE 20-14   The noise/grunge pass

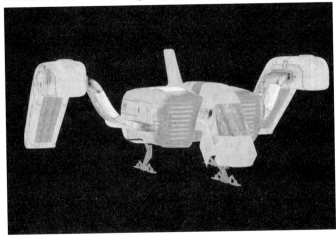

Turn off all of the check boxes in the tmRenderPass Options window and turn on the Incandescence option. Also, turn off the light in the scene by hiding it or setting its Intensity to **0**. The render should look like Figure 20-14. Save the scene as **MCR_JYL_RP_LUM_noiz.mb**.

Facing Ratio Mask

In Chapter 14, you learned a method of achieving Fresnel type effects by using the Sampler Info node's Facing Ratio attribute to control the color gain of the texture connected to the Reflectivity attribute. The result was that the object was more reflective around the edges that were facing away from the camera and not reflective at all where the surface was perpendicular to the view. Now, instead of setting this up on the reflectivity channel, we will do it on the incandescence channel.

> **NOTE** *For the purpose of this tutorial, we will disconnect the existing textures that are connected to the Incandescence attribute of the materials. However, if you were going to be rendering a few different passes using this attribute, you might want to create layered textures and connect all of the different textures for the separate Incandescence passes in there. That way, you could just turn on and off a specific texture in the layered texture node. Remember, though, that the more nodes Maya has to evaluate, the longer the render may take.*

1. You need to create one Sampler Info node to control all of the materials. Select all of the materials and then right-click their incandescence channel and choose Set Driven Key from the marking menu.

2. Create the Sampler Info node. In the Set Driven Key window, load the Sampler Info as the driver and choose the Facing Ratio attribute.

3. SHIFT-select all of the driven materials and choose the Incandescence R, G, and B attributes. (Refer to Chapter 14 in the section called "The Fresnel Effect" for more details on how to do this.)

4. It doesn't matter how you key the relationship between the Facing Ratio and the Incandescence. You could have a Facing Ratio of 1 equal to an Incandescence value of 0, or you could set both to 1. Whatever you choose can be inverted later on. It's probably easiest to set both to 1 so that a Facing Ratio of 1 equals an Incandescence value of 1 and a Facing Ratio of 0 equals an Incandescence value of 0. Render and save this pass, shown in Figure 20-15.

FIGURE 20-15 *Facing Ratio mask pass*

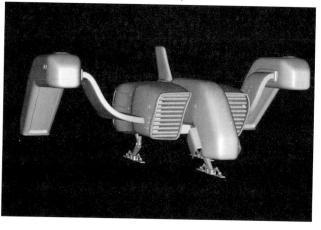

Occlusion Pass

When we are faking reflections by mapping textures to the Reflection Color attribute, areas in little holes and creases will sometimes still produce a reflection. Raytracing will solve this problem, but the render time will suffer. However, you can make a simple raytrace pass that will accurately determine what areas should be occluded, which means that they are not reflected back to the camera. While the end result may be subtle, this pass adds contrast that can be necessary for realistic results.

You can download a host of occlusion shaders from the Internet. If you find that you need more control over the occlusion, do some research and find the one that works for you. Here we will use a quick "hack" that will provide some very basic occlusion.

1. Create a new sphere in the scene, and scale it up so that it completely surrounds the ship throughout the entire animation. In the Attribute Editor, turn off the Primary Visibility in the Render Stats section. This will keep the sphere from being rendered, but it will still be able to cast reflections. In the Hypershade, create a new surface shader material and set its Out Color attribute to white.

2. We need to set the Reflected Color to black so that the only reflections visible in the render will be from the raytracing, not the environment reflection. Instead of disconnecting the existing reflection map from all of the materials, we can just set the Color Gain attribute on the file texture that is connected to the EnvBall_junkyard node to black. Then, in the Render Global Settings window, turn on Raytracing. Set the Reflection Limit to **1**.

3. Test render and save. It should look similar to Figure 20-16.

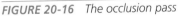
FIGURE 20-16   The occlusion pass

Shadow Pass

The shadow is probably the most important thing that ties together elements of a scene. A shadow tell us whether an object is floating above the ground or resting on it. It also gives us an idea of how far away the object is from the camera.

You can spend a lot of time perfecting the shadow, and in still renders, accurate shadowing may be very important. However, in animation you can get away with a lot less. A simple, low-resolution shadow can be blurred and colored in the compositing stage. In this step, we'll make a pass that will render a Depth Map Shadow of the ship on a ground plane.

1. Select the light in the scene and turn on Depth Map Shadows. The default setting should be OK for this stage of the process.

2. Now we need a ground plane. The camera-mapped plane would do, except that it is in another layer right now. In this case, it is easier to add a plane that will cover the shadow area and use that.

NOTE   *At the time of printing this book, the tmRenderPass.el script does not support a separate shadow pass. You can check to see whether a new version is available by going to* http://www.datasynthi.com/maya/scripts.html. *For now, we will use Maya's built-in multipass rendering features to render the shadow.*

3. In the Render Global Settings window, select the Maya Software tab and scroll down to the folder called Render Layer/Pass Control.

4. Check the box next to Enable Global Passes and then turn off all of the render passes in the globalRender fields except for Shadow, as shown in the illustration.

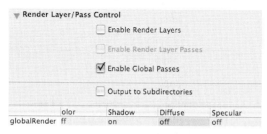

FIGURE 20-17   *The shadow in the alpha channel*

5. Save this scene as **MCR_JYL_RP_ shadow.mb**. Beware that against the black background, the shadow will be visible only in the alpha channel. Figure 20-17 shows the shadow pass in white in the alpha channel.

Engine Glow

While the ship's main engine is on the rear of the engine block, the thrusters on the sides of the ship help it to steer as it hovers in a planet's atmosphere. These particular engines operate on some science fiction–based ionic reaction and therefore do not need to look like something we might see on Earth today. Instead, we will give them self-illumination by creating a material with its incandescence turned all the way up. We will use this pass to create a glow effect.

1. Create a new Lambert material.

2. Map a Ramp texture to its incandescence channel. Set up the ramp to have four colors with blue on both ends and white in the middle. Your ramp should look like this illustration.

3. Map this material to the geometry on the bottom side of the thrusters. Name the pieces **pEngineIllum_LT** and **pEngineIllum_RT**.

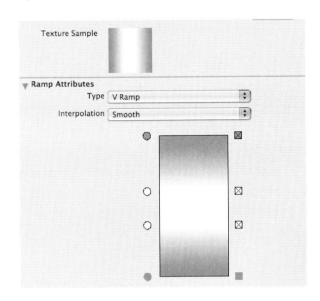

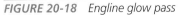
FIGURE 20-18　Engine glow pass

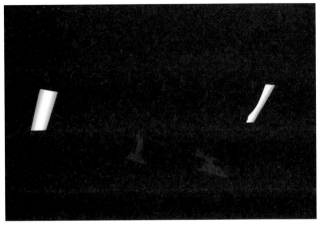

4. Turn off all of the check boxes in the tmRenderPass Options window. Since this MEL script works only on Blinn materials, the incandescence of this Lambert material will not be affected.

5. Save this pass as **MCR_JYL_RP_LUM_EngGlow.mb**. Figure 20-18 shows how it should look.

Engine Reflection

If the engines are glowing, the ship's material must reflect this light. We will hide the geometry with the glow material on it and replace the glow material with area lights. Area lights will emit the light from a rectangular area, so by placing two area lights on each thruster, we can simulate the light emitting from the glow.

1. Create an area light, and then translate, rotate, and scale it so that it fits inside the thruster and faces down toward the ground.

2. Set the Decay Rate to Linear and turn off the Emit Diffuse check box.

3. Duplicate this light and place it on the upper part of the thruster, pointing down.

4. Duplicate both lights and move the copies to the opposite thruster. Add them to the thruster group so that they will animate with the ship.

5. Hide the original pieces of geometry, and then in the tmRenderPass Options window, turn off everything except the Specularity option.

6. Verify that the Specular Roll Off and Eccentricity are set for a hard reflection, as they were when we did the hard specular pass earlier.

7. Save the scene as **MCR_JYL_RP_SPC_engin.mb**; this pass is shown in Figure 20-19.

FIGURE 20-19   *Engine reflection pass*

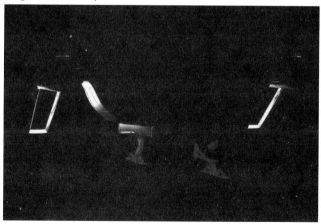

Heat Ripples

The air around a hot object heats up on contact and expands. When you are looking at some-thing that is behind such a heat emission, it appears distorted due to the refraction of the light. A simple way to replicate this effect is to render red and green particles and then use this pass as a displacement map in your compositing program.

To set this up, we will place a few volume emitters on different places of the ship. The thrusters are the most likely place to add them.

1. Create a volume emitter and set it so that it emits downward, in the –Y direction at a value of about **–0.25**. Set the Emission Rate to 300 particles per second.

2. Set the Along Axis attribute to **–5**. All the rest of the emitter's attributes can remain at their default settings.

3. Parent the emitter to the Thruster group.

4. For the particle shape, set the Render type to MultiPoint, with a Multi Count of **10** and the Multi Radius set at **0.54**.

5. Add a per particle attribute for the Color and Opacity. Create a ramp for each attribute.

6. On the color ramp, the particles should be set so they are red on birth and green at death. The opacity ramp should control them so that they are opaque for about 90 percent of their life and then go transparent.

7. Set their Lifespan to **1** with a **0.2** Randomness. The Conserve attribute should be set to **0.5** so that they no longer respond to the emitter after they are born.

FIGURE 20-20   *Heat ripples pass*

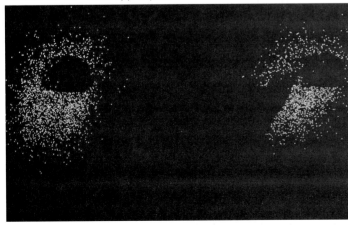

8. An Air field can then be added to blow them upward. When you create the Air field, turn off the Max Distance attribute. Set the Magnitude to about **8**.

9. Use Playblast to view the animation in real time. Make any tweaks necessary.

10. Duplicate the emitter and move it to the other thruster, and parent it to that group.

11. To emit the same particle group from that duplicate emitter, open the Dynamic Relationship Editor and connect the emitter and the particle group together.

12. Use the hardware renderer to render the animation. In the Render Global Settings window, turn on Enable Geometry Mask. This will render only the particles while masking out areas obstructed by geometry.

13. Save this scene as **MCR_JYL_RP_PRT_heat.ma**. Figure 20-20 shows a sample of what the pass might look like.

Background

This last pass has nothing to do with the ship at all. For this one, we will turn off the ship's display layer and turn on the environment. Make sure that all of the scene lights are turned off. Save the scene as **MCR_JYL_RP_Background.mb**. A frame from this pass is shown in Figure 20-21.

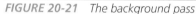

FIGURE 20-21 The background pass

Batch Rendering

So far in this book, we have been rendering with the Batch Render command found in the Render menu. This command provides a quick way to render a project without you having to leave Maya. However, if the batch renderer is already working on a certain scene or pass and it is invoked again with the Batch Render command, you will need to abort the rendering in progress to render your new scene.

By saving each scene that is set up for a specific pass in our render scenes directory, we can start the batch renderer through a command-line interface without even having to launch Maya. Even more useful is creating a text file containing a list of all of the scenes you'd like rendered and then using the `render` command to open the file. When rendering is done in this way, the batch renderer will render the first scene in the list and then move on to the next until every scene in the list has been rendered. You can set this up and then leave the machine to do all of the work. Rendering is best done when nobody will be working on the computer (such as while you're asleep), so that the computer's resources are freed up just to render.

To create the file, use a text editor such as BBEdit. On the first line, type **render**. Then enter the rendering flags—rendering flags are available for pretty much every attribute in the Render Global Settings window. You could specify a frame range or image resolution here if you wish. If the flag is not set in the text editor, the batch renderer will use the settings from the scene file. The only flag we'll use here is the `-n` flag. This sets the renderer to use a specified number of processors. If this flag is set to 0, the batch renderer will use all available processors. After the flags, type the path to the scene file and the scene filename. (If this text file is placed in the same directory as the render scenes, it is not necessary to enter the path.) The text file for this project should look similar to the following.

> *NOTE* **The following lines are shown with line breaks to accommodate the size of the page. However, when the script is read by Maya, Maya will read everything before the semicolon (;) as one command line, so it does not really matter where or if you break the lines.**

```
render -n 0 /Users/tmeade/Documents/maya/projects/Chapter20/renderScenes/
MCR_c20_JYL_RP_Dif_hard.mb;
render -n 0 /Users/tmeade/Documents/maya/projects/Chapter20/renderScenes/
MCR_c20_JYL_RP_Dif_soft.mb;
render -n 0 /Users/tmeade/Documents/maya/projects/Chapter20/renderScenes/
MCR_c20_JYL_RP_REF_Hard.mb;
mayarender_with_mr -file/Users/tmeade/Documents/maya/projects/Chapter20/
renderScenes/MCR_c20_JYL_RP_REF_soft.mb;
```

> *NOTE* **When rendering with Mental Ray from the command line, you must use the `mayarender_with_mr` command.**

```
render -n 0 /Users/tmeade/Documents/maya/projects/Chapter20/renderScenes/
MCR_c20_JYL_RP_SPC_soft.mb;
render -n 0 /Users/tmeade/Documents/maya/projects/Chapter20/renderScenes/
MCR_c20_JYL_RP_SPC_hard.mb;
render -r hw -n 0 /Users/tmeade/Documents/maya/projects/Chapter20/renderScenes/
MCR_c20_JYL_RP_PART_heat.mb;
```

```
render -n 0 /Users/tmeade/Documents/maya/projects/Chapter20/renderScenes/
MCR_c20_JYL_RP_SPC_Engin.mb
render -n 0 /Users/tmeade/Documents/maya/projects/Chapter20/renderScenes/
MCR_c20_JYL_RP_LUM_EngGlow.mb;
render -n 0 /Users/tmeade/Documents/maya/projects/Chapter20/renderScenes/
MCR_c20_JYL_RP_LUM_FacRat.mb;
render -n 0 /Users/tmeade/Documents/maya/projects/Chapter20/renderScenes/
MCR_c20_JYL_RP_LUM_noiz.mb;
render -n 0 /Users/tmeade/Documents/maya/projects/Chapter20/renderScenes/
MCR_c20_JYL_RP_LUM_Occlud.mb;
render -n 0 /Users/tmeade/Documents/maya/projects/Chapter20/renderScenes/
MCR_c20_JYL_RP_Shadow.mb;
render -n 0 /Users/tmeade/Documents/maya/projects/Chapter20/renderScenes/
MCR_c20_JYL_RP_Background.mb;
```

> **NOTE** *The heat ripple pass uses the hardware renderer to render the particles. You need to specify this by including the* `-r` *flag with the* `hw` *option.*

Now you need to save the file and change its permissions so that it can be used as an executable. I named the file **mcrRender.txt**. To change its permissions in a UNIX-based OS, you can open a shell and use the `cd` command to navigate to the location of this file. Then type the following:

```
chmod a=rwx mcrRender.txt
```

Press RETURN (ENTER) and this text file is now an executable. To begin rendering, type `./mcrRender.txt`.

The file will open and send the commands to the renderer. If you are using the Microsoft Windows operating system, making the file executable is much easier. Simply change the text file's extension to *.bat*. To launch the script, just double-click the .bat file. At this time, you can get up and take a break—or go to sleep, eat, drink, and be happy—because in a few hours, your scene will be rendered in multiple passes. To complete the project, you need to composite them together.

Summary

In this chapter, we've combined a lot of the information you've learned so far in this book, introduced a few new tricks, and rendered all of our passes. Hopefully, this has served as a good review and demonstrated how all of the elements of a visual effects shot come together inside Maya.

In the next chapter, you will learn how to put all of these renderings together in a final composite using Abode After Effects.

Compositing in Post-Production

Compositing is the process of putting

together all of the elements of a scene into one

cohesive piece. The compositing stage of any

production is the central process into which all the

other parts of production flow. In many situations,

these parts might come not just from Maya, but

from many different programs. In this chapter, we

will composite the different passes of our spaceship

onto the background and then do some color

correction and make other small adjustments to

integrate the production. Before you begin this

chapter, however, you will need access to a compositing application. We use Adobe After Effects here, because it is a widely available and relatively inexpensive application. After Effects is more than capable of doing everything we need for this shot. If you don't own After Effects, you can download a free trial version from the Adobe web site at *http://www.adobe.com/support/ downloads/main.html.*

You can also use many other compositing applications, such as Discreet's Combustion (*http:// www4.discreet.com/combustion/*) and Apple's Shake (*http://www.apple.com/shake/*), two high-end compositing applications widely used in visual effects production. While these two applications work a little differently from After Effects, both of them are fine to use as you work through this chapter. If you have one of these or another application, and you think you can translate the following materials, go for it. But if compositing is something new to you, you might be better off using After Effects as you work through the tutorials.

Compositing the Ship Passes

Let's begin by compositing all of the spaceship's passes that we rendered in Chapter 20. The process will be similar to the one we used in Chapter 14 to build up materials in the Hypershade, except that now we'll be able to get real-time feedback instead of waiting for renders. We will use the grunge pass as a mask on one of the main passes and then use one of the layer blend modes to affect the layers underneath.

Set Up After Effects

We'll start by setting up After Effects.

1. Launch Adobe After Effects. You'll see the project window and a few floating pallets. Choose File | Import | Multiple Files. Navigate to the folder with the QuickTime movies of all of the passes (you can use your own or use the files provided on the CD). Select them all and click the Import button. All of the movies will appear in the project window.

2. Choose File | Project Settings. Set the Time Base to 24 frames per second.

3. Now we'll set up our ship's composition. Choose Composition | New Composition, and you'll see the Composition Settings window. Name this composition **Ship_Main**. Since we rendered the movies at 600×399, we will match this resolution here. Set the Width to **600** and the Height to **399**, and set the Duration to **5** seconds. We will be editing this a bit at the end of the tutorial, but for now we'll stick to matching our renders. The Composition Settings window should look like Figure 21-1.

FIGURE 21-1   *The Composition Settings window*

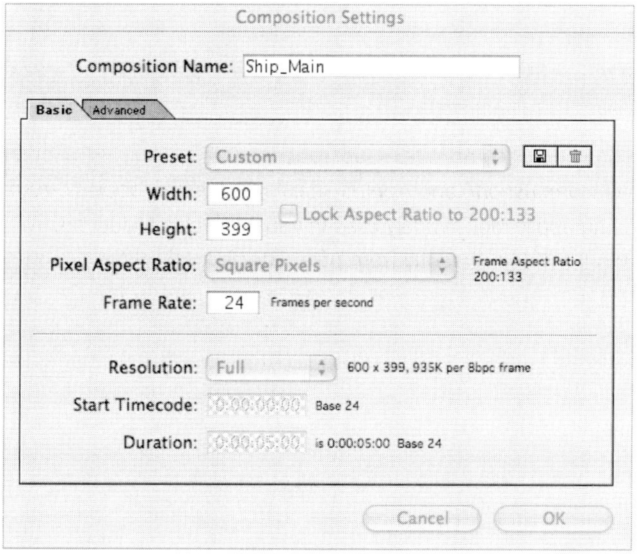

4. Click the OK button and the composition will be created. The Ship_Main Composition window and Timeline will also appear on your screen.

Diffuse Surface

We rendered two passes for the diffuse color of the spaceship. The first, the soft diffuse pass, is used to describe the ship's basic surface color in the even lighting situation of the background plate. It was rendered with Mental Ray's Final Gather rendering engine. The second diffuse pass, the hard diffuse, was created with one light turned on so that only the surfaces facing upward were being lit, while the surfaces on the sides and facing the ground were much darker, almost black. We want to combine these passes to create a spaceship surface that has been "beat up" a bit. We will use the grunge pass to mask out areas where the shiny, reflective paint has been chipped away to reveal the surface underneath, which is the hard diffuse layer. We will play with the contrast of the grunge layer to control the amount of wear we desire.

1. Drag the MCR_JYL_RP_Dif_Soft.mov into the Timeline window, or the composition window, so that it snaps into the center. Drag the MCR_JYL_RP_grunge.mov into the layer above that so that it sits on top.

2. At the bottom of the Timeline window, make sure that the modes are visible by clicking the Switches/Modes button.

3. Click the TrkMat pull-down menu in the MCR_JYL_RP_Dif_Soft.mov layer and set it to Luma Matte "MCR _JYL_RP_grunge.mov." This will use the dark areas from the grunge layer to mask out the diffuse layer, making the soft diffuse layer a little more beat-up looking. We will continue to use this same technique of using the grunge layer as a mask for most of the passes rendered for the ship's surface.

4. The beat-up look might be a bit too subtle. To sharpen it, we will increase the contrast of the grunge layer by adjusting the levels: select the grunge layer and then choose Effect | Adjust | Levels. We are going to "clamp" the image so that the darkest color is black and the brightest color is white.

5. In the Effects window, move the sliders at the bottom of the Histogram so that they clamp the levels shown. Your levels should look like those in Figure 21-2.

FIGURE 21-2   *Clamp levels in the Histogram*

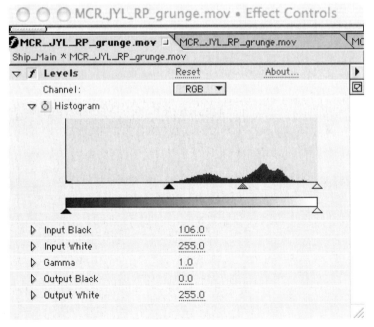

6. The masked-out areas in the soft diffuse layer appear black. However, the areas that are receiving more direct light from above should be a bit brighter. This is where our hard diffuse layer will come into to play. Place the MCR_JYL_RP_Dif_hard.mov layer under the soft diffuse layer. Now the masked-out areas on the surfaces facing up will be a bit lighter than those facing down. The layers in the Timeline window should now look like the illustration.

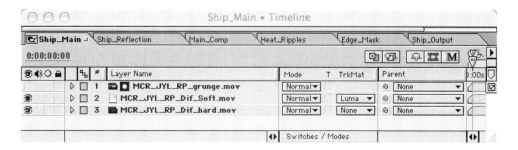

7. Now we can fine-tune everything so far by adjusting the opacity of the different layers. We will continue doing this throughout the compositing process. The settings we choose now may be changed later, but realize that this is part of the beauty of building your images in this way. You can continue changing the look of everything by adjusting a slider instead of re-rendering the entire image. For now, let's decrease the amount of the hard diffuse layer. Click the little triangle to the left of the layer name in the Timeline window to see its default transform attributes. The attribute at the bottom is called Opacity. Set it to **40** percent. This will make the composited layers appear dark, but not quite black. Figure 21-3 shows the composition window with these three layers composited.

FIGURE 21-3   Our spaceship with the soft diffuse, hard diffuse, and grunge layers composited together

TIP   *If you are new to using After Effects, you can access all of a layer's attributes in the Timeline by clicking the little triangle on the left side of the layer's name. This will list the transform attributes, including Opacity and many others, such as Position, Scale, and Rotation.*

Reflections

For the most part, our spaceship is made from highly reflective surfaces. Reflections will be duller in the areas where the paint has been chipped away and the underlying surface is visible. Some of these areas will not be reflective at all due to dirt and the creases in the ship's surface. We rendered several different passes to control the reflections: the hard reflection pass, soft reflection pass, occlusion pass, and facing ratio pass. And, of course, we will once again make use of the grunge pass. We will composite the reflections inside a separate composition because so many different layers are involved. This reflection composition will then be added to the Ship_Main composition to affect the diffuse layer underneath it. Finally, we'll go through all of the layers and adjust their opacity levels until everything is working together to make the ship look like it is made of the material we want.

1. Choose Composition | New Composition. All the settings in the Composition Settings window should be the same as those of the Ship_Main composition; name this new composition **Ship_reflection**.

2. In the Timeline window, add the MCR_ JYL_RP_RFL_hard.mov file to the new composition. Place MCR_JYL_RP_grunge.mov in the layer above that.

3. Choose Multiply from the blend modes pull-down menu (under the Modes column) on the grunge layer. This operation will multiply the pixels' brightness values between the images on the different layers. This will darken all of the dark areas in the grunge map, making the highly reflective surface look dirty and beat up—much more realistic looking than a perfectly reflective chrome ship.

4. Once again, clamp the levels of this grunge layer to increase the contrast. Watch the effect that this has on the image. Select the grunge layer and then choose Effect | Adjust | Levels. The Levels settings should be similar to those set for the diffuse surface in step 5 of the preceding section.

5. Next we'll add the soft reflections for the dirty or worn parts of the surfaces. In the Timeline window, add MCR_JYL_RP_RFL_soft.mov on top and then add another MCR_ JYL_RP_grunge.mov layer on top of that.

6. Set the TrkMat for the soft reflection layer to Luma Invert "MCR_JYL_RP_grunge.mov," and set its blend mode to Screen. Screening adds the pixel values together while constraining the brightest value in either layer.

7. Now we need to adjust the levels of the grunge layer that are affecting the soft reflections. Once again, choose Effect | Adjust | Levels. Adjust the light values, dark values, and midtones (known as the *Gamma*) so that the levels look similar to Figure 21-4.

FIGURE 21-4   Adjusted light, dark, and midtones

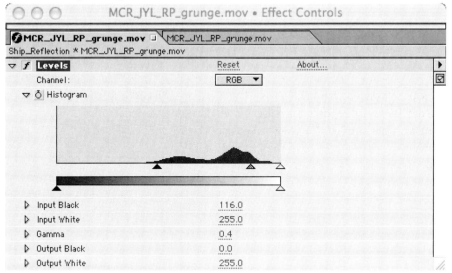

8. As you may remember from Chapter 14's discussion of the Fresnel Effect, most surfaces aren't as reflective when viewed straight on as they are when viewed at an angle. In this step, we'll use the facing ratio pass to attenuate the reflections. Add the MCR_JYL_RP_LUM_FacRat.mov to the top of the Timeline and set its blend mode to Multiply.

9. The initial effect the layer is having on the layers below it is the opposite of what we need. Currently, the addition of the facing ratio pass makes the surface more reflective at the angles close to perpendicular to the viewing camera. It should be the other way around. We can therefore invert it by selecting it and choosing Effect | Channel | Invert.

10. We rendered this pass so that the relationship between the facing ratio and incandescence was linear. However, we really need the falloff to occur exponentially. Choose Effect | Adjust | Curves to bring up the Curves control for this layer.

11. Grab a point near the middle of the curve and drag it so that it looks similar to Figure 21-5. You should also adjust the bottom output so that the curve begins above a value of 0 for its output.

12. Some areas on the ship should not be reflective at all, including any crevices or seams in the ship's hull. Add MCR_JYL_RP_occlude.mov on top of the other layers in the Timeline. Set its blend mode to Multiply.

FIGURE 21-5 *Drag the curve like this.*

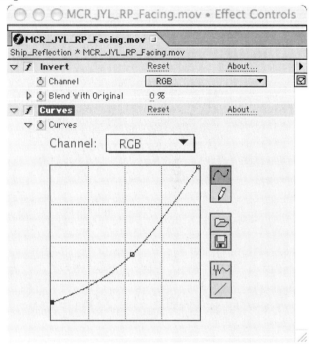

13. Apply a small blur to the layer, just to soften it as you would a shadow. Choose Effect | Blur And Sharpen | Gaussian Blur and set the Blurriness value to **1**. Your reflection composition should look similar to Figure 21-6.

FIGURE 21-6 *The reflection composition*

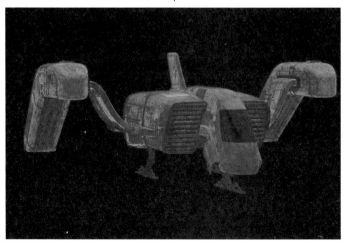

14. In the Timeline, switch back to the Ship_Main composition by clicking the Ship_Main tab. From the project window, drag the Ship_Reflection composition icon into the Ship_Main composition and place it on the top layer. This is called a *nested composition*. The entire composition can now be adjusted as a single layer. In the Timeline, set the Ship_Reflection layer's blend mode to Screen. You will now see the reflections on top of the diffuse surface.

15. A shiny metallic surface such as this ship's surface should be emitting its color mostly from the reflections around it, not much from its diffuse color. In the Timeline, we need to turn down the opacity levels of the diffuse layers, which is pretty much the same thing as turning down the Diffuse attribute in the material attributes in Maya. Set the Opacity setting at 20 percent for both the hard and soft diffuse layers. Use your own judgment to find the exact values that work. The result should look similar to Figure 21-7.

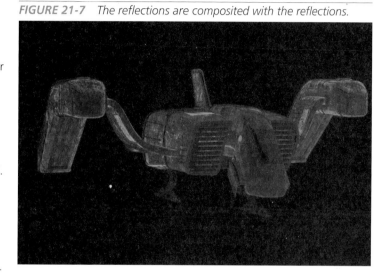

FIGURE 21-7   The reflections are composited with the reflections.

16. Now preview the animation to make sure that everything looks OK from various angles as the ship lands.

Specular Highlights

Now we'll add the specular highlights to the existing composition. We rendered two separate specular passes—one hard and one soft. The specular highlight is one of the most important characteristics of a surface, because it accentuates how soft, smooth, hard, or rough a surface is.

This soft specular pass is meant to pick up the subtle highlights in the dull areas, while the hard specular pass will reflect the main, shiny, highly reflective parts of the surface.

FIGURE 21-8   The soft specular pass is added and masked with the grunge layer.

1. Add MCR_JYL_RP_SPC_soft.mov and the MCR_JYL_RP_grunge.mov into the Ship_Main composition. Since we want this pass to affect the worn areas of the ship, set TrkMat to Luma Inverted Matte "MCR_JYL_RP_grunge.mov." Add the Levels effect to the grunge layer and adjust the contrast. Figure 21-8 shows a close-up of parts of the ship where this specular highlight is most noticeable.

2. Set the blend mode of the soft specular layer to Screen.

3. Now let's handle the hard specular highlights. Add the MCR_JYL_RP_SPC_hard.mov and the MCR_JYL_RP_grunge.mov to the layers above the soft specular layers. This time, set TrkMat on the hard specular layer to Luma, rather than Luma Inverted as we last used.

4. Once again, adjust the contrast of the grunge layer by adding the Levels effect and tweaking it until it looks right. The specular highlights should look fairly rough and beat-up.

5. When hard specular highlights are exposed onto a piece of film, the light bleeds around the existing overexposed area. To simulate this, we'll use another copy of the hard highlight and blur it. Make a copy of the hard specular layer and place it on top of the other layers. Choose Effect | Blur And Sharpen | Gaussian Blur. Set the Blurriness value to 15 pixels.

6. Obviously, this is a bit too bright. Set the Opacity to about 30 percent.

7. Select the hard specular layer in the Timeline window and press ENTER (RETURN). You can rename the layer so that you do not confuse it with the non-blurred version of the layer. Name it **specular hard blur**.

8. One final tweak would be to select this version of the blurred specular highlight and choose Effect | Adjust | Curves, and tweak the curves so that the falloff of this "blooming" specular is very round. Again, this is a subtle effect, but little tweaks like this can make images look really good. Figure 21-9 shows the Curves control for this layer.

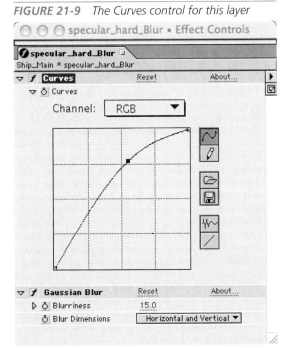

FIGURE 21-9 *The Curves control for this layer*

Thruster Effects

The thrusters need to produce a glowing effect. To achieve this, we rendered two passes: an incandescence pass, with the incandescence turned up on the material for the parts that need to glow, and a specular pass to simulate the light emitting from the thrusters. Now we need to put them together and produce a glowing effect.

1. Add MCR_JYL_RP_SPC_Eng.mov on the top layer, and then add MCR_JYL_RP_grunge.mov on top of that. Set the MCR_JYL_RP_SPC_Eng.mov to Screen and use the Luma of the grunge layer as the matte. Once again, add the Levels effect to the grunge layer and adjust it to suit you.

2. Add MCR_JYL_RP_LUM_Eng.mov on top of the other layers in the Ship_Main composition. Set the blend mode to Add.

3. Duplicate this layer and choose Effect | Blur And Sharpen | Gaussian Blur. Set the Blurriness of this duplicate to **25**. Rename the layer **engine glow**.

4. Now everything it too bright, and some of the bluish color is being lost. Play with the Opacity settings for both layers. The original layer's Opacity should be set low, about 40 percent. The glow layer's Opacity should be set at about 75 percent. But, as is always the case, you'll find that you can experiment to find the settings that you like best. The final effect should look like Figure 21-10.

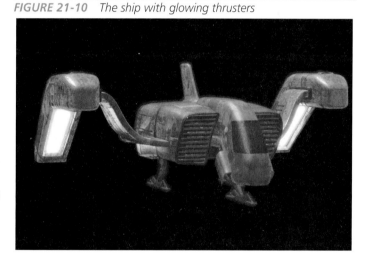

FIGURE 21-10   The ship with glowing thrusters

5. Do another preview of the animation to make sure that everything looks good as the ship comes down for its landing.

Masking the Edge

When the passes were imported into After Effects, they were set to ignore their alpha channels. Otherwise, the edges would be anti-aliased against black or some other color. When this composition is placed on top of the background layer, it is possible that the black edges will show up. For this reason, we will use a single layer with an alpha channel as a stencil over the entire composition.

1. Select the pass that contains the ship. The soft diffuse pass will work fine.

2. Place this layer on the top of the Ship_Main composition.

3. Set the blend mode to Stencil Alpha. Notice that the edges around the ship soften a bit.

Now we are ready to begin integrating the ship into the background.

Compositing the Ship into the Background

Now we can really begin bringing this shot together. A few areas need attention. First, we need to add some elements that tie the ship to the background—adding a shadow and adding pools of light where the thrusters illuminate the ground. We'll also use our particle pass to distort the background so that it appears as if the ship were emitting heat by using this pass as a displacement map against the background layer. Some color correction is also needed for the ship and the background so that the levels of both elements match. And we can do some tricks to soften the edges around the ship just a bit more.

Initial Color/Contrast Adjustment

Let's start by making major adjustments to the background. We need to use the background as the basis for many other operations yet to come. First we'll create a new composition that contains the ship and the background. From there, it will be a little more obvious which way the colors and contrast need to shift.

1. Create a new composition. In the Composition Settings window, be sure that all of the same settings of the other compositions in the scene are used, but name it **Main_Comp**.

2. Add the MCR_JYL_RP_background.mov to this composite, and then nest the Ship_ Main composite into this composition. Right away, you should be able to see that the ship is dark with a lot of contrast, while the background is light and the contrast is flat.

3. Select the background layer and duplicate it. Select this duplicate and change its blend mode to Overlay. Overlay will screen the light areas and multiply the dark areas of the two images, increasing the contrast and color intensity of the background image.

4. Select both background layers and choose Layer | Pre-Compose. In the Pre-compose window, name the new composition **background_Overlay** and choose the option to Move all attributes into a new composition. Now we have a single layer for the background, for which we can make subtle adjustments later on, as well as use for some other things.

5. Select the Ship_Main layer and duplicate it. Screen the duplicate layer over the original. This will brighten all of those darker colors and make the ship a little less contrasting.

6. Select both Ship_Main layers and choose Layer | Pre-Compose. In the Pre-compose window, name the new composition **Ship_Screen** and choose the option to Move all attributes into a new composition.

Shadow

In this section, we will composite the shadow of the ship onto the ground. Instead of just applying the shadow pass to the layers underneath and using a blend mode such as Multiply or Darken, we will use the shadow pass as a mask over a copy of the background layer and adjust the midtones of this background. This will make the ship appear to be shading the ground, not just darkening it.

1. In the Main_Comp composition, duplicate the Background_Overlay and name it **Background Shadow**.

2. Add MCR_JYL_RP_shadow.mov on the top layer of this composition. Set the Background Shadow layer to use the shadow pass as an alpha matte by setting the TrkMat on the Background Shadow layer to Alpha Matte "MCR_JYL_RP_shadow.mov."

3. Select the Background Shadow layer and choose Effect | Adjust | Levels.

4. Adjust the Gamma slider in the Histogram (the slider in the center) by sliding it to the right. Watch the composition window as you slide this. You want to match the shadow areas of the ship with the shadow areas under the bins in the background. A Gamma value of about **0.7** looks right.

5. Now, to soften the shadow, select the shadow pass layer and blur it. Try a Blurriness setting of **10**. This composition should look similar to Figure 21-11.

FIGURE 21-11   The background with the ship's shadow added

Heat Ripples

When we rendered the particles in Chapter 20, you probably were a little concerned about how we were going to integrate these brightly colored particles into the scene. The secret is finally revealed in this section. Basically, we will use these particles as a displacement map to distort the background image. This will simulate the light refraction that occurs when you look through heated air. Just like a shadow, this is another good technique for tying together different elements.

1. Create a new composition and name it **Heat_Ripples**.

2. Add MCR_JYL_RP_PART_heat.mov. Select it, add a Gaussian blur, and blur it about 12 pixels.

3. Return to the Main_Comp Timeline and select the Background_Overlay layer. Choose Effect | Distort | Displacement Map.

4. In the Effect Controls window for the displacement map, set the Displacement Map Layer to Heat_Ripples. This will tell the displacement filter to get its values from the Heat Ripples layer. It will displace the background layer by the number of pixels specified in the Maximum Horizontal Displacement and Max Vertical Displacement. Set these values low—2 pixels in either direction should be enough. The effect is subtle enough that you will have to play the animation to notice it. If you are still having trouble, view the final movie on the CD to see the effect example.

Pools of Light

The thrusters on the ship emit quite a glow, surely enough that you should be able to see them illuminate the ground a bit. We could have rendered a pass out of Maya that contained just the illumination of the ground plane from the area lights in the engine. However, it can be tough to get the area of illumination to be as rectangular as the thrusters. Plus, their effect on the ground should be noticeable only as the ship gets very close. For these reasons, we will "fake it" by masking out a solid color layer and using that as a mask for another copy of the background. Instead of using the levels to darken this area, as we did for the shadow, we will use them to lighten the ground.

1. In the Main_Comp Timeline, create a new solid layer by choosing Layer | New | Solid. Make the solid layer white and set the Width and Height so that it covers the entire composition window.

2. Select the Pen tool and draw a box with six points whose ends connect somewhere near the bottom of the screen, where the ground might be. See Figure 21-12 to get an idea of how it should look.

FIGURE 21-12 The masks are created over the solid layer.

3. After you draw the first shape, draw another one on the other side under the opposite thruster. It can be fairly rough, as we are going to blur it quite a bit.

4. Now select the solid layer and add a blur to it of about 30 pixels.

5. Make a duplicate of the Background Overlay layer and place it above the MCR_c20_JYL_RP_LUM_Shadow.iff layer. Rename it **Engine_Light**.

6. Move the solid layer so that it is right on top of that layer, and below the Ship_Screen layer.

7. Select the Engine_Light layer and set its TrkMat to Luma Matte "Solid1."

8. Add a Levels effect to the Engine_Light layer, and pull the Gamma and the Input White sliders to the left to lighten the area of the background matted by the blurred solid. Your composition should look similar to Figure 21-13.

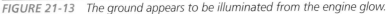

FIGURE 21-13   The ground appears to be illuminated from the engine glow.

Edge Feathering

As of now, the outer edges of the ship are a little too hard. They need to blend into the background better. We will create a new composition that is nothing more than a mask of the inner edge of the ship. This can then be used as a mask for another copy of the background layer. This layer is then placed on top of the ship. The result is that the background appears to "spill over" onto the edges of the ship.

1. Create a new composition, and name it **Edge_Mask**.

2. Add a layer that contains an alpha channel of the entire ship. The file MCR_c20_JYL_RP_DIF_soft.mov will work fine.

3. Duplicate this layer.

4. Select the layer on the bottom, and choose Effect | Render | Fill. Fill this layer with a white color.

5. Choose the layer above the bottom one, and change its blend mode to Silhouette Alpha.

6. Now apply a blur to this layer of about 2 pixels. The composition should look like Figure 21-14.

7. Add this Edge_mask layer to the Main_Comp and place it on the top layer.

8. Make a duplicate of the Background_Overlay layer and move it under the Edge_Mask layer. Rename it **Background_Spill**.

9. Set the TrkMat of the Background_Spill layer to Luma Matte "Edge_Mask." You should notice that the edge around the ship softened just a bit.

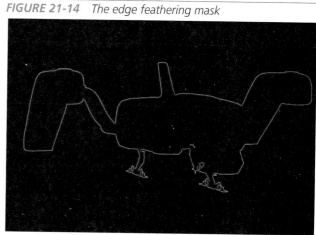

FIGURE 21-14 *The edge feathering mask*

Color Correction

In this section, we will correct the color in two ways: First, we will make some subtle adjustments to the levels of the background and the ship so that they match more closely. Judging from the specular highlights on the ship, the background should look as if it were shot on a fairly bright day. Therefore, we need to brighten it up a bit more. Next, we will create a new composition, add the main composition to it, and do some color manipulation to the entire image as a whole. In this final color correction, the image becomes stylized. Only a few things are suggested here, but you are encouraged to play around and create your own "look" for the final animation.

1. Select the Background_Overlay layer and add a levels effect to it. Pull the white input slider down to about 220. This will brighten the lighter colors.

2. Select the Ship_Screen layer. Add a levels effect to this layer and pull the input white slider down a bit until it looks right. Scrub through the animation and try scrubbing it at different places on the Timeline.

TIP **It may sound silly, but it can help to stand back from the monitor and squint your eyes. This can soften the defining edges in the composition and let you judge the overall color of the image.**

3. Create a new composition and name it **Ship_Output**.

4. Add the Main_Comp into this new composition.

5. Choose Effect | Hue/Saturation. Move the Master Saturation Slider down to desaturate the colors in the entire image. Set it at about **–40**.

6. Duplicate this layer. Unfold its attribute list and double-click its Hue/Saturation layer under the Effects group.

7. In the Effect Controls window for this effect, click the Colorize check box, and then use the Colorize Hue setting to change the hue to a bluish color, a hue value of **200**. Set the Colorize Saturation attribute to **50**.

8. Now set the blend mode for this layer to Hard Light.

9. Decrease the Opacity value to about **20**. We now have a somewhat desaturated image with a slightly bluish tint to it. Again, play around with this some more. Try other colors and saturation levels, and then experiment with different blend modes.

Final Touches

We can do just a few more things to this image to get it looking like it came from a single frame of film. We can soften the entire image just a bit to get rid of any edges that are too hard. We can also add some noise to simulate film grain. You'll find some plug-ins that do a great job simulating film grains of different film stocks, but we'll set it all up manually here.

1. With the Ship_Output composition loaded in the Timeline, create a solid white layer on top. We are going to use this as an adjustment layer.

2. Click the Switches/Modes button at the bottom of the Timeline window and enable the adjustment layer for the solid.

3. Now apply a Gaussian blur to this adjustment layer. A value of **1** should be good.

4. Return to displaying the blend modes in the Timeline and set the solid's blend mode to Lighten.

5. Adjust the Opacity value of the solid layer to about **50** percent.

6. To add the noise, create another solid white layer on the top of this composition.

7. With this layer selected, choose Effect | Stylize | Noise. Deselect the Use Color Noise and Clip Result Values check boxes.

8. Set the Amount of Noise to **1.6** percent. Turn on the animation channel for the Amount Of Noise channel and set another key at the end of the animation for the same amount.

9. Select both the first and last keys, and choose Window | The Wiggler. The Wiggler pallet appears. In this pallet window, set the Noise Type to Jagged, and set the Frequency to **24** and the Magnitude to **0.3**. This will cause the amount of noise to be from 1.3 to 1.9, changing randomly every frame.

10. Apply a Gaussian blur to this noise layer of about 1 pixel. Set its blend mode to Multiply and turn the Opacity down to about **6** percent.

Figure 21-15 shows the final image. Be sure to check out the color insert section of this book to see the image in color.

FIGURE 21-15   The final composite

At this point, you may wish to go back and make small adjustments to various layers inside the nested compositions. Make sure to take a look at the color insert pages in this book to see a still from this animation. And don't forget to look at the final animation on the CD.

Keep playing with this exercise if you want. Not only can you keep tweaking it to perfection, but you can try to change the image completely. If you are feeling comfortable, you could go back into Maya and render some more passes, such as additional particle effects and other grunge maps or color maps. As long as you don't need to change the animation, you can easily re-render any pass or make additions to it. Have fun with it!

Appendix

MEL Scripting

MEL (Maya Embedded Language) is
Maya's internal scripting language. While the
word *scripting* might send many artists away
screaming, learning to use MEL is an important
aspect of learning Maya. To learn it well, you'd
need to study an entire book devoted to the
subject of MEL or programming in general.
However, for many users, just understanding
the basics is enough to create short scripts that
make working in Maya very efficient. This
appendix serves as a guide to understanding
the basic framework of MEL.

We'll wrap up this appendix by examining the process of writing a short script. In the "Case Study" section of this appendix, we will write a short script that was mentioned back in Chapter 10.

What Is MEL?

MEL is a scripting language. Scripting is a simple form of programming. Unlike languages such as C and C++, MEL does not require that the script be *compiled* before it can be run—in other words, the script you write does not have to be translated into machine code to be executed by the computer. In fact, you can think of MEL as a layer between the Maya GUI (graphical user interface) and C++. Any time you click a button in the Shelf or choose a command from a menu, that action sends a MEL command to the main Maya program, which then talks to the operating system of your computer that controls the hardware.

What Can MEL Scripts Do?

MEL can assist you in almost everything you do in Maya. One of the most basic things you can do with MEL is string together several commands and run them in sequence. For instance, the time it takes to convert a multi-patch NURBS model into polygons and clean it up could be minimized by creating a script that runs each command to convert, combine, merge vertices, freeze transformations, and delete history. As an artist, any time you identify a repetitive task, such as the one in this example, you should consider writing a MEL script to handle the task.

Some other uses for MEL are

- To redo previous tasks
- To create custom controls, windows, and GUIs
- To control particle systems
- To create, connect, and control multiple attributes (what the tmRenderPass script that was used in Chapter 20 does)
- To align transform attributes of different objects (covered in the tutorial at the end of this appendix)

MEL Commands

To master MEL scripting completely, you will probably want to research and practice basic programming. Pick up a book on C, C++, Perl, Java, or any other programming language so that you can become more familiar with how programming works and what you can do to optimize and write better scripts.

If you don't want to go that far, a handful of great books on the market are dedicated to MEL scripting. One of the best resources for learning MEL can be found in Maya's online documentation, in the "MEL Command Reference" section. Learning about commands and how to use them is a great starting point to learning MEL. This online section is a dictionary of every MEL command available in Maya, detailing every option for each command and providing examples of how to use it.

TIP *Every time you open Maya, press F1 on the keyboard to open Maya's online documentation, and then go to the "MEL Command Reference" section. Get in the habit of choosing a command of interest, or even at random, and reading about it. Sooner or later, it will all start to make sense. That's how this author learned basic MEL scripting.*

Most of the MEL command names are fairly intuitive. The command to add an attribute, for example, is called `addAttr`. In addition to searching the reference alphabetically, you can browse the commands by category. Either way, the names of MEL commands were designed to be as close to English as possible.

The Script Editor

Perhaps the easiest way to find a MEL command is to execute a command from one of the menus in the main Maya user interface and then look at the Script Editor (Window | General Editors | Script Editor) to see what is journaled. Every time you select an object, open a window, or execute a command from the menus or Shelf buttons, these actions fire off a MEL command, which is then journaled, or listed, in the Script Editor. If you have been working in Maya for a few hours, it may surprise you to see that every operation you've done since you launched Maya appears in the Script Editor.

NOTE *Some commands are not journaled in the Script Editor by default. Such commands usually have to do with loading certain parts of the UI. You can see these in the Script Editor by choosing Script | Echo All Commands from the Script Editor menu bar.*

Figure A-1 shows the Script Editor and its contents after Maya was launched, the online documentation was opened, and a polygonal cube was created. The top part of the Script Editor that contains all of the journaled commands is called the History window, and the bottom section is called the Input window, where commands can be typed in and executed.

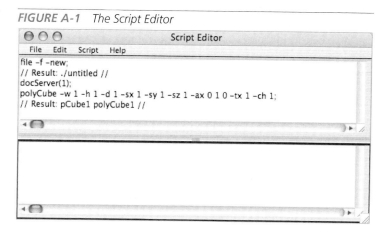

FIGURE A-1   The Script Editor

Let's step through the commands journaled so far and figure out what is going on. The first line says

```
file -f -new;
```

The command used here is `file`. This command will create a new Maya scene file and is executed automatically when Maya is launched. The text that follows the dash (–) is called a *flag* (`-f`, `-new`). Flags are the options, or settings, for the command. When you set options for a command in its Options window, these options, or attributes, will appear as flags in the script. So what do `-f` and `-new` do? We could look up the `file` command in the "MEL Command Reference," but while we are in the Script Editor, we can run the `help` command for the `file` command: in the Input window of the Script Editor, type this:

```
help file ;
```

Then press CTRL-ENTER (CONTROL-RETURN) to execute the command. A synopsis for the `file` command is listed, and all of the available flags are listed and show what the flags stand for. Find the `-f` flag in this list, and the History window tells you that it stands for *force*. For a more precise definition of this flag, look up the `file` command in the "MEL Command Reference." You'll learn that *force* means to force an action to take place (such as new, open, and save). The `-new` flag creates a new scene named *untitled*. Finally, the line ends with a semicolon (;), which marks the end of a command.

The next line in the script tells us the result of the `file` command, which in this example is a scene called *untitled*. This result is just feedback from the program telling us what has happened; it is not executing an actual command. Any line preceded by double slashes (/ /) is a *comment* and is not executed. Comments are often used to document, explain, or comment the script.

FIGURE A-2   *The Options window showing command options*

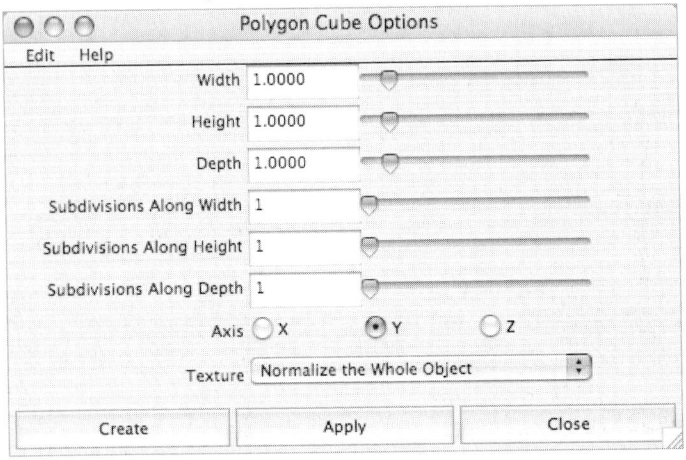

The `docServer` command on the next line opens the online documentation. Next, the command to create the polygonal cube, `polyCube`, is followed by a bunch of flags and their values. Once again, you could use the `help` command in the Script Editor or look up the `polyCube` command in the "MEL Command Reference" section of the documentation. What you will find is that the flags represent all of the command's options that you will see in the Options window, as shown in Figure A-2.

As you can see, while many options are available, MEL commands are quite simple to read. At this point, you could string together a few commands in the Input window and execute them without too much trouble.

Using MEL Scripts

One of the most wonderful things about MEL is that additional tools and functionality can be added to Maya without having to wait for Alias to release a new version of the software. However, many of us would rather spend time using tools than making them. The Maya community has generously organized a library of MEL scripts, available at *http://www.highend3d.com,* that are available as free downloads. Before you decide that you need to build a new tool, it is a good idea to check this web site to see whether you can find a MEL script that does what you need. Chances are, someone has already written it and you can download, install, and use it.

Another good source for MEL scripts is Alias's web site (*http://www.alias.com*). Also, many of the training DVDs available from Alias contain MEL scripts. The "Integrating a Creature Rig into a Production Pipeline and Fast Animation Rigs" DVDs contain dozens of great scripts to assist in character rigging and animation. The author of these DVDs, Jason Schliefer, also offers many of these MEL scripts as downloads from his own web site, at *http://www.jonhandhisdog.com*.

Where Do Scripts Go?

OK, so you've just been to Highend3d.com, found the MEL script you were looking for, and downloaded it. So now what? The most common way to use MEL scripts is to place them in one of the scripts directories on your hard drive. Three scripts directories are created when you install Maya.

One of the directories is located in the same directory as the Maya application. Inside this scripts directory, you'll find several subfolders that contain hundreds of scripts. Remember that the entire Maya user interface is programmed in MEL. The scripts found in these subdirectories are those that control the Maya UI. Unless you need to modify the existing UI, it is best to stay out of this directory.

Another scripts directory can be found at Documents and Settings*<your user name>*\ My Documents\Maya\Scripts (on the Macintosh, this can be found at /Users/*<your user name>*/ Library/Preferences/Alias/Maya/Scripts). This scripts directory is a good place to store scripts that are in development or that are loaded in manually.

Scripts that will be frequently executed from Maya should be placed in Documents and Settings\ *<your user name>*\My Documents\Maya\6.0\scripts (Users/*<your user name>*/Library/Preferences/ Alias/Maya/6.0/Scripts on the Mac). Any time a script is called, Maya scans this directory, finds the script, and executes the procedures found inside it.

Definition   *Procedure*   *A user-defined function similar to Maya's built-in functions. Discussed in the "Procedures" section.*

Executing MEL Scripts

Once you have downloaded a script, it is always a good idea open it in a text editor and read any instructions that might be included. These instructions will often tell you what the script does, how to use it (such as what things need to be selected before executing), and how to execute it. Sometimes, scripts are written *modularly*. In other words, several scripts may be needed to run a procedure. In the case of the tmRenderPass script, a separate script called tmRenderPassUI.mel builds a window that then calls procedures in the tmRenderPass.mel script.

If the script is well documented, it will often tell you what you need to do to execute it. To execute a script, you can type the name of the command you need into either the command line or the Input window of the Script Editor. If the script has no documentation, chances are it is a global procedure script.

Most of the scripts that are downloaded are known as *global procedure scripts*. This means that the procedures contained within the scripts can be called from anywhere: from a script, a Shelf button, the Script Editor, or elsewhere. A global procedure script needs to be named after the global procedure. If the global procedure is called tmRenderSpec, then the script should be named tmRenderSpec.mel. When **tmRenderSpec** is typed into the command line or the Script Editor, Maya searches all of the script paths for a script name that matches the command. If it finds the script, it declares all of the global MEL procedures with that file and executes. Most of the time, it is most helpful if you make a Shelf button that contains the name of the command so that you can readily use it without having to look up the name.

Writing MEL Scripts

Earlier in this appendix, we discussed MEL commands and introduced the idea of stringing several commands together. While this may save you some time in some cases, as you become more proficient with Maya, you will undoubtedly need to take things a bit further. Specific problems or workflow issues will arise and can usually be solved through using MEL. The tmRenderPass script, for example, was written to provide a specific rendering workflow that is very time-consuming to set up manually in Maya's interface. This section covers some of the basic elements of MEL scripts.

Syntax

Every language has its own syntax. In English, every sentence ends with a period. In MEL, we conclude a command with a semicolon (;). Learning the punctuation or special characters is one of the first things you'll need to do. If the syntax is incorrect in a MEL script, Maya will return an error. Therefore, it is important that you use the correct syntax as you type in your script. The following table shows some common characters and gives a description of each.

//	A double slash is used as a comment indicator.
;	A semicolon is used to indicate the end of a command.
( )	Parentheses are used for grouping math equations of strings.
[ ]	Square brackets are used to bracket an array index.
{ }	Curly brackets are used for grouping commands and arrays.
" "	Quotation marks are used to indicate that the text contained within is to be treated as a text string for the command line so that any special characters used will not have an effect on the execution of the script.

Variables

Variables are the cornerstone of any programming language. They are used to store a piece of information temporarily for use anywhere within your script. For Maya to be able to differentiate between a variable and the name of another object or node in a scene, the $ symbol is placed at the beginning of the variable's name.

Variables can hold different types of data. The variable could hold a whole number, text, or a vector. (Refer to Chapter 18 for definitions of the different types of variables.) Before using a variable, it is important that you declare it in the script by naming it and its data type. Here's a simple example of declaring a variable:

```
float $tmVal = 5 ;
```

This declares that the variable called $tmVal is of a float data type and is equal to 5. Now that this variable has been defined, we can use it in a math equation. In this line, we use the print command to tell Maya to return the result in the History section of the Script Editor and in the feedback line:

```
print ($tmVal + 1) ;
//Result : 6
```

Instead of defining the variable with a constant number, it could be defined using a MEL command:

```
string $tmMaterials[] = `ls -mat` ;
```

In this example, we have defined the $tmMaterials variable as a string data type (meaning it can store text). The [] that follows the variable name indicates that the variable can store a list of objects. This variable is then defined with the `ls -mat` command that will list all of the materials in the scene.

Conditional Statements

As you are scripting, you often want to perform a certain function only when a certain condition is met: if "this" do "that" else do "the other." Here is an example:

```
if ($x > 1){
print "X is greater than 1";
} else {
print "X is not greater than 1";
}
```

Procedures

Procedures enable you to encapsulate a frequently used piece of code into a single function that can be executed by entering the function's name. For example, you may have a script that performs several different tasks, but each task requires finding out what materials are in the scene (as in our variable example shown earlier). Rather than writing the piece of code for listing all materials in each task, you would make a procedure that does nothing but find and list all of the materials in the scene and return their names in a list. You would then call that procedure at each task.

First, we will declare the procedure using the `proc` statement:

```
proc string[] getMaterials()
{
    string $materials[] = `ls -mat`;
    return $materials;
}
```

This procedure will return an array of values that contains the names of the materials in the scene. Now, instead of having to use this entire piece of code every time your scripts needs this information, you can simply call `getMaterials()`.

Two different types of procedures can be used, local and global. By default, procedures are known only locally. This means that if you have a procedure that is written in MEL, it can be called only from within that MEL script. If you were to type the name of the procedure into the Script Editor, Maya would return an error. If you put the word *global* in front of your procedure, you make it known to all of Maya. This means that it can be called from the Script Editor, a Shelf icon, or even another MEL script. You should use local procedures whenever possible and use a global procedure only for the procedure that is called by the user from the Script Editor or Maya UI.

Case Study: Using MEL to Enhance IK to FK Switching

Back in Chapter 10, you learned how to set up a switchable FK/IK arm. While that section covers the actual setup of the skeleton and controls for switching, it leaves out one detail that many animators will need if they want to have the position and orientation of the IK skeleton match that of the FK skeleton. This would prevent any jumping or skipping of the arm when the switch is made.

Work Through a Solution

So what is a scriptable solution to this issue? When confronted with a problem like this, the first step is to figure out what the process is—ask "what are the steps involved to accomplish the task manually?" The best way to do this is simply to perform all of the necessary actions in the main Maya UI.

How would this work manually? We could move and snap the wrist IK control to the FK wrist control, but this would solve matching only the translations, not the rotations. We need to figure out a way that we can do this in script. Snapping just enables the Move tool to snap to specified components and is therefore not something we can do in script. Copying the translation and rotation values won't work because each object's transforms will differ slightly relative to their parent objects.

A good solution would then be to point and orient constrain the IK control to the FK wrist joint and find out what the transform values of the IK control are at that position; then we could copy those values, delete the constraint, and paste those values back in.

Since this will be scripted, a good idea would be to make a duplicate of the IK control and constrain it to the FK wrist. This way, we can easily store the target transform values in a variable, and when we are finished setting them to the original IK control, we can delete the entire duplicate. This solves the problem of having to figure out which constraints need to be duplicated.

Write the Script

Step through the following script. Each line has been commented to document the entire process. Note that some lines have been broken here because of page-width constraints.

```
//Moves armCTRL to LT_Wrist_FK
//This line makes a duplicate of the LT_WristCTRL and stores the
//object in a variable named $dup.
$dup = `duplicate "LT_ WristCTRL"` ;
//The select command is used to select the LT_Wrist_FK object and
//the $dup in this specific order
select  "LT_Wrist_FK" $dup[0] ;
//The $dup is point and orient constrained to the LT_Wrist_FK
pointConstraint ;
orientConstraint ;
//The translations from the $dup are stored in a variable called
//$pos and the rotations are stored in a variable called $rot
$pos = `getAttr ($dup[0] + ".t")` ;
$rot = `getAttr ($dup[0] + ".r")` ;
//The values in $pos are used to set the translate and rotate
```

```
//attributes for the LT_WristCTRL
setAttr ("LT_WristCTRL" + ".t") $pos[0] $pos[1] $pos[2];
setAttr ("LT_WristCTRL" + ".r") $pos[0] $pos[1] $pos[2] ;
//The $dup, along with its constraints, is deleted from the scene.
 delete $dup[0] ;
//We print the result to confirm that it worked
print ("//Result:"+" LT_WristCTRL"+" to " +"LT_Wrist_FK" + "\n");
// finished


//Moves IKPole to FKPole
$dup = `duplicate "FKPole"`;
    select  $dup[0] "FKPole";
    pointConstraint;
    $pos = `getAttr ($dup[0] + ".t")`;
    setAttr ("LT_ElbowCTRL" + ".t") $pos[0] $pos[1] $pos[2];
    delete $dup[0];
    print ("// Result: " + "LT_ElbowCTRL" + " moved to the position
    of " + "FKPole" + "\n");
    // finished
```

Once you have written this script, you can select all of it in the Script Editor and drag the selection onto the Shelf along with any other character controls that you may have. This way, you can quickly execute the script while you are animating your character.

Index

INTERNATIONAL CONTACT INFORMATION

AUSTRALIA
McGraw-Hill Book Company
Australia Pty. Ltd.
TEL +61-2-9900-1800
FAX +61-2-9878-8881
http://www.mcgraw-hill.com.au
books-it_sydney@mcgraw-hill.com

CANADA
McGraw-Hill Ryerson Ltd.
TEL +905-430-5000
FAX +905-430-5020
http://www.mcgraw-hill.ca

**GREECE, MIDDLE EAST, & AFRICA
(Excluding South Africa)**
McGraw-Hill Hellas
TEL +30-210-6560-990
TEL +30-210-6560-993
TEL +30-210-6560-994
FAX +30-210-6545-525

MEXICO (Also serving Latin America)
McGraw-Hill Interamericana Editores
S.A. de C.V.
TEL +525-1500-5108
FAX +525-117-1589
http://www.mcgraw-hill.com.mx
carlos_ruiz@mcgraw-hill.com

SINGAPORE (Serving Asia)
McGraw-Hill Book Company
TEL +65-6863-1580
FAX +65-6862-3354
http://www.mcgraw-hill.com.sg
mghasia@mcgraw-hill.com

SOUTH AFRICA
McGraw-Hill South Africa
TEL +27-11-622-7512
FAX +27-11-622-9045
robyn_swanepoel@mcgraw-hill.com

SPAIN
McGraw-Hill/
Interamericana de España, S.A.U.
TEL +34-91-180-3000
FAX +34-91-372-8513
http://www.mcgraw-hill.es
professional@mcgraw-hill.es

**UNITED KINGDOM, NORTHERN,
EASTERN, & CENTRAL EUROPE**
McGraw-Hill Education Europe
TEL +44-1-628-502500
FAX +44-1-628-770224
http://www.mcgraw-hill.co.uk
emea_queries@mcgraw-hill.com

ALL OTHER INQUIRIES Contact:
McGraw-Hill/Osborne
TEL +1-510-420-7700
FAX +1-510-420-7703
http://www.osborne.com
omg_international@mcgraw-hill.com

Sound Off!

Visit us at **www.osborne.com/bookregistration** and let us know what you thought of this book. While you're online you'll have the opportunity to register for newsletters and special offers from McGraw-Hill/Osborne.

We want to hear from you!

Sneak Peek

Visit us today at **www.betabooks.com** and see what's coming from McGraw-Hill/Osborne tomorrow!

Based on the successful software paradigm, Bet@Books™ allows computing professionals to view partial and sometimes complete text versions of selected titles online. Bet@Books™ viewing is free, invites comments and feedback, and allows you to "test drive" books in progress on the subjects that interest you the most.

LICENSE AGREEMENT

THIS PRODUCT (THE "PRODUCT") CONTAINS PROPRIETARY SOFTWARE, DATA AND INFORMATION (INCLUDING DOCUMENTATION) OWNED BY THE McGRAW-HILL COMPANIES, INC. ("McGRAW-HILL") AND ITS LICENSORS. YOUR RIGHT TO USE THE PRODUCT IS GOVERNED BY THE TERMS AND CONDITIONS OF THIS AGREEMENT.

LICENSE: Throughout this License Agreement, "you" shall mean either the individual or the entity whose agent opens this package. You are granted a non-exclusive and non-transferable license to use the Product subject to the following terms:
(i) If you have licensed a single user version of the Product, the Product may only be used on a single computer (i.e., a single CPU). If you licensed and paid the fee applicable to a local area network or wide area network version of the Product, you are subject to the terms of the following subparagraph (ii).
(ii) If you have licensed a local area network version, you may use the Product on unlimited workstations located in one single building selected by you that is served by such local area network. If you have licensed a wide area network version, you may use the Product on unlimited workstations located in multiple buildings on the same site selected by you that is served by such wide area network; provided, however, that any building will not be considered located in the same site if it is more than five (5) miles away from any building included in such site. In addition, you may only use a local area or wide area network version of the Product on one single server. If you wish to use the Product on more than one server, you must obtain written authorization from McGraw-Hill and pay additional fees.
(iii) You may make one copy of the Product for back-up purposes only and you must maintain an accurate record as to the location of the back-up at all times.

COPYRIGHT; RESTRICTIONS ON USE AND TRANSFER: All rights (including copyright) in and to the Product are owned by McGraw-Hill and its licensors. You are the owner of the enclosed disc on which the Product is recorded. You may not use, copy, decompile, disassemble, reverse engineer, modify, reproduce, create derivative works, transmit, distribute, sublicense, store in a database or retrieval system of any kind, rent or transfer the Product, or any portion thereof, in any form or by any means (including electronically or otherwise) except as expressly provided for in this License Agreement. You must reproduce the copyright notices, trademark notices, legends and logos of McGraw-Hill and its licensors that appear on the Product on the back-up copy of the Product which you are permitted to make hereunder. All rights in the Product not expressly granted herein are reserved by McGraw-Hill and its licensors.

TERM: This License Agreement is effective until terminated. It will terminate if you fail to comply with any term or condition of this License Agreement. Upon termination, you are obligated to return to McGraw-Hill the Product together with all copies thereof and to purge all copies of the Product included in any and all servers and computer facilities.

DISCLAIMER OF WARRANTY: THE PRODUCT AND THE BACK-UP COPY ARE LICENSED "AS IS." McGRAW-HILL, ITS LICENSORS AND THE AUTHORS MAKE NO WARRANTIES, EXPRESS OR IMPLIED, AS TO THE RESULTS TO BE OBTAINED BY ANY PERSON OR ENTITY FROM USE OF THE PRODUCT, ANY INFORMATION OR DATA INCLUDED THEREIN AND/OR ANY TECHNICAL SUPPORT SERVICES PROVIDED HEREUNDER, IF ANY ("TECHNICAL SUPPORT SERVICES"). McGRAW-HILL, ITS LICENSORS AND THE AUTHORS MAKE NO EXPRESS OR IMPLIED WARRANTIES OF MERCHANTABILITY OR FITNESS FOR A PARTICULAR PURPOSE OR USE WITH RESPECT TO THE PRODUCT. McGRAW-HILL, ITS LICENSORS, AND THE AUTHORS MAKE NO GUARANTEE THAT YOU WILL PASS ANY CERTIFICATION EXAM WHATSOEVER BY USING THIS PRODUCT. NEITHER McGRAW-HILL, ANY OF ITS LICENSORS NOR THE AUTHORS WARRANT THAT THE FUNCTIONS CONTAINED IN THE PRODUCT WILL MEET YOUR REQUIREMENTS OR THAT THE OPERATION OF THE PRODUCT WILL BE UNINTERRUPTED OR ERROR FREE. YOU ASSUME THE ENTIRE RISK WITH RESPECT TO THE QUALITY AND PERFORMANCE OF THE PRODUCT.

LIMITED WARRANTY FOR DISC: To the original licensee only, McGraw-Hill warrants that the enclosed disc on which the Product is recorded is free from defects in materials and workmanship under normal use and service for a period of ninety (90) days from the date of purchase. In the event of a defect in the disc covered by the foregoing warranty, McGraw-Hill will replace the disc.

LIMITATION OF LIABILITY: NEITHER McGRAW-HILL, ITS LICENSORS NOR THE AUTHORS SHALL BE LIABLE FOR ANY INDIRECT, SPECIAL OR CONSEQUENTIAL DAMAGES, SUCH AS BUT NOT LIMITED TO, LOSS OF ANTICIPATED PROFITS OR BENEFITS, RESULTING FROM THE USE OR INABILITY TO USE THE PRODUCT EVEN IF ANY OF THEM HAS BEEN ADVISED OF THE POSSIBILITY OF SUCH DAMAGES. THIS LIMITATION OF LIABILITY SHALL APPLY TO ANY CLAIM OR CAUSE WHATSOEVER WHETHER SUCH CLAIM OR CAUSE ARISES IN CONTRACT, TORT, OR OTHERWISE. Some states do not allow the exclusion or limitation of indirect, special or consequential damages, so the above limitation may not apply to you.

U.S. GOVERNMENT RESTRICTED RIGHTS: Any software included in the Product is provided with restricted rights subject to subparagraphs (c), (1) and (2) of the Commercial Computer Software-Restricted Rights clause at 48 C.F.R. 52.227-19. The terms of this Agreement applicable to the use of the data in the Product are those under which the data are generally made available to the general public by McGraw-Hill. Except as provided herein, no reproduction, use, or disclosure rights are granted with respect to the data included in the Product and no right to modify or create derivative works from any such data is hereby granted.

GENERAL: This License Agreement constitutes the entire agreement between the parties relating to the Product. The terms of any Purchase Order shall have no effect on the terms of this License Agreement. Failure of McGraw-Hill to insist at any time on strict compliance with this License Agreement shall not constitute a waiver of any rights under this License Agreement. This License Agreement shall be construed and governed in accordance with the laws of the State of New York. If any provision of this License Agreement is held to be contrary to law, that provision will be enforced to the maximum extent permissible and the remaining provisions will remain in full force and effect.